Armchair Cinema

T0379722

This book is dedicated, with love and gratitude, to my mam, Maureen, and to the memory of my dad, Tom. They gave me control of the remote and allowed me to stay up late, which is how it all started.

Armchair Cinema

A History of Feature Films on British Television, 1929–1981

Sheldon Hall

EDINBURGH
University Press

Edinburgh University Press is one of the leading university presses in the UK. We publish academic books and journals in our selected subject areas across the humanities and social sciences, combining cutting-edge scholarship with high editorial and production values to produce academic works of lasting importance. For more information visit our website: edinburghuniversitypress.com

© Sheldon Hall, 2024

Grateful acknowledgement is made to the sources listed in the List of Illustrations for permission to reproduce material previously published elsewhere. Every effort has been made to trace the copyright holders, but if any have been inadvertently overlooked, the publisher will be pleased to make the necessary arrangements at the first opportunity.

Edinburgh University Press Ltd
13 Infirmary Street
Edinburgh EH1 1LT

Typeset in Ehrhardt
by Cheshire Typesetting Ltd, Cuddington, Cheshire, and
printed and bound by CPI Group (UK) Ltd,
Croydon, CR0 4YY

A CIP record for this book is available from the British Library

ISBN 978 1 3995 2013 3 (hardback)
ISBN 978 1 3995 2015 7 (webready PDF)
ISBN 978 1 3995 2016 4 (epub)

The right of Sheldon Hall to be identified as the author of this work has been asserted in accordance with the Copyright, Designs and Patents Act 1988, and the Copyright and Related Rights Regulations 2003 (SI No. 2498).

Contents

Illustrations

Figures

List of Tables

INTRODUCTION

Meet Mr Lucifer –
Cinema, Television and Films on TV

It is Saturday night. Midnight has passed, and in sitting rooms all over Britain figures are slumped almost horizontally in front of television sets. A remarkable number of them have just finished grumbling 'Oh not another one of those awful old black and white films' as BBC2's *Midnight Movie* comes on. Quite a few have even complained with airy expertise 'Good grief, another of those wartime United Artists efforts.'

Moans and groans thus dutifully delivered for the benefit of sleepy companions headed towards bed, the horizontal masses snuggle down into their armchairs with profound content-ment to watch the 36-year-old movie.

(Chris Dunkley, 'The Magic of the Movies', *Financial Times*, 18 May 1977, 3)

Last week, for the price of about 30 Consulate Extra Mild, you could have seen a double bill of *The Omen* and *The Bizarre and the Beautiful*.

Alternatively, you could have sat comfortably in an armchair and watched Fred Astaire in *The Band Wagon*, with no more effort than it requires to walk to the fridge for a fresh supply of soda-water.

(Laurence Marks, 'Can Sir Harold Ride to the Rescue in the Last Reel?',
Observer, 2 October 1977, 3)

This book is not a history of television in the United Kingdom. Nor is it another history of the British film industry. It is, rather, about the interface between the film industry and TV in one particular respect: the showing on television of feature-length films made for the cinema. This study, conceived as the first of two companion volumes, is confined to the UK, partly for reasons of economy and partly because a full-length account of this topic specifically in relation to Britain has not been attempted before. There have been at least two substantial monographs about films on television in the United States, yet there has been no comparable, over-arching study for the UK since Ed Buscombe's slim pamphlet *Films on TV*, initially undertaken as a report for UNESCO and published by *Screen* more than half a century ago.[1]

This is not to say that no substantial scholarly work has been done since then on the relationship between film and television; indeed there have been a number of notable works in the field. Buscombe has also written a book chapter charting the UK film industry's past hostility to television, particularly focusing on the formation in 1958 of the Film Industry Defence Organisation (FIDO) to fight the sale of British films to TV. FIDO itself has also been touched on by a number of other writers, often in relation to British cinema in the 1950s. Su Holmes's monograph *British TV and Film Culture in the 1950s* examines television's coverage of cinema in that decade, while Paul Kerr has discussed more broadly the subject of TV programmes about the cinema in his contribution to an edited collection whose subtitle is *The Relations between Film and Television*.[2] More recently, the University of Portsmouth's research project 'Channel 4 Television and British Film Culture' (2010–14) has resulted in three doctoral dissertations, a special issue of the *Journal of British Cinema and Television* and a monograph, among other outputs.[3]

These latter works are as much concerned with the involvement of UK broadcasting organisations (the BBC as well as Channel Four) in theatrical film production as with the programming of films on TV, twin concerns that also inform Hannah Andrews' 2014 monograph, *Television and British Cinema: Convergence and Divergence since 1990*. The present book restricts itself to the period up to 1981, before the advent of the fourth channel the following year; but Andrews nevertheless offers some useful ideas with which we can begin to answer why the film-television nexus had hitherto attracted so little academic attention. She posits, on the one hand, the bewildering number of possible angles ('multiple points of entry') it offers, and on the other, the 'disciplinary rivalry' between film studies and television studies. The essentialism underlying much traditional film theory and its preoccupation with 'medium specificity' – the notion that art forms and communications media are characterised by particular properties that fundamentally distinguish them one from another – may have made scholars wary of phenomena that blur the lines between them. More recently, however, concepts such as 'convergence', 'intermediality' and 'remediation' have been gaining traction; in a multi-platform but all-digital world, the separateness of art forms and media technologies now appears increasingly untenable.[4]

I would however take issue with one aspect of Andrews' argument, when she claims that greater cultural prestige invariably accrues to cinema rather than to television, which has often been seen as the artistically inferior medium.[5] This is so to only a limited degree, as I hope to show.

From Essence to Convergence

Although the scanning and transmission of images from film was a part of television from its experimental beginnings, this was usually regarded as different in kind from the transmission of 'live' images (see Figure 0.1). 'One should resist the temptation to compare television too closely with the stage or films', said the BBC's first Director of Television, Gerald Cock, in 1939. 'The charm of television', he believed, 'lies in its intimacy and immediacy.'[6] For these qualities, the domestic environment in which TV was usually consumed was crucial. A 1937 *Radio Times* article identified cinema with the physical presence of a large

Figure 0.1 Technicians checking film before completing loading into one of the Cintel telecine machines at BBC Lime Grove Studios, March 1951. BBC Photo Library © BBC.

audience in a theatrical auditorium, using this as an explanation of the inherent incompatibility of film and TV:

> The ordinary commercial film is not suitable for transmission by television. The reason? Because in television the most important part of any film is lacking: the audience. A film appeals to several hundred people at the same time; a comedian cracks a joke and there are several hundred laughs; the heroine sheds a tear and several hundred eyes are moist; at the sight of a gun several hundred hearts stop beating. Mass emotion. It is far, far easier to make a crowd of people laugh or cry than to produce the same effect on a solitary person.[7]

BBC producer Dallas Bower went further: 'The transmission by television of "feature" films is neither desirable nor appropriate', he wrote the same year.[8] For Bower, film was primarily of use as an adjunct to television production (through, for example, the addition to a studio-based play of scenes shot on location), not a separate programme category, unless it meant newsreels and other short subjects. John Swift, writing in 1950, emphasised this limited but important functionality of film in television, noting that it had 'a very definite and vital role to play as an integral part of any television service'. For Swift, film served three purposes:

(a) as a stop-gap between 'live' studio programmes, or as a substitute for pro-
    grammes unexpectedly postponed or cancelled ...
(b) as a 'convenience,' such as continuity shots to link action (if necessary)
    between studio scenes. Also to establish scenes other than in the studio ...
(c) to bring to the screen something that can only be shown by film, including
    news – news of events, that is, taking place outside the range of the O.B.
    [Outside Broadcast] units, or where it is inconvenient for the O.B. cameras to
    operate.[9]

However, hostile attitudes persisted into the postwar era, when attempts at cooperation between the cinema and television were mooted. 'Wiser is the film producer who allows TV to show parts of his latest films in *Current Release*, making use of TV with a Trojan Horse in the shape of a trailer for his film!', wrote Christopher Barry in 1952, referring to the BBC's regular film magazine show. But Barry also argued that 'whenever TV resorts to film as part of an otherwise live performance it is losing some of its essential qualities of spontaneity and immediacy and prostituting itself into the bargain'.[10] Some observers argued that films on television were against the interests of both the film industry and broadcasting. 'The television set, with its small screen and relatively poor definition, is not a suitable medium for the reception of films', commented S. Seeman in 1949. So unsuitable, in fact, that 'the ultimate effect of showing commercial films would undoubtedly be to discredit the entertainment value of a film to the televiewer'. Seeman, like many another pundit, foresaw the threat television would eventually pose to the cinema: 'there can be no doubt that in the not distant future, when transmission stations give a nationwide service, this new medium will prove a serious competitor to the film industry'.[11]

Much of the early commentary on the relationship and perceived rivalry between cinema and television is concerned not so much with the superiority of one medium over the other as with the extent to which they are (or were) different, have different aptitudes, and consequently offer different types of appeal to both practitioners and viewers. The chapters on television in the three annual anthologies on *The Cinema*, edited by Roger Manvell for Pelican Books in the early 1950s, are all concerned with the degree to which the new medium was capable of performing the same functions as cinema along with others held to be beyond the latter's reach. Thus, in a 1950 group discussion, 'Television's Challenge to the Cinema', George More O'Ferrall – both a producer of television drama and a director of feature films – averred: 'The public looks for an intimacy in television that it does not look for or expect to find in films.' When Manvell responded that 'the simple, two-dimensional moving picture which both mediums share makes people think it is the same thing in the end', More O'Ferrall countered: 'People may think that. But television and films are emphatically not the same.'[12] Writing in *Sight and Sound* the same year, in a new but short-lived regular column on 'Television', the National Film Archive's director Ernest Lindgren itemised what he claimed to be the three main differences between cinema and TV: 'immediacy', 'scale' and 'viewing conditions'; to which he subsequently added a fourth, 'freedom of time' ('freedom to stretch itself leisurely and unhurriedly').[13]

These differences-in-similarity underpinned the profusion of contemporaneous writings on the relationship between the two media, which often expressed concern about what the advent of television might mean for the future of the commercial cinema. The nature of their anxieties is clear enough from their very titles: 'Television – the End of Film?'; 'TV Launches a Film Offensive'; 'How Goes the Enemy?'; and so on.[14] Observers immersed in the older medium inevitably stressed its virtues. Thus, film director René Clair claimed: 'Television is a new means of transmission, but nothing to date has encouraged us to find in it a means of expression with which we are not already familiar.' He added: 'The television screen shows us nothing which the cinema screen cannot show.'[15]

But the Young Turks of television had their own strong feelings too. Andrew Miller Jones, who in 1947–48 produced the earliest BBC TV series on the cinema, *The Film*, hosted by Roger Manvell, put the case for the home screen:

> Television will ultimately develop into an art form in its own right, capable of being judged by its own standards of criticism, as the theatre and the cinema are. And, when it is more widespread, it will become in the dramatic field as much a rival, but no more, of the cinema and the theatre as they are of one another. But as a medium for the expression of ideas, and as a social force, it will have no rival.[16]

With this latter point, Miller Jones was largely concerned with documentary, instructional and 'non-entertainment' television rather than with drama. In discussing the quality of immediacy, the BBC's first postwar Controller of Television, Maurice Gorham, stressed that this was most obviously advantageous in respect of 'actuality' broadcasting; for fiction its importance was less certain. But he nevertheless emphasised television's advantages over the cinema in the field of drama production, partly through the context of viewing in the home and partly through TV's technical facilities, primitive though they presently seemed:

> Compared with the film, television has more flexible means of production. The television producer can do things instantaneously that the film director has to do piecemeal, and he has the vital advantage of seeing his pictures while the camera sees them instead of only when the film developed. If television had happened to be invented before the cinema, one can imagine how television producers would have scoffed at the laborious, synthetic process by which films are built up.[17]

Thus, convictions of superiority existed among advocates of both media. As for the institutions that supported them, Gorham's successor as Controller, Norman Collins, had no doubt about where the weakness lay: 'The film industry contains a large proportion of the stupidest men in the world, particularly on the exhibitors' side.'[18]

By the time the BBC faced a competitor of its own in the shape of Independent Television (ITV), which began broadcasting in 1955, the opposition included both feature films and TV programmes made on film, or 'telefilms'. Writing on the twenty-first anniversary of 'the Corporation', the BBC's new Director of Television, Gerald Beadle, implicitly contrasted the young upstart with his own organisation, which at that time was limiting its use of film material:

> The overriding impression BBC Television has left with me is the way it has remained faithful to the idea of television as against the film picture. True, the BBC service uses film on occasions; but the vast majority of its programmes are done 'live,' as we say in the business. In this sense, the BBC has preserved the character of television.[19]

Other commentators expressed similar views. While celebrating television as 'an impure medium – thank goodness', Hilary Corke placed, at one end of a notional spectrum, '"actuality"', the split-second transmission of what is happening somewhere else in the world but at this very moment'. At the other was 'a little cinema in the home, at which one can enjoy, without having to brave the queues and blizzards and fork out two-and-ninepence, a forgotten Humphrey Bogart or an early Astaire-and-Rogers. This is of course "not television", though it can be most enjoyable.'[20] The novelist John Braine demurred on the last point. Discussing his least favourite domestic viewing, he said: 'I don't like re-issues of old films, even when the films are good. This isn't TV at all.'[21]

The development of videotape recording (VTR) in the late 1950s gave increased flexibility to TV production even while it lacked the cachet of both live drama and film. As producer Kenith Trodd and others have attested, film as a physical medium in television drama came to enjoy a higher status than VTR, especially among aspirant filmmakers. But that was not necessarily because of its cinematic associations; rather it was due to its greater flexibility and higher resolution.[22] The participants in a 1963 debate at the Edinburgh Film Festival pondering the question 'What is a Television Film?' were mainly concerned with the practical utility of film as a physical medium in the context of broadcasting, though they could not help straying into questions of aesthetics. The discussion anticipated convergence, as in the remark of a Belgian contributor who stated that the differences between cinema and television in respect of 'production economics and diffusion' would soon lessen. He added that 'many people have talked about [television] screens getting larger and consequently transmission conditions are nearer to those now applying in the cinema. So I think that the only difference which is likely to remain is the nature of the audience.'[23] Among a conference gathering mainly comprising TV practitioners, the sole participant identified in the published proceedings as an academic – John Shepherd, a 'University Student' – echoed this latter point:

> Television is a versatile bastard born of the full range of the national press of the critical weeklies of the cinema and of the theatre; and covers virtually all the things that all these things cover. Therefore in each individual programme it can aim at a particular sort of audience. The cinema, on the other hand, is throwing its products into a wilderness and tends, naturally, to go for a lowest common denominator.[24]

In the 1970s, a new generation of media scholars brought fresh attention to the differences between viewing 'platforms'. Without departing altogether from the themes of previous discussions, some of their interventions imply a more open acceptance of what would now be called intermediality. Raymond Williams, in a passage devoted to films as one of the 'forms of television', emphasised the disparity in visual quality between the theatrical and domestic screens while acknowledging the pleasure of viewing films on TV and its cultural importance as a form of repertory cinema; to lose this, he argued, 'would be disastrous for the future of our most popular modern art' (by which one assumes he meant the cinema rather than television).[25]

Stuart Hall enlarged on the 'bastard' quality of television quoted earlier from Shepherd:

> Television is a hybrid medium. In part, this is because it is so extraordinarily heterogeneous in content and subject-matter. But, in terms of its formal properties, television also appropriates and cannibalises a variety of forms and techniques from other sources, including other media.

Cinema films on television, Hall argued, were a prime example of the 'small but significant transformations' occurring in the passage of material from one medium to another, manifested most obviously in the scaling down of the image and the editing of films for one reason or another. But rather than pointing to the incompatibility of the two media, he saw this as simply one instance among many of '(a) the relatively low level of the type of transformation which television operates on the great bulk of its contents; and (b) the very high proportion of cases in which the raw material is itself the content of another medium'. According to Hall, 'Television uses up – indeed, exhausts – the contents of other media and of everyday life; but it does not characteristically, decisively impose its forms upon that material.'[26]

Echoing Hall's analysis, journalist and media commentator Chris Dunkley – writing in, of all publications, the BBC's programme journal, *Radio Times* – observed: 'Not only is there a general tacit assumption that you can put absolutely any sort of art, entertainment or information on television successfully but there also seem to be very few questions asked about the comparative suitability of individual items within those categories.' Declaring that his purpose was precisely to ask such awkward questions, Dunkley identified cinema films as one instance of an art form being diminished through its re-presentation on TV. Although he mainly focused on the obvious case of CinemaScope films, such as *Bad Day at Black Rock* (1955/26.12.1970), when they were 'optically rationalised' for TV, he extended his argument to encompass even those masterworks designed to fit a similarly shaped but larger screen: 'I still believe that people who see *Intolerance*, *She Wore a Yellow Ribbon* or *Ivan the Terrible* only on television miss so many of the intentions and achievements of their makers that although they may have been entertained it is true to say they have never really seen the films at all.'[27]

If the remediation of films through broadcasting represents a dilution of their cinematic properties and a diminution of their cinemascopic proportions, it is equally for some observers a corruption of the host medium. Acquired material bought in from outside a broadcasting organisation, no matter how prestigious in its own right, generally enjoyed a lower status than in-house productions (or 'originations' in TV jargon). In 1983, Leslie Halliwell – ITV's film buyer for the past fifteen years – expressed his disappointment at the negligible space routinely given to acquired programmes and films in the annual handbook published by the Independent Broadcasting Authority (IBA) to celebrate the network's output and achievements. In a letter to the Authority's Director of Television, Halliwell referred to having had 'fruitless conversations over many years with IBA people about the curious mental block' he believed they had about purchased films shown on ITV:

> It is as though they are ashamed to admit that they play any, whereas in fact, as you and I know, films often get the biggest ratings, and there must be some satisfaction in reporting at the end of each year that ITV has beaten its opposition to the best selection of features, series, and other material made outside our organisation. This office, for instance, which spends so many millions of pounds a year, is never mentioned under Granada and does not seem to warrant even a paragraph in the general section of the book. Everybody on my staff has come to think this very eccentric.[28]

The persistence of prejudice against television and in favour of cinema is perhaps most evident in the realms of film theory. Jacques Kermabon, the co-editor of *Cinema and Television: Fifty Years of Reflection in France*, a 1991 collection of translated articles, opened the case for the prosecution:

It seems to be taken for granted that television does not offer scope for creation, that it is but a means of transmission, and that the conditions of viewing are such that it cannot encourage any ambitious artistic endeavour. Rarely is television given continued attention. It is a tap from which images drip endlessly into a corner of the house, while the members of the household go about their daily business. The lights are on, people walk to and fro in front of it, the telephone rings, a child cries … When the entire family settles itself before the set – more often than not, for a feature film that is being telecast – rarely does the film go by without a running commentary from those present: a practice which is gradually spreading to cinema halls, much to the displeasure of those who love cinema.[29]

Lest it be suspected that Kermabon is here playing devil's advocate – he does acknowledge that, despite its conditions of reception, television permits 'a living history of the Seventh Art, cinema' – he intensifies the attack, going on to accuse TV of an 'atrophy of intelligence':

Everything flows along in a tide of tepid water. Everything is reduced to the dimensions of a bland spectacle, without asperity, without collisions, without imagination. Television levels everything to the lowest common denominator. The space shown bears no comparison to the cinematographic space. Even as it blurs emotional lines with a plethora of images that telescope the distant and the proximate, the sensitive and the insensitive, the simple and the complex, television plunges the spectator into an absence of spatial distinctions, far poorer than in the case of cinema, and therefore that much more impoverishing in terms of the visual imagination it can evoke … it has been proved that the memory of a film seen on television is less enduring than that of a film seen in a cinema hall. To quote Godard once again: 'Cinema leaves memories. Television manufactures oblivion.'[30]

In a 1985 anthology surveying the state of *British Cinema Now*, Martyn Auty contributed a chapter on the rising tide of films backed by broadcasting organisations, whose title spoke eloquently of a new set of worries: 'But is it cinema?'[31] In the nearly four decades since, film and television scholars have offered some robust answers, ranging from an emphatic 'Yes!' to 'Who cares?' Work as rich and diverse as Jason Jacobs' analysis of early television drama, Dave Rolinson's defence of filmed TV 'plays' as the product of 'the last studio system', and Hannah Andrews' aforementioned exploration of convergence and divergence in the treatment of films by television has quashed any such simplistic notions of the inferiority of television to cinema or the separateness of media forms.[32] Yet despite the rise of what we might call intermedia studies, the essentialist discourse is maintained even in some modern accounts. Mark Aldridge, in his fine history of early television, asked how Mickey Mouse – a frequent visitor to prewar BBC schedules – fitted into the picture.

In its broadest sense, the Disney creation can be justified as a public service broadcast as he would entertain a general audience and supply some wholesome family entertainment. Nevertheless, he is not a creation original to television, nor did he have any educational purpose or even have his roots in British culture. This, perhaps, makes him less interesting to the television historian.[33]

Not British, not BBC, not television – even though a Disney cartoon closed the prewar BBC service and opened the postwar one (see Chapter 2).

The simplest explanation of not only the neglect of films on television as an object of serious inquiry by scholars, but also the hostility towards them that has often been a marked feature of institutional discourse within the film and TV industries, press journalism and film theory, is that they are neither one thing nor another. If films on TV are 'not television', they are assuredly 'not cinema' either. They have therefore suffered, from both sides, the contempt born of illegitimacy: the bastard child of a bastard medium. This is a condition that the present book seeks to redeem.

I start from the position that the showing of cinema films on television was and is, quite simply, an empirical fact: that, however inadequately from a technological or an aesthetic standpoint, films have been seen on television by many more viewers than would have seen them in cinemas (the differential in the size of theatrical and TV audiences makes this inevitable); and that, whatever filmmakers or film theorists might prefer to believe, this viewing experience must have had some positive value, otherwise broadcasters would not bother to show them or viewers to watch them. My method is far from theoretical; I have no interest in identifying what is uniquely cinematic or specifically televisual, or in blaming television for not being cinema. Rather, I aim to examine the *mechanisms* by which films came to be shown on television: both the institutional contexts of TV and the cinema that underpinned them, and the practices and priorities internal to broadcasting organisations that led them to make use of films in particular ways. In setting out, as clearly as I can, the 'how' of films shown on television, I hope also to arrive at the 'why'; and, indeed, the 'Why not?'

The Shape of This Book

Armchair Cinema is divided into two sections, each comprising six chapters. While covering the same period, up to the end of 1981, the sections approach the subject of films on television from different angles. The first half is a roughly chronological history of how British television organisations dealt with the commercial interests of the film industry, and on occasion with the Government, in the acquisition of feature films for broadcast. The second part explores, in a more synoptic fashion, the ways in which those films appeared on air: their role as programme material, the manner and purpose of their scheduling, and the institutional structures and priorities that shaped their use. Here I set out some of the concerns and contents of each chapter and relate them to the broadly theoretical issues just outlined.

Chapter 1 begins by sketching the pre-history of films on television, from early experiments in transmitting film to the use of cinema material in the BBC's prewar television service. Worries about competition, present from the beginning, led the film industry to refuse cooperation and the BBC's attempt to secure material from the largest UK film company, Gaumont British, ended in frustration. After the war, this non-cooperation developed into a policy of organised opposition, as discussed in Chapter 2. Frustrated in their attempts to mount theatre television as an alternative to the BBC's monopoly on domestic broadcasting, the major film interests responded with boycotts and other punitive actions. They relented, to a degree, only when television offered opportunities to promote new theatrical releases through the use of clips, star interviews and coverage of premieres. But distributors still withheld feature films from regular use, and what few films slipped through the net were mostly minor.

As the BBC in the early 1950s scaled back its use of cinema films in favour of made-for-TV telefilm series, the advent of ITV in 1955 added competition for the few features available for broadcast. As Chapter 3 explains, the new commercial network had success in acquiring several major film 'packages', and this spurred the BBC on to do similar deals. Opposition to films on television, orchestrated by the cinema owners' representative body, the Cinematograph Exhibitors' Association (CEA), reached a peak in 1958 with the formation of FIDO, funded by cinemas and dedicated to keeping British films in particular off the air. The story behind this organisation is told in Chapter 4. But it was eventually thwarted in 1964, following further large deals made by both the BBC and ITV, after which the CEA conceded that it would not stand in the way of films being sold to television so long as they were at least five years old. FIDO subsequently dwindled into the background as the way was cleared for a backlog spanning several decades to be unleashed onto the small screen. This is discussed in Chapter 5, which also includes an account of the mixed press and public reaction to this rush of vintage celluloid (see Figure 0.2).[34]

Films have subsequently been seen on television by far larger audiences than ever saw them in cinemas. In the period covered by this book, most viewers at home had a very limited choice of only one, two or three channels. These were all free-to-air services, aside from a brief, limited experiment in cable television from 1966–68, also discussed in Chapter 5. But while choice was limited, audiences for even averagely-popular programmes, including films, could be very large. The gradual release to television of the cinema's biggest hits, discussed in Chapter 6, led to huge ratings for certain titles. They included the James Bond films, culminating in 1980 when *Live and Let Die* (1973/20.01.1980) was seen by an audience estimated as either 23.5 million or 28 million viewers, depending on which set of figures one believes. By that year, annual cinema admissions had fallen from an all-time peak of 1,635 million in 1946 to 101 million (and would nearly halve again within the next four years). The fact that a single screening on television could be seen by an audience one-quarter the size of all audiences for all films at all cinemas in the space of the year emphasises the unequal contest that the relationship between cinema and television had become. Throughout the 1970s and into the 1980s, therefore, opposition from the film industry continued in the form of calls for legislation both to limit the use broadcasters made of feature films and to make them pay more, even while film production became increasingly dependent on TV investment.

Opening the book's second section, Chapter 7 includes a more expansive

Figure 0.2 In 1971, BBC1 presented 'The Movie Crazy Years', a Friday-night season of Warner Bros classics launched with an American TV documentary of the same name.
Radio Times © Immediate Media Co. Artwork © Frank Bellamy.

discussion of ratings and audience research, along with scheduling strategies for the effective 'placing' of films. Once feature films became established in the late 1950s as a regular, rather than an occasional, part of television programming, their placement within the schedules became more standardised. Films were often shown in regular weekly slots under umbrella titles that signalled their status as a particular type of programme. This chapter also includes a section on films for children and concludes with an examination of the programming of films at Christmas, when they often had the status of special events, different from the weekly norm. Chapter 8 is a detailed case study of a highly specialised group of films: those made in foreign (non-Anglophone) languages and usually shown with subtitles. Such films have been broadcast since the very earliest days of television, but they have often met with resistance from viewers and sometimes caused controversy over their content. Nevertheless, this type of 'cultural' programming has been found even on commercial stations, and the chapter examines several of the broadcast 'strands' in which they have been presented.

Chapter 9 explains the regulatory procedures adopted by the key broadcasting institutions: the BBC ('the Corporation'); the Independent Television Authority (ITA), which in 1972 became the IBA, the Independent Broadcasting Authority (both commonly referred to as 'the Authority'); and the companies comprising ITV, collectively represented by the Independent Television Companies Association (ITCA) as well as by a host of committees, panels and groups with more specific remits. The internal systems of rules and practices adopted by all of these agencies exerted considerable force over the form in which films appeared on screen. The question of how to present films previously exhibited before age-restricted audiences in cinemas to an undifferentiated audience at home was always contentious. The chapter therefore includes a discussion of the relationships between television structures and the industry body responsible for regulating films in cinemas: the British Board of Film Censors (BBFC). Chapter 10 is a further extended case study, exploring television's treatment of one genre that has on occasion caused concern but also developed a large fan following: the horror film. After treating the genre guardedly for years, broadcasters embraced it in the 1970s with imaginative scheduling strategies exploiting their distinctive appeal, most notably a long-running annual series of late-night double bills on BBC2.

As we have already noted, feature films were not always shown on television in the form in which they were first seen in cinemas; arguably, they could never be. Chapter 11 examines how they were subject to various types of editing and re-presentation, including differences of format. Sex, violence and 'bad language' were all often modified or removed from films prior to transmission, when they had been accepted for broadcast at all. The various compromises inflicted on films by television, often for scheduling purposes rather than content, was one of the complaints articulated in Ed Buscombe's aforementioned 1971 booklet *Films on TV*. This is discussed at length in Chapter 12 along with Lynda Myles's 1979 report for the BBC's General Advisory Council, 'The BBC and the Film Industry'; these two accounts comprise wide-ranging critiques of television's treatment of films, but were themselves subject to a critical reception. The chapter concludes with a case study of a sample year, 1975, offering an assessment of the successes and failures of the BBC and ITV in their presentation of feature films in the light of the criticisms made by Buscombe, Myles and others.

The choice of 1981 as the point to end this study was not arbitrary. On the first day of the following year, new franchise periods began for the ITV programme contractors, some of which were new arrivals to the network. Even more importantly, Channel Four began broadcasting in November 1982. The new network (and its Welsh counterpart, S4C), as well as new cable television services and the increasing spread of home video machines, brought major changes to the programming of films on television. The book therefore concludes with a brief Epilogue looking at some of the developments emerging at the start of the 1980s and commenting on what has been called a 'televisualised' film culture.

The text is supplemented by numerous charts and tables, and general film statistics are provided at the end of the book in Appendices 1 (BBC) and 2 (ITV). Appendix 3 provides details of the films acquired by FIDO, Appendix 4 is a list of abbreviations and acronyms and Appendix 5 is a guide to the key television personnel mentioned in the text.

The book's main title has been attached to it since I first began thinking seriously about the subject in 2011. The subsequent publication of Joe Moran's history of TV-watching in Britain, *Armchair Nation* (2013), led me briefly to consider *Fireside Cinema* as an alternative, to avoid suspicion of direct influence. But *Armchair Cinema* has other precedents too. It was used in 1974–75 as an umbrella title by Thames Television for a group of made-for-TV movies from its subsidiary Euston Films. The reference point was clearly ITV's long-established drama strand *Armchair Theatre*, the key difference being that Euston's 'plays' were shot on film.[35] More recently, in his 2022 booklet *British Cinema: A Very Short Introduction*, Charles Barr has identified 'armchair cinema' as a middle phase in the history of public access to old movies, coming between 'repertory cinema' as it once existed in the form of specialised exhibition halls and 'desktop cinema' in the sense of streaming films online.[36]

Although I cannot claim to have coined the phrase, *Armchair Cinema* therefore still seems to me the most apt title for my project. As the passages by Chris Dunkley and Laurence Marks quoted as epigraphs to this Introduction make clear, the armchair image evokes the casualness, comfort and convenience of domestic film-viewing along with the possibility of rapt, intimate engagement in the isolation of a private space. One aspect of the convergence of cinema and television that I have not seen addressed in print is the way that many modern cinemas, especially those claiming to offer a 'luxury' service, have been replacing their traditional theatre seating with larger, more elaborately upholstered and sometimes reclining armchairs, apparently modelled on those to which spectators are presumed to have become accustomed in their own homes. Part of the attraction of moviegoing in the past – during the 1930s Depression, say – was the notion that cinemas were infinitely more comfortable places to spend one's leisure time than the houses of most ordinary people. Today, the standard of theatrical comfort is set by a symbol of the transplanted middle-class home rather than by an exotic picture palace. Armchair cinema has thus become the benchmark for going out to the movies; but it began, and arguably belongs, in front of the telly.

Sources and Acknowledgements

The book has been a long time in gestation. As noted above, I began active preparation and research in 2011; after several interruptions for other projects, writing and editing were completed in 2023. But my interest in the subject had been fomenting long before. I date it originally from September 1974, when, aged nine, I started buying *Radio Times* as a way of discovering in advance what films were due to be shown by the BBC. I began keeping lists of films on TV, an enlarged version of which should in time have an online showcase of its own. The idea of turning this lifelong interest into a full-scale research project occurred to me while helping staff at my university library sort through its vast collection of off-air recordings on VHS. There's a story here, I thought. My grateful thanks therefore go to the librarians at Sheffield Hallam University (SHU), especially Linda Purdy and Mags Boot, for indulging and inspiring me.

I have relied very largely on primary sources to construct this history. The most important are housed in three major archives: the BBC Written Archives Centre (BBC WAC) in Caversham; the ITA, IBA, ITC and Cable Authority Archives (hereinafter IBA Archives) in the Sir Michael Cobham Library at Bournemouth University; and British Film Institute Special Collections, now based at the Reuben Library at BFI Southbank. At the latter, I drew particularly on the FIDO Collection, the Michael Balcon Collection and the IBA Clippings Files. Staff at all three institutions facilitated access and provided helpful advice. I am grateful especially to Katie Ankers and Jessica Hogg at BBC WAC, Stephen Parton, Phil Stocks, Louise Tucker and Clare West at Bournemouth University, and Sarah Currant, Jonny Davies and Nathalie Morris at the BFI.

This study has necessarily been shaped by the strengths and limitations of these sources. The BBC material is richest in the earlier part of the period covered, from the 1930s to the 1950s. It thins out in the 1960s and 1970s, and aside from some later Broadcasting Research reports the relevant files end in 1979. The IBA material, by contrast, is strongest from 1965 onward and there is a wealth of material for the 1970s and 1980s. If the book's coverage of these two organisations seems uneven, that is partly attributable to the material I have been able to access. No doubt there is a great deal more that I have missed and I may well return to these magnificent archives for follow-up studies.

Besides unpublished documents, I have also trawled newspaper and trade-paper sources. SHU's online library gateway gave me access to several digital newspaper archives, including those of *The Times* and *Sunday Times*, the *Guardian* and *Observer* and the *Daily Mail*, and to ProQuest's Entertainment Industry Magazine Archive (EIMA), embracing journals such as *Variety*, *The Stage and Television*

Today and *Screen International*. In the basement stack of SHU's Adsetts building, housing its library, I have also ploughed through many reels of analogue microfilm, scouring trade journals such as *Kinematograph* (*Kine*) *Weekly* and *Variety*. But no publications have been more useful than the weekly programme listings magazines, *Radio Times* and *TV Times*, along with the latter's various regional predecessors. I now have my own archive of these journals sitting behind me at home as I type this. I am grateful to their current copyright controllers for permission to quote extracts and reproduce images from them: Ralph Montagu at Immediate Media Co and Phoebe Castledine and Claire Shepherd at Future Publications Ltd.

Quotations from and references to most primary and major secondary sources are cited in abbreviated form in the endnotes. Full details of books, book chapters and journal articles are listed in the Bibliography, along with a list of the archival files consulted. Articles in newspapers and trade-papers are cited only in the notes; those cited without page numbers are usually from the IBA Clippings Files.

Several people involved with television in an executive, editorial, technical or creative capacity kindly submitted to interviews or sent me personal communication. While in most cases they have not been quoted in the text, they nevertheless gave me an enhanced understanding of television's internal operation and helped undergird the archival research: Geoff Brown, Kevin Brownlow, Alex Cox, Jon Dixon, Allen Eyles, Sir Paul Fox, Sir Christopher Frayling, Bill Gilbert, Tim Highsted, the late Derek Hill, the late Veronica Hitchcock, Steve Jenkins and David Robinson. They are not, of course, responsible for any misunderstandings, which are mine alone. Reg Roberts helpfully provided access to internal records of the BBC's film acquisitions and transmissions from 1967 onwards.

I am indebted to all the artists, graphic designers, illustrators and photographers whose work enriches the book. For granting, arranging or helping with permissions, besides those already mentioned, I thank Tessa Bellamy, Norman Boyd, Mick Brownfield, Jeff Cummins, Sir Christopher Frayling, Ellen Graham, Kate Powell at BBC Photo Archive, Cameron Sterling, Mark Thomas and Sadie Williams. I am most especially grateful to Steve Kirkham of Tree Frog Communications for his cover design and for going above and beyond the call of duty in advising on design matters.

My personal thanks also go to the many friends and colleagues who, over the years, have expressed an interest in the progress of this project and offered encouragement or material help. Richard Farmer unearthed a pertinent joke from the BBC radio show *Educating Archie*, Jenny Stewart found a useful article about the ratings of films on television and Julian Upton kindly loaned me a copy of his research on the broadcast of widescreen films. My random posts on social media have resulted in valuable ideas and feedback; for example, the title of Chapter 8 was provided by Brad Stevens following an appeal for suggestions. I have also had several more formal opportunities to share work in progress. Sergio Angelini asked me to write an article for *Viewfinder*, the journal of Learning on Screen (formerly the British Film and Video Council); Nicky Smith persuaded me to give an online presentation in the seminar series she organised for Westminster Libraries; Andy Medhurst and Melanie Williams invited me to deliver guest seminar papers at the universities of Sussex and East Anglia, respectively; and there have been several opportunities to speak on the subject at SHU.

The Shiers Trust gave me a small grant that covered BBC licensing costs; I am grateful to the members of the awarding panel, who have waited a long time to see the results. SHU supplemented this by reimbursing other research, licensing and publication expenses, as well as providing intermittent remission from teaching and a semester of research leave, without which the book would have taken several more years to complete. I am indebted for support of many kinds to fellow SHU staff, especially Doug Hamilton, Chris Hopkins, Lisa Hopkins, Suzanne Speidel and David Waddington. I took the photographs of film prints featured in the illustrations at our projectionist Daniel Judge's winding bench. I also thank my editors at Edinburgh University Press, Sam Johnson, Gillian Leslie and Kelly O'Brien, for their understanding, patience and forbearance. The anonymous readers appointed to peer-review both my original proposal and the draft manuscript made many useful suggestions that I have incorporated or adapted when producing the final version. My previous publisher, Bruce Sachs at Tomahawk Press, waited so long for the book that he decided to retire before the manuscript could be delivered. I thank him for his belief in me and for agreeing to waive the contract and allow the project to be passed on to EUP.

My final, most heartfelt thanks go to my cat, Barney, my constant companion throughout the writing of this book, who died shortly before its publication. Farewell, dear friend.

Image Credits

Most of the illustrations in this book were scanned directly from contemporary television listings magazines: *Radio Times*, *TVTimes* (no space) and the latter's predecessors, *TV Times* (with space), *Look Westward* and *The Viewer*. They are intended to evoke the creative ways in which films on television were once promoted and to pay tribute to the lustrous artwork and imaginative designs that might otherwise seem ephemeral, unseen after their first publication. Every effort has been made to identify, contact and acknowledge the rights holders of the original images. In the event that any have been inadvertently overlooked, they are invited to contact the publisher so that appropriate credits can be added to any subsequent editions.

Figures 0.1, 1.1, 1.4, 6.1, 13.2: BBC Photo Library © BBC copyright content reproduced courtesy of the British Broadcasting Corporation. All rights reserved.

Figures 0.2, 6.4: *Radio Times* © Immediate Media Co. Artwork © Frank Bellamy.

Figures 1.2, 1.3: *Television* © Television Press Ltd.

Figures 2.1, 11.1, 11.2: Author's copyright.

Figures 2.2, 2.3, 3.4, 4.2, 5.2, 7.1, 11.2a, 12.1, 12.3b: *Radio Times* © Immediate Media Co.

Figures 3.1, 3.2, 3.3, 4.1: *TV Times* © Associated-Rediffusion Ltd.

Figures 4.3, 8.2, 12.2: *Radio Times* © Immediate Media Co. Artwork © Mick Brownfield.

Figure 5.1: *Look Westward* © The Dickens Press Ltd.

Figure 5.3: *Halliwell's Television Guide* © Granada Publishing Ltd.

Figure 5.4: *The Viewer* © The Dickens Press Ltd.

Figures 6.2, 6.3, 7.2, 9.3, 10.1, 11.4b: *TVTimes* © Future Publishing Ltd.

Figure 7.3: *Radio Times* © Immediate Media Co. Artwork © Ralph Steadman.

Figure 7.4: The TV Museum.

Figure 8.1: *Radio Times* © Immediate Media Co. Artwork © Robert Micklewright.

Figure 8.3: Photograph courtesy of Christopher Frayling. Photographer unknown.

Figure 9.1: *Radio Times* © Immediate Media Co. Artwork © David da Silva.

Figure 9.2: IBA Archives, Bournemouth University.

Figure 10.2: *Radio Times* © Immediate Media Co. Artwork © Mark Thomas.

Figure 11.3: *TV World* © Aston Publications Ltd.

Figure 11.4a: *TVTimes* © Future Publishing Ltd. Artwork © Giannetto Coppola.

Figure 12.3a: *Radio Times* © Immediate Media Co. Photograph © Ellen Graham.

Figure 13.1: *Radio Times* © Immediate Media Co. Artwork © Jeff Cummins.

Notes

1 Besides Porst, *Broadcasting Hollywood*, and Segrave, *Movies at Home*, the literature on the use of feature films by American television is far more extensive than that on UK television. See, for example: Davis, 'Small Screen, Smaller Pictures: Television Broadcasting and B-Movies in the Early 1950s'; Gomery, *Shared Pleasures*, 247–75; Hilmes, *Hollywood and Television*, 156–67; Hoyt, *Hollywood Vault*, 142–77; Klinger, *Beyond the Multiplex*; Lafferty, 'Feature Films on Prime-Time Television', in Balio, *Hollywood in the Age of Television*, 235–56; Litman, 'The Economics of the Television Market for Theatrical Movies', in Kindem, *The American Movie Industry*, 308–21; Pierce, '"Senile celluloid": Independent Exhibitors, the Major Studios and the Fight over Features on Television, 1939–1956'; and Schnapper, 'The Distribution of Theatrical Feature Films to Television'.

2 Kerr, 'Television Programmes about the Cinema: The Making of *Moving Pictures*', in Hill and McLoone, *Big Picture, Small Screen*, 133–47. Disappointingly, the book contains no chapter about film programming on television.

3 The three dissertations, all based at the University of Portsmouth, are: Keene, 'Channel 4 Television: Film Policy and Film Programming, 1982–2011'; Mayne, 'Channel 4 and British Film: An Assessment of Cultural Impact, 1982–1998'; and Woods, 'A Critical Survey of BBC Films, 1988–2013'. See also *Journal of British Cinema and Television* 11, no. 4 (2014), eds. Paul McDonald and Justin Smith; Mayne, *Channel 4 and the British Film Industry, 1982–1998*.

4 Andrews, *Television and British Cinema*, 2–3.

5 Ibid, 7–18.

6 Alan Hunter, 'Television Is for the Home', *Radio Times*, 10 February 1939, 10. On the notions of immediacy and intimacy that characterised early television discourse, see Jacobs, *The Intimate Screen*, 28–32.

7 S. John Woods, 'Looking at Television', *Radio Times*, 23 July 1937, 10.

8 Dallas Bower, 'Television and the Films', *Radio Times*, 15 January 1937, Television Supplement, 5.

9 Swift, *Adventures in Vision*, 185.

10 Christopher Barry, 'We're Not Doomed Yet', *Television Weekly* 5, no. 7 (October 1952): 23.

11 S. Seeman, 'The Cinema and Television', quoted in 'An Insight into the Cinema–Television Conflict', *Scan* 2, no. 1 (May 1949): 15.

12 More O'Ferrall, et al, 'Television's Challenge to the Cinema', in Manvell, *The Cinema 1950*, 171. See also Gorham with Neilson Baxter, 'Television: A Medium in Its Own Right?', in Manvell and Baxter, *The Cinema 1951*, 131–46; and Clarke, 'Television Prospect: Some Reflexions of a Documentary Film-maker', in Manvell and Neilson Baxter, *The Cinema 1952*, 174–87.

13 Ernest Lindgren, 'Television', *Sight and Sound* 19, no. 7 (November 1950): 302; and 19, no. 8 (December 1950): 340.

14 Peter D. Cross, 'Television – the End of Film?', *Sight and Sound* 17, no. 67 (Autumn 1948): 131–2; Ware, 'TV Launches a Film Offensive', in Noble, *Movie Stars: A Film World Book*, 19; 'The Front Page: How Goes the Enemy?', *Sight and Sound* 23, no. 4 (April–June 1954): 175.

15 René Clair, 'Television and Cinema', *Sight and Sound* 19, no. 9 (January 1951): 372.

16 Andrew Miller Jones, 'Television and Cinema', *The Penguin Film Review* 6 (April 1948), 50–1.

17 Gorham, 'Television: A Medium in Its Own Right?', 140. Of course, the availability of instant playback to later generations of filmmakers is a result of importing TV technology into film production.

18 Quoted in Ware, 'TV Launches a Film Offensive'.

19 Gerald Beadle, 'Opening the Window on the World', *Radio Times*, 25 October 1957, 3.

20 Hilary Corke, 'Not Quite Innocent Deceptions', *The Listener*, 31 December 1959, 1172.

21 John Braine, 'Life at the TV Top', *TV Times* (Northern), 26 October 1962, 9.

22 See Trodd, 'Introduction to Trodd Index', in Pilling and Canham, *The Screen on the Tube: Filmed TV Drama*, 53; and Sexton, 'Celluloid Television Culture'.

23 Robert Stéphane-Clausse, editor of *Les Cahiers RTB* of Radiodiffusion Télévision belge – Institut des Services Communs, in the Edinburgh Film Festival publication *What Is a Television Film?*, 36.

24 *What Is a Television Film*, 30.

25 Williams, *Television: Technology and Cultural Form*, 64.

26 Stuart Hall, 'Television and Culture', *Sight and Sound* 45, no. 4 (Autumn 1976): 247. The article was adapted from Hall's own 1971 report for UNESCO, *Innovation and Decline in the Treatment of Culture on British Television*. An alternative extract, also containing the material quoted here, was published as 'Technics of the Medium', in Corner and Harvey, *Television Times: A Reader*, 3–10.

27 Chris Dunkley, 'Review', *Radio Times*, 6 March 1975, 66. Despite these caveats, later the same year Dunkley listed *The Ox-Bow Incident* (1943/21.06.1972) and *Carry on Cleo* (1964/26.12.1972) among his recommendations for the week ('Preview', *Radio Times*, 23 October 1975, 19). Note: films are identified on first mention in each chapter by citing in parenthesis the year of their theatrical release, followed by the date of their first known transmission on free-to-air terrestrial television.

28 Leslie Halliwell to Colin Shaw, 30 March 1983, IBA/01021: 3996312.

29 Kermabon, 'Introduction', in Kermabon and Shahani, *Cinema and Television*, 13. The book includes pieces published between 1935 and 1988 by such distinguished critics and theorists as Rudolph Arnheim, Guy Gauthier, Pascal Bonitzer and Serge Daney. Not all their contributions are as hostile to TV as the co-editor's. See also Serge Daney, 'From the Large to the Small Screen' (1987), online at *Serge Daney in English*, http://sergedaney.blogspot.co.uk.

30 Ibid, 14–15. Jean-Luc Godard is also said to have 'once declared that showing a cinema film on television was tantamount to showing a painting on a postcard' ('Technological, Aesthetic and Technical Approaches', 61).

31 Auty, 'But Is It Cinema?', in Auty and Roddick, *British Cinema Now*, 57–70.

32 Jacobs, *The Intimate Screen*; Rolinson, 'The Last Studio System: A Case for British Television Films', in Newland, *Don't Look Now*, 163–74.

33 Aldridge, *The Birth of Television*, 142.

34 My archivist friends would no doubt wish me to point out that modern film prints (those produced since about 1950) are not in fact made from cellulose nitrate stock, so their description as 'celluloid' is a misnomer. Nevertheless, the term persists in colloquial usage.

35 The *Armchair Cinema* series was released as a DVD collection by Network Distribution.

36 Barr, *British Cinema: A Very Short Introduction*, 4–12.

Part One

Organisations and Acquisition

CHAPTER 1

The Magic Box – Television, Tele-cinema and Tele-talkies (1929–39)

> There will scarcely be a home in England to-morrow which will not have its own television screen. You will sit in your armchair after you come home from 'the city,' put a pipe on, switch on your wireless and look at the screen which will be hanging like a picture before your eyes. On that screen you will see perhaps a curtain as in a theatre. The curtain will roll up. ... *C'est tous!* After a minute or so, when you have properly tuned in your televisor, the entertainment, both visible and audible, will commence.
>
> (Shaw Desmond, 'Seeing round the World: What Television Will Mean to YOU',
> *Television* 1, no. 6 [August 1928]: 12)

> In many cases a person who owns a wireless set goes to see the talking films, but he does so only because, at the moment, he has nothing else better to do. He would, indeed, be a very brave man who would venture to predict that when televisors are readily obtainable, and can be attached to an existing wireless receiver, the wireless enthusiast would go to see a talking film when *he will be able to see them* in his own home. It simply will not be done.
>
> (Cyril Sylvester, 'Talkies versus Television', *Television* 2, no. 16 [June 1929]: 169;
> original emphasis)

> I listened to two women armed with shopping baskets, who had dropped in [to a public viewing room] quite as much for a rest as to see the television demonstrations. One of them ... turned to her friend and exclaimed: 'Blimey, Lil, this is too good! If ever we get one of those things at home, we shan't have an excuse to go out to the pictures.'
>
> ('What Viewers Are Saying', *Radio Times*, 26 March 1937, Television Supplement, 4)

Shortly after 9.00pm on Sunday, 14 August 1938, following the news headlines, the BBC Television Service introduced the remainder of the night's broadcast with the following announcement, read by presenter David Hofman:

> Good evening, this is the BBC Television Station at Alexandra Palace. For the first time, and as an experiment, we are televising tonight the whole of a feature film, *The Student of Prague*. Unfortunately we are unable at present to run through this film continuously, and there will therefore be an interval of about three minutes while the film is being shown. Very soon the need for intervals will disappear, but tonight we can only ask for your indulgence.[1]

The need for an interval was due to the fact that the television service currently had only one telecine, the machine required to convert a film image into an electronic signal that could be transmitted over the airwaves (see Figure 1.1). The telecine

Figure 1.1 The Telecine Room at Alexandra Palace, showing the duplicate equipment for televising films, February 1938. BBC Photo Library © BBC.

could handle two 2,000-foot reels at a time, each running around twenty minutes and spliced together, before the reels had to be changed. At 9.43pm, therefore, following the first half, viewers saw two superimposed captions: the film's title and 'Interval of Three Minutes'. A gramophone record of the Overture to Heuberger's *The Opera Ball* was played over the caption until the telecine engineer had completed changing reels and was ready to resume transmission. The music and caption were then faded out before a further announcement introduced the second part of the film. Here Hofman read out the names of the story's original author, Henrik Galeen, the film's director, Arthur Robison, and its principal cast members, including Anton Walbrook and Dorothea Wieck. After a fade-out to a blank screen and silence for five seconds, the film then continued to its conclusion.

Aside from the news, the announcements and the interval music, *The Student of Prague* (1935/14.08.1938) was the only programme televised in regular hours on that date. Normally a day's television broadcasts – which then occupied only one hour in the afternoon on weekdays and up to two in the evening, including weekends – comprised a selection of shorter items, linked by a continuity announcer like Hofman. Some items were transmitted live from the studio at

Alexandra Palace; others were pre-recorded on 35mm film and relayed via tel-ecine. The broadcast of *The Student of Prague* was remarkable not only for its length (a total of nearly 90 minutes including the introductions and intermission) but also for the fact that it was a foreign production, with German dialogue trans-lated by subtitle captions. Yet despite the prefatory announcement, and contrary to most available accounts, it was not in fact the first feature film to be shown on British television – though it was the first to run longer than an hour.[2] Television's first fiction feature originally made for the cinema had been broadcast almost exactly one year before, without fuss or fanfare and without becoming the start of regular or even occasional full-length film broadcasts as *The Student of Prague* was intended, however tentatively, to be. We shall come to these films in due course. Before then, we must see what else went before them.

Early Experiments in Televising Film

Attempts at the television transmission of motion-picture film had begun much earlier than the British Broadcasting Corporation's relatively high-definition broadcasts in the late 1930s. According to Bruce Norman, producer of a BBC documentary on *The Birth of Television*, 'a Boston radio station, WLEX, used film in its occasional telecasts as early as 1928'.[3] The Hungarian electrical engineer Dénes von Mihály developed a method of scanning and transmitting both still and moving images, the former demonstrated at the Berlin Radio Exhibition in September 1928, though he claimed to have first achieved this in July 1919. Reporting in 1929 on a private demonstration of Mihály's motion-picture trans-missions, which scanned each frame with 900 elements (thirty rows of thirty lines), the British journal *Television* described the results as not 'actual television but tele-cinema'.[4] This was a distinction that underpinned a good deal of early research and which persisted long after.

The leading British pioneer of television technology was John Logie Baird, who in 1925 and 1926 had given the first press and public demonstrations of the trans-mission of live images by means of television. Baird achieved a practical telecine setup by adapting his 'flying spot' scanning device for use in conjunction with a film projector. His biographer Russell W. Burns explains:

> In this method of generating televised images, a standard cinematograph projector was adapted so that the individual film images were scanned by an aperture disc scanner/photocell arrangement. The method has the advantage that the sensitivity and colour response of the photocell are less critical than for direct television, since the cell has to distinguish between black and white only, and the flux of the cell can be very large.[5]

The different mechanisms involved in producing cinematic and televisual moving images required the use of a continuous-motion projector (one which does not involve each individual film frame being momentarily held static, as is the case in cinema projection). A German-made Mechau projector was acquired by Baird for this purpose from a cinema in Charing Cross Road and adapted for him by D.R. Campbell. According to fellow engineer T.H. Bridgewater, Campbell 'made a small projector that shone its beam into the gate of this film machine where the image appeared and, lo and behold, through the disc on the receiving end, was a continuous image and from that moment on we had the means to show film on television'.[6]

The earliest transmission of film images in Britain for which details are available occurred on 19 August 1929, at a Baird press demonstration in London; the film used was a record of the stage comedian George Robey's drag act. Variously referred to in published sources as *The Bride* or *The Blushing Bride*, this seven-minute short apparently consisted entirely of head-and-shoulder close-ups, Baird's scanning mechanism being too insensitive to variations in light and, at 30 lines, too low in resolution to permit the clear, detailed representation of a more complex image.[7] The *Daily Telegraph*'s correspondent commented that, despite its technical limitations, 'the demonstration was sufficiently convincing to evoke a vision of the not-so-distant future when a television cabinet and an armchair at home might take the place of the cinema itself'.[8]

Most notable about the Robey film was that it had a synchronised soundtrack, using the variable-area system in which the sound information is striped along the left-hand edge of the 35mm film strip and is read by a photo-electric cell on the film projector. Another reporter, for *The Times*, commented of the demonstration: 'The voice transmission was clearer than is usual in the cinema theatres, and the synchronised pictures were of the standard which has so far been attained in television development.' That this was not the first time that film material per se had been scanned and transmitted by Baird is evident from other remarks made in this report: 'The broadcasting of films unaccompanied by sound proved in practice, however, to have very little entertainment value, and efforts have for some time been directed to the realization of the "tele-talkie".'[9]

The Robey demonstration took place six weeks before the start of a series of experimental transmissions by the Baird Television Development Company using the studio facilities of the BBC ('the Corporation'). These had been arranged by order of the Postmaster-General, though the transmissions were primarily for the purpose of technical development and engineering tests and were not part of the Corporation's regular programme output due to its reservations about the technology. Nevertheless, members of the public who had purchased or built their own domestic 'televisors' could receive the signals, transmitted outside normal broadcast hours for half an hour at a time, five days a week. They began at 11.00am on 30 September 1929 and continued, in one form or another, until 11 September 1935 (see Figure 1.2). Although it was envisaged from the start that the television broadcasts would be in sound as well as vision, because of limited available bandwidth it was not until 31 March 1930 that both could be transmitted simultaneously and synchronously, with the dual signals on different wavelengths carried by two separate broadcasting stations and combined at the point of reception. *The Times* commented:

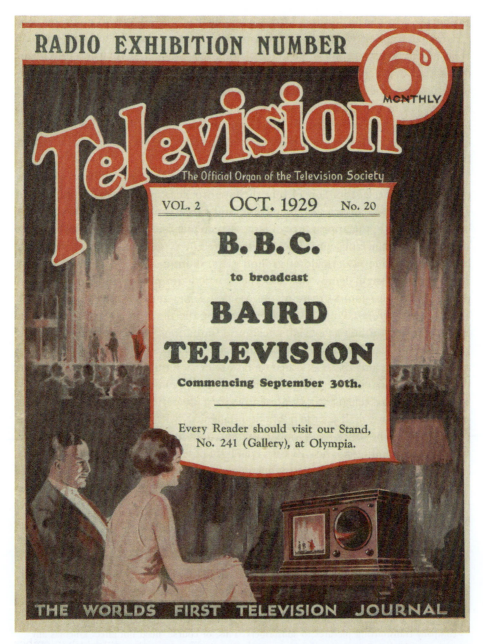

Figure 1.2 The Television Society's magazine *Television* marks the start in 1929 of Baird's experimental broadcasts via the BBC. *Television* © Television Press Ltd.

A particularly noteworthy feature of the dual transmission was that there was no lag between vision and sound such as often destroys the illusion of the 'talkies'. Such exact synchronism is, of course, brought about automatically by the practically simultaneous transmission of both television and sound signals.[10]

Sydney A. Moseley, a leading advocate of television development and later also a Baird biographer, wrote that 'Germany in particular sees in "tele-cinema" or "tele-talkies" the stepping stone to television proper', again invoking the common distinction between the televising of live subjects and of pre-recorded material, with the former considered superior in kind to the latter. Moseley commented further: 'For myself I look forward to a leading personage *being televised direct* and not second-hand from a film.'[11] *The Times*'s report on the Robey demonstration had made a similar point when it referred to 'true television' as distinct from 'transmitting moving transparencies'.[12]

In the summer of 1930, Baird had two further opportunities to demonstrate the potentialities of television: on 14 July, the first broadcast of a live play, Pirandello's *The Man with the Flower in His Mouth*; and three times daily for three weeks beginning 28 July, the appearance of large-screen television as an 'act' at a London variety theatre, the Coliseum. The screen erected on stage, measuring six feet high by three feet wide, was made of ground glass, illuminated from behind by over 2,000 separate small lamps that together carried the picture information. Two prominent critics, James Agate of the *Sunday Times* and Robert Herring of the *Manchester Guardian*, could not help comparing the new medium to the cinema. Both remarked on how television's technical limitations, notably the conspicuous visual 'flicker' caused by the slow frame rate and low resolution, recalled early motion pictures, and also speculated on how television might develop in relation to the contemporary cinema. Agate commented: 'There can be no doubt in all unprejudiced minds that television will presently attain the perfection of the talkie – that, in other words, we shall see the talkie simultaneously with its creation.'[13]

Herring, on the other hand, hoped that it would 'not repeat the mistakes of the talkies' by depending too heavily on trivial light entertainment for its material: 'we do not need another disseminating channel for things of which there are already too much'. Herring also echoed comments made by Baird, that television as a transmission medium would one day come to replace theatrical film projection. His words were prescient in anticipating the prospect of direct competition as well as influence:

> It is because I think television is likely to be a development of kinema [*sic*] more than a thing in itself that I consider it here; in America the film people are in panic about television, which they regard as a menace only to be opposed by wide screen. But Mr Baird himself has stated that in his opinion 'television will be the final method of supplying films' – a master film company transmitting pictures to subscribers. This, of course, need not affect kinemas any more than have home projectors. The public, lacking television, can see televised films on big screens in the theatres, some of which may be run for showing of concurrent events, just as the Avenue Pavilion is now devoted to news reels.[14]

The performances at the Coliseum included not only the Robey film but at least one other tele-talkie: a filmed record of a speech by the aforementioned Sydney Moseley, now 'Director of Baird's Television Programme', who appeared live on stage while the film was being presented on screen. The significance of this first *theatrical* presentation of a film transmitted by means of television was apparent to the *Sunday Times*, which commented, again echoing Baird: 'The talkie fore-shadows the day when all cinemas will be equipped with television screens, and will receive their programme televised from a master film from a central studio.'[15] A notable feature of the tele-talkie was that the picture not only appeared clearer than one of a live subject, but also potentially enlarged the range of subjects that television could represent, when both the low resolution of the television scanner and the narrow wavelength available for broadcast placed severe restrictions on image content: 'The Tele-talkie makes possible the transmission of any subject within the capabilities of the cinema camera, and its reception by anybody having the necessary receiving apparatus.'[16]

Mystery surrounds another tele-talkie circa 1930. The BFI National Archive holds a short film, labelled 'Baird Television', featuring the actor Seymour Hicks speaking direct to camera. He states in his three-minute speech:

> We're all of us assisting at an epoch-making event. It's the first talking film to be televised in the history of the world. Think of that. And it is all British. Cheers from all parts of the house. It's a film, I may tell you, ladies and gentlemen, that's been made by British International Pictures and has been directed by our greatest producer, Alfred Hitchcock. And it's being transmitted from the Baird Television Company's studio in Long Acre, London, England.

The 35mm film stock dates the material to 1930; it was apparently donated to the Archive in 1959 by BIP's successor, the Associated British Picture Corporation. But no contemporary records have thus far been unearthed to confirm the exact date or manner of its transmission or those of the Hitchcock film apparently being introduced. The BFI's records note that the latter is 'believed to be' the film commonly thought of as the first British sound feature, *Blackmail* (1929/07.11.1976).

However, the authors of a recent book on Hitchcock's 'lost' films speculate that Hicks might be introducing not a feature but specially-shot footage made for test purposes, possibly presented at one of the Coliseum performances – though no known press reports refer to it, unlike Moseley's own speech film.[17] The manner of Hicks's address and the remark about 'all parts of the house' suggest that it was intended for presentation in a theatre or cinema. It's possible that the first part of the speech – framed in a vertical aspect ratio and blurrier in quality than the rest, which is shot conventionally – was photographed from a large screen during a test transmission of the pre-filmed footage and then spliced together with the latter part. But this is only an attempt to read what is on the screen, there being no available documentation to confirm one way or another. In any event, unless this footage was actually shot and the accompanying film transmitted in 1929, before the Robey demonstration (and prior to being printed onto the 1930 stock held by the BFI Archive), it was certainly not 'the first' sound-film transmission and is highly unlikely to have preceded a full-length broadcast of an entire feature, whatever the occasion.

I had begun to think this mystery unsolvable until I asked for clues on the Facebook page of Kaleidoscope, the organisation that seeks to retrieve and conserve lost TV material. A plausible explanation was offered by group member Phil Nichols:

> The [Hitchcock] book refers to Hicks INTRODUCING a film. But if you read Hicks' own words as quoted, he may be referring to the very film that Hicks is in. (In other words, he might be saying: what you are watching RIGHT NOW is the first piece of talking film ever to have been shown on TV.)[18]

If Nichols is correct, as seems likely to me, the solution was literally in front of our eyes! Of course this still does not answer the question of how, where and when the film was shown publicly (if it ever was). But at least it has the potential of identifying the 'missing' film itself – and adding a rediscovered work to Hitchcock's filmography.[19]

BBC Broadcasts Baird

Another claim of a first was made by Sydney Moseley, again in the pages of *Television* magazine, in an article entitled 'The First Tele-Cine Broadcast' (see Figure 1.3). Moseley referred to the transmission of 'a piece of test film' from the Baird studios via the BBC, which took place in the regular experimental broadcast at midnight on Friday, 6 March 1931 (that is, at the end of Friday's radio programmes). He writes: 'I do not think I am betraying any secret when I say that the BBC engineer in charge of the transmissions at Savoy Hill himself rang up and informed the Baird engineer how successful he thought the transmission had been.' A further, 'more formal transmission' took place in the 11.00am test slot on the following Monday, 9 March, and about this Moseley is more specific: 'a piece of an old Charlie Chaplin film was shown'. He goes on:

> Readers will want to know what special technical considerations this needed. First of all, let me make it clear that no special film was used. A film-renting company was asked in the ordinary way to lend the Baird Company a film, and from three that were sent, two were used. The film was transmitted through the tele-cine projector, which has been in the Baird laboratories for the past three or four years.
>
> The projector, however, is, of course, an improvement on that hitherto used for experimental purposes.
>
> The projector is situated in one little room and from there a landline couples it up with the ordinary television transmitter. Reports received from various parts of the country are unanimously in praise of the innovation.

Moseley himself comments that the picture quality of the transmission was variable due to the material not having been shot with the needs of television in mind:

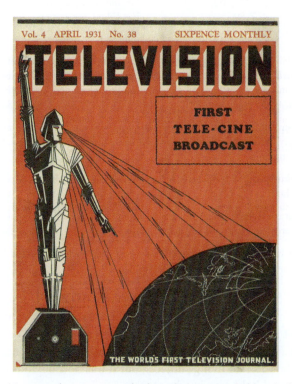

Figure 1.3 *Television* magazine announces the first telecine transmissions via the BBC in 1931. *Television* © Television Press Ltd.

Take the case of the Chaplin film. When he was chasing or being chased by his inevitable, implacable foe round the park seat, this was clearly seen, together with Charlie's inimitable methods of 'downing' those who have the misfortune to cross him, and, of course, when there was a 'close-up' this was far better still. Charlie's every action was clearly portrayed, but when one was asked to look at a church steeple, for instance, miles in the background, it became quite evident that this part of the film would be of no use for television production at its present stage.[20]

It ought to be possible to identify the unnamed Chaplin film using this description of the action, but there are at least half a dozen Chaplin shorts set partly or wholly in parks, and none that I have looked at contains a shot recognisable as a church steeple. However, in *A Jitney Elopement* (1915/27.09.1975), the second reel of which begins in a park in which Chaplin ingeniously 'downs' several opponents around a bench and is shown smoking a cigarette in medium close-up, a climactic car chase includes several buildings in the background. Could one of these have been mistaken by Moseley for a church?[21]

A third and final telecine test on 13 March featured a boxing match. Moseley quotes from a dozen letters received from viewers situated as far afield as Worthing, Southall, Rochdale, Sunderland, Bristol, Acton and Guildford, all of whom had written in praise of the tele-cinema transmissions:

The short television film came through almost, if not quite, as clearly as the rest of the programme. A most promising experiment and it should be repeated.

I have witnessed one of the biggest strides in the science of television, namely the tele-ciné [*sic*] film. I was thrilled at the first part of the programme, but when the boxing match appeared I became spellbound. Every little detail stood out on the screen and was quite equal in purity to a cinema film.

For a film transmission I should consider this reception very fine. The close-up picture of 'Charlie' was very clear and as good as many direct pictures I have received. Oh, how I long for all-day transmissions!

I hope that in future, you will be able to transmit cinematograph pictures once or twice a week for the full half hour.

Without a doubt these films would be a greater interest to the public than the usual head and shoulders, as there is more idea of movement, and we hope you will continue with them.

The audience I had was extremely appreciative and much impressed, and hoped that you would give us some more films in your future transmissions.

Moseley summed up by noting that 'a new source of entertainment by television has been discovered', though he could not help adding the by-now standard rider that 'it must not be forgotten that television proper is likely to be more attractive in the long run'. Tele-cinema was still regarded as being of secondary importance to the 'direct television' of living subjects, but it was now obvious that it could not be ignored and even held certain advantages:

Tele-cinema was, in the first instance, regarded by Mr Baird as a retrograde step. When I first saw a demonstration in the laboratories some years ago I agreed with Mr Baird that it was not half so interesting as seeing the image which was actually there – in the flesh. But I have to confess that the technical progress of tele-cinema has been so rapid that there may be no alternative but to offer the public films in their homes as well as images first-hand.[22]

Baird's was not the only British company to experiment with television in this period, or with the transmission of films. In early January 1931, His Master's Voice Gramophone Company (HMV) gave a demonstration of its own equipment for projecting 'scenes from kinema films' at an exhibition by the Physical and Optical Society in South Kensington.[23] In August 1932 the BBC itself took over responsibility for providing the programme content of the Baird test transmissions, initially produced by the Baird Company at its Long Acre studio, but the broadcasts remained experimental.[24] In December, another rival to Baird, Electric and Musical Industries (EMI), provided the Corporation with a demonstration of its own television apparatus, built by the Marconi radio company.[25] In contrast to the portrait-shaped screen first used by Baird, EMI's system produced an image 'in the landscape proportions of 5:4, an aspect ratio of 1.25:1'.[26] The following year, the BBC announced that it had set up a new ultra-short-wave transmitter on the roof of Broadcasting House as part of its own 'regular experimental work', which involved 'using both sound and visual signals, including cinematograph films'.[27]

On the same day that this was reported, the Baird Company itself demonstrated the successful 'reproductions of films and various cartoons' in an exhibition for the British Association (for the Advancement of Science) in Leicester. This demonstration was notable for the use of an eight-inch-square screen on a cathode-ray tube (CRT). The CRT gave increased clarity and luminosity to the image and 'showed very considerable improvement ... in the matter of detail and absence of flicker' compared to previous demonstrations.[28] The screen employed 120 lines of resolution; according to the *Observer*'s film critic C.A. Lejeune, the company had 'chosen films in which the peculiar black-and-white quality of the photography has been particularly suitable for demonstration, and the experiment was remarkably successful'. Lejeune considered that 'the films that lend themselves most readily to television are cartoons', but gave particular mention to what she considered 'a more significant indication of what television may do for the entertainment world in the near future': the transmission of the last reel of a British feature film currently on release in the West End, *I Was a Spy* (1933/21.02.1987). Lejeune ended the report with her own prognostication:

> Television, as a common form of entertainment, will not come to-day or to-morrow or even the next day. Too much British and American money is tied up in the talkies for that. But when the next world slump in moving pictures arrives, as it is bound to arrive sooner or later, the companies that have equipped themselves with television are going to have things all their own way. The next entertainment will be the telefilm, and it will go into a million homes where the silent film and the talking film have never been able to penetrate. It will create a new audience and demand a new type of production. There will be a whole new set of art dogmas and a whole new batch of funerals in the industry. But we can no more stop it than we can stop the steady march of the seasons. Entertainment never looks back.[29]

Baird had taken out a long lease on Crystal Palace as his own broadcast station; further 'high-definition' transmissions from there were also initially to be from films. Meanwhile, the BBC announced that it would experiment on its own account with the possibilities of high-definition television by carrying out two series of tests, using equipment provided by the Baird Company and Marconi-EMI respectively. But it was also open to approaches by other companies, and furthermore planned to discontinue transmissions using Baird's 30-line system after its contractual arrangement expired in March 1934 (though in fact they continued until 11 September 1935).[30]

Summing up the state of technological developments in August 1934, Professor E.V. Appleton commented that 'high-definition television broadcast from an elevated sender [i.e., a high mast] by ultra-short waves and interpreted as a picture on the screen of a cathode-ray tube is likely to provide a service of real entertainment value'.[31] Early the following year, the report of a Government committee chaired by Lord Selsdon concurred and gave the go-ahead for a regular public television service to be delivered by the BBC.[32] It was to be funded by the existing radio licence fee of 10 shillings per annum and overseen by an independent

'Advisory Committee appointed by the Postmaster-General', also to be chaired by Selsdon. The report recommended a resolution of 'not fewer than 240 lines a picture, with a minimum picture frequency of 25 a second'. It gave no direction on the type of programmes to be offered but recommended time restrictions on the service: 'An hour's transmission in the morning or afternoon which will give facilities for trade demonstration, and, say, two hours in the evening will probably suffice.' Television was seen as 'a natural adjunct to sound broadcasting' and the Selsdon Report envisaged that 'the time may come when a sound broadcasting service entirely unaccompanied by television will be almost as rare as the silent film is to-day'.[33]

As for the type of television system to be used, the report recognised that in the current state of ongoing development and research it would have been inappropriate to choose one over the others, and that an entirely unrestricted 'patents pool' would have been impracticable. Instead it recommended 'an extended trial of two systems, under strictly comparable conditions, by installing them side by side at a station in London where they should be used alternately – and not simultaneously – for a public service'.[34] As the two most advanced systems in use at that time, Baird and Marconi-EMI were chosen for the 'extended trial', each being used on alternating weeks. Baird's system, as previously noted, had a resolution of 240 lines; Marconi-EMI's one of 405 lines. In an ironic twist, while the Marconi-EMI Emitron camera was entirely electronic, the Baird process now used a mechanical technique that involved the use of film, as Andrew Martin explains:

> Baird had two methods of capturing pictures. The Intermediate Film System, for long and medium shots, involved filming action on 17.5mm stock, quickly developing it and then scanning it, a continuous process that meant pictures were only slightly behind the original live performance. Shots were taken from a fixed position film camera and a soundproofed glass booth. The Spotlight Studio, for close-ups, was properly 'live' but involved scanning by infra-red light in an enclosed booth, which was effectively in darkness as far as the performer was concerned. The delay in scanning the film in the former process made it very difficult to synchronise with the Spotlight studio.[35]

Baird's telecine system, on the other hand, was claimed to produce superior picture quality to that of its rival. According to Bruce Norman,

> All that EMI could do to provide a telecine picture was to try to adapt one of their electronic studio cameras and point it at the gate of a standard film projector with the film travelling at the rate of 25 frames a second – the same rate as television pictures are built up. If the film was bright then the pictures were reasonable. If the film was dense then they were terrible.[36]

In the event, Baird was not to last the course; by the time a feature film was transmitted in full by the BBC, his company had lost the race to Marconi-EMI.

The BBC and the Film Industry

When, in early 1935, the BBC was authorised to set up the world's first regular, high-definition television service, it was by no means inevitable that feature films made originally for cinema release would find a place in the schedules.[37] Gerald Cock, the Corporation's first Director of Television, gave the public version of his rationale in a special Television Issue of the BBC's proprietary programme journal *Radio Times*, marking the imminent start of the regular TV service on 2 November 1936:

> Obviously, the film provides the newest and most varied form of entertainment, ready 'canned' for television purposes. From the practical point of view, in saving rehearsal time, studio space, and production difficulties, films ought to be of great value to a pioneer entertainment service such as television.
>
> But televised programmes should be personal to the viewer, and there is something impersonal about films. It may be because they are meant to be shown on a large screen, or because the person who is intended to see them is envisaged as one of a large audience, or there may be some other subtle psychological distinction; but I suggest that feature films are not really suitable broadcast ammunition. As an extreme case, I believe viewers would rather see an actual scene of a rush hour at Oxford Circus directly transmitted to them than the latest in film musicals costing £100,000 – though I do not expect to escape unscathed with such an opinion.[38]

Thus both the immediacy and the intimacy of television were thought to militate against the incursion onto the airwaves of the products of its large-screen cousin. These qualities offered, as Cock suggested, the advantages that television could boast in the absence of the big budgets enjoyed by the film industry (in relative terms, even as far as the always-in-crisis British cinema was concerned). The restricted daily broadcasting hours also meant that a balanced programme of short items would provide more varied fare for the limited audience available than a single long one.

As we shall see, there were other reasons for not showing theatrical features on television besides those Cock outlined or the mechanical difficulties of transmitting long-form films. But in his article Cock also hinted at the potential utility of film material. The strain, as well as the cost, of rehearsing and staging live studio broadcasts night after night, day after day, could be relieved if an alternative form of programming was available, especially in the event of emergencies such as technical breakdowns. A proportion of pre-recorded output was therefore essential both for practical purposes and for programme variety, while the cost of producing filmed material meant that, especially at the outset of the television service, much of it had to be bought in instead.

Cock and his staff were therefore faced with the task, only eighteen months before broadcasts were due to begin, of acquiring such pre-existing material as might be needed for programming purposes. The most likely source was the commercial film industry, which, as well as producing and distributing features, also dealt in a wide range of short films with which cinemas could themselves construct a varied programme to satisfy their diverse audiences. Shorts each comprised one or two reels (around ten or twenty minutes in length) and typically included, for example, comedies and musical novelties; 'interest' films of a documentary nature, such as travelogues; animated cartoons; and, most importantly as far as television was concerned, newsreels.

In the 1930s, five different companies produced fortnightly newsreels for distribution to British cinemas. Each was a subsidiary or an affiliate of one of the major film renters: British Movietone (co-owned by Twentieth Century-Fox and the Rothermere news organisation), Gaumont British, Pathé, Paramount and Universal. For the BBC to set up from scratch its own film news service would have been prohibitively expensive (Cock estimated the likely start-up cost as £25,000), so it was deemed essential to contract with one or more of these companies in order to gain access to their news output. As their parent companies also produced and distributed other types of film such as those just mentioned, the BBC needed an arrangement that would enable the television service to use as much filmed material as it might require on the most reasonable terms possible.

Cock and the Corporation's Director of Business Relations, V.H. Goldsmith, exchanged estimates over the projected costs of the 1,040 programme hours to be scheduled annually (three hours on weekdays, two on Sundays). A total annual budget of £180,000 had been allocated to cover the first year of the service, evenly divided between the cost of programmes and overheads. Cock pointed out that the average cost per hour of programme material could not be estimated accurately. He predicted that film use would be heaviest at the start of the service, making up around three-quarters of the schedule, and that this would 'gradually be reduced to two-thirds or less, as direct televising improves technically. But no "production" will ever compete with a good film, economically or on programme value grounds. We could never afford £15,000 on an individual hour's show!'[39]

As early as February 1935, the BBC's Director General, Sir John Reith, had asked Goldsmith to contact all the major film companies with a view to sounding out the possibility of hiring various kinds of material but without going into the specifics of their planned use. 'I could see no way of speaking to any film interest and attempting to obtain any price agreement when we not only knew little of what we wanted', commented Goldsmith, 'but were unable to disclose to them the reason for our interest. Film people are much too wide awake to be caught napping by a request for prices of films without knowing how and where they are to be shown.'[40]

Two alternative routes for acquiring films presented themselves: either what would now be called an 'output deal' with one or more companies, in which case the BBC would have a blanket contract allowing it to use as much material controlled by a supplier as it desired without having to negotiate separate deals for individual items; or a number of more 'ad hoc' arrangements in which the Corporation bought in only the specific items that it needed on separate terms with different renters. The former option offered convenience and a steady flow of product as long as the supplier delivered the goods; the latter would allow the BBC to pick and choose from a wider range of material, but on less straightforward terms, with no guarantee of availability and possibly at greater expense. It was therefore deemed expedient first to approach one of the majors with a view to striking a blanket deal. As the largest British-owned firm, with the most highly-regarded newsreel service, Gaumont British (G-B) was selected as the first prospective client.

Cock remarked that the G-B scheme amounted 'to buying a call or option on film supplies. Hence the organisation which has the greatest supply available, and the one likely to be least unsympathetic to Television, has been chosen.' He felt that an initial approach to more than one company would result in a greater likelihood of concerted opposition. Cock acknowledged that G-B could not supply all the material needed, but informed Goldsmith that he wanted to ensure 'the largest possible pool to draw upon from *one* (the largest) organisation. That this is the only way to get others in later.' He hoped that 356 hours of material would be made available through the G-B deal and was particularly concerned to acquire the American-produced shorts the company controlled.[41] Cock estimated that, in total,

> 600 hours of film programme, with each film shown three times, half Gaumont-British, and half outside films, would cost £20,000, which gives a considerable margin with which to play if we take £40,000 or even £30,000 as the limit to be spent on film. The figures I have given combine the unusual characteristics of conservatism and speculation![42]

In April 1935, following an informal telephone conversation with Cock, G-B representative Ian Crémieu-Javal received a list of the sorts of material that the BBC required. At this early stage, feature films were considered a real possibility for television showing, along with specially extended versions of newsreels; shorts on topics 'of current interest' as well as on nature and 'educational talks'; TV editions of trailers for new theatrical releases; films for use as experimental test transmissions; and even the preparation of a 'Special Tuning-in Film' to be supervised by Michael Balcon, then head of production at G-B. To reassure the company about the modest extent of the competition the television service would pose to cinema business, Goldsmith explained:

> The effective range of the London television transmitter is limited to about 25 miles. There will only be a limited exhibition both as regards audience and the number of showings. We suggest that the provision of these films should be agreed on a rental basis.[43]

Here Goldsmith was referring specifically to films that had completed their general release in the London area, and had therefore in effect exhausted their commercial value within the region to be covered by TV. As a sop, he also suggested that the Corporation might like to feature the stars of new and forthcoming films in occasional television appearances. Whatever agreement might be arranged, he suggested, should last for an initial period of one year.

The management of G-B at this time was controlled by the Ostrer brothers, Isidore, Maurice and Mark, with another brother, David (the eldest), handling distribution.[44] Any agreement would need to be approved by them, and for this they would need to be assured that their business interests were protected. The Ostrers were also concerned about the reaction the rest of the film industry might have to any dealings G-B entered into with television, and in particular what action might be taken by the three powerful trade associations that defended the interests of the different factions: the Cinematograph Exhibitors' Association (CEA), representing cinema owners; the Kinematograph Renters' Society (KRS), representing distributors; and the film section of the Federation of British Industries (FBI), representing producers. However, among G-B's subsidiaries was Baird Television, which owned the patent on one of the two alternative transmission systems to be used once the television service started, so G-B had some incentive to work with the BBC in helping to set it up.

With the G-B deal set in motion, Goldsmith then approached the next-largest UK-based company, British International Pictures (BIP). He informed its managing director John Maxwell that the BBC's aim was 'to establish a general basis of cooperation with the film industry, and not to confine our activities to the output of any one organisation'.[45] Maxwell, however, thought the proposal raised 'a very big question fraught with repercussions from all branches of the business'. Before agreeing to any cooperation, he wanted first to discuss the matter with the CEA and 'to know what the other producers and distributors intend to do, as if we took action on our own we might find ourselves completely at loggerheads'.[46] Goldsmith suggested a joint approach by G-B and BIP to the film trade associations, and Crémieu-Javal reported that Mark Ostrer and Maxwell had met over lunch:

> Mr Ostrer had been successful in persuading Mr Maxwell to adopt a sympathetic attitude towards the use of films in television. Mr Maxwell even went so far as to say that films might be supplied on what are known technically as re-issue terms. These are the terms applied to good-class films that have been stored for a few years and are re-released, e.g. the [1925] film *Ben-Hur*.[47]

Before the trade bodies could be dealt with, however, another obstacle arose. Goldsmith was informed by Louis Sterling of EMI that Western Electric and the Radio Corporation of America (RCA), the American companies that owned the copyright on the two most widely used sound recording and reproduction systems (respectively, Westrex and Photophone), had 'refused to release their licencees from the condition that films made under their patents must not be used for television broadcasting'.[48] As well as the Hollywood studios, most British production companies, including three of the five newsreels, used one or other of these two systems, though G-B had its own patented system, British Acoustic, and BIP used

Capco. However, the default ban imposed by Western Electric and RCA threatened to deprive television not only of almost all US-produced material, but also those portions of G-B's newsreels that had been filmed in America (the company used Western Electric's Westrex system for such footage). Goldsmith noted that the sound companies' position meant that the ban, if maintained, would probably place up to 90 per cent of film material off limits. He felt that it struck 'at the root of television' and set a bad precedent for other companies that might also choose to restrict the use of films.[49] For example, G-B might insist on using only the Baird transmission system, rather than EMI's rival Marconi system, which the BBC preferred for its higher resolution. EMI was itself controlled by RCA.

Cock informed the Deputy Director General, C.C. Graves, of the serious implications of this situation for the television service:

> It is obvious that the policy of these two companies [Western Electric and RCA] is collusive, and probable that it emanates from their USA headquarters, the idea being that Television can never do them or the picture industry any good, and may do a good deal of harm later on. ... Heavy limitation in film supply would not only make the programmes insufferably dull and unenterprising but would increase the total cost very considerably, and put us completely at the mercy of perhaps one or possibly two organisations.[50]

Although Cock advocated investigating the ramifications of the US duopoly's stance for the illegal restraint of trade, he doubted 'whether the mobilisation of public opinion, questions in the House, etc., would be effective. People would not be able to appreciate the importance of the whole matter; I expect, indeed, that many people with the "Buy British" complex would be delighted'.[51]

Cock had anticipated having G-B itself clear the 'mechanical' (sound reproduction) rights of the US features it controlled, and had been willing to pay a fee of £3 per film or £1 per showing to cover this, on top of the blanket agreement.[52] However, with the ban in place no American material could be provided by G-B at all. The situation only found a precarious resolution when Reith personally approached the head of RCA, David Sarnoff, who thereupon agreed that his company would not object to the BBC's use of sound films on television.[53] Shortly before Christmas 1935, the BBC also obtained a twelve-month waiver from Western Electric, conditional upon the television service still being at an experimental stage, which was renewed annually for the next three years. With these barriers removed, Cock proceeded to attempt to close the deal with G-B. That, however, stalled over the terms and conditions both parties wished to impose to safeguard their own rights.

Negotiating with Gaumont British

Isidore Ostrer's first proposal, made in April 1935, was for an annual payment to G-B by the BBC of £15,000 plus a charge of £6 12s 6d per 1,000 feet of film supplied, to cover the cost of making prints. He stipulated that 'only feature films a year old would be released, but this restriction would be liberally interpreted so that a certain amount of flexibility would be allowed'.[54] Ostrer was not averse to making films specifically for television use, including footage of news events not already covered by the G-B newsreel along with test and tuning-in films. Cock did not think G-B's figure unreasonable, as the 'rock bottom figure' of £10,000 he had anticipated did not include the cost of newsreels. He estimated that the BBC's total exposure on the deal would be about £20,000.[55] In September Cock nevertheless suggested to Goldsmith an arrangement involving the payment of £10,000 per annum plus print costs of 1½d per foot in order to receive two newsreels per month and the use of all features, magazine films and shorts the company controlled. With the addition of material he hoped to acquire from other companies, Cock envisaged spending around £30,000 per annum in total on films, of which at least £13,000 would go to G-B.[56] However, Ostrer's initial figure turned out not to include the G-B theatrical newsreel. For this, the company wanted an additional £10,000 per annum.

Even with the fee thus increased to £25,000, this package was estimated to cost only £1 per minute of air time, whereas the cost of live programmes was put at £31 10s 0d per minute.[57] If no other company could be persuaded to strike a deal with the BBC – and BIP had still not responded to the Corporation's overtures, preferring to wait until the film trade had made some definite ruling on co-operation with television[58] – the G-B films would be used almost exclusively for prerecorded programming and its average cost per minute would therefore effectively be reduced even further. Reith personally authorised the payment of £25,000 as the maximum sum permissible, but did not think G-B would settle for any less.[59] This outlay, while hefty, was felt essential to ensure the availability of film material in general and the newsreel in particular.

It was now January 1936, and the television service was due to start broadcasting in October. But for the next ten months wrangling continued over the precise terms and conditions of the proposed deal and what the Corporation would be getting for its money. Particular concerns included the value placed on the separate items comprising the package (feature films, shorts and the newsreel); the BBC's rights of control over its use of the material; the 'television age' of the films supplied; and G-B's wish to be indemnified against the possibility of hostile action by the trade associations. In July 1935, the CEA and KRS had both resolved not to sell films to television on the grounds that the new medium 'might be regarded as a serious menace' to the cinema.[60]

G-B was willing to supply features only after they had completed their London general release. This normally meant an exclusive engagement in a West End theatre for a month or two, followed by a blanket booking in the suburbs. After this, prints were circulated to cinemas around the country, which the television service would not reach for some time (indeed it was not to do so until the 1950s). Negotiations focused on what in America was known as the period of 'clearance' or in Britain the 'time bar' after which a film would become available for booking.

Cock wanted films to be made available to the BBC three to six months after release; G-B was only willing to offer a window of nine to twelve months. Cock considered this excessive, as in his opinion 'the value of a feature film which has exhausted its London showing is nothing within that area unless it happens to be a particularly celebrated picture capable of re-showing, such as *Cavalcade*. None of G-B's films really come into this category.'[61]

Cock took the view that the television service had the status of a single West End cinema, with 'an audience equivalent to a week's attendance'.[62] The limited, 25-mile range of the Alexandra Palace transmitter and the small, mostly suburban, middle-class audience likely to be at its disposal meant that the service should not be seen as a significant competitor for the business attracted by first-run houses. Indeed, a television broadcast would most likely mean pure profit for G-B. While the possibility of an ad hoc rental arrangement had been under discussion, Cock had proposed a fee of £100 per feature film for three showings each. G-B rejected this figure as too low, but Cock remarked:

> Even at £100, their value to us is overrated. If Gaumont will not accept a compromise, there-fore, we must do without their features, which in any case are on the long side for Television purposes, and if only on account of their age, would be dull programme material. Some of them would probably be unsuitable. In my view, £2,500 per annum for the call on these films is ample.[63]

Nevertheless, a counter-offer was made of £150 each for selected films; but here G-B responded with its proposal of a flat fee of £25,000. This would give the BBC unrestricted access to around 1,000 shorts, including comedies, educational films and American material distributed by the company, as well as features on a similar basis.[64] While this offer was under discussion, Cock asked to see a catalogue of all the material available, which G-B promised to deliver once it had clarified the rights situation on each title under its control. Contracts with individual artists had varying terms that rarely took the possibility of television broadcast into account, so it could not guarantee to supply any particular items until all possible contractual barriers had been lifted.

Pending this, G-B delivered a draft of the proposed blanket agreement in May 1936 – whereupon it was dismissed by Cock as 'obviously an impossible document'.[65] Among other restrictions, G-B sought to prevent the BBC from editing the company's films at its own discretion; demanded approval of the way films were described in broadcasts; obliged the BBC to pay for rights clearances; prohibited the Corporation from making its own news films or contracting with any company other than G-B for news footage, but could not guarantee to provide coverage of crucial sporting events like the Grand National; and imposed charges of 1s 6d per foot of film to cover print costs with a minimum of £10 per print, which Cock considered 'an outrageous overcharge'. But the major sticking point was a 'force majeure' clause protecting G-B in the event of hostile action by the industry 'so strong that they are unable to resist it'.[66] This clause allowed G-B in such circumstances to renege on its contractual obligations and cease its supply of films altogether, but still required the BBC to pay the full annual fee without any right of redress. Cock was appalled:

> G-B has sought completely to safeguard itself against any trouble with the KRS or CEA (and there is almost certain to be trouble), in an arrangement carrying a large sum agreed only because of such risks, and equivalent to the normal News Reel rentals of more than eighty hypothetical West End Theatres! ... We cannot organise and prepare a Service with the possibility that at any moment the whole of our film supply (approx. 50% of our programmes) might suddenly cease. If G-B retains this right we should insist on a similar right of termination, but this clause in any case makes the arrangement hardly worth bothering about.[67]

The BBC's Business Manager, Jardine Brown, subsequently met David Ostrer and G-B's legal representative to resolve some of these issues. According to Brown, G-B refused to give the Corporation an 'unfettered right to eliminate any part of the films supplied' because 'from their experience with the Baird Co., they know that practically every feature film will require to be cut as the strain of "viewing" on a television receiving set is [at] present too great for anyone to concentrate much more than 30 minutes at a time'.[68]

David Ostrer insisted that broadcast comments on new films could not be critical but should offer only praise or neutral description. He was also concerned that the BBC should not scoop G-B in making its own films of news events that G-B itself was unable to cover. (Cock added in a handwritten note in the margins: 'Why? If we get an event which they cannot, that is our affair! If G-B get an event which we cannot they are not including them in their television news reels! He cannot have it both ways.') But Ostrer could not guarantee newsreels of major sporting events being delivered for broadcast before they had been seen in West End cinemas, as 'there was a special circle of half a dozen large cinemas in the West End where rush editions were specifically featured and which were attended by people who came up from the suburbs and who would not continue to come in to the West End theatres if they could view the event by sitting at home'.[69] The discussion also covered the BBC's desired right to cut newsreels to remove material that might be objectionable. As for relations with the film trade bodies, Ostrer suggested not approaching the CEA and KRS before any agreement with the BBC was signed but instead presenting them with a fait accompli, to which they would be less likely to object.

Goldsmith, who regarded David Ostrer as 'impossible', remarked that G-B was 'one of the hardest commercial crowds we have ever had dealings with, whose money is in hundreds of thousands, and to whom therefore this £25,000 is not of great consequence'.[70] Nevertheless, it was clear that the BBC needed the material that at present only G-B could provide (something of which Ostrer was well aware), and if a deal could not be concluded somehow then the television service would be seriously handicapped from the outset. Negotiations continued, with compromises being sought on both sides. The BBC insisted on a 'diminution clause', in which an agreed amount was refunded from the annual rental fee for every important sporting or news event omitted from the newsreels. G-B agreed to individual abatements of up to £500 for each of the Grand National and Derby horse races, but capped them at £5,000 in total. Further BBC stipulations included at least three months' notice to be given if the supply of films was to be suspended and no increase in the annual payment in any circumstances. At G-B's suggestion, the initial term of the deal was to be extended to three years instead of one, which would at least allow the BBC sufficient time to make its own arrangements for in-house filmmaking units while keeping the service supplied with product.

By early September, when Goldsmith felt that a signed agreement was imminent, Cock was becoming increasingly concerned to find a possible alternative to what he called 'this appalling contract'.[71] He advocated approaching all the other major companies to suggest the kind of ad hoc hire agreements that had earlier been rejected. In April, Cock had compiled a list of the eight major distributors, 'in approximate order of their importance', though he considered that only the first two released films that were 'a credit to the British film industry': London Film Productions, Gaumont British, Associated British Picture Corporation, Associated British Film Distributors, British and Dominions, Twickenham Film Studios, Capitol Film Productions and Criterion Film Productions.[72] Now he wanted also to approach the British offices of some of the American companies, including MGM, Paramount and Pathé, which as well as controlling their own newsreels also handled the type of American-produced short films that he hoped to acquire but which G-B was unable to deliver. Cock argued that the G-B deal would 'not provide us with anything approaching our requirements; ties us up in an almost uninterpretable commitment for up to three years; is grossly inequitable; and costs us far too much for what we shall get'.[73] Seeing G-B now only as a last resort, he instructed Goldsmith to write at once to all eight American-owned majors (the others being Columbia, Fox, RKO Radio, United Artists and Warner Bros) in the hope of securing suitable shorts. Meanwhile, he was privately engaged in negotiations to secure the British Movietone newsreel at a much lower price than G-B was demanding for its own. Cock argued: 'This is valuable to us whether or not we are compelled to conclude the G-B contract, but as soon as we have this Movietone agreement in our pocket, it will be nothing short of a crime to proceed with Gaumont-British on the present basis.'[74]

Support for Cock's position came when it was eventually revealed what material G-B actually had available. It was not until mid-September, just six weeks before regular broadcasts were now due to begin, that G-B at last furnished its long-promised catalogue. It included fifty-six features released between 1934 and 1936, the most recent titles being withheld until after they had completed their London release. In Cock's absence, BBC producer Dallas Bower noted in a memo that he had always understood 'that the transmission of feature length films will not be part of the television service for a considerable time, if ever'. Bower considered most of the G-B features 'unsuitable programme material' because, though none was more than three years old, their age still meant that they were all 'dead from an entertainment point of view': they had 'been widely released and they are consequently, very well known'. In terms of quality, he considered only seven of the films on the list 'to be really first-rate (technically, based on Hollywood standards and as entertainment)'. Bower also pointed out: 'Not one feature in the catalogue is American; they are all British.' As for the short films so important to Cock, because they were mostly of a magazine type and were no longer topical, Bower opined: 'the overall bulk of the material I consider to be useless'.[75]

On his return, Cock added his own thoughts on the catalogue, which he considered 'an even more depressing document than I had anticipated'. In respect of the fifty-six full-length films, he reiterated his previously expressed position, that

> old features were of no real value but as they were to be included in the 'bag' for the money, it did not seem necessary to exclude them specifically. From those I have seen in the attached catalogue, about ten seem to me up to a certain possible standard, and about six can, I think, be classified as good films. GBD have, however, already said they would not condense features to twenty minutes or half an hour (even were this possible) except at extra cost to us, and even then all sorts of difficulties would be raised, and we have not the facilities for doing it ourselves.

Cock estimated the combined rental value of the feature package as no more than £500 and put the total worth of the short films G-B offered at £195. He dismissed the whole catalogue as 'a list of almost entirely valueless footage' and pointed out that he had now secured the British Movietone news for only £820 per annum, compared to the £15,000 demanded by G-B for its own newsreel. He summed up by recommending,

> with all the emphasis of which I am capable, that GBD be now informed that the contents and nature of their catalogue makes [sic] it quite impossible to proceed further with the contract (specific reasons can be given if necessary), but that we should be agreeable to taking selected films at a fair rate, based on their present commercial value.[76]

On 26 October, the blanket deal with G-B was finally dropped. Exactly one month later, it was agreed that the BBC would hire its newsreels at a rate of £15 15s 0d per week and shorts at £5 5s 0d per film, though G-B's Ian Crémieu-Javal considered these rates 'extraordinarily low'.[77] It had taken a full eighteen months of negotiation to arrive at this resolution, largely due to the recalcitrance and opportunism of G-B in the person of David Ostrer. By this time broadcasts had already begun, so the need to secure sufficient film footage to fill the schedules was more pressing than ever.

Of the other film companies approached by Goldsmith, most had not even bothered to reply, but Fox (through its subsidiary, Movietone), G-B, Pathé and Radio Pictures (RKO) all agreed to supply shorts. Indeed, Radio offered them free of charge only three months after they had been seen in West End cinemas. Cock insisted on the BBC paying a nominal fee of £5 per film to keep things above board; the renter claimed to regard this only as insurance, 'to cover wear and tear' on the prints.[78] Radio's UK manager R.J. Hanbury did, however, strike one cautious note: 'It is impossible for us to say at present what effect this new art may have upon our business, so that the permission we are giving you by this letter must be subject to cancellation on our part at any time.'[79]

While Cock had found G-B's similar proviso intolerable in a blanket contract, in the context of a more flexible arrangement such as this it was acceptable. Hanbury also enquired after the number of television sets in operation, information which Jardine Brown stated (and internal correspondence confirms) the BBC did not yet know.[80] Radio Pictures was a particularly important renter as far as television was concerned, as it controlled the bulk of the short animated cartoons produced by Walt Disney. These were shown extensively on BBC Television from 1937 to 1939, and when the outbreak of war halted the service, the BBC agreed to store all the Disney prints it had borrowed (some 118 titles, many in Technicolor though broadcast only in black and white) for the duration, free of charge, on the distributor's behalf.

First Broadcast Features

The television service was due to begin regular daily broadcasts from Alexandra Palace at the end of October 1936. Before then, however, experimental transmissions were seen publicly during the annual Radio Show at Olympia from 26 August to 5 September. This event, popularly known as Radiolympia, was a public exhibition designed to demonstrate and promote the latest technological developments in broadcasting equipment, and thereby to increase sales of radio and television sets. The two different systems, Baird and Marconi-EMI, were used for broadcasts on alternate days.

The event was preceded by two days of press previews, with a Gaumont British newsreel and a live transmission of presenter Leslie Mitchell on Monday, 24 August, followed the day after by televised extracts from three new feature films: *Rembrandt* (1936/01.02.1958), *Show Boat* (1936/11.09.1973) and *It's Love Again* (1936/16.10.1989). The exhibition itself included a varied bill of items lasting up to two hours. Though the contents of each programme were essentially the same, the order in which the items appeared varied slightly from day to day. Each broadcast began with a tuning signal: the image of a 'watching eye' with accompanying music, to 'allow both sight and sound to be tuned in satisfactorily before the public is admitted'.[81] The programmes themselves began fifteen minutes after this, with announcements by Mitchell. The subsequent sequence of items included, on some days only, a live half-hour variety show, *Here's Looking at You*, produced by Cecil Madden and George More O'Ferrall (later a producer-director of cinema films), plus singer Helen McKay performing two songs in the Spotlight studio, guest appearances by other performers and outside pictures from Alexandra Palace. But most of the items were on film: Gaumont British and British Movietone newsreels; a short documentary directed by Paul Rotha, *Cover to Cover* (1936/26.08.1936), in which Leslie Mitchell also appeared; and excerpts from eight new feature films, including the three already mentioned plus *The Amateur Gentleman* (1936/08.03.1949), *As You Like It* (1936), *First a Girl* (1936/28.02.1988), *Two's Company* (1936) and *When Knights Were Bold* (1936/21.12.1989).[82] The exhibition as a whole was judged a considerable success, and though technical breakdowns occasionally interrupted the transmissions from Alexandra Palace, they were reportedly seen by 123,683 people, more than half the total number of visitors to the event.[83] However, according to a BBC report cited by television historian Jamie Medhurst, 'it became clear during the exhibition that the public were not interested in film transmissions. They were not considered to be television.'[84]

Subsequent test transmissions began on Thursday, 1 October and continued until 28 October, excepting Sundays. They included a number of short documentary films, among them Harry Watt's *Droitwich, the World's Most Modern Long Wave Transmitter*, Mary Field's *This Was England* and Paul Rotha's *The Face of Britain* (all 1935), as well as the feature-length *The Voice of Britain* (directed by Stuart Legg, 1935) and *Wings over Everest* (Ivor Montagu and Geoffrey Barkas, 1934).[85] Both *Droitwich* and *The Voice of Britain* were about the BBC radio service (see Table 1.1).

When the regular television service finally opened on Monday, 2 November, slightly later than planned, it was announced that the first month would also be experimental in nature, in effect a 'dress rehearsal' seen by the public.[86] The opening day also included a variety show produced by Madden and More O'Ferrall. Film material this time included a British Movietone newsreel and a BBC short, *Television Comes to London*, featuring presenters Leslie Mitchell and Adele Dixon and a commentary written by Cecil Lewis. The two transmission systems now alternated on a weekly basis until the Television Advisory Committee finally settled on Marconi-EMI as the superior system in February 1937.[87] Two hour-long broadcasts were made each day from Monday to Saturday, beginning at 3.00pm and 9.00pm, typically comprising a balance of live shows and short films. There were at first no transmissions on Sundays, though outside regular hours broadcasts were often shown of *Television Survey*, a specially-made compilation of representative programme material, shot on 35mm film for test and demonstration purposes.[88]

The limited broadcasting hours meant, as Cock had maintained, that full-length feature films were simply not practicable programme items, though excerpts of new theatrical releases occasionally appeared with the consent of their distributors. These included, for example, clips from G-B's *The Great Barrier* (1937/04.02.2002) on 6 February 1937 and London Films' *Fire over England* (1937/28.03.1950) on 20 February. However, an opportunity arose with the 1937 Radiolympia exhibition, on what was very nearly the anniversary of the first BBC TV broadcasts.

The exhibition lasted from 25 August until 4 September 1937. For the duration of the event, a live outside broadcast unit was established at Pets' Corner in

Table 1.1 Feature films and selected shorts transmitted on prewar BBC Television.

Film	Source	Year	Country	First TX date
Cover to Cover (documentary short)	Associated British Film Distributors	1936	UK	26.08.1936
Droitwich, the World's Most Modern Long Wave Transmitter (documentary short)	GPO Film Unit	1935	UK	01.10.1936
The Voice of Britain (documentary)	Associated British Film Distributors	1935	UK	01.10.1936
Wings over Everest (documentary)	Gaumont British Picture Corporation	1934	UK	19.10.1936
Television Comes to London (documentary short)	BBC	1936	UK	02.11.1936
The Last of the Clintons	Exclusive Films	1935	USA	23.08.1937
Tell Me If It Hurts (short)	Denning Films	1934	UK	14.03.1938
The River (documentary short)	US Farm Security Administration	1938	USA	30.05.1938
The Student of Prague	Denning Films	1935	Germany	14.08.1938
Aces Wild	Exclusive Films	1933	USA	17.08.1938
Jack Ahoy	Gaumont British Picture Corporation	1934	UK	24.08.1938
Aunt Sally	Gaumont British Picture Corporation	1933	UK	26.08.1938
Man of the Moment	Metropolis Films	1937	France	12.09.1938
La Kermesse héroïque	Unity Films	1935	France	07.10.1938
So Ended a Great Love	Denning Films	1934	Germany	21.10.1938
The Edge of the World	Denning Films	1937	UK	22.03.1939
Chaplin's First Films (compilation)	British Film Institute	1939	UK/ USA	16.04.1939
The Plow That Broke the Plains (documentary short)	US Resettlement Administration Film Unit	1936	USA	21.05.1939
The Fighting Texan	Exclusive Films	1937	USA	29.05.1939
Deuxième Bureau	Denning Films	1935	France	21.06.1939
Whistling Bullets	Exclusive Films	1937	USA	04.07.1939
Le Patriote	Denning Films	1938	France	04.08.1939
Galloping Dynamite	Exclusive Films	1937	USA	07.08.1939

Regent Park, with daily transmissions from there between 4.00pm and 5.00pm and more orthodox programming as usual in the evening. An additional daily hour, from 11.30am to 12.30pm, involved the transmission of the demonstration film. Booths had been set up at Radiolympia to allow visitors fifteen minutes of viewing at a time. *Radio Times*'s television columnist 'The Scanner' noted wryly: 'It is too much to hope that on the strength of, at most, a quarter-of-an-hour's viewing you will buy a television set. Conversely, on the strength of a mere quarter-of-an-hour's viewing, it is to be hoped that you will not decide *not* to buy a television set.'[89] In order to provide cover to move all the necessary equipment from Alexandra Palace and set up in time for the start of the exhibition, all live programmes were replaced entirely by film material for two days. Television executive Major L.G. Barbrook, whose responsibility it was to book short films, therefore had to find a film of suitable length to fill the evening of Monday, 23 August and to be repeated the following afternoon.[90]

Rather than approach one of the major renters, Barbrook turned to a small British company that had already proved a reliable source. Exclusive Films had supplied a number of shorts from the very beginning of the television service and was prepared to make available features at a very reasonable rental price. Barbrook at first arranged for the booking of *Wild Mustang* (1935), starring Harry Carey, one of a number of low-budget American 'B' Westerns that Exclusive distributed in the UK; but after attending a trade show of another Carey vehicle, he preferred that one instead. So it was that, for a fee of £10 per showing, BBC Television presented its first full-length fiction feature: *The Last of the Clintons* (1935/23.08.1937).[91] The hour-long transmission, beginning at 9.00pm, included a three-minute interval while the telecine operator changed reels and was followed by a Mickey Mouse cartoon, *Mickey's Orphans* (1931/30.03.1937). The repeat broadcast of *The Last of the Clintons* at 3.00pm next day was accompanied by a different cartoon, *Touchdown Mickey* (1932/28.05.1937), while the remaining daytime and evening slots on both days were filled by a selection of shorts, including more Disney material.

These screenings were the invention of necessity, not the start of a change in policy; but less than two months later, discussions were opened about the possibility of regular feature-film showings. A memorandum circulated at an executive meeting on 15 October included a proposal by the Controller of Programmes, B.E. Nicholls: 'In view of the small number of sets sold and the necessity to increase sales, the BBC should augment the transmission hours from three to four per day by the introduction of a regular daily feature film (75–85 minutes) to follow immediately the present 9–10pm transmissions.' This was an ambitious hope. Supporting documentation summarised the state of relations with the film industry, including past experience in the use of shorts and the likelihood of acquiring features. More realistically, it was suggested that either an occasional feature film would replace a live studio programme or a regular feature might be used once or twice weekly if a sufficient supply of suitable material could be guaranteed for a year or two in advance. The signs, however, were not propitious:

> There is without question strong opposition on the part of the industry in this country to the principle of televising feature films. The main troubles are probably that, for the price we could pay, it would not be worth the film companies while [*sic*], and also that the industry is not anxious to assist what it regards as a possible future competitor. Privately D. Tel. [Cock] has been warned of the possibility that if we attempt to use feature films on any scale, the trade associations may very likely get together and ban all films from television, including news

reels, 'shorts', and excerpts for illustration purposes. This is possibly correct, and, if so, would be very serious. In any case it seems clear that an attempt to use feature films regularly at the present juncture would have some serious repercussions in the film industry at a time when we are cultivating a better mutual understanding.

There were concerns also about the technical difficulties of maintaining extended broadcast hours, as it had been reported that 'two hours' continuous viewing is far too great a strain on the attention in present conditions' and would serve to alienate viewers rather than attract them: it was 'believed that there should be a minimum interval of one hour between programmes, especially between those that require concentrated attention'.[92]

Nevertheless, on 25 October, letters from Cock ('with great trepidation and with the conviction that it is the wrong move'[93]) were sent to all the major distributors, including Gaumont British, asking whether they would be 'prepared to negotiate for the televising of selected feature films which have already completed their general release. The features we have in mind are those that date from not earlier than about 1932, provided copies in good condition are available.' The letters explained that the BBC wished to select those most appropriate to TV; to show each one between two and four times, each screening separated by at least a week; and possibly to transmit the longer films in two parts on separate evenings.[94] Without exception, all the renters declined or, in the case of most of the American companies, replied only to say that they had referred the matter to their head offices in New York, which amounted to the same thing. The managing directors of the British branches of two such companies, however, explained their reasons for declining, and these shed light on some of the prevailing attitudes in the trade towards the prospect of films on television.

J.C. Graham, Managing Director of the Paramount Film Service, issued a reply in which, while trying to assure Cock that he had 'no definite desire to be antagonistic to your television developments', he stated:

[We] are definitely opposed to any attempt to push old product onto the public. We claim to be a progressive firm and are making every effort possible to increase the quality and standing of our product. We retire our films from circulation after a certain age, and we see nothing whatever to be gained by going back and picking up old product after same has been retired and attempting to show same to the public again through some other method, such as television.

Furthermore, in our humble opinion, after you make a few attempts of this kind you will find that the public will laugh at you, as they will not waste their time either in the theatre or by means of television to look at films which are four or five years old.[95]

In his own reply, Cock explained to Graham:

Naturally we do not want to make idiots of ourselves or of film producers, and I can assure you that our idea was to choose as far as possible outstanding films which had become almost classics in people's memories, as recent, of course, as possible. I could mention, for example, at least half a dozen of your films which, in my conviction, people would enjoy seeing again.[96]

Joseph Friedman of Columbia Pictures also cited the age of films for television:

> [We] deem it inadvisable to broadcast films which are anywhere from three to five years old, because of the difference in the quality of the films as compared with the present time and those of even only two years back. The technical and other qualities improve so rapidly each year that we believe we would be doing the film industry, as such, considerable harm by projecting for television purposes, very old films.
>
> Further to that, we do not believe that the technical qualities of television at this time are of a high enough standard to maintain the projection quality which the public is accustomed to seeing in the Cinemas. This too would be detrimental to the Cinema Industry.[97]

The sharp differential in visual quality between films as screened in cinemas and as broadcast on television was also a concern expressed in the document circulated among BBC Controllers, albeit with the emphasis on their effect on public perceptions of the television service rather than of the film industry.

In November, Cock reported that the situation was at a standstill, with none of the major distributors willing to negotiate a deal.[98] Even the deplored Gaumont British package was unavailable, control of the company's distribution arm now being in the hands of C.M. Woolf, who was unremittingly hostile to television. Requests from BBC executives for the acquisition of particular films – Programme Organiser Cecil Madden wanted G-B's *Rhodes of Africa* (1936/13.08.1981), while Assistant Director of Television R.E. Rendall hoped for London Films' *The Private Life of Henry VIII* (1933/28.09.1957) – therefore had to be rebuffed.[99] Even though London Films' chief executive Alexander Korda was sympathetic to television, his distributor, United Artists, was not and there the final decision lay. Summing up the state of play with regard to each company, Barbrook reported that even executives who wished to help, like Hanbury of Radio Pictures, had their hands tied and had been specifically instructed not to make films available to television. In the case of many films, television rights might not even be owned by the distributors and the position of artists' rights (such as those of actors and musicians) in relation to television showing was unclear.

Even if rights could be cleared, good-quality prints of films only a few years old were often scarce and the cost of making new copies at upwards of £40 each was prohibitive. However, Barbrook did raise one note of cautious optimism: if the British and American majors were unwilling to cooperate and it was therefore impossible to ensure a regular supply of films in quantity, it might yet be feasible to acquire a number of foreign ('continental') films through either the (London) Film Society or the various small distributors that specialised in such product. He did not anticipate more than around a dozen such films a year being available, insufficient for a regular slot but perhaps the basis for an occasional special screening of something that would be 'good entertainment, and new to many viewers'.[100]

In January 1938, Cock duly reported to Madden, who was especially keen on showing a feature film:

it looks as if we can obtain some very good foreign feature films with English sub titles at a reasonable cost, although the number is likely to be limited. I propose to try one as an experiment in the ordinary hours, if you approve, choosing it with great care. This will relieve studio congestion occasionally, and be very valuable both as an experiment and for other reasons.[101]

The following month, Barbrook opened formal negotiations with J.S. Fairfax-Jones, representing a small distributor, Denning Films, with the aim of televising selected films at the rate of up to one per week; each would most likely be repeated and booking fees were offered of £50 for a first transmission and £25 per repeat. Barbrook listed thirteen films controlled by Denning that might be suitable, including *The Student of Prague*, and asked Fairfax-Jones to investigate the TV rights situation and the condition of the available prints. In reply to a query similar to the one made earlier by Hanbury, Barbrook explained that it was difficult to be sure of the number of viewers for the television service but that 5,000 sets were thought to be in operation.[102]

While the rights situation was being explored, Barbrook booked a British comedy short distributed by Denning, starring and directed by Richard Massingham: *Tell Me if It Hurts* (1934/21.03.1938). Before being televised it was trimmed of a scene involving a dental operation, about which some BBC executives had expressed concern. Though this was not the first televising of a live-action fiction film, as is claimed in some quarters, at twenty minutes it was one of the longest shorts screened to that date and may well have been the first cinema film to be censored for television (permission for the excision of material had been given by Massingham himself).[103]

Another important, longer-than-usual short film was brought in from the United States. At 28 minutes, *The River* (1937/20.05.1938) was technically a 'featurette', but the BBC's record of Programmes as Broadcast (PasB) described it as a 'Specially imported feature film'.[104] Directed by Pare Lorentz and produced by the Farm Security Administration and the US Department of Agriculture, *The River* is a documentary about the disastrous floods in the Mississippi Valley the previous year. Its importation was arranged through the BBC's North American representative, who described it as 'one of the most beautiful films I have seen'. *The River* was shown by the BBC before it could be seen theatrically in the UK; it's likely that it would not have been commercially released anyway.[105] Cock thought it 'magnificent' and following uniformly favourable audience reactions the film was repeated three times within the month.[106] An earlier documentary by Lorentz, *The Plow That Broke the Plains* (1936/21.05.39), was shown three times the following year.

The opportunity to screen a major feature did not arrive until the summer of 1938, when Madden asked Barbrook if he could find 'a good feature film for the Sunday night programme on this day, August 14th – possibly a continental film, or a [Robert] Flaherty film'.[107] Regular Sunday broadcasts had begun in April, usually in the evenings only, while night-time hours had been extended beyond 10.00pm, allowing for longer programmes. After first considering either *La Kermesse héroïque* (1935/07.10.1938) or *Gribouille* (1937/03.07.1987) for the inaugural transmission, Barbrook and Cock finally settled on *The Student of Prague*, of which a good-quality print happened to be available.[108] Cock himself wrote the introductory announcement quoted at the head of this chapter. Further foreign-language screenings ensued in the next few months: the aforementioned historical satire *La Kermesse héroïque*, directed by Jacques Feyder; *Man of the Moment* (1937/12.09.1938), starring Maurice Chevalier; and a second German film, *So Ended a Great Love* (1934/21.10.1938). All four films were repeated within a month. By this time, new telecine equipment had been received, which enabled *So Ended a Great Love* to be run continuously, without planned interruption (see Figure 1.4).[109]

Aside from the two sponsored documentaries, the only American features televised at this time were four more 'B' Westerns starring Harry Carey or Kermit Maynard, also supplied by Exclusive. This company, along with its better-known subsidiary, Hammer Film Productions, was to play a major role in providing films for television in the postwar era. As for British-produced features, Gaumont British agreed to supply two films, both musical comedies, for Radiolympia week

Figure 1.4 An operator adjusting one of the film projectors in the Telecine Room at Alexandra Palace, January 1939. The Emitron camera can be seen on the left. BBC Photo Library © BBC. Photographer unknown.

in 1938. Both *Jack Ahoy* (1934/27.08.1938), starring Jack Hulbert, and *Aunt Sally* (1933/27.08.1938), starring Cicely Courtneidge, were shown first on the opening Saturday afternoon of the exhibition and then repeated on alternating days from Monday to Thursday before being double-billed again on the Friday. The only other British feature to be televised in this period was an independent production, Michael Powell's *The Edge of the World* (1937/22.03.1939). Despite the low audience-approval rating of foreign-language films (see Chapter 8), two more were shown in 1939: the French *Deuxième Bureau* (1935/21.06.1939) and *Le Patriote* (1938/04.08.1939). There would undoubtedly have been more had not the imminence of war brought the whole television service to a premature, if temporary, end on 1 September.

Evidence of concerted industry hostility to television, as opposed to the intransigence of particular companies, had emerged as early as February 1937, when Cock attended a meeting of the CEA at which the formation of a TV Liaison Committee was discussed. Its apparent aim was to 'control the development of television'. Cock warned that 'although there were the usual mutual and violent antagonisms between members, the only thing they did agree upon was this desirability of cramping television as far as was in their power'.[110] A *Radio Times* article tried vainly to suggest that in fact the industry had nothing to fear from its supposed rival:

> For the last five years, while television was being developed and finally made practicable, the magnates of this industry have been having periodic heart-attacks at the thought of this unforeseen danger. Now that television has started and is rapidly finding its feet, we are beginning to realise that the film magnates don't have to worry; that television will have little effect on films, for between television and films there is a vast No Man's Land.

> At first sight this may seem odd, because both are viewed on a screen in black and white, and accompanied by sound. There, however, the similarity ends. The ordinary commercial film is not suitable for transmission by television. The reason? Because in television the most important part of any film is lacking: the audience. A film appeals to several hundred people at the same time; a comedian cracks a joke and there are several hundred laughs; the heroine sheds a tear and several hundred eyes are moist; at the sight of a gun several hundred hearts stop beating. Mass emotion. It is far, far easier to make a crowd of people laugh or cry than to produce the same effect on a solitary person.[111]

In November 1938, Barbrook wrote to Alexander Korda to explain that for the first time he had been refused a request to view a film, *Love from a Stranger* (1937/16.10.1985), by its distributor, United Artists, in its preview theatre. This was a courtesy usually afforded within the industry, but the renter now announced that its 'directors had decided that they were unwilling to co-operate in any way with television'.[112] Barbrook noted that in subsequently refusing the possibility of televising the evidently uncommercial documentary *Land of Promise* (1935), made by the Zionist Association, or any other of its films, United Artists could 'only be regarded as deliberately antagonistic'.[113] While Korda had always been willing to allow extracts from his company's films to be televised for purposes of comment, illustration and review, the KRS had rejected 'out of hand' an application for the similar use of its members' product. 'I wish the film industry had more of Mr Korda's imagination and enterprise', Cock wrote to London Films' J.B. Myers. Myers regretfully replied that he thought it 'a great pity that there is not more tolerance and vision in our industry'.[114] These experiences were but a foretaste of the organised opposition that television was to face from the film trade in the postwar era.

Notes

1   The text of the announcement was dictated in a memo from Gerald Cock, 29 July 1938, BBC T6/110. On the early history of British television see: Aldridge, *The Birth of British Television*; Briggs, *The History of Broadcasting in the United Kingdom*, Volumes 2 and 4; Medhurst, *The Early Years of Television and the BBC*; and Norman, *Here's Looking at You*. Background information for this chapter was also gleaned from the website Teletronic, http://www.teletronic.co.uk, especially the extracts from Kenneth Baily, *Here's Television: A Personal Account of Television's Early Days* (Vox Mundi, 1950).

2   See, for example, Buscombe, 'All Bark and No Bite: The Film Industry's Response to Television', in Corner, *Popular Television in Britain*; Hayward, 'Films on TV', in Speed, *Film Review 1983–1984*, 29; and Robertson, *The Guinness Book of Film Facts and Feats*, 260.

3   Norman, *Here's Looking at You*, 64.

4   Dr Alfred Gradenwitz, 'Mihály's Tele-Cinema', *Television* 2, no. 14 (April 1929): 61.

5   Burns, *John Logie Baird, Television Pioneer*, 193. Further background material on Baird's experiments can be found in Anon., *John Logie Baird*; Baird, *Sermons, Soap and Television*; and Slater and Lobban, *All Shapes and Sizes*.

6   Quoted in Norman, *Here's Looking at You*, 65.

7   Robertson, *The Guinness Book of Film Facts and Feats*, 260; Hayward, 'Films on TV', 29. The film is not held in the BFI National Archive and may not survive.

8   Quoted in Burns, *John Logie Baird, Television Pioneer*, 193.

9   'Talking Films by Television', *The Times*, 20 August 1929, 10. Further technical details of tele-talkies (apparently Baird's own coinage) are provided in Norman J. Nicolson, 'Tele-cinematography', *Television* 2, no. 19 (September 1929): 361–3.

10   'Television Broadcast with Sound', *The Times*, 1 April 1930, 28.

11   Sydney A. Moseley, 'The Future of Television', *Television* 2, no. 20 (October 1929): 407; original emphasis. The same issue contains an extensive report by the magazine's editor on the Berlin Radio Exhibition, including a comparison of different systems of transmitting film by television: A. Dinsdale, 'Television at the Berlin Radio Exhibition', 379–89.

12   'Talking Films by Television', *The Times*, 20 August 1929, 10.

13   James Agate, 'The Dramatic World: Television and the Theatre', *Sunday Times*, 3 August 1930, 4. According to Slater and Lobban, the Coliseum show included the transmission of a short cinema film featuring George Robey (*All Shapes and Sizes*, 188).

14 R.H. (Robert Herring), 'The Week on the Screen: Television', *Manchester Guardian*, 9 August 1930, 8. Baird again demonstrated theatre television in the West End in 1932, with a transmission of the Derby at the Metropole Cinema on a screen 10 feet wide by 8 feet high; and in 1935, at the Dominion, using a screen 24 feet wide: Captain Ernest H. Robinson, 'Television and the Cinema: A Demonstration in London; Challenge to the "Movies"; Baird Experiment', *Observer*, 3 November 1935, 14.

15 'Talking Film by Television', *Sunday Times*, 10 August 1930, 12.

16 Capt. Ernest H. Robinson, 'Television: IV – The Tele-Talkie', *Observer*, 17 August 1930, 16.

17 Kerzoncuf and Barr, *Hitchcock Lost & Found*, 85–88. Parts of the speech are transcribed at greater length in the book, which also includes two frame enlargements and a discussion of the film's possible origins.

18 Phil Nichols, reply to the author's Facebook post, 17 January 2020: https://www.facebook.com/groups/kaleidoscopearchive/permalink/10162626968855198/

19 Slater and Lobban appear to confirm this interpretation (*All Shapes and Sizes*, 189). When I conveyed it to Charles Barr, he too was convinced of its veracity.

20 Sydney A. Moseley, 'The First Tele-cine Broadcast', *Television* 4, no. 38 (April 1931), 48.

21 Andrew S. Martin's comprehensive listing of pre-war transmissions in *Sound & Vision, Volume 1: 1928–1935* confirms the dates of these telecine experiments and notes that the Chaplin film was a Keystone production.

22 Moseley, 'The First Tele-cine Broadcast', 49.

23 'Big Advance in Television: "Entertainment Value" – Films Shown by New Apparatus', *Manchester Guardian*, 7 January 1931, 6. On HMV's system, see Norman, *Here's Looking at You*, 97–9.

24 'Television: Broadcasts Begun by the BBC', *The Times*, 23 August 1932, 12.

25 'High-definition Television: BBC Experiments', *The Times*, 13 October 1933, 12.

26 Slater and Lobban, *All Shapes and Sizes*, 189.

27 'Television Tests with Cinema Films', *Manchester Guardian*, 13 September 1933, 10.

28 'Development of Television: Proposed Experiments at Crystal Palace', *The Times*, 13 September 1933, 5.

29 C.A. Lejeune, 'The Pictures: The Picture's Progress – the Telefilm', *Observer*, 17 September 1933, 14.

30 'High-definition Television: BBC Experiments', *The Times*, 13 October 1933, 12; Norman, *Here's Looking at You*, 109.

31 Professor E.V. Appleton, FRS, 'Television: Translation of Light and Shade', *The Times*, 14 August 1934, 46.

32 Home Office, *Report of the Television Committee*.

33 'Television: Advice on Trial Service – Selsdon Committee Report', *The Times*, 1 February 1935, 8.

34 Ibid.

35 Martin, *Sound & Vision, Volume 1*. On the limitations of the Baird system for drama production, see Jacobs, *The Intimate Screen*, 32–4.

36 Norman, *Here's Looking at You*, 134.

37 In March that same year, 180-line broadcasts were begun by the German Post Office.

38 Gerald Cock, 'Looking Forward: A Personal Forecast of the Future of Television', *Radio Times*, 23 October 1936, 7.

39 Cock to V.H. Goldsmith, 9 May 1935, BBC T16/73/1.

40 Goldsmith to C.E., 12 February 1935, BBC T16/72/1.

41 Cock to Goldsmith, 9 May 1935, BBC T16/73/1.

42 Cock to Goldsmith, 27 May 1935, BBC T16/73/1.

43 Goldsmith to Ian Crémieu-Javal, 10 April 1935, BBC T16/73/1.

44 A fifth Ostrer brother, Harry, was a script editor for G-B. For a family history, see *The Ostrer Brothers & Gaumont British*, written and self-published by Maurice's son Nigel.

45 Goldsmith to John Maxwell, 11 June 1935, BBC T16/72/1.

46 Maxwell to Goldsmith, 25 June 1935, BBC T16/72/1.

47 Jardine Brown to Goldsmith, 30 August 1935, BBC T16/72/1.

48 Louis Sterling to Goldsmith, 2 October 1935, BBC T16/72/1.

49 Goldsmith to L. Lochhead, 3 October 1935, BBC T16/72/1.

50 Cock to C.C. Graves, 4 October 1935, BBC T16/72/1.

51 Ibid.

52 Cock to Goldsmith, 29 April 1935, BBC T16/73/1.

53 David Sarnoff to Sir John Reith, 26 October 1935, BBC T16/72/1.

54 Record of interview, Brown with Crémieu-Javal, 26 April 1935, BBC T16/73/1.

55 Cock to Goldsmith, 29 April 1935, BBC T16/73/1.

56 Cock to Goldsmith, 4 September 1935, BBC T16/72/1.

57 Leonard F. Schuster, January 1936, BBC T16/72/2.

58 BIP to Brown, 22 January 1936, BBC T16/72/2.

59 Handwritten note on Cock to Lochhead, 15 January 1936, BBC T16/73/2.

60 Quoted in Michael Jackson, 'Cinema versus Television', *Sight and Sound* 49, no. 3 (Summer 1980): 178.

61 Cock to Goldsmith, 10 October 1935, BBC T16/73/1.

62 Cock to Goldsmith, 15 October 1935, BBC T16/73/1.

63 Ibid.

64 Cock, January 1936, BBC T16/73/2.

65 Cock to Brown, 8 May 1936, BBC T16/73/2.

66 Goldsmith to Lochhead, 13 February 1936, BBC T16/73/2.

67 Cock to Brown, 8 May 1936, BBC T16/73/2.

68 Brown to Goldsmith, n.d. (1936), BBC T16/73/2.

69 Ibid.

70 Goldsmith to Lochhead, 25 August 1936; Goldsmith to Brown, 2 July 1936, BBC T16/73/3.

71 Cock to Goldsmith, 2 September 1936, BBC T16/72/2.

72 Cock to Goldsmith, 2 April 1936, BBC T16/72/2.

73 Cock to Goldsmith, 7 September 1936, BBC T16/72/2.

74 Cock to Goldsmith, 9 September 1936, BBC T16/72/2.

75 Dallas Bower, 18 September 1936, BBC T16/73/4. The films Bower considered acceptable were *The 39 Steps* (1935/01.01.1968), *The Constant Nymph* (1933),

Evergreen (1934/26.04.1978), *Jew Süss* (1934/23.04.1988), *Little Friend* (1934), *The Man Who Knew Too Much* (1934/19.09.1969) and *Tudor Rose* (1936/31.03.1988).

76 Cock to Goldsmith, 21 September 1936, BBC T16/73/4.

77 Record of interview, Brown with Crémieu-Javal, 26 October 1936; Crémieu-Javal to Brown, 26 November 1936, BBC T16/73/4.

78 Brown to Schuster, 20 November 1936, BBC T16/72/2.

79 R.J. Hanbury to Brown, 26 November 1936, BBC T16/72/2.

80 Brown to Hanbury, 31 December 1936, BBC T16/72/2.

81 'First Television Broadcast', *The Times*, 26 August 1936, 12.

82 In 1981, in response to a *Radio Times* article (Philip Purser, 'The Pally Pioneers', 2 July 1981, 11, 13), Paul Rotha wrote to the magazine to claim that *Cover to Cover* was 'the first actual film, other than newsreels, to be transmitted by BBCtv' ('The First Television', 23 July 1981, 70). Contemporary newspaper reports indicate that a second documentary short, Humphrey Jennings's *Post-Haste* (1936/14.11.1952), was also shown at Radiolympia, but there is no mention of this film in Martin's listing, based on the BBC's PasB records, in *Sound & Vision, Volume 2*.

83 'Radiolympia Closed', *The Times*, 7 September 1936, 10.

84 Medhurst, *The Early Years of Television and the BBC*, 122.

85 Martin, *Sound & Vision, Volume 2*.

86 'Regular Service in October', *The Times*, 8 September 1936, 10.

87 'One Television Year', *The Times*, 7 January 1938, 13.

88 A 35mm print of the *Television Demonstration Film* is held in the BFI National Archive.

89 The Scanner, 'Prelude to Radiolympia', *Radio Times*, 13 August 1937, 16.

90 Barbrook also headed the fledgling BBC film production unit, shooting film inserts on outdoor locations for live programmes. The same twin duties also fell to his successor, Greeve del Strother (see Chapter 2). On Barbrook's work, see The Scanner, 'News for Televiewers', *Radio Times*, 3 July 1937, Television Supplement, 1. For further details of early BBC in-house films, see Martin, 'Appendix D: Films for Television', *Sound & Vision, Volume 7: Appendices B*, 635–9.

91 L.G. Barbrook to Mrs Burnham, 22 and 28 June 1937, BBC T6/135/1.

92 'Use of Feature Film', memo for Controllers' Meeting, 15 October 1937, 1, BBC T6/138. The first ninety-minute continuous broadcast was in December 1937.

93 Cock to B.E. Nicholls, 25 October 1937, BBC T6/138.

94 Standard letter to Associated British Picture Corporation, Columbia, Gaumont-British, MGM, Paramount, Pathé, RKO Radio, Twentieth Century-Fox, United Artists, Universal and Warner Bros, 25 October 1937, BBC T6/138.

95 J.C. Graham to Cock, 26 October 1937, BBC T6/138.

96 Cock to Graham, 27 October 1937, BBC T6/138.

97 Joseph Friedman to Cock, 8 November 1937, BBC T6/138.

98 Cock to Nicholls, 4 November 1937, BBC T6/138.

99 Cecil Madden to R.E. Rendall, 15 November 1937, BBC T6/138; Rendall to Barbrook, 26 January 1938, BBC T6/194.

100 Barbrook to Cock, 25 October 1937, BBC T6/138.

101 Cock to Madden, 20 January 1938, BBC T6/138.

102 Barbrook to J.S. Fairfax-Jones, 4 February 1938, BBC T6/138.

103 Fairfax-Jones to Barbrook, 15 February 1938, BBC T6/138. See also The Scanner, 'Film Comedy That Was Banned', *Radio Times*, 11 March 1938, 24. The Internet Movie Database erroneously states that *Tell Me if It Hurts* was the 'first film (apart from cartoons and newsreel) to be shown on British Television' (http://www.imdb.com/title/tt0290892/trivia).

104 Photographic copies of these typewritten documents, stored on 16mm film, are held at the BBC Written Archives Centre and at the BFI Reuben Library.

105 N.A.R. to Cock, 28 February 1937, BBC T6/138.

106 Cock to Madden, 27 April 1937, BBC T6/138.

107 Madden to Barbrook, 28 June 1938, BBC T6/138.

108 Madden to Cock, 28 June 1938, BBC T6/138.

109 'Showing How It's Done', *Radio Times*, 14 October 1938, 17. For further details of pre-war features on BBC Television, see Hall, 'The First 15 Feature Films Broadcast on British Television'.

110 Cock to Nicholls, 25 February 1937, BBC T16/72/2.

111 S. John Woods, 'Looking at Television', *Radio Times*, 23 July 1937, 10.

112 Barbrook to Alexander Korda, 4 November 1938 (draft), BBC T16/72/2.

113 Barbrook to Cock, 11 November 1938, BBC T16/72/2.

114 Cock to J.B. Myers, 8 March 1939; Myers to Cock, 9 March 1939, BBC T6/194.

CHAPTER 2

The Smallest Show on Earth –
Cinema versus Television (1945–52)

Conscious that it holds the master medium, it is understandable that the BBC should have taken a firm stand in face of the terms offered by the Cinematograph Exhibitors' Association. The cinema representatives have shown their reluctance to co-operate with the Television Service on any terms but their own. New films will not be made available, as the competition of the home talking picture is feared. It is even possible that a state of 'cold war' will break out between the two interests.

(John Archdeacon, 'Television and the BBC Charter', *Scan* 2, no. 6 [October 1949]: 5)

Indeed cinema films are *the* raw material for television, and provide it with from one- to two-thirds of its programmes, according to the country and the company. One obvious reason why this is anything but a satisfactory state of affairs is because of the cold war between the film industry and television, a war led by the exhibitors and bluntly referred to in a recent issue of a trade paper as: 'Theatre v. TV'.

(Jean Quéval, 'Cinema and Television', *Sight and Sound* 19, no. 3 [May 1950]: 141)

Cold War

From the officers' mess at RAF Broadstairs in Kent, where he was stationed on active service, three months after the cessation of hostilities, Group Captain Philip Dorté OBE drafted a letter to the man who had by 1945 emerged as the leading figure in the British film industry: J. Arthur Rank. Dorté, the BBC's new Head of Television Outside Broadcasts and Film Supervisor, was concerned at reports that the Rank Organisation, which had interests in film production, distribution and exhibition, wanted to move into theatre television by installing large-screen TV projection in its two major national cinema circuits, Odeon and Gaumont. Although the BBC had no direct interest in theatre television itself, if Rank were given the go-ahead by the Government this would nevertheless place him in competition with the Corporation in the field of broadcasting. Dorté's draft letter asserted that

although Television in its initial stages can do little either to help or harm the cinema, an agreement made between the BBC and the film trade – and operative when television actually recommences – will do much to establish the co-operation which will be essential when the Television Service is extended to the provinces and when television receivers will be installed in millions of private homes.

Dorté outlined several propositions for arrangements that he claimed would be of mutual benefit to films and television:

1. Television should transmit, free of charge, trailers for upcoming theatrical releases.
2. Television should permit the transmission in theatres of outside broadcasts of certain sporting events in exchange for sharing the cost of the fees charged by their promoters.
3. The film trade should permit television appearances by film stars and directors, either in TV productions or in film studio visits by outside broadcast units.
4. The film trade should make available to television current newsreels (of which the Rank Organisation operated two, Gaumont British and Universal), short subjects and feature films of around five years old, for a rental 'which would take into account the probable number of home-viewers to such film transmissions'.[1]

Following the publication in March 1945 of the Report of the Television Committee, chaired by Lord Hankey, the BBC was at this time preparing to reopen the television service in the summer of the following year. The Director General was now Sir William Haley, and the Head of Television, Maurice Gorham (whose tenure in the post was to be brief); Cecil Madden retained his prewar role as Programme Organiser. On 30 April 1946, less than six weeks before the scheduled resumption of the TV service, Gorham arranged an informal meeting with Rank. The film industry generally remained wary of television and Gorham, like Dorté, hoped that the mogul would take the lead in establishing a new spirit of amity and co-operation. But while Rank claimed that he had no immediate plans for theatre television until higher-definition transmission was possible, he made no firm offer of help to the BBC.[2]

Other approaches to film trade bodies proved similarly fruitless. Negotiations were opened with the newsreel companies in March 1946 over a proposal to televise all five regular newsreels in rotation and to use library footage for another demonstration film, Television Is Here Again, to be directed by Dorté (see Figure 2.1). Although the companies were willing to discuss the proposal individually, they were deterred by their representative body, the Newsreel Association, from actively co-operating with the BBC and all five ultimately backed away.[3] At the beginning of August, Dorté and Gorham attended a meeting of the Renters', Exhibitors' and Producers' Committee (REP), an all-industry body chaired by Rank and including representatives of all the major trade associations – now comprising the Cinematograph Exhibitors' Association (CEA), the Kinematograph Renters' Society (KRS), the British Film Producers' Association (BFPA) and the Association of Specialised Film Producers (ASFP). There they reiterated the proposals conveyed by Dorté in his letter to Rank, but again left without obtaining

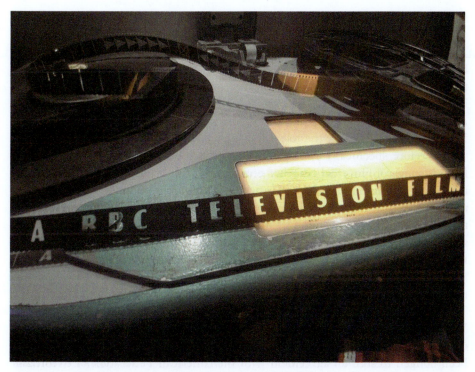

Figure 2.1 The BBC's Outside Broadcast and Films Unit was responsible for film inserts and other in-house productions, including the postwar demonstration film *Television Is Here Again* (1946), shot on and transmitted from 35mm. Author's copyright.

either an agreement or a definite refusal of assistance.[4] 'These people', noted Haley, 'are afraid of shadows in more senses than one.'[5]

The following month, the REP put its own set of proposals before the Government-appointed Television Advisory Committee (TAC). They envisioned two separate spheres of television influence: the BBC broadcasting programmes to homes and the film industry transmitting its own productions direct from studios to cinemas. The TAC had informed Rank that the Government's main priority was to ensure 'that the public television service shall be assured of conditions favourable for its development and growth' and sought to reassure him that the 'regular televising of full-length feature films would be regarded for the present as outside the programme policy of the BBC'. Though the TAC recognised the potential benefits of cinema television, it did not subsequently endorse the plan, leading the REP to conclude that it had 'produced a deadlock which cannot fail to be prejudicial both to the future of television in this country and to the interests of cinemagoers'.[6] For much of the next decade the film trade repeated its requests to be allowed to involve itself in television while it continued with technical research and experimentation; but the Government's persistent withholding of permission in order to protect the BBC's broadcasting monopoly fuelled the industry's resentment and its fear of competition for the loyalty of its own audience.

This hostility contrasted markedly with the positive attitude shown by Walt Disney Mickey Mouse Ltd, the UK branch of the Disney company, whose cartoons had been a regular fixture of prewar television and which had been stored in Alexandra Palace for the duration of the war. One such cartoon, *Mickey's Gala Premiere* (1933/26.11.1937), had in fact been the last programme broadcast on 1 September 1939 before the television service closed down on the eve of war. It was therefore specifically chosen to reopen the service on 7 June 1946, though Film Manager Greeve del Strother noted that 'this particular cartoon is slightly more "dated" than most since it caricatures a number of Hollywood stars who are now just memories'.[7] Disney proved agreeable to continuing the prewar hire arrangement with only a nominal increase in fees. Both *Mickey's Gala Premiere* and another cartoon, *The Dognapper* (1934/15.05.1939), were indeed broadcast on reopening day, with a further six shown in the first week of transmissions.[8]

With little other cinema material available, even more extensive use was made of Disney cartoons over the next six months than had been the case in the 1930s. But on 21 November 1946, the very day after Maurice Gorham had met Walt Disney himself during the latter's personal visit to London, Gorham was informed that the Disney company had, along with other Hollywood producers, been obliged to sign an agreement with the American Federation of Musicians (AFM) that prevented it from making any films available to television in any territory in the world. As a result, all the company's cartoons were withdrawn from TV use after 31 December 1946. AFM subsequently gave its permission for the BBC to use extracts from selected Disney cartoons in a programme celebrating Mickey Mouse's twentieth anniversary, broadcast in two parts in January and March 1948, but the ban on showing the cartoons in their entirety remained in force. The prints were still held at Alexandra Palace until April 1949, when pressure of space caused them to be removed for storage by RKO Radio Pictures, Disney's current distributor.[9]

Television Liaison Officer David Wolfe-Murray was assigned to investigate the 'sub-standard' distribution sector, which supplied 16mm prints for non-theatrical use by film societies, schools, hospitals and the like. But after a visit to Wallace Heaton, the largest 16mm film library, Wolfe-Murray reported that 'unless the KRS are agreeable to films being televised, no film, whether 35, 16 or 9mm, handled by any commercial organisation will be made available to us, since if this is done, the film libraries [sic] supplies will be cut off at source'.[10] He suggested instead trying not-for-profit outlets like the Central Office of Information (COI) and other Government organisations. But even the COI was reluctant to lend its short educational and informational films for fear of alienating commercial interests (they were often included in cinema programmes) and specialised distributors were also afraid to risk the wrath of the CEA. The suppliers of shorts, both commercial and non-commercial, would provide television only with material that did not interest a theatrical distributor or exhibitor or that had exhausted all possible cinema bookings.

Thus, at the start of 1947, the BBC's film programming was in an even more parlous state than it had ever been, with no cinema newsreels or cartoons available and no regular supply of shorts or features in sight. In order to provide a regular news service, the BBC produced in-house a twice-weekly Television Newsreel from the first week in January. Replacing the Disney cartoons as breaks between studio programmes were specially filmed 'interludes' of around three minutes each. These were also made for television by the BBC's outside broadcast unit under Dorté, whose more usual function was to provide film inserts and links for live shows. While they were fondly regarded by many viewers, interludes were essentially functional rather than having their own definite 'programme value', unlike cartoons. As Gorham noted, 'although we don't count largely on films for programme purposes, there are many occasions when we have to use a film to cover a studio change'.[11]

It was not only the film industry that declined to co-operate with the television service. *The Times* reported a House of Commons debate in which the Labour member for Bolton, John Lewis, summed up the situation now faced by those trying to operate the television service with 'out-of-date equipment in inadequate accommodation':

> They were trying to keep alive this twentieth-century child which was struggling against the opposition of large vested interests running the entertainment in this country. ... The film interests were quite frankly terrorized by what was regarded as a new monster, and thought it was against their interests to allow films to be shown on the television screen. Gradually, day by day opposition to this very important service was becoming so acute as to make the pro-grammes virtually unattractive to those who might wish to buy television sets.[12]

A further meeting with Rank and his increasingly dominant lieutenant, John Davis, was arranged by Maurice Gorham's successor as Head (now Controller) of Television, Norman Collins, on 1 March 1948. Unlike the guarded Davis, Rank himself was candid in acknowledging the general view among exhibitors, which he claimed not to share, that television was 'a menace which will eventually put them out of business altogether'. He saw the televising of sporting events in cinemas as a way of replacing revenue that would inevitably be lost to home viewing. While wishing to produce his own TV material, Rank said he also wanted to draw on the BBC's valuable production experience in a field new to his company.[13]

Internal BBC correspondence indicates the Corporation's anxiety that the film industry should not be permitted to encroach on its own territory, as the influx of commercial interests into television would threaten its public-service remit and use up scarce resources as well as becoming a direct competitor. For these reasons it was opposed to the production of television material by Rank or other cinema concerns and held to the principle that the film industry should stay out of televi-sion and the BBC should stay out of the film business. It was, however, willing to compromise to the extent of allowing BBC-produced material available 'as outside broadcasts for a limited experimental period in a limited number of cinemas'. In return, it would expect the film industry to make feature films available for broadcast, albeit again on a limited basis, as it was 'no part of the Corporation's intention to convert the BBC Television Service into a home cinema, showing mainly commercial films'.[14]

At the urging of the Government, a series of meetings, held at and chaired by the Post Office (which was responsible for issuing broadcasting licences), was arranged between the BBC and the REP in order to work out a basis of co-operation pending resolution of the film industry's requests to be allowed to participate in television. A provisional agreement was made in November 1948 to allow 'the television [showing] of selected films and the showing of selected BBC television items in cinemas'.[15] This *quid pro quo* agreement was to last twelve months from 1 January 1949. A list of 'commercial film requirements' for the year was drawn up by the BBC, which included requests for the following: twelve British 'first features', six produced in 1948 and six produced earlier; up to six American first features, if available for hire from UK distributors; fifty-two second features (i.e., 'B' pictures), 'of any nationality and not necessarily modern'; twelve children's films, also of any provenance; an unspecified number of short interest and educational films; and such newsreel and library material as might be required for programme purposes. Specific titles listed as examples of suitable features included *Snow White and the Seven Dwarfs* (1937/03.04.2016), *The Wizard of Oz* (1939/25.12.1975), *Meet Me in St. Louis* (1944/13.07.1969), *Brief Encounter* (1945/11.10.1965), *The Red Shoes* (1948/14.11.1965) and *Hamlet* (1948/22.09.1973).[16]

This list turned out to be a major tactical error, as it confirmed the industry's fears that the BBC wanted to draw audiences away from the cinema and to deprive exhibitors of valuable material by showing recent, current and commercially important product. Commented John Archdeacon in *Scan* magazine:

> In exchange for very limited facilities in television the BBC expects permission to show new films of the highest quality. These productions are the bread and butter of the film trade, and at times when it is difficult to recover production costs, it is surely a little unreasonable to give away a few hundred thousand potential free tickets to televiewers and their numerous friends. If this is so, then it is equally unreasonable for the film trade to expect to establish a claim to be granted licences to transmit programmes exclusively to certain cinemas for paying audiences with which the BBC would be unable to compete on anything like equal terms.[17]

Already by March 1949, it was apparent that the agreement was not working out. Television apparatus had been installed in only a single Rank-owned cinema, the Palais de Luxe in Bromley, where experimental transmissions had lasted only until December 1948.[18] While Rank was still keen to produce and exhibit his own television material in cinemas, other film interests had no urgent concern to do likewise and adopted a wait-and-see stance. Nor were most of them yet prepared to offer films to television, including Rank. In January the CEA had decided to oppose this idea and in June it went further than it had ever gone before, by declaring that any film shown on television would be denied further cinema bookings by its members.[19] The Association was the industry's leading opponent of television. Producers and distributors were mainly concerned about the threat to copyright protection if their films were made available through a public medium other than licensed cinemas, but they could at least see the broadcast service as a source of (modest) additional revenue. Exhibitors gained nothing except competition for audiences. The prospect of being able to show BBC programmes already available to home viewers was not a sufficient inducement for cinema operators to go to the expense of installing transmission equipment. As the exhibition sector was the means by which films were able to make a profit, it held the whip hand over the rest of the industry, which generally bowed to its wishes.[20]

The agreement was therefore effectively a dead letter before the experimental period was even half over. With one partial exception (dealt with below), no major renter had agreed to supply the BBC with any of the types of product it had requested. So draconian was the CEA's policy that the Corporation found it 'impossible to book any reputable English film through the normal channels' and even foreign-language films could only be booked when their theatrical prospects were nil.[21] Smaller companies that entered into negotiations for the broadcasting of films found themselves intimidated into withdrawing before deals had been signed. Sir Henry French of the BFPA summed up the industry's position:

> It is impossible to co-operate with the BBC while they insist on monopolising every aspect of television. We have no wish to encroach on domestic entertainment, but we do feel that we should be allowed to transmit to large cinema screens the more important 'outside' events, such as the opening of Parliament by the King, the Oxford and Cambridge boatrace [sic], and so on. It should be borne in mind that the film industry has far more experience of providing entertainment than the BBC.

> On no account can we loan our films to the BBC so long as they insist on a one-way traffic. There is no effective means of protecting copyright. What is there to prevent a film being seen on a public-house television set by people who would otherwise pay to see it in a cinema?[22]

The ban on co-operation even extended to the televising of film extracts, though the Rank Organisation had been agreeable to this for the sake of free publicity for new films. Eventually the KRS consented to its members providing clips for purposes of review, though this was subsequently regretted when many of the reviews proved unfavourable.[23]

Film Deals and Contract Disputes

The principal BBC executive responsible for sourcing film material suitable for television use was now Greeve del Strother, the Corporation's Film Booking Manager. His regular clients for the supply of short and non-fiction films included the National Film Board of Canada, Australia House, the United States

Information Service, the Czech Ministry of Information, the British Council and the French Embassy. While noting that he was also attempting to explore other avenues, del Strother reflected ruefully in July 1947 that none of them would 'provide sufficient films to ease our problem which is becoming more and more difficult every week'.[24] Despite the industry's best efforts, some theatrical features did slip through the net to appear on television. The first to be televised after the war was *Marie-Louise* (1944/28.10.1946), a Swiss production that had won the American Academy Award for Best Original Screenplay of 1945. This was in fact the *only* full-length film broadcast in the first twelve months of postwar television.

In June 1948, del Strother compiled a list (slightly incomplete) of films longer than three reels transmitted by the BBC over the preceding year. The list included twenty-four films, eleven of which had been shown more than once. Four were foreign-language titles, including the German version of *The Blue Angel* (1930/01.12.1947); two French films, *Poil de carotte* (1932/12.09.1947) and *Bataille du rail* (1946/12.04.1948); and a shortened, hour-long version of Sergei Eisenstein's Soviet epic *Alexander Nevsky* (1938/21.05.1948). A second German film, not listed by del Strother, was the silent documentary *Berlin: The Symphony of a Great City* (1927/12.12.1947), abridged to 40 minutes and accompanied by gramophone records. D.W. Griffith's silent epic *The Birth of a Nation* (1915/07.07.1947) was also presented in truncated form, in an extract of 55 minutes; the print was borrowed from New York's Museum of Modern Art and the broadcast, introduced by film historian Roger Manvell as part of his regular television series *The Film*, had live musical accompaniment by Louis Voss and His Orchestra.

Six British features were also televised in the period covered by del Strother's list. Four of these were Government-sponsored wartime drama-documentaries supplied by the COI, which by that time were of neither box-office nor propagandist utility: *Coastal Command* (1943/03.06.1947), *Target for To-night* (1941/28.08.1947), *Western Approaches* (1944/14.12.1947) and *Close Quarters* (1943/20.04.1948).[25] The only products of the commercial British industry to be shown were two independent productions, *The Mill on the Floss* (1937/02.10.1947) and *Secret of Stamboul* (1936/16.03.1948), both featuring James Mason. Most of the remaining films on the list were American 'B' Westerns; but at Christmas 1947 the BBC achieved a coup with the first British television showing of any full-length film by a major Hollywood producer: David O. Selznick's *The Young in Heart* (1938/24.12.1947). This was one of three Selznick pictures acquired for multiple screenings over several years (an arrangement known as 'long rights'); the others were *Little Lord Fauntleroy* (1936/24.06.1948) and *Made for Each Other* (1939/19.07.1948). They had been acquired from a sub-distributor that had in turn leased the rights from Selznick (of which more later).

This group of films indicates in microcosm the narrow range of feature material available to the BBC in the postwar years: foreign-language and silent films, documentaries, independent productions and 'B' movies. Those shown were a selection from the limited supply available. Most of the films offered by those few distributors willing to sell to television were judged to be unsuitable on grounds of quality or for other reasons; del Strother stated of his list of twenty-four titles: 'To obtain these films, I have viewed or have had viewed, well over 100 full length films and approximately 500 short films.'[26]

The one deal to be made with a major renter during the period of the provisional agreement discussed earlier had actually been initiated before the agreement was struck. In April 1948, after contracting to supply some short films for broadcast, Gordon Rayner of Associated British Film Distributors (ABFD) had tentatively suggested to the BBC that, if the industry was amenable, he would like to offer some of the prewar George Formby and Gracie Fields vehicles the company controlled.[27] Despite its name, ABFD was not affiliated to the vertically-integrated Associated British Picture Corporation (ABPC) but was instead the distribution arm of Associated Talking Pictures (ATP), also the parent company of Ealing Studios. Ealing's head of production, Michael Balcon, was favourably disposed to television and described himself as 'a keen and critical viewer'.

Over lunch with the BBC's Robert McDermot, Balcon and Ealing's managing director, R.P. (Reginald) Baker, expressed their enthusiasm for the medium. According to McDermot:

> When talking about television in general, both Balcon and Baker said that, off the record, they thought the KRS and REP Committees were being stupidly obstructive towards us and that from their own point of view they would welcome our being allowed to show films which had exhausted their major revenue from the circuits. I murmured polite agreement and Balcon then went on to say that he would personally like to see us televise some of his best films such as *San Demetrio, London* and *Dead of Night*, saying that he regarded these as pictures that he was proud of, that would have a lasting appeal and that television viewers should be given the chance to see. As they were both of them films that I had thought of myself I again said how nice this would be, and Baker said off his own bat that he was going to find out if there wasn't some loophole through which we could acquire them. Balcon also mentioned the large number of George Formby, Will Hay and Jack Hulbert comedy films made under his aegis in the old G-B [Gaumont British] days and that he would like to see us use them if the snags could be got round.[28]

However, trade approval of the ABFD deal was not forthcoming and it was called off in July 1948. Philip Dorté remarked to Rayner that he had never been optimistic about it, 'particularly as the CEA seem, of late, to have been stepping up their adverse propaganda about those firms which are still continuing to make short and feature films available to Television'.[29] But with the provisional agreement as incentive, discussions resumed in December. When, the following month, the CEA again decided against supporting the agreement, Reginald Baker intervened privately. According to Dorté, Baker 'very sportingly told me that if we liked to sign a more or less blank agreement forthwith, he would be prepared to honour it and to take such abuse as he knew would be hurled at him by the KRS of which he was a past president – and in fact there was ultimately such a scene that Baker offered to resign from the KRS'.[30] With the approval of Norman Collins, a contract was signed 'over a dateline which came within the lifted-ban period'. When the deal was announced, it was said in the trade press to have hit the industry like a bombshell, though no details of the films involved were mentioned.[31]

Although Rayner had initially suggested the possibility of leasing more than two dozen films, Dorté cautiously limited the booking to twelve for a total hire fee of £3,600. Each film was to be screened up to three times over a period of twelve months, with the possibility of more to follow if they were favourably received by viewers.[32] The task of picking the films fell to Greeve del Strother. His choice was limited, as several plums were withheld in order not to antagonise exhibitors who might still wish to show them. Del Strother eventually chose three George Formby vehicles, three Gracie Fields films and six 'miscellaneous' titles. All but two were ATP/Ealing Studios productions. 'From the point of view of the general viewer,' del Strother remarked, 'I think the Formby's [sic] are the best, the Gracie Fields fair and the miscellaneous poor.'[33] The Head of Television Programmes, Cecil McGivern, was concerned that del Strother had recommended most of the films for afternoon rather than evening transmissions and that their average length was only 75 minutes, necessitating the addition of one or more shorts to make up a full programme slot. When the deal was first mooted, McGivern had insisted that the BBC was 'in *desperate need* of some full length feature films', but later he was of the opinion that they had 'rushed into this scheme too precipitately'.[34]

No Limit (1935/08.02.1949) and *Sally in Our Alley* (1931/08.03.1949) were the first of the ABFD films to be televised, both in evening slots (see Figure 2.2). The latter was accompanied by McDonald Hobley's live interview with its still-active director, Maurice Elvey. Dorté summarised the audience reaction: 'some people have enjoyed them for auld lang syne's sake – others have disliked them because they have never liked either George Formby or Gracie Fields as visual entertainers'.[35] The popular weekly film magazine *Picturegoer* was less than impressed, considering that *Sally in Our Alley* 'just did not stand up, even on curiosity value'. The journal's editorial commented:

> The truth is that films of this kind, which are totally unsuited to the small screen, can do a great deal of harm to all concerned.

> This is a thing which film people, in their own interests, should watch closely. The public – whether picture-going or television – will not put up with this out-of-date stuff for long.[36]

Nevertheless, and despite the reservations of both McGivern and del Strother, Dorté was confident that the batch would prove acceptable. All twelve films were duly shown three times each in the course of the year (see Table 2.1). Del Strother noted with muted satisfaction that the BBC had thus enjoyed 'maximum value from this deal. Whether our audience's appreciation would be quite so great is another matter!'[37] However, when he broached with ABFD the possibility of hiring a further group of films, del Strother was politely rebuffed: Rayner 'said he

TUESDAY—March 8

11.0-12.0 Demonstration Film

★   ★   ★

3.0-4.0 Douglas Fairbanks Jr.
as Barnabas Barty
in the film
'THE AMATEUR GENTLEMAN'
A romantic story of swash-
buckling. The cast includes
Margaret Lockwood and Gordon
Harker

★   ★   ★

8.30 THEATRE ORGAN
Reginald Foort takes viewers on
a second visit to the famous BBC
Theatre Organ, shows how the
various combinations are used,
and plays some of his popular
music

8.50   Gracie Fields
in her first film
'SALLY IN OUR ALLEY'
Directed by Maurice Elvey
The story which is based on the
(*Continued in next column*)

play 'The Likes of 'Er,' takes
place at the end of the first world
war. The cast includes Ian
Hunter and Florence Desmond

10.0-10.15 NEWS (sound only)

'OUR GRACIE'
*You will hear her singing her famous
song 'Sally' in tonight's presentation
of her first film*

Figure 2.2 A day on BBC Television in 1949, consisting mainly of filmed material, including the first transmission of *Sally in Our Alley* (1931). *Radio Times* © Immediate Media Co.

Table 2.1 The ABFD package, 1949.

Film	Year	Transmission dates
No Limit (George Formby)	1935	08.02.1949, 01.04.1949, 29.08.1949
Sally in Our Alley (Gracie Fields)	1931	08.03.1949, 04.05.1949, 14.09.1949
Trouble Brewing (Formby)	1939	19.03.1949, 11.06.1949, 13.10.1949
Look Up and Laugh (Fields)	1935	22.03.1949, 27.05.1949, 07.12.1949
Young Man's Fancy	1939	05.04.1949, 22.07.1949, 07.11.1949
The Ware Case	1938	06.04.1949, 16.05.1949, 14.10.1949
The Beloved Vagabond	1936	03.05.1949, 12.07.1949, 26.10.1949
Let's Be Famous	1939	10.05.1949, 25.07.1949, 01.12.1949
The Missing Million	1942	13.05.1949, 31.07.1949, 16.11.1949
Keep Fit (Formby)	1937	18.05.1949, 29.07.1949, 19.12.1949
Looking on the Bright Side (Fields)	1932	13.06.1949, 25.08.1949, 03.11.1949
Java Head	1934	22.06.1949, 16.09.1949, 24.11.1949

would like to help, but that the trade attitude made it impossible for him to do so. He would bear in mind that we would still like to do business and if he could find any sort of loophole he would let me know.'[38] No such loophole was found and the arrangement was not repeated. Nevertheless, this was television's first substantial film 'package' from a major distributor.

For American and British independent features, del Strother turned to renters that were not members of the KRS or CEA. He thought that the ABFD deal would 'make things a little easier and there are signs that one or two smaller companies who have so far been holding out will want to cash-in where ABFD have led the way'.[39] These included New Realm, Grand National, Anglo Amalgamated and Exclusive. They and others acted as distributors for many US producers who had no permanent agency of their own in Britain and who therefore sold or leased their films to locally-based firms. Dorté pointed out to Norman Collins that 'the position vis-à-vis the supply of films is such that we just have to take a chance and deal with a company which can offer us reasonable films, even if we suspect that the company is financially unstable'.[40] The complicated business of rights ownership resulted in the BBC becoming involved in several legal disputes.

A case in point concerned the three David O. Selznick productions previously mentioned. *The Young in Heart*, *Little Lord Fauntleroy* and *Made for Each Other* had each been televised three times by August 1950. But a fourth screening of *The Young in Heart* had to be cancelled at short notice when the BBC was contacted by lawyers acting for the films' current American owners, Auerbach Film Enterprises, claiming that the television rights had been sold without their authorisation. The BBC had leased the films from the E.J. & S.A. Fancey Syndicate, which had bought them from London & Overseas Film Services, which had in turn acquired them from the International Optima Corporation.[41] Although the matter was cleared up within two months and the fourth transmission of *The Young in Heart* eventually went ahead, this case served as a warning of the risks involved in dealing with what the trade press referred to as the black market. Del Strother observed:

> While 'black market' is perhaps a little too strong, the manager of a renting company described it more accurately the other day in conversation, as the 'sub-strata' of the commercial business. This, unfortunately, is true, and it should be realised that I am often dealing with companies who are up to every possible sharp practice, and who are not viewed with favour in normal trade circles.[42]

The demand to fill gaps in even the limited airtime available (an average total of thirty-seven hours weekly until 1955) meant that del Strother was under constant pressure to find new sources for material of acceptable quality. 'I often feel that this excessive number of indifferent films does lower the quality of our programmes,' he reflected. 'It seems a great pity that we have to depend so much on film when the supply situation is so bad.'[43]

Most of the feature-film slots were placed on weekday afternoons, either around 3.00pm (which on other days was occupied by programmes in the strand 'Mainly for Women') or in the children's hour from 5.00pm, in which series 'B' Westerns were most often shown. As del Strother pointed out, the danger of including poor-quality material in the afternoons was that these were the hours when transmissions were likely to be seen on the premises of retailers of television sets by prospective customers, with the attendant risk of putting them off purchasing a set.[44] In evening broadcast hours, beginning at 8.30pm, more substantial fare should ideally have been offered as an occasional alternative to live programmes; but when major films proved unavailable these slots were typically occupied by 'B' movies of general appeal, such as the Dr Christian and Scattergood Baines series (both of which had been released theatrically by RKO Radio but were produced independently and no longer controlled by the Hollywood major). In May 1949 Cecil McGivern complained to Collins:

> We are once again in a very bad position. We have *no* films which are worth an evening showing if they are to be the only item in the evening. Some of the film spaces we have scheduled are acts of rather ridiculous optimism, as there is no sign of our being able to get hold of any decent films. I am having to take out film spaces and am, consequently, spending more money. ... At times I wonder how we accomplish a week's schedule at all![45]

The continuing hostility of the trade associations, both to the Corporation and to any film distributors that dealt with it, meant that negotiations for television rights were unpredictable, as del Strother described: 'One company may well come on the telephone tomorrow and say they have a large batch of films available; on the other hand another company may take fright and call off promising negotiations at short notice.' Changes to programme patterns meant that demand for films became particularly heavy in early 1949, which del Strother said had 'eaten into my reserves and also caused me to schedule films which I had previously marked as rather below standard and not really suitable'.[46] By May the supply had slowed to a trickle:

> At the present moment I am being offered pretty well no acceptable feature films; only indifferent Westerns and third rate British quota efforts. If it was not for the 2 or 3 contract deals for long rights in a number of films I should not even now be able to supply the week-to-week demand. ... For evening showings, apart from odd continental films, the outlook is very bad; if possible they ought to be cut out entirely because the quality of the films can do our programmes no good.[47]

Despite the odds, a small number of 'quality' British films from independent sources was shown from 1949–50, including *The Stars Look Down* (1940/29.07.1949), *South Riding* (1938/17.01.1950), *Fire over England* (1937/28.03.1950) and the documentaries *90° South* (1933/01.11.1950) and *The True Glory* (1945/17.02.1950). Some of the 'quota quickies' transmitted are now regarded as semi-classics, such as *The Last Journey* (1936/27.02.1950), as are several Tod Slaughter melodramas, including *The Face at the Window* (1939/28.04.1952). But an example of apparently inferior material being forced into the schedules to fill air space is *Discoveries* (1939/15.07.1949). This was a vehicle for Carroll Levis, a talent-spotter of new variety performers, whose subsequent television series was the forerunner of the TV talent show. However, the Head of Television Light Entertainment, Pat Hillyard, raised objections to the film being screened:

Carroll Levis, who plays the chief part, and can *not* act, is never off the screen. The production is bad, and the gags, with which the show is liberally sprinkled, are of the corniest variety. The 'discoveries' themselves are pretty poor, and the whole show is, in fact, one glorious plug for Levis.[48]

Del Strother's response to McGivern indicated the awkward position he was in:

I know the film is third rate, but what can I do about it? As you know, I obtained the film as one of a batch, some of which were quite good value. I could not reject more than one or two of the titles or the whole deal would have been called off. I think under present circumstances the film is showable and I have purposely put it in on a mid-week summer afternoon. So long as the heavy afternoon demand for films continues and our supply sources are so very limited, I must unfortunately schedule pictures of this sort, as far as I can see...[49]

Among the better-regarded American bookings were a number of films produced by Hal Roach, including *Of Mice and Men* (1939/28.01.1951) and a selection of the Stan Laurel and Oliver Hardy comedies. Roach's films were the subject of several disputes over distribution rights that intermittently prevented them being televised. Indeed, the film chosen to replace the cancelled screening of *The Young in Heart* soon after became itself the subject of a rights dispute. *Pack Up Your Troubles* (1932/14.08.1950), a Laurel and Hardy feature, was one of a number of films produced by Roach that were shared among several different UK distributors. The package in which the film was leased to the BBC came from Anglo Amalgamated; but another company with which the Corporation had regular dealings, New Realm, claimed that it owned the film instead. This problem was quickly resolved, leading del Strother to remark that the 'bark of many of these small Wardour Street companies is much worse than their bite'.[50]

However, New Realm had previously been involved in yet another dispute over television rights, albeit as defendant rather than plaintiff. On that occasion del Strother had faced 'a drastic and very sudden dwindling' in the supply of Westerns:

Until recently I could always rely on that company for a fairly regular flow of this type of picture, but I gather they have run into trouble, probably for supplying us with films to which they had no clear rights, and the result is that only a very few Westerns are now coming through. Quite a number of old films of other types are being offered me, but they are much less rewarding from my point of view since I may have to see six to find one acceptable, whereas Westerns have the great advantage that they do not really date much and so can generally be used.[51]

Grand National was also hit by a claim from the owners of the Hopalong Cassidy series that the company had no authorisation to lease these films for broadcast, as its contract specified only the transfer of theatrical rights. In this case the BBC had paid out £2,000 to screen a dozen of these 'B' Westerns and had to sue for restitution. As a result of this and other disputes, Norman Collins set aside £10,000 as a reserve for dealing with rights claims if and when they arose.[52]

The most notable contract dispute involved a property originated by the BBC itself. Film rights to the popular radio series *Dick Barton – Special Agent* had been sold to Hammer Film Productions with the condition that the resulting films should be made available for television showing (for an agreed fee) after their theatrical release. Hammer also purchased other BBC properties, such as the radio character PC 49 (used for two films in 1949 and 1951) and later the Quatermass television serials (adapted as features in 1955, 1957 and 1967), but in these cases the Corporation did not hold on to any broadcast rights. Hammer's distribution arm was Exclusive, the company that had supplied some of television's earliest features before the war and which del Strother had been dealing with since early 1948. In a report on the film booking situation at that time, he noted that Exclusive was 'a bit nervous about the film trade reaction if they supply us with pictures'.[53] A number of booking deals went ahead anyway, albeit mostly of non-Hammer material. *Dick Barton – Special Agent* (1948/10.09.1982) was the first of three films that Hammer made from the radio show, but del Strother rejected this as unsuitable for television because of its poor production values.[54] Reports on the sequel, *Dick Barton Strikes Back* (1949/15.01.1951), were more favourable. It was contracted and scheduled for broadcast in a prime slot, on Christmas Eve 1949 beginning at 7.30pm. The booking fee paid by the BBC was only £100, plus £50 each for any subsequent showings.

However, one month before the planned transmission, Exclusive's managing director James Carreras asked for the company to be relieved of its obligation, in fear of the industry's reaction to the broadcast of a film less than six months after its London release. Carreras produced a letter from the CEA confirming that a boycott of future theatrical bookings of the film would be the likely result, though he was also concerned that takings from existing bookings in Birmingham, where the first television transmitter outside London had recently begun operation, would be affected by the broadcast.[55] The BBC insisted on carrying the deal through, but Carreras failed to respond to its entreaties and the print was not delivered. The scheduled screening had to be cancelled after *Radio Times* had gone to press and was replaced by a repeat of *Little Men* (1940/07.08.49), for which the BBC held unlimited rights.

Despite further attempts at persuasion, Exclusive did not finally deliver *Dick Barton Strikes Back* for broadcast until more than a year later. The BBC declined to press its legal rights in the matter because the financial hardship necessarily inflicted on the company by a damages suit would have left an adverse impression on the industry at a difficult time. However, the Corporation's Head of Programme Contracts observed that this incident would render it 'impossible to make any further deals for film rights' to BBC properties while the CEA maintained its ban on theatrical bookings of films shown on television.[56] Exclusive's offer to make the third Dick Barton adaptation, *Dick Barton at Bay* (1950/17.04.1987), available for Christmas 1951 was not taken up; nor were any of the company's other films that it submitted by way of compensation.[57]

Fear of Competition

Worries that the advent and spread of television would spell serious competition for – even the end of – the popular cinema were nothing new. Speculations to that effect were already being aired in the late 1920s, even before the BBC had begun Baird's experimental transmissions, so it was not surprising that the film industry quickly came to share this view. As long as television remained in a relatively 'primitive' state technically and was confined to a small geographical area, these fears could easily be dismissed. But in the postwar era, when the greatest box-office boom in the film industry's history subsided and turned to irrevocable decline, such speculations began to take on a new quality of immediacy. The peak year for cinema attendance in Britain, as in the United States, was 1946, with an estimated 1,635 million tickets sold in that year. They fell slightly to 1,462 million in 1947 before rising again to 1,514 million in 1948. But thereafter they dropped steadily, in 1957 falling below one billion admissions for the first time since before the war.[58]

This decline was, from an early date, widely blamed on the influence of television, only increasing with the advent in 1955 of ITV. According to media historian Burton Paulu, writing in 1961:

> One statistician estimated that three fourths of the drop in attendance between 1950 and 1952 was due to increased television viewing. He assumed an average loss of sixty-five admissions per year for each new television license, while another observer put it as high as a hundred for each new license. British Board of Trade figures show that in the areas within range of the London, Birmingham, and Manchester ITA [ITV] stations, cinema admissions fell by 23 per cent between the first quarter of 1956 and the third quarter of 1957, while admissions for the country as a whole fell only 17½ per cent. Cinema admissions fell more in those regions that had television first, while those areas with both ITA and BBC stations experienced the greatest decline of all.[59]

Even while cinema admissions remained high and the television service was still under-developed, there were solemn portents of what might soon follow. A booklet published in 1949 by the managing director of Capital and Provincial News Theatres, *The Cinema and Television*, warned the film industry not to be complacent, arguing that while 'television in Great Britain holds no immediate threat to the cinema, there can be no doubt that in the not distant future, when transmission stations give a nationwide service, this new medium will prove a serious competitor to the film industry'.[60]

On 17 December that same year, the BBC Television service began to be extended to the regions with the opening of the first transmitter outside London, located near Sutton Coldfield and serving the Midlands. Early experience of regional television provided mixed evidence of what to expect. According to a newspaper report in February 1950, 'The effect of television on cinema attendance figures in Sutton Coldfield is negligible, state the managers of three local cinemas. The attraction of watching a screen by one's own fireside has not caused patrons to forego their visits to the films.'[61] This was attributed by one manager to the poor quality of TV programmes currently available. However, other surveys around the same time contradicted this view. John Ware, the author of an article entitled 'TV Launches a Film Offensive', also warned the industry against taking its audience for granted and dismissing the threat of television based on its present quality rather than its future potential. He asked the manager of a London suburban electrical goods store for his customers' opinions:

'Without exception', said the store manager, 'the married people who want to buy television sets by hire-purchase, say that they will save the first year's instalment by not going to the cinema.

'I do not recall selling a low-priced set to what you would call working-class people where this remark about saving the cost on cinema-going has not come into the discussions.'[62]

Ware also cited a recent report in the *Daily Express* interviewing 'nine people in three income groups' about the effect of actually owning a television on their leisure habits, all of whom said they now went to the cinema less often, if at all.

The public survey organisation Mass-Observation reported in September 1949 on an investigation in which it asked its national panel of mainly middle-class observers 'not only about their general feelings towards television but also about the effects that they think it would have on them had they a set in their own home'. According to the results, published in the *Journal of the Television Society*, 'Two-thirds of the Panel expect that with a television set their filmgoing will suffer. Why, after all, should they go out when the cinema and theatre can be brought to their own front room?' The journal noted that 'the survey reveals that even after the initial "craze" has worn off television set owners for the most part adjust their leisure hours to include television at the expense of such former activities as reading and the cinema'.[63]

The BBC conducted its own survey of television use in December 1948, though the results were not published until the spring of 1950. At a time when TV ownership was approaching 100,000, a sample of householders was interviewed about their viewing and other leisure habits. A 'control group' of householders without TV sets was also surveyed, and both groups were asked to keep log books of their evening activities over a three-week period:

The final report was based on a TV Group of 873 TV households, with a population of 2,724, and a Control Group of 856 non-TV households, with a population of 2,628, while the total number of evening 'logs' completed by the adults of the TV Group was 15,869 and by those of the Control Group was 11,434.

The survey confirmed that television ownership had spread rapidly and substantially to the lower-middle and working classes: 'whereas 57 per cent of those families which possessed TV sets when the TV Service was resumed in 1946 were well-to-do or upper middle class and the remaining 43 per cent lower middle or working class, the corresponding proportions of 1948 buyers were 39 per cent and 61 per cent'. Most significant for the theme of this chapter was the effect of TV ownership on cinemagoing:

> If possessing a TV set causes substantial modifications in the habits of those who are at home, it appears to have comparatively little power to keep at home those who would otherwise go out. Thus, whereas the average proportion of the Control Group who were not at home between 8.30 and 10.00pm was 22 per cent, the corresponding proportion of the TV Group was 19 per cent – only 3 per cent less. Among the many activities in which those not at home were engaged was cinema-going. This did not in fact account for more than a small proportion, but this is of less significance than the fact that the differences between the Control Group's and the TV Group's cinema-going was substantial. Whereas an average of 3.3 per cent of the Control Group were at the cinema during TV transmission hours, the corresponding proportion of the TV Group was only two-thirds of this figure – 2.2 per cent.

The report noted that television viewing waned over time as the novelty of TV ownership wore off and older leisure habits returned among the TV Group to a level comparable with those of the Control Group. However:

> Even if, as this evidence suggests, cinema-going habits are only temporarily disturbed by the acquisition of a TV set, and that in a comparatively short time viewers are going to the movies as frequently as they ever did, viewers are week by week exposed to TV for far longer than they are at the cinema. The enquiry shows that even the veteran viewers whose cinema-going habits had almost reverted to normal, were on the average watching sixteen evening TV transmissions for every visit to the pictures. The social implications of this fact are too obvious to need stressing.[64]

It should also be recalled that, at the time this survey was taken, nightly TV transmissions occupied on average only 90 minutes per evening.

Relations with the Film Industry in the Early 1950s

Subsequent developments in relations between television and the film industry took place in the light of new legislation. In June 1949, the Labour Government had set up a Committee of Inquiry on the future of broadcasting, chaired by Sir William Beveridge. Presented to Parliament in January 1951, the Beveridge Report on Broadcasting recommended the renewal of the BBC's Charter to operate as a publicly-funded service.[65] Arguments in favour of the film industry being licensed to participate in television had been placed before the Committee by a representative body, the Film Production and Cinema Industries (FPCI), and while the Report had not ruled out this possibility, it laid down as a condition that any TV programmes produced for showing in cinemas should also be made available for home broadcast by the BBC, on financial terms approved by the Postmaster-General. These were recommendations that the industry was not prepared to accept, considering them 'extraordinary, arbitrary and unjust'.[66]

By effectively prohibiting the production of material exclusively for theatre television they made unviable the expense of technological experimentation and cinema installations. At a meeting with George Barnes, the BBC's new Director of Television (the third incumbent in close succession since the service had resumed after the war), Associated British-Pathé's Howard Thomas (later a television executive) explained 'that the Industry did not want to install expensive machinery in order to put BBC programmes on [the] big screen – except for the very rare outside event. The cinema trade is in need of a boost. It will not get that by relaying programmes which an increasing number of people can see at home.'[67] He might well have added: 'for nothing'.

A dissenting Minority Report by one of the Beveridge Committee's members, the Tory MP Selwyn Lloyd, was published in May 1952 as a White Paper by the new Conservative Government. Contrary to the main report, it proposed setting up a commercially-funded alternative to the BBC, the first step in establishing what was ultimately to become Independent Television. But in respect of the film industry's application for permission to narrow-cast television to cinemas, the White Paper had noted 'that any scheme should take account of the interests of the BBC in regard to the showing of films on the home television programme'.[68] This too seemed designed to reduce the capacity of cinemas to compete with television. The FPCI argued that distributors allowing films on current release to be shown by domestic television would be 'tantamount to signing one's own death warrant'; and that even if this were to go ahead it would result in film artists, musicians and technicians demanding of the BBC additional fees that it would find prohibitive. William Haley remarked to Barnes that the Corporation had never asked to televise films while they were still on initial release and observed: 'what they say about artists' demands is a pointer to the way in which the Unions might be mustered to be sure films are denied to BBC Television'.[69]

Despite these ominous signs, there were various attempts from both sides at a rapprochement, as the film trade tried to find ways of accommodating its rival and the Corporation tried to address some of the industry's main concerns. Aside from the 'suicidal' idea of allowing current films to be televised (based, as BBC executives were at pains to point out, on a misunderstanding of the poorly-formulated list of film requirements it had submitted for 1949), these concerns can be summarised briefly as follows: the venerable age of the films the BBC did show; the low hire fees it was willing or able to pay; and the threat to the theatrical box office posed by the counter-attraction of television, especially when cinema films formed part of that attraction. The industry did however consent to allow film extracts and trailers, as well as personal appearances by and interviews with stars and directors, to be used for a 'magazine' programme highlighting new and forthcoming releases.

This programme eventually emerged as *Current Release*, which began broadcasting fortnightly from January 1952, offering news, reviews, interviews, studio visits and coverage of premieres and other industry events (see Figure 2.3).

Figure 2.3 BBC Television covered the London premiere of Charlie Chaplin's *Limelight* (1952). The cover still is from *City Lights* (1931) but neither film was broadcast in full until the late 1970s. *Radio Times* © Immediate Media Co.

In an article for *Radio Times*, Philip Dorté described this programme as showing that, 'for the first time since the war, the film industry and the BBC are wholeheartedly co-operating in a project which should not harm film interests and yet be of undoubted entertainment value to viewers'. He warned, however, that although *Current Release* can rightly be regarded as a 'combined operation' by the BBC and the film industry, it does not mean that the gates of the English and American film studios have been opened wide so that television can help itself to the latest, biggest, and best motion pictures which have been made expressly for viewing in the cinema. On the contrary, only a few of the older films made for the cinema will remain available for showing in full on television.[70]

The covert purpose of the programme, however, was precisely to prise open the studios' gates by offering the industry access to the television audience. *Scan and Television News* commented:

The BBC will receive no direct return for giving this free publicity to the film industry. But it is hoped that such a gesture by the Corporation will help to break down the violent animosity to TV harboured by many film men, and may result in a lifting of the present ban on modern full-length films for TV showing.[71]

If this attempt seems cynical, it was matched by the attitude of the industry:

There is a lot of bad feeling among TV men about the meanness of film producers in not allowing TV to show their best or more recent films. But why should the film men weaken their hand by giving to TV some of their own advantages – their star appeal, production values and, frankly, their professional quality? No. Wiser is the film producer who allows TV to show parts of his latest films in *Current Release*, making use of TV with a Trojan Horse in the shape of a trailer for his film![72]

The age and quality of the films available for televising were of course the direct result of the industry's own action in denying the BBC access either to more recent releases or to past classics. Dorté pointed out in his article that, 'as television endeavours to present all that is best in the other branches of art, it is only right that it should, from time to time, televise a specimen of the best that the film industry produces. It is to be hoped that our future relations with the film industry will one day allow us to fulfil that ambition.'[73]

But while cinema owners were undoubtedly relieved at the antiquity of most televised features, some producers and distributors were dismayed at the showing of 'old films', which they felt would 'give viewers a poor opinion of the quality of British pictures and may even give those viewers who are not normal cinemagoers a totally wrong impression of present day film technique and entertainment quality'.[74] John Archdeacon of *Scan* magazine concurred:

It is unfortunate that the Cinema has so far failed to make better quality films available to television. At the moment the owner of a television set is reminded of the cinema only by seeing dated films of poor all-round quality. This is, surely, the worst possible form of advertisement for the cinema.[75]

The schedulers were themselves often embarrassed by the quality of the product they could lay their hands on. In October 1951 Greeve del Strother wrote apologetically to Cecil McGivern to say that he had 'nothing that could be called "highlight films" to offer for the near future' and that he was now reduced to 'giving third showings to some prewar Paramount-British subjects; these are very poor offerings and I reject three out of four of them. I would not show any of them if I could help it, and I am sure they do the service no good.'[76] When McGivern in desperation asked Dorté for 'a good film for Boxing night', adding that he hoped the response would 'not be the usual "we cannot find one"', he was informed that the best film available was only suitable for an afternoon slot because of its age.[77] *Something to Sing About*, a low-budget musical James Cagney had made independently, dated from 1937. It was nevertheless transmitted at 7.45pm on 26 December 1951.

Sir Arthur Jarratt of the British Lion Film Corporation told Dorté that he was prepared to offer up to a dozen films per year for televising in afternoon slots, albeit not in the evenings except in case of emergency, if the Corporation would cease screening 'aged films of which the industry is really ashamed'. He was prepared to defy the CEA because he feared that the image of the cinema created by the material shown on television would be so off-putting as to deter TV owners from going out to pay for their film entertainment. Dorté explained that the service would need more than just a dozen pictures and remarked to McGivern: 'in view of the restrictions that would be imposed we should not be able to offer even as much money as we now offer for inferior films which we can bill when and how we like, but this angle did not seem to worry Jarratt at all. His main purpose seemed to be to stop us televising aged pictures.'[78]

The biggest obstacle remained the attitude of exhibitors, as represented by the CEA. They were convinced that films shown on television would compete directly with those in cinemas and that, once televised, a film would lose all its attraction for future cinema release and even non-theatrical screenings. Hundreds of bookings for *Pack Up Your Troubles* were reportedly cancelled after it was broadcast in 1950.[79] When a Western was erroneously billed in *Radio Times* as *Stage Coach*, exhibitors cancelled bookings worth a total of £400; the film transmitted was not in fact John Ford's 1939 classic but a Hopalong Cassidy adventure, *Stagecoach War* (1940/18.01.1950).[80] Rank's John Davis later informed the BBC that a 'good' five-year-old film still had the potential to earn between £5,000 and £20,000 in cinemas and added that as television was 'statistically doing harm' to cinema attendance there was no incentive for the industry to help the enemy by improving its service.[81]

From May to July 1952, BBC executives held a series of meetings with senior industry figures and representative bodies, beginning with the principal officers of the CEA. George Barnes tried to reassure them that the Corporation did 'not wish to televise any feature film until general release is completed'. He said the BBC wanted 'two afternoon showings per week and would like one prestige film a month for evening showing'. If it could not use British films for these purposes the BBC would need to look further afield, to 'foreign feature films or films specially made for television here or abroad'. In response, the CEA's president,

W.J. Speakman, 'denied that there is any period in which a film is not on exhibition between the end of its general release and its first re-release; showing the BBC would therefore take the bread out of the mouths of some exhibitors'. As well as referring pointedly to the Beveridge Report (in which it was widely believed that the BBC had had a hand), the members also expressed concern at 'the use made of television in attracting customers to cafés and in holding evening parties in private homes', which Speakman described as a 'public form of home television [that] was a great menace to the industry'.[82]

Subsequent meetings between the BBC and representatives of Associated British-Pathé, the Rank Organisation and the BFPA confirmed that it was mainly the CEA's intransigence that prevented them from offering any feature films to television. Arthur Rank advised Cecil McGivern not to try dealing with producers and distributors but to get the new Director General, Sir Ian Jacob, to work on persuading the five CEA officers who were the policy makers of the organisation.[83]

However, in the midst of these talks the CEA held its annual conference at Llandudno. There, a motion was proposed by Cecil Bernstein (whose company Granada Theatres was to play a major role in television only a few years later) and passed by its members that represented a significant worsening of the situation. Whereas previously exhibitors had been advised not to book films that had been shown on television, now they agreed to boycott *all* films made by producers and distributors who allowed their films to be televised. Companies could choose between supplying films to cinemas or to television; they could not do both.[84] This was a categorical statement of non-co-operation with the BBC and an open threat to any dissident factions in the film industry. The landmark 'Llandudno Resolution' of 9 July 1952 had an immediate effect: Dorté reported that 'film distributors who have done business with us in the past are now even scared to talk to us on the telephone'.[85] As a tit-for-tat retaliatory measure, he suggested announcing that *Current Release*, which had proved popular with both viewers and the industry itself, would be dropped at the end of the current quarter to see what reaction it would provoke. In fact it remained in the schedules until March 1953 before being withdrawn.

In May 1950, Dorté had offered a projection of what he hoped the situation regarding the television showing of feature films would be two years hence: 'Only two or three of these will be transmitted each week and these will be the "Hamlets" and "Red Shoes" of this world which have finished their general release and which we will televise because they are classics of their types and thus worthy of television screen time.' However, Dorté knew that unless relations with the film industry improved substantially this was unlikely to transpire:

> All that I can hope is that enough really good first-feature films will be forthcoming to make possible the rejection by us of what are really second-feature pictures, and that we shall be in such a position that when we show, say, a Western it is because we want to transmit a Western and not just because we want to transmit a film.[86]

A radical plan was put forward three months later in a five-page memorandum by David Kingsley, Secretary of the National Film Finance Corporation (NFFC). Kingsley envisaged a future in which a nationwide, high-definition television service (perhaps utilising the 1,200-line transmission standard proposed by Rank's subsidiary Cinema-Television, which incorporated Baird Television) had matched the cinema in technical quality of presentation and superseded it in popularity. Kingsley regarded films 'or similar pre-recorded material', rather than live shows, as 'the best television entertainment' and argued that 'television is not in competition with the film industry but only with the exhibition side of that industry'. As a film financier, he was aware that it was in the interests of film producers to have their work seen by the largest possible audience:

> At present the average film is seen by only 10% of the potential audience; the very best films by only 30%. Television as a means of exhibition will enable films to reach a much larger audience, including groups who do not at present visit the cinema. ...
>
> If television is to replace, or co-exist with, the cinema as a means of exhibiting films, it is as well, from the national standpoint, that the process should be accelerated. If, as some people still maintain, there are aspects of television which will always make it inferior to the cinema, then there can be little ultimate danger to exhibitors in giving the BBC an opportunity to show good recent films.
>
> Immediate efforts must be made to obtain the best and latest films for television; eventually to encourage the production of films specially designed for television.[87]

Kingsley proposed two ways of enabling television to acquire suitable recent films: by legislation, requiring all British and even foreign films to be offered to the BBC on reasonable terms within an agreed period; and by the payment of significantly higher fees, as much as £50,000 for several screenings of a particular film rather than the £300 that had been the typical price for two showings of a feature. Over time, he argued, rental payments at this level (to be paid for by a levy on the sale of television sets) would enable producers to break even through the TV market alone, while the development of new production techniques specific to television films would enable the British film industry to forego its generally unsuccessful attempts to break into the overseas theatrical market, particularly America.

These were extraordinary proposals coming from a leading figure in the film industry, especially the representative of a major Government-backed organisation, and it is not clear how widely circulated they were (it seems unlikely that the confidential memo was meant to be seen by anyone in the exhibition sector). Both the BBC and other officers of the NFFC were sceptical about some of its more extravagant ideas. George Barnes considered that 'live productions and films made for television would be the staple ingredient of any television broadcasting service'.[88]

An unsigned set of notes addressing each of Kingsley's main points was prepared for the attention of Lord Reith, the former BBC Director General who was now chairman of the NFFC. Their author doubted that television would ever be the equal of the cinema technically ('The immediacy of the medium is against this') or that it would replace the cinema entirely as a medium of popular entertainment. Doubt was also cast on the affordability of producing films mainly or exclusively for television unless they were extremely low in cost, and on the practicability of the hire fees Kingsley had urged. Instead, the notes suggested that a sound basis of co-operation between television and the film industry would help both. Not only could they learn from one another's production techniques, but the proper use by television of theatrical films would help stimulate a revival of interest in cinemagoing: 'Every good film on television will remind viewers how attractive a piece of entertainment the current cinema can be.'[89]

Meanwhile, the practical position for BBC Television was encapsulated in a 1951 comedy sketch on BBC Radio, featuring ventriloquist Peter Brough and his doll Archie Andrews:

> Archie: There's a smashing film at the local. Can we go?
> Peter: No, I'm sorry. Besides, you can see exactly the same film at home on television.
> Archie: I know, but who wants to wait twenty years?[90]

Notes

1 Draft letter, Philip Dorté to J. Arthur Rank, enclosed in letter to Maurice Gorham, 25 November 1945, BBC T16/76/1. For other accounts of postwar television's relationship with the film industry, see: Buscombe, 'All Bark and No Bite: The Film Industry's Response to Television', in Corner, *Popular Television in Britain*; Peter D. Cross, 'Television – the End of Film?', *Sight and Sound* 17, no. 67 (Autumn 1948): 131–2; Jean Quéval, 'Cinema and Television', *Sight and Sound* 19, no. 3 (May 1950): 141–2; and Michael Jackson, 'Cinema versus Television', *Sight and Sound* 49, no. 3 (Summer 1980): 178–81.

2 Record of interview, Gorham with Rank, 30 April 1946, BBC T16/76/1.

3 'Television: Negotiations with Newsreels', n.d. (1946), BBC T16/76/1. The postwar demonstration film directed by Dorté is *Television Is Here Again* (1946); like its prewar predecessor, a 35mm print is held by the BFI National Archive.

4 Record of interview, Gorham with REP, 1 August 1946, BBC T16/76/1.

5 Sir William Haley, note appended to memo from Gorham, 30 May 1946, BBC T16/76/1.

6 Representations from the Cinema and Film Production Industries to the Television Advisory Committee, 3 October 1947, BBC T16/75/1. An earlier memorandum on this subject had been submitted to the Committee by the film industry on 22 August 1946.

7 Greeve del Strother, 17 April 1946, BBC T6/334. For discussion of the myths regarding the last prewar broadcast, see Teletronic, 'The Day the BBC Closed Down'. Contrary to popular legend – already present in internal BBC correspondence in 1946 and perpetuated, many years later, by Cecil Madden in articles such as Philip Purser, 'The Pally Pioneers', *Radio Times*, 2 July 1981, 11, 13, and Robert Ottaway, 'Look What Happened in the Old Days', *Radio Times*, 2 October 1986, 16 – the Service

was not shut down midway through *Mickey's Gala Premiere* but shortly after it had finished transmission. This is confirmed by PasB records held at the BBC Written Archives Centre. Details of film transmissions mentioned in this chapter also derive from this source. See also Teletronic, 'The Day the BBC Closed Down', at http:// www.teletronic.co.uk/bbcclosedown.htm

8 Dorté to W.B. Levy, 26 March 1946; del Strother to Walt Disney Mickey Mouse Ltd, 19 June 1946, BBC T6/334.

9 J.E. Ricketts to Gorham, 21 November 1946; Ricketts to Norman Collins, 18 December 1947; Ricketts to del Strother, 11 April 1949, BBC T6/334.

10 David K. Wolfe-Murray to Dorté, 19 February 1946, BBC T6/151.

11 Gorham to Bernard Smith, 25 November 1946, BBC T6/334.

12 *The Times*, 24 January 1947, 8.

13 Collins to Haley, 2 March 1948, BBC T16/75/1. John Davis's name is misspelt Davies throughout this memorandum.

14 Draft paper by Collins for the Board of Governors, 'Television and the Film Industry', 11 July 1948, BBC T16/75/1.

15 'Cinema Television', *The Times*, 13 November 1948, 4. The basis of the talks and the reasons for their breakdown are discussed in Sir Henry French, 'Television and Cinema', 26 January 1950, BBC T16/76/2.

16 Estimate of BBC's Commercial Film Requirements for Television for 1949, 18 November 1948, BBC T16/76/1.

17 Archdeacon, 'Television and the BBC Charter', 5–6.

18 See Eyles, *Gaumont British Cinemas*, 201; Nigel A. Rainbow, 'First Hand Report of the J. Arthur Rank Big Screen Test', *Scan* 1, no. 10 (February 1949): 9. The television equipment from the Palais de Luxe was subsequently moved to the Odeon, Penge. In 1939, six West End cinemas had shown sporting events via large-screen television and in 1953, a larger number of theatres installed equipment to transmit the BBC's coverage of the Coronation: see T.A. Thompson, 'Television in the Cinema', *Picture House* 6 (Spring 1985): 3–9. On Rank's postwar television ambitions, see Macnab, *J. Arthur Rank and the British Film Industry*, 205–13.

19 Collins to H.J.S. Baker, 13 June 1949, BBC T16/76/2.

20 These points were made by Collins in memos of 4 July 1949 and 19 July 1950, BBC T16/76/2.

21 Collins, 19 July 1950, BBC T16/76/2.

22 Quoted in 'Is This the Best They Can Do?', *Television Weekly* 1, no. 53 (17 February 1950): 11.

23 Madden, re: conversation with Mr Crockford of the Rank Organisation, 13 June 1950, BBC T16/76/2.

24 Del Strother, 'Hire of Films from Outside Sources', 11 July 1947, BBC T6/169.

25 The first of these broadcasts was introduced by Air Chief Marshal Sir Philip Joubert de la Ferte, KCB, CB, CMG, DSO. The COI was established as a Government department in 1946 and closed in 2012.

26 Del Strother to Cecil McGivern, 4 June 1947, BBC T6/144/1. In addition to the films mentioned, del Strother's list included *Tennessee Valley Authority* (1946/22.07.1947) and two Soviet productions, *Land of Toys* (date unknown/04.04.1948) and *Russian Salad* (1941/09.05.1948).

27 Dorté to Wolfe-Murray, 7 April 1948, BBC T6/13.
28 Robert McDermot to Collins, 5 October 1948, BBC T6/122.
29 Dorté to W.G. Rayner, 5 July 1948, BBC T16/76/1.
30 Dorté to McGivern, 10 March 1949, BBC T6/13.
31 'Ealing, BBC Deal on 12 Features Bombshell to Brit. Pix Industry'.
32 Dorté to Rayner, 7 December 1948, BBC T6/13.
33 Del Strother to McGivern, 4 February 1949, BBC T6/13.
34 Note by McGivern, appended to memo, Dorté to Collins, 23 April 1948; McGivern to Dorté, del Strother, et al, 7 February 1949, BBC T6/13.
35 Dorté to McGivern, 10 March 1949, BBC T6/13.
36 'Don't Waste Time on These Films!', *Picturegoer*, 9 April 1949, 15. The magazine estimated that, 'at the moment, out of about twenty hours' viewing there is an average of up to nine hours of films in some shape or form – and they will be used more and more as the programmes expand'.
37 Del Strother to Dorté, 30 December 1949, BBC T6/13.
38 Record of interview, del Strother with Rayner, 30 November 1949, BBC T6/13.
39 Del Strother to Dorté, 17 January 1949, BBC T6/144/1.
40 Dorté to Collins, 29 March 1950, BBC T6/169.
41 Sundry correspondence in BBC R12/217/2.
42 Del Strother to McGivern, 17 February 1950, BBC T6/144/2.
43 Del Strother to Dorté, 17 January 1949, BBC T6/144/1.
44 Del Strother to McGivern, 8 December 1950, BBC T6/144/2.
45 McGivern to Collins, 27 May 1949, BBC T6/144/1.
46 Del Strother to Collins, 3 March 1949, BBC T6/144/1.
47 Del Strother to McGivern, 31 May 1949, BBC T6/144/1.
48 Pat Hillyard to McGivern, 27 June 1949, BBC T6/144/1.
49 Del Strother to McGivern and Madden, 28 June 1949, BBC T6/144/1.
50 Del Strother to Assistant Solicitor, 10 November 1950, BBC T6/144/2.
51 Del Strother to Collins, 3 March 1949, BBC T6/144/1.
52 Del Strother to McGivern, 31 May 1949, BBC R12/217/2; Dorté to del Strother, 13 April 1950, BBC T6/144/2.
53 Del Strother to McGivern, 20 February 1948, BBC T6/138.
54 Del Strother to W.L. Streeton, 1 September 1948, BBC T6/135/2.
55 Streeton to James Carreras and Streeton to del Strother, 30 November 1949; W.H. Fuller to Carreras, 13 December 1949; Streeton to BBC Solicitor, 19 December 1949, BBC T6/138.
56 Streeton to Collins, 5 January 1950, BBC T6/138.
57 Streeton to del Strother, 13 December 1950, BBC T6/138.
58 Figures are derived from the chart of UK Cinema Admissions at http://www.terra media.co.uk/reference/statistics/cinema/cinema_admissions.htm
59 Paulu, *British Broadcasting in Transition*, 167. For further speculations on the influence of television on cinema attendance, see: Kelly with Norton and Perry, *A Competitive Cinema*; Political and Economic Planning, *The British Film Industry*, 290–1; and Spraos, *The Decline of the Cinema*, 19–31. As Kelly et al note, Spraos considered the spread of television ownership to working-class households more important than the spread of ITV per se.

60 S. Seeman, 'The Cinema and Television', quoted in 'An Insight into the Cinema-Television Conflict', *Scan* 2, no. 1 (May 1949): 15.

61 'Television's Effect on the Film Industry', *Television Weekly* 1, no. 53 (17 February 1950): 3.

62 Ware, 'TV Launches a Film Offensive', in Noble, *Movie Stars*, 19.

63 'Mass Observation and Television', *Journal of the Television Society* 5, no. 11 (September 1949): 334.

64 Robert Silvey, 'The BBC Looks into Viewing', *Scan and Television News* 2, no. 12, April 1950, 4–6.

65 Home Office, *Report of the Broadcasting Committee, 1949*.

66 'Television and the Cinema', Film Production and Cinema Industries, 16 July 1951, BBC T16/75/1.

67 Record of interview, George Barnes with Howard Thomas, 3 August 1951, BBC T16/76/2.

68 Quoted in ibid.

69 Haley to Barnes, 25 July 1951, BBC T16/75/1.

70 Philip Dorté, 'Feature Films for Television', *Radio Times*, 11 January 1952, 42. *Current Release* and other cinema programmes are discussed in Holmes, *British TV & Film Culture in the 1950s*.

71 'Film Trailers Are on the Way', *Scan and Television News* 3, no. 12 (April 1951): 18.

72 Christopher Barry, 'We're Not Doomed Yet', *Television Weekly* 5, no. 7 (October 1952): 23.

73 Dorté, 'Feature Films for Television'.

74 Streeton to Dorté, 29 April 1949, BBC T6/169.

75 Archdeacon, 'The Function of Film in Television', 8.

76 Del Strother to McGivern, 2 October 1951, BBC T6/144/3.

77 McGivern to Dorté, 8 November 1951; Dorté to McGivern, 9 November 1951, BBC T6/144/3.

78 Dorté to McGivern, 4 March 1952, BBC T16/76/2.

79 Jackson, 'Cinema versus Television', 179.

80 Del Strother to McGivern, 17 February 1950, BBC T6/144/2.

81 Note of luncheon with John Davis and Sidney Wynne, 23 April 1953, BBC T16/75/1.

82 Note of meeting with CEA, 13 May 1952, BBC T16/76/3.

83 Note of talk with Rank, 24 July 1952, BBC T16/75/1.

84 'CEA Boycott Threat Snarls Chance of BBC-TV, Brit Pix Industry Tie', *Variety*, 16 July 1952, 11.

85 Dorté to McGivern, 25 July 1952, BBC T16/76/3.

86 Dorté to Collins, 12 May 1950, BBC T16/72/4.

87 David Kingsley, 'Television', 30 August 1950, BBC T16/75/1.

88 Note by Barnes on meeting with Mr Lawrie of the NFFC, 20 March 1951, BBC T16/75/1.

89 Notes for Lord Reith on David Kingsley's memorandum, 2 October 1950, BBC T16/75/1.

90 *Educating Archie*, Light Programme, 19 October 1951. I am grateful to Richard Farmer for discovering and passing on this item.

CHAPTER 3

Network –
The BBC at Bay, ITV Begins (1952–58)

I know Korda was a great producer. I know he dragged British films from a rut. I know his work often reaches classical heights. But Korda was working for films, not TV. It may be pleasant to blow off the dust and see again Laughton in *The Private Life of Henry VIII*, Olivier and Leigh in *Lady Hamilton*, Sabu in *The Drum*, and the epic *Shape of Things to Come* [*sic*], but when all is said and done it is not helping that struggling infant, TV, in the least. ... All these miles of film which the ITV companies foist upon the viewer day after day make the medium nothing more than the handmaiden of very poor cinema.

(John Marshall, '25 Old Films for TV – and Why?', *Yorkshire Post*, 10 May 1957)

Feature Films to Telefilms: Changes in BBC Programming

A sticking point for the film industry in the debate over whether or not to sell films to television was the low prices the BBC was willing to pay. By the end of 1952, the highest fee the Corporation had yet paid for a single showing of a feature seems to have been a mere £400 for *Storm in a Teacup* (1937/31.12.1949). It had paid £500 for two showings for each of the foreign-language titles hired from London Films (discussed in Chapter 2) and also for Robert Flaherty's *Louisiana Story* (1948/27.07.1951); but it was more usual to pay £300 for two or three showings of most features and only half that for two showings of a Western. For most renters, rates like these would hardly be sufficient to offset their risk, as allowing them to be shown on television would result in the Cinematograph Exhibitors' Association (CEA) boycotting them in cinemas. Film Booking Manager Greeve del Strother was offered three British films – *To-morrow We Live* (1943/18.07.1950), *Candlelight in Algeria* (1942/03.09.1956) and *The First of the Few* (1942/16.09.1956) – for a fee of £750 per title for three showings each. He explained the suppliers' dilemma: 'If films of this type are televised, so the owners say, all chances of further commercial revenue are killed. They are not willing to make them available, therefore, unless the revenue from the BBC will exceed what they might expect from commercial sources.'[1] In this instance the terms of the deal were not accepted: *To-morrow We Live* was acquired by the BBC but the other two were declined. All three were picked up six years later by the soon-to-be rival, ITV. However, it was rapidly becoming clear that prices were rising across the board and that eventually the Corporation would have to be prepared to pay them. A package of six American

'B' movies that had been turned down at £400 each in 1952 was accepted at the same price the following year simply because nothing else was available.[2]

More than once, del Strother asked to be sent to the United States to 'prospect the market' there.[3] But such a visit was turned down as an unacceptable expense, partly because the cost would have had to come out of the Corporation's limited dollar allocation, the result of the Government's Anglo-American Agreement of 1948, which placed restrictions on currency exports. There was in any case no guarantee that an American expedition would have been successful, as the major Hollywood studios were still just as opposed to allowing their films to be shown on television as were the British companies (though the latter did release films to American television from as early as 1948). Bookings from independent US suppliers, which became increasingly common as British sources continued to shrink, had to be done at a distance, with most of the product acquired sight unseen. These deals too were restricted by the amount of dollars available.[4]

Possibly as much out of pity as self-interest, the Rank Organisation, Associated British-Pathé and the Association of Specialised Film Producers (ASFP) all offered the BBC documentary and educational shorts for broadcast. Along with an increase in budget for live studio productions and the addition of extra floor space (including the former Gaumont British studio at Lime Grove, purchased by the BBC in 1950 and converted for television use), the availability of this material was one of a number of factors that helped substantially reduce reliance on feature films to fill afternoon slots. It was just as well, as the already restricted flow of features was contracting even more as the film industry entered what would prove to be a period of decline lasting more than three decades. In 1951, Head of Programmes Cecil McGivern explained to Director of Television George Barnes:

> The supply of feature films has once again lessened to the most meagre amount, and there is little hope of matters in this respect improving. This is to be expected, however, because of the present state of the British Film Industry and one must sympathise with the Exhibitors' difficulties in finding enough British films to keep going. It is inevitable in these circumstances that they are forced to use more old films and that therefore our very few sources of supply have become practically non-existent.[5]

McGivern pointed out that although the number of film slots was progressively being reduced he still needed some films to place in children's programmes. He would have liked to use more 'telerecordings' – film recordings of television programmes, photographed from large monitors during live broadcasts – but according to the terms agreed with the various performers' unions, such as Actors' Equity and the Musicians' Union, programmes could not usually be recorded or repeated except in emergencies because the artists were paid per performance. Telerecording on 35mm, a practice made possible in 1947, was expensive, costing around £130 per hour, so even if negotiations with the unions were successful in changing the regulations, it would still have been very costly by comparison with the hire of feature films.[6] For pragmatic reasons, McGivern also wanted to have more cinema films available for showing in the evening:

> A full length feature frees a studio and staff and it is constantly surprising even to those of us who are well versed in the manipulation of television facilities what an effect even one full length feature film can have on programme planning and the use of studios. *The regular use* of a full length feature film a week could considerably alter our rather rigid programme planning system. Two such films a week could alter it almost completely. Because of our inability to obtain films of sufficient standard, I have tried continuously to plan so that we need not use full-length films in our evening transmissions. The effort has been successful but all our studio and programme finance plans are based at present on a television service which does not use full-length films in the evening.[7]

In August 1953, the Corporation arranged a first: the simultaneous world premiere of a film in a cinema and on television. A documentary feature sponsored by UNESCO, *World without End* (1953/31.08.1953), was shown at the Edinburgh Film Festival on the same evening that it was transmitted by the BBC. Before the event, press reports explained that this arrangement meant the film would be banned by the CEA from commercial exhibition: 'The ban would be quite automatic, and unless a successful appeal is made, the film, co-directed by Paul Rotha and Basil Wright, would go on the "black list".'[8] In an article the following year, Rotha – by that time the BBC's Head of Documentary – explained the rationale behind the choice of simultaneous exhibition:

> When Unesco decided to let its film *World Without End* be premièred on British TV, thereby at one stroke precluding it from being booked into any cinema in the United Kingdom, it did so in the belief that through such a single screening (plus a later repeat) its picture would reach a wider and possibly more receptive audience (in the quiet of the home) than via a second-feature commercial cinema release. Unesco was proved right. Added to which, the warm and wide reception given to the film by its TV audience quickly stimulated the subsequent non-theatrical release which followed immediately on the TV screening. Many people having seen the film on their own TV set wanted to see it again on a film screen.

He estimated the film's TV audience as 3.5 million viewers. Thus the possibility existed of an alternative release circuit, with television as, in Rotha's words, 'a transmitter of celluloid, where every receiver becomes a little movie-screen either for film made specially or film acquired'.[9]

Despite the CEA's hostile actions, other industry bodies were still willing to try for a positive working relationship with the BBC. Towards the end of 1953, Sir Henry French of the British Film Producers' Association (BFPA) approached Barnes with a request for information. He wanted to know how many films the Corporation needed for the television service, categorised by features and other types of material, including films made for television; how much it might be prepared to pay for each type; and whether it intended to make television films of its own.[10] 'Television films' did not mean features, but any TV programmes made directly on film, including episodic series, as opposed to live productions

telerecorded on film for posterity. Made-for-TV film series were now being produced in considerable numbers in the US, though they had not yet been shown
by the BBC. French's letter, which was copied to the other trade associations, may
well have been prompted by an awareness of this development and a fear that the
Corporation might bypass the British film industry altogether to acquire TV films
from abroad or produce them in-house.

An estimate of annual feature-film requirements was forwarded to the BFPA
and a preliminary meeting was held on New Year's Day 1953. These requirements
were later announced to the press, where it was reported that the BBC 'would pay
higher rates for the hire of films only if much more modern and better quality films
were made available than those at present offered'. It wanted '12 feature films for
the evening performances, 26 feature films for the afternoons, 26 films suitable for
children, and two short films every week'. Representatives of the Corporation said
that fees between £750 and £1,000 might be offered for suitable, recent feature
films. These fees were to be for two showings for each of the twelve major features
required for evening slots, with the second screening of each to be in afternoons;
the combined audience for two such showings was estimated as four million
viewers, based on the two million TV sets thought to be in operation. When
asked by the BFPA 'if the corporation would be interested in hiring programmes
specially produced for television by the film industry', the BBC confirmed 'that
its policy was to consider films from all available sources, but again it had to take
account of quality and cost'.[11]

No agreements were signed, promises made or conclusions reached; but in
March 1953, the industry stated its current position in a memorandum signed by
the presidents of the four major trade associations and submitted to the Television
Advisory Committee (TAC):

> The day may come when the financial resources of the BBC may be increased and the terms
> above-mentioned may be revised, but basing ourselves on the information given at the meeting
> of the 1st January, we have no doubt whatever that all sections of the film industry (to say
> nothing of the Exchequer through reduced Entertainments Duty) would suffer heavy financial
> loss through reduced attendances at cinemas if they agreed to lend films to the BBC for inclu-
> sion in its Public TV Programme.

This memorandum also reiterated the industry's desire, first put before the
Committee in 1946, to be allowed to transmit its own programmes via television
to cinemas, without this being conditional on sharing such material with the BBC.
It added that the industry might also want to submit 'projects consequent on the
introduction of (i) sponsored television in this country and (ii) the developments
which are taking place in the United States in regard to the transmission of films
by TV'.[12]

The first made-for-TV fiction film shown by the BBC was *Dinner Date with
Death* (1950/28.09.1950), a half-hour British production, though it had no
immediate follow-up. But from the second quarter of 1954, 'telefilms' became a

staple of the schedules, largely taking the place of feature films in both afternoon and evening slots. Among the earliest TV film series broadcast by the BBC in 1954–55 were the British-produced *Orient Express* and *Fabian of Scotland Yard*, the American *Amos 'n' Andy*, *I'm the Law*, *I Married Joan*, and episodes of the US anthology shows *Gruen Guild Playhouse*, *The Pepsi-Cola Playhouse* (omitting their sponsors' names from UK billing) and *Disneyland*.

When news first broke that the BBC was to import American telefilms rather than make its own, George Elvin, General Secretary of the Association of Cinematograph Technicians (ACT), commented that the union had 'never agreed with the attitude of those British film interests who have resisted competition and cooperation with British television' but that it was 'no solution for the BBC to try to overcome this situation by importing foreign programmes, which ... are completely unsuited to transmission on the British television network'. Elvin claimed even to have asked the President of the Board of Trade to withhold import licences for the films.[13]

In May 1954, admonishing a technician who had complained about the poor condition of prints received, Greeve del Strother's assistant Daphne Turrell noted: 'Considering the general film situation, we are fortunate to obtain any films at all for television.' That summer, del Strother himself warned that it might 'well be impossible to fill future quarterly schedules at any price unless the film spaces are cut down', due partly to the CEA blockade ensuring the 'almost complete impossibility of obtaining any British films'.[14] Statistics provide a clear picture of the changing situation. In 1949 and 1950, despite the difficulties facing del Strother, there had respectively been 172 and 148 feature-film transmissions on BBC Television, the highest numbers since the start of TV broadcasting. Over the next three years, the number of such showings fell by around one-third, with repeats outnumbering first 'placings' by three to one. In 1954, there were only sixty-one feature-film transmissions, of which forty-five were repeats, and in the following year a mere twenty-one, of which twelve were repeats and only one – *Land without Music* (1936/27.05.1955), a Richard Tauber operetta – was in an evening slot. No newly-acquired films were transmitted at all in the first quarter of the following year.

Instead, the number of imported telefilms rose significantly. In the last week of September 1955, the BBC showed episodes of only two American series; by the summer of 1957 it was showing sixteen weekly, amounting to 10.7 per cent of total airtime.[15] From the autumn of 1956, 'B'-feature Westerns were largely dropped from children's hour in favour of in-house programming and acquired telefilm series such as *The Cisco Kid*, *The Range Rider* and *The Lone Ranger*. The Corporation also substantially increased the amount of film footage produced for use in its own programmes, having recently purchased the former Ealing Studios lot to provide additional floor space. In April 1958, it was estimated that the BBC's own film output (including pre-recorded sequences inserted in otherwise live productions) accounted for 20 per cent of its transmission time: the annual equivalent of 400 feature films when the same studio facilities had once produced six feature films a year for Ealing.[16] But by that time the Corporation itself had a rival, which after a slow start was soon to make more extensive use of feature films, telefilms and telefilm series than the BBC ever had.

The Competitor

The proposal for an alternative television service to provide competition for the BBC, first mooted in Selwyn Lloyd's minority report for the Beveridge Committee in 1951, was given concrete form in the Television Bill of 1954. The subsequent Television Act, creating the Independent Television Authority (ITA) as a public body to provide the service, was passed on 30 July of that year. The Authority met for the first time five days later and the first ITV station was on the air just over thirteen months after that: an astonishingly short period from conception to birth for a major broadcasting organisation.[17] Internal correspondence at the BBC rarely called this new service 'independent television', which would have implied that the Corporation's service was *not* independent (of the Government – an implication BBC staff deeply resented), or by the acronym ITV, which only later gained popular acceptance. It was instead usually referred to by a euphemism such as 'the Opposition' or, better still, 'the Competitor'. Newspapers referred to the new service as simply ITA, but for clarity this book will use that acronym for the Authority and refer to the programme providers as ITV.

Within the loose framework of the Act, the Authority determined how this competitor was to be constituted. Rather than a single national broadcaster, ITV was to be a network of regional franchises operated by separate companies. The country was carved up into fourteen regions and companies were invited to apply for a contract to provide the service in a particular area. The successful franchisees were to be independent of one another as well as of state control and, in theory at least, were in competition with each other as well as with the BBC: a company that produced a programme would seek to sell it to contractors in other regions. The Authority's own principal functions were fourfold: 'the appointment of companies, the control of programme output, the control of advertising, and the building and operation of the transmitters'.[18]

The three largest regions in terms of population – London, the Midlands and the North (the latter encompassing Lancashire and Yorkshire) – together served around three-fifths of the potential national audience. The ITA split each of these areas between two contractors, with different companies providing weekday and weekend services. One company, Associated TeleVision (ATV), was awarded both the London weekend and the Midlands weekday contracts; another, Associated British Corporation Television (soon renamed ABC Television), was given the weekend services for both the Midlands and the North. The London weekday franchise was awarded to Associated-Rediffusion (A-R) and the Northern weekday contract to Granada Television (see Table 3.1). These 'Big Four' – known as

Table 3.1 ITV programme companies (September 1955–July 1968) and their service opening dates.

Contractor	Franchise Region	Service Days	Service Start Date
Associated-Rediffusion (A-R, Rediffusion London)[a]	London	Monday–Friday	22.09.1955
Associated TeleVision (ATV Network)	London	Saturday–Sunday	24.09.1955
Associated TeleVision (ATV Network)	Midlands	Monday–Friday	17.02.1956
ABC Television (ABC-TV)	Midlands and Northern England	Saturday–Sunday	18.02.1956 (Midlands) 05.05.1956 (North)
Granada Television	Northern England	Monday–Friday	03.05.1956 (Lancashire) 03.11.1956 (Yorkshire)
Scottish Television (STV)	Central Scotland	All week	31.08.1957
Television Wales and the West (TWW)	South Wales and West England	All week	14.01.1958 (service ended 03.03.1968)
Southern Television	South East England	All week	30.08.1958
Tyne Tees Television (TTT)	North East England	All week	15.01.1959
Anglia Television	East of England	All week	27.10.1959
Ulster Television (UTV)	Northern Ireland	All week	31.10.1959
Westward Television (WTV)	South West England	All week	29.04.1961
Border Television (BTV)	English-Scottish borders	All week	01.09.1961
Grampian Television	North Scotland	All week	30.09.1961
Channel Television (CTV)	Channel Islands	All week	01.09.1962
Wales West and North Television (Teledu Cymru)	North and West Wales	All week	14.09.1962 (service ended 26.01.1964)
Independent Television Service for Wales and the West (ITSWW)[b]	Wales and West England	All week	04.03.1968 (service ended 20.05.1968)
Harlech Television (HTV Wales / HTV West)	Wales and West England	All week	20.05.1968

Note: see Table 5.5 for franchises operating from 29/30 July 1968.

a Renamed Rediffusion London on 6 April 1964.

b Interim service following the early termination of TWW, operated by the ITA until HTV could take over the franchise.

'networking' companies – were to produce the majority of original programming. They were also the first to go on the air, all commencing transmissions between September 1955 and May 1956, though the Manchester-based Granada did not extend its coverage to Yorkshire until November 1956, nearly six months after beginning its Lancashire service. The remaining eleven contractors – known as 'regional' companies – were appointed gradually over the next few years, opening their services between September 1957 and September 1962, as transmitters were built. Although the ITA was supported by a Government grant, all the franchise holders were private enterprises with their own staff and studios. All services were financed by the sale of on-air advertising time in the form of 'spot' advertisements inserted between programmes or in clearly demarcated breaks within them. This was quite different from the American model of commercial network television, in which programmes were directly sponsored by advertisers.

The main fear of the film and theatre worlds regarding ITV was that the commercial companies would be heavily dependent on acquired and, especially, imported programmes, including feature films, rather than on new material originated in-house. While revisions to the Television Bill were being drafted in March 1954, a deputation of representatives from fourteen showbusiness organisations, led by British Actors' Equity, met members of the House of Commons 'to discuss safeguards for commercial television and particularly methods of preventing a flood of cheap American films and recordings to the exclusion of British material'.[19] The Bill stipulated only, rather vaguely, that 'proper proportions of the recorded and other matter included in the programmes [should be] of British origin and of British performance'.[20] The delegation wanted this rule tightened up to require at least 80 per cent of any station's transmission time to be devoted to British programming. It was not patriotism that motivated this call, but the threat of work being denied to the organisations' members if ITV were to rely on programmes made outside the UK or on pre-existing material such as films made for the cinema. To this end, the delegation also requested that the following clause be inserted in the Bill:

> That there shall be no transmission of any film or other recorded programme which has been publicly exhibited at home or abroad at any time before the date of the first public transmission from any station under the control of the Authority, provided the Authority may except material from the provisions of this paragraph on cultural or educational grounds.[21]

In the event, neither of the proposed amendments was included in the Act; but discussions on broadcasting policy between the ITA and the trade organisations continued until the end of September 1955, after transmissions had begun. The resulting 'gentleman's agreement', set down in writing but not to be made public, was in some respects more advantageous to Equity and the other organisations than even their original proposals had required. The agreement called for no more than seven hours from the maximum permitted airtime of fifty hours per week (equivalent to 14 per cent) to be devoted to pre-recorded programmes of foreign origin, averaged over periods of three months but not to exceed ten hours in any one week. The initial term of this agreement was to be for one year from the start of each station's transmissions. Though these requirements were apparently restrictive, the initial programme plans of the new companies revealed that only 'slightly more' than five weekly hours of 'foreign filmed material' had in fact been scheduled. The trade organisations' request that, for the purposes of the agreement, 'material filmed here [in the UK] which had been publicly exhibited *anywhere* before the Authority's service opened, or which had been made here but was intended primarily for the American market, should be classified as foreign', was dropped as 'unreasonable'.[22] Despite the amicable negotiations over these arrangements, which did much to instil mutual confidence among the various parties, the film industry's resistance to the very notion of cinema films being broadcast on television inevitably led to confrontation before very long.

Commercial broadcasting from London began with A-R on Thursday, 22 December 1955, the weekend contractor ATV taking over two days later. No full-length feature films were shown in the first four weeks of operation. There were, however, episodes of a number of American telefilm series, including *Dragnet*, *Roy Rogers*, *I Love Lucy* and *Four Star Theatre*, along with three made in Britain and partly intended for export: *Colonel March of Scotland Yard*, *The Adventures of Robin Hood* and *The Scarlet Pimpernel*. One American series partly comprised films originally made for the cinema but edited down from around an hour to fill half-hour slots, inclusive of commercials. They were Hopalong Cassidy 'B' Westerns, beginning with *The Devil's Playground* (1946/29.09.1955), shown in children's hour (5.00–6.00pm). The BBC had been showing other Hopalong Cassidy films at their full original length, also in children's viewing time, since 1949 and continued to do so while ITV's abridged versions were on the air: the very day after the first ITV transmission of the series, the Corporation showed a repeat of another Cassidy feature, *Stagecoach War* (1940/18.01.1950), in the same time slot.[23] A-R and later ATV in the Midlands also showed a small selection of Laurel and Hardy shorts, a number of which had previously been shown by the BBC (see Figure 3.1). Such was the shortage of features available to television that at least twenty-five other films that the BBC had already televised were to be repeated by ITV stations in their first few years of operation.

Unlike the BBC, which aside from minor regional variations generally operated a single national service (at least as far as those parts of the country that it then reached were concerned), all of the ITV contractors separately made up their own programme schedules, coming together mainly for certain live programmes. Schedules could vary considerably from region to region. Although some programmes were shown by all or most local stations at the same time (especially in peak evening hours and including, for obvious reasons, live productions such as plays, variety shows and national news bulletins), others were shown on different days or at different times in each region. Feature films were shown regularly on ITV from the summer of 1956, though rarely more than one or two a week by each station. Like other recorded programmes, they usually varied considerably among regions, even when the days and time slots were the same (notably Sunday afternoons, which from September 1956 became a regular fixture for film matinees).

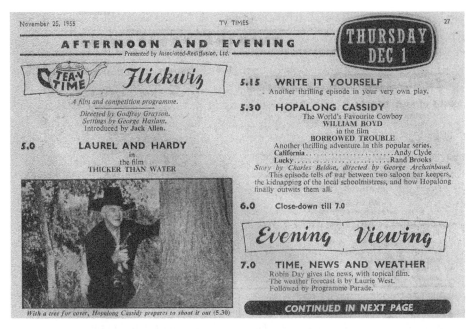

Figure 3.1 Children's hour on Associated-Rediffusion in 1955, including a Laurel and Hardy short previously shown by the BBC and a cut-down Hopalong Cassidy 'B' Western. *TV Times* © Associated-Rediffusion Ltd.

Like programme production, film acquisition was decentralised. Films were purchased by each company according to its needs, either individually or in packages; the broadcast rights acquired might be only for the region covered by that station or for the whole country. In the latter case, the films could be sub-contracted to other ITV companies for a fee to offset the acquisition cost. Not surprisingly, the larger companies typically bought the most films, particularly ATV and ABC. Granada acquired many films particularly suited to its Northern regional audience that would not have gone down well in London. These included the cinema vehicles of Arthur Lucan's Old Mother Riley character and the locally-produced comedies of the Mancunian Film Corporation, starring the likes of Frank Randle and other Northern music-hall performers. In his memoirs of working in the film acquisition team at Granada, Bill Gilbert recalls that his boss, Cecil Bernstein, used the scores awarded by reviews in the CEA's monthly Film Reports as a quality benchmark: 'Any film that had been rated above 7½ out of ten in the CEA reports seemed to satisfy CGB as to its suitability for showing on television.' Gilbert states that the company typically paid a hire fee for seven years of £200 to £250 for local rights or £1,000 to £1,200 for UK rights. He also notes that Granada acquired films for Television Wales and the West (TWW) when that station began transmissions in 1958.

The first ITV film to be 'networked' – that is, shown simultaneously in all or several of the regions currently operating (a mere three at that juncture) – was the Hammer production *Stolen Face* (1952/08.11.1956), released by Exclusive Films. The Exclusive library of 'B' pictures had been acquired by Granada, which particularly favoured a scheduling strategy that adapted features to the serial form now favoured by British television. Gilbert explains:

> Someone came up with the idea of the 'split feature'. I screened a number of features around 60–70 minutes in length, then arranged for them to be edited down to 54 minutes and split into two commercial half-hour episodes to be programmed over two evenings. For a while, this worked and other ITV regions contracted for split features.[24]

More than a dozen films, beginning with Exclusive/Hammer's *Lady in the Fog* (1952/27.02.1957), were networked in this way, and Granada continued to serialise films well into the 1960s. Such films were typical of those shown by ITV companies in this early period. Whereas the BBC tended to show American 'B' pictures, ITV generally opted for their British equivalents. Besides Exclusive, they came from small companies such as Adelphi, Apex, Archway, British National, Butcher's, Eros, Grand National, Monarch and Renown; or independent producers and distributors such as George King, Steven Pallos, Raymond Stross and Herbert Wilcox.[25] In many cases ownership had reverted to producers who were no longer active and rights had then been sold on to companies with no cinema interests but which specialised in supplying films for television, such as M. and A. Alexander, National Telefilm Associates, Orb Productions and Television Programmes (Distributors). Only occasionally in the 1950s did an American picture find its way into the ITV schedules. Among those that did were a group of 'B' features produced by William Pine and William Thomas for Paramount and the Sherlock Holmes series made for Universal, which had been disposed of to television distributors (see Chapter 7).[26] Prestige films of any kind were rarely available, but one block purchase by ABC in 1957 made newspaper headlines. A deal described by the *Daily Mirror* as 'the biggest of its kind since television began' helped the commercial companies gain an advantage over the BBC.[27]

The Korda Deal

The BBC's reluctance to pay higher fees lost it the most prestigious package of features yet to hit the market. In April 1952, Alexander Korda's London Film Productions proposed to supply up to twenty-six Korda-produced features at a fee of £2,000 each for two or three showings over two years. The company was willing to do this because it had recently resigned from the BFPA and was 'prepared to face the music' from the other trade associations if it could get the right price. Greeve del Strother (himself a former employee of London Films) thought the package 'far and away better than anything else available' and the proposal 'quite the most encouraging thing that has happened on the film booking front for a very long time'.[28] He suggested a counter-offer of £1,500 per title but was unable to get permission to pay more than £1,250 each for twenty selected films or

£1,000 each for all twenty-six, either way barely half what Korda hoped to make on the deal. London Films would not lower its price or guarantee to supply prints free of charge, so the cost of striking new copies would have made the package even more expensive. Despite the urging of both del Strother and Philip Dorté, who considered that a deal with Korda would set an important precedent for future dealings with the industry, as he was too important a figure for the CEA to blacklist, senior Corporation staff considered the deal neither economically nor politically worthwhile.[29] George Barnes and Cecil McGivern argued that its only effect would be to drive up the cost of films from other suppliers. McGivern was even sceptical about the programme value of the films themselves, 'some of which are good, some fair only, all old, and very few really exciting for viewers'.[30] The deal fell through.

Korda himself died in 1956, after which London Films ceased to engage in active production. The following year, the press reported that ABC had purchased twenty-five Korda films for over £50,000 – though in fact twenty-six films were involved, almost certainly putting the price at precisely that which the producer had earlier wanted from the BBC. All these films had been made between 1933 and 1942. Twenty-four of them were among those offered in the earlier package. Withheld from the deal were *The Four Feathers* (1939/23.03.1975) – presumably to protect the recent remake *Storm over the Nile* (1955/29.10.1960), which was still in theatrical circulation – and the semi-documentary *The Conquest of the Air* (1936/28.06.1975), which del Strother had considered the weakest of the batch. Substituted for them were two other, lesser titles that had not been offered to the BBC – *Forget Me Not* (1936/11.05.1958) and *21 Days* (1940/25.10.1958).[31]

Most of these films were ultimately shown up to three times by most ITV stations (again on a regional rather than a national network basis) between September 1957 and September 1962. They were usually presented in Saturday late-night or Sunday afternoon slots labelled with such titles as 'The Great Pictures of Alexander Korda' and 'Korda Classics'. These themed series, the first on British television devoted to a particular individual, were preceded by a networked documentary, *Alexander Korda the Great*. ITV's listings magazine *TV Times* promoted the Korda series on the cover with the strapline 'Great British Films', confirming that their critical reputation, perceived classic status and indeed their Britishness were the films' major selling points (see Figure 3.2). The same issue carried an article in tribute to Korda by the film critic of the *Observer*, C.A. Lejeune.[32]

The deal did not however escape adverse press comment, as the epigraph to this chapter demonstrates. An editorial in *Sight and Sound* quoted George Singleton, President of the CEA: 'the films are 20 years old at least and they have exhausted their value as film entertainment ... perhaps the public will now appreciate how good modern films are, after watching 25 weeks of these old ones'. Also quoted was sometime Labour MP Tom Driberg, then TV reviewer of the *New Statesman*, who commented that it was 'a retrograde step to rely at all substantially in programme-building on films made for the cinema. To pay this large sum for 25

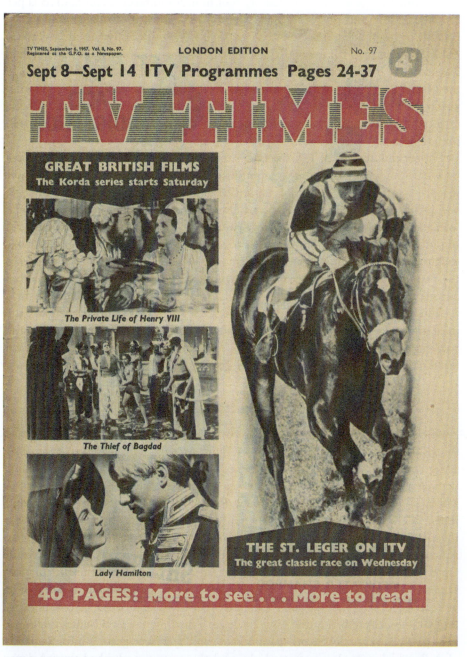

Figure 3.2 *TV Times* promotes ATV's Saturday-night series 'The Great Pictures of Alexander Korda' in 1957. *TV Times* © Associated-Rediffusion Ltd.

old movie films, and to feature them so prominently for 25 weeks running, is to confess, or to imply, that there is a shortage of live, or specially filmed, TV material.'[33] Despite such harangues, which were to become commonplace in the public discussion of films on television (see Chapter 5), viewers responded positively to the first of the Kordas, with an estimated 2.2 million London homes tuning in to watch *The Thief of Bagdad* (1940/14.09.1957). This compared favourably with the ratings for other films shown in the area earlier in the year, which averaged 1.46 million homes.[34]

The second quarter of 1957 was the subject of a case study in *Sight and Sound* by Duncan Crow. A self-confessed enthusiast of films on TV, Crow pointed out that the total of thirty-nine films shown on all channels between April and June, occupying an average of three and a half hours per week, could hardly be deemed 'considerable compared with the total weekly screening time of BBC and ITA stations'.[35] The maximum total weekly broadcasting time normally permitted for each station was fifty hours, the BBC's airtime being increased to that figure from the date of ITV's first broadcast.[36] Crow noted that, as the ratings indicated, a cinema film in the schedules was generally 'a fairly popular item, although even the most popular film will not attract as great an audience as, say for instance, the most popular variety programme'.[37] He observed that the high cost of the Korda package – an average of £2,000 per film – was anomalous when the more typical fees would scarcely enrich a producer or distributor.

The BBC Films Agreement

Although it had lost out on the Korda package, in the second half of the decade the BBC renewed its efforts to acquire more prestigious film product. In June 1955, Greeve del Strother was approached by James Carreras of Exclusive Films with an offer of up to two dozen American features for which he was acting as the UK agent through a subsidiary company, Saturn Films. This package consisted of independent productions, most of them produced by Walter Wanger and released theatrically by United Artists. The films had been purchased four years earlier by American TV distributor Motion Pictures for Television, owned by Matty Fox.[38] On behalf of his client, Fox, Carreras wanted a fee of £2,000 per title; this was four times as much as the BBC had ever paid for a single film, and so the offer was declined. Six months later Carreras reopened negotiations, now offering fifteen titles selected from the same package. This time the deal went through, at least partly because del Strother wanted to avoid the films getting into the hands of A-R, which was also interested. Around the same time he had turned down thirteen of Exclusive's own low-budget productions, which had then been picked up by ITV.[39]

The Saturn package included several high-profile titles, among them Ernst Lubitsch's *To Be or Not to Be* (1942/02.04.1956), John Ford's *Stagecoach* (1939/29.04.1956) and *The Long Voyage Home* (1940/24.01.1957), Alfred

Hitchcock's *Foreign Correspondent* (1940/06.08.1956) and Fritz Lang's *You Only Live Once* (1937/29.11.1956). These were by far the most important Hollywood pictures yet acquired for British television, licensed for up to three screenings each over a period of nearly three years. They were typically shown by the BBC as occasional 'specials', usually in evening slots or on bank holidays, beginning with *To Be or Not to Be* on Easter Monday 1956. It was presented as a posthumous tribute to its co-producer, none other than Alexander Korda.

The following summer, the BBC once again approached the four key trade associations – the CEA, BFPA, ASFP and Kinematograph Renters' Society (KRS) – with a proposal for a scheme that would address the concerns of all sides. One of the major fears in the trade was the flooding of the airwaves with films now controlled by US-owned TV distributors such as Motion Pictures for Television. The *Daily Express* speculated that the BBC would most likely be the 'main target' of salesmen 'because of its national audience, and because its programmes allow for 90-minute films'.[40] The Corporation proposed voluntarily to limit the number of films it showed if some relatively recent titles of good quality could be made available at a reasonable price. It submitted a modest request to be allowed twenty films per annum, all of which would have completed their theatrical release by the time they were broadcast. These twenty were to comprise twelve English-language films (including both British and American titles), four foreign-language pictures and four feature-length documentaries. Despite this major concession by the BBC, the CEA stuck to its guns and after months of negotiation declared in September 1956 that it would not agree to the televising of any feature films whatsoever. However, talks with the remaining three associations continued and after a meeting between their presidents and the BBC's Director General, Sir Ian Jacob, on 16 November an agreement was announced. The requested number of films could be supplied provided they were made not later than 1948 (the cut-off point used by the major studios in America). The agreement was to last for an initial period of twelve months commencing 1 January 1957.[41]

Immediately following this announcement, before any formal contract had been signed (in fact no such written document was ever signed – it was to remain another gentleman's agreement), Cecil Madden, Assistant to the Controller of Television, began making phone calls and writing letters to each of the major distributors requesting lists of the films available and the prices asked. The agreement did not directly provide for the supply of particular films, as this was something the trade associations could not offer themselves; they could only promise not to oppose the supply by their respective member companies and to encourage them to co-operate in the best interests of all parties (the CEA alone still refusing to concede this point). However, the hoped-for goods were not to be delivered. Without exception, the British branches of the American majors once again declined to offer any films at all, just as they had done twenty years before at the outset of television. This time their excuses were either that their US head offices still maintained a policy of not selling to television or that all their pre-1948 films had already been sold to third-party distributors and were consequently no longer under their control. Of the ten British companies approached, most would offer only titles that were either too old or too minor to meet the quality threshold that was one of the BBC's main reasons for seeking a formal arrangement. Others requested fees that the Corporation considered unreasonably high. London Films, whose deal with ABC had not yet been consummated, wanted £75,000 for twenty-three titles, more films than the BBC wanted under the terms of the agreement and even more expensive than the package that had been turned down as too costly five years before.[42]

Only the Rank Organisation was able to provide a short list of desirable titles; but the company wanted £25,000 for one transmission of each of *Henry V* (1944/25.12.1972), *Great Expectations* (1946/04.07.1965), *Hamlet* (1948/22.09.1973) and *The Red Shoes* (1948/14.11.1965); £10,000 for *Caesar and Cleopatra* (1945/04.02.1975); and £5,000 each for *In Which We Serve* (1942/12.11.1972), *The Way to the Stars* (1945/13.04.1975) and *Miranda* (1948/18.02.1965). Even the lowest price was far beyond the Corporation's range, and when asked to compromise the best deal Rank could offer was a package of six films for £35,000. The company's argument was that the considerable residual value of these films for theatrical reissue would be wiped out following a TV screening, especially as the CEA would block its member cinemas from showing them; Rank therefore wanted to be compensated for this loss of future business.[43]

To put these proposed charges in perspective, the overall cost of running BBC Television in 1956–57 was claimed by the Director of Administration (and future Director General), Hugh Carleton Greene, to be 'just over £3,250 an hour, of which £1,500 an hour represented actual programme costs', the rest overhead.[44] Acquired material was expected to be significantly cheaper than original programming. Thus, within two months of making the agreement it became apparent that it was not going to work. Further negotiations with the distributors, particularly Rank, continued for several more months, but still not a single suitable film was offered at an acceptable price and ultimately the agreement was brought to a premature end on 1 June 1957.[45]

These developments did not leave the BBC entirely empty-handed. At the beginning of the year, it had twenty-three films already in stock from previous deals: the fifteen Saturn titles and eight more besides, only one of which was British: *Tall Headlines* (1952/02.06.1956). Most of these had already been shown once or twice each by mid-1956 and all the contracts were set to expire by November 1958. If the Films Agreement had gone through as planned these remaining contracts would most likely have had to be scrapped, as they already exceeded the number of films permitted under the Agreement. Thus, from one angle, the BBC had saved itself a loss of £21,300 in cancelled bookings.[46] But there was still no prospect of a more regular supply of any features at all, much less films of the quality that the Corporation had hoped to secure.

Hollywood Deals, Major and Minor

The only possible sources of such material lay outside the mainstream of the film industry, from companies distributing to television films that had been acquired from the majors, either by outright purchase or by leasing for a fixed term. These companies had already supplied thousands of features to American television and had been the source of the films the BBC had booked through Saturn. James Carreras was keen to broker another deal on a larger scale and pushed for one with Associated Artists Productions' (AAP), which in 1956 had acquired the rights to all Warner Bros' films produced before 1950. AAP offered some 200 features at around £3,000 each.[47] According to Cecil Madden, Carreras promised that the BBC 'only had to ask for one big film, fix a price and he will get it in. Then he says all the others will come tumbling in.' John Huston's *The Maltese Falcon* (1941/10.06.1957) was provisionally pencilled in for Easter Monday 1956, before *To Be or Not to Be* was eventually fixed. But this was while the Films Agreement still seemed a live proposition. Madden argued that if it had been pursued the BBC 'would be dealing in an open market outside the Film Companies and that if we bought in this way our agreement was not strictly necessary, especially if our Opposition were refusing a similar agreement'.[48]

Madden also claimed that the ITV companies were 'stockpiling' films, and indeed they were striding ahead with package deals.[49] The trade press reported that the heads of the major ITV contractors – 'the four wise men of commercial TV, Lew Grade of ATV, John MacMillan of A-R, Howard Thomas of ABC and Sidney Bernstein of Granada' – had recently visited the United States in order 'to nibble at the extensive film libraries' of the Hollywood majors (though new government restrictions on dollar expenditure might have made their trip futile).[50]

In August, ATV bought a package of thirty-three Warner Bros titles from AAP for $250,000 (£89,300, or around £2,700 per title). This fee was paid from the dollar earnings of ATV's successful telefilm exports, such as the series *The Adventures of Robin Hood*.[51] The purchase was described in press reports as 'the first large-scale deal for the showing of feature-length American films on British television'.[52] On Whit Monday in May ITV networked, as a one-off special, *The Maltese Falcon* (see Figure 3.3). The package deal followed soon after this, with *Rhapsody in Blue* (1945/22.12.1957) the next title to be broadcast. The initial package was renewed and expanded, and over the next decade some 400 Warner films were transmitted on ITV stations, representing most of the studio's major titles of the 1930s and 1940s along with a great many minor ones that have not been broadcast since.[53]

Around the same time, other ITV companies picked up lesser packages of Hollywood product. In January 1957, while the Corporation was trying to make its trade agreement work and after acquiring the Korda library, ABC bought a group of John Wayne 'B' Westerns. These had been made in the 1930s for the now-defunct Republic Pictures and distributed by its television offshoot, Hollywood TV

Figure 3.3 ITV's networked treat for Whit Monday 1957 was the UK television premiere of
The Maltese Falcon (1941). *TV Times* © Associated-Rediffusion Ltd.

Service.[54] Similarly, Granada purchased twelve pre-1950 Columbia titles through
the studio's television arm, Screen Gems, after ABC had acquired a smaller group.
According to Bill Gilbert, the fee was £940 per film for two transmissions.[55]

The obvious disparity between the numbers of films scheduled by ITV and the
BBC was noted in both internal Corporation memoranda and the trade papers. In
the first quarter of 1957, the BBC had shown only two feature films: one American
(*The Long Voyage Home*), the other Italian (*Bicycle Thieves*, 1948/05.03.1957). The
four commercial stations, by contrast, had shown twenty-eight features amongst
them, all but two of which were British. In the second quarter, as previously noted,
film transmissions by the BBC and ITV were seven and thirty-nine, respectively.[56]
Unsurprisingly, therefore, when the independent companies were approached by
the trade associations to consider a self-restrictive agreement similar to the BBC's,
they declined.[57]

In March 1957, by which time it was widely known that the BBC had not been
able to secure any films under its trade agreement, the press was speculating that
the Corporation would seek films from other sources such as the TV distributors.
Internal BBC documents confirm that this was exactly what was about to happen.[58]
However, Deputy Director of Television Broadcasting Cecil McGivern stressed
the need for caution in any prospective deals: as the issue of cost was one of the
reasons for the collapse of the Films Agreement, prices should be reasonable and
preferably not in the upper range of what the BBC typically paid; the number of
American films should be carefully monitored. But McGivern also insisted that

films were particularly needed for occasions such as holidays, as well as to ease the pressure on in-house resources, and that they had 'a definite and valuable place in television provided they are good'. He commented pointedly: 'ITA might have gained audiences by the number of feature films it has transmitted but it has not gained respect by doing so.'[59]

The month after the Films Agreement had been dropped, the BBC's Director of Television Broadcasting, Gerald Beadle, was approached with a most unusual offer. Two years earlier, Howard Hughes, billionaire owner of the ailing Hollywood studio RKO Radio Pictures, had sold the company to General Teleradio (a division of the General Tire and Rubber Co), which owned a small group of US television stations. This company in turn sold the bulk of the studio's film library to C&C Television (a division of the C&C Super Corporation), headed by Matty Fox, whose company Motion Pictures for Television had also been bought by C&C. The loan of $15.2 million used to buy the library was guaranteed by the International Latex Corporation (itself a subsidiary of the Stanley Warner Corporation, owners of the former Warner Bros theatre chain). Fox's unorthodox practice was to licence his stock of features to commercial broadcasters, not for cash but in return for advertising time for corporate clients; he therefore set about bartering the RKO library for ad time on behalf of International Latex, typically offering local stations TV rights in perpetuity to the studio's entire inventory of 740 features made between 1928 and 1955. Fox had cleared the broadcast rights of the post-1948 RKO titles with the American talent guilds and unions by agreeing residual payments, so the library contained a significant number of films of relatively recent vintage.[60]

These activities had been confined to the American market until Beadle was contacted in July 1957. It remains unclear whether the ITV companies had been approached first, as would seem logical, because of course the BBC itself had no broadcast advertising time to exchange. It did, however, own the most widely read periodical in the country in the listings magazine *Radio Times*, which had a circulation of around 8,000,000.[61] The magazine carried programme details only of BBC TV and radio schedules, and as the Corporation retained the sole copyright in its listings, no other publication could carry similar details. C&C's proposal, relayed through a sales agent, Robin International, was for the exchange of two weekly pages of advertising in *Radio Times* over three years in return for unlimited rights to the RKO library for a period of ten years. Included were the rights not only to broadcast the films but to reissue them theatrically and even to re-sell them to other broadcasters in the Eastern hemisphere, including the rival ITV. In theory, then, the BBC could make a significant profit on the deal for no cash up front, while gaining a large stock of Hollywood films that would last it for the next decade and could even be exploited for revenue. They would be particularly useful in the event of emergencies such as strikes or studio blackouts or of broadcasting hours being further extended, as seemed likely. Beadle also noted, with recent events in mind: 'The possession of such a library would greatly strengthen our bargaining position with the owners of British films.'[62]

He elaborated on these arguments in a later memo attempting to overcome objections that had been made to the deal:

1. We shall have a lot of valuable material ready made for our own showing and a lot of rubbish too admittedly.
2. We shall gain much prestige with the business community who think that only ITV have the sagacity to operate these sort [*sic*] of deals.
3. We shall bring the British Film Industry to heel. At the moment they think we are in a weak position and can be trifled with.
4. It is not impossible that we might make quite a lot of money.

For all these reasons Beadle was keen on pursuing the proposal; but its unconventional nature proved a deterrent for his colleagues. The BBC's General Manager of Publications, G. Strode, considered the idea unethical, partly because one of the two pages of advertising would be taken for an unnamed client besides International Latex. Strode insisted: 'it is a firm practice of all publications of repute that they never sell advertising space "blind". Every order placed by an advertising agent or advertiser is always for a particular client.'[63] The Controller of Finance, T. Lochhead, expressed concern at what the Public Accounts Committee might think of the deal, and also pointed out that the acquisition of so many American features, and their likely frequent use, would substantially increase the proportion of non-British material transmitted by the BBC.[64]

There was also the issue of cost: the cash value of two pages of advertising for three years at current rates was put at £1,372,800; but if space could not be found each week, four pages would have to be added to the magazine at a present cost of £750,000 for the three years.[65] Unless the vendor would agree to pay these additional production costs, equivalent to half the estimated cash value of the library, they would have to be met by the BBC. The alternative, of providing space only when it was available, was estimated by Hugh Carleton Greene as likely to take up to fifteen years to reach the equivalent value; Strode put the period at twenty-four years. But it was concern about 'the effect of such a deal on the reputation (and the profits) of the *Radio Times*' that finally decided the matter.[66]

It was left to Beadle to suggest instead what the vendor had previously refused to contemplate: 'a contribution of real cash value from the Television Service to pay for the showing of the best of the RKO films'.[67] This more straightforward block purchase arrangement resulted in a deal announced to the press in December 1957:

The BBC has acquired the television rights of a hundred of the best films in the RKO library, ranging from pre-war productions such as the famous Astaire-Rogers musicals to films made as recently as 1954 and 1955. They were all selected individually by the BBC and have been acquired for the sum of £215,000 sterling. This is the biggest film deal that has been made in British television.[68]

The hire period was seven years. The cost of the deal, based on a rate of £2,150 per title, was carried by the programme allowance budget until each film had been played at least once and the full amount thereby absorbed. The fact that no dollars had been spent on the package was a significant point in the Corporation's favour when purchasing a large block of American material. Anticipating criticism, the press office supplied ready answers to likely questions. On the matter of live versus pre-recorded material: 'The BBC intends to continue to provide a comprehensive service with predominantly "live" material. The agreement will, however, enable us to show better quality films, including some more recent films, than we have been able to hitherto.' On why the Corporation had not bought British films: 'We couldn't. We made sincere efforts to reach agreement with the British film industry, but could not get their cooperation.'[69]

Aside from the size of the package deal (which was later extended with the addition of twenty more titles), the biggest ructions were created by the news of how the films would be scheduled: around 9.00pm on Saturday evenings, alternating fortnightly with live drama. According to one trade observer, this programming strategy 'could virtually ruin the film industry'.[70] Saturdays were traditionally 'the cinema's best night' and for one cinema owner, 'the renters having put the exhibitors in their coffins, the BBC are now going to screw it down'.[71] The trade paper *The Daily Cinema*, estimating that the potential loss of admissions 'could be counted in millions', was clear where the blame lay:

> The CEA should not be surprised by this blow. They had warnings aplenty – not least from this journal. Knowing that two thousand films were held outside the industry they nevertheless preferred to act like ostriches, burying their heads not in the sand but in the ridiculous Llandudno resolution. ... This is a crisis affecting the whole industry. Since it has been brought about largely by the CEA's recalcitrance it is to that association that the industry will look for flexibility, adroitness and acumen to resolve it.[72]

The RKO package was used strategically and with some success by the BBC to help improve its share of the viewing audience, which had been markedly inferior to ITV's since the competitor's inception. The first RKO film to be placed was the comedy *Bachelor Knight* (1947/11.01.1958), starring Cary Grant. It launched 'The Saturday Film', BBC Television's first regular programme slot devoted to feature films in peak-time hours (see Figure 3.4).[73] The initial RKO titles were each seen by an estimated nine or ten million viewers, around half the potential audience, and ranked 'about third or fourth on the BBC list of top attractions'.[74]

When shown irregularly on weekday nights against weaker competition, they could perform even better. On a Tuesday evening in 1959, ITV networked a live play, *The Skin of Our Teeth*, produced by Granada and starring Vivien Leigh in her first television performance. The BBC had scheduled a Western, *Rachel and the Stranger* (1948/07.08.1961), as opposition but at the last minute it substituted a stronger attraction, the Fred Astaire-Ginger Rogers musical *Follow the Fleet* (1936/17.03.1959), which reportedly 'drew a record audience'.[75] Another RKO title shown midweek, *The Big Steal* (1949/17.08.1959), starring Robert Mitchum, was placed at number 7 in the weekly national ratings, being seen in an

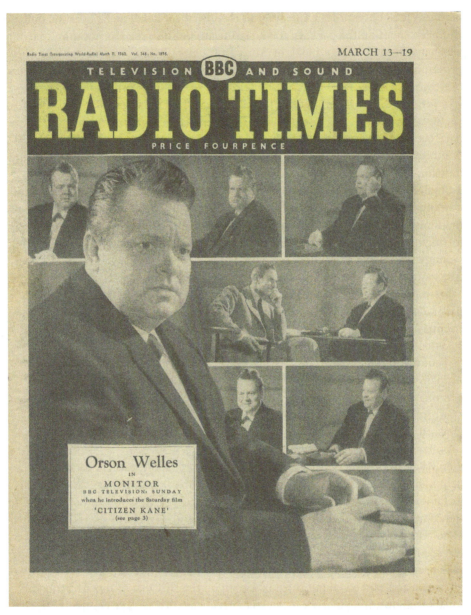

Figure 3.4 Orson Welles was interviewed for the BBC's flagship arts show *Monitor* in 1960, in the same week that his RKO-Mercury production *Citizen Kane* (1941) made its British television debut on 'The Saturday Film'. *Radio Times* © Immediate Media Co.

estimated 3.6 million homes. This was one of the few occasions when any BBC show made the ratings top ten in the latter half of the decade. The ITV stations' usual practice of scheduling on a regional basis meant that films rarely figured in the national charts except on the few occasions when they were networked.

My Favorite Wife (1940/06.10.1959), another Cary Grant comedy, was one of about forty RKO films bypassed by the BBC that ITV bought instead; when part-networked in four of the six regions then operating, the film achieved a 74 per cent audience share.[76]

The Ealing Deal

The Korda, Warner and RKO deals constituted a series of serious blows for the film industry. The Korda package occupied most of the major ITV film slots in the 1957 autumn schedules, usually starting shortly after 10.00pm on Saturdays, at which time cinemas would be finishing their last performance of the night. But after the BBC announced its plans for the RKO package, ITV schedulers moved their Saturday film slots earlier in the evening (8.30pm for ATV, 9.15pm for ABC) in order to compete directly for audiences. The Warner titles alternated with the remaining Korda pictures. Thus cinemas were faced with film competition on two fronts simultaneously.[77]

Yet another ITV package deal hailed from much closer to home than Hollywood: Ealing, to be precise. In October 1957 news broke that Michael Balcon was preparing to sell 100 features produced at Ealing Studios before 1945 to ABC Television for £200,000. We saw in Chapter 2 that Balcon and his studio manager Reginald Baker had been sympathetic to the idea of the company's films appearing on television as far back as 1948, but that the wariness of its subsidiary Associated British Film Distributors (ABFD) toward the mood in the industry had prevented any more than a dozen films from being televised. In December 1956, with the BBC Films Agreement in the air, ABFD had offered the Corporation a further selection of titles from the prewar period, requesting 'favoured nation status' based on the previous deal, but these had been turned down by the BBC as too old.[78] The package now being offered to ABC contained titles thirteen or more years old; but such a large block of films from such a respected source threatened to set a dangerous precedent. *Kine Weekly* speculated that 'if the Ealing deal goes through the flood gates will be opened by the greatest torrent of old British films ever seen on television'.[79] Although Balcon stated that the purchase fee the company received would be put back into film production to the ultimate benefit of cinemas, the announcement provoked threats from the CEA to boycott Ealing films.

Balcon doubted whether boycotts were 'logical, possible or legal' and the BFPA was powerless to intervene because Ealing was not a member company.[80] It was, however, a member of another trade association, the Federation of British Film Makers (FBFM), which had been formed in January 1957 to represent the smaller production companies and the British branches of the major American producer-distributors. After selling its production facilities to the BBC in 1955, Ealing Films had moved base to MGM's studio lot in Borehamwood and most of its later productions were financed and distributed by that company. The FBFM was as concerned as any other industry body with the 'problem' of selling films to television, but it was also acutely aware that an absolute ban, closing off a potential source of revenue, might cause filmmakers difficulties in raising finance for future pictures. It therefore sought a compromise: 'that for any release of films to television there should be a formula of control covering the age of films and the times of showing'.[81] Such a formula was first proposed by, of all bodies, the CEA. It suggested that for a trial period of one year, producers and distributors should agree not to offer films to broadcasters unless at least ten years had elapsed since their initial theatrical release. It also proposed contractual restrictions on the days and times when films could be broadcast: in afternoons, excepting Saturdays and bank holidays, to finish by 5.00pm; and on one or two nights per week (one midweek, the other at the weekend), to start after 10.00pm. Furthermore, no station would be permitted to show more than two films in any one week. All broadcasters would be required to agree to these terms and conditions for any films they wanted to show; any breach of them and the contracts for all films would be cancelled.[82]

Ealing had demurred from the first of these proposals when they were discussed at an FBFM council meeting in September 1957. The Federation had proposed raising the age limit of films from ten to twelve years but Baker, who was also FBFM's vice chairman, pointed out that 'the Government, in the Regulations arising under the new Films act, had prescribed a period of twelve months as being an appropriate period between the initial showing of a film and its showing on television'.[83] The sale of Ealing films to ABC was at this stage already on the cards. By January 1958, following the news of the RKO, Warner and Ealing deals, the CEA formula appeared utterly redundant, events having passed it by. But another plan was in the offing – one that would have a crucial influence on relations between the film trade and television for the next seven years and beyond.

Notes

1 Greeve del Strother to Cecil McGivern, 14 February 1950, BBC T6/138.
2 Daphne Turrell to McGivern, 4 September 1953, BBC T6/144/6.
3 McGivern to George Barnes, 13 December 1951, BBC T6/144/3.
4 Del Strother to McGivern, 20 November 1951, BBC T6/144/3; McGivern to Barnes, 3 March 1952, BBC T16/76/3; del Strother to McGivern, 28 April 1953, BBC T6/144/6.
5 McGivern to Barnes, 1 January 1951, BBC T16/76/2.
6 On the genesis of telerecording, see Jacobs, *The Intimate Screen*, 10–24, 79–80.
7 McGivern to Barnes, 13 December 1951, BBC T6/144/3.
8 'No TV or...!', *TV News* 6, no. 18 (16 October 1953): 7.
9 Paul Rotha, 'Documentary: Is Television Affecting Its Future?', *Film* 2 (December 1954): 14–15. These pages also contained readers' responses to a proposition, put in *Scan*'s launch issue, that television might serve as a form of repertory cinema, an adjunct to the Film Society movement that the new magazine was created to serve.
10 Sir Henry French to Barnes, 4 December 1952, BBC T16/75/1.

11 'Film Hiring Fees for Television', *The Times*, 9 January 1953, 6.

12 Memorandum from the Film Industry to the Television Advisory Committee, 26 March 1953, BBC T16/75/1.

13 'BBC Plan to Use US Programmes', *The Times*, 29 January 1954, 3. In an article written for a popular film magazine, Elvin later complained: 'The film industry is doing nobody any good by continuing to adopt the King Canute-like attitude of trying to halt progress by refusing to let its films be shown on television screens unless the print is so old as to be almost a museum piece' ('How Cinema Might Die', *Films and Filming* 1, no. 11 [August 1955]: 8).

14 Turrell to H.H. Hall, 31 May 1954; del Strother to Joanna Spicer, 19 August 1954, BBC T6/144/6.

15 'Statistics on Films', quarterly report, 25 September 1957, BBC T16/311/1.

16 Ronald Waldman, 21 April 1958, BBC T16/72/5.

17 On the creation and the early years of ITV, see: Briggs, *The History of Broadcasting in the United Kingdom*, Volumes 4 and 5; and Sendall, *Independent Television in Britain*, Volumes 1 and 2.

18 Independent Broadcasting Authority, 'Evidence to the Committee on the Future of Broadcasting under the Chairmanship of Lord Annan' (September 1974), quoted in Potter, *Independent Television in Britain*, Volume 3, 230.

19 'Television Bill "Dangers"', *The Times*, 23 March 1954, 5.

20 Television Act 1954, Section 3(1)(d).

21 'Television Bill: Draft Amendments', enclosed with ITA Paper 54(24), 10 December 1954, IBA/422: 3997073.

22 'The Use of Imported Films: Final Agreement at Last', ITA Paper 87(55), 30 September 1955, IBA/422: 3997073.

23 On the TV afterlife of Hopalong Cassidy, see Kelly Boyd, 'Cowboys, Comedy and Crime: American Programmes on BBC Television, 1946–1955', *Media History* 17, no. 3 (2011), 233–51; Glancy, *Hollywood and the Americanization of Britain*, 199–204; and Michael Kackman, 'Nothing on but Hoppy Badges: *Hopalong Cassidy*, William Boyd Enterprises, and Emergent Media Globalization', *Cinema Journal* 48, no. 4 (Summer 2008), 76–101.

24 Bill Gilbert, 'Films on TV: Before the Flood', *The Veteran* 120 (Autumn 2008), 11.

25 For discussion of some of these films, companies and producers, see: Chibnall, *Quota Quickies*; and Chibnall and McFarlane, *The British 'B' Film*.

26 On the Hollywood studios' practice of quietly selling off some of their least important titles, even prior to the start of their official dealings with television, see David Pierce, '"Senile Celluloid": Independent Exhibitors, the Major Studios and the Fight over Features on Television, 1939–1956', *Film History* 10, no. 2 (1998): 141–64.

27 Clifford Davis, 'ITV Gets 25 Top Films', *Daily Mirror*, 7 May 1957, 3.

28 Del Strother to McGivern, 18 April 1952, BBC T6/194.

29 Del Strother to Barnes, 30 April 1952; Barnes to Philip Dorté, 6 June 1952; Dorté to Barnes, 9 and 16 June 1952, BBC T6/194.

30 McGivern to Barnes, 12 June 1952, BBC T6/194.

31 A number of films originally distributed by London Films but no longer under its control had previously been televised: *Storm in a Teacup*, *Fire over England* (1937/28.03.1950) and *South Riding* (1938/17.01.1950) had been shown by both the

BBC and ITV; *Dark Journey* (1937/06.08.1956), *Action for Slander* (1937/26.12.1956) and *The Shop at Sly Corner* (1946/13.01.1957) by ITV alone.

32 C.A. Lejeune, 'Korda as I Knew Him', *TV Times*, 6 September 1957, 6–7.

33 Quoted in 'The Front Page', *Sight and Sound* 27, no. 1 (Summer 1957): 3; ellipses and interpolations in original. Tom Driberg's article was 'The Resurrection Men', *New Statesman*, 11 May 1957.

34 Teletronic, TAM ratings. These figures were for the spring quarter. The six films shown by BBC in this period averaged 1.2 million homes and ITA's twenty-one, 1.52 million.

35 Duncan Crow, 'From Screen to Screen: Cinema Films on Television', *Sight and Sound* 27, no. 2 (Autumn 1957): 62.

36 Cecil McGivern, 'New Pattern in BBC Television Programmes', *Radio Times*, 16 September 1955, 15. Educational, religious and political programming was allowed additional time.

37 'From Screen to Screen', 64. Crow erroneously cites the figures as millions of viewers, when in fact they referred to the number of homes tuning in.

38 Pierce, '"Senile Celluloid"', 150.

39 Del Strother, 24 June 1955, 18 January 1956, 22 March 1956 and 15 May 1956; James Carreras to del Strother, 19 April 1956, BBC T6/135/2.

40 Robert Cannell, 'BBC Plans Deal to Put Newer Films on TV', *Daily Express*, 14 May 1956.

41 '"Films on Television" Ban to Stay', *The Times*, 14 September 1956, 8; 'Film Agreement with the BBC', *The Times*, 17 November 1956, 6.

42 Gordon Smith, 24 January 1957, BBC T6/350/1.

43 K.N. Hargreaves to Smith, 7 January 1957, BBC T6/360/1.

44 'Cost to BBC of Competitive Television', *The Times*, 13 March 1958, 14.

45 BBC press release, 6 June 1957, BBC T6/360/1.

46 Smith, 3 January 1957; Spicer, 7 January 1957, BBC T6/360/1.

47 List of sample product available from AAP and other distributors enclosed with Madden to McGivern, 25 January 1957, BBC T6/360/1. AAP was itself soon to be acquired by United Artists.

48 Madden to McGivern, 3 January 1957, BBC T6/360/1.

49 Madden to Sir David Griffiths, 4 February 1957; Madden, 7 February 1957, BBC T6/360/1.

50 *Daily Film Renter*, 8 February 1957.

51 'Warner Films for Television', *The Times*, 30 August 1957, 3.

52 'ATV to Pay £89,300 for US Films', *The Times*, 29 August 1957, 3.

53 Former Granada and BBC film buyer Bill Gilbert states that ATV, A-R and Granada all bought into the Warner library, Granada for thirty titles at £1,000 apiece for five years' unlimited rights (Gilbert, 'Films on TV: Before the Flood', 12).

54 *Daily Film Renter*, 1 February 1957.

55 Gilbert, 'Films on TV: Before the Flood', 12.

56 Waldman, 21 April 1958, BBC T16/72/5; 'Many More Features on TV in Second Quarter', *Kine Weekly*, 18 July 1957.

57 'Unions Want Total Ban on Films for TV', *Kine Weekly*, 4 April 1957.

58 *Daily Film Renter*, 8 March 1957; McGivern to Gerald Beadle, 28 March 1957, BBC T6/360/1.

59   McGivern, 'Feature Films in Television', 11 June 1957, BBC T6/360/1.

60   Pierce, '"Senile Celluloid"', 156–7; Segrave, *Movies at Home*, 40–2. On the background to the TV deals for the RKO library, see also: Hoyt, *Hollywood Vault*, 142–77; Jewell, *Slow Fade to Black*, 188–94; and Porst, *Broadcasting Hollywood*.

61   *Radio Times*'s weekly circulation figures peaked at 8,801,895 in 1955 and declined year-on-year thereafter (Currie, *The Radio Times Story*, 242).

62   Beadle to Sir Ian Jacob, 9 July 1957, BBC R44/1,350/1.

63   G. Strode, 14 August 1957, BBC R44/1,350/1.

64   T. Lochhead, 4 September 1957, BBC R44/1,350/1.

65   'Comments on D.Tel.B.'s Memorandum', 4 September 1957, BBC R44/1,350/1.

66   Record of meeting by Hugh Carleton Greene, 26 September 1957, BBC R44/1,350/1.

67   Beadle to Greene, 7 October 1957, BBC R44/1,350/1.

68   BBC press release, 18 December 1957, BBC R44/1,350/1. According to Bill Gilbert, the RKO package was 'known as the Window Package after the RKO B film *The Window* included within it' ('Early Days of TV Acquisition', *The Veteran* 136, Autumn 2012, 19). *The Window* (1949/04.01.62) was not in fact included in the original acquisition list, so the 'Window Package' may actually have been the later selection of twenty additional titles mentioned below.

69   Notes to BBC press release, ibid.

70   Sir Arthur Jarratt, quoted in Madden to McGivern, 20 December 1957, BBC T6/360/1.

71   Letter from G. Ranger, *Daily Cinema*, 7 January 1958.

72   *Daily Cinema*, 19 December 1957.

73   An earlier strand, 'The Friday Western', running in children's hour from September 1955 to August 1956, included nine feature films but mainly consisted of TV Western series episodes.

74   'Keeping Films off TV', *Financial Times*, 6 February 1958, 6. Allen Eyles reports that *Bachelor Knight* was one of a number of films shown by the Classic chain of repertory cinemas after they had been broadcast and specifically promoted on that basis, with such taglines as 'Recently televised – now see it on the BIG screen' ('Classic Repertory Cinemas', *Picture House* 45 [2020]: 30).

75   'Profits, Culture and the Great God TAM', *Sunday Times*, 28 May 1961, 28; Leslie Halliwell, 'Top of the Film Pops', *TVTimes*, 11–17 February 1984, 55.

76   'More Feature Films for the Small Screen', *Financial Times*, 7 January 1960, 14.

77   'ITV Can't be Bound While BBC are Free', *Daily Cinema*, 20 December 1957; 'ATV Sets 8.30pm for Film Shows', *Kine Weekly*, 2 January 1958.

78   Rayner to del Strother, 11 December 1956; del Strother to Rayner, 17 December 1956, BBC T6/360/1.

79   *Kine Weekly*, 19 December 1957.

80   'Possible Films for Television Deal', *The Times*, 12 October 1957, 4.

81   FBFM Council Report no. 4, 10 December 1957; Minutes of the Federation of British Film Makers, MBC 1/91c.

82   'Control of Supply of Feature Films to Television: Proposals of CEA for Discussion with other Sections of the Trade', 18 December 1957, MBC 1/92.

83   Reginald Baker to A.W. Filson, 1 October 1957, MBC 1/91c.

CHAPTER 4

The Empire Strikes Back –
The FIDO Saga (1958–64)

The cinema with its new and progressive forms of technical production and presentation could withstand the competition of live TV shows as such, but when TV programmes are likely to devote most of their viewing time to film presentation it simply means that there will be a cinema in every home which has a television set.

(Sir Tom O'Brien, quoted in 'O'Brien Calls for TV Film Talks', *Daily Cinema*, 1 January 1958)

We know that films on TV are not the only adverse influence on the cinema box office. Better housing, more motor cars, dancing, long playing records and TV itself even without films are all serious factors. But films on TV have demonstrably a most disastrous effect on the box office and they are the only competition that the industry can counter directly. Producers, distributors and exhibitors are all hurt by this particular competition and it is in the interests of the whole industry that this competition be eliminated if possible. Any organisation in the industry which elects not to join in the effort to remove this competition will therefore be highly unpopular and lose influence.

(Letter, Lord Archibald to Reginald Baker, 15 July 1958, MBC I/91)

The Industry Watchdog

The British film industry has always seemed to be in crisis, one way and another, and in 1958 that word was widely being used to describe its current situation.[1] This particular crisis was occasioned by a deepening box-office recession caused by a number of factors, not least the spread of commercial television, which had by then reached central Scotland, South Wales and the west and south-east of England. It was manifested in plummeting cinema admission figures. As we have seen, attendances had been in steady but gradual decline since the peak year of 1946, but by the late 1950s the fall was accelerating. The third quarter of 1957 marked a 20 per cent drop in admissions from the corresponding period the year before; in the last quarter of the year the decline was 25 per cent, and over the whole period 1946-58 it was more than 50 per cent, while costs continued to mount. A long-standing grievance in the trade was the punitive Entertainments Tax on box-office takings, a penalty suffered by no other leisure industry; the campaign against it resulted in a reduction in 1957 but not in abolition until 1960. A further portion of the exhibition gross was taken by the British Film Production Fund, better known as the Eady Levy, which after being introduced on a voluntary basis in 1951 was made statutory in 1957. Cinemas increased their ticket prices to compensate for falling sales and rising operating costs, but were unable to halt the slide in both admissions and earnings and the concomitant rise in the rate of cinema closures.

It was in this context that the large package deals discussed in Chapter 3 were seen by the industry as a threat, offering audiences a similar type and quality of entertainment at home, free of charge at the point of consumption, to that which they would have to pay to see in cinemas. This concern prompted the industry to take action. The Radio and Television Safeguards Committee, comprising representatives of sixteen unions and trade associations and chaired by Sir Tom O'Brien, General Secretary of the National Association of Theatrical and Kine Employees (NATKE), issued a statement:

> While the committee welcomes the exhibition of classic films on television from time to time, it draws a big distinction between such restricted and controlled showing and the recent bulk arrangement. The latter is against the public interest because it means the automatic showing of a cheaply acquired product without any necessary regard for its entertainment value, and means the showing in one medium of a product specially produced for another.[2]

One of the peculiar aspects of the situation was the fact that several film companies had a stake in independent television contractors. Having been frozen out of theatre television by the Government and the BBC, the majors had instead found their way into commercial TV. As the American academic Burton Paulu noted in 1961, 'Of the first eight [ITV] program contractors 20 per cent of the stock was held by cinemas.'[3] ABC Television was wholly owned by Associated British Picture Corporation (ABPC), a vertically-integrated combine with interests in production, distribution and exhibition. Six of ABPC's directors, including its chairman, vice-chairman and managing director, also sat on the board of ABC TV. Both Granada Television and the Granada Theatres circuit were owned and run by brothers Sidney and Cecil Bernstein. The latter was also on the board of Humphries Laboratories along with its chairman, Paul Adorian, who was managing director of Associated-Rediffusion (A-R). The Rank Organisation had a controlling interest (37.5 per cent) in Southern Television, whose chairman was Rank managing director John Davis; Rank's assistant MD, Kenneth Winckles, also sat on the board. Independent film producers and executives involved in other present and future ITV companies included Sidney Gilliat (Television Wales and the West), Sydney Box (Tyne Tees Television), John Woolf (Anglia Television), Frank Hoare (Westward Television), William MacQuitty, Betty Box and Laurence Olivier (Ulster Television), and Michael Balcon (Grampian Television). All these were powerful figures in the film industry, carrying considerable influence in their respective fields. Their potential conflicts of interest – or convergence of interests, depending on one's point of view – were made much of by the film unions, who claimed that the individuals and companies involved could easily have done more to protect the cinema from the competitive threat of television.[4]

One of these figures devised a plan that he hoped would do exactly that. Cecil Bernstein has generally been overshadowed by his better-known brother Sidney, but Cecil played the more decisive role in the relationship between the company's cinema and television interests.[5] It had been Cecil, as managing director of Granada Theatres, who motioned the Llandudno Resolution at the CEA conference in July 1952; yet it was Cecil also who subsequently had the main responsibility for acquiring films to show on Granada Television. (The TV company was based in the north, its studio being in Manchester, whereas the sixty-odd Granada cinemas were mainly located in Greater London and the south.) He envisioned a trade body that would protect the interests of both filmmakers and exhibitors, claiming to have had this idea after the TV showing of one particular film to great ratings success.

Sydney Box's production *The Seventh Veil* (1945/08.01.1958), which had broken UK box-office records when originally released, was networked in the four regions then comprising ITV, at peak time on a weekday evening. The broadcast proved so popular that cinema admissions reportedly fell that night by 15 per cent. 'The producer got about £2,700 for two nation-wide showings', Bernstein recalled. 'Why not, I thought, pay the producer his money and keep it off TV?'[6] He pitched his plan at a meeting of 'industry leaders' a mere two days after the televising of *The Seventh Veil*. It called 'for the establishment of an Industry Trust which would be financed by a voluntary levy along the lines of the Eady levy'.

> This Trust would acquire the television rights of films at their market value and would then control the issue of films to television in accordance with policies which would be agreed by the industry. To help with the Trust in its early days the Rank Group and ABPC had agreed to withhold most, if not all, of their backlog (and it was believed that British Lion would also agree) so that the Trust would not have to acquire the rights of these films at the outset. It was hoped that the income from licensing films would be sufficient, after a few years, to make the continuation of the levy unnecessary.[7]

Yet another proposal, supported by the Federation of British Film Makers (FBFM), suggested instead setting up 'a producers' Co-operative Agency' that would lease film rights to television on producers' behalf and negotiate 'on the general principle that the fee for a film should be relative to the audience that viewed it'.[8] This move was motivated by a fear that Bernstein's 'Industry Trust' would be dominated by the major film companies that also had a stake in television. However, after a meeting of the five trade associations on 15 February 1958 it was decided, subject to safeguards against the major distributors gaining advantage over the producers, to implement the Bernstein scheme, described in FBFM's Council Report as a switch 'from a "controlled release" plan to a "no release" plan'.[9] Bernstein's scheme had initially also been for controlled release, albeit one that was 'more severe and limiting in its effects than the CEA scheme and required no defence contribution'; however, it was changed to 'no release' in order to appease the CEA.[10]

Bernstein had set out written proposals on 22 January, which he revised on 30 January following further discussions. They included:

1. An Authority to be set up consisting of producers, distributors and exhibitors to operate the scheme.
2. A defence Fund contribution to be made by exhibitors of one farthing per admission, estimated to raise in the first year a sum in the region of £500,000, such contribution to be a charge on takings for the purposes of film hire. Any exhibitor whose net takings in any one week are less than £200 would be free from the contribution for that week.
3. The Rank Organisation, Pathé, British Lion and other major distributing organisations to undertake not to press upon the Authority to purchase their product.
4. The Authority to be empowered to purchase the UK television rights of all British feature films in the market at the then existing market rates.
5. If after the setting up of the Authority a producer or distributor (British or foreign), directly or indirectly sells a film or films to UK television, exhibitors will refuse to book any of his future product.
6. Intimation to be given to Banks and others responsible for the financing of films in England and the United States, who for any reason obtain the rights to sell films to television, that exhibitors would be compelled to refuse to show any future product they might finance should they dispose of such films to television.[11]

The name of this new body first appeared in the press in June 1958: the Film Industry Defence Organisation (FIDO).[12] A drafting committee worked for several months to iron out the details of the plan, which was finalised on 31 July. The minutiae included making exceptions of earnings from 'children's matinees, charity performances and all programmes at News Theatres which do not exceed ninety minutes in running time and which do not include any film of three thousand feet or more in length'. The owners of films who approached 'the Authority' (hereinafter FIDO or 'the Organisation' to avoid confusion with the ITA) agreed to withhold them from television (including 'toll television' or 'pay TV', when it was introduced at some point in the future) and instead to assign the TV rights to the Organisation for an agreed period. FIDO would accept these rights only when satisfied 'that the film in question would otherwise be offered to television' and 'that the showing of the film in question on television would be injurious to the legitimate commercial interests of the Film Industry'. Only films at least ten years old would be considered, as this was the period for which it was assumed that owners would prefer to keep their films in theatrical circulation. As for the sanctions to be applied in the event of non-compliance, the CEA was called upon 'to recommend to all Exhibitors that they should refuse to book films produced, distributed or financed by a person who directly or indirectly permits any British or foreign film to be made available to a television contractor'. A similar entreaty recommended the KRS to cut off the supply of films to any exhibitor who failed to comply with this requirement or who had supplied films to television.[13]

FIDO's initial chairman was Sir Arthur Jarratt, president of the KRS and managing director of British Lion. 'If anyone can lead the Industry out of its troubles he is the man', the BBC's Cecil Madden had once said of him. 'Jarratt has always been friendly and helpful to us and will, I am sure, emerge as what has been needed for a long time, the leader of the Industry.'[14] However, Jarratt was not to remain long in post: he died on 14 December 1958 and was replaced by W.F.W. Ram. FIDO's board of directors, numbering initially eighteen, first met on 21 August. They included the presidents and other representatives of the trade associations as well as several film and television executives, among them Cecil Bernstein, John Davis of Rank and Southern Television, and D.J. Goodlatte of ABPC and ABC Television. The fund-raising levy went into operation on 31 August. The lay press exhibited some scepticism about the plan, *The Times* commenting:

> The cinema industry presumably takes the view that if old British films are not shown on television so many more people will go to the cinema that what film producers lose by not renting or selling their old films for this purpose will be more than made up by additional cinema takings. It is not self-evident that this must be so.[15]

In the Doghouse

Even while FIDO was in the process of being established, a potential crisis arose. From 1955, all the major Hollywood studios had become involved in making their older films available to US television, either by selling them outright to independent distributors, as RKO Radio and Warner Bros had done, by leasing them for a fixed term to sub-distributors, or by forming subsidiary divisions that would syndicate them to the major networks and, more often, local stations. In February 1958, Paramount Pictures, the last of the studios to hold out on releasing its backlog to TV, announced that it had sold around 750 pre-1949 sound features to the Music Corporation of America (MCA), which would distribute the films to television. Cecil Bernstein telephoned his brother Sidney while the latter was in New York on business to ask him to obtain from both Paramount and MCA an assurance that the films would never be offered to British broadcasters.[16] MCA also had a controlling interest in Universal Pictures, whose films were distributed in the UK by the Rank Organisation; these too were to be kept off the air in Britain, with the exception of a small number of independent productions and 'B' pictures, such as the Sherlock Holmes series (1942–46), that had now fallen outside Universal's control. Other American companies were also enjoined to include a clause in film distribution contracts barring Britain from potential TV sales.[17]

Although FIDO undertook to purchase rights only for British productions, the UK distributors of foreign (including American) pictures were warned that they were subject to the same sanctions if they sold to television, including via third-party distributors. For this reason, the BBC increasingly dealt directly with the European-based producers or distributors of continental films rather than with British-based renters. Gala, UK owner of a chain of specialised cinemas as well as a distributor in its own right, announced that it would refuse to show any film from a European company that had supplied films to British television in this way.[18]

FIDO's founders hoped that those television companies with interests in the film industry would demonstrate their support for the scheme by undertaking not to acquire any more films for TV use. Unsurprisingly, given that the Bernsteins were its chief sponsors, Granada took a lead in this, though its TV station did in fact continue to show the films that it had previously acquired and still held under contract, along with films sourced from other ITV companies.[19] ATV, which at that time had no cinema interests of its own but which was the principal buyer and seller of films for the network, equally unsurprisingly announced its opposition to the plan and declared that it was 'taking advice as to whether such an agreement would constitute a restriction under the provisions of the Restrictive Trade Practices Act of 1956'.[20] ABC Television, which had been expected to support the scheme, also refused to guarantee not to show or acquire other films or not to show networked films originated by other stations. Its parent company ABPC did, however, agree not to supply its own backlog of films to the TV subsidiary or to sell them to other ITV companies.[21] Rank gave a similar assurance regarding Southern Television and both film companies, along with British Lion, agreed not to ask for payment for withholding their old films for three years, while FIDO was establishing itself. Instead, the watchdog was to concentrate its efforts on those independent producers and smaller distributors that had more financial incentive to seek television buyers for their product.

However, within a few days of the levy on cinema seats coming into effect, news broke of yet another potential crisis that threatened to destabilise FIDO before it had even got started. In early September 1958, ABPC was revealed as the bidder for a controlling interest in Associated Talking Pictures (ATP), the parent company of Ealing Films, which held the rights to an estimated 200 titles. If this went through (as it did), the sale announced the previous August of 100 prewar Ealing pictures to ABPC's subsidiary ABC Television would not only be augmented by an equal number of more recent films, but the whole package would be available to ABC in perpetuity and through it to the ITV network.[22]

Emergency talks were held between ABPC and FIDO, chaired by the president of the BFPA, former chief censor and FIDO board member Arthur Watkins. Watkins flew out from Venice, where he had been attending a summit about films on television organised by the International Federation of Film Producers, and where it had been 'declared that feature films, when shown on video [i.e., TV], caused great damage to the artistic and technical value of motion pictures and their authors'.[23] Putting weight behind the negotiations was the implication of a threatened industry-wide boycott to ABPC and all its affiliates, including the theatrical distributor Warner-Pathé, which owned a 37.5 per cent stake in the company. After six weeks, a settlement was reached in which ABC agreed to limit the exposure of the Ealing films to its own stations serving only the Midlands and the North on weekends. No more than sixty of the films would be shown, only on Sunday afternoons, and they would not be networked or made available to other ITV stations (see Figure 4.1). This damage-limitation plan, a 'controlled release'

Figure 4.1 ABC agreed a deal with FIDO to show its Ealing library only on Sunday afternoons and exclusively in the Midlands and North regions. *The Foreman Went to France* (1942) was first broadcast in 1959. *TV Times* © Associated-Rediffusion Ltd.

rather than a complete ban, nevertheless received the approval even of the CEA and was regarded as an auspicious start for FIDO.[24]

Not all exhibitors actively supported FIDO, though only a tiny handful declined to contribute to the fund. A breakaway body, the Association of Independent Cinemas (AIC), opposed the plan but had little choice but to go along with it when its members were faced with the possibility of being denied films from the major distributors. AIC's president, Harry Mears, claimed that telefilm series were a bigger threat to the cinema than televised feature films and asserted that if the broadcasters 'had put on 15 old films a week they would have killed TV stone dead. The public would have got tired of them.'[25]

For their part, senior Ealing personnel had registered their opposition to FIDO from the beginning and did not change their minds. In private correspondence with Lord Archibald, the chairman of FBFM, during the early stages of discussion of Bernstein's plan, Michael Balcon asked whether the Government had a view on the scheme and whether it would be likely to come under the Restrictive Trade Practices Act. Archibald's view was that it would not, as 'the Act applies fundamentally to goods, whereas this Scheme does not deal with goods but "licences to perform"'.[26] Archibald later commented to Reginald Baker that he would have preferred the less restrictive FBFM plan but now that the industry had put its support behind FIDO, the Federation (including Ealing) ought to as well, 'because of the enormous importance the industry attaches to the menace of films on TV':

> If the Federation rejects FIDO, it will still go on with the backing of the other four trade associations. The producer representation on FIDO will be weakened. The struggle to get reasonable terms for producers who do wish to make deals with FIDO will be less energetic and less effective.[27]

Any organisation rejecting the FIDO scheme would, Archibald argued, 'lose its influence inside the industry. To put it colloquially it will "be in the doghouse".' More positively, and perhaps contradictorily, he predicted that FIDO's operation would create a 'scarcity value' for films that would ultimately benefit those producers who wished to sell out their film interests to television. Neither Baker nor Balcon was convinced by these arguments and they continued to oppose FIDO. Balcon wrote privately to Baker: 'In his letter Archibald says "none of us like the Defence Scheme". This seems to me to be a very good reason for not going forward with it.' Balcon refuted the suggestion that FBFM's opposition would put it 'in the doghouse' – 'on the contrary, I think their standing and status [would be] considerably enhanced'. With regard to Ealing's own position and that of other producers who might wish to demur from the scheme, Balcon noted wryly:

> The reference to 'accepting a democratic majority decision' of the Federation really is a gross over-statement. It is rather like a 'democratic majority' being arrived at on a question of drink by seven teetotallers and one person who likes an occasional alcoholic beverage.[28]

In the event, when ABPC's purchase of ATP went through in November 1958, it made Ealing a wholly-owned subsidiary of a company with involvement in cinema exhibition. According to the terms of the Federation's Constitution this represented a 'disqualifying interest', and Ealing was therefore obliged to resign from the FBFM.[29]

FIDO's MO

Although it is commonly assumed that FIDO purchased the television rights of the films it acquired or even bought the films outright, neither was in fact the case.[30] Rather, in return for a compensatory fee to a 'vendor' or controller of a film, it acquired a 'negative covenant' on the TV rights: a legally binding assurance that for a specified period (which might be a fixed number of years, the term for which the rights were held by the vendor or the full copyright life of the film) these rights would not be exercised. FIDO simply sat on the rights, withholding the films from both broadcasters and TV distributors; it did not own them or control their theatrical distribution, which was not affected by the covenants. It did not even request copies of films from their owners, though it did require a certificate from a laboratory stating that an acceptable print for theatrical or television use could be made from the negative. In the event of any attempt to show a covenanted film on television in the UK or the Republic of Ireland, FIDO would have an injunction served, the costs of this action being charged to the copyright owner. On occasion FIDO permitted broadcasters to show extracts from the films it controlled, for a fee that would be donated to industry charities.

The acquisition fees that FIDO paid to vendors were determined on an individual basis by negotiation. The Negotiating Committee (subsequently renamed the Executive Committee and then the Purchasing and Finance Committee) was typically composed of around seven members of the board of directors, with W.J. (Bill) Speakman as secretary. It usually met monthly and negotiations could drag on for months at a time, depending on the stubbornness of the vendors. Although FIDO was obliged to treat with any vendor who approached it, there was no obligation actually to acquire a film. The importance of reaching a deal was proportionate to the likelihood of the film being offered and taken for television broadcast. Exceptions were sometimes made to the stipulation that titles should be at least ten years old when owners had liquidated their business, in which case they would have an incentive to dispose of their assets for a quick financial return. There was pressure also to reduce the acquisition age for 'second features' to four years, the term of a film's 'quota life', after which 'B' pictures were deemed less likely to remain in commercial circulation than first features. It was also assumed that most films made before 1939 would be too old to be attractive to broadcasters, so FIDO could exercise greater selectivity with titles more than twenty years old. In practice, then, many pre-1939 titles were rejected for covenants and many post-1948 ones were accepted.

If a vendor approached FIDO and was turned down for a covenant, they were free to offer their film to television. But if an offer was made by FIDO and the vendor refused it, any subsequent sale to television would result in the application of sanctions. For lesser films, derisory sums were offered, and presumably accepted by the vendors, either because no better offers were likely to be forthcoming from TV companies or because the owners were eager to dispose of their goods as quickly as possible. The cheapest FIDO acquisition was *Captain's Orders* (1937/08.02.1954), which had at first been turned down by the Committee before being accepted for a payment of only £75. A ceiling was set at £7,500 for any one film. This maximum was paid in only a small number of cases, including *Morning Departure* (1950/13.07.1974) and *The Browning Version* (1951/06.11.1975). Some films were turned down because the vendor demanded an amount in excess of any fee a British broadcaster had yet been known to pay; this happened in the case of two Korda productions, *Anna Karenina* (1948/15.01.1958) and *Bonnie Prince Charlie* (1948/25.03.1973), which were eventually acquired by FIDO for a joint outlay of £4,500.

Anna Karenina had by this time already been shown once on the ITV network. As well as paying to prevent films reaching television at all, FIDO also sought to prevent those that had previously been broadcast from being shown again. For this reason, some 250 titles were the subjects of covenants *after* they had been televised. These also included *The Seventh Veil*, for which Sydney Box received a payment from FIDO of £4,500 – almost twice Cecil Bernstein's estimate of what he had been paid by ITV – and the bulk of the Korda library, comprising thirty films acquired for a total of £45,000 in two batches in October 1961 and May 1962; ITV's lease on its Korda package expired in September 1962.

Despite his disapproval of FIDO, Ealing's Reginald Baker nevertheless submitted four films, two of which were turned down purely on grounds of age: *For the Love of a Queen* (1935/21.04.1957) and *The Beloved Vagabond* (1936/03.05.1949). The latter had been shown by the BBC as part of its twelve-film ABFD package in 1949, when the Corporation had itself turned down the former title, later picked up by ITV. Of the two other films submitted by Baker, the Negotiating Committee offered £1,500 for the 'B' picture *Headline* (1944/28.04.1957) despite its having been 'extensively televised'; but it considered that Will Hay's final vehicle *My Learned Friend* (1943/02.12.1969) had 'little entertainment value left'.[31] Also rejected were the horror film *Dark Eyes of London* (1939/22.05.1970), 'in view of the reaction of certain Television Companies to "H" Certificate films', and Jill Craigie's *Blue Scar* (1946), 'in view of the very ordinary star value and the limited appeal of the film'.[32] Nevertheless, a *Daily Cinema* columnist reported:

> [The FIDO board] insists that any film which has the slightest chance of a TV outlet must be bid for. 'Our exhibitor members insist, and I agree with them, that even a poor picture on TV can be a competitor to the cinema,' [Arthur] Watkins told me.

> 'We are perfectly entitled to tell an owner that we consider his property to be worthless and that he is welcome to try to place it with the opposition. But we would rather acquire the rights of the most dubious film than allow it to hamper our operations in the slightest way'.[33]

FIDO issued periodic press releases to announce the sums it had raised from the cinema levy or had spent on acquiring covenants. It specified the cumulative number of films it had acquired and often claimed that it had prevented thousands more from being sold to TV simply through its very existence. However, FIDO rarely named the films or identified the vendors and acquisition prices. An exception was made in April 1960 when it announced that a sum of £400,000 was to be paid in instalments to British Lion for around seventy films (the exact amount eventually paid was actually £417,506 15s 11d for eighty films).[34] This was no doubt publicised to address trade speculation that the films FIDO was acquiring were largely minor and commercially insignificant. In fact, the vast majority of the films for which covenants were issued did indeed meet this description, having come mostly from independent sources rather than the major producer-distributors.

However, in January 1961 Lord Archibald devised a plan by which these bigger companies – which, as we have noted, had initially agreed voluntarily to withhold their films rather than seek payment – would be paid somewhat earlier than planned for their complete backlogs. These were to be acquired in stages. The Backlog Acquisition Programme, which would also cover the British-made output of the UK branches of the American majors, was introduced at least partly to avoid FIDO having to pay tax on uncommitted revenues:

> Lord Archibald explained to the Board that the Negotiating Committee had worked out a scheme to spend a considerable sum of money before the end of the financial year, in order to safeguard the tax position of FIDO. The only logical way of doing this was to start buying in backlogs of films beginning with the year 1939/40 and continuing from year to year so far as the money available would permit, so that possibly the following two or three years would be included.[35]

In this way, the annual output of, for example, Rank from 1938–39 to 1942–43 was acquired in 1961, that from 1943–44 to the end of 1946 in 1963, and for 1947 and 1948 in 1964. A total of £450,000 was paid to Rank for 124 films, the greatest amount received in covenants by any single company. Of the other largest recipients, Associated British-Pathé and ABPC together received £267,450 for a total of ninety-seven films, including forty-two Ealing titles; Twentieth Century-Fox received £75,250 for forty-two films; the National Film Finance Corporation, £70,000 for twenty-two films, all made by Group 3; Columbia, £67,900 for eighteen titles; and James Carreras's Exclusive Films and Saturn Films, £62,000 for forty-five titles between them. Smaller companies receiving payments for large blocks of films (in most cases also transacted in bundles over a period of years) included: Ambassador Film Productions (£12,400 for eighty-four titles); Border Film Productions (£8,500 for twenty-two titles); Butcher's Film Distributors (£42,900 for sixty-five titles); Grand National Pictures (£11,150 for twenty-four titles); and Television Programmes (Distributors) (£32,300 for forty-five titles).[36] This last group was, unusually, covenanted in a single package on 20 April 1960. Twenty-three of the films involved were subsequently the subjects of further covenants with other vendors who presumably owned the copyrights and had reclaimed them from the TV distributor.

All these package deals were exceptions to the norm, however: most films were offered to FIDO singly or in much smaller groups. In total, 974 films were the subject of 217 covenants with 106 vendors. Between April 1959, when the first covenants were signed, and February 1965, FIDO spent £2,005,196 on acquiring films. Additional monies went towards operating expenses and, when not spent immediately, revenues were invested on the stock market. The total amount raised from the cinema levy over this period was £2,162,316.[37]

The Selznick Deal

While FIDO had secured the agreement of the American majors not to supply films to British television, it could do little about US independents. From time to time, Hollywood films made by small production companies (some of them originally released by United Artists or other majors but no longer under their control) found their way onto both BBC and ITV screens. These rarely caused a stir in the cinema community, but one package from a major producer did. In September 1959, it was announced that producer David O. Selznick had sold a package of his old movies to BBC Television. The number of films involved and the exact amount paid were the subjects of speculation; unconfirmed press reports had the fee pegged at £50,000 or £100,000 and the number of films involved as between seventeen and twenty-two.[38] In fact, the BBC had purchased twenty-four films for an average fee per title of £4,820 (a total of £115,680), with the right to show each of them twice (a third showing was later negotiated for ten of the titles).[39]

The package apparently included the three films that the BBC had previously screened between 1947 and 1950 (see Chapter 2), but these were not repeated. Four other pictures – *Topaze* (1933), *Becky Sharp* (1935/10.09.1994), *The Dancing Pirate* (1936) and *Nothing Sacred* (1937/08.07.1983) – were also not shown. The reasons for this are unclear: possibly it was due to the films' age or the condition of available prints. But the remaining seventeen included such titles as *Little Women* (1933/23.12.1962), *The Adventures of Tom Sawyer* (1938/03.04.1961), *The Spiral Staircase* (1945/24.11.1962), *Portrait of Jennie* (1948/03.07.1961) and four directed by Alfred Hitchcock: *Rebecca* (1940/25.12.1961), *Spellbound* (1945/09.04.1961), *Notorious* (1946/23.12.1961) and *The Paradine Case* (1947/28.04.1962). Most of these films had been distributed theatrically by either United Artists or RKO, but the rights had now reverted to Selznick. The first of the package to be televised was *The Prisoner of Zenda* (1937/25.12.1960).

This was an opportunity for the long-standing Llandudno Resolution to be put into practice. The CEA Executive Committee passed a motion recommending members 'not to book any film or films in which Mr Selznick is concerned'.[40] A list of thirty-seven Selznick pictures was duly circulated to CEA members, but the producer was now semi-retired and the only film of his still in active UK release, *A Farewell to Arms* (1957/08.04.1973), was owned and distributed by Twentieth Century-Fox.[41] Selznick's magnum opus *Gone with the Wind* (1981/26 & 27.12.1981), the industry's greatest money-maker, was owned by MGM and currently withdrawn. There were further obstacles to the successful application of a boycott. American companies that were members of the KRS were concerned that any unified action on their part would constitute a breach of US antitrust laws and leave their parent companies open to prosecution. In consequence, FIDO was obliged to delete from the terms of its agreement the calls for sanctions to be imposed by the CEA and KRS, potentially depriving it of any direct power.[42] FIDO also pointed out that it could simply not afford to issue covenants to prevent American films from reaching television, which would multiply its financial commitments tenfold.[43] Essentially, however, despite making a serious dent in the industry's defences, the Selznick deal was not seen as FIDO's fault. A more severe threat to the organisation's credibility instead transpired only a few months later, in highly unusual circumstances.

The IFD Deal

Unlike ATV and ABC, the London weekday contractor Associated-Rediffusion (A-R) was not usually in the habit of acquiring large numbers of feature films. But in early January 1960, it announced a remarkable deal: A-R had bought out Independent Film Distributors (IFD), which handled the output of John and James Woolf's Romulus Films and the independent producer Daniel M. Angel, as well as some London Films productions. Not only had A-R acquired the entire backlog of fifty-five films controlled by IFD but, in purchasing the company outright, it also took over these films' theatrical distribution. Thus A-R now owned a full portfolio of rights to a large catalogue of major product that it could lease to cinema exhibitors and indeed to other broadcasters, including the BBC. The films had all been made between 1946 and 1956, so in television terms they were relatively recent and therefore highly desirable. Among them were a number of famous, acclaimed and popular pictures; the titles invariably cited in press reports were *The African Queen* (1951/15.03.1961), *Moulin Rouge* (1952/01.03.1961), *Richard III* (1955/27.10.1961) and *Storm over the Nile* (see Figure 4.2). The cost of the deal was not publicly revealed, though press speculation put it at £200,000 or £250,000. In fact, A-R had paid £500,000, by far the largest sum any UK broadcaster had yet spent in acquiring a library of films.[44]

When news of the deal broke, it was described as a 'major breach in the protective curtain which film exhibitors and distributors have sought to use against television'.[45] A columnist in the American trade journal *Motion Picture Exhibitor* described the UK industry reaction:

Figure 4.2 Whether by chance or design, *Radio Times*'s still for the 1960 transmission, in 'letterboxed' format, of IFD's *Storm over the Nile* (1955) preserved its approximate CinemaScope aspect ratio. *Radio Times* © Immediate Media Co.

Not since the Labor [*sic*] Government, without warning, slapped on the iniquitous ad valorem duty over 12 years ago has the film industry been so incensed or shocked as it has been by the sale of Independent Film Distributors and its product to Associated Rediffusion TV. Big and small men alike have blown their tops in their indignation while the producers' associations in cold, soberly couched statements have been no less to the point.[46]

The *Daily Telegraph* observed that not only did the IFD package constitute the 'first big batch of post-war British films to be released for television' but that it also came at an opportune moment, 'when there has been a drop in the production of British filmed series for television' due to 'the difficulty in selling British series abroad'.

It was Daniel Angel and the Woolf brothers, rather than A-R management, who provoked the most vituperation within the trade. They were reprimanded by the CEA General Council for 'callous indifference to the future of the film industry and their action is to be condemned in the strongest possible terms'.[47] But some of the blame was passed on to FIDO, which was accused of having failed to take action to prevent the deal going through. The organisation itself blamed the producers for having failed to make an approach; they in turn attacked FIDO:

John Woolf says FIDO did not respond 'to an invitation to contact them on the subject'. The letter he received from FIDO in January 1959 required him to approach them with his under-taking not to sell to TV; he invited them to approach him, which they did not. FIDO normally did not acquire films less than ten years old.

Major Angel said he had always insisted that under no circumstances would he ever offer his films to FIDO. He considered money from that source as nothing more than a bribe. He had acted completely honestly and had done the deal with Associated-Rediffusion quite openly and under his own name.[48]

Records of FIDO's board meetings include a note of Cecil Bernstein making the point that 'Mr [John] Woolf was known to everyone on the Board and there would have been nothing to stop him telling one of the Members that he was dissatisfied and was considering selling to TV'.[49] Nevertheless, the undisclosed cost of the deal to A-R was such that FIDO's resources would have fallen far short of the sum that Woolf and Angel evidently wanted, even if they had been approached. Angel subsequently did approach FIDO to ask it to acquire other films not involved in the A-R deal, and was turned down on both occasions for wanting too much money.

The CEA circulated a list of sixty-five films produced by Romulus or Angel to be boycotted, ten of which had not been involved in the IFD sale. Three of these were subsequently 'whitewashed' when it was determined that the producers no longer had a financial interest in them.[50] Their plans for future productions were also the targets of sabotage. Angel declared in December 1960 that he had been unable to make a film for the last year because of action against him, and that he was taking his case to the Restrictive Practices Council. When it was reported that CEA general secretary Ellis Pinkney had scotched a deal for James Woolf to produce a film for Warner Bros, Woolf threatened to sue.[51] The possibility of legal action from both Woolf and Angel ultimately led to a climb-down. Woolf withdrew his suit after the boycott of Romulus Films was lifted and an open letter Pinkney had written to Jack Warner notifying him of the ban was retracted. By March 1961, the boycotts against both Angel and David Selznick had also been dropped.[52]

One of the most extraordinary aspects of the situation was a unique deal between an ITV company and the BBC. Within a few days of A-R announcing its purchase of IFD, the head of BBC Promotions, Ronald Waldman, was told by the company's managing director, Paul Adorian, that the films would in principle be available to the BBC.[53] To help defray the cost of the buy-out, Adorian agreed to a sharing arrangement. The Corporation was invited to divide fifty-two of the fifty-five IFD films into two groups of twenty-six, each containing an equal proportion of what it considered strong and weak films. A-R would then choose which group of films it wanted to screen first, the other group going to the BBC. After all fifty-two had been played off in 'first placings' on the respective channels, the groups would be swapped over and the films repeated on the opposing channel. The BBC could then pick thirteen of its initial group for a further rerun. In between each of these runs, A-R would make the films available for theatrical distribution, should any exhibitor be willing to take the risk.

The BBC paid A-R a fee of £260,000, slightly more than half A-R's initial outlay. This meant an average of £5,000 per title, which the Corporation considered a fair expense in view of the films' prestige value. The only restriction placed on the BBC was an agreement to show most of the films on Saturday evenings, when A-R's London weekday service was not broadcasting. On ITV, the films were not nationally networked but were leased by A-R to other stations to show on a regional basis in the usual way. The three films excluded from the BBC split were televised first: *The Galloping Major* (1951/25.05.1960), *She Shall Have Murder* (1950/06.07.1960) and *Never Take No for an Answer* (1951/20.07.1960). They were followed by the first of A-R's group, *Angela* (1954/31.08.1960), and then by the first of the BBC's, *The Sea Shall Not Have Them* (1954/15.10.1960). The swap took place after eighteen months. By April 1964, all the films bar one had received at least one transmission on both the BBC and an ITV station; the BBC's further selected repeats were shown in 1965 and 1966, mostly on Saturday afternoons on its new second channel, BBC2 (see Table 4.1).[54]

The major effect of the IFD affair was to throw into serious doubt the effectiveness of FIDO; already there were calls for it to be disbanded. There were worries that the sale might set a dangerous precedent for other television companies to attempt similar takeovers of film interests. It was also reported that 'four leading independent producing companies have begun negotiating with A-R to sell their backlog to commercial television'.[55] FIDO's decision in April 1960 to pay British Lion £400,000 for part of its backlog – the first time it had 'offered really big money to producers to stop them selling films to TV' – was very likely an attempt to address such concerns and to demonstrate a more proactive attitude by taking

Table 4.1 The IFD package, shared by Associated-Rediffusion/ITV and the BBC, 1960–66.

Group A Titles (shown by ITV first)	Release Year	First ITV TX	First BBC TX	
Dancing with Crime	1947	30.11.1960	16.11.1963	
Corridor of Mirrors	1948	24.05.1961	03.08.1963	
The Guinea Pig	1948	26.12.1960	15.04.1963	
William Comes to Town	1948	27.12.1960	14.03.1964	
Murder at the Windmill	1949	18.09.1961	15.02.1964	
Private Angelo	1949	11.01.1961	01.12.1962	
The Romantic Age	1949	21.12.1960	15.12.1962	
The Body Said No!	1950	11.12.1961	09.03.1963	
Tony Draws a Horse	1950	24.05.1961	14.07.1962	
The African Queen	1951	15.03.1961	25.12.1962	
Another Man's Poison	1951	26.04.1961	17.08.1963	
Mr. Drake's Duck	1951	26.10.1960	23.03.1963	
Gift Horse	1952	17.05.1961	21.07.1962	
Moulin Rouge	1952	01.03.1961	26.12.1962	
Women of Twilight	1952	none	29.02.1964	
Beat the Devil	1953	02.08.1961	11.05.1963	
Three Steps to the Gallows	1953	16.11.1960	21.09.1963	
Angela	1954	31.08.1960	28.07.1962	
The Good Die Young	1954	15.02.1961	06.04.1963	
To Dorothy, a Son	1954	28.09.1960	18.05.1963	
The Bespoke Overcoat	1955	04.08.1961	27.03.1964	
A Kid for Two Farthings	1955	12.10.1960	22.06.1963	
The Reluctant Bride	1955	05.04.1961	18.04.1964	
They Can't Hang Me	1955	10.05.1961	22.02.1964	
Sailor Beware	1956	14.09.1960	11.06.1962	
Three Men in a Boat	1956	12.04.1961	27.10.1962	
Group B Titles (shown by BBC first)	**Release Year**	**First BBC TX**	**First ITV TX**	**Second BBC TX**
A Girl in a Million	1946	18.02.1961	01.07.1962	
Just William's Luck	1947	25.12.1961	26.12.1962	
The Interrupted Journey	1949	21.03.1961	06.04.1962	
Miss Pilgrim's Progress	1949	07.05.1961	02.08.1962	
Chance of a Lifetime	1950	27.01.1962	06.09.1962	
Shadow of the Eagle	1950	04.02.1961	15.03.1962	
I'll Get You for This	1951	14.10.1961	31.05.1962	
The Late Edwina Black	1951	13.08.1961	23.03.1962	
Pandora and the Flying Dutchman	1951	02.07.1961	17.04.1962	08.01.1966
Treasure Hunt	1952	23.04.1961	16.03.1962	29.01.1966
Albert R.N.	1953	27.12.1960	28.06.1962	14.02.1965
Cosh Boy	1953	08.09.1961	18.07.1963	
Innocents in Paris	1953	21.01.1961	11.04.1962	04.04.1965
Abdullah the Great	1954	16.07.1961	26.12.1962	
Passing Stranger	1954	30.09.1961	12.09.1963	
The Runaway Bus	1954	22.05.1961	17.04.1962	21.02.1965
The Sea Shall Not Have Them	1954	15.10.1960	24.05.1962	07.02.1965

Table 4.1 (continued)

Group B Titles (shown by BBC first)	Release Year	First BBC TX	First ITV TX	Second BBC TX
Time Is My Enemy	1954	03.03.1962	11.12.1963	
Cast a Dark Shadow	1955	24.09.1961	27.04.1962	06.06.1965
Escapade	1955	27.08.1961	20.04.1962	22.01.1966
I Am a Camera	1955	07.01.1961	20.03.1962	15.01.1966
Richard III	1955	27.10.1961	06.11.1963	03.07.1965
Storm over the Nile	1955	29.10.1960	13.03.1962	05.02.1966
Windfall	1955	24.02.1962	19.09.1963	
Dry Rot	1956	26.11.1960	13.04.1962	
The Iron Petticoat	1956	28.05.1961	01.05.1962	28.02.1965

Not included in shared package:

ITV-only titles	Release Year	First ITV TX
She Shall Have Murder	1950	06.07.1960
The Galloping Major	1951	25.05.1960
Never Take No for an Answer	1951	20.07.1960

the initiative in a deal rather than waiting to be approached for covenants.[56] However, FIDO's most severe reprimand came from the film unions, which now adopted a more militant line on films for television than even the CEA.

Industrial Action

An unsigned article in *Sight and Sound* commented on the implications of the IFD deal: 'Coming at a time when British production of TV series was at a particularly low ebb, the sale and implications (more material on TV; less work in current TV filming) seemed to hit at the technicians as well as the obvious exhibitor interests.'[57] On 25 January 1960, the Federation of Film Unions (FFU), representing 100,000 members, issued a formal response to the IFD sale and the wider issues it raised in the form of a lengthy statement, headed 'Exhibition of Cinema Films on Television'. Pointing out that the recent deal was but the latest instance of a much larger, ongoing problem, the FFU stated categorically:

> It is not in the interests of the cinematograph industry, the television industry, the public who patronise both forms of entertainment, and of the employees who work in both media, for such transactions to take place. The issue is much more complex than the simple erection of a protective wall around the film industry. We think it wrong for the television service to acquire cheaply already existing old material instead of directing its energy and resources to providing new programmes for the viewing public. We think it unfair for the public to be foisted off with old material not only on that account but also because for technical and other reasons

many cinematograph films are not ideal for showing on television. And we think it is to the detriment of the workers in both film and television if by such transactions they are deprived of employment.

The FFU argued that the failure to act of both FIDO and the film and television interests that supported it had 'allowed a situation to develop which will mean that, as in the case of some of the outstanding films in the recent batch purchase ... many cinemas will be practically empty at the time these films are shown on television'. It stated that 'FIDO has been inept and there has been complete incompetence or inability in the trade as a whole to deal with the matters which have now come to a head'.[58]

The statement made a number of recommendations to rectify the situation. It called for an urgent meeting between FFU's own representatives and those of the BBC, the ITA and the ITV companies, with a view to reaching 'agreement for the drastic curtailment both in overall numbers and frequency of the showing of cinematograph films in television'. It suggested that until then the commercial companies with a stake in the cinema should cease all transmissions of feature films and encourage the other companies to do likewise. It added: 'Fundamentally we do not want films made for the cinema to be a regular part of television programmes. But we do not object to films of great merit being shown on television from time to time under ordered selection.' Looking further into the future, FFU recommended establishing a permanent official body, similar to the Cinematograph Films Council (CFC), which controlled 'the extension of quota life of British films',[59] to advise on the supply of films for TV. This body would have an independent chairman and its members would include 'representatives of film and television production interests, the trade unions and the public'.

The terms of reference should indicate that it is against public policy for cinematograph films to be shown on television and that the granting of permission should only be occasional and for very special reasons. The films to be shown should firstly be in the category of classics and secondly should in any case be of an agreed age, and there must be a definite limit to the number of films which can be shown in any one year and in any one week.

To ensure compliance, FFU also recommended that future film contracts with union members should contain a clause requiring their permission for the film to be televised. In the shorter term, regarding the IFD deal, it made a threat of disruption: 'If necessary the Unions will consider instructing their members in television not to work on any intended transmission of these films.'[60]

Making its own statement in response, A-R drew particular attention to FFU's neglect of the public interest while claiming to have it at heart. Rather than recognise the popularity of films on television as a legitimate expression of audience taste, the unions instead sought only to protect their own 'narrow interests'. A-R summarised what it saw as the implications of the unions' position:

> The public are either not competent to judge for themselves or they must be told what they should not like. The contention that the cinemas will be empty when the films are being shown on television is accepted by the Unions neither as a sign nor a portent; it is taken as an excuse for any action the Unions may take to impose their point of view.[61]

The official body that FFU advocated would in effect 'decide what films are good for the public to view', thereby abrogating not only the right of broadcasters to schedule programmes as they saw fit but that of the audience to choose what it wanted to see. A-R asserted: 'Programming is and must be a function of management but in the last resort it is the public that decides.' The result of FFU's proposed course of action would be to deprive both film producers of legitimate financial benefit and the public of the opportunity to view 'British films of outstanding merit, many of international fame and acknowledged as masterpieces of British skill and craftsmanship'.

In a discussion paper canvassing members of the ITA on their own views regarding the FFU proposals, the Authority's Director General, Sir Robert Fraser, summed up the situation that the unions found so objectionable:

> Since 1957, there have been included in Independent Television programmes, on the average, about two or three feature films a week, the number varying from season to season, year to year, and place to place. A fair way of putting it would be to say that about five films are transmitted every fortnight, including repeats, four of normal length, and one shorter, with a combined running time of about seven hours. At present, in the London service area, there are being transmitted two feature films a week, with a combined running time of slightly over three hours, accounting for five per cent of the total weekly running time of all programmes transmitted, this being just under 64 hours, comprising a total of about 120 programmes. This is almost identical with the position in the BBC's transmissions, even down to the two films in each service on Saturday evenings and Sunday afternoons respectively.[62]

The paper drew attention to the contradictions in the unions' position. On the one hand, they wished to see the suppression of programme material for which there was a demonstrable public appetite: 'Feature films are invariably very well liked by viewers. The audiences for them are always very large. The experience of years has shown that very few programmes indeed attract and hold so many viewers.' Instead of old films, FFU wanted there to be more original material produced directly for television, yet it seemed confused about how this would help attain its ultimate objective: 'Presumably people would then be even less likely to go out to the cinema.' From both the public's and the broadcasters' point of view, the report acknowledged that the present film supply was not all that it might be: 'If better films were available the public would probably like to see even more on television. It is likely that both the BBC and the [ITV] companies would use rather more if they could get them.' However, films were something of a straw man for the unions' real grievance: 'it is not the use of old feature films on television that is hurting the film trade, but television itself'. Fraser considered that the FFU's threat to obstruct the transmission of the IFD films was 'grievously wrong' and its disregard for public taste 'gravely improper'. He trusted that the ITA's cordial relationship with the Radio and Television Safeguards Committee would prevent the situation resulting in a stand-off.

As it turned out, all the FFU proposals were rejected by the five trade associations, which instead chose to reaffirm their support of FIDO's role in protecting the industry. Lacking wider support, strike action did not therefore materialise and TV showings of the IFD films went ahead unhindered. The Government also declined to intervene in the matter and proposals by Stephen Swingler MP to amend the Cinematograph Films Bill 1960 with the addition of a statutory quota of British material for TV stations, along with censorship regulations, tax and levy to bring television under the same controls as theatrical exhibitors, were also withdrawn as unworkable.[63]

While FFU objected primarily to the showing of cinema films on television, British Actors' Equity worried that the circulation of all recorded performances 'capable of infinite repetition to audiences all over the world', whether on film or videotape, threatened its members' livelihood. By its reasoning, if a recording of an existing performance was regarded as an acceptable substitute for a new, live one, then actors and other entertainers would be called upon to perform less often. Equity therefore campaigned for 'standard contractual provisions safeguarding performers by controlling the use of their recorded performances and in particular the use of cinema films made in other media'.[64] The union's general secretary, Gerald Croasdell, complained that neither the underfunded BBC nor the apparently more prosperous commercial companies were prepared to invest properly in new programmes; he referred to the IFD deal as being part of a 'growing flood of old cinema films, the use of which in television has increased sixfold in the last three years. These have been acquired at knock-down prices as cheap fillers of programme time to the exclusion of material created for the medium, whether on film or in the TV studios.'[65]

In March 1961, Equity opened pay negotiations with the ITV companies, but on 1 November the union joined a strike by the Variety Artistes' Federation (VAF) in protest at the low wage rates the commercial companies offered to performers. The VAF had asked for a 200 per cent increase in fees from the Big Four contractors and a 100 per cent increase from the regional companies. Equity demanded a sliding scale of fees proportionate to the number of potential viewers in each region, but when the contractors offered only a flat-rate increase the union stopped work, in a strike that ultimately lasted five months.[66] This action did not result in any station going off the air; instead, the companies stepped up the number of pre-recorded programmes, including feature films, in their schedules to fill the gaps left by shows that had been cancelled, postponed or disrupted. Live programming was reduced by more than a third; from being scheduled on only one or two evenings, films, often part-networked, now occupied prime slots on three, four or five nights weekly. In one week in February 1962, Television Wales and the West (TWW) alone showed eight features.

FIDO's Secretary Bill Speakman observed that in this way the companies were using up their stock of films 'at an unprecedented rate'.[67] But he neglected to mention that they had also recently replenished supplies by buying up the back-logs of two British distributors that had gone into liquidation: Renown Pictures Corporation and Eros Films. Though these films were mostly undistinguished and their use was heavily criticised in the press as a lazy option on the part of schedulers, they often did as well in the ratings as the programmes they replaced. For example, in the week before Christmas, the comedy *Carry on Admiral* (1957/21.12.1961) – unrelated to the later *Carry On* series – was placed first in the ratings charts for three out of the eight regions in which it was screened, appearing in the top ten of all eight.[68] The following month, *The Gelignite Gang* (1957/12.01.1962), a 'B' crime picture, 'topped the ratings in London'.[69]

In a letter to FIDO, F.L. Thomas of the Rank Organisation noted that 'while the strike lasts it clearly enhances the value of feature films. Indeed, I am not too sure that the end of the strike will materially lower the higher value that [ITV] obvi-ously places on feature films because they might be encouraged to stock-pile them. It seems, does it not, that FIDO may have to approach Covenants with their sights set a little higher.'[70] When the strike did end in early April 1962, with a victory for the unions at an estimated annual cost to ITV of £2 million, ATV's Val Parnell remarked tartly of the return to regular programming: 'Some of the viewers seem to prefer the old films to the new rubbish.'[71]

Equity, flushed with success but angry at ITV's scheduling policy during the dispute, planned a similar campaign not only against the BBC but against all films on television 'anywhere in the world'. It called for the insertion of a clause in contracts stipulating that in Britain a film could be shown either in cinemas or on television but not both; that actors' consent was required for the latter; and that for TV showings overseas every actor should be paid the equivalent of at least one day's fee.[72] In this instance, the threat of action did not materialise. But further strife lay ahead for the commercial companies. On 1 July 1964, the Association of Cinematograph Television and Allied Technicians (ACTT) began a strike against ITV following the breakdown of negotiations over the union's demand for a pay increase amounting to 25 per cent over five years, along with improved conditions. Although ACTT's general secretary George Elvin 'said that he suspected "tatty and shabby old films" would replace the scheduled programmes', on this occa-sion most of the ITV stations went off the air altogether.[73] Three of the smallest companies continued to broadcast for several days using non-union labour, before Westward Television and Ulster Television capitulated in order not to obstruct talks, leaving only Border Television to be run by management and administrative staff.[74]

The strike was ended after a week, following the intervention of Labour Party leader Harold Wilson. On the night transmissions resumed they included a net-worked feature film, *Room at the Top* (1958/07.07.1964), which had not previously been scheduled. This broadcast achieved a record audience to date for any film on

British television, with an estimated 8.339 million homes tuning in.[75] *Room at the Top* was produced by Romulus Films, though it was not part of the IFD deal. It had instead been sold to A-R as part of another package of five films that had this time been offered by John Woolf to FIDO, but which was turned down when the price he wanted (£75,000, ten times FIDO's maximum) was considered too high.[76] Nevertheless, no punitive action seems to have been taken for this sale. On the day the ACTT strike began, the *Daily Cinema* claimed: 'Through the efforts of FIDO, the TV boys cannot draw on many cinema films that have not already been shown over and over again. ITV is left with repeats. The TV audience is unlikely to do other than to watch more of BBC until normal services are resumed.'[77]

Repeat transmissions of films had been a subject often raised in the press over the past two years – repeatedly, in fact. The exchange of the IFD package between ITV and the BBC brought complaints from both critics and viewers, especially when the Corporation chose two pictures that had already been shown by most of the commercial stations, *The African Queen* and *Moulin Rouge*, as its chief film attractions for Christmas 1962.[78] Its RKO stock was also running down, all 100 films in the original package having been shown at least once by 1963 and several three or four times. The matter of repeats even reached the House of Commons. The Postmaster-General, Reginald Bevins, was asked about the number of times some films had been televised, including *She Wore a Yellow Ribbon* (1949/06.06.1960): 'It is shown so often that the ribbon has become faded.' Bevins was asked but declined to set a limit on the number of times any film could be tel-evised.[79] The John Ford/John Wayne Western had been televised four times in less than two years, and as a result of these parliamentary questions the BBC's Board of Management asked for details of its viewing figures. The Board was told that the successive repeats had drawn audiences 'of about 3, 6 and 9 million, respectively', and that the 'same pattern emerged in the case of many other repeated films'.[80] In ratings terms, therefore, repeats were justified, as audiences tended to build rather than diminish over time. Nevertheless, there was pressure on both the BBC and ITV to refresh their stocks; when they did so it caused an even greater fuss, which ultimately spelled the end of FIDO as an active force.

The Goldwyn and MCA-Paramount Deals

In June 1964, rumours surfaced in the trade that the BBC was in the process of negotiating the purchase of a selection from the 750 pre-1949 titles that had been sold by Paramount to MCA six years earlier. The CEA, reporting this deal, pointed out that Paramount and MCA had previously agreed not to allow them to be televised in the UK. Both MCA and the BBC denied that any such purchase had taken place, but the Corporation stated: 'We are always in touch with compa-nies who may have films to offer.'[81]

Two months later, Lew Grade's ATV announced that it had purchased fifty films from one of Hollywood's leading independent producers, Samuel Goldwyn, for £500,000. All the films were more than ten years old and some had been made as long ago as 1930, but Grade remarked: 'What are ten years, fifteen years for a good feature film – nothing.'[82] The CEA duly recommended its members not to book any Goldwyn films, but none of the titles involved in the deal was still in theatrical circulation. The only film that might have been affected by a boycott was Goldwyn's final production, *Porgy and Bess* (1959/26.12.1973), which had not opened in Britain until 1963 and was still in theatrical circulation. But rather than accept the consequences, as David Selznick had done five years earlier, Goldwyn protested the ban on principle. He wrote an open letter to Prime Minister Alec Douglas-Home, Board of Trade President Edward Heath and the leaders of the opposition parties, Harold Wilson and Jo Grimond, in which he stated:

> The action flies in the face of the economic fundamentals upon which trade and industry in your country as well as in ours are based. A boycott such as has been recommended is nothing short of an attempt at economic blackmail which cannot be condoned in any society which believes in free competition.[83]

While this controversy was still fresh, the BBC admitted that its rumoured deal with MCA had now in fact gone through: a block purchase of 140 Paramount films for £550,000. Many of these were to be shown on its new second channel, BBC2, which had struggled to find audiences since beginning transmissions in April. Until November, the channel's reach was confined to London and the south-east, and it had fewer than one million viewers tuning in. Other films, however, were to be given prime slots on the Corporation's main channel, now known as BBC1.[84]

Faced with two such bombshell announcements in the space of a fortnight, with indications from other distributors that they were likewise willing to sell to television, the CEA was forced to concede defeat and back down, not only on the boycott but on its general policy. On 10 September, the Association stated that it would henceforth no longer recommend action against the producers or distributors of 'any feature film the first televising of which takes place after the expiration of five years from the date of its first general availability to exhibitors in the United Kingdom'.[85] The same proviso applied to foreign-language films after a lapse of three years following their release. The CEA now accepted 'that with the passage of time circumstances, including in particular the attitude of the public to television, have changed and in the case of older cinema films the element of competition with current box-office attractions for the leisure time of the public has lessened'.[86]

Some CEA members, including Granada Theatres, registered protests at this change of attitude, fearing that capitulation to the enemy might spell further cinema closures and that 'the floodgates for films for television had been thrown open'.[87] But its secretary Pinkney pointed out: 'The Executive felt it would be completely unrealistic to say "no" to films on TV. We have to face the facts of life.'[88] *The Daily Cinema* quoted from a letter that it had received from the respected film critic Jympson Harman regarding what he called the 'statesmanlike' decision of the CEA:

It surely reflects a conclusion that television cannot be stemmed by undignified opposition, that it has to be lived with, like Bingo, Bowling, Wimpy Bars, motor cars, works trips to the theatre, Continental holidays organised by the shop steward and other by-products of the Welfare State which have unhappily reduced the importance of the cinema to well-filled pockets.[89]

Aside from the implications of this policy change for exhibitors, there remained a question mark over what it would mean for FIDO. Now that it no longer had any teeth for the enforcement of sanctions and had conceded the inevitability of the sale of films to TV, the Organisation was faced with obsolescence. There was also pressure from within the industry to refund the more than £2 million in funds received from exhibitors that had been used for the purchase of covenants. The levy on cinema seats was discontinued from 26 December 1964 and the last covenant was signed, somewhat belatedly, in February 1965, five months after they had ceased generally to be used. In November 1964, FIDO decided to approach all its vendors with the offer of an opportunity to buy back the TV rights of their films for the same amounts that it had paid for them. Letters went out in December and January, but on 16 March 1965 it was reported, at what proved to be the last FIDO board meeting, that of the more than 100 companies with which it had concluded deals, '15 did not reply or acknowledge the communications, 33 definitely declined to exercise their options, ONE has agreed to exercise the option and the remaining 57 have intimated that they may exercise their options in the future, or if the existing circumstances should change'.[90]

Although FIDO no longer sought control of more TV rights, it was still charged with maintaining those it had acquired. Its secretary, Bill Speakman, carried on what was virtually a one-man operation until the late 1970s. He monitored the sale of films to television, kept records of their broadcasts and, where necessary, intervened to ensure compliance with the terms of covenants. For example, FIDO reported the 'successful prevention' of *Never Take No for an Answer* being shown by the Irish state broadcaster Raidió Teilefís Éireann (RTÉ) on 26 December 1964 following the serving of an injunction, the costs of which were charged to the rights owner. This was A-R, as the film had been included in the IFD purchase.[91] Speakman made plain his own feelings about films on television when he commented on ATV's Goldwyn deal:

Producers who sell to TV are just kicking their own industry in the teeth.

Goldwyn made quite a lot of money out of his pictures in the past – now, by selling them to TV, he may be helping to destroy the cinema today.

Some of the films may have been great – at the time they were made.

But show them now and they are awful. TV will bill them as great epics, and people will stay at home to see them: younger people because they have heard tell of names like Eddie Cantor; older people out of sentimental interest, perhaps.

But, after seeing them on TV, they'll think – the younger people, especially – 'Heavens, is that the best that films can do?' And they'll go to the cinema even less than they do now.[92]

Over time, many of the films entrusted to FIDO were eventually reacquired by their owners or their successors in interest, and refunds were regularly made to exhibitors as monies became available. But a survey of FIDO's holdings conducted in 1970 reported that covenants for 531 films would still be held after September 1973, more than half of those originally acquired, representing 'a total outlay of £615,285'.[93] The last of these covenants were not due to expire until 1986. The effect of this was to keep many films that could have been made available to television off the air and largely unseen for more than two decades (see Figure 4.3). One exhibitor remarked of the nearly 1,000 films on which cinema owners' money had been spent over a period of more than six years: 'It might have been better for the cinema trade if three-quarters of them had been shown on television.'[94]

Writing in 1980, the future television executive Michael Jackson asked: 'But why did FIDO die?' He attributed the cause to the twin desires of American distributors to exploit the British market and the corresponding need of broadcasters, BBC2 in particular, to source programme material. Jackson concluded: 'The sudden end of FIDO provoked a desperate rush to the market-place, which created a buyers' market for almost ten years afterwards.'[95] This will be the starting point of the next chapter.

Figure 4.3 BBC2's season of 1940s British films, all TV premieres shown on 'Midweek Cinema' in 1978, was comprised of titles previously kept off television by FIDO covenants. *Radio Times* © Immediate Media Co. Artwork © Mick Brownfield.

Notes

1 See, for example, 'Cinema Crisis', *News Chronicle*, 16 January 1958, and Penelope Houston, 'Time of Crisis', *Sight and Sound* 27, no. 4 (Spring 1958): 166–75. On the historical decline in cinema attendance, see Docherty, Morrison and Tracey, *The Last Picture Show?*; and Hanson, *From Silent Screen to Multi-screen*, 87–143. For other discussions of FIDO, see: John D. Ayres, 'The Two Screens: FIDO, RFDA and Film vs. Television in Post-Second World War Britain', *Journal of British Cinema and Television* 14, no. 4 (2017): 504–21; Buscombe, 'All Bark and No Bite: The Film Industry's Response to Television', in Corner, *Popular Television in Britain*; Derek Hill, 'Defence through FIDO', *Sight and Sound* 28, no. 3/4 (Summer–Autumn 1959): 183–4; and Michael Jackson, 'Cinema versus Television', *Sight and Sound* 49, no. 3 (Summer 1980): 178–81. For a TV film buyer's three-part account of the period, see Bill Gilbert, 'Films on TV: Before the Flood', *The Veteran* 120 (Autumn 2008): 11–14; 'Early Days of TV Acquisition', *The Veteran* 136 (Autumn 2012): 18–21; and 'Overcoming FIDO', *The Veteran* 141 (Winter 2013): 15–18.

2 'Unions Oppose TV Film Deals', *Manchester Guardian*, 4 January 1958, 3.

3 Paulu, *British Broadcasting in Transition*, 168.

4 Federation of Film Unions, 'Exhibition of Cinema Films on Television', 25 January 1960, BBC T36/5; also included as an appendix to ITA Paper 30(60), 12 February 1960, IBA/034: 3997074.

5 On the Granada companies and the Bernsteins, see Eyles, *The Granada Theatres*; and Forman, *Persona Granada*.

6 'Watchdog', *Daily Cinema*, 10 June 1959.

7 FBFM Council Report no. 5, meetings of 7 and 14 January 1958, MBC I/91c.

8 Ibid.

9 FBFM Council Report no. 6, meetings of 30 January and 11 February 1958, MBC I/91c.

10 FBFM Annual Report, 30 April 1958 (draft), section C(6), MBC I/91c.

11 Attached to ibid.

12 'War Chest vs. Video', *Variety*, 18 June 1958, 3.

13 Memorandum of Agreement between the Five Associations, 31 July 1958, MBC I/92.

14 Cecil Madden, 'Crisis in the Cinema Industry', 7 January 1958, BBC T6/360/1.

15 'Old Films on Television', *The Times*, 26 July 1958, 7.

16 'Granada Joins British Industry Boycott vs. Features-to-TV Sale; Seen Blocking Par Pix Sales by MCA', *Variety*, 19 February 1958, 3.

17 '2 Sour Notes Heard as British Pix Biz Okays Defense vs. Tele Films', *Variety*, 30 July 1958, 13.

18 Clifford Davis, 'Fireside Films Cause Trouble', *Daily Mirror*, 22 February 1963; 'O'seas Producers Get a Red Light on Deals with TV', *Daily Cinema*, 20 February 1963.

19 'Granada Stops Feature Films', *Manchester Evening News*, 6 February 1958.

20 ATV press statement, quoted in 'Cinema-TV films battle', *Financial Times*, 6 February 1958, 9.

21 '2 Sour Notes'.

22 'Assoc. British Pix Bids $1,344,000 for Assoc. Talking Pictures Capital', *Variety*, 3 September 1958, 11; 'British Ain't Talkin' on Strategy to Keep Feature Pix off TV', *Variety*, 17 September 1958, 29.

23 'FIAPF Hot for "Summit" vs. Sale of Pix to Video', *Variety*, 17 September 1958, 10.

24 'Peace at Last between ABP, Brit. Film Biz', *Variety*, 15 October 1958, 11.

25 '"Drop FIDO Levy for a Year"', *Kine Weekly*, 14 May 1959, 120.

26 Lord Archibald to Michael Balcon, 11 March 1958, MBC I/91.

27 Archibald to Reginald Baker, 15 July 1958, MBC I/91.

28 Unsigned memo, 'FIDO', MBC I/36.

29 Letter from Reginald Baker, cited in minutes of FBFM Council Meeting (no. 21), 4 November 1958, MBC I/91d.

30 This discussion of FIDO's activities has been compiled from numerous files in the BFI Reuben Library's FIDO Collection.

31 Minutes of FIDO Board Meetings, January 1961, FIDO/17.

32 Minutes of the Negotiating Committee, 5 January 1961, FIDO/14.

33 Bernard Charman, Brighton Conference report, *Daily Cinema*, 22 May 1959.

34 Peter Evans, '70 Films Barred to TV', *Daily Express*, 22 April 1960.

35 Minutes of Board Meetings, 19 January 1961, FIDO/17.

36 These figures are my own calculations based on information contained in FIDO/12-13.

37 Balance Sheets, FIDO/17.

38 William Pay, 'Selznick-BBC TV Film Deal Is Completed', *Motion Picture Daily*, 16 September 1959; 'BBC's Old Films Deal Starts Rumpus', *Daily Express*, 17 September 1959.

39 Minutes of Television Controllers' Meeting, 19 January 1960, FIDO/17. A Selznick press release, reported in 'BBC to Show Selznick Films at Peak Viewing Times', *Kine Weekly*, 24 September 1959, 7, listed twenty-two of the titles in the package but omitted the two most recent: *The Wild Heart* (1952/30.12.1961), a re-edited version of *Gone to Earth* (1950/05.11.1988), and *Terminal Station* (1953/07.10.1961), which had been made in Britain and Italy, respectively.

40 'TV: CEA/FIDO Action', *Daily Cinema*, 9 October 1959.

41 'FIDO to Consider BBC Selznick Deal Tomorrow', *Motion Picture Daily*, 22 September 1959; 'British Are Seeking Booking Clause against TV Sales', *Motion Picture Herald*, 21 November 1959.

42 William Pay, 'CEA Board Ask Boycott of Selznick', *Motion Picture Daily*, 8 October 1959; 'FIDO Change: CEA Boycotts All Selznick Films', *Kine Weekly*, 15 October 1959, 4.

43 'FIDO to Consider BBC Selznick Deal Tomorrow', *Motion Picture Daily*, 22 September 1959.

44 Ronald Waldman to Kenneth Adam, 5 January 1960, BBC T36/5.

45 'TV Deal Shocks Trade', *Daily Cinema*, 6 January 1960.

46 Jock MacGregor, 'London Observations', *Motion Picture Exhibitor*, 20 January 1960.

47 'Why GC is Recommending a Woolf/Angel Films Boycott', *Daily Cinema*, 15 January 1960.

48 'TV Deal Shocks Trade'.

49 Minutes of Board Meetings, 12 January 1960, FIDO/17.

50 William Pay, 'Meet Friday on British Sales to TV', *Motion Picture Daily*, 8 February 1960; Pay, 'Four Pictures Removed from CEA Banned List', *Motion Picture Daily*, 15 February 1960.

51 'Producer Angel Fights CEA Ban on His Films', *Evening Standard*, 5 December 1960; 'Woolf Suing CEA over Film Deal with WB', *Motion Picture Herald*, 26 November 1960. Pinkney's letter to Warner, dated 4 May 1960, was published in *Kine Weekly*, 9 June 1960, 35.

52 'CEA Boycott against James Woolf Withdrawn', *Motion Picture Daily*, 22 December 1960; 'CEA Lift Ban on Producers – Pass a New TV Restriction', *Daily Cinema*, 10 March 1961.

53 'BBC to Show 52 Features', *Kine Weekly*, 15 September 1960, 3. According to Bill Gilbert, the idea for proposing the arrangement to Adorian came from the BBC's Head of Purchasing, Gordon Smith ('Early Days of TV Acquisition', 20).

54 Adam, 18 January 1960; Waldman, 18 March 1960 and 19 June 1960; S.G. Williams, 7 June 1960; BBC press release, 13 September 1960, BBC T36/5. The only film in the IFD package not transmitted by any ITV station was *Women of Twilight* (1952/29.02.1964), though it was shown by the BBC (see Chapter 11).

55 Editorial, *Boxoffice*, 1 February 1960.

56 Peter Evans, '70 Films Barred to TV', *Daily Express*, 22 April 1960.

57 'In the Picture: Action Stations', *Sight and Sound* 29, no. 2 (Spring 1960): 67–68.

58 Federation of Film Unions, 'Exhibition of Cinema Films on Television'.

59 'Control by Consent', *Kine Weekly*, 28 January 1960, 4.

60 Federation of Film Unions, 'Exhibition of Cinema Films on Television'.

61 Associated-Rediffusion Ltd, 'Exhibition of Cinema Films on Television', 4 February 1960, included as an appendix to ITA Paper 30(60), IBA/034: 3997074.

62 ITA Paper 30(60).

63 'TV as "Cinema Exhibitor"; Quota Plea Fails', *Daily Telegraph*, 8 March 1960; 'MPs Reject Quota and Levy for TV', *Kine Weekly*, 17 March 1960, 6; 'The Five Trades Reject FFU's TV Plan', *Kine Weekly*, 31 March 1960, 3.

64 'Actors' Concern over Effect of Television on Jobs', *The Times*, 6 April 1959, 5.

65 Gerald Croasdell, 'Television Profits' (letter), *The Times*, 11 January 1960, 13.

66 'Strike Threat by Variety Artistes', *The Times*, 16 October 1961, 16; 'Strike against ITV Today', *The Times*, 1 November 1961, 10; 'TV Artistes' Pay Agreement', *The Times*, 10 March 1962, 5; 'TV Actors End Strike Today', *The Times*, 3 April 1962, 12. VAF reached a settlement one month earlier than Equity.

67 'This Is Where You Came In!', *Daily Sketch*, 23 February 1962.

68 'TAM's Top 20 Programmes', *Television Mail*, 5 January 1962.

69 'The Growing Use of Films on TV', *Financial Times*, 13 March 1962.

70 Letter from F.L. Thomas, 19 December 1961, enclosed with minutes of FIDO Negotiating Committee, 25 January 1962, FIDO/14.

71 'Regulars Return', *The Times*, 18 April 1962, 5.

72 'Equity Now Calls on the Film Industry', *Sunday Times*, 15 April 1962, 17.

73 'Commercial TV Strike Tomorrow', *The Times*, 30 June 1964, 10.

74 '2 TV Stations Beat Strike', *The Times*, 2 July 1964, 12; 'Two Stations Ending TV Service', *The Times*, 4 July 1964, 8.

75 'The Struggle to Keep Films off TV', *Financial Times*, 20 August 1964, 13; TAM press release, 'Film Attracts BBC2's Biggest Audience', 25 November 1964.

76 Minutes of the Purchasing and Finance Committee, 25 July 1963, FIDO/14.

77 'Commentary', *Daily Cinema*, 1 July 1964.

78 '55 Film Swop: It Means More of the Same Old Thing', *Daily Express*, 5 March 1962; 'Like ... Those Old Films on the Telly', *Daily Mail*, 27 December 1962.

79 'TV Film Repeats: *Yellow Ribbon* a bit Faded', *Daily Telegraph*, 13 March 1963; 'Have You Seen Any Old Films Lately?', *Daily Herald*, 13 March 1963. As I was writing a draft of this chapter, the same film was again being shown on BBC2.

80 Minutes of BBC Board of Management, 25 March 1963, BBC T16/72/5.

81 'TV Films Storm', *Evening News*, 15 June 1964, 1.

82 'The Struggle to Keep Films off TV'.

83 'Goldwyn Hits CEA's Boycott of His Films', *Motion Picture Daily*, 10 September 1964.

84 'New Programmes for BBC2', *The Times*, 2 September 1964, 6; 'New, New, NEW, on BBC2!', *Daily Mail*, 2 September 1964, 7. Bill Gilbert describes the process of selecting and placing the Paramount titles in 'Overcoming FIDO'.

85 Quoted in Elizabeth Sussex, 'Buyer's Market', *Sight and Sound* 34, no. 2 (Spring 1965): 62.

86 'CEA Say Old Films Not So Competitive on TV Today', *Daily Cinema*, 11 September 1964.

87 'If FIDO Goes Should CTBF Benefit from Sale of Rights?', *Daily Cinema*, 23 September 1964.

88 'CEA Executive Had to "Face Facts of Life"', *Daily Cinema*, 14 September 1964.

89 Commentary, *Daily Cinema*, 14 September 1964.

90 Minutes of the General Purpose Committee, 16 March 1965, FIDO/14.

91 Ibid, 21 January 1965, FIDO/14.

92 Quoted in Donald Gomery, 'Don't Let These Ghosts Walk Again!', *Daily Express*, 21 August 1964.

93 Covenants that will still be held by FIDO after September, 1973: compiled November 1968, revised August 1970, FIDO.

94 'If FIDO Goes Should CTBF Benefit from Sale of Rights?', *Daily Cinema*, 23 September 1964.

95 Jackson, 'Cinema versus Television', 181. Jackson was at the time the organiser of the Channel Four Group, advocating control of the upcoming fourth channel on behalf of independent producers. He later became, in turn, Controller of first BBC2, then BBC1, and Chief Executive of Channel Four.

CHAPTER 5

The Great Escape –
Emptying the Vaults (1964–73)

Once upon a time there was a new television channel called BBC2.

It was newer than new, whiter than white, and purer than pure.

Unfortunately, scarcely anybody watched it.

The audience dwindled to a million. Even they watched less than an hour a week.

So a great change was planned. Steps were taken. Great thoughts were thought. No brain was left unpicked.

And suddenly there was an IDEA. They said (very softly no doubt at first):

LET US SHOW SOME OLD FILMS.

And as no one objected they said it louder:

OLD FILMS

The idea caught on and all at the BBC were happy at the Great Leap Forward.
(Douglas Marlborough, 'New, New, NEW, on BBC2!', *Daily Mail*,
2 September 1964, 7)

The Vault Doors Open

The decision in September 1964 of the Cinematograph Exhibitors' Association (CEA) no longer to oppose the showing of films on television, so long as an interval of five years had passed following their release, had an immediate effect on film buying and scheduling. The broadcasters now had an embarrassment of riches to choose from, with the available backlog of American and British films estimated by one source as some 9,000 features.[1] The major distributors, which had been sitting on their wares for so long, were now more than happy to offer them to television, even at hire fees which some in the industry found derisory.

Announcements of further large deals followed soon after the MCA-Paramount and Goldwyn purchases. In October 1964, ABC Television bought 100 films from Warner Bros, while ATV acquired seventy-five from United Artists for a fee 'estimated at between £375,000 ($1,050,000) and £500,000 ($1,400,000) or approximately £5,000 ($14,000) a picture'.[2] The following January the press reported that ATV had bought fifty British films from the Rank Organisation (see Figure 5.1) and that A-R had 'acquired an interest in Bryanston Films, a company with assets including 30 feature films'.[3] While muted trade protests often accompanied news of these transactions, by March 1965 reports that Twentieth Century-Fox had sold 200 films to the BBC for £500,000 (the actual number was 150) provoked little response. According to the *Daily Cinema*, the fall in cost also represented 'the decline in industry excitement that covers such sales to TV today; for hardly a breath has been stirred in any quarter by this BBC purchase of 200 pictures, although some big titles of yesterday are included in the list'.[4] This was a sign that, just over six months after the CEA's concession, the sale of films to television had already become a matter of routine, an accepted and indeed inevitable fact of life, no longer in itself newsworthy. Viewers also had never had it so good, as the quality, range and variety of films on air increased markedly. So, in time, did the number of regular scheduled film slots on each channel. But despite the unions' and exhibitors' fears, there was no sudden deluge of celluloid saturating the airwaves and forcing out other kinds of programmes. Both the BBC and the ITA imposed strict limits on the use of acquired material, with quotas for overseas imports and for the number of feature films broadcast in any given period (see Chapter 9). Even had there not been written guidelines, the professional instincts of schedulers would have told them not to overload viewers with too much of the same kind of material, variety being of the essence in television, and to give priority to in-house rather than to bought-in programming. What the relaxation of the CEA's ban did was give them far more latitude in their scheduling and drive up the quality of films shown.

Beginning a regular monthly column on 'Cinema-TV' in the popular magazine *Films and Filming*, Allen Eyles summed up the transformation in July 1965:

> For a long time now it has been impossible for me or any film addict worthy of the name to stay clear of television. One by one we've found our way to an up-to-date set with all three channels, and tuned in to the good things that only the box can offer. It's true that the picture is disturbingly small, the definition poor, half the image can disappear from a 'scope film, and anything in colour is reduced to black and white. Yet I remember seeing *Rancho Notorious* some eighteen months ago at one of the remaining repertory cinemas where it was cropped at top and bottom by a wide screen. I don't know that being able to view the whole image though without the colour ... is very much worse.
>
> But more often television is indispensable for reviving films that have been totally unavailable. It pays enough money to get new prints, which an individual cinema would be hard put to arrange. The National Film Theatre has been heavily borrowing from the television companies.[5]

Eyles's column, which lasted until 1973, became a regular source of advance information and critical but generally supportive comment for readers at a time when the subject of films on television continued to attract a good deal of hostile attention. One newspaper columnist described BBC2 as being 'ready and

Figure 5.1 Westward Television's programme journal promotes the local broadcast of the Rank Organisation's *Malta Story* (1953), starring Alec Guinness, on 12 June 1965.
Look Westward © The Dickens Press Ltd.

willing to become a home cinema'.[6] This implicitly disparaging view was clearly shared by the *Daily Mail* correspondent quoted in the epigraph to this chapter. The Corporation's second channel had officially begun broadcasting, initially to London only, in April 1964. It would be several years before the new channel would be rolled out to the rest of the country. Feature films played a key role in its programmes and also assumed increasing importance on BBC1.

The upgrade in the quality of films available to television was immediately apparent in BBC1's regular Sunday-evening film strand, which had been running since June 1964. Beginning with *Rancho Notorious* (1952/28.06.1964), a distinguished but at the time under-valued Western directed by Fritz Lang, the strand had for several months mainly offered routine action films from minor studios such as Republic, Eagle-Lion or the latterday RKO. But from September it began also to draw on the BBC's MCA-Paramount package, with titles such as Billy Wilder's *Double Indemnity* (1944/27.09.1964) and *Five Graves to Cairo* (1943/06.12.1964), William Wyler's *The Heiress* (1949/27.12.1964) and many sturdy vehicles for studio contract stars such as Alan Ladd and Bob Hope. The following year, the BBC Board of Governors noted 'that the enormous popularity of old feature films was in itself sufficient justification for showing them' and that 'the feature films being currently screened were good films of some considerable artistic merit, much better, indeed, than they had ever been since showing of feature films began'.[7]

The Corporation's chief film buyer, Gordon Smith, did not always share the high view of these films held by his boss. Controller of Programmes Kenneth Adam suggested to Smith that information on upcoming schedules could profitably be shared with film societies, in order 'to make a virtue of [the films'] age, where it was a virtue, rather than try and disguise it'. Publicity, he felt, could place more stress on their 'almost "classical"' qualities.[8] Yet Smith was unconvinced:

> The Sunday feature films presented on BBC1 have no 'classic' significance, and although some are of an advanced age, an early production date has no merit in itself. These offers stand or fall on their entertainment and not historical value. Whilst these films make sound, popular and strong peak viewing offers, they are not likely to be of particular interest to students of the cinema or members of film societies.[9]

Posterity might not agree.

Press and Public Opinion

The steady rise in the number of films on television and their increasing prominence in the schedules led to a good deal of snide critical comment in the press. 'Old' films on television were a gift for newspaper columnists and headline writers: 'The Old Film Gravy Train'; 'Old Contemptibles'; 'Here We Go, Back to the Tuppenny Crush'; 'Stop Me if You've Seen This One Before'; 'Ah, Hello Again Mr Chips'; 'Not That Old Film Again!'; 'Cut the Awful Oldies!'; and of course, the inevitable 'Play It Again, Sam'.[10]

There was a remarkable consistency to the press coverage: the curiosity or amusement value of seeing stars, now elderly or deceased, suddenly revived in their monochrome youth; creakiness and scratchiness, in reference to supposedly dated production values or imperfect prints; the laziness and stinginess of programme planners who exploited 'captive audiences' and preferred to buy up old celluloid on the cheap rather than invest in TV production; the spectre of films 'taking over' the schedules and pushing out new material; the frequency of repeats; and, where the 'classic' quality of some older films was conceded, the inferior standards of more recent films available to television, from the years of the cinema's commercial decline. Some commentators noticed the peculiarly British practice of showing old films in peak viewing time, rather than in the middle of the night as was common in America.[11] Others deplored the broadcasters' habit of deliberately scheduling their film slots against one another, squeezing out choice on particular evenings. The following selection of comments is representative.

An anonymous reporter for the *Leicester Mercury*:

One is almost tempted to believe that it has at last sunk home in the necessary quarters that the viewing public has had all it can take of prewar films, the vast majority of which present the most extreme mental stress, to say the least. ... But if they can occasionally slip in a film made after 1950 viewing life would be much brighter by far.[12]

James Thomas in the *Daily Express*:

Sunday has become a projectionists' desert with ITV and BBC1 struggling after 9 pm to turn television into an old peoples' [*sic*] home, a dustbin of old ideas with a good proportion of the casts long since rowdily interred at Forest Lawn.[13]

Rosemarie Wittman in the *Sun*:

If I ever get divorced, I shall blame old movies on television. I am so sick of them I could scream.

It seems to me that there is nothing else on television. Nothing that I get to see, anyway.

The other night was typical. I get home late. I make supper. I dish it up, 'How's your day been, darling?'

'Shhhh.' Doris Day is slapping Rock Hudson on the face. Or is it Jimmy Stewart nearly getting shot again? I can't remember.

The plots are so transparent, it's a wonder they don't fall out of the screen. Eventually, it's over.

I open my mouth to say something, but already the knob is being switched over to the other channel. We're just in time to catch the last three-quarters of the other film.

And this winter there will be on average 10 to 12 films a week on television. I can't bear the thought.[14]

Certain columnists, most notably Milton Shulman of the London *Evening Standard*, Ivor Jay of the *Birmingham Evening Mail*, Bill Smith of the *Wolverhampton Express and Star* and James Thomas of the *Daily Express*, returned so often to the theme that some readers were led to point out that they were as prone to repeats as any broadcaster.[15] Shulman in particular seemed determined to conduct a personal crusade against the prevalence of films on television. In doing so he often echoed the arguments made by the talent guilds and craft unions, though he seemed unsure who was most to blame: the schedulers, the viewers or the Americans. Here are three samples of Shulman's wit:

> Most of these films are about 15 years old and when they made up an occasional item on the schedule, they could obviously have no influence on the taste of the viewers.

> But I can see nothing but complacency and inertia emerging from this creeping cinematic take-over of the small screen ... the pummelling of the audience with these old-fashioned techniques and plots is sure to further reduce that area of intelligent receptivity in the viewer and create a public even less capable of enjoying anything fresh, different or obscure.[16]

> [In America] TV tycoons have found it much easier to make profits by dishing up the leaving and droppings of the cinema business than by bothering to make programmes that have some relevance to the potential, the excitement and the uniqueness of a medium that makes them rich. ... And since what happens in America has an insidious way of creeping into our own TV scene, it is going to be difficult to prevent old films taking over more and more of the small screen over here.

> Both the ITV and BBC1 now transmit four old films per week in the London area. Almost five of these hours are at peak viewing time. Sundays and Tuesdays are now almost unviewable because of the concentration of dated celluloid. We are promised no fewer than *ten* old films on three channels over Christmas.[17]

> If I had to blame a single factor for the paralytic pace of visual innovation in British TV over the past six or seven years, I suppose it would be the creeping take-over of the small screen by the cinema industry.

> Old films are no longer a joke; they are a menace. Gradually they are edging into so many crevices of the TV schedules that there is becoming a serious shrinkage of opportunities for TV technicians and artists to originate very much of their own.[18]

Even the broadcasters themselves sometimes seemed to share these views. ITV's programme journal *TV Times*, of all publications, joined in the kicking with an entry in an 'A–Z of Television' on 'Rotten Old Movies', co-written by comedian (and noted film buff) Bob Monkhouse and playwright Willis Hall.[19] The *Daily Sketch* reported a BBC announcer's unfortunate remark, live on air:

> Of Saturday night's midnight movie, *The Vanishing American*, he commented: 'That was The Vanishing American, and he's taken until nine minutes to one to do it.

> 'I hope it takes him even longer to come back. Next week's film *has* to be better...'[20]

Yet for each of the articles expressing contempt for old films on television, there was another communicating enthusiasm and even passion for them. Favourable observers pointed out how the home screen provided unique opportunities to view films long forgotten or inaccessible, and all in the relaxing comfort of one's own living room. Again, the titles of articles give away their sentiments: 'I Say Give

Us More Old Films'; 'Still Joy in the Old Film'; 'Switch on the Home Movies'; 'When Telly Can Be Better Dead than Alive'.[21] Among the most vociferous enthusiasts was Vincent Mulchrone of the *Daily Mail*:

> [A]nytime now, the critics' complaints about oldies on the TV are going to lose their validity. Because, for the millions of customers the cinema lost 15 and more years ago, the oldies aren't old anymore.
>
> I think what brought it home to me was a film called *Suddenly*, screened a few weeks ago. It was a wonderful, taut film about an attempt on the life of the President of the US, a case of art anticipating life.
>
> It starred Frank Sinatra, a person for whom I wouldn't cross the road if he were giving away gold clocks *rattling* with jewels. But the film was good. And I saw it in slippers, in the best armchair in the house, central heating going full tilt, children sticky with sweets, and a glass of beer handy. For nothing.
>
> It was followed, more recently, by Humphrey Bogart in *The Treasure of the Sierra Madre*. It was great, wasn't it? And I didn't even have to shave to see it.
>
> They *were* oldies, I suppose. But only if you'd seen them all those years ago. I hadn't. And I'll lay there are millions more for whom they were fresh and exciting and tremendous entertainment.

Mulchrone urged broadcasters, 'in the name of everything that is middle-aged, middle-class, and the main support of your pay cheque, please keep screening the oldies'. He elaborated: 'Those of us who gave up the cinema because of the queues and the rain and the chivvying management a long time ago, have at least *15 years'* backlog to make up at our own firesides. And I, for one, am looking forward to it.'[22]

Mulchrone spoke for many. Films that former cinemagoers had not been able to see on their first release were now easier to catch up with. Younger viewers had rarely had the chance to see such films at all, having only read or heard about them at second hand. Some argued that the production values and entertainment value of old films put to shame both current releases and material made directly for television. For others there was simply the nostalgia of revisiting past favourites, reliving a lost era or relishing the contrast with modern permissiveness. As Sean Day-Lewis noted, the chance 'to see again the movies of the 1930s, 1940s and 1950s is as sweet a reminder of lost youth as any television producer could devise'.[23] A further sampling of quotations follows.

An anonymous scribe for the *Daily Sketch*:

> Why 'films' should be a dirty word when applied to television has always mystified me.
>
> They take months to make and staggering sums are lavished on stars and production.
>
> TV directors count themselves lucky if they can rehearse their actors for a few weeks.
>
> Budgets are tied either to licence fees (BBC) or the money left over from profits (ITV) so movies are often better than genuine TV material.
>
> Given the choice of a corny old movie or a corny old TV programme, I know which I'd choose. ...

Anyone who believes movies are taking up time which might be filled by new, dynamic television techniques is suffering from a massive dose of wishful thinking.[24]

Philip Phillips in the *Sun*:

I do not care how old a feature movie is, provided it is good entertainment. I would much rather have it than some of the weird, kinky, incomprehensible (and all too frequently inefficiently-produced) plays we are getting on all three networks. ...

I am not advocating that BBC or ITV network should become what Pay TV really is today – a home cinema. But I would not object to a feature film a night on one of the three networks.

I refuse to believe that this would affect the livelihood of our actors or writers, but it might put them more on their mettle to reach the standards of a good British or American film.[25]

Cecil Wilson in the *Daily Mail*:

What was it these old films had that eludes so many films today? Sheer craftsmanship, for one thing; simplicity for another, plus a flattering belief that the audience could use its imagination without having all the sex and violence spelt out in capital letters. ...

Yes, there were some bad old movies but there were also some good ones that can never be bettered and let us thank 'the box' for bringing them so deservedly back.[26]

Chris Dunkley in the *Financial Times*:

It is high time that television people stopped taking extreme umbrage every time they hear the term 'old movies' used to describe feature films on television. 'Good gracious us' (they cry) 'nobody talks about old operas or old symphonies, and when we do a Shakespeare production no one would dream of calling it an "old" play'. But the word 'old' in this context is no more pejorative than in the phrase 'Good grief, there is old Charlie'. In both cases 'old' is an expression of affection rather than aversion, and just as old Charlie may very well be pushing 22, so the 'old' in old movies is not necessarily an insulting reference to the age of the films.

At worst it indicates that the public knows the film to be second hand – unlike old symphonies or old plays, of which each performance is new – and at best, when applied to films that really are very old, it can imply a deep respect and a pleasant nostalgia for both the movies themselves and the great era of cinema when the Regal changed programmes three times a week, and matinees meant two full length features with tea on a tray and the Wurlitzer in the interval.[27]

Viewers often wrote in to voice their own opinions, which sometimes echoed those of professional commentators. There were occasional complaints about 'the ceaseless flood of old films' or broadcasters who 'rummage among dustbins' for them.[28] Some drew attention to the number of films shown in black and white when they were paying for a colour licence, or to the number of repeats. But by far the majority of readers' letters on this theme appearing in newspapers and programme journals were in praise of old movies on television, frequently expressing irritation or resentment at critics' carping. Some wrote to ask for more or to name particular films that they would like to see broadcast.

Take, for example, Mrs Joan Elkins's letter to *Radio Times*:

I am sick to death of the critics who keep sniping at the old movies shown on TV. In the past people have queued to see these pictures, and even today some join clubs and travel miles to watch them at special shows.

Not all of us have been around since the birth of the cinema, and many have only recently discovered such all-time greats as Dietrich, Bogart, Edward G. Robinson, Bette Davis, and others.

If their early films are available to the general public now through TV viewing, why should we be denied the right to see them and form our own opinions?[29]

Tony White in the *Birmingham Evening Mail*:

The film enthusiast is catered for by TV. He can never afford to see all the films on release and TV helps him to fill in the gaps.

Many people, including my parents, missed years of cinema-going while they were spending every available penny on rearing their children.

Television is giving them the chance to see the films that they have only heard about.[30]

Ken Horton in the *Sunday People*:

When will TV critics stop criticising old films on the box?

It just shows they are out of touch.

The stars of these films are more handsome and beautiful than today's undersized and croaking-voiced lot.

We get so much drabness in life, and in modern films and TV plays, that Clark Gable, Greer Garson and Gregory Peck give us the escape to romance that we need. A Claudette Colbert film, like *Midnight* on BBC2 the other night, has more comedy and up-to-date wit than the sick excuses of *The Clockwork Orange* [sic].[31]

Miss A. Winckworth, again in *Radio Times*:

A few months ago, I am sorry to say, the Marx Brothers meant very little to me. Now, thanks to the BBC's repeat showing of 11 of their films, I would walk a hundred miles to see Groucho, Harpo and Chico, and the chaos that always accompanied them.

I now consider them to be the greatest comedians the world has ever known or will ever know. To think that *Animal Crackers* was made 25 years before I was born! Thank you for giving me so much pleasure by introducing me to the mad Marxes.[32]

Perhaps most remarkable about this show of support is how much of it came from young people, who often stressed their own youth in contrast to the age of the movies and testified to how television had helped them to discover the cinema of the past. In July 1973, the *Daily Mail* published one letter from a 15-year-old objecting to the 'boring old films which dominate weekend television, especially on Sundays', but three from other teenagers who 'welcome[d] the chance of seeing some of the excellent films made before our time'.[33]

Finally, what might the actors appearing in these 'old' films have thought about seeing their younger selves resurrected? In 1966, the popular film magazine *Photoplay* surveyed British stars and found that 'they're not crazy on it – *but all without exception admitted that they always watched themselves!*' These are a few of the comments elicited:

I'd like to stop them showing these fifteen and twenty year old films. They are behind the times technically and – far more serious – draw attention to an actor's dated style.

An actor must always be looking forward, always progressing. How can he, when his early apprentice work is shown to millions of potential box-office-payers in one evening?

(Stanley Baker – see Figure 5.2)

I simply feel awkward. I think a lot of actors do. I'm frankly embarrassed by the amount of 'up-periscope' – 'down-periscope' stuff I used to do.

Look at the titles of some of my pictures – *In Which We Serve*, *We Dive at Dawn*, *The Way to the Stars*. That's a phase of my career that's now over. I don't particularly want to be reminded of it, however fine the films may have been at the time.

(John Mills)

I think there are times when they show the public how much you've *improved*. What I object to on TV are films I made just five years ago. They're *too* recent. I'm trying to establish a new image for myself – as an actor who picks his roles with a good deal of care and has an interest in production. Showing my fairly recent films on TV does rather confuse the public's view of me. …

Odd scenes stir memories, some of them painful, some nostalgic. It's playing a part of your life over again. People say you should never go back. Every time I vow I won't watch them, but I do.

(Dirk Bogarde)

Of course I watch them – and I *love* 'em. So does every actor, really – though he'll pretend not to. We've all got king-size egos. Look, television gives us free publicity, so why on earth should we complain?

Do any of the films make me curl up? No more than when I first made them. Whenever I see *Our Girl Friday* on the box, I want to weep, and TV couldn't make it worse.

But I consider it a stroke of genius on somebody's part to show *Reach for the Sky* on Battle of Britain Sunday. It was the *right* occasion and the *right* film. Even I was moved by it.

(Kenneth More)

It's a fascinating exercise, watching one's development as an actor. Time brings detachment and it's possible to study your performance without being emotionally involved. I find this very valuable. I can relate what I see to my work today.

Mind you, I've been very lucky. I don't think I've ever been in one really bad film. And none of them look *too* out of date. *Light up the Sky*, I believe, got into the Top Ten ratings in the London ITV area and the Boulting Brothers comedies – *Private's Progress*, *Lucky Jim* – are

Figure 5.2 The first presentation of BBC2's 'Midnight Movie' strand, on 20 August 1966, was Joseph Losey's *Blind Date* (1959), starring Stanley Baker and Hardy Kruger. *Radio Times* © Immediate Media Co.

as popular as ever on the small screen. So I can look at myself without wincing – and I learn a good deal.

(Ian Carmichael)

[*The Wicked Lady*] was a comic-strip story and never pretended to be anything else. I played my part in that spirit and I'm as pleased with it today as I was then.

I do wish, though, they'd show some of my other films on TV – people think I never played anything else but the wicked Lady Skelton.

(Margaret Lockwood)

The old days were a hoot. The films were nearly all dreadful, so I see no reason why they shouldn't be equally dreadful on television. I'd really rather not see stuff like *Fanny by Gaslight* and *Madonna of the Seven Moons*. The very titles make me wince.

(Phyllis Calvert)

Any shopkeeper who put his products of ten years ago in the front of his window would be thought a nut. Why should our early selves be taken out of store, dusted down and put on show again? It's just as mad.

(Anonymous)[34]

BBC Film Purchasing Policy in the 1960s

By 1964, film acquisition at the BBC had been incorporated into the Television Enterprises department, with Gordon Smith as Head of Purchasing. In January 1965, Director of Television Kenneth Adam asked Smith to compile a report on the comparative states of the film stocks held by the Corporation and by the ITV companies. In the space of only four months following the CEA's capitulation, the broadcasters had vastly increased the size of their respective holdings. Smith's report showed that the BBC currently had 504 English-language features accruing from six major deals already completed, awaiting approval or under negotiation, while the combined ITV stock was estimated as being up to three times as many, partly because of the 'many hundreds' of films notionally available to the network through Associated British-Pathé, the distribution arm of ABC Television's parent company Associated British Picture Corporation (ABPC) (see Table 5.1).[35]

Making up the bulk of these totals were packages from all the major distributors, each varying in size from twenty features to as many as 150. The contents of each package were to some extent determined by the suppliers, but it was up to the buyer to negotiate a satisfactory balance of material. Amongst them, the BBC and the main film-buying companies in the commercial network had purchased material from nine American majors and seven large British corporations. Over the next few years they would acquire further selections, virtually clearing the shelves of everything considered suitable for peak-time broadcast. The two factions were locked in competition with one another for the most worthwhile material. Smith wrote to Adam about waging a 'war of nerves' and playing a 'waiting game' in holding out for the best possible deals: 'I trust you will agree we are right in pursuing with vigour all prospects which might result in really attractive product, whilst resisting attempts to be stampeded into making large commitments for average only films in what is, for the moment, something of a buyer's market.'[36]

The BBC's total financial commitment to film hire at this point was some £2 million (three-quarters of which had been spent on American films), with a further £645,000 pending on a deal in progress. The costs of purchases were

Table 5.1 Broadcasters' estimated film stocks as at March 1965.

American	BBC	ITV	ITV buyer
Columbia	80		
MGM		100	ABC
Paramount		50	ABC
Paramount (MCA/Bob Hope/Koenig)	104		
Republic		50	ATV
Samuel Goldwyn		50	ATV
Twentieth Century-Fox	132		
United Artists		75	ATV
Universal	40		
Warner Bros.		100	ABC
Miscellaneous	72		
Totals	**428**	**425**	
British	**BBC**	**ITV**	**ITV buyer**
Anglo Amalgamated		40	ABC
Associated British-Pathé		Not available	ABC
British Lion	54		
Bryanston		24	A-R
Columbia	20		
Ealing		150	ABC
Eros		100	A-R
Rank	50	40	ATV
Twentieth Century-Fox	18		
Miscellaneous		50 (approx.)	
Totals	**142**	**404+**	
Grand Totals	*570*	*829+*	

Note from Gordon Smith re: ABC Television: 'Also has access to many hundreds of their own A.B. Pathé films.'

Sources: Adapted from memos by Gordon Smith, 'Feature Films', 28 January 1965, and Joanna Spicer, 'BBC1 and BBC2 Feature Film Deals', 18 March 1965, BBC T16/72/6.

parcelled out over a number of years, with cash payments to distributors usually made in instalments. For budget purposes, the expenditure was charged to each channel's programme allowance at standard fixed rates for each first transmission of a film. These 'recovery rates' were reviewed and adjusted in each financial year: for 1965/66 they were set at £4,300 per film on BBC1 and £4,680 for English-language films on BBC2 (foreign-language films were charged at only £1,250 each, reflecting the differential in their hire costs).[37] Repeat screenings were treated as cost-free – that is, films were deemed to have paid for themselves after their first transmission – so a balance of first placings and repeats was required to make the schedules both attractive and economical. A minimum number of first placings each year was therefore agreed with channel controllers in advance to ensure a reasonable speed of recovery on purchases, but the number could be increased on an ad hoc basis according to programming needs; it was thus permissible to 'over-recover' costs. This in turn made further acquisitions more affordable, as past purchase costs were progressively written off and the stock was replenished. From 1966 –67, the policy was simplified: the recovery rate for both BBC1 and BBC2 was set at a standard £4,470, with minimum first placings for each channel of ninety and sixty respectively; both targets were again comfortably exceeded.

However, contracts with distributors stipulated that the number of films transmitted from each package had to keep pace with cash instalments, and that additional payments would be required if more films were shown than had yet been paid for. Each film in a package had a specified start and end date when it would be available for screening, but these dates and the duration of each film's licence period could vary widely even within a single package. A maximum number of transmissions for each film was normally specified, typically three times over the course of the hire period, which was most often five or seven years. To ensure flexibility in programming and adherence to contracts, schedulers therefore alternated films selected from several different packages rather than playing off one package in its entirety before opening another. By July 1968, the BBC's total inventory had grown to nearly 700 films and the investment to over £3 million (see Table 5.2).

Besides their cash value, Gordon Smith was clear about the importance of acquired feature films to the television service, in terms of both viewing numbers and audience appreciation, as he explained in a memo to BBC1 Controller Paul Fox:

> As a generalisation, it is safe to predict that an 'average' film will perform 'very well indeed' on television both in terms of the number of viewers it attracts and the extent of their enjoyment. A 'first class' film will achieve an outstanding success on television judged on the same terms. ...

> Currently we are holding a very attractive and well stocked library, but supplies of feature films from the cinema will eventually be less plentiful as the backlog is used up and because fewer are now being produced. It is fairly certain however that they will be a part of BBC Television programming for some years to come. A part that, although deliberately limited in quantity, will be widely popular and comparatively economical, and whilst we continue to select only those films of quality and in which we have confidence and which we can present effectively in the ways described, is one of which we need not feel in any way ashamed.[38]

The figures cited above excluded an additional, particularly expensive block of films from British Lion which alone had cost £1,750,000.[39] As this was the single most expensive film deal made by any British broadcaster to that date, it is worth looking more closely at the British Lion package as an example of how the acquisition system worked in practice.

Table 5.2 BBC film purchases as at September 1968.

Package	Number of films	Package cost (£)	Average cost per film (£)
Universal A	40	180,300	4,508
Columbia	100	457,000	4,570
British Lion A	51 (54)	220,000	4,314
Rank A	50	245,000	4,900
Twentieth Century-Fox	150	636,300	4,242
Balance of miscellaneous deals	176	784,660	4,458
Sub-totals	**567**	**2,523,260**	**4,450**
Edward Small	8	24,000	3,000
Warner-Pathé	25	120,000	4,800
United Artists	20	81,000	4,050
Universal B	25	120,250	4,810
Monarch	14	55,000	3,929
Rank B	22	100,000	4,545
Raymond Stross	1	5,000	5,000
Miscellaneous further deals	3	8,000	2,666
Sub-totals	**118**	**513,250**	**4,349**
Totals	*685*	*3,036,510*	*4,433*
British Lion B	136	1,750,000	12,868
Grand Total	*821*	*4,786,510*	*5,830*

Note: The British Lion B deal is not included in the original chart, though it had been finalised in March 1968. Also excluded is a package of MGM titles purchased in 1967.

Source: Adapted from 'Feature Film Deals', enclosed with memo from W.G. Dovey, 'Feature Films', 18 September 1968, BBC T16/72/6.

The British Lion Deal

In the 1950s and 1960s, British Lion Films was the third-largest domestic production-distribution company, behind the Rank Organisation and Associated British Picture Corporation. It distributed the films of John and Roy Boulting, Frank Launder and Sidney Gilliat, Herbert Wilcox and Anna Neagle, and Alexander Korda's London Film Productions, among other leading filmmakers and companies. Nevertheless, it regularly experienced financial difficulties. Newspapers reported in January 1968 that the company had turned down an offer of £600,000 from London Weekend Television (LWT) for a package of 118 films. LWT was one of several new ITV companies that had been introduced with the shakeup of regional franchises. It was set to begin broadcasting in July that year, and one of its aims in trying to make the purchase was to put itself in the same league as the other major companies that had bought films for the network. Frank Launder, one of British Lion's board of directors as well as a filmmaker himself, stated publicly that LWT's offer (an average price per film of just over £5,000 when the going rate was now £6,000 to £7,500) was 'far too low' in relation to the advertising revenues the ITV companies would generate from showing the films (up to £200,000 in peak time, he estimated). It also made for unfavourable comparison with the monies spent on in-house production or on the rights to show live events such as sporting fixtures, or indeed with the much higher rates paid for films by US TV networks.[40] LWT then raised its offer to £875,000, but that too was refused.

The BBC had offered £900,000 for a slightly larger package and that also had been turned down, as had two further bids by ITV companies of over £1 million each. Instead, British Lion let it be known that it would not accept anything less than £1,750,000 for the whole library. This was for a fixed-term lease, not an outright sale.[41] Rather than try to negotiate the price down and risk losing the package to a possible rival bid from ITV, the BBC's purse-holders pondered the wisdom of paying the full amount. The alternative, of joining forces with the opposition and splitting the cost of the package with one or even two commercial companies for shared rights, as had been done with A-R for the IFD package in 1960, was rejected. One incentive for buying the films was simply to get them away from the opposition and thereby gain a 'competitive advantage' over ITV.[42] The cost was also worthwhile, staff reasoned, because the British Lion library was the last major unsold package of British films on the market and the BBC had relatively few such films in stock. A deal at the price proposed would not have the effect of driving up market rates because there were no comparable packages waiting to be put up for sale.

The available library consisted of approximately 136 films (give or take one, according to conflicting BBC memos), but staff thought it likely that only 120 would be acceptable for broadcast. On that basis, the average cost per film worked out at nearly £15,000, or two-and-a-half times the standard market price. But if each showable film was transmitted twice over an extended period, the cost per hour of screen time was only £5,000 (assuming an average length of 90 minutes), compared to £16,000 per hour for original drama productions. Satisfying itself with these justifications, in mid-March the BBC made a flat offer of £1,750,000, with the stipulation that an answer was required by the end of the financial year on 31 March. The offer was accepted and announced to the press in June, with Controller of Programmes Huw Wheldon describing it as 'the biggest and easily most important package-deal for British films ever made by a television organisation'.[43] The sale price was not officially disclosed, both parties to the deal being sworn to confidentiality. Press reports speculated that it was £1 million, a figure publicly denied by British Lion's John Boulting, while one journalist claimed to know that it was actually £1,200,000; apparently no-one guessed the full, massive cost.[44]

This 1968 deal was in fact the second that the BBC had made with British Lion. A previous deal for £220,000 had resulted in a package of fifty-four films (of which three proved unacceptable for broadcast) that had begun transmissions in September 1965. At least forty of these earlier titles had been broadcast by the time films from the new package began appearing in the autumn of 1968, and they continued to be played off as the newer acquisitions were being shown. All those titles that can be confirmed as belonging to the second, larger package were made between 1947 and 1967. As usual with block purchases, their contract periods began and ended at different times, the first films being available from 1 September 1968 and the last not until 23 June 1981. This was *Anna Karenina* (1948/15.01.1958), which had previously been shown by ITV and was still under contract to the commercial network when acquired by the BBC. Hire periods typically lasted seven to ten years, but there was considerable variation: some were as long as sixteen years – the 'B' feature *Stolen Assignment* (1953/18.06.1976) was held under contract until June 1985 – and one as short as three (*Anna Karenina* again). The most popular or highly regarded films were played up to three times, including the Wilcox-Neagle collaborations *Spring in Park Lane* (1948/30.05.1972), *Maytime in Mayfair* (1949/23.05.1972) and *Derby Day* (1952/06.06.1972). But many were shown only once, often close to the end of their hire period – *Beautiful Stranger* (1954/19.06.1981), for example, was given its only transmission five days before its lease was due to expire – and at least ten not at all.[45]

The rationale for this scheduling strategy was explained by purchasing assistant Alan Howden, in a memo resisting a suggestion from Finance staff that, to help with cost recovery, a quota be set for the minimum number of films to be shown from the package over a given period, irrespective of programming requirements:

> It has always been the policy to achieve at least one transmission of each feature film acquired – hence the simplicity of the present system of cost recovery. Thereafter, any particularly weak films and/or those not particularly well suited to our presentation themes and needs can be discarded, except in dire emergency, while the really outstanding titles can be screened three or even four times over a number of years, thus exploiting them fully, effectively, and with maximum prestige.
>
> In the present case, of the total of 136 films, it has already been agreed that because of the special nature of this deal involving the purchase of a whole library, costs should be spread over 120 films, in anticipation that some 16 may be unsuitable for transmission. However, of these 120 films, a further 20 are likely, by our normal standards, to be only worth a single transmission, though, on the other hand, some 30 may expect to receive three or more transmissions. It seems absurd if we are obliged to show less suitable films twice in order to fulfil the needs of a particular costing system when at the same time superior films (either third transmissions in the British Lion group, or second transmissions elsewhere in our stocks) may be languishing unseen.[46]

The cost-recovery system eventually devised specifically for the British Lion package was that each and every screening of any of the films should be counted as a 'first' (cost-bearing) placing, including repeats, up to a total of 240 transmissions, thus spreading the cost of the films over a longer period than with the standard arrangement. The fixed recovery charge for all films, not just British Lion titles, was raised to £5,560 to distribute the expense further. There was no obligation to schedule a quarterly minimum from the package in an arbitrary way, as Alan Howden had feared.[47] Howden also made several further important points:

> The exceptionally high price of the British Lion films reflects not so much the quality of the films as the peculiar competitive necessity of cornering a number of prestige films in the group, and the need to secure our future supply of British films. However, from a programme point of view, when viewed in comparison with present stocks, the high price cannot be justified except for a minority of the films concerned.

In order to present these films 'with maximum prestige', several were first transmitted as 'specials' on bank holidays and other exceptional occasions. Thus *The Colditz Story* (1955/30.03.1970) was shown on Easter Monday; the Boultings' *I'm All Right Jack* (1959/26.05.1969) and Carol Reed's *The Third Man* (1949/25.05.1970) on successive Spring Bank Holidays; Reed's *The Fallen Idol* (1948/31.08.1970) on August Bank Holiday; the documentary *The Conquest of Everest* (1953/26.12.1968) on Boxing Day; David Lean's *The Sound Barrier* (1952/31.12.1968) on New Year's Eve; and the Alec Guinness comedy *The Captain's Paradise* (1953/01.01.1971) on New Year's Day. Others were included in established regular film strands where appropriate, such as 'British Film Night' and 'British Film Comedy', or in special seasons such as 'Best of [Peter] Sellers', 'Anna Neagle Stars' and 'The Saga of St. Trinian's' (all four films in that series having been acquired under the deal). However, only a few of the British Lion films appeared in TAM's weekly ratings Top Ten, which estimated the number of homes in which programmes were seen. The most highly rated title from the deal was the comedy *What a Carve Up* (1961/28.01.1969), seen in 7.3 million homes. This was comparable with the best figures scored by any BBC films to that date, the Corporation's only larger audience before 1970 being achieved by a title from the earlier British Lion package – *The Green Man* (1956/09.01.1968) – seen in an estimated 7.7 million homes (see Chapter 7).

ITV Film Purchasing Policy

From its inception, film acquisition at ITV had been conducted by representatives of individual companies. Having acquired UK rights to the films, they could then sub-lease them to other local stations in the network in order to defray their acquisition costs. The largest companies (ATV, ABC, A-R and Granada, in that order) did most of the buying, just as they made most of the network programmes, because, serving the largest regions and earning the largest amount of advertising revenue, they had the greatest capital resources. The smaller regional companies could acquire other films independently for their own use through the Film Purchasing Consortium, a division of their representative body, the British Regional Television Association (BRTA), but mostly they bought from the Big Four. This at least was the situation until the summer of 1968, when a number of changes took place both to the composition of ITV and to its film-buying arrangements.

The regional franchises entered a new licence period beginning in July (see Table 5.3). Most of the existing companies' contracts were renewed by the ITA

Table 5.3 ITV programme companies (29/30 July 1968–31 December 1981) and the start of their colour services.

Contractor	Franchise Region	Service Days	Start of Colour Service
London Weekend Television (LWT)	London	Friday 7.00pm–Sunday	15.11.1969
Thames Television	London	Monday–7.00pm Friday	17.11.1969
ATV Network	Midlands	All week	15.11.1969
Granada Television	Lancashire	All week	15.11.1969
Yorkshire Television (YTV)	Yorkshire	All week	15.11.1969
Scottish Television (STV)	Central Scotland	All week	13.12.1969
Southern Television	South East England	All week	13.12.1969
HTV Wales / HTV West	Wales and West England	All week	06.04.1970
Tyne Tees Television (TTT)	North East England	All week	20.06.1970
Ulster Television (UTV)	Northern Ireland	All week	14.09.1970
Anglia Television	East of England	All week	01.10.1970
Westward Television (WTV)	South West England	All week	22.05.1971
Border Television (BTV)	English-Scottish Borders	All week	01.09.1971
Grampian Television	North Scotland	All week	25.09.1971
Channel Television (CTV)	Channel Islands	All week	26.07.1976

but some were not, and there was some alteration to the way the regions were constituted. ATV, which since 1955 had held the weekday franchise for the Midlands and the weekend franchise for London, had the latter withdrawn but the former extended to cover the whole week. Two new companies now divided up the week in the capital: Thames Television, formed from the merger of Rediffusion (as A-R had been renamed in 1964) and ABC, had the London franchise from the start of Monday to Friday evening, and LWT from Friday evening to the close of Sunday. Granada held on to its licence for the North West but the former Northern region (geographically the largest, if not in demographic terms) was subdivided into Lancashire, where Granada had studios in Manchester, and Yorkshire, which came under the remit of another new company, Yorkshire Television (YTV), based in Leeds. Finally the Wales and West England franchise, which had been financially the least stable in the network, was awarded to a fourth new company, Harlech

Television (HTV), which provided complementary but distinct services for either side of the border: HTV West and HTV Wales, the latter including programmes in the Welsh language. Thus, fourteen regions were split among fifteen companies, and the Big Four was replaced by a Big Five: Thames, ATV, LWT, Granada and YTV.

Around the same time, the task of purchasing films and other outside programmes for the network was centralised by the formation of the Network Purchase Committee (NPC) and the Film Purchase Group (FPG). The latter included the heads of the Big Five plus a single representative of the regional companies, a post rotating from year to year. The key member of the group was the film buyer and scheduler for Granada, Leslie Halliwell, who acted as, in his own words, 'an information filter and negotiator for the companies' (see Figure 5.3).[48] As Network Film Buyer it was Halliwell's role to source likely deals, select suitable films (along with TV programmes made by outside companies), negotiate hire terms and act as an advisor to the FPG, which would then make a decision whether or not to endorse proposed purchases. The group met irregularly but at least once a month to consider the latest round of possible deals along with other items for discussion as they arose. Halliwell described the process in a 1975 trade-press article:

Figure 5.3 In addition to being ITV's network film buyer from 1968 to 1987, Leslie Halliwell (1929–1989) was a prolific author of film and television reference books.
© Granada Publishing Ltd.

The group usually finds on its agenda twenty-five or thirty items, which I have negotiated to the point where I feel they are worthy of consideration. This means that no distributor's 'package' is even discussed in the form in which it was originally presented to me: it has been carefully worked on before I enter upon final negotiations.

I naturally turn down many offers, indeed the vast majority, without discussing them with the Film Purchase Group at all; others are initiated by me in the sense that I decide which distributors are currently likely to have good films to sell, and approach them with a tentative offer (hopefully before the subject occurs to the opposition). In this way it is we and not the distributors who dictate the group of films to be discussed.[49]

Purchases were financed by each ITV company paying an amount relative to its share of the overall advertising revenue earned by the network (a proportion termed the NARAL – Net Advertising Revenue After Levy, in reference to the tax on excess profits that the companies were each obliged to pay the Treasury); hence each contributor paid according to its size and wealth. Granada made down payments on the cost of purchases, and for this and Halliwell's services the other companies paid it an annual fee (as of 1970, this was £10,000). Once deals had been approved – which usually had to be with a unanimous decision by FPG members – and contracts issued, details of new acquisitions would be circulated in the form of regular Network Film Information (NFI) bulletins. Publicity material was acquired from distributors and provided both to local stations and to the press for promotional purposes. Separate information sheets were also made available for each film, carrying the dates of availability, number of runs permitted, plot synopsis, cast list and so forth. By the end of the 1970s, film data were made available to local schedulers in the form of three computer logs, listing all available titles alphabetically, in order of expiry date and in order of running time. When a film was coming to the end of its licence period, extensions to the contract could be requested through Halliwell's office if frequent use merited renewal.[50]

Bookers at the local stations could draw whatever they needed from the pool of available films to suit their own schedules. No special privileges seemingly attached to the larger companies and a film's first transmission could as well be on one of the smaller stations, such as Grampian, as one of the majors; but on the rare occasions when a film was 'networked' nationally or part-networked in two or more regions simultaneously, the transmission would invariably originate with one of the Big Five (see Figure 5.4). Particularly important titles were added to a regularly updated list of 'Films Reserved for Networking', which meant that they could not normally be booked for regional showing (although it was not unknown for companies to breach this custom). In the case of the two London contractors, the inventory was subdivided so that a film designated for Thames's use could not be shown in a weekend slot in the London area, and one earmarked for LWT likewise could not be shown during the week. This arrangement was colloquially known as the 'London split'.

We have seen that, even before the withdrawal of the CEA's ban, ITV had been a prolific buyer and scheduler of films, much more so than had the BBC;

Figure 5.4 Tyne Tees Television and ATV in London shared the British TV premiere on 20 November 1966 of Howard Hawks's *Rio Bravo* (1959), starring John Wayne and Ricky Nelson. *The Viewer* was the ITV listings magazine for the North East of England and Central Scotland. *The Viewer* © The Dickens Press Ltd.

by the start of 1965, the network had already acquired a very substantial stock, totalling more than 800 titles. But from 1966 to 1968, according to Halliwell, the companies were not in a position to negotiate and ITV lost out to the BBC in the making of deals. The reasons for this are unclear, but it is most likely because of the uncertainties around franchise renewal. With the advent of the FPG and the lead taken by Halliwell, ITV regained ground and between October 1968 and May 1969 acquired seven major packages, comprising 458 films for a total cost of £2,311,400 (see Table 5.4).[51] Although the received wisdom was that package deals 'traditionally contain half a dozen good 'uns, half a dozen stinkers and ten to twenty medium grade', Halliwell nevertheless claimed: 'We've never bought a film that didn't have a reasonable function.'[52] ITV's vaults became so well-stocked that in early 1970 the regional companies asked for a review of the purchase arrangements so that they were not obliged to participate in every acquisition and thereby tie up scarce funds in more films than they had programme time to show, but could instead pay only for the films that they needed. On this basis, Tyne Tees and Ulster Television seem to have excluded themselves from certain purchases.[53]

The use of newly-struck 35mm prints rather than 16mm, the international standard, and the Authority's rigorous application of its technical standards allowed Halliwell to claim in 1975 'that the result of all this will be to make our print quality the best in the world' (although the same claim could no doubt have been made by the BBC).[54] Normally two prints were ordered of each title, in order to ensure flexibility in bookings. The availability of two copies also limited the effects of wear and tear as the film made its way around the system over the course of its licence period. Once prints had been received, checked and accepted, they became bookable by local stations according to their scheduling needs. In order to avoid delays in delivery caused by crossover from one station to another, bookings were not usually accepted less than two weeks apart. Prints were initially stored at facilities provided by the film company EMI, and shipped to regional stations from there; but from mid-1976 a dedicated service unit was operated for ITV by a subsidiary, Independent Storage and Cleaning Ltd. This was based at the Film Centre, situated at Park Royal in northwest London, which had 3,500 square feet of storage space 'and was designed to hold up to 42,500 cans of 35mm film'.[55]

The key figure in ITV's film operations, from 1968 to his retirement in 1987, remained Leslie Halliwell. Paul Fox, the former BBC executive who became chair of the FPG after joining Yorkshire Television in 1973, often accompanied him on buying trips to Los Angeles. Fox said of Halliwell:

> He was incredibly knowledgeable, I mean really, truly, a true professional, and extremely well received in Hollywood, because they knew him as someone who was deeply knowledgeable about film. I loved [BBC film buyer] Gordon Smith, lovely bloke, but Leslie knew much more about the film business than Gordon, and knew his way around Hollywood and was totally independent. By 'independent' I mean he cared for ITV, obviously, that was his first thought, but he knew his views in a very trenchant way. Hollywood is a very corrupt world; Leslie was totally, 100 per cent above all of that. The sums involved when we were dealing with Columbia,

Table 5.4 ITV network film purchases, 1968–71.

Company and Period	Number of films (with adjustments)	Package cost (£)	Average cost per film (£)
June 1968–May 1969:			
Paramount	89 (90)	421,500	4,736 (4,683)
Paramount	30	100,000	3,333
Screen Gems	90	432,000	4,800
Screen Gems	67 (68)	491,900	7,342 (7,234)
ABC Films (David O. Selznick)	2	15,000	7,500
United Artists	80 (84)	350,000	4,375 (4,167)
Warner-Seven Arts	100	501,000	5,010
Totals for year	**458**	**2,311,400**	**5,047**
June 1969–May 1970:			
MGM	51	259,000	5,078
ABC (*Movie of the Week*)	9	33,800	3,756
MGM	61	400,000	6,557
MCA (Universal horror)	20	60,000	3,000
NBC (*Heidi* – TV movie)	1	10,400	10,400
RKO Radio	12	18,000	1,500
Screen Gems (*Goal! World Cup 1966*)	1	17,500	17,500
Warner-Seven Arts	51 (50)	250,000	4,902 (5,000)
Totals for year	**208**	**1,048,700**	**5,042**
June 1970–May 1971:			
Darville	15	17,500	1,167
ABC (*Movie of the Week*)	10	33,300	3,330
Paramount (*Movie of the Week*)	8	26,700	3,338
Twentieth Century-Fox	36	167,000	4,639
MGM	37	270,000	7,297
Warner Bros	36	180,000	5,000
Paramount	44	250,000	5,682
NPTA (*Oklahoma!*)	1	18,000	18,000
Totals for year	**187**	**962,500**	**5,147**
Grand Totals	*853*	*4,322,600*	*5,068*

Note: Figures in brackets indicate deductions or adjustments. All purchases for 1970–71 except *Oklahoma!* were marked as 'ex-TTT' or, in the case of the Darville package, 'ex-TTT for 12, ex-UTV for 3'. These notes presumably mean that Tyne Tees Television and Ulster Television were excluded from the purchases.

Source: Adapted from 'Film Purchases', NPC Paper 29(71), and memo from Leslie Halliwell, 26 May 1971, IBA/01023: 3996311.

Warners, MCA, were hundreds of millions of dollars. The chairmen of those studios didn't come out and greet us because they liked the colour of our suits! They came out because they knew it was good business. But they also knew that with Leslie there was no nonsense ... he was 100 per cent incorruptible. That says a great deal about his integrity, above all.[56]

Reflecting on his first three years as network film buyer – in which time he and the FPG had spent a total of £4,322,600 – and surveying the present situation, Halliwell himself noted in 1971:

> by keeping close watch on the situation we have secured all the deals we wanted with the exception of the British Lion package, for which the BBC paid an enormous amount of money, the Anglo-EMI package last year, and an MCA package which was withdrawn from us in such a way that we felt bound to ban that company's remaining product. With this exception we are on very good terms with all our suppliers, and it is safe to say that all future packages will be offered to us at least simultaneously and usually first.[57]

However, Halliwell also pointed out that future deals were 'likely to be comparatively small and choice ... especially as we shall be less interested in the flood of "permissive" films which will shortly come onto the market'. As Gordon Smith had anticipated three years earlier, the market was already shrinking, leaving mainly films considered unsuitable for broadcast. Thus, only seven years after the floodgates had opened, the torrent was beginning to slacken and dry up.

Films on Pay-TV, 1966–68

Although this book is primarily concerned with mainstream, free-to-air broadcasters, there was another provider of films on television in the period under discussion, which merits some attention. Since the mid-1950s, the British press had reported on North American experiments in what was variously called 'pay-TV', 'toll-TV' and 'pay-as-you-view television' (henceforward, toll-TV for the concept and Pay-TV for the relevant company name). Such services did not become a realistic prospect in the UK until 1960. In that year, coinciding with the Government's setting-up of the Pilkington Committee on the future of broadcasting, several companies were formed in anticipation of a third television channel being awarded, independent of both the BBC and ITA. They included: British Telemeter Home Viewing (or Telemeter Programmes), an offshoot of a US company backed by Paramount Pictures, supported in the UK by British Lion, the Granada Group and associates including Michael Balcon; Choiceview, co-owned by the Rank Organisation and Rediffusion; and British Home Entertainment (BHE), whose board of directors included Laurence Olivier and the film producers John Brabourne, Anthony Havelock-Allan and Daniel Angel.[58] By 1962, the contenders also included PayVision, backed by Marconi, and Toll Television, a subsidiary of British Relay Wireless and Television, supported by ATV and Pye. PayVision's programme advisory board included many film-industry figures, among them Stanley Baker, Charles Crichton, Carl Foreman and Joseph Losey.

Toll Television subsequently allied with BHE and the Associated British Picture Corporation (ABPC), changing its name to Pay-TV Ltd.[59]

Rediffusion and British Relay were the two largest companies involved in cable networks. Coaxial cables were used in some areas to deliver existing television services to homes situated where reception by aerial was poor.[60] It was generally assumed that this would be the means of diffusing any future toll-TV service, along with a coin-in-the-slot box attached to TV sets. Cinema owners expressed predictable concerns about competition, even while other interests, including talent and labour unions, were looking forward to new opportunities.[61] But when the Pilkington Report was published in June 1962, it rejected the idea of toll-TV tests, strongly criticised the public service offered by ITV and recommended a second channel be awarded to the BBC (which was of course soon realised in the form of BBC2).[62] A member of the Pilkington Committee, the academic and author Richard Hoggart, thought that toll-TV would impoverish existing services and reduce the public's freedom of choice rather than increase it.[63] Nevertheless, a Government White Paper, published in December 1962, proposed experimental toll-TV services in a small number of areas for a limited period of two to three years, to test public reaction and determine 'whether pay-television could find enough new programme material to justify itself'.[64]

In March 1963, the Postmaster-General, Reginald Bevins, invited expressions of interest in tendering for the experimental services. However, any such service was to operate under tight restrictions. These included: the service had to be provided by landline cables, not the airwaves; effective control of a company must not be held by any current ITV contractor; there would be only one toll-TV channel in any area selected for the experiment but the service also had to offer BBC and ITV programmes; there was to be no advertising, commercial sponsorship, high-value prizes or exclusive televising of sporting and other national events, which would deny them to the majority of the public; and a 30 per cent quota of British-produced programmes would apply.[65] Objections were made to these rules in some quarters: if experimental services were on too small a scale they would not attract the large investments needed; offering only one channel would oblige it to compete directly with the existing broadcasters; and delivery only by wire meant confining services to those areas with established cable networks. Nevertheless, ten companies submitted expressions of interest.[66]

The Film Industry Defence Organisation (FIDO) naturally greeted the prospect of cinema films being shown on toll-TV with the same hostility as it regarded other services. But it faced the dilemma that all the leading candidates were tied up with major film interests, including Paramount, British Lion, Rank and ABPC, which were likely to want to provide films for the new service. Prominent figures, including Rank's John Davis, British Lion's David Kingsley and ABPC's Robert Clark, voiced their opposition to the idea of FIDO forbidding their films from being shown on toll-TV, under the threat of boycotts. Producers saw toll-TV as an additional market, helping them recoup losses from cinemas and distributors contemplated toll-TV availability simultaneous with theatrical release. But following consultation with the Association of Independent Cinemas (AIC), the Board of Trade announced that films shown on toll-TV within twelve months of cinema release would lose their eligibility for the Eady Fund, as was already the case with regular TV.[67] The AIC wanted it to go further and ensure 'that while a film has any cinema commercial value an exhibitor should have the opportunity to show it before it goes on Pay television'.[68] In response, the Post Office instituted a ban on any film being shown on toll-TV within six months of its local theatrical opening, along with a fund to help any cinema whose takings for a film had demonstrably been harmed by its showing on toll-TV.[69]

The Post Office announced franchise allocations in December 1963, for experimental services expected to start a year later. It granted five companies three-year contracts to provide programmes in eight regions: Caledonian Television in Penicuik, near Edinburgh, and Dundee; Choiceview in Leicester, with the option of an extension to an unspecified London area; Pay-TV in Sheffield and certain London boroughs, beginning with Southwark and Westminster; Telemeter in a London area comprising Merton, Morden, Mitcham and Wimbledon, plus an unspecified area in the North of England; and Tolvision in Luton, Bedford and another unspecified London area. The London suburbs were expected to be the most lucrative franchises and the provincial ones more burdensome, so all operators were obliged to take one of these.[70] Reflecting in *Television Mail*, John Hughes wrote:

> Based on experience in the United States, it is difficult to see how any Pay TV company can possibly come out of this small operation without losing a pile of money. The whole essence of the Pay TV concept is that a minority audience can be catered for and the process cannot make a profit until when the minority is of a reasonably absolute size. It seems to me that the testing of Pay TV in small areas must, to some extent, be self defeating and certainly extremely costly, since the programming content must presumably be the same for the small areas (and costs the same) as it would be on a national basis.[71]

Telemeter was expected to be first on the air in the autumn of 1964 with its South London service, to be delivered via the Telefusion cable network and consisting mainly of feature films. The company's Ivor Smith argued that toll-TV would not close cinemas but would 'restore producers' lost audiences', people who would pay to see a film in their own home rather than go out to see one.[72] In a further attempt to placate exhibitors, the toll-TV companies collectively offered to contribute to the Eady Fund according to a formula to be devised after a year's operation. The CEA and AIC in turn took the view that each toll-TV station was the equivalent of a cinema and that companies should therefore pay levy on every viewer's payment to watch a film.[73]

Such opposition from the film industry having already delayed the issuing of licences, the Board of Trade was unwilling to jeopardise the toll-TV experiment when the companies stood to make a collective loss of at least £2 million over the trial period. It therefore proposed the Cinematograph Film (Distribution of Levy) (Amendment) Regulations 1964, to exempt British films less than twelve months old from ineligibility for Eady money when shown on toll-TV services, though they could not be shown until at least six months following the start of their theatrical release. This gave toll-TV favoured treatment over the established broadcasters but recognised that the new services, being small in scale and therefore lacking the capital for much in the way of programme origination, would be highly dependent on the showing of feature films. The companies would also pay a voluntary, non-statutory levy of 6 per cent of their gross income, less than that paid on average by cinemas (7.2 per cent).[74]

The first toll-TV licence was granted to Telemeter in July 1964.[75] Further licences were delayed due both to legal complications in drafting them and to the General Election in October that year, which replaced a Conservative Government with a Labour one. But there were other problems, including a dispute with Equity over payments to actors. Reports appeared of low profits made by toll-TV companies in America and Canada. Most importantly, the concession, in September 1964, of the CEA to the showing of films on regular television as long as they were at least five years old meant that one of the chief selling points of toll-TV – its ability to provide relatively recent films at a cost to the viewer – was significantly diminished. Five-year-old films could now be, and soon were, acquired in large numbers by the BBC and ITV, which of course offered them free at the point of viewing. The first major crack in the new system appeared in April 1965, when Choiceview, the only company not to have a London-area franchise allocation, dropped out. Within a month, Telemeter had also withdrawn, citing unfavourable conditions. The licences to Caledonian and Tolvision, the two smallest companies, had not yet been granted, leaving Pay-TV the only player still in the game.[76]

Nevertheless, the Pay-TV service for Southwark and Westminster duly opened at 7.00pm on Friday, 7 January 1966. The 625-line service (the same line standard as BBC2), reaching around 3,000 homes, was launched by a pre-recorded speech from the Postmaster-General, Anthony Wedgwood (Tony) Benn. The opening night's film offers were *Father Goose* (1964) and *The Ipcress File* (1965), both released by Rank/Universal, and Pay-TV co-owner BHE's initial production, *An Evening with the Royal Ballet* (1963).[77] The latter incurred a charge to the viewer of 7/6, the others the standard price of six shillings each. Other titles subsequently available were from MGM, United Artists and Warner-Pathé, mostly made within the past five years. Films from other major studios were added later. The regular Pay-TV service operated from 7.00pm to midnight on weekdays and 11.00am to midnight at weekends. Sets equipped to receive the new service had to be rented from British Relay.[78]

In its first six months, besides films (which comprised over 83 per cent of programming and which were repeated at occasional intervals – see Table 5.5 for examples), Pay-TV offered subscribers filmed theatre, ballet and opera productions along with sporting events, including a live transmission of the World

Table 5.5 Sample Pay-TV offers, May–July 1967.

TX Date	Day	London	Sheffield
20.05.1967	Sat	*Big Deal at Dodge City* (*A Big Hand for the Little Lady*, 1966) *Live Now – Pay Later* (1962)	*The Masque of the Red Death* (1964) *Repulsion* (1965)
21.05.1967	Sun	*Love & Kisses* (1965) *Red Line 7000* (1965)	*Buffalo Bill – Hero of the Far West* (1964) *Operation Crossbow* (1965)
27.05.1967	Sat	*Madame X* (1965) *The Naked Prey* (1966)	*The Curse of the Mummy's Tomb* (1964) *The Pleasure Girls* (1965)
28.05.1967	Sun	*Beau Geste* (1966) *Daleks' Invasion Earth 2150 AD* (1966) *Jack the Ripper* (1959)	*Fluffy* (1965) *The Pure Hell of St Trinian's* (1960)
03.06.1967	Sat	*I Was Happy Here* (1966) *Intimacy* (1966)	*The Black Torment* (1964) *Of Human Bondage* (1964) *Walk, Don't Run* (1966)
04.06.1967	Sun	*The Moving Target* (*Harper*, 1966) *The Sandwich Man* (1966)	*King Rat* (1965) *The Son of Captain Blood* (1962)
10.06.1967	Sat	*Southwest to Sonora* (*The Appaloosa*, 1966) *This Property Is Condemned* (1966)	*Dead Image* (*Dead Ringer*, 1964)
11.06.1967	Sun	*The Early Bird* (1965) *The Lost Kingdom* (1961) *The Tomb of Ligeia* (1964)	*Arabesque* (1966) *Hercules Attacks* (1963)
17.06.1967	Sat	*The Flesh and the Fiends* (1960)	*Assault on a Queen* (1966) *The L-shaped Room* (1962) *Rasputin – the Mad Monk* (1966)
18.06.1967	Sun	*The Beauty Jungle* (1964) *Lost in Alaska* (1952) *Nevada Smith* (1966) *The Young Warriors* (1967)	*Mysterious Island* (1961) *Paradise – Hawaiian Style* (1966)
24.06.1967	Sat	*Mr Sardonicus* (1961)	*The Chase* (1966) *Doctor in Love* (1960) *Strait-jacket* (1964)
25.06.1967	Sun	*The Adventures of Scaramouche* (1963) *Death Is a Woman* (1966) *The Great St Trinian's Train Robbery* (1966) *Marriage on the Rocks* (1965)	*Captain Blood* (1960) *Lost Command* (1966)
01.07.1967	Sat	*Kismet* (1955) *The Thing from Another World* (1951)	*The Day of the Triffids* (1962) *The Naked Prey* (1966)
02.07.1967	Sun	*Batman* (1966) *Hold On!* (1966) *Murder Most Foul* (1964)	*Live Now – Pay Later* (1962) *Morgan – a Suitable Case or Treatment* (1966) *Son of a Gunfighter* (1965)

Source: *CEA News Letter*, no. 99, 7 July 1967.

Heavyweight Championship boxing match between Cassius Clay (Muhammad Ali) and Henry Cooper. The latter gave the channel its largest viewing figure, with 80 per cent of the potential audience tuning in. *Television Mail* later remarked that the most popular films on the service were 'the action-packed thrillers which are least suited to a television screen'.[79] The most-viewed titles were *The Great Escape* (1963, 48 per cent), *The Magnificent Seven* (1960, 46 per cent), *The Birds* (1963, 41.5 per cent) and *The Guns of Navarone* (1961, 38 per cent).[80] Although two of these were already five years old, none was shown on free terrestrial television until the 1970s. According to company manager Michael Frostick, Pay-TV could 'restore some of the lost life to Britain's film industry' by bringing 'films to people who either can't get to, or do not want to go to the cinema'. This constituted 'a new audience which the cinema can reach at home'. He said that 40 per cent of films shown on the channel were British.[81]

Pay-TV's Sheffield service did not begin until 17 November 1966. From newly-built studios on Northfield Road, the channel offered fifty hours of programmes weekly to an estimated 2,500 viewers in the Crookes, Hillsborough and Walkley areas. They included 'lifestyle' shows (hobbies, cookery, education) hosted by local presenters, as well as the established line-up of films and culture. The opening night's features were *Charade* (1963) and *The War Lord* (1965), again both supplied by Rank/Universal. The Sheffield system had some differences from the London one, notably in the design of the set meter, which did not give the viewer cash credit if a programme was switched off before it was over, as was the case in London. Both, however, allowed the company to see exactly how many viewers were watching a programme at any given time.[82]

While allowing the trial period to run its course, the Government decided against extending the experiment to other areas until after it was completed, despite calls from the British Film Producers' Association (BFPA) to make Pay-TV a national service.[83] *Television Today* observed that Pay-TV mostly offered 'material from other media (principally the cinema)', and while it did not offer much original work to those in the entertainment business it also, due to its limited scale, posed little threat to their livelihood either. Even if it were to be extended further, the prices charged (ranging between 7/6 and 2 shillings per programme) meant that few families could afford to tune in more than a few times each week.[84]

But by early 1968, the future of Pay-TV was in doubt. The company now had around 7,500 subscribers (households) in London – the target was 10,000 – and 1,800 in Sheffield. It had invested about £1 million in the scheme and without expansion it could not commit to further expenditure.[85] Then, in October, the Government announced that the experiment was not to be expanded but instead terminated. The reason given was that it would not consent to the development of a full service but had offered to continue the trial until 1976. The Government wanted to limit the service to 125,000 subscribers in London and 25,000 in Sheffield, whereas Pay-TV had wanted a total of 250,000 to remain viable. When the two sides could not agree, Pay-TV decided to shut down the service without delay on Saturday, 8 November 1968.[86] Toll-TV services offering feature films did not emerge again until the early 1980s.

Notes

1 'Fox Will Not Sell Film Backlog to British TV', *Daily Cinema*, 19 October 1964.
2 William Pay, 'UA Sells 75 Features to British TV', *Motion Picture Daily*, 27 October 1964.
3 'Rank Sells Films to British TV', *Motion Picture Daily*, 19 January 1965.
4 *Daily Cinema*, 17 March 1965.
5 Allen Eyles, 'Boxed-in', *Films and Filming* 11, no. 10 (July 1965): 38.
6 Ivor Jay, 'I Prefer Longer Plays to Old Films…', *Birmingham Evening Mail*, 11 September 1964.
7 Minutes of BBC Controllers' Meeting, 23 March 1965, BBC T16/72/6.
8 Kenneth Adam, 'West Regional Advisory Council', 18 January 1965, BBC T16/72/6.
9 Gordon Smith, 'Presentation of Feature Films', 22 January 1965, BBC T16/72/6.
10 Respectively: *Birmingham Evening Mail*, 10 June 1966; *Wolverhampton Express and Star*, 20 June 1969; *Evening Standard*, 3 September 1969; *Daily Mail*, 8 February 1971; *Sun*, 2 December 1972; *Sun*, 11 August 1973; *Daily Mirror*, 22 March 1971.
11 This observation was also made by veteran Hollywood actor George Raft during his appearance on ITV's variety show *Sunday Night at the London Palladium* on 31 October 1965, a rare episode that survives in the archives. For contrasting views of films on television by American writers, which lie beyond the scope of the present study, see: Kael, 'Movies on Television', in *Kiss Kiss Bang Bang*, 217–26; and Thompson, 'TV Favorites', in Nobile, *Favorite Movies*, 246–53.
12 'Welcome Trend in TV films', *Leicester Mercury*, 24 August 1966.
13 James Thomas, 'Old Contemptibles', *Daily Express*, 31 May 1968.
14 Rosemarie Wittman, 'Why Dig Up the Bad Old Films?', *Sun*, 7 September 1970.
15 'Surely the Heading of Shulman's Article Should Have Been "Stop Me if You've Read This One Before." We Have – Many Times' (W. Kane, 'TV and Old Films' [letter], *Evening Standard*, 10 September 1969).
16 Milton Shulman, 'If You're Quick on the Switch You Can See 12 Old Movies from Your Armchair This Week', *Evening Standard*, 1 June 1966.
17 Milton Shulman, 'You May Watch *Ten* Old Films for Christmas. Why?', *Evening Standard*, 21 December 1967.
18 Milton Shulman, 'Stop Me if You've Seen This One Before', *Evening Standard*, 3 September 1969.
19 Bob Monkhouse and Willis Hall, 'A–Z of Television', Part Five, *TV Times*, 11 November 1971, 21. The previous week's issue had included an entry on 'Old Movies' that was less judgemental.
20 'BBC Bites the Dust', *Daily Sketch*, 23 June 1969.
21 Philip Phillips, 'I Say Give Us More Old Films', *Sun*, 5 October 1966; 'Still Joy in the Old Film', *The Times* supplement on Independent Television, 2 July 1968, X; John Spencer, *Sun*, 17 April 1971; John Spencer, *Sun*, 28 August 1971.
22 Vincent Mulchrone, 'Ah, But for Me Those Oldie Films Are Brand New!', *Daily Mail*, 19 January 1966, 8; original emphasis.

23 Sean Day-Lewis, 'Catching up with the Old Movies', *Daily Telegraph*, 24 May 1971.

24 'I'll Always Settle for Stella', *Daily Sketch*, 3 September 1964.

25 Philip Phillips, 'I Say Give Us More Old Films', *Sun*, 5 October 1966. See below in the present chapter for a discussion of Pay-TV.

26 Cecil Wilson, 'Vintage Vision…', *Daily Mail*, 29 April 1973, 7.

27 Chris Dunkley, 'Old Ones, Loved Ones…', *Financial Times*, 11 April 1973, 3.

28 Letters from Robert Harper, *Radio Times*, 16 July 1970, 54; W. Innes, *Daily Mirror*, 17 April 1972.

29 Joan Elkins, 'Ever-green Oldies' (letter), *Radio Times*, 2 June 1966, 4.

30 Tony White, 'TV and the Film Enthusiast', *Birmingham Evening Mail*, 26 March 1969.

31 Ken Horton, 'Give Me the Old-time Stars!' (letter), *Sunday People*, 30 April 1972.

32 A. Winckworth, 'Getting to Know the Marx Bros' (letter), *Radio Times*, 27 July 1972, 51.

33 Letters, *Daily Mail*, 21 July 1973 and 28 July 1973.

34 Francis Peters, 'Those Old Films on TV and What the Stars of Them Really Think', *Photoplay*, December 1966, 42–3, 56; original emphases. None of the three films mentioned by John Mills was shown on British television until the 1970s.

35 Smith, 'Feature Films', 28 January 1965, BBC T16/72/6. Smith's report concerned only American and British titles, excluding the foreign-language films that had been acquired.

36 Ibid.

37 Dennis Scuse, 'Hired Film Investment', 12 March 1965; Joanna Spicer, 'BBC1 and BBC2 Feature Film Deals', 18 March 1965, BBC T16/72/6.

38 Smith to Paul Fox, 2 January 1968, BBC T16/72/6.

39 Financial information taken from: W.G. Dovey, 'Feature Films', 29 November 1965, and 'Feature Films', 19 April 1966; P.A. Findlay, 10 May 1966; W.J. Bridges, 'Feature Film Deals: Recoveries from Programme Allowance 1965/66', 10 May 1966; Smith, 'Feature Film Costs', 1 February 1968; Alan Howden, 'Feature Film Deals', 4 July 1968; Dovey, 'Feature Films', 18 September 1968, all BBC T16/72/6.

40 Nicholas Travers, 'British Lion Battles TV Network over Fees for Old Films', *The Times*, 13 January 1968.

41 Minutes of BBC Board of Management meeting, 11 March 1968, BBC R78/1,123/1.

42 Lord Hill of Luton to Sir Robert Bellinger, 12 March 1968, BBC R78/1,123/1; original emphasis.

43 Huw Wheldon (or his press release) was quoted in several newspapers, including the *Daily Mail*, *Daily Telegraph* and *Financial Times* of 25 June 1968.

44 'Talking of Money…', *Daily Mirror*, 8 July 1968.

45 BBC records kindly provided by Reg Roberts enabled me to determine the hire periods of films in the British Lion package.

46 Howden, 'Feature Film Deals'.

47 Dovey, 'Feature Films'.

48 Leslie Halliwell, 'Film Purchases', NPC Paper 29(71), 26 May 1971, IBA/01023: 3996311.

49 Leslie Halliwell, 'How We Buy the Films for ITV and What the Problems Can Be', *The Stage and Television Today*, 10 July 1975.

50 Halliwell, 'ITV Working Rules for Film Purchase and Handling', attached to Network Film Information 8(80), 20 October 1980, IBA/01024: 3996310.

51 Ibid. These totals do not include three small packages listed (in an appendix to an earlier memo) as having been bought since October 1968: eleven Tarzan films, twelve films from the Rank Organisation and one, *The Wages of Fear* (1953/26.10.68), from Connoisseur Films (Frank Copplestone, 'Review of Network Film Purchasing Arrangements', NPC Paper 5[70], 30 January 1970, IBA/01023: 3996311).

52 'More Movies to Be Shown on TV', *Sunday Times*, 31 January 1971, 40.

53 Copplestone, 'Review of Network Film Purchasing Arrangements'.

54 Halliwell, 'Network Film Purchase', 11 December 1975, IBA/01024: 3996310.

55 Halliwell, 'ITV Working Rules for Film Purchase and Handling'.

56 Author's interview with Sir Paul Fox, 3 September 2012.

57 Halliwell, 'Film Purchases'.

58 'British Company Is Formed to Promote Telemeter', *Kine Weekly*, 7 July 1960, 1, 26; 'Paramount's Bid for Toll System in Britain', *Television Mail*, 8 July 1960, 3; 'Coin-in-slot TV Company', *The Times*, 8 October 1960, 4; 'Toll Television', *Kine Weekly*, 17 November 1960, 14, 19; 'British-controlled Telemeter Pay-TV Company Is Set Up', *Kine Weekly*, 24 November 1960, 6; Duncan Crow, 'Pay Television', *Sight and Sound*, Spring 1961, 96–7.

59 Wilfred Altman, 'Pay TV', *Contrast* 2, no. 2 (1 January 1962): 81–90 ; 'New Pay-TV System Gets Support from Entertainment Industry', *The Stage and Television Today*, 29 March 1962, 9; 'Pay as You View Firm Changes Its Name', *The Stage and Television Today*, 22 August 1963, 9.

60 Lewis, *Community Television and Cable in Britain*, 12.

61 'KRS Comes Out in Favour of Toll-television', *Kine Weekly*, 16 February 1961, 1, 42.

62 Home Office, *Report of the Committee on Broadcasting, 1960*; 'Pilkington Blow to ITV', *Television Mail*, 29 June 1962, 6, 9.

63 Editorial, *Television Mail*, 12 October 1962, 3.

64 'No New ITV Channel – but Power for ITA', *The Stage and Television Today*, 20 December 1962, 9.

65 'No Advertising or Significant Prizes on Pay-TV', *The Times*, 7 March 1963, 6; 'Terms of Reference Given for Pay TV', *Television Mail*, 8 March 1963, 7.

66 'Film Producers Are Concerned over the Scope of Pay-TV', *Television Mail*, 15 March 1963, 9; 'PMG's Policy Wrong for Pay TV', *Television Mail*, 3 May 1963, 14.

67 'FIDO Prepares to Fight Pay-TV Interests', *Television Mail*, 30 August 1963, 10; 'Pay TV is TV', *Television Mail*, 25 October 1963, 6.

68 'Pay-TV Safeguards', *Television Mail*, 27 March 1964, 9.

69 'Feature Films and Pay-TV: PMG's Assurance', *Television Mail*, 8 May 1964, 4.

70 'Coin-box TV to Start Next Autumn', *The Times*, 9 December 1963, 10; 'Licences for Five Pay-TV Groups', *The Times*, 12 December 1963, 4; 'Rank, Rediffusion, ABPC Win Pay-TV Contracts', *Television Mail*, 13 December 1963, 4; 'Five Groups to Take Part in Pay TV Experiment', *The Stage and Television Today*, 19 December, 11.

71 John Hughes, '1963: Year of Indecision', *Television Mail*, 27 December 1963, 5.

72 'Looking at Pay-TV with Ivor Smith', *Television Mail*, 22 May 1964, 22.

73 'Pay-TV Companies will Pay Levy on Features', *Television Mail*, 29 May 1964, 4; 'Pay TV Protection', *Television Mail*, 19 June 1964, 4; 'The Pay-TV Debate', *Television Mail*, 26 June 1964, 18.

74 'New British Films Will Be Shown on Pay TV', *The Stage and Television Today*, 16 July 1964, 9; John Mountjoy, 'Pay Television 1965', *Television Mail*, 17 July 1964, 7.

75 'Pay-TV Licence', *Television Mail*, 31 July 1964, 4.

76 'More Delays for Pay TV', *The Stage and Television Today*, 22 April 1965, 9, 16; 'Telemeter Drops Out', *The Stage and Television Today*, 6 May 1965, 13.

77 To avoid confusion, films cited in this section are not identified by first terrestrial transmission date.

78 'PMG to Open Pay-TV', *The Stage and Television Today*, 9 December 1965, 9; 'Pay TV's Opening Night', *The Stage and Television Today*, 6 January 1966, 19; 'Right Time for Pay TV Experiment – PMG', *The Stage and Television Today*, 13 January 1966, 10; 'The Quarter: Happened…', *Contrast*, 5: 5/6, 1 April 1966, 148.

79 Patricia Tisdall, 'Will Subscription Television Pay?', *Television Mail*, 20 March 1968, 22–3.

80 Marjorie Bilbow, 'Six Months of Pay-TV', *The Stage and Television Today*, 16 June 1966, 10; 'What Pay-TV Subscribers Spend and on What', *The Stage and Television Today*, 23 June 1966, 13.

81 'Pay-TV can "Restore Life to Film Industry"', *Television Mail*, 2 September 1966, 5.

82 'Sheffield to Have Pay-TV in November', *The Stage and Television Today*, 1 September 1996, 9; 'Pay TV Comes to Sheffield', *The Stage and Television Today*, 17 November 1966, 12; 'Pay TV Reports', *Television Mail*, 24 November 1967, 5. See also David Laine, 'Pay-TV – 1960s Style', *Transdiffusion Broadcasting System*, 23 November 2006, at https://www.transdiffusion.org/2006/11/23/paytv_1960s_sty?fbclid=IwAR33rDx_obb5WFa1sJZbLw7ixC9xoPnOoFoCSVsYeJYScvURHYN pChqS7tY

83 'Call to PMG to Extend Pay TV', *The Stage and Television Today*, 20 April 1967, 9.

84 'Pay TV No Threat at the Moment', *The Stage and Television Today*, 24 November 1966, 10.

85 'Pay TV Future Now in Doubt', *The Stage and Television Today*, 4 January 1968, 17.

86 'Pay-TV Is Rejected – Then Talks Give New Hope', *The Stage and Television Today*, 31 October 1968, 9; 'Pay-TV Finishes', *The Stage and Television Today*, 14 November 1968, 9. For recollections of Pay-TV's services, see Laine, 'Pay-TV – 1960s Style'.

CHAPTER 6

The Sound of Wind –
Blockbusters on the Box (1973–81)

The general excellence of British television compared with the television services of other countries explains in large part why the decline in cinema admissions is more dramatic in Britain than in every other country in the world for which figures are available. One reason for its excellence, in the eyes of its audience, is the large number of feature films shown. In Italy, television is restricted in the number of films it can show; in France, certain days are free of movies; in Germany, the television service pays a Danegeld to the film industry. But in Britain, television has sucked up the mass audience using the vacuum cleaner of the mass audience's mass entertainment – and gives precious little in return. Eventually, television could kill off the feature film made for the large screen – and its audience will have to make do with those very inferior made-for-television movies.

(David Gordon, 'Ten Points about the Crisis in the British Film Industry',
Sight and Sound 43, no. 2 [Spring 1974]: 70)

BBC Film Purchasing Policy in the 1970s

When Gordon Smith retired as the BBC's chief film buyer in 1970, his role was filled by Gunnar Rugheimer, a combative Swedish-born veteran of Canadian and Irish television (see Figure 6.1). As General Manager, Purchased Programmes (Television), Rugheimer pursued an aggressive strategy determined partly by the increasing scarcity of product suitable for peak-time family viewing. In July 1972, the Corporation's Director of Finance, H.P. Hughes, had expressed concern about the level of film stocks (the number of films held and their value) and the lack of a clear policy on acquisition. Rugheimer therefore prepared a report in which he set out the present stock situation and drew up a projection of future film needs as far ahead as 1980 (see Tables 6.1.1–6.1.4).[1] Based on current levels, Rugheimer estimated annual programme requirements as 200 first runs and 200 repeats. Films were classified in five quality grades, and their annual usage was broken down as follows:

First showing Specials (Bank Holidays): 6 per annum
First showings Grade A: 33 per annum
First showings Grade B: 74 per annum
First showings Grade C: 87 per annum
Re-runs (all quality grades): 200 per annum

Figure 6.1 Gunnar Rugheimer (1923–2003) was the BBC's chief film buyer from 1970 to 1983. BBC Photo Library © BBC.

He also pointed out:

> In scheduling Feature Films consideration must, of course, be given to a number of factors other than quality grading such as, for instance, running time, suitability of theme and treatment in relationship to the hour of scheduling and possible duplication of our own originations.
>
> This means that Controllers, in order to make up viable schedules, must have a reasonable choice of alternative Feature Films on hand for selection. In practice, two year's [*sic*] supply has been found to be the minimum.[2]

At present rate of use based on stock currently held, Rugheimer foresaw that first-run films in the top two grades would be exhausted by the 1974–75 financial year and in the lower two grades by the year after. They could be replenished by new films coming onto the market, but these would inevitably be the subject of competition with ITV. Rugheimer anticipated that only 40 per cent of available product would typically be bought by the opposition. But even if the BBC bought all the films theoretically available to it (that is, 60 per cent of those on the market), an assessment of the major studios' unsold inventories suggested that there would still be a shortage of suitable product in years ahead. Rugheimer therefore antici- pated that in future, first runs of films in Grade C would have to be replaced by re-runs; but stocks already under licence would be depleted by 1976–77. They could, however, be refreshed by acquiring films already shown by ITV after their

Tables 6.1.1–6.1.4 'Proposed Feature Film Stock Policy'. Source: memo from Gunnar Rugheimer, 7 July 1972, BBC R78/1, 123/1.

Table 6.1.1 Projected use of films available for first transmission.

Quality grade	Colour or mono [-chrome]	Films under license	Annual use	Films available for transmission at 31st March								
				1972	1973	1974	1975	1976	1977	1978	1979	1980
New films												
Special	C	13	5	3	4	1	-4	-10	-16	-22	-28	-34
	M	1	1	1								
A	C	67	27	27	18	6	-18	-49	-82	-115	-148	-181
	M	16	6	16	10	4						
B	C	158	47	98	76	44	12	-55	-129	-203	-277	-351
	M	83	27	83	56	29	2					
C	C	129	41	103	81	40	4					
	M	147	46	143	101	55	9					
Total	C	367	120	231	179	91	-6	-114	-227	-340	-453	-566
	M	247	80	243	167	88	11					
		614	200	474	346	179	5	-114	-227	-340	-453	-566
Re-runs	C	66		14	16	25	33	31	-10	-51	-92	-133
	M	98		27	34	45	64	61	15	-31	-77	-123
		164		41	50	70	97	92	5	-82	-169	-256
Total	C	433	120	345	195	116	27	-83	-237	-391	-545	-699
	M	345	80	270	201	133	75	61	15	-31	-77	-123
		778	200	515	396	249	102	-22	-222	-422	-622	-822

Note (1): Films under license include the contracts negotiated at 31st March 1972 plus the 20th Century Fox and United Artists contracts approved by D.G. Meeting 5th May 1972. [Rugheimer's note]

Note (2): It is assumed that Re-Runs will be used in place of New Grade C films after March 1975. [Rugheimer's note]

Table 6.1.2 Availability of suitable new films.

Production year		Total	Pre 1968	68/69	69/70	70/71	71/72	72/73	73/74	74/75
Year available to television			72/73	73/74	74/75	75/76	76/77	77/78	78/79	79/80
Total supply of suitable new films										
	Special	56	5	13	7	11	5	5	5	5
	A	294	9	16	40	66	43	40	40	40
	B	672	43	59	82	102	101	95	95	95
	C	12	1	2	6	2	1			
		1034	58	90	135	181	150	140	140	140
Available to BBC if ITV buy 40%										
	Special	35	3	8	5	7	3	3	3	3
	A	176	6	10	24	40	24	24	24	24
	B	394	25	36	50	62	62	53	53	53
	C	5	1	1	1	1	1			
		610	35	55	80	110	980	80	80	80
Films available 31st March if BBC buy all new films available (i.e. 60% as above plus Table 1)										
New films	Special		7	12	12	13	10	7	4	1
	A		34	26	22	31	22	13	4	-5
	B		157	134	125	118	106	85	64	43
	C		183	97	16					
			381	269	175	162	138	105	72	39
	Re-runs		50	70	97	96	10	-77	-164	-251
	Total		431	339	272	258	148	28	-92	-212

Table 6.1.3 Availability of suitable re-runs.

Production year		Total	Pre 1968	68/69	69/70	70/71	71/72	72/73	73/74	74/75
Year available to television			72/73	73/74	74/75	75/76	76/77	77/78	78/79	79/80
Total supply of suitable re-runs										
	Special	18			1		6	3	5	3
	A	153	40	10	13	14	14	7	37	18
	B	420	204	41	42	28	29	6	48	22
		591	**244**	**51**	**56**	**42**	**49**	**16**	**90**	**43**
Available to BBC if ITV buy 40%										
	Special	12			1		4	2	3	2
	A	95	26	6	8	9	9	5	23	11
	B	253	123	25	25	17	18	4	28	13
		360	149	31	34	26	31	11	54	26
BBC purchases restricted to number of new films bought		**360**	**35**	**55**	**80**	**68**	**31**	**11**	**54**	**26**
Films available 31st March if BBC buy all available new films and re-runs										
New films	Special		7	12	12	13	10	7	4	1
	A		34	26	22	31	22	13	4	–5
	B		157	134	123	118	106	85	64	43
	C		183	97	16					
			381	269	175	162	138	105	72	39
	Re-runs		85	160	267	334	279	203	170	109
	Total		**466**	**429**	**442**	**496**	**417**	**308**	**242**	**148**

Table 6.1.4 Estimated payments, recoveries and stock values.

Estimated cost of purchases at current prices £000	Price	Total £000	72/73 £000	73/74 £000	74/75 £000	75/76 £000	76/77 £000	77/78 £000	78/79 £000	79/80 £000
New films										
Special	£17,700	620	53	142	89	124	53	53	53	53
A	£12,200	2148	73	122	293	488	293	293	293	293
B	£8,200	3131	205	295	410	508	508	435	435	435
C	£5,900	30	6	6	6	6	6			
		5029	337	565	798	1126	860	781	781	781
Re-runs	£2,500	900	88	137	200	170	78	27	135	65
Total		6929	425	702	998	1296	938	808	916	846
Assume 8% increase p.a.		9346	425	758	1164	1633	1276	1187	1453	1450
Stock values										
Opening stock		3064	3064	3295	3551	4135	4424	4054	3463	2996
Add future payments:										
Present commitments		2952	1086	842	844	180				
Estimated purchases		9346	425	758	1164	1633	1276	1187	1453	1450
		15362	4575	4895	5559	5948	5700	5241	4916	4446
Less programme recoveries		12990	1280	1344	1424	1524	1646	1778	1920	2074
Closing stock		2372	3295	3551	4135	4424	4054	3463	2996	2372

contracts had expired or by renewing the licences of films previously bought by the BBC.

Supplying the BBC's own film needs was one priority; denying ammunition to the enemy was another. Rugheimer reasoned that if he didn't buy up new films as they became available, ITV certainly would. Anything left over would then be offered at inflated prices later. He therefore proposed that, as a matter of course, the BBC should aim to acquire all new films as soon as they came onto the market, along with all acceptable re-runs. If this were done, then an appropriate balance could be maintained for years to come (assuming the 60/40 split with ITV remained steady). This policy would of course come at a price. Each quality grade was assigned an approximate purchase cost. As most films were usually bought in packages that varied considerably in size and whose contents did not always come with individual price tags, these costs were perhaps notional, but they reflected the relative valuation of films at current market rates as of 1972:

Specials: £17,700
Grade A: £12,200
Grade B: £8,200
Grade C: £5,900
Re-runs: £2,500

Although maintaining a constant stock of at least two years' worth of first-run films would insure against the effects of inflation due to the increasing scarcity and cost of new product, this would also mean that a considerable amount of money would be tied up in 'unrecovered' investment. Hughes therefore suggested imposing certain restraints to limit risk: the number of films available for first run should not exceed 450 at any one time, and the unrecovered value of the stock should not exceed £4 million. With these strictures observed, according to Hughes, any new proposed purchase coming before the Board of Governors for approval could be readily assessed within the terms of the framework provided by this stock policy.[3] The Director General, Charles Curran, assented to the policy as being in the BBC's best interests, although a combination of factors (including intensified competition with ITV for the most desirable films) caused the upper limit on stock value to be progressively increased, reaching £7,200,000 by the end of 1977–78.[4] Moreover, costs mounted rapidly; in that financial year, the cost of an average feature was twice what it had been only two years before.[5]

Re-runs became increasingly important to the film-scheduling economy. From 1964 to 1974 inclusive, the BBC showed 2,000 first-run films across its two channels (see Appendix 1). Repeat transmissions outnumbered premieres for the first time in 1972 and the balance was never again to shift the other way; by the end of the decade, repeats exceeded first runs by more than three to one. The same year saw the first transmission in significant numbers on both the BBC and ITV of titles previously shown by the other channel. The increasing reliance on re-runs was not, however, to the liking of every BBC executive. Director of Television Programmes Alasdair Milne took a particular interest in film acquisition and scheduling, often issuing policy papers on the subject and stressing the distinct appeal of films for the viewing audience. 'It is the rare film', he noted, that could 'beat *The Generation Game* or *The Two Ronnies* or *Match of the Day*' in the ratings. However, he argued, 'there is no doubt that viewers enjoy the different texture and the "long view" offered by feature films and that is why they are a valuable ingredient in any television schedule'.[6]

In August 1974, Milne expressed publicly some of his concerns about current trends:

> Recently the number of first run movies – films seen for the first time on TV – has dropped to only 40 per cent. That is not good enough.
>
> I decided that more money should be allocated for newer and better films. I'd like to see first run films increased to 60 per cent. And I hope to achieve 50 per cent this autumn.[7]

He acknowledged that television schedules could not subsist entirely on first runs, either from a practical standpoint (not enough suitable new films were being made to replenish stocks fully each year) or from that of audience appreciation. Some films retained their appeal over multiple showings, despite the slide in popularity of many older titles, as Milne later explained:

> Except for the classics of cinema history, films made in monochrome are now at a serious disadvantage. This fact, combined with changes in public attitude since they were made, makes it now difficult to get big audiences for films like *Spring in Park Lane* while even the audiences for a classic like *Mrs Miniver* are not what might have been expected some years ago.
>
> However, the audiences for re-runs of films made in colour, between – say – 1955 and 1970, have not fallen off. Nor have those for the planned second and third transmissions of original runs. Thus, the first BBC transmission of *The Wizard of Oz* on Christmas Day, 1975 on BBC1 was seen by 20 million. The second showing on Boxing Day, 1976, was seen by 15 million. The third showing on Christmas Day, 1977, attracted 14½ million. There are clearly not 49½ million potential viewers of such a film in the country. So it was clearly enjoyed by many for a second or even a third time, within quite a short period.[8]

The BBC's largest single deal in the first half of the decade was with United Artists in early 1974, involving no fewer than 377 titles. Rather than being offered a pre-packaged selection, buyers were given virtually complete freedom to choose the films they wanted from the company's inventory, which at that time included Warner Bros' pre-1949 library as well as UA's own releases, mostly made from the 1950s onwards. The only off-limits titles at this time were the company's biggest hit to that date, the musical *Fiddler on the Roof* (1971/18.12.1977), which the BBC later acquired in another block purchase, and the James Bond films, which were bought by ITV. The resulting package comprised mostly re-runs but also included first runs of such major films as *The Magnificent Seven* (1960/26.12.1974), *It's a Mad, Mad, Mad, Mad World* (1963/26.08.1974), *The Graduate* (1967/23.12.1974),

Chitty Chitty Bang Bang (1968/26.12.1974), *Battle of Britain* (1969/15.09.1974), *Midnight Cowboy* (1969/21.12.1980) and the three Clint Eastwood/Sergio Leone Spaghetti Westerns. This was described in the trade press as 'the biggest ever feature picture deal made in the British TV industry', at an estimated cost of at least £4 million.[9]

Package deals, while often maligned in the press for causing the networks to buy a number of mediocre films as well as good ones, had their advantages in helping to justify the high prices attached to the most desirable items. As Milne explained:

> When in 1975 MCA/Universal offered the BBC a package of nine films, the notional cost of one of them, *Anne of the Thousand Days*, was really quite high, some tens of thousands of pounds, much more than the BBC likes to pay. In fact purchase of the package was only possible because the nine films taken together could be averaged out at a reasonable figure.[10]

The total cost of this package was £216,000, or an average £24,000 per film, but the price tag for *Anne of the Thousand Days* (1969/21.12.1975) individually had been set as £70,000 (see Table 6.2).[11] Yet only three years after the deal had been done, Milne noted ruefully: 'What is rather frightening now is that the BBC would be lucky if it could acquire the same package for twice as much money.'[12]

Turned down by the BBC as 'outrageously expensive', a package of the first six James Bond films formed ITV's most costly purchase in the first half of the 1970s.[13] The sale of these films by UA stirred particular resentment in the film industry and highlighted what had long been a bone of contention: what many in the trade considered the low prices paid by broadcasters for films, relative both to their production costs and to their theatrical earning potential. Despite the record fee paid for the Bond pictures, it was still deemed insufficient by exhibitors, who felt that these films would now be devalued for further cinema use. The protests that ensued formed part of a larger debate on finding a fairer way for television to pay for the films it used; these are discussed further below, following a section on the Bond pictures themselves.

Table 6.2 BBC film purchases, 1976.

Source	No. films in package	Average cost per film	Total cost of package
EMI	37	£24,648	£911,976
British Lion	11	£18,181	£199,991
Paramount	22	£17,681	£388,982
CIC/MGM	33	£14,712	£485,496
MCA/Universal	9	£24,000	£216,000
Warner Bros	24	£14,229	£341,496
Totals	136	£18,908.50	£2,543,941

Source: Adapted from Alasdair Milne, 'Film Purchasing Policy', 27 May 1976, BBC R78/1, 123/1.

Views to a Kill: The James Bond Films

Over the six decades since their inception, the James Bond films have regularly topped UK box-office charts. Not only were they immensely successful on first release, but in the 1960s, 1970s and 1980s they were often brought back to cinemas as reissues, double-billed in various combinations either with one another or with other past hits from their original distributor, United Artists. Their ongoing earning power was a boon for exhibitors, especially independent cinemas and those not receiving new circuit releases. When press reports surfaced in January 1974 that a deal was about to be made to sell the first six of the series to ITV, there was, therefore, considerable alarm in the film industry.

This first ITV Bond deal fetched a UK record price of £850,000 for two showings of each of the first six films in the series; some newspapers speculated that it was as much as £1,500,000. Internal BBC documentation indicates that the package had first been offered to the Corporation at the same price. According to journalist David Lewin, who broke the story in both the *Daily Mail* and the trade paper he edited, *CinemaTV Today*, protests were lodged with both UA and the Department of Trade and Industry by the Cinematograph Exhibitors' Association (CEA) and the Association of Independent Cinemas (AIC).[14] They drew attention to the fact that over the years the films had received large sums from the Eady Levy. There were also objections from the technicians' union ACTT, whose general secretary Alan Sapper invoked a familiar fear: 'I'm appalled. If it goes through, it makes the production of original TV material even more unnecessary.'[15] Protesting to both the Independent Broadcasting Authority (IBA) and the Minister of Posts and Telecommunications, Sapper said that 'If television wants such films it should make them for itself' – thus missing the point that it was precisely their commercial track record in cinemas that made the films so attractive to ITV.[16]

Lewin also quoted one of the Bond series' co-producers, Albert R. 'Cubby' Broccoli, as saying: 'Personally I am against the sale of Bond films to television at this moment. They still have a very long way to go in cinemas.'[17] However, according to Paul Fox, then chair of ITV's Film Purchase Group (FPG), the films only became available to television because Broccoli's partner, Harry Saltzman, was broke and needed a quick injection of cash (Saltzman was soon to sell out his entire interest in the franchise to UA). The FPG had also baulked at the cost, with the heads of two of the five major companies, Lew Grade of ATV and Sidney Bernstein of Granada, initially refusing to participate in the proposed purchase. Fox recalled that his own boss at Yorkshire Television, Ward Thomas,

> was away at the time on holiday and it had to be decided in twenty-four hours. So I went to my chairman, who was James Hanson, and said this is the situation, we've been offered these films. He said, what do you think of them? I said, 'Greatest films ever'. He said, tell the negotiators, if the deal isn't done, Hanson Trust will buy the films and lease them out to ITV! That was what he thought of them. So the deal was done, and eventually of course Lew came along and paid his share and Granada paid their share, and they were winners.[18]

After ITV had made public denials, the sale was agreed by the end of January. At an average cost per film (according to BBC calculations) of £141,666, or £37,390 per hour of total transmission time, the package was the most expensive yet acquired for British television (see Table 6.3). But for ITV it made sound business sense: the high ratings that the films were sure to command guaranteed that advertising time during the commercial breaks would be sold at a premium. According to *Broadcast*, 'one estimate is that the total amount at card rate for one prime time showing of each movie could be in the region of £1,300,000 – shared between the companies – with another £1 million available for a second showing straddling early and prime or prime and late time'.[19] One of the unions' main objections had been that the price paid was too low in view of the films' theatrical earning potential. It was later reported that during 1974, the first eight Bond films, all still in reissue circulation, 'took enough money to have placed them ninth' on the year's box-office chart. Their all-time total rental revenue for the UK was estimated to be more than £10,250,000.[20] Depriving the exhibition sector of continuing income from the Bonds was claimed to be 'a disaster',

Table 6.3 Cost per hour of blockbusters.

BBC purchases	Number of TX runs	TX running time (mins)	Total licence fee	Cost per hour	Release year	First TX
The Bridge on the River Kwai	5	155	£125,000	£9,677	1957	1974
Butch Cassidy and the Sundance Kid	3	105	£125,000	£23,809	1969	1975
Murder on the Orient Express	3	126	£125,000	£19,841	1974	1979
Oliver!	3	140	£250,000	£35,714	1968	1976
ITV purchases	Number of TX runs	TX running time (mins)	Total licence fee	Cost per hour	Release year	First TX
First Bond package:						
Dr No	2	101	£850,000	£37,390	1962	1975
From Russia with Love	2	111			1963	1976
Goldfinger	2	105			1964	1976
Thunderball	2	120			1965	1977
You Only Live Twice	2	111			1967	1977
On Her Majesty's Secret Service	2	134			1969	1978
Second Bond package:						
Diamonds Are Forever	2	115	£540,545	£44,307	1971	1978
Live and Let Die	2	116			1973	1980
The Man with the Golden Gun	2	120			1974	1980
Average cost per film in first Bond package			£141,666			
Average cost per film in second Bond package			£180,181			
Average cost per film in both packages combined			£154,545			

Source: Adapted from Alasdair Milne, 'Film Purchasing Policy', 27 May 1976, BBC R78/1, 123/1.

especially with the prospect of empty cinemas on the evenings when the films were eventually broadcast.[21]

Reports also appeared that the same package had been, or was about to be, sold to US network television for the equivalent of £7,000,000.[22] At this time only one Bond film – the third, *Goldfinger* (1964/03.11.1976) – had yet been shown on American television, as a one-off special in 1972; three more followed, out of chronological order, in 1974.[23] The BBC had previously shown *Casino Royale* (1967/25.12.1973), an independently-produced spoof of the first Bond novel, whose screen rights had eluded Broccoli and Saltzman. However, ITV planned to show the 'official' films in their original sequence, beginning in the autumn of 1975. This delay, along with their spacing at lengthy intervals over several years, may have been a deliberate concession to cinema interests. It meant that exhibitors had a temporary 'reprieve' period in which they could continue to exploit the films on the big screen.[24] A further, self-imposed restriction on ITV schedulers was the 'London split', whereby the two contractors for the London area had to be given equal consideration in the use of valuable properties. Rather than each company being allocated exclusive use of a number of the six films, as was done with other packages, the first and second transmissions of all six alternated on weekdays and weekends so that both Thames and LWT had one showing of each title.

There were special conditions attached to the deal. Unusually, the entire sum had to be paid in advance rather than in instalments over several years. Only two runs were licensed of each film, and no more than two transmissions of any Bond films were allowed in any one year (though in fact this rule was soon broken). When *Dr No* (1962/28.10.1975) finally made its UK television debut (see Figure 6.2), the advertising trade journal *Campaign* reported that the participating broadcast companies' ad slots 'were fully sold throughout the evening, but none was tempted to exceed the IBA's limit of seven minutes advertising an hour'.[25] Audience figures justified ITV's investment, with the independent body Joint Industry Committee for Audience Research (JICTAR) claiming that the film had been watched in 10.5 million homes and BBC Audience Research reporting that it had been seen by as many as 27 million viewers (see Chapter 7).[26] Either way, this was by far the largest audience for any film on British television to date, despite the fact that *Dr No* was not fully networked: Ulster Television had opted out of the initial broadcast but instead showed the film exactly two months later, as a Christmas attraction.

The second Bond film, *From Russia with Love* (1963/02.05.1976), followed seven months after and again topped the ratings, as did *Goldfinger* six months after that.[27] In between was an early repeat of *Dr No* in July 1976 as a spoiler for the BBC's coverage of the Olympic Games Opening Ceremony. The second transmission of *From Russia with Love* was also very soon after the first, at Christmas 1976: this was the fourth broadcast of a Bond film that year, contrary to the initial reports of scheduling restrictions. However, the IBA was unhappy at the lapse of only nine and seven months, respectively, between the first and second showings of the first two films, so the transmissions of the remaining four occurred at

Figure 6.2 ITV's television premiere on 28 October 1975 of the first James Bond film, *Dr No* (1962), drew the largest TV audience for any feature film to that date, despite its not being shown in the Ulster Television region. *TVTimes* © Future Publishing Ltd.

intervals of between fifteen months and two years. The premiere of *Thunderball* (1965/26.02.1977) presented an unusual situation in that, while most companies had agreed to schedule it for a Saturday evening, four – HTV, Westward, Channel and Border – preferred a Sunday night instead. This may have had an adverse effect on viewing figures, which fell slightly below the level of the preceding three premieres; unlike them, *Thunderball* failed to lead the monthly ratings charts. But *You Only Live Twice* (1967/20.11.1977) bounced back to the top: JICTAR, which now estimated the number of individual viewers rather than homes tuning in, put the audience figure at 20.8 million, its highest rating for any film transmission in the 1970s.

Nearly a year passed before the premiere of the sixth and final film in the initial package, *On Her Majesty's Secret Service* (1969/04.09.1978). But in September 1976, ITV acquired the remaining three Bonds for a combined fee of $1 million or £540,545; at an average of £180,181 per film, they were slightly more expensive than the earlier purchase.[28] A condition of this deal was that ITV should also buy $200,000 worth of additional material from the distributor. As the BBC had already cleared United Artists' shelves of virtually everything suitable for peak time, Halliwell suggested a group of minor vintage titles from Warner Bros, whose pre-1948 library was then controlled by UA. The rest of the package was filled out with cartoons.[29]

Diamonds Are Forever (1971/25.12.1978) was the first Bond film to be scheduled on a Christmas Day. Its relatively early start at 6.45pm caused some concern at the IBA, along with the fact that this was a holiday, when large numbers of children would have been watching no matter what time the film started. The Authority insisted on cuts to two particularly violent sequences (a fight in an elevator, and the climax, in which a would-be assassin is set on fire), and these cuts were retained even when the film was subsequently repeated in later time slots. However, the only complaint the IBA received about the premiere transmission was for a bedroom scene with implied nudity.[30] Over the years, as the Bond films have been shown repeatedly on ITV, fans often expressed dismay at the cutting of scenes, whether for violence as in this case or for length, as occurred with the third transmission of *Dr No* (originally certificated Post-7.30pm) on Christmas Day afternoon, 1981. On that occasion, network film buyer Leslie Halliwell was authorised to make cuts at his discretion; an IBA officer stated that the film had 'the usual quota of sanitized violence peculiar to these films and, of course, every child will want to see it. I do not, myself, believe that it will do any harm (except possibly to parents).'[31]

Further transmission rights to the Bond films were acquired in early 1978. This purchase also had to be approved by the IBA, which did so only with some reluctance, as it discouraged excessive repeats of films. The deal was agreed only on condition that it was exceptional and did not set a precedent for future re-acquisitions.[32] Halliwell noted: 'the Bonds are rather a special case at a special price! Because of the latter we do intend to take up all the runs we have bought, which ... is seldom the case with our normal deals where even though four runs may be available we do not take them more than once in thirty or forty cases.'[33] The first showing of Roger Moore's debut as 007, *Live and Let Die* (1973/20.01.1980), achieved the largest audience of any film on British television, according to both the new ratings body Broadcasters' Audience Research Board (BARB) and BBC

Audience Research: they estimated the number of viewers as 23.5 million or 28 million, respectively. By this time, two more Bond films had been made and they, along with all subsequent films in the series, were in due course acquired by ITV.

Broadcast columnist William Phillips claimed in 1988 that the 'Bond films have been indisputably the best bargain ever bought by a British network'.[34] Paul Fox agrees: 'Of all the film coups, the Bond package was the best ever.'[35] In terms of their ratings impact and sheer longevity, this was demonstrably the case, with even the repeats earning high audience figures: *Goldfinger* appears three times in BARB's list of the all-time most-watched films, with three of its first four transmissions achieving over 17 million viewers. Despite the occasional, temporary loss of the broadcast rights to cable and satellite services, there have been at least two screenings of a Bond film on ITV every year since 1975, and at time of writing they continue to be re-run. In the summer of 2022, all the films from *Live and Let Die* onwards were shown in succession by ITV at peak-time on Saturday nights, with earlier episodes running in parallel on Sunday afternoons. At the same time, and in the same weeks, the films were being revived in UK cinemas to considerable box–office success.[36]

Waiting on the Levy

In February 1973, Bernard Delfont, chairman of EMI Film and Theatre Corporation, the second-largest British film company after the Rank Organisation, announced that he planned to set up an all-industry consortium to drive up the prices paid for films by British broadcasters. Four years earlier, the music company EMI had taken over the assets of the Associated British Picture Corporation, including the ABC chain of cinemas and a 50 per cent stake in Thames Television, the successor to ABC Television. Despite this interest in a major broadcasting company, Delfont wanted the BBC and ITV to increase their spending on film acquisition to around £10 million per year. This was estimated by trade paper *CinemaTV Today* to be about twice the current level, though Delfont said he wanted an increase of three or four times on present prices. The additional revenues this earned for EMI would be ploughed back into film production. But Delfont also wanted broadcasters to pay a levy of around 20 per cent on acquired films, which would go to exhibitors to help keep cinemas in business.[37]

Industry trade associations and unions were quick to voice their support, though Delfont's brother, ATV's Lew Grade, predictably argued against him: 'We already pay high prices for films. What happens is that the film companies sell us films in batches. In order to get a few films which are any good we may have to buy 20 which are rubbish.'[38] Delfont retorted that Grade still screened the rubbish anyway. He later stepped up his campaign by blocking the sale of a batch of films from his own company because the prices offered by both ITV and the BBC were, in his estimation, not high enough.[39]

Paramount Pictures' president Frank Yablans waded in from across the Atlantic, arguing that the British broadcasting duopoly was partly responsible for keeping film prices artificially low. As reported in *Variety*, he was in favour of the consortium idea but opposed to the CEA's five-year rule, which he called an 'obsolescent and unrealistic embargo'. The fact that the product was 'aged' by the time it was available for television screening meant that the broadcasters were resistant to paying more for it and the market was consequently 'soft'.[40] In the US, films typically became available to network television within two years of their theatrical release, though prices paid were considerably higher because of the size of the market and the value of potential advertising revenue.

It was widely reported that the maximum sum to have been paid by British television for a film at this time was £30,000, the lowest as little as £2,000 and the average about £10,000. Modest as these prices were by the standards of the US (where blockbusters could fetch millions of dollars for one or two transmissions), they were nevertheless higher than for most other world markets. Vincent Porter pointed out in 1974: 'In most countries of the EEC, the purchase price for films reflects a market price of between $50 and $100 per hundred thousand viewers', but that in the UK, despite there being only two competing buyers, 'the price is nearly twice as high'.[41] *Variety* estimated the typical price range per film for the UK in 1973 to be $18,000–$30,000. Only two other countries were in a similar bracket: Australia, where the range was $12,000–$30,000, and Japan, $15,000–$40,000. Even Canada's top figure was $12,000 and West Germany's $16,000. So by this measure at least, UK broadcasters seemed to pay reasonable prices for the size of their market.[42]

In a letter to *The Times*, producer Michael Relph, chairman of the Film Production Association of Great Britain (FPA), claimed that a film screened by ITV in peak viewing time could earn up to £300,000 in advertising revenue, none of which would be shared with the film industry. Noting the continuing decline in earnings and attendance at cinemas coupled with rising audiences for films on television, he proposed two alternative solutions of his own:

(1) A share of the 4th television channel must be allocated to the film industry for the commercial showing of new, or nearly new, films which could be confined to this channel and earn full advertising revenue, or

(2) An immediate extension of pay TV must be authorised on which new films can be shown to a paying public.[43]

Thus, potential increases in prices and earnings were associated not just with new outlets for the domestic exhibition of films – though both the fourth channel and country-wide subscription television were still in the future – but also with a reduction in the age of the films available to the home viewer. Relph told *Cinema TV Today*:

I think the cinema takings have reached such a low level that a native industry cannot be supported on them alone.

We can't any longer go on with a situation where more people than ever before are watching films [on television] and there is no revenue coming from them.[44]

Relph then made a further intervention by calling for a Government 'tax' on the sale of films to television, of either £1,000 per film or 10 per cent of the purchase price, whichever was higher. The resulting projected revenues of around £1 million per year would go to the state-owned National Film Finance Corporation (NFFC), which had an annual production fund of £1.5 million but was currently in deficit by £6.5 million. The proposal was advocated in the House of Commons by the actor and Labour MP Andrew Faulds, who cited the recent ITV Bond deal to stress the urgency of the situation. Additional pressure came from industry trade unions. The Association of Cinematograph, Television and Allied Technicians (ACTT) proposed that in future technicians' film contracts should guarantee residual payments when the films were sold to TV, including provision for repeat fees. Added to the prospect of both a levy on the TV sale of films and an increase in the prices paid for them, this was welcomed as potentially leading to a reduction in the number of cinema films transmitted and a consequent increase in television production, thus guaranteeing more work for members. Another union, the National Association of Theatrical, Television and Kine Employees (NATKE), proposed a stricter quota than currently existed on the broadcasting of both feature films and overseas television productions.[45]

The Minister for Trade, Eric Deakins, lent his support for a levy, arguing: 'Films now play such a major part in television programmes that television should be asked to help the film production industry, rather than the other way round.'[46] The Minister for the Arts, Hugh Jenkins, added: 'It is about time television, both the BBC and ITV, realised that they are living on the film capital. They show old films almost every night. Television will have to take a far greater responsibility.'[47] However, other concurrent developments complicated the debate. Passing through Parliament was a bill designed to change the basis on which the ITV network was taxed, from a levy on revenues (as had been the case since 1964) to one on profits; ultimately the companies had to pay to the Government 66.7 per cent of their annual surplus. Gwyneth Dunwoody, secretary of the FPA and also a Labour MP, suggested that this money could be used to support both film and television production. But the possibility of an additional tax threatened to place too heavy a financial burden on the commercial network.[48]

The Ministry of Posts and Telecommunications wrote to both the BBC and the Independent Broadcasting Authority (IBA, as the ITA had now been renamed) in April 1974 to set out and solicit their responses to proposals devised by the Cinematograph Films Council (CFC), 'a statutory advisory body for many years responsible for advising the President of the Board of Trade on the state of the film industry'. The proposed statutory levy on the showing of films on television was intended as an extension of the existing British Film Production Fund (the Eady Levy), imposed on cinema revenues in order to plough back money into domestic film production; this was administered by the British Film Fund Agency, which would most likely also be responsible for the films-on-TV levy. The latter was projected to be an average of £3,000 per film, though the Department of Trade allowed for some flexibility:

> They envisage a sliding scale of charges depending on the time of day at which the film was shown and an estimate of the population in the area where the film was shown. Part of the objective of the proposals is to discourage the showing of films on television, since it is argued that the decline in cinema audiences is due in part to the large number of films shown on television in Britain, as opposed to the Continent of Europe where the number of films shown is much more restricted.[49]

Thus the CFC wanted to limit the supply of funds it considered vital to the industry because of the perceived threat of competition to that industry from its own products when shown via another medium. The naïveté of the film trade itself can perhaps be gauged by the suggestion of 'one leading cinema exhibitor', cited in the Ministry's letter, that the broadcasters could absorb the cost of the levy simply by paying less to the films' distributors in order to acquire them.

Further details of the CFC's case were given in two reports to the Department of Trade. Among their assertions were the following:

> The showing of feature films forms a significant part of all television programmes screened in the UK and these films are among the most popular programmes watched on television. ... A very high proportion of these films was of foreign origin [i.e., predominantly American] and a very high proportion was shown at peak viewing hours, when viewers might otherwise be tempted to go to the cinema. ...

> The broadcasting authorities in considering what is a proper proportion of British material do not appear to take into account the effect of their policy on particular categories, such as feature films. The result is that the proportion of foreign films shown on television is considerably higher than that relating to foreign material as a whole. Moreover this heavy concentration of imported material has depressed earnings from the showing of films to a very low level. ...

> There can be no doubt that the economic benefits accruing to the television industry from the showing of cinematograph films on television greatly outweigh the economic contributions made by that industry to the film production industry, and that this state of imbalance is prejudicial to the film production industry, and should be corrected by one means or another.

Claiming that the expensive deal for the Bond films, none of which had yet been transmitted, proved that 'old films can still have very considerable appeal', the CFC noted:

> The showing of such films on television adversely affects the film industry in three ways: it keeps viewers away from the cinema; it takes away from them what would otherwise have been a very saleable product [in cinemas] – at a time when saleable product is in short supply; and it deprives the British Film Fund of the considerable levy which would have been paid on the lost business.

It therefore concluded that a 'levy on the showing of cinematograph films on television which varies according to the time of showing would encourage the television authorities to restrict the showing of films at peak periods'.[50]

Detailed responses to the proposals were drafted over the next few months by Gunnar Rugheimer and others at the BBC and by Howard Thomas of Thames Television on behalf of ITV. Following a meeting in November with representatives of the CFC, in January 1975 a joint formal reply was issued by the Independent Television Companies' Association (ITCA, the contractors' representative body), IBA and BBC, represented respectively by signatories Thomas, Bernard Sendall and Alasdair Milne. They sought to refute the claims on which the CFC's proposals were based and to argue against the levy on the grounds of both practicality and principle. The following account summarises their objections.[51]

Although the broadcasters accepted that competition from television was in part responsible for the crisis in the film industry, they denied that this was due to the broadcasting of feature films in particular. The postwar decline in cinemagoing had begun well before features had been transmitted in significant numbers or indeed before television itself was widely available. Between 1946 and 1964 (when the CEA had relaxed its position on films on TV), the cinema had lost some 75 per cent of its audience; although numbers continued to fall, with admissions by the mid-1970s at only one-tenth of their 1946 peak, clearly other factors, such as alternative leisure pursuits, were also to blame, as even the unions had admitted. The broadcasters argued that there was no concrete evidence that the transmission of particularly attractive films in peak viewing hours led to a drop-off in cinema attendance; indeed it was pointed out that there had been a box-office boom over the Christmas period of 1974, despite an unprecedented number of major first-run features broadcast during the holiday season. Nor was there any evidence to show that in the absence of films available to watch at home viewers would go more often to the cinema; the demographics of typical cinemagoers and TV viewers were very different, the latter being somewhat older. The fact that distributors agreed to supply films to television after they had been in release for five years or more suggested that their theatrical value was exhausted by this time and that their being broadcast was not considered a danger to present business, otherwise they would not have been sold. As for television screenings ruining films for cinema reissue purposes, the BBC produced figures to show that the box-office performance in subsequent theatrical runs of the first six *Carry On* films had actually improved after broadcast (see Table 6.4).

Figures also showed that in 1974, feature films occupied only 12 per cent of airtime on the two BBC channels and 7 per cent on ITV (the disparity partly being due to the greater number of made-for-TV films shown by the commercial network, a figure which was excluded from the data). Films accounted for an average 15 per cent of peak viewing time (between 7.00pm and 11.00pm) on all channels. The BBC observed discretionary limits on the use of films, while ITV abided by IBA quotas on the number of films shown per week. The larger proportion of features being of foreign (largely Hollywood) origin was attributed to the limited availability of British films in comparison with American; even so, in 1974

Table 6.4 Carrying on: distributors' gross in two years before and after television showing.

Carry on–	Release Year	First TX	£ before TX	£ after TX
Sergeant	1958	01.10.1966	4,508	9,451
Nurse	1959	25.03.1967	5,913	9,650
Teacher	1959	24.12.1966	4,020	8,839
Constable	1960	24.06.1967	5,191	8,089
Regardless	1961	26.08.1967	3,581	8,375
Cruising	1962	23.12.1967	3,516	12,463

Source: 'Home Movies, New Style', *The Economist*, 7 September 1974, 78.

British features occupied 25.8 per cent of the BBC's film output and 46 per cent of ITV's (the imbalance again being due to the exclusion of US TV movies from the total). BBC viewing figures showed that average audiences for in-house television productions were typically twice as large as for acquired films, and only a handful of feature films matched the number of viewers attracted by the most popular home-grown shows.

Claims that restrictions on the televising of films in continental Europe benefited cinema attendance were, according to the broadcasters, based on inaccurate information: France, West Germany and Italy could not be directly compared with the UK because 'set penetration' (the number of television sets owned per head of population) varied considerably amongst these markets – it was highest in Britain and lowest in Italy, which had the healthiest theatrical exhibition and production sectors. While West German television invested directly in the making of theatrical features, it also had early access to them for broadcast, whereas in the UK an artificial embargo was imposed in the form of the five-year rule. This, the broadcasters argued, was largely responsible for keeping purchase prices lower than the cinema industry liked: the prices paid reflected market value, but if artificial restrictions on the TV age of films were lifted, the networks would be willing to pay more for them. Meanwhile, the fact that features could be acquired at relatively low cost meant that more money was available to make productions in-house; adding to outgoing costs without any increase in revenue would mean fewer such productions, not more, or the replacement of feature films in the schedules with low-cost imported made-for-TV material.

As for the proposed levy, the broadcasters were against it in principle. For the BBC it would have represented an 'improper use' of the licence fee, requisitioning as risk capital for private industry public funds intended for the maintenance of a public utility; a levy on films on television would in effect be a 'concealed subsidy', over the use of which the BBC would have no control.[52] For ITV, added to the existing Levy on its profits it would have meant a reduction in those profits, hence also a reduced flow of money to the Exchequer; the Government would be funding the film industry with an additional tax instead of using the ITV revenues already at its disposal and channelling them to existing state-controlled sources of film finance in the forms of the British Film Fund and the NFFC. For both organisations also a levy would have meant a heavy financial burden at an unstable time when they were trying to save money and in the BBC's case were in deficit.

In any event, they argued, why should the television industry be responsible for supporting a rival medium by paying a tax on the goods the film industry had voluntarily sold to it? If the industry were to stake a claim for subsidy on the basis of unfair competition from television, what was to stop other businesses from doing the same, such as sporting organisations aggrieved at TV coverage of sports events? To some extent, it was claimed, television already supported the film industry through the employment of film technicians in various capacities, the nurturing of talent such as directors and writers who went on to make cinema films, and the provision of source material such as the current, highly successful cycle of big-screen adaptations of television situation comedies.

The broadcasters had already bought up most of the available stocks of feature films to last them for the next few years; the number of films bought each year was falling, in line with the decline in cinema production, so a levy on the showing of films yet to be acquired would be unlikely to produce the kind of sums (between £2.5 and £3 million annually) the CFC anticipated. Imposing a levy on the showing of films already acquired (often from British industry sources) would amount to an unfair change in the terms and conditions under which they had been purchased, upsetting budget calculations. Imposing a levy on foreign (American) films for the benefit of UK production might result in retaliatory action by the US suppliers, whose British theatrical revenues were already taxed by the Eady Levy.

For all the foregoing reasons, the BBC, ITCA and IBA rejected the proposed levy on films. The CFC nevertheless persisted with its case, still hoping for a mutually agreeable compromise that would result in a plan for action in furtherance of the Government's declared aim of protecting the future of the film industry.[53] A further meeting was therefore held on 21 March 1975 with representatives of all concerned parties, where many of the arguments were rehearsed, along with some new attempts at flexibility. The broadcasters considered the prospect of a levy imposed at the point of sale, payable by either the buyer or the seller and possibly in the form of a 'withholding tax' (in which a portion of the purchase cost was held back from the vendor), more acceptable than one at the point of transmission; in this way commercial decisions could be made before the films were purchased, thereby preventing any incursions on the independence of schedulers. The BBC in particular was prepared to invest directly in film production, so long as it had some editorial control over the choice of subjects to help ensure their suitability for broadcast and it was entitled to show the films on television soon after their theatrical release was over. But this had to be on a voluntary basis, modestly scaled, and not the result of statutory compulsion.[54]

The Government had hoped for a joint report from the CFC and the broadcasters with concrete proposals for a way forward, but there was so little agreement between the two sides that the television representatives elected instead to prepare a collective report of their own. Two reports, one from the CFC and another from the broadcasters, were thus submitted to the Minister for Trade in early May 1975, each setting out a case respectively for and against the proposed levy.[55] However, they were subsequently overtaken by the announcement by Prime Minister Harold Wilson of a new Working Party to be formed to make policy proposals on the future of the film industry. The Working Party had a broad remit but among the matters to which it would address itself were two closely related issues at the heart of the levy debate: the involvement of television money in film production and the time bar on cinema films reaching TV.

Bucking the Five-year Rule

Often referred to as a 'gentleman's agreement' between the film and television industries, the five-year rule was in fact nothing of the kind. The rule was internal to the film industry: a policy for the protection of exhibitors, comparable to the 'clearances' observed by US cinemas and the 'barring' practices of their UK equivalents. It was maintained by distributors when specifying licence periods to their clients but resented by the broadcasters, who regarded it as an unreasonable restrictive practice. The rule applied primarily to English-language films that had been given theatrical release in the UK; foreign-language films were subject to a similar three-year rule, though in practice they were treated more flexibly. In principle, if a film had been commercially exhibited in Britain, it was embargoed for showing on television for five years from the date of its trade show. However, if a film had not been given a commercial release, either because it had not been offered to UK exhibitors or had been turned down by them, then it was available for broadcasting without such restrictions.

For this reason, a number of so-called 'lost films' that had escaped UK distribution found their way onto the small screen before they were five years old.[56] They included, for example, the Elvis Presley vehicle *Change of Habit* (1969/24.08.1971) and Francis Ford Coppola's *The Rain People* (1969/18.04.1973), both acquired by the BBC; as well as Sidney Lumet's *Blood Kin* (1970/03.11.1972) and Samuel Fuller's *Shark* (1969/21.04.1973), purchased by ITV. A short season of such films, including the latter two, was presented at the BFI's National Film Theatre in October 1973, programmed by Leslie Halliwell under the title 'Films That Nearly Got Away'. Feature-length films made for American television but given theatrical release in the UK counted as cinema films for purposes of the rule, though several 'TV movies' of this kind nevertheless appeared on British television before their embargo period was up, apparently without causing objections. One such example is *The Autobiography of Miss Jane Pittman* (1974/02.01.1976), the subject of a letter to a trade paper pointing out what appeared to be a double standard after it was televised without protest from the exhibition sector.[57] In general, however, the broadcasters abided by the rule because they had little choice in the matter; in that respect it was an effective protectionist measure from the exhibitors' point of view.

The first significant breach of the rule came in May 1974, when BBC2 transmitted *The Ruling Class* (1972/25.05.1974) two years to the day from its London opening. Despite a long premiere run in the West End, the film – a satirical fantasy starring Peter O'Toole – had received no circuit general release. The original distributor, United Artists, sold the theatrical rights to Avco Embassy, which could make no headway with it either. Its producer, Jules Buck, who had retained the TV rights, sold the film to the BBC for a reported £20,000 with only a two-year bar, in what the FPA's Gwyneth Dunwoody called 'a vicious body blow to an industry struggling to survive'.[58] The CEA subsequently imposed a lifetime ban on its members exhibiting films made by Buck, whose production company Keep Films was co-owned by O'Toole. According to Michael Relph, Buck had 'struck a blow at the unity which the film industry has maintained on this point and he has threatened to remove one of the major negotiating factors [with television]'.[59] As no major national chain had rushed to show the film when it first became available it was clearly not the loss of *The Ruling Class* itself to the small screen that irked the exhibitors, but the precedent it set for flouting the five-year rule. Coinciding with the debate about a potential levy on film transmissions, it stoked the growing hostility between television and the film industry.

The following year, a novel experiment was tried which, while apparently also in breach of the rule, did not attract the same opprobrium. Director Peter Hall's rural saga *Akenfield*, made on a low budget with a largely non-professional cast, premiered in Ipswich in October 1974 and was shown at the London Film Festival the following month; but when it opened commercially in London on Sunday, 26 January 1975, it was transmitted the very same evening on the ITV national network. This was claimed to be the first time that a film had been simultaneously released in cinemas and shown on television in the UK (forgetting 1953's *World without End*, discussed in Chapter 3). A sum of £40,000 (around one-third of the film's total cost, including deferments) had been invested up front by London Weekend Television (LWT) in return for the TV rights. *Akenfield* had always been intended for theatrical release and was shot in the Techniscope widescreen process (which meant that it had to be 'panned and scanned' for the broadcast version).

It was the fact that it had been given such an early television showing, rather than the financial investment by a TV company, that made *Akenfield* a 'television film' under Government regulations.[60] Only films made specifically for the cinema could benefit from Eady money. British Film Production Fund regulations specified that a television film was one for which an agreement to broadcast existed at the time the film was registered with the Board of Trade, or one which was broadcast within twelve months of the date of registration, irrespective of any theatrical showing. This meant that *Akenfield*'s producers were not entitled to receive any money from the fund.[61] In fact, the BBC's premature transmission of *The Ruling Class* had prompted Hugh Orr, president of the Association of Independent Cinemas, to propose to the Department of Trade that the regulations be extended to define any film broadcast within five years of registration as a television film for the purposes of the Eady Levy.[62]

Akenfield performed reasonably well in its exclusive London run but failed to gain much of a wider release; the disappointing public response in its few cinema showings was attributed by its makers to the fact that so many people – around 14.5 million – had already seen the film on television, making it a success in TV terms but a failure theatrically.[63] Nevertheless, several further experiments in simultaneous cinema/TV exhibition followed in the next few years. They included the British-produced documentary about the Great Depression, *Brother, Can You Spare a Dime?* (1975/22.03.1975), in which the BBC had invested a sum reported as £20,000–25,000 and which was presented as a 'world premiere' on BBC2 four days before its West End opening; and Alain Resnais's *Stavisky...* (1974/18.05.1975), sold to the BBC by its UK distributor Gala Films in advance of a cinema booking and also broadcast four days prior to its London premiere. Both these deals were able to circumvent hostile industry action on a technicality: the five-year rule was measured from the date of a film's trade show before an audience of prospective exhibitors; but in these cases neither of the two films was shown to the trade until after they had been broadcast. For the cinemas that presented them in their public engagements, the television screenings were seen as promotional previews, saving on advertising costs, rather than as competition for audiences.[64]

This kind of 'dual-platform' arrangement was one that BBC drama producer Tony Garnett wanted for his television productions, which despite being shot on film were prevented from having any commercial theatrical exposure. He said in early 1975: 'I would like to see *Days of Hope* open on BBC2 and at the Academy Cinema in London. It has been the thing I've been fighting hardest for for the past eight years. But the BBC will not allow it.'[65]

Other films subsequently broadcast in advance of, or concurrent with, their UK theatrical runs included Eric Rohmer's *Die Marquise von O...* (1974/23.10.1976), Costa-Gavras's *Section spéciale* (1975/12.03.1977), the comedy gala *Pleasure at Her Majesty's* (1976/29.12.1976) and two Merchant Ivory productions, *Hullabaloo over Georgie and Bonnie's Pictures* (1978/15.07.1978) and *Jane Austen in Manhattan* (1980/06.07.1980), both premiered in LWT's arts programme *The South Bank Show*. These were all specialised or art-house releases; their transmissions were unlikely to affect the business of mainstream commercial cinemas because few such cinemas were likely to show them. Hence, aside from flurries of critical comment in the press, no formal protests were apparently made over them. But when LWT showed the British horror film *Tales from the Crypt* (1972/06.12.1975) only three years after its release, a spat broke out. Despite threats from the CEA, no action was taken because Cinerama Releasing, the film's original theatrical distributor, which had licensed the film to ITV, had since gone out of business. ITV stations were slow to pick the film up, only two other regions showing it before 1977 despite the hire contract allowing earlier transmissions.[66] *The Vault of*

Horror (1973/05.09.1977), a companion film from the same production company, Amicus, was first broadcast (again locally, this time by Westward Television and Channel Television) when only four years old, but this seemed to pass unnoticed.

At the time of the *Ruling Class* row, an offer made by Gunnar Rugheimer meant partly to placate the film industry ended up having the opposite effect. The BBC announced in June 1974 that it was prepared to invest up to £25,000 in selected film projects at the development stage in exchange for the future option on first UK television rights. The catch, as far as exhibitors were concerned, was that the right to broadcast could be exercised as soon as the films had completed their theatrical runs or at least after an interval earlier than five years – most likely two or three unless the film continued to do well in cinemas. While some in the trade welcomed the initiative for bringing the film and television industries into a closer relationship and supplementing existing sources of development money, others mocked the sums involved as paltry or were concerned at the precedent that would be set by producers agreeing to a comparatively early broadcast date.[67]

Rugheimer himself admitted that the scheme was partly driven by the desire to break down the five-year rule and gain access to cinema films more quickly. He argued that the scheme was nevertheless in line with government film policy, namely 'that British audiences, whether of *cinema or television*, shall be able to enjoy a continuing supply of films from British sources' (emphasis Rugheimer's) and 'that British films can stand up to the requirements of the world market'. He was insistent that the BBC should continue to act as a broadcasting organisation first and foremost, seeing the films it supported primarily as potential future programme material:

> The support which the Corporation could give to the making of feature films in this country must be dictated by the broadcasting use which can be made of such films. There should be no financial involvement on the part of television without a corresponding editorial involvement.
>
> The degree of financial involvement by the Corporation in the making of feature films must relate in scale to the economics of producing other popular television programmes.
>
> Our involvement must be determined by our broadcasting requirements and cannot be justified by speculative expectations of future commercial profits. ...
>
> For this to make sense it would be necessary that the film industry abandoned its restrictive practices at least in regard to such films in which there was a BBC production investment.[68]

The terms of the scheme, with a revolving fund of £250,000, entitled the BBC to recover its investment from theatrical receipts, but any profits would be ploughed back into the fund. The risk was that there was no firm guarantee that the end results, if a completed film emerged at all, would be suitable for broadcast. If they were, and assuming the initial outlay was recovered, at least a further £25,000 would then be paid for the TV rights. The first beneficiary of the BBC's 'seed money' scheme was revealed in August 1975 to be a Jules Buck production, *Aspects of Love*. Several other film projects had also received backing in the first year of the fund's operation, but Rugheimer declined to name them publicly lest they become subject to the sort of discriminatory action that Buck had faced over *The Ruling Class*. Because the money was being offered at a relatively early stage of pre-production, usually in aid of script development, a number of the projects did not finally see the light of day – among them, *Aspects of Love*.[69]

The Thirty-nine Steps: The Prime Minister's Working Party

The involvement of television in film finance was among the matters discussed by the Prime Minister's Working Party on the Film Industry, which began to hold meetings and take evidence in August 1975. Chaired by John Terry, head of the NFFC, its members included filmmakers Richard Attenborough, John Brabourne, Michael Deeley, Carl Foreman and John Woolf; EMI's Bernard Delfont; the ACTT's Alan Sapper; and representing the broadcasters, the BBC's Alasdair Milne and Thames Television's Brian Tesler.[70] Submissions from the film industry included the suggestion by the Writers' Guild of Great Britain that the five-year rule, rather than being reduced, should be extended to fifteen years and that 'the price of any feature film to television should be not less than one-half the cost of mounting a dramatic programme of similar length'.[71] Such unrealistic extremes were not, however, likely to be accepted as official recommendations.

While these discussions were ongoing, the ITCA was approached on the Working Party's behalf by the Department of Trade to ask the ITV companies' views on proposals arising from one of the Party's declared aims: 'the desirability of a closer integration between the cinematograph and television industries in respect of the resources and the film entertainment and information which they afford'.[72] These proposals were, firstly, for the Treasury to divert a proportion of the ITV Levy payments that the companies paid on their profits into a fund that would be used to support film production; and secondly, to incentivise direct financial involvement by the companies by allowing any sums invested in film production or revenues derived from it to be deducted from their payments. The companies' response, summarised by LWT's John Freeman in a letter to the Home Office, indicated their willingness to accede to the first proposal but also their concern that such an arrangement would 'institutionalise the [ITV] Levy at its existing high rate without – as we see it – regard for the needs of broadcasting or, for that matter, of the taxpayers in general'. Freeman was ambivalent also about the second proposal, despite its obvious advantages, based on much the same principles and priorities that had been articulated by Rugheimer at the BBC:

> I hope it does not sound pompous to express the view that the high quality of British television is achieved at least partly because both broadcasting services are single-minded in the pursuit of good broadcasting and have no incentive to take decisions directed to any other end. Of course, some of the ITV companies have diversified interests and some of these are in film production. But they are entirely separate from the operation of the television contracts and therefore unaffected by the [ITV] Levy. They are, in other words, business operations based

on commercial judgment. Once remission of levy is related to investment in film production, the companies have the incentive to base their television decisions on considerations other than those of good broadcasting.

More generally, in a stinging remark, Freeman suggested a fundamental reservation about what appeared to be the Working Party's underlying assumption: 'that the television industry (which we believe to be economically and efficiently run) has an obligation to rescue the film industry (about which we hold different beliefs)'.[73]

As Freeman noted, a number of the ITV programme companies had already invested directly in the making of cinema films through the formation of theatrical production arms, with mixed results (see Table 6.5). Granada Film Productions made *All the Way Up* (1970/12.09.1975), directed by BBC drama producer James MacTaggart. Sunny Productions, a subsidiary of Yorkshire Television (YTV), made *The Best Pair of Legs in the Business* (1973/01.03.1980), an expansion of a TV play. Trident Television, parent company of both YTV and Tyne Tees Television,

Table 6.5 ITV contractors and subsidiary companies producing theatrical films, 1970–82.

ITV contractor	Production companies	Films
ATV Network	Associated General Films	*The Cassandra Crossing* (1976), *The Eagle Has Landed* (1976), *Voyage of the Damned* (1976), *Capricorn One* (1977), *The Domino Principle* (1977), *March or Die* (1977)
ATV Network	Black Lion Films	*Porridge* (1979), *To Russia . . . with Elton* (1979), *Bloody Kids* (1980), *The Long Good Friday* (1980), *Rising Damp* (1980), *Looks and Smiles* (1981)
ATV Network	Chips Productions	*George and Mildred* (1980), *Hawk the Slayer* (1980), *The Monster Club* (1980)
ATV Network	Incorporated Television Company	*Mister Jerico* (1970), *Desperate Characters* (1971), *The Firechasers* (1971), *Baffled!* (1972), *Madame Sin* (1972), *The Possession of Joel Delaney* (1972), *Moses* (1976)
ATV Network	ITC Entertainment	*92 in the Shade** (1975), *The Count of Monte-Cristo* (1975), *Farewell, My Lovely* (1975), *Great Expectations* (1975), *Man Friday* (1975), *Russian Roulette* (1975), *Spot* (*Dogpound Shuffle*, 1976), *Virginity** (1976), *Autumn Sonata* (1978), *The Big Sleep* (1978), *The Boys from Brazil* (1978), *The Medusa Touch* (1978), *Firepower* (1979), *From the Life of the Marionettes* (1980), *Saturn 3* (1980), *The Great Muppet Caper* (1981), *Green Ice* (1981), *The Legend of the Lone Ranger* (1981), *The Dark Crystal* (1982)
ATV Network	ITC Films	*Movie Movie* (1978), *Love and Bullets* (1979), *The Muppet Movie* (1979), *Raise the Titanic* (1980), *On Golden Pond* (1981), *Barbarosa* (1982), *The Last Unicorn* (1982), *Sophie's Choice* (1982)
ATV Network	ITC Films International	*The Salamander** (1980)

Table 6.5 (continued)

ITV contractor	Production companies	Films
ATV Network	Marble Arch Productions	*All Quiet on the Western Front* (1979), *Borderline* (1980), *Hard Country** (1981)
ATV Network	Pimlico Films	*The Tamarind Seed* (1974), *The Return of the Pink Panther* (1975), *Escape to Athena* (1979)
Granada Television	Granada Films	*All the Way Up* (1970)
HTV		*Diagnosis: Murder* (1974), *Deadly Strangers* (1975)
London Weekend Television (LWT)		*Akenfield* (1974), *Hullabaloo over George and Bonnie's Pictures* (1978)
Scottish Television (STV)		*Gregory's Girl* (1980)
Southern Television	Southern Pictures	*Richard's Things** (1980), *Bad Blood** (1981)
Thames Television	Euston Films	*The Best of Benny Hill* (1974), *Sweeney!* (1977), *The Sailor's Return** (1978), *Sweeney 2* (1978)
Trident Television (YTV/Tyne Tees Television)	Trident Films, Southbrook International Programmes	*The Bushido Blade** (1978), *The Four Feathers* (1978), *Oliver Twist* (1982)
Yorkshire Television (YTV)	Sunny Productions	*The Best Pair of Legs in the Business* (1973)

Note: Many of these films were made in co-production with other companies. Titles marked * did not receive a UK theatrical release.

formed Trident Films; it made *The Four Feathers* (1978/25.10.1981) and *Oliver Twist* (1982/19.03.1994), both released in UK cinemas but aimed primarily at the American television market. HTV produced two modest thrillers, *Deadly Strangers* (1974/10.10.1981) and *Diagnosis: Murder* (1975/12.10.1981), and Scottish Television (STV) invested in the 'sleeper' hit *Gregory's Girl* (1980/08.01.1985). From 1969, Thames Television made a number of television dramas shot on 16mm or 35mm film, several of them forming an occasional series, *Armchair Cinema* (1974–75). In 1973, Thames set up a subsidiary, Euston Films, principally to make drama series on film, including the cop show *The Sweeney*, but also its big-screen spin-offs, *Sweeney!* (1977/22.12.1980) and *Sweeney 2* (1978/17.09.1983). Thames also co-produced Polish director Andrzej Wajda's film about Joseph Conrad, *The Shadow Line* (1976/01.07.1976), for broadcast in the UK and cinema release overseas. Euston's period drama *The Sailor's Return* (1978/09.12.1980) was meant for theatrical release, but after a London Film Festival premiere it failed to find a distributor; two years later, it finally emerged on ITV (see Figure 6.3). Southern Television formed Southern Pictures, but neither of its two productions, *Richard's Things* (1980/16.08.1981) and *Bad Blood* (1981/21.10.1981), received a UK theatrical release and they too went direct to television.[74]

Figure 6.3 Shope Shodeinde and Tom Bell in Euston Films' production *The Sailor's Return* (1978), which was intended for theatrical release but went straight to television, premiering on 9 December 1980. *TV Times* © Future Publishing Ltd.

By far the most prolific producer in this field was Lew Grade's Incorporated Television Company (ITC), a subsidiary of ATV, which since 1955 had, like Euston, mainly been making telefilm series. ITC began producing feature films for theatrical release in 1969, and this activity was stepped up in 1974 with more ambitious films on bigger budgets, including the highly successful *The Return of the Pink Panther* (1975/14.09.1980). Some of ITC's films were intended for alternate markets – television in some countries, cinemas in others – with, of course, the prospect of eventual TV sales either way. Grade announced that he would respect the five-year rule but would prefer it to be reduced to three or even less; he also contemplated the prospect of simultaneous cinema and TV release, should agreement on it be reached with the industry.[75] ITC had several other film-production subsidiaries, including Black Lion Films and the American-based Associated General Films and Marble Arch Productions, and it also established theatrical distribution companies in both the US and UK (respectively, Associated Film Distribution and ITC Film Distributors). Among the many films ITC produced at this time was another Jules Buck picture starring Peter O'Toole, *Man Friday* (1975/31.01.1984).

Despite the differences of opinion it encountered, the Working Party completed its deliberations in double-quick time and delivered its thirty-three-page report to 10 Downing Street in December 1975; it was published as a White Paper on

14 January 1976. The Terry Report, intended to lead to 'a new era of cooperation between the cinematograph and television industries', included thirty-nine
proposals and hence was often referred to jokingly (by John Terry himself as well
as the press) as the Thirty-nine Steps. Those points which concern us here relate
primarily to the involvement of the broadcasting organisations in film production
and to regulating the supply of cinema films for showing on television. The former
included the BBC's commitment to its seed-money scheme and, more vaguely,
the ITV companies' expressed willingness to invest in film production on the
terms discussed above. Both broadcasting groups also agreed that none of their
permanent staff would be involved in any of the productions they financed, thus
safeguarding jobs in the film industry. Importantly, as an incentive for filmmakers,
the Report recommended that films funded by the broadcasters 'should be eligible
for Eady payments even if, at their registration date, there is an agreement for television exhibition in existence'. The Government production fund to be derived
from the ITV Levy amounted to £5 million per annum, interest-free.

Regarding the age of films available to television, the Report recommended
that the present five-year embargo should be reduced to three years from the
date of registration with the Board of Trade; to ensure that this was enforceable
and not merely a 'gentleman's agreement', the rule was to be made statutory.
This measure was partly in recognition that other new proposed legislation,
the Restrictive Practices (Service) Order 1975, which had not yet gone through
Parliament, threatened to make any such time bar illegal unless explicitly protected by statute. These recommendations were clearly offered as a compromise
designed to placate both exhibitors and the broadcasters, as it was in their interests
as investors for the films they financed to benefit from the maximum profitable
period of cinema exposure. By allowing a particular, albeit modified, restrictive
practice and enshrining it in law, the Report was proposing to safeguard cinemas;
but it stopped short of imposing a punitive levy on the broadcasters' use of films,
instead encouraging voluntary investment in the theatrical sector. The Report
argued that 'so far as possible restrictions should be avoided' but that 'the current
controls over the number of feature films shown on independent television
imposed by the IBA and the similar self-imposed restrictions observed by the
BBC should be maintained'. It added: 'it is only if these plans fail to operate successfully in practice that the CFC's recommendation for the imposition of a levy
should be implemented'.[76]

These proposed measures, along with most of the rest of the Report, were
unanimously endorsed by all members of the Working Party. But Milne and Tesler
pointedly dissociated themselves from two other proposals, both less attractive to
existing television interests:

> One calls for greater efforts by producers and distributors of British films to get better prices
> for them from United Kingdom television companies. The other recommends sympathetic
> consideration for a subscription television service, transmitting feature films by cable televi-
> sion and providing a new and perhaps substantial source of revenue for film makers.[77]

Reactions to the White Paper varied widely. The London *Evening Standard* opined that the 'much freer interchange of cinema films and television is to be commended'. The *Financial Times* also considered the 'gradual blurring of the lines between film and television' to be a good thing. The *Daily Mail* described the plan for greater cooperation as 'the White Paper's major proposal. For too long the film industry has regarded TV as the villain of the piece. Now it could be the hero.' Taking the point of view of television, *Broadcast* judged: 'If the Report really is anything more than a palliative papering over of the cracks, then TV stands to benefit as much as the film industry does. If it isn't, well the TV industry won't come to much harm either.'[78]

There were, however, more contrary voices. Bob Camplin, General Secretary of the CEA, deplored the proposed reduction of the embargo from five to three years as a 'time bomb ... designed to go off almost immediately, which will decimate the subsequent run exhibitor in addition to doing some injury to exhibition as a whole'. The CEA's official response welcomed the call to increase the sums paid by broadcasters for films, but noted that 'resolutions of this sort are meaningless unless they attempt to propose charges based [on] and related to the size of the audience as they are in cinemas'. Michael Relph approved the moves to make television 'integrated more with the film industry' but argued that 'there must be a severe restriction on the number of films shown on TV and a restriction on the hours and days on which they are shown'. This was a view echoed by other producers. David Puttnam, who in his own evidence to the Working Party had suggested that films be banned entirely from the existing channels and shown only on a Post Office-controlled cable network, regretted that 'no restriction had been suggested on the number of cinema films shown on television'. Michael Klinger argued: 'We need restrictions to protect us, such as films on television only two nights a week, then maybe the film industry would have a better chance of standing on its own feet without coming across as a lame duck asking for a hand-out.' Their point seemed to be reinforced by ITV's television premiere, at peak-time on a Sunday, of *The Italian Job* (1969/25.01.1976): according to various trade-paper reports, theatrical box-office revenues fell that evening by 40 to 60 per cent from normal levels.[79]

In the months and indeed years that followed the White Paper's publication, it became increasingly clear that the groundswell of film-industry opinion was against its recommendations for films on television. According to a joint statement from Equity and the Musicians' Union (MU), the proposals for the greater involvement of broadcasters in film finance would 'result in hybrid films lacking the best features of either medium and aimed at an amorphous international audience'.[80] The CEA reaffirmed its commitment to the five-year embargo and made demands for greater controls on television's use of films. Other industry bodies echoed them, including the Performers' Alliance, formed by Equity and the MU; the Association of Directors and Producers (ADP); the All-Industry Standing Committee, convened by the Film Production Association (FPA); the

All-Industry Committee on the Film Industry, organised by the Association of
Independent Producers (AIP); the Association of Independent Cinemas (AIC);
and the Film Industry Council (FIC), another all-industry body, chaired by the
ACTT's Alan Sapper, a signatory of the Terry Report. As of 1977, there were no
fewer than nineteen trade associations, unions and collective bodies. Through
them, and through the letters columns of newspapers, calls for increased prices,
fewer film transmissions, restrictions on the days and times of transmissions, and
either a levy on transmissions or for the broadcasters to contribute to the existing
Eady Levy, were reiterated into the 1980s; but none was ever enacted.[81]

In the event, other than the BBC's already-existing seed-money scheme, none of
the Terry Report's proposed measures was put into practice either. Within weeks
of its publication, Harold Wilson had resigned as Prime Minister; with his departure, the impetus behind the White Paper was lost. Wilson, a staunch advocate of
the film industry at whose instigation the NFFC and Eady Fund had originally
been created, was subsequently invited to chair an Interim Action Committee
following up the Terry Report, to consult with film and television interests and
to make further recommendations of its own. Eight of its eighteen members had
also sat on the Working Party, including Terry himself. But the Committee did not
meet for the first time until May 1977, nine months after it had been announced;
and aside from producing periodic reports over a number of years, it achieved
nothing resulting in anything that could be called action.[82]

The 1977 Report of the Committee on the Future of Broadcasting, chaired
by Lord Annan, was the first report by a Government broadcasting committee
to include a section (indeed, an entire chapter) on 'Films on Television', though
much of it was taken up with general discussion of acquired and foreign programming rather than feature films specifically. Some of Annan's findings and
recommendations are discussed in other parts of this book, so it is not necessary
to attempt a full summary here. It is, however, worth noting that the report recognised the popularity with viewers of feature films. In the years preceding the report
they had comprised from 10 to 13 per cent of broadcast output, and often drew
high ratings. Evidence submitted by viewers the committee found 'bewildering'.

> Some objected to the number of films shown. Others complained, not that the films shown
> were too numerous, but that they were too old and too often repeated. Others clearly liked
> watching films regardless of how old they might be. ... People like to see an expensive produc-
> tion with well known actors in a film which they know will be enjoyable because they remember
> its reputation when it was distributed to the cinemas. Nor should it be ignored that some of the
> most popular films are the glossiest American productions.[83]

Though the committee recognised the objections made to films on television by
unions and other trade associations, it declined to recommend statutory remedies
for their grievances in the form of measures such as levies and quotas. Instead, it
urged more cooperation between the film and television industries through TV
investment in film production, and hoped that broadcasters would 'concentrate

more on increasing the range rather than the amount of material which they buy from abroad, particularly by drawing on the distinguished film making traditions in some European countries, even if it means a reduction in the cheaper American output'.[84]

And what of the films that had benefited from TV money? By 1978 the BBC had provided funding for thirteen projects still in development and two that had been successfully produced: *Agatha* (1979/05.12.1982) and *Murder by Decree* (1979/01.01.1984). When *Agatha* was being readied for release, the CEA announced that its members, including the major cinema circuits, Rank's Odeon chain and EMI's ABC, would decline to book it because of the BBC's intention to broadcast the film only three years after its release. This was despite the fact that *Agatha* was distributed in the UK by Columbia-EMI-Warner, in which EMI was a partner. EMI's Bernard Delfont, who as a signatory of the Terry Report had endorsed its view that the time bar should be reduced, explained:

> We are doing this because films are made to be seen in the cinema and not on television ... I myself am not against a three-year instead of a five-year rule. But I cannot go against my colleagues [in the CEA], who would feel badly let down if the rule was broken.[85]

The CEA had tabled an amendment to its rules, recommending to its members 'that a licence agreement should not be entered into if [they are] unable to obtain satisfactory assurances that a film will not be televised before the expiry of five years from the date of its trade show'. The BBC's response was to serve a High Court writ on both the CEA and EMI, charging them with illegal restrictive practices in refusing to consider *Agatha* for exhibition.[86] The film eventually opened in May 1979 at the Prince Charles Cinema off Leicester Square, part of the Star Cinemas group, and was subsequently shown in independent cinemas around the country.

The CEA did make one concession, in February 1978, when it agreed to remove altogether the three-year bar on the transmission of foreign-language films, so long as they were broadcast in subtitled rather than dubbed versions. The rationale for this was that 'if a foreign film has any box-office potential, it is likely to be exhibited in the UK in a dubbed version'.[87] As previous instances of foreign-language films being broadcast after less than three years had not resulted in any hostile action from the CEA, this was merely formalising what was already a fait accompli. This applied also to specialised films in the English language. In early 1980, the BBC's established practice of showing recent films that were unreleased or given limited release in the UK was prominently displayed with an entire season of such films on BBC2, entitled 'Movie Showcase'. In several instances, the BBC had actively encouraged their producers and distributors to open the films commercially before they were shown on television, on the principle that theatrical exposure, however minimal, and its attendant publicity and press coverage gave them an increased cachet when finally broadcast; their *Radio Times* billings included quotations from critical reviews. In the case of *The Stepford Wives* (1975/22.01.1980), which had not been taken for UK release until 1978, three years after it was made, the BBC had voluntarily postponed an earlier planned transmission in order to give the UK distributor, Contemporary Films, more time to exploit it in cinemas.[88]

The five-year rule was finally reduced to three years, but not because the CEA had relaxed its stance or because new legislation had been passed. In March 1980, Lew Grade, whose purchase of the Goldwyn package in 1964 had effectively led to the rule, announced that films made by his Associated Communications Corporation (ACC, the parent company of ATV and ITC) would be made available for broadcast after only three years rather than five. Grade argued that most films had realised all their potential revenues after three years and allowing an earlier sale to television would be a boon to their producers. The CEA's response was unusually muted and delayed in coming. Commented Grade, with characteristic bullishness: 'I have had no reaction to my decision from anybody and I don't expect any. I have made a decision and that's it.'[89] He had previously indicated his willingness to make this concession, but it was speculated that Grade's move at this time was due to cash-flow problems caused by the commercial failure of a number of ITC productions.[90]

Grade's brother Bernard Delfont expressed his reservations about the decision, as it had not been agreed with the CEA first; he also admitted that the broadcasters now paid 'respectable figures' for films.[91] The following month, EMI announced that it would adopt the same three-year policy. Its CEO, Barry Spikings, argued: 'The way in which films are marketed today is such that they reach the UK cinema audience quickly and efficiently. It is simply not possible to justify withholding them from the [TV] audience for five years.'[92] With two such major players – both Grade/ACC and Delfont/EMI were members of the CEA through their respective ownership of the Classic and ABC cinema chains – making a change of policy, it was no longer possible for the Association to maintain its stance and in May 1980 it reluctantly conceded to the introduction of a three-year rule.[93] In time, all the other major suppliers followed this example. Thus, just as he did in 1964, Lew Grade – not coincidentally both a broadcasting mogul and a film tycoon – had again broken the power of the CEA to set the terms by which the film industry did business with television. Though not strictly a rule, and with other exhibition platforms now intervening, a window of around three years between theatrical release and broadcast on free-to-air terrestrial TV remains the norm to this day.

Bidding for Blockbusters

By the middle of the 1970s, as Gordon Smith, Gunnar Rugheimer and Leslie Halliwell had all predicted, most 'classic' and routine mainstream product had been sold up to the limit of the five-year rule. Indeed, many newer films had been sold beyond this, with the proviso that they could not be broadcast until the embargo period was up. There were, however, a number of older films that had not been made available to television as they continued to be of commercial importance to the film industry due to their theatrical reissue potential. It was these that the broadcasters now sought to acquire.

At this point, only a few 'blockbusters' – the breakaway box-office hits on which the industry had increasingly come to depend since the early 1950s – had been shown on British television, usually scheduled as special events for Christmas and other public holidays. They included, for example, *Around the World in Eighty Days* (1956/25.12.1971), *Oklahoma!* (1955/26.12.1971), *Giant* (1956/29.12.1973) and *The King and I* (1956/31.12.1973) on ITV; and *The Alamo* (1960/28.12.1970), *West Side Story* (1961/24.12.1972), *How the West Was Won* (1962/23.12.1973) and *Cleopatra* (1963/29 & 30.12.1973) on the BBC. Valuable as these big-screen properties had been in their day, they had sufficiently exhausted their residual theatrical value by the early 1970s to be sold to television at what seemed to many in the film industry to be knock-down rates. *Oklahoma!*, for example, was acquired by ITV in a one-off deal of £18,000 for two showings, though in 1971 that was apparently the highest fee the network had yet paid for a single film. Bigger prizes remained on the shelf, out of reach; but they could yet be brought down for the right price.

The TV premiere in October 1975 of the first Bond film, *Dr No*, to a then-record audience has been called the start of the 'great age of films on television' in the UK.[94] However, a case could also be made for the previous Christmas as being a watershed moment. In the US, 'the birth of the big picture TV special' had occurred in 1966, with the sale to ABC Television of *The Bridge on the River Kwai* (1957/25.12.1974) for $2 million for two showings. The year after, Paul Fox, then Controller of BBC1 and hoping for 'some real blockbusters' in his autumn schedules for the following year, had told Gordon Smith: 'Somehow or other, we must go for a *Bridge on the River Kwai*, if possible.'[95] But it was not until after the departure from the Corporation of both Fox and Smith that the BBC was at last able to acquire *Kwai*, for a fee of £125,000 for five showings over ten years (see Figure 6.4). The price was kept confidential: publicly, the BBC denied as 'exaggerated' reports that it was £120,000.[96] The same, actual, amount was subsequently paid for three showings of *Butch Cassidy and the Sundance Kid* (1969/25.12.1975), the sale of which had to be personally authorised (due to a clause in his contract) by its star, Paul Newman. The outcome was promoted in *Radio Times* as a 'world television premiere', as the film had not yet been sold to television anywhere else, including the US.[97] The BBC's purchase of *Oliver!* (1968/25.12.1976) for three showings over five years cost as much as both these films combined: a new UK record of £250,000. Its producer John Woolf had agreed to the sale only on condition that the film would be shown, at least for its first transmission, on Christmas Day, when cinemas were closed and it would therefore not be competing with new films.[98] Woolf's mauling by FIDO probably still left scars; his own response to the Terry Report had been that he 'would stop films going on TV for at least ten years'.[99] Woolf also pointed out that *Oliver!* had 'earned very little on its last two or three cinema releases. It is finished as far as the cinema is concerned.'[100]

Figure 6.4 The long-awaited British television premiere of *The Bridge on the River Kwai* (1957) was presented by BBC1 on Christmas Day 1974. *Radio Times* © Immediate Media Co. Artwork © Frank Bellamy.

These three films were BBC1's prime Christmas Day attractions in successive years (see Chapter 7). The scale of the BBC's investment in film acquisition did not go unnoticed by ITV and the IBA; nor did its success in the ratings. An Authority board member observed in a December 1976 meeting that 'the BBC's promotion of their Christmas schedules had brought it home to him how many more good films they seemed to have than ITV' and he queried the availability of funds for the commercial network's buyers. Leslie Halliwell and Paul Fox, now chair of the Film Purchase Group, made buying trips to Los Angeles two or three times a year. They were given discretionary powers to make deals on the spot without referring them back to the FPG. The IBA's Bernard Sendall reported that although Halliwell and Fox had 'virtually been given a blank cheque to buy films, it would be a long time before they caught up with the BBC, who had seemed to be more prepared to pay whatever had been asked for films over recent years'.[101]

In his own report that year to the BBC Board of Governors, Alasdair Milne claimed the same for the opposition. Citing the recent ITV deal to acquire the remaining three Bond films, Milne stated that it was 'clear from the figures that ITV have been and are paying by far the higher prices for top films'. However, he denied that it was competition between the broadcasters that was responsible for the escalation in fees: 'the price level is determined by the revenue expectation from continued cinema distribution – or the potential reduction of such revenue caused by a television showing'. This was the case, he argued, with both the Bond deals and the BBC's own acquisitions: 'If we had insisted on lower prices, we simply would not have got the films. I am quite satisfied that collusion with ITV, in whatever form, would not have made the slightest difference to the price.' The justification for such purchases, at a time when the Corporation was heavily in debt and making cutbacks to staff and production budgets, was that the cost per hour of acquired films, no matter how expensive, was always lower than that of new drama made directly for television. Milne concluded his argument:

> I am certain that when it comes to 'special buys' of topline films, we are going to have to pay prices which will seem extravagant until the number of licensed transmissions and hence their cost per hour ratio put them in proper perspective against the effects of rising costs on our own output.[102]

The costs per hour of *The Bridge on the River Kwai*, *Butch Cassidy and the Sundance Kid* and *Oliver!* were calculated as £9,677, £23,809 and £35,714 respectively (see Table 6.3), compared with an hourly cost for original drama production (at 1976 rates) of £40,000. One month after the *Oliver!* deal had been settled, Bryan Cowgill, Controller of BBC1, claimed that a cost-per-hour limit of £60,000 had been set for further film purchases. On this basis, the BBC reportedly rejected approaches from Twentieth Century-Fox to buy *The Sound of Music* (1965/25.12.1978) for £300,000 and from MGM to buy *Gone with the Wind* (1939/26 & 27.12.1981) for £500,000.[103] ITV had been offered a single run of the latter for $1 million, which it had declined as 'astronomical'.[104] But other high-priced deals followed in the next few years. ITV paid $800,000 – equivalent to £457,000, or in the BBC's preferred terms, nearly £65,000 per hour – for two runs of *Ben-Hur* (1959/07.05.1978) and £1 million for *Doctor Zhivago* (1965/01.01.1981). The BBC paid £450,000 for *The Godfather* (1972/28.05.1978) and around £1 million for each of *The Poseidon Adventure* (1972/23.12.1979), *The Sting* (1973/25.12.1979), *The Towering Inferno* (1974/26.12.1980) and *The Deer Hunter* (1978/01.01.1985).[105]

Most of these purchases included additional films besides the named titles, but many were re-runs that had essentially been thrown in by the distributors as 'sweeteners'. For example, the deal for *The Godfather* comprised a package of thirty-eight features, mainly repeats but also including first runs of *Three Days of the Condor* (1975/13.12.1980) and *Nashville* (1975/28.12.1980). This gave an average cost per hour for the whole package of only £5,123, allowing Gunnar Rugheimer to claim that the effective cost to the BBC of acquiring *The Godfather* was 'less than £45,000', or one-tenth of the total package price.[106] Nevertheless, as Milne had anticipated, all of these deals attracted wide criticism. The press made particular sport of a fee of £1.6 million for a package of 104 features from EMI, whose main item was the flop Village People musical *Can't Stop the Music* (1980/17.12.1983).[107]

However, the major controversies arose over the extraordinary sums paid for the biggest prizes of all. In June 1978, Peter Plouvier, General Secretary of Equity, wrote to BBC Director General Ian Trethowan, asking him to confirm or deny unofficial reports of the Corporation's purchase for over $4 million of *The Sound of Music*. Trethowan replied to confirm, saying that the film was 'one that we particularly wished to acquire because of its broad family appeal, and because the rights were available over ten years'.[108] A sum of $4,150,000 (equivalent to around £2 million) was paid for up to ten transmissions of the nearly three-hour film. This allowed Alasdair Milne to claim a cost per hour of £83,375, compared to current drama production costs of £85,000 per hour: 'In terms of cost per viewer we are talking about 1.5p per viewer every time the film is shown.'[109] He argued that inflation over the unusually long licence period would close the cost-per-hour gap further. However, Leslie Halliwell's biographer Michael Binder argues that this was somewhat disingenuous, as it 'did not take into account re-runs [of television drama], and the question remained whether the BBC was serving its licence fee payers better by repeating an old movie ten times over instead of making ten new dramas, each of which would have an added sell-on value to foreign networks'.[110]

As it happens, only seven of the ten licensed transmissions were taken up, so the eventual cost to the public of *The Sound of Music* was slightly greater than Milne had allowed. Although the deal with Twentieth Century-Fox had been provision-ally agreed on 6 June, it had not been concluded and signed until six days later, the day on which the story broke in newspapers. Internal correspondence shows concern among executives about the deleterious effect on the BBC's reputation of allowing details of the deal to leak out unofficially, thus placing the Corporation in a defensive position, rather than taking the initiative of making a formal announcement. But it was not the Programme Acquisition department's policy to publicise deals and so the Corporation was left on the back foot, having to justify its purchases after they had been brought to light by the press and its own rivals.[111] Meanwhile, Plouvier publicly attacked the 'competition of desperation' between the networks, arguing that 'they should be spending more money on home grown products that would provide our members with work'.[112]

Unlike previous big-money deals, which had not placed the BBC and ITV in direct competition for particular films or packages, the *Sound of Music* purchase was the outcome of competitive bidding. Rugheimer supplied Milne with a detailed breakdown of the rival bids:

26 May 1978: the BBC offered $3,750,000 ('the lowest price Fox would accept') for ten trans-missions, with 10 per cent of the fee payable on signature and the rest in three annual instal-ments of 15, 35 and 40 per cent, respectively.

30 May: ITV offered $3,875,000 for ten transmissions on similar payment terms; the BBC counter-offered $3,900,000.

31 May: ITV offered $3,950,000; the BBC counter-offered $4,000,000.

1 June: ITV offered $4,100,000.

2 June: the BBC offered $4,150,000.

6 June: ITV withdrew from the bidding and Fox agreed to accept the BBC's last offer, 'subject to further discussion of payment terms'.

12 June: Payment terms were finalised as '15% on signature, 10% on April 5th 1979, 35% on April 5th 1980 and 40% on April 5th 1981'.

Rugheimer further commented of the process: 'If ITV sources persist in their suggestions that they abandoned the bidding at US $3,875,000 corroboration of the above timetable can if required be obtained from Fox.' He estimated the difference between the bidders' final offers as $2,175.[113]

Rumours surfaced in the press in April 1980 that *Gone with the Wind* was about to be offered again to British television. This was a difficult time for both broadcasting organisations. The BBC had been asking the Government for an increase in viewers' TV licence fees to address its record deficit for the year just ended, and had recently axed five orchestras to cut costs, leading to a musicians' strike. The ITV companies were approaching the next period of franchise renewal, with new contracts to be announced at the end of the year for terms beginning on 1 January 1982. They were also threatened with an increase of the government Levy on ITV profits.[114] But the most successful film ever made, in terms of ticket sales, was too big a prize to pass up and the buyers again found themselves involved in a bidding war. In 1976, the American network NBC had paid the equivalent of £3 million for a single showing of *Gone with the Wind*; in 1978, the rival CBS spent around £18 million for the rights to show the film twenty times over twenty years.[115] Both were record sums for the US market and whatever was paid for the film in the UK would clearly break records also.

This time the BBC announced the start of the auction directly to the press in November 1980, with bidding opening at $8.7 million (around £3.6 million). *Wind* was offered for ten runs over fifteen years; but also included in the deal, on more regular limited terms up to seven years, were fifty-five other MGM films, all repeats. At the base price the BBC thus calculated the real cost per hour of the package as £12,000.[116] ITV buyers, however, cried foul, as the package had originally been put up for auction in the summer, when both sides had declared a year's moratorium due to their financial hardships. In publicising its opening offer before the opposition had even been informed that the package was back on the table, the BBC had apparently broken a gentleman's agreement in order to seize a publicity advantage.[117]

The commercial network also accused the Corporation of a 'dirty tricks' campaign, as stories of ITV bids for other major films, quickly denied, also began appearing in newspapers. The BBC, in turn, argued that ITV had an unfair advantage because, as previously noted, the Government Levy on the network now taxed its profits rather than its revenues. An unusual expense such as a large film buy would therefore reduce its profits and hence the size of the Levy payments. According to 'a BBC spokesman' (probably Alasdair Milne, as it was consistent with other comments attributed to him):

What it means is that ITV actually only pays one third of the price they offer for a film. The other two thirds is paid by the taxpayer [*sic*].

The result is that ITV can always outbid us on everything. We think this causes an unhealthy inequality. If ITV gets all the best movies it would threaten our survival.[118]

Leslie Halliwell responded that he had been 'mildly cross' at the BBC's renewal of the *Wind* bidding but was 'absolutely furious' at its profligacy:[119]

But they want to be top so they spend the money. It forces us to offer more.

Then they have the gall to say we're pushing the prices up. The truth is that we are appalled by the way the BBC spends money on films. We simply do not regard feature films as worth it. Most of them are minority viewing and many of even the biggest blockbusters are out of date.[120]

Counter-accusations of ITV's own alleged profligacy flew back from Milne, prompting further denials and a repudiation from Paul Fox of the BBC's 'gutter tactics' and 'the sort of lunatic auction that goes on when the BBC is determined to buy something'.[121] Halliwell was in no doubt where the blame lay for the current artificial escalation in prices: 'Mr Rugheimer is responsible single-handed for much of what has happened' – a claim swiftly refuted by the BBC.[122]

Before the *Wind* storm had blown over, yet another high-priced film package came on the market, and again the BBC seemed determined to throw in a spoiler. In January 1981, Rugheimer leaked to the press the news that ITV had offered $9,750,000 for thirty-one films from MCA-Universal, headed by *Jaws* (1975/08.10.1981) and *Jaws 2* (1978/09.01.1983). Whereas the MGM package contained only re-runs besides the main attraction of *Wind*, MCA's also included a number of other first-run features. Halliwell and Fox had made the deal in Hollywood, where Rugheimer was also on a buying trip. He boasted about not having responded to ITV's bid with a counter-offer: 'We do not believe the programme value of this particular package is sufficient to warrant this sort of money.' What Rugheimer did not say was that, according to trade journal *Broadcast*, he had earlier put in a bid for a different MCA package of thirty-three films, including *Jaws*, when it had been offered the previous year. The film at that time had an individual price-tag of $3 million, subsequently raised to $4 million, and Rugheimer had 'then asked for a moritorium [*sic*] on the sale because it was politically difficult to be seen spending such an amount of money when several orchestras were being cut back'. Later in Hollywood, MCA had gone back to Rugheimer, who at the last minute declined, thereby allowing ITV's buyers to step in and make the purchase.[123]

The auction for the *Gone with the Wind* package finally took place in London the following week. It lasted just over an hour, with the rival bidders, Rugheimer and Halliwell, respectively ensconced in the Atheneum Hotel and in Granada's Golden Square offices, fielding the bids by telephone. Bill Davis of MGM's overseas distributor Cinema International Corporation (CIC) acted as sales agent.

The ITV buyer opened with an offer of $9 million, and for the next 61 minutes a series of bids and counter-bids followed in increments of $50,000 (BBC) and $100,000 (ITV) until Rugheimer closed the deal at $10,550,000 (£4,400,000).[124] Halliwell later claimed: 'In a way I was glad the BBC got it because it kept them quiet. It left them short of money so we did much better in the following months when films came up.'[125] In a further display of sour grapes, he said that the BBC was 'going for broke on it, so we put in a token bid only'; but clearly he was serious enough at the time to have tendered slightly more than ITV paid on the *Jaws* deal, bowing out at $10.5 million.[126] For its part, the BBC trumpeted the total package's value for money as 300 hours of family entertainment at a cost per hour of £14,700, against current hourly averages of £120,000 for new drama, £31,000 for all in-house production and £9,000 for outside purchases.[127]

Halliwell's ITV colleague Paul Fox recalled to me: '*Gone with the Wind* for television was frankly too long, and certainly for a commercial network too long, because it would have had to be shown over two nights. So we got involved in the bidding basically to drive the BBC up, make the BBC pay more. Alasdair Milne said, we're going to beat these bastards, and they did.'[128] The film was indeed first shown in two parts, over successive nights on BBC1 at Christmas 1981, a scheduling decision that drew further press criticism. *Gone with the Wind* was subsequently broadcast by the BBC seven more times over the fifteen years of its licence period. But its ratings never matched the 23.25 million viewers estimated to have tuned in to ITV two months earlier for the premiere of *Jaws*.

Notes

1 H. Hughes, 'Feature Film Stock Policy', 20 July 1972, BBC R78/1,123/1.
2 Gunnar Rugheimer, 'Proposed Feature Film Stock Policy', 13 July 1972, BBC R78/1,123/1.
3 Hughes, 'Feature Film Stock Policy'.
4 Charles Curran, 'Feature Film Stock Policy', 25 July 1972; Hughes, 'Feature Film Purchasing Policy', 27 February 1975, and 'Feature Film Recovery and Money Outstanding', 27 August 1976, BBC R78/1,123/1.
5 Alasdair Milne, 'BBC Television: The Purchase and Transmission of Feature Films, 1978–79', n.d. (1978), BBC R78/1, 123/1.
6 Alasdair Milne, 'The Purchase and Transmission of Feature Films', 25 November 1975, BBC R78/1, 123/1.
7 Quoted in 'Good News if You're Fed up with Ancient Movies', *Daily Mail*, 24 August 1974.
8 Milne, 'The Purchase and Transmission of Feature Films, 1978–79'.
9 'BBC Buys Hundreds of United Artists Pictures', *Broadcast*, 1 February 1974, 5.
10 Milne, 'The Purchase and Transmission of Feature Films, 1978–79'.
11 Milne, 'Film Purchasing Policy', 27 May 1976, BBC R78/1,123/1.
12 Milne, 'The Purchase and Transmission of Feature Films, 1978–79'.

13 Milne, 'Film Purchasing Policy'.

14 David Lewin, 'Storm over Bond Movies for ITV', *Cinema TV Today*, 7 January 1974, and '007 Goes to ITV in a Record £850,000 Deal', *Daily Mail*, 7 January 1974, 11.

15 Aldo Nicolotti, 'Bond in Licence to Screen TV Row', *Evening News*, 7 January 1974.

16 'Union Protests at TV Deal on Bond Films', *Daily Telegraph*, 8 January 1974.

17 Lewin, '007 Goes to ITV'.

18 Author's interview with Sir Paul Fox, 3 September 2012.

19 'ACTT Joins Opposition to UA Bond Movies TV Sale', *Broadcast*, 11 January 1974, 6.

20 C.H.B. Williamson, 'The Year's Box Office Winners', *Cinema TV Today*, 21 December 1974, 2.

21 'Bond TV Deal Attacked', *Daily Mail*, 8 January 1974, 11; Roderick Gilchrist, 'Film Union Threatens Bond Deal', *Daily Mail*, 10 January 1974, 11.

22 'No Bond Deal – ITV', *Cinema TV Today*, 10 January 1974.

23 'James Bond on TV', *MI6: The Home of James Bond 007*.

24 Clifford Davis, 'My Word – It's Bond', *Daily Mirror*, 12 January 1974; David Lewin, 'Bond's TV Debut Is Off for a Year', *Daily Mail*, 18 January 1974, 13.

25 'James Bond Tops Ratings for ITV', *Campaign*, 14 November 1975.

26 '*Dr No* Pays off with 10 Million Homes Rating Bonus', *Broadcast*, 17 November 1975.

27 BARB later recalculated the number of viewers for the premieres of *From Russia with Love* and *Goldfinger* as 16.55 million and 17.65 million, respectively.

28 Milne, 'Film Purchasing Policy'; Sue Summers, 'Three Latest Bonds for TV', *Screen International*, 11 September 1976, 1.

29 Halliwell, 'Film Purchase Matters', 15 March 1976, item 077 (044), IBA/01024: 3996310.

30 Dermot O'Hagan, 19 October 1978 and 23 October 1978; letter from Mr S.M., 1 January 1979, and reply, 12 January 1979, IBA/01024: 3996310; letter from Mr A.C.C., 16 March 1984, and reply, 28 March 1984, IBA/01022: 3996312; IBA Paper 260(78), Television Programme Intervention Report, September-November 1978, 16 November 1978, IBA/01021: 3996313.

31 O'Hagan, 8 October 1981, IBA/01022: 3996312.

32 Chris Rowley, 12 January 1978, IBA/01021: 3996313.

33 Leslie Halliwell to Rowley, 1 February 1978, IBA/01021: 3996313.

34 William Phillips, 'Are Films TV's Fatal Attraction?', *Broadcast*, 20 May 1988, 20. My thanks to Jenny Stewart for bringing this article to my attention.

35 Author's interview, 3 September 2012.

36 For alternative accounts of the Bond films on television, with transmission and ratings data, see 'James Bond on TV', *MI6: The Home of James Bond 007*, 13 October 2007 (updated 5 April 2011), at https://www.mi6-hq.com/sections/articles/history_bond_on_tv and Kevin Harper, 'James Bond on the Small Screen', *Double-O-Seven Magazine*, n.d., at http://www.007magazine.co.uk/bond_on_tv.htm.

37 John Deighton, '"Pay up" for Those Movies on Television', *Cinema TV Today*, 17 February 1973.

38 Quoted in Arthur Sandles, 'Delfont Starts Film Price Battle with Television', *Financial Times*, 17 February 1973, 14.

39 "'We'll Back You, Bernie'", *CinemaTV Today*, 24 February 1973; 'Delfont Halts Films for TV', *CinemaTV Today*, 5 May 1973; Tim Ewbank, 'TV Films Price War Hots Up', *Daily Mail*, 17 November 1973, 10.

40 Abel Green, 'British Terms Rile Par Chief', *Variety*, 14 March 1973, 3.

41 Vincent Porter, 'TV Strategies and European Film Production', *Sight and Sound* 43, no. 3 (Summer 1974): 163.

42 'Global Prices for Films on TV', *Variety*, 4 April 1973, 66.

43 Michael Relph, 'Film Industry Attitude to Television' (letter), *The Times*, 30 October 1973, 17.

44 Quoted in C.H.B. Williamson, "'We Want Channel Four'" says FPA', *CinemaTV Today*, 3 November 1973.

45 Tim Devlin, 'Call for £1m Levy from Old Films on TV', *The Times*, 30 November 1973, 20; Arthur Sandles, 'For Want of a Godfather', *Financial Times*, 14 January 1974, 25; Dennis Barker, 'Levy on Every Film Shown on TV Planned', *Guardian*, 15 January 1974, 30; 'ACTT Action to Restrict Old Films', *CinemaTV Today*, 11 April 1975; 'ACTT Yes to "Repeat Films on TV" Levy', *CinemaTV Today*, 18 April 1974.

46 'Minister Would Consider Levy on Television Films', *The Times*, 26 April 1974, 2.

47 'Jenkins Hits out at "TV Living on Film Capital"', *CinemaTV Today*, 27 April 1974.

48 Sue Newsom-Smith, 'Commons Call for TV Tax on Cinema Films', *CinemaTV Today*, 5 April 1974; 'Minister Ready for Tax on TV Films', *Guardian*, 26 April 1974, 24; Robin Page, 'News from Parliament', *CinemaTV Today*, 25 May 1974.

49 Nigel Johnson, 'Proposals of Cinematograph Films Council for a Financial Contribution from Television to the Film Production Industry', 11 April 1974, BBC R78/1, 123/1.

50 Reports of Cinematograph Films Council to Secretary of State for Trade on future prospects for the British film industry, extracts enclosed with letter from A.W. Mallinson, 20 September 1974, BBC R78/1, 123/1.

51 This account is based on the following: Howard Thomas, 'Screen Split', *Guardian*, 20 July 1974, 9; S.G. Williams to Colin Shaw, 24 April 1974; Thomas, 'The Use of Feature Films on British Television', 26 April 1974; Williams to Shaw, 7 May 1974; Shaw to Johnson, 8 May 1974; Rugheimer to Hugh Jenkins, 31 May 1974; Shaw to M.A.G. Veal, 26 June 1974; Rugheimer, 'Comments on Extracts from Reports of Cinematograph Film Council to Secretary of State for Trade on Future Prospects for the British Film Industry', 13 November 1974, and 'Meeting with CFC Delegation', 13 November 1974; D.L. Lamberth to Rugheimer, 14 November 1974; joint statement from ITCA, IBA and BBC, 22 January 1975, BBC R78/1,123/1.

52 Minutes of BBC Board of Management, 'Subsidising the Film Industry', 13 May 1974, BBC R78/1,123/1. The legal implications of a levy for the BBC's Charter were addressed in a brief memo from R.J. Marshall to Shaw, BBC 1 May 1975; Marshall's view was that it would not require amendments to the Charter.

53 This had been set out in J. Dromgoole to Curran and Brian Young, 19 September 1974, BBC R78/1,123/1.

54 The discussion that took place at the meeting of 21 March 1975 was summarised in an undated note, with additions, corrections and comments in memos from Rugheimer to Shaw, 27 March 1975, and Shaw to J. de Quidt, 30 April 1975, BBC R78/1,123/1.

55 Draft letter from the chairmen of the BBC and IBA, enclosed with memo from Shaw, 5 May 1975; Mallinson to Eric Deakins MP, 9 May 1975, BBC R78/1,123/1.

56 The term 'lost films' was used in several issues of the magazine *Films Illustrated* in 1972, including letters from readers referring to shelved films that in some cases had turned up on television.

57 Derek R. Threadgall, 'Television Letter of the Day' (letter), *Screen International*, 17 January 1976.

58 Quoted in 'Ruling Class Hits Back', *Daily Express*, 30 May 1975.

59 Quoted in Dennis Barker, 'Filmdom's Ruling Classes up in Arms', *Guardian*, 31 May 1974, 6.

60 James Thomas, 'Everyone's a Film Star in *Akenfield*', *Daily Express*, 17 August 1974; John Higgins, 'A Life Style in *Akenfield*', *The Times*, 9 October 1974, 11; Quentin Falk, '*Akenfield* Spans TV and Film', *CinemaTV Today*, 23 November 1974; Mike Bygrave, 'Why LWT Went into the Film Business', *Campaign*, 6 November 1974; 'The *Akenfield* Experiment', *CinemaTV Today*, 2 February 1975. See also Gareth Jones, '*Akenfield*', *Sight and Sound* 42, no. 4 (Autumn 1973): 192–3.

61 The Cinematograph Films (Distribution of Levy) Regulations 1970, S.I. 1970/1146 (1970), 2–3.

62 Veal to Shaw, 27 June 1974, BBC R78/1,123/1.

63 ITV had the rights to show *Akenfield* twice but it was not in fact repeated; the film-makers discuss the reasons for its commercial failure in the special features on the BFI's DVD and Blu-ray release.

64 In the week of transmission for *Brother, Can You Spare a Dime?*, Barry Took's 'Preview' column in *Radio Times* acknowledged the BBC's recent 'bumpy ride' from the film trade over *The Ruling Class* and quoted Gunnar Rugheimer: 'Films on TV generate a curiosity and an interest which expresses itself in the cinema box office' (*Radio Times*, 20 March 1975, 5). See also: Quentin Falk, 'After *Akenfield*... Brother, Can We Spare the Time?', *CinemaTV Today*, 15 February 1975; Philip Jordan, 'Attempt to Lift TV Film Blackout', *Guardian*, 5 March 1975; 'End of the Film Feud?', *Daily Mail*, 8 March 1975, 17; Martin Jackson, '£250,000 Film Bid by BBC', *Daily Mail*, 21 March 1975, 27; 'Feature Film Cash Boost from BBC', *CinemaTV Today*, 22 March 1975; Chris Petit, 'TV Spares a Dime', *Time Out*, 28 March–4 April 1975; 'BBC-TV Preems *Stavisky* before Theatrical Run', *Variety*, 20 May 1975, 3; 'BBC Showing 1970s Films', *The Stage and Television Today*, 17 July 1975, 11; 'New Movies – and There's No Need to Go out and Catch Them', *Daily Mail*, 17 July 1976, 13; Arthur Thirkell, 'Cinema Suicide!', *Daily Mirror*, 18 March 1977.

65 Quoted in Joan Bakewell, 'Review', *Radio Times*, 20 February 1975, 66. *Days of Hope* (1975) is a series of four feature-length films, produced by Garnett and directed by Ken Loach for the BBC.

66 'Film Men in Battle to Stop a TV Movie', *Daily Mirror*, 6 December 1975; 'Muddle over Showing of Three Year Old Film', *The Stage and Television Today*, 11 December 1975, 16.

67 Philip Jordan, 'BBC Ready to Invest in British Feature Films for Cinema' and 'Ruling Brass', *Guardian*, 1 June 1974, 4, 9; Sue Summers, 'BBC Will Back Movies, but – and It's a Big But...', *CinemaTV Today*, 8 June 1974; Sean Day-Lewis, 'BBC £30,000 Film Advances Scheme Laughable, Says MP', *Daily Telegraph*, 10 June

1974; Sean Day-Lewis, 'BBC Defends £300,000 Film Plan', *Daily Telegraph*, 12 June 1974; Sue Summers, 'More "New" Films on BBC', *CinemaTV Today*, 15 June 1974.

68 Rugheimer to Milne, 13 November 1974, BBC R78/1,123/1.

69 'BBC Makes a New Move into Feature Films', *CinemaTV Today*, 16 August 1975; 'BBC Makes First Risk Investment in Feature Film', *Broadcast*, 18 August 1975; Roderick Gilchrist, 'TV Goes into the Cinema', *Daily Mail*, 19 August 1975, 6; Sue Summers, 'BBC Honours Pre-production Cash Pledge for Features', *Screen International*, 22 January 1977, 4.

70 According to Penelope Houston, the inclusion of TV executives Milne and Tesler in 'what is basically a film industry enquiry is a realistic move, a recognition that they are all together in motion pictures' ('Working Party', *Sight and Sound* 44, no. 4 [Autumn 1975]: 219).

71 'Writers Want New 15-year Rule', *The Stage and Television Today*, 8 January 1976, 11.

72 F. Morris Dyson to Mary Lund, 27 October 1975, reproduced in IBA Paper 312(75), 17 November 1975, IBA/00014: 3997086.

73 John Freeman to Robert T. Armstrong, 14 November 1975, attached to IBA Paper 312(75).

74 See Sulik, *A Change of Tack*; Sue Summers, '*The Sailor's Return*', *Sight and Sound* 47, no. 1 (Winter 1977–78), 26; Simon Perry, 'Finance for Local Talent', *Sight and Sound* 49, no. 3 (Summer 1980): 144–8, and the accompanying production report on *Richard's Things* by Richard Combs, 149–51; Alvarado and Stewart, *Made for Television*; and Roddy Buxton, 'Cinema for Television', *Transdiffusion Broadcasting System*, 8 January 2008, at https://www.transdiffusion.org/2008/01/08/cinema_for_tele

75 'ATV Films Will Observe "Rule"', *The Stage and Television Today*, 4 September 1975.

76 Home Office, *Future of the British Film Industry: Report of the Prime Minister's Working Party, 1976*. For a detailed summary, see 'What That Report Means to Britain', *Screen International*, 17 January 1976.

77 Kenneth Gosling, 'Television Should Be Important New Source of Finance for Film Industry, Report Says', *The Times*, 15 January 1976, 4.

78 'Help for Film-makers', *Evening Standard*, 14 January 1976; Arthur Sandles, 'A Little TV Oil for UK Films', *Financial Times*, 17 January 1976, 13; Julian Graff, 'TV & the Film Industry', *Broadcast*, 19 January 1976, 6–7. See also David Gordon, 'British National Pictures Rides Again', *Sight and Sound* 45, no. 2 (Spring 1976): 81–82.

79 R.S. Camplin, 'Watch the Time Bombs among the Crumbs Warns CEA's Bob Camplin' (letter), *Screen International*, 24 January 1976, 4; 'CEA News', *Screen International*, 6 March 1976; 'Relph Speaks out on the Terry Report', *Screen International*, 14 February 1976, 1, 21; Michael Owen, 'How TV Could Save Cinema', *Evening Standard*, 27 October 1977; 'Carry on Hoping', *Guardian*, 15 January 1976, 13; Michael Klinger, 'No Mr Wilson! Don't Lower the "Films to TV Ban" to Three Years' (letter), *Screen International*, 28 February 1976; 'Film Exhibitors Want "Time Ban" on BBC and ITV', *The Stage and Television Today*, 12 February 1976, 13.

80 Quoted in 'Never Mind about the PM – What about His Film Working Party Report?', *Broadcast*, 22 March 1976, 6.

81 '5 Year Ban Will Stay Pledge CEA', *Screen International*, 10 April 1976, 1; 'Feature Films – the Countdown to Action', *The Stage and Television Today*, 14 October 1976, 12; 'Industry Demand for Fewer Films on TV', *Screen International*, 30 October 1976, 20; Rod Allen, 'Film Industry Committee Presents Canute-like Stance vs TV to Interim Action Committee', *Broadcast*, 1 November 1976, 6; 'Film Industry Committee Calls for Further Restrictions on TV's Use of Feature Films', *Broadcast*, 13 December 1976, 4; 'Levy on Films on TV', *Screen International*, 9 April 1977, 20; 'Government Aid Sought in Admissions Battle', *Screen International*, 23 April 1977, 4; 'Film Industry Pleads with Home Office to Limit Number and Time of Showings of Features on TV', *Broadcast*, 25 April 1977, 3; Sue Summers, '"Save UK Cinema" Plea to State', *Screen International*, 30 July 1977, 1, 36; 'Film Industry Committee Calls for Higher Prices and Massive Restrictions on TV Feature Film Transmissions', *Broadcast*, 1 August 1977, 3; Laurence Marks, 'Can Sir Harold Ride to the Rescue in Last Reel?', *Observer*, 2 October 1977, 3; '936 Features a Year on TV', *Film and Television Technician*, January 1978; Robert Bolt, et al., 'New Life for British Film Making' (letter), *The Times*, 10 April 1981, 17; Keith Nurse, 'TV's Cheap Buys Blamed for Crisis in Film Industry', *Daily Telegraph*, 2 July 1981; Gunnar Rugheimer, 'TV Film Levy' (letter), *The Times*, 28 October 1982, 11.

82 Sue Newsom-Smith, 'Wilson's Film Brief', *Screen International*, 31 July 1976, 1; 'At Long Last – Wilson's Team in Action', *Screen International*, 7 May 1977, 4, 54; Philip Jordan, 'Wilson Seeks the Film Successes', *Guardian*, 3 February 1978, 4; Penelope Houston, 'Interim Inaction', *Sight and Sound* 50, no. 3 (Summer 1981): 150.

83 Home Office, *Report of the Committee on the Future of Broadcasting*, 338.

84 Ibid, 339–40. See Penelope Houston, 'Annan and the Cinema', *Sight and Sound* 46, no. 3 (Summer 1977): 150–1.

85 Quoted in 'Cinemas Bar Films Co-financed by BBC', *Evening Standard*, 6 October 1978. Two other films named in this and other articles as beneficiaries of the scheme, *The Class of Miss MacMichael* (1978/11.05.1980) and *The Cat and the Canary* (1978/02.04.1983), were later dissociated from it.

86 'BBC Writs over Five Year "Bar"', *Screen International*, 11 November 1978, 1–2.

87 'CEA Lifts Bar on TV Sales of Foreign Pix', *Broadcast*, 20 February 1978, 8.

88 '*Stepford Wives* Set for TV Next Year', *Screen International*, 12 August 1978, 1; Elkan Allan, 'Screen Scoops', *Now*, 11 January 1980; Paul Donovan, 'Why TV films Are Getting Younger', *Daily Mail*, 12 January 1980, 20.

89 'Grade Breaks "Rule"', *Show Biz*, 23 March 1980.

90 Martin Jackson, *Media World*, June 1980. On Grade's problems with ITC's films, see Falk and Prince, *Last of a Kind*.

91 Quoted in *Observer*, 'Men and Matters: Grade Sets off TV Time Bomb', *Financial Times*, 1 April 1980.

92 Quoted in 'EMI Bust 5-year Bar', *Screen International*, 26 April 1980, 1.

93 Adrian Hodges, 'CEA Concedes to Three-year TV Bar', *Screen International*, 17 May 1980, 1.

94 William Phillips, 'Are Films TV's Fatal Attraction?', *Broadcast*, 20 May 1988, 20.

95 Paul Fox to Gordon Smith, 23 October 1967, BBC T16/72/6.

96 Ron Boyle, 'As the Real Life Drama behind Your Small Screen Christmas Movies Gets under Way', *Daily Express*, 24 December 1974.

97 Milne, 'Film Purchasing Policy'. In an earlier memo (2 January 1976, BBC R78/1,123/1), Milne had claimed the deal for *Kwai* involved £100,000 for three showings.

98 Martin Jackson, 'BBC Splashes £250,000 in Secret Deal for *Oliver!*', *Daily Mail*, 23 August 1976, 8; 'The Man Who Won't Let Oliver into Your Home', *Daily Mail*, 14 February 1976, 15.

99 Quoted in Martin Jackson, 'Cinema Ban on New Films for TV May Be Illegal', *Daily Telegraph*, 16 February 1976.

100 Quoted in Sue Summers, '*Oliver!* to TV – Who Could Really Ask for More?', *Screen International*, 28 August 1976, 4.

101 Minutes of IBA Meeting 198, 16 December 1976, IBA/01024: 3996310.

102 Milne, 'Film Purchasing Policy'.

103 Martin Jackson, 'TV Deal Has Gone with the Wind', *Daily Mail*, 2 September 1976, 3.

104 Leslie Halliwell, 'Film Purchase Matters', 15 March 1976, item 078(046), IBA/01024: 3996310. In this FPG agenda item, Halliwell claims that he has 'seen proof that the BBC paid £170,000 for one run of *The Wizard of Oz*'. Internal BBC documentation indicates that the film was bought in a package of thirty-five titles, most of them first runs. The FPG agenda includes details of another MGM package, including one run of *Seven Brides for Seven Brothers* (1954/31.12.1976) for £160,000, but this too went to the BBC.

105 Milne, 27 May 1977; Rugheimer, 1 June 1977 and 24 November 1977, BBC R78/1,123/1; Charles Catchpole, 'The Dear Deer Hunter', *Daily Mail*, 13 May 1980; Judith Judd, 'TV Chiefs Are up in the Air over *Gone with the Wind*', *Observer*, 7 December 1980, 2; Ivan Waterman, 'BBC in TV Film Deals Rumpus', *News of the World*, 14 December 1980.

106 Rugheimer, 28 November 1977, BBC R78/1,123/1.

107 Londoner's Diary, 'BBC Buys the *Can't Stop* Flop', *Evening Standard*, 30 October 1980; David Stevens, 'True Facts' (letter), *Evening Standard*, 3 November 1980.

108 Peter Plouvier to Ian Trethowan, 9 June 1978; Trethowan to Plouvier, 13 June 1978, BBC R78/1,123/1.

109 Milne, 12 June 1978, BBC R78/1,123/1.

110 Binder, *Halliwell's Horizon*, 168.

111 Michael Bunce, 21 June 1978, BBC R78/1,123/1.

112 Quoted in 'BBC "Paid $4m for a Film"', *The Times*, 12 June 1978, 2.

113 Rugheimer to Milne, 13 June 1978, BBC R78/1,123/1.

114 Patrick Stoddart, 'TV in Battle for *Gone with the Wind*', *Evening News*, 30 April 1980; Peter Fiddick, 'Millions Gone with the Wind', *Guardian*, 28 November 1980, 24; 'ITV Hit Back at BBC Film "Lunacy"', *Evening Standard*, 10 December 1980.

115 'Going, Going, Gone!', *Sun*, 16 October 1976; Tony Purnell, 'The Hit That's Too Pricey', *Sunday People*, 20 January 1980.

116 Fiddick, 'Millions Gone with the Wind'; Sean Day-Lewis, 'BBC Wants *Gone with the Wind*', *Daily Telegraph*, 22 November 1980; Arthur Sandles, 'BBC Bids £3.6m for *Gone with the Wind* Package', *Financial Times*, 22 November 1980, 3.

117 'BBC Money Goes with the Wind', *Broadcast*, 1 December 1980, 8.

118 James Murray, 'Who Really Wins in the Great Movie War?', *Daily Express*, 6 December 1980.

119 Quoted in Judith Judd, 'TV Chiefs Are up in the Air', and Murray, 'Who Really Wins in the Great Movie War?'

120 Murray, 'Who Really Wins in the Great Movie War?'

121 Kenneth Gosling, 'BBC Chief Attacks High ITV Film Bids', *The Times*, 10 December 1980, 4; 'ITV Denies Profligacy in Programme Deals', *The Times*, 11 December 1980, 4.

122 Quoted in Waterman, 'BBC in TV Film Deals Rumpus'.

123 Quoted in 'Just as You Thought It Was Safe to Bid Again', *Broadcast*, 2 February 1981, 4.

124 Peter Lennon, 'Going... Going... Gone with the Wind', *Sunday Times*, 8 February 1981, 13. For an alternative account of the *Jaws* and *Gone with the Wind* auctions, see Binder, *Halliwell's Horizon*, 167–72.

125 Quoted in 'Halliwell's Screen Test', *Yorkshire Post*, 19 December 1981.

126 Quoted in Doug Gardner, 'The Not-so-festive Star War', *Wolverhampton Express and Star*, 24 December 1981.

127 Peter Knight, '*Gone with the Wind* Film Deal Costs BBC £4.4m', *Daily Telegraph*, 3 February 1981.

128 Author's interview, 3 September 2012.

Part Two

Programming and Regulation

CHAPTER 7

Saturday Night and Sunday Afternoon – Scheduling Films on Television

We continue to exploit this area of programming to a limited extent only, but in a manner that we think makes feature films even more enjoyable and meaningful to the viewer and which shows respect for the work itself, by presenting them with the framework or context of their original production (e.g. The Vintage Years of Hollywood) and/or to a given presentation theme (e.g. British Film Comedy: The Thriller: High Adventure). This, in preference to the indiscriminate presentation of what might otherwise be described as 'old movies'.

(Memo, Gordon Smith to Paul Fox, 2 January 1968, BBC T16/72/6)

Most people must now see more films on television than they do in the cinema. And on television there is far more of a structure to be found in the scheduling of films than there ever was in the haphazard programming of the cinema circuits.

(Edward Buscombe, *Screen Pamphlet* 1: *Films on TV*, 24)

Slots, Strands, Series and Seasons

The first part of this book was largely concerned with the changing historical relationships between the broadcasting organisations and the various factions of the film industry, particularly regarding the acquisition of films for broadcast. The second half now focuses more specifically on the uses made of films, through discussion of their 'placing' in the schedules. It also examines the broadcasters' internal structures and the regulatory mechanisms that shaped and controlled such uses. I begin by tracing some patterns in film programming by the BBC and then by ITV, for which it will be useful first to define four common terms.

Slot means a particular time or time band within the daily schedules, most often one that is regularly devoted to a particular programme or type of programme. *Strand* is a general term for the grouping of (in this instance) films, which can embrace either or both of the remaining two, more specific categories. *Series* indicates a run of films, usually placed in a particular time slot and given an umbrella title, which may or may not have common features to link them beyond the simple fact of their appearing in a given slot. *Season* usually implies a more specific thematic link among a group of films: common factors such as genre, star, director, studio or country. Confusion may arise because in practice these four terms tend to be used interchangeably. Whereas 'slot' and 'strand' more often appear in broadcasters' internal communications than in the public sphere, 'series' and 'season' are commonly used in listings magazines, publicity materials and on-air announcements to brand a particular group of films for promotional purposes.

It is also worth noting two other applications of the term 'season' in television circles, which muddy the waters still further. One is the common-or-garden meaning of the word: the quarterly periods into which the broadcasting year is divided. The autumn, as the major launch pad for new shows, lasts seventeen weeks, including Christmas week. The UK TV autumn season now begins in early September (until about 1968 it was the end of September). The winter season begins in the first week of the New Year and the spring season starts around Easter. Both the latter two seasons typically last thirteen weeks; the summer season, traditionally the least prestigious and often dominated by a mixture of repeats and sporting events, usually lasts nine weeks, ending with the August Bank Holiday week. The significance of these periods for film programming is that film strands were often specific to particular quarters; thus, a new quarterly *season* might see the start of one or more new film *strands* or *series*.

The second common use of 'season' is specifically in relation to episodic television, but has in the past been used differently by American and British broadcasters. US networks refer to successive annual runs of a particular *series* (show) as *seasons*: thus, a given show has Season 1, Season 2 and so on. British television has traditionally used 'series' to mean *both* the episodic show itself *and* successive sequential runs of that show; more recently, however, the American usage of 'season' has been increasingly adopted in the UK to distinguish between these two things. In relation to films on television, therefore, we may say that a *strand* of films placed in a particular time *slot* forms a *series*, often recognisable as such by being billed under an umbrella title used in programme listings, and that this series may run to several *seasons* appearing at periodic intervals. It was also common for a series in a given slot to incorporate mini-seasons on a particular theme over several weeks.

However they were described, the act of regularly placing films at or around the same times on the same days, with umbrella titles to mark them out, in on-screen billing and in press listings, as a distinct type of programming, evinced a commitment on the part of the broadcasters to integrate feature films fully into the schedules. Rather than being used as mere time-fillers or occasional special events, they became part of the standard bill of fare alongside other regular types of show, thus shaping viewers' expectations of what a particular day on air would offer.

BBC Film Scheduling

In January 1958, the BBC for the first time began scheduling films in a named evening slot, thus forming a regular series. 'The Saturday Film', mainly showcasing titles from the recently-acquired RKO package (see Chapter 3), alternated fortnightly with original drama productions. Gradually, over the next few years, BBC schedulers added other regular film strands. A Sunday afternoon slot, featuring mostly repeats, was introduced in October 1959; after a year, *Radio Times* began billing films shown at this time under the title 'Film Matinée', a rubric that lasted (with periodic breaks, often for film series under different titles) until as late as April 1990. A Sunday evening slot, billed as 'The Sunday Film', was introduced in April 1961, alternating, like its Saturday equivalent (then on temporary hiatus), with single plays. Initially this strand lasted only one season before plays returned full-time from September 1961. But when a new season of 'The Saturday Film' began that same month it was now on a weekly rather than a fortnightly basis as previously.

It was the 1964–65 programme year that really set the pattern for the BBC's placing of feature films for the next two decades and beyond. Paul Fox, Controller of BBC1 from 1967 to 1973, recalled: 'The man who looked after films at that time was the lovely Gordon Smith. A little film department was born, separate from the department that was shooting films. Gordon was put in charge of it because he knew something about films – so he said. And he did, actually!'[1] As Head of Purchased Programmes, Smith led a team that also included Jeff Edwards, David Francis, Bill Gilbert, Alan Howden, Peggy Miller, Dora Nirva and Daphne Turrell, each of whom negotiated purchases, proposed programming ideas to channel controllers and scheduled film strands, as well as writing promotional blurb and billing copy to appear in *Radio Times*.[2] Following Smith's retirement in 1970, former Controller of Programmes Kenneth Adam wrote:

It is because of him that almost always nowadays, BBC films are better than ITV's.

Gordon Smith did much more than that, because he happens to be a 'cineaste' and historian as well.

Movies are an important part of our past, but, jumbled together out of any old stable at any old time, they cannot have the same impact or meaning for the new generation. ...

With great care and patience, Smith for years combed through his library as it grew, purposefully discarding the junk to offpeak hours, and providing umbrella titles and successive weekly showings that really were sequential.

He had the courage to see there is no inevitable virtue in newness, and often a special charm in the dated. ... It is only the snobs who do not enjoy movies on TV, but we, with our simple pleasures, do need a guiding hand.[3]

The BBC exploited thematic series to a far greater degree than the ITV companies; in the early years this may have been due to the coordination of film scheduling by Smith. Regular slots at key points throughout the week, not just the now-familiar Saturday nights and Sunday afternoons, allowed frequent opportunities for the sequential groupings of films, often around a particular linking attribute. 'Presentation themes' were determined partly by Smith's perception of their suitability for particular days and nights of the week. According to Paul Fox, 'He knew what sort of film would work on a Sunday evening, or would work on a Tuesday evening or late at night. He was usually right – the great thing about Gordon was that he had good taste.'[4]

Saturdays on BBC1 were typically the province of action and adventure films: the main series rubrics Smith introduced here were 'The Western', 'High Adventure' and 'The Saturday Thriller'. Launched in 1965, 1966 and 1967, respectively, their first seasons each ran for over a year with no more than a week's break at a time. Thereafter these series tended to alternate at shorter intervals. Adventure films were also a frequent choice for Sunday afternoons or midweek evenings, as were Westerns for early Friday evenings and Saturday afternoons. Sunday evenings were the occasion for weightier material, with major premieres of prestige films, often grouped around particular stars (indeed, 'The Great Stars' began a long run in 1968 – see Figure 7.1) or genres, such as British war films in 1970 and 1975. A notable series of 'All Time Greats', including many older titles receiving their first transmission on the BBC after being shown previously by ITV, ran at peak-time on Sunday evenings for thirty-one weeks in 1972–73.

For early weekday evenings, before the watershed marked by the evening news, more lightweight fare was favoured. Comedies (most often British) and family films were a frequent choice for Tuesdays or Wednesdays, along with more action-adventure. 'The Love Affair' also had a long run from 1966. More adult attractions were scheduled for later in the evening, either immediately following the main news bulletin or at the end of the night, before closedown. One series of 'major films made in the 60s for adult audiences', beginning in September 1973, occupied a new, post-news slot on Mondays; one year later, it became known simply as 'The Monday Film'. Typically showing more recent films unsuitable for an earlier hour, this strand ran, with occasional breaks, until 1987.

The advent of BBC2 in April 1964 presented opportunities for more specialised film choices than on BBC1. The new channel was described as 'a television equivalent of the Third Programme' (that is, the future Radio 3), able to provide a more rarefied diet by addressing upmarket, intellectual audiences.[5] Programming was designed to be complementary to BBC1 and feature films were rarely scheduled against one another; if both channels presented films on a given evening, interlocking schedule 'junctions' would allow a viewer to switch over directly from one channel's film to the other's, so that they didn't miss either the end of the earlier film or the start of the next.

The first regular film strand on the new channel was called 'Cinema 625' in reference to the 625 lines of resolution that made BBC2 a higher-definition service than BBC1 or ITV. This series was used mainly to present foreign-language films, a function BBC2 eventually took over almost entirely from BBC1 (see the next chapter), along with select British and American titles. But the channel really made its mark with 'The Vintage Years of Hollywood', showcasing classics and popular hits of the 1930s and 1940s. The vast majority of these were drawn from the Paramount package that the BBC had purchased from MCA in 1964 (see Chapter 4). It was claimed in the press that this package had been specifically acquired to help BBC2 boost its disappointing early viewing figures.[6] If so,

Figure 7.1 BBC1's Sunday-night series of mini-seasons, 'The Great Stars', included a run of three Clark Gable films in September 1971. *Radio Times* © Immediate Media Co.

it worked: the initial film in the series, Cecil B. De Mille's *Reap the Wild Wind* (1942/10.11.1964), gave the channel the single highest audience rating of its first year of operation.[7]

'Vintage Years' ran on midweek evenings for nearly two years. In October 1966, it was replaced by 'The Hollywood Musical'. This series also drew on the pre-1949 Paramount library, along with the vaults of other major studios, including MGM, the company most closely associated with the genre. Its second season was launched in the inaugural week of colour broadcasts with *Singin' in the Rain* (1952/06.12.1967). Nearly two dozen more seasons of musicals followed over the next two decades, more often on BBC2 than BBC1, perhaps in recognition of what may have been perceived as their specialised appeal. In the 1970s, a midweek evening slot around 9.00pm (periodically occupying Tuesday, Wednesday or Thursday) often presented short themed seasons or assorted major films without thematic portfolio.

Groups of films built around particular directors, writers or even studios were also more likely to be found on BBC2, but the first of many tributes to Alfred Hitchcock appeared on the main channel in 1969. An American series of director biographies, *The Men Who Made the Movies*, prompted eight accompanying film seasons between 1975 and 1977, beginning with Hitchcock (again on BBC1) and also including, on BBC2, Howard Hawks, William Wellman, Frank Capra, George Cukor, Raoul Walsh, King Vidor and Vincente Minnelli. Three seasons of a home-produced documentary series, *The Hollywood Greats*, written and presented by Barry Norman, were followed in 1980 by a single season of *The British Greats*; these were linked to film screenings on BBC1. But most film series needed no programme tie-ins to justify themselves. Among the stars accorded multiple retrospectives from the late 1960s to the end of the 1980s were Bette Davis, Elvis Presley, John Wayne (seven seasons apiece), Bob Hope (six), Humphrey Bogart and Greta Garbo (five each). Such series often carried generic titles identifying the nature of their subjects' appeal: 'Wayne in Action', 'Laugh with Hope', 'Garbo the Great' and so on.

BBC2 also created new strands at weekends. A Saturday matinee slot, offering an alternative to afternoon sport on both BBC1 and ITV, began in January 1966, most often presenting repeats of films previously shown in evening slots. From November 1968, this strand was known as 'Saturday Cinema', running under that title (again with occasional breaks) until 1990; but even today, Saturday film matinees remain a staple of BBC2 programming. From August 1966, Saturday late nights were occupied by 'Midnight Movie'. This was promoted as the first programme slot on British television scheduled to run into the early hours of the morning, though the films usually started slightly before rather than after midnight. Titles chosen for this series were often crime thrillers and melodramas, but from 1975 onwards a season of horror double bills in summer months became beloved of a generation of genre fans (see Chapter 10). Late Sunday-night film strands, introduced in April 1971, typically offered more challenging fare than in peak-time slots, often grouped in themed seasons.

In early 1978, Director of Television Alasdair Milne explained to the BBC's Board of Governors the rationale behind the Corporation's then-current film strands, based on the prevailing economic situation as well as programming needs:

The principal outlet for those feature films that can be shown before 9.00pm is at the moment the Sunday night placing on BBC1, starting at 8.15pm. BBC1 has a second, lesser opportunity to show such films starting at c.7.20pm on a Friday. The prime BBC2 placing for films suitable for showing after 9.00pm is currently the 9.25pm placing on a Monday evening. The late film placing on Friday starting at c.11.20pm provides a second opportunity, which at the moment is generally used for good re-runs.

BBC2 can only just afford one strand of new feature films. This is the 'Screen 2' placing on a Sunday evening starting at c.10.20pm. This strand has lately been maintained by including in it more off-beat films than would normally be transmitted on BBC1. Some of these can subsequently be shown for a second time on BBC1's late night Friday placing. In future BBC2 may have to rely more on re-runs for this strand. However, for other placings it continues to do well by scouring the market for important feature films in foreign languages. Some of these were made with English sub-titles already; some have benefitted by having English sub-titles added. Some have available their own dubbed English versions. Others require dubbing and success depends on how well this task is carried out.[8]

Because films were usually acquired for a number of screenings (typically two, three or four over a hire period of five or seven years), repeat transmissions allowed for some variation in the way they were programmed. Premieres of major films would typically be given a peak-time evening slot, though it was not at all unknown for first transmissions to appear in afternoon or late-night slots. This was true also of the first BBC showings of films previously screened by ITV; BBC scheduling policy seems to have been to wipe the slate clean and pretend that the ITV transmissions had never happened, whereas at ITV films that had previously been shown on the BBC would normally be relegated to off-peak slots unless they were particularly important titles. Many films deemed to be of lesser importance were transmitted once only, even when rights were held for more. But repeat screenings would normally be at a different time, on a different day or on a different channel from the first, partly in order to reach audiences with different viewing habits. This meant, of course, that films would normally appear in several different programme strands over their hire period, each of which might emphasise a different facet. To take but one example, Hitchcock's *Saboteur* (1942/24.05.1967) was shown first in BBC2's 'The Vintage Years of Hollywood' series, starting at 9.05pm on a Wednesday; secondly in BBC1's 'The Saturday Thriller', at 8.35pm on 20 April 1968; and thirdly in BBC1's 'The Films of Alfred Hitchcock', at 10.50pm on Friday, 25 July 1969.

ITV Film Scheduling

At ITV, from its inception, films tended to be programmed locally rather than nationally networked. Nevertheless, there were recurrent patterns across all the companies so that, despite regional variations in both series titles and the films shown, the days and time slots chosen for film placings were often the same. Indeed, commercial stations got into the habit of scheduling weekly, named film strands some two years before the BBC did. Typically these slots included Saturday and/or Sunday evenings and Sunday afternoons. Common umbrella titles in the 1950s and early 1960s included 'Film Festival', 'The Film Show', 'Great Movies of Our Time' and 'Movietime'. Often series titles evoked a theatrical experience, one that was rapidly disappearing: 'All Our Yesterdays', 'First House Friday', 'Seat in the Circle' and 'Your Seat in the Stalls'. Others emphasised the domestic environment: 'Fireside Cinema', 'Fireside Film Show' and 'Fireside Hour'. As old films became commonplace and schedules prone to repeats, newness to television itself was often used as a promotional tool, as in 'Film Premiere', 'First Time on TV' and later even 'First Time on TV Western'.

From 1964, as the number of films available for broadcast increased, the weeknights most often chosen were Tuesdays, Thursdays and Fridays, especially between 7.00pm and 9.00pm. Some ITV companies also scheduled late-night screenings at around 10.30pm or later, following the networked news, especially on Mondays and Fridays. Statistically, the number of cinema films shown by ITV and the proportion of broadcasting time that they occupied peaked in the early 1970s, when it was common to find companies showing a feature film on five evenings per week (see Appendix A2.2). Following deregulation of broadcasting hours in 1972, most companies also scheduled at least one weekday matinee, again typically on a Monday or Friday, aimed at housewives and shift-workers. In holiday weeks, weekday morning films might be added. Regular Saturday-morning films, with younger viewers in mind, were also introduced at this time, though the smallest companies (such as Channel) often skipped morning broadcasts altogether. By this time, however, American made-for-TV movies were increasingly being programmed in place of theatrical features.

Films were chosen by the executive responsible for them at each station. The selection varied greatly from company to company, based either on the tastes of particular schedulers or, more likely, on their estimation of local audiences' interests. There were observable trends at each station and there was wide variance in both the number and the types of films shown. Granada, for instance, being network film buyer Leslie Halliwell's own patch, scheduled more than any other company and was more likely to show older titles from the 1930s and 1940s, many of them acquired only for local rather than network use. These were often arranged in themed series, a concept that Halliwell pioneered at ITV and understood better than most of his counterparts at other stations. This is reflected in the often quirky series titles he chose, again evocative of cinema nostalgia: 'Tuppenny Rush' (children's matinees); 'Famous Monsters' (horror films); 'And the Villain Is...' (mystery thrillers); 'Close Encounters of Various Kinds' (science fiction); and, most distinctively, 'Red Roses Every Night' (recreating cinema programmes redolent of World War Two).

Among the other companies, HTV and Southern Television were the most adventurous, both presenting seasons of art-house and experimental films (see Chapter 8). Scottish Television (STV) and Ulster Television were the most conservative. STV's staff were more likely than most to object to the sexual content of films and programmes originated south of the border. Ulster scheduled films in evening slots that the rest of the network – even Granada – would have consigned to the daytime, such as vintage British comedies starring Arthur Askey or the Crazy Gang. The Northern Irish contractor also repeated films more often, with shorter intervals between the repeats than any other company. Some stations linked up to share broadcasts of particular films, especially in off-peak slots. Yorkshire, Tyne Tees and Border most often joined forces in this way for weekday matinees (see Table 7.1 for a snapshot of scheduling trends in the Yorkshire region from August–November 1973), while Channel generally shared Westward's film output along with other scheduled programmes.

The (mostly male) company bookers seemed more comfortable with action-adventure fare than with musicals, which rarely appeared in ITV schedules. Of the 300 or so films that ITV acquired from MGM in the 1960s and early 1970s, only a handful were 'tuners' and they were among the titles least often selected for transmission. Among the most frequently screened MGM films were the costume epics *Ivanhoe* (1952/27.06.1970), *Knights of the Round Table* (1953/29.08.1970) and *The Adventures*

Table 7.1 Age, country of origin and types of films shown on television, 4 August–2 November 1973.

Age of Films Shown on Television		
	BBC	ITV (Yorkshire)
Pre-1939	17	2
1940–1949	19	13
1950–1959	26	31
1960–1969	37	54
1970 on	1	0
Country of Origin of Films Shown on Television		
	BBC	ITV (Yorkshire)
Great Britain	21	30
United States	74	70
Other Countries	5	0
Types of Films Shown on Television		
	BBC	ITV (Yorkshire)
Comedy	22	14
Drama	28	19
Adventure Drama	4	14
Crime and Melodrama	9	16
Musicals	12	7
Westerns	15	12
War	7	7
Horror	3	11

Note: All figures are percentages.

Source: 'Appeal of Old Films Keeps Growing', *The Stage and Television Today*, 29 December 1973, 10.

of Quentin Durward (1955/08.08.1970), transmitted thirty-six, thirty-four and thirty-one times respectively over their seven-year hire periods. By contrast, the musicals *Easter Parade* (1948/08.04.1965), *On the Town* (1949/22.03.1966) and *An American in Paris* (1951/29.08.1970) were transmitted seventeen, eleven and nineteen times respectively, missing out some stations altogether. It may have helped that the epics were also classed as British productions: whereas American films rarely had more than one or two screenings each per station, British films – which were in shorter supply – often had three, four or even more transmissions each.

Network scheduling was the province of the Programme Controllers' Group, which included representatives from each of the Big Five companies. Networking of films was reserved for special occasions such as Christmas and other bank holidays (sometimes not even then) or for strategic counter-programming, such as competition for the annual Royal Variety Performance, which alternated between BBC1 and ITV biennially. Thus, the network offered *Duel in the Sun* (1946/24.11.1968), *South Pacific* (1958/05.11.1972) and *The Professionals* (1966/24.11.1974) as alternatives to the three-hour show in those years when it was hosted by BBC1. The last-named was the first occasion on which any Royal Variety Performance had failed to top the ratings. Rather than crowing, as might be expected, ITV staff sounded almost guilty at having toppled a TV origination with a cinema film:

> 'Those of us who care for variety,' said one senior executive in charge of light entertainment output, 'must be disturbed that a bill of very good, established acts could be disturbed that far by a film. ... We suspected, of course, that they would like the film, but obviously I cannot be too pleased that they liked it that much.'[9]

A growing concern in the latter half of the 1970s and after was the increasing shortage of first-run films suitable for peak-time. When blockbusters became available to television it was particularly important to take full advantage of them. From 1974 onwards, therefore, networking and part-networking became more frequent, as the companies made greater efforts to coordinate schedules and share transmissions of the few 'big' and 'new' films now available. Networking allowed the coordination of publicity and promotion for major films, on air, in the national press and in ITV's programme journal *TVTimes*. When the opportunity arose, the magazine could run tie-in articles and cover stories on films as well as splash out on elaborately illustrated listings displays. A case in point is *Spartacus* (1960/20.10.1973). Despite its importance, the all-star, three-hour epic was not fully networked on its first ITV transmission. Instead, it was shown regionally on four separate dates, three of them involving part-networking, as follows:

20 October 1973: LWT, Granada, HTV, Southern, Anglia, Grampian
12 January 1974: Yorkshire, Tyne Tees, Border
23 March 1974: ATV, STV, Westward, Channel
6 April 1974: Ulster

Because these were not national showings, *TV Times* was unable to devote much space to the film on the listings pages of its regional editions and the broadcasts did not appear in the combined national ratings chart. The result, according to Halliwell, was 'a waste of a good deal of money'.[10] However, for its second run, on Saturday, 7 August 1976, *Spartacus* was fully networked. *TV Times* ran background articles on star/producer Kirk Douglas and co-star Peter Ustinov, featured Douglas on the cover and used a three-quarter-page programme listing with a colour illustration, the largest page display the magazine had ever used for a film (see Figure 7.2). The film was also trailed on air several weeks in advance, along with other highlights of the summer season, which was dominated by blockbuster films. On this occasion, *Spartacus* just scraped into the JICTAR ratings top twenty for the week; but according to BBC Audience Research, it gained the largest audience of any programme shown on any channel that month, with an estimated 15 million viewers.[11] Either way, networking helped the film to make an impact through coordinated promotion.

The same year, 1976, the BBC's Alasdair Milne attempted to rationalise his rivals' strategy of scheduling networked films to skew the ratings:

> As far as we can judge, ITV are placing the Bond and other big films to 'compensate' for big BBC audiences upsetting the advertising average for given weeks – *The Guns of Navarone* being placed on the night after the Eurovision Song Contest, *From Russia with Love* on the day after the FA Cup Final, the repeat of *Dr No* to be placed on the opening night of the Olympic Games.[12]

As they informed programming choices and helped shape scheduling decisions, the next section explains methods of audience research and the gathering of viewing figures in relation to films.

Ratings and Audience Research

Although the BBC had been conducting research on public response to its television output since before the war, data on viewing patterns did not become a matter of wide trade or public interest until the advent of competition. Besides the question of who was watching what, it was the presence of commercial breaks on ITV that made trade knowledge of viewing figures imperative. The potential number of viewers determined the rate cards set by the companies, whose charges for carrying commercials varied greatly depending on the day and time of transmission and the catchment of a particular region. Thus, an advertisement at peak-time on a Sunday evening in London would be charged at a higher rate than one during a weekday afternoon in the North East. To be sure that they were getting value for money, buyers of ad space wanted to know how many people were watching at the exact time their commercials went out, and for that they needed to know about the relative popularity of the programmes into which ads were inserted.

Figure 7.2a–b *TVTimes*'s spectacular promotion for the networked repeat of *Spartacus* (1960) on 7 August 1976 included a full-colour, three-quarter-page illustrated listing. *TVTimes* © Future Publishing Ltd.

Even before the first ITV stations began broadcasting in September 1955, research companies were pitching their services to broadcasters and advertisers. There were three main contenders: Television Audience Measurement Ltd (TAM), part of the Attwood Group of Companies; the A.C. Nielsen Company, an overseas branch of the main supplier of ratings information to US television; and the British Institute of Public Opinion, which produced the Gallup Poll. The systems of audience monitoring offered by both TAM and Nielsen were based on data from meters installed in television receivers, which recorded on paper tape data about the station to which the TV set was tuned at any given moment (and indeed whether it was turned on at all). This information was supplemented by a 'viewing diary', listing each family member's viewing activity, to be completed by a householder and mailed weekly to the research service along with the TV tape recording. Gallup's method was instead based on 'assisted recall', which involved conducting interviews with members of the public about what they had watched the day before.[13] BBC Audience Research used an approach similar to Gallup's, and until 1981 the Corporation continued to rely on its own in-house unit to gather both quantitative and qualitative information on viewership rather than subscribe to any of the competing alternatives.

For several years, broadcasting trade papers printed, often side by side, top-ten charts from both TAM and Nielsen. Both used their metered samples to estimate the total number of homes viewing, whether nationally or in a particular region. Despite their similar methods, the companies produced datasets with considerable differences between them. Feature films rarely appeared in TAM charts but did so more often in Nielsen's. However, in 1959 the two companies merged to form United Broadcast Audience Research Ltd, a joint venture which continued to operate as TAM. For the next nine years, this remained the principal source used by ITV companies, the advertising industry and broadcasting journals for 'official' audience data, published weekly (albeit a fortnight after the week being reported on). In 1961, a governing body, the Joint Industry Committee for Audience Research (JICTAR), was formed to represent the interests of advertisers, agencies and commercial broadcasters. BBC Audience Research released its own figures to the press and the discrepancies with TAM's were often both marked and widely remarked-upon.

These discrepancies can be attributed to a number of different factors. TAM confined its metering to households with access to both BBC and ITV transmissions (older sets had to be converted to receive the new services, including BBC2 when it arrived); BBC-only homes were excluded, so the total audience for BBC programmes was likely to be under-estimated. BBC Audience Research made no such discrimination, interviewing viewers from all types of household and researching all programme sources. BBC researchers asked interviewees how much of a programme they had watched and only reported their reactions when at least half of it had been viewed; whereas TAM's meters recorded data minute by minute so that precise use of the TV set could be monitored. This included whether, for example, it remained tuned to a given channel throughout a particular programme or only for parts of it, and exactly when the channel was changed. But as BBC representatives often pointed out, TAMmeters (*sic*) recorded the status of the TV set but not whether anyone was actually watching a programme; published data did not show how much of a programme had been viewed. Although the meter recordings were supplemented by viewing diaries, these too were an imperfect way of measuring attention, as Gallup's Doctor Durant had explained:

> A sudden swoop on them would discover a number not up to date. They tend to get completed at the end of the recording period, so that reliance upon memory proves to be much greater in practice than with aided recall. Filling in the columns the diarist is anxious to oblige and so inflates the information.[14]

Because BBC interviewers asked about programmes viewed the day before, they were drawing on fresh recollection. On the other hand, as TAM's defenders often noted, because Corporation researchers identified themselves as such, interviewees might be tempted to claim more loyalty to BBC programmes in order to appear 'helpful'; thus the BBC's information could be 'inflated' too.

There were also differences in the number of people surveyed, hence questions about the statistical representativeness of the samples. According to one 1959 report, TAM and Nielsen (when they were still separate) each reported on a total of 600 homes, whereas BBC research panels interviewed 4,400 people daily.[15] Two years later, it was reported that TAM now monitored 1,000 TV homes, though company owner Bedford Attwood admitted that this was still a 'small sample'.[16]

In 1968, when the ITV system was refreshed with the start of new regional franchises, the provider of ratings services also changed. JICTAR dropped TAM's contract and appointed TV Ratings, a company operated by Audits of Great Britain (AGB), effective from 30 July 1968. The new system operated along lines similar to TAM, albeit using a larger sample: 2,650 homes, the number in each region being roughly proportionate to its share of viewers for the country as a whole. Thus, JICTAR (as the service was usually referred to, rather than AGB or TV Ratings) monitored '350 homes in London, 300 homes each in Midlands, Lancashire and Yorkshire, and 200 homes in each of the next five regions', with 100 homes in the next four.[17] These households were said to provide a regular sample of 7,790 individuals.[18] According to the BBC at this time, its own researchers interviewed 2,250 people daily (the interviewees changing each day). The Corporation limited its research to the hours when both BBC and ITV services were on air (about 47 hours weekly), whereas JICTAR tracked all output over about 80 hours weekly.[19]

JICTAR estimated the number of homes tuned in until the week ending 7 August 1977, after which it estimated individual viewers – as did the BBC. However, major discrepancies remained between BBC figures and JICTAR's. Both organisations claimed that their method was appropriate to the purposes for which it was used; it was their purposes that differed, hence their methods. The BBC stated:

'The systems inevitably produce apparently divergent results – indeed it may be said that they are deliberately designed to do so, since they set out to measure different things.'[20] Reporting JICTAR's latest figures, the journal *Television* put it this way: 'In reality, both organisations are providing answers to two different questions. The BBC provides "percentage audience shares" in terms of the average individual, whilst JICTAR provides "percentage audience shares" in terms of the average household viewing.'[21] Put yet another way, the BBC monitored individuals whereas JICTAR monitored households – or TV sets. Nevertheless, both provided estimates of the likely size of audience for particular programmes. And it was here that the discrepancies became most embarrassingly apparent.

In July 1976, the BBC reported that the film *Bonnie and Clyde* (1967/05.07.1976) was the most-watched programme of the month, with an audience of 18.5 million viewers (see Figure 7.3). But JICTAR placed it only fifth for its week of broadcast, seen in 6.2 million homes – equivalent to about two-thirds as many viewers as the BBC estimated. Adding fuel, the Corporation also claimed that audiences throughout the month watched in a ratio of 63 per cent for the BBC to 37 per cent for ITV, giving it 'the highest monthly lead since ITV started 21 years ago'. JICTAR, on the other hand, reported a straight 50:50 split between the BBC and ITV, with 41 per cent watching BBC1 and 9 per cent watching BBC2.[22] Commented one newspaper: 'Clearly the differences between the two claims are so considerable as to make any comparisons worthless.'[23] Such massive differences had wider implications too. According to *Broadcast*, 'whereas JICTAR believes that the average British viewer spends a colossal 32.31 hours a week in front of

Figure 7.3 To mark the American Bicentennial in July 1976, BBC1 showed a week of Hollywood classics, including the TV premiere of *Bonnie and Clyde* (1967), under the rubric 'The Great American Picture Show'. *Radio Times* © Immediate Media Co. Artwork © Ralph Steadman.

the box, the BBC thinks that the average viewer only spends 15.90 hours a week watching TV – or almost exactly half of the JICTAR estimate'.[24]

The different methods of audience measurement used by the BBC and JICTAR may have had inbuilt biases, but not necessarily in favour of one channel over another. A 1979 report commissioned by the IBA argued that JICTAR's method of recording the number of viewers for each quarter-hour and then averaging the numbers to arrive at the audiences for particular programmes effectively discriminated against longer programmes (such as feature films) in favour of shorter ones. Viewers might not stay with a long programme for the whole of its length but might see substantial parts of it; the sum of viewers seeing any part of the programme would thus be greater than the number watching at any one time, but this would not be reflected in JICTAR figures. The BBC's method of asking viewers what they had watched typically resulted in higher numbers than JICTAR's, but this was not necessarily an exaggeration if it reflected the cumulative number of viewers tuning in throughout a show, rather than the number at a given moment.[25]

Minute-by-minute tracking did have its advantages, although it did not always show that viewers behaved as the ITV companies might have hoped. 'BBC films tend to generate more audience loyalty than those shown by ITV', reported *Campaign* in 1970. 'On Tuesday, November 17, for example, the ITV film, which had a 20 minute start on the BBC film, lost a large part of its audience once the BBC film started at 7.30pm.'[26] In this case, the BBC film was *633 Squadron* (1964/17.11.1970), watched in 8.2 million homes, according to JICTAR, or by 20.5 million people, according to the BBC. Either way, this was the Corporation's largest audience for a feature film to date and the second highest for any channel. Local films were ITV's main opposition that night.

Kine Weekly's TV columnist Tony Gruner remarked on the increasing popularity of films on television in the early 1970s, with the BBC in particular regularly scoring big audiences for them. Three features made it into the Top Twenty ratings for the week ending 6 June 1971, with Hitchcock's *The Birds* (1963/06.06.1971) placing first. This was only the third time that the national chart had been topped by a film; there was not to be another until three years later. Gruner also recognised the BBC's superior film scheduling: 'Of the fifteen [ITV] companies, only two, who shall be nameless, are successfully able to cope and compete with the BBC in feature film slotting.'[27] Five years later, save for occasional networked blockbusters, which achieved higher viewing figures than ever, ITV films were struggling to win audiences away from regular programming. *Television Today* reported in 1976 that 'for the week ended September 26, not one feature film appeared among the top ten titles in any ITV region; a phenomenon which, if repeated too often, could cast doubts upon the validity of the claim that the films are there because they are what the viewer wants'.[28]

From collating and interpreting ratings, it was only a short step to anticipating and trying to predict them. This was the function of a system called Television Audience Programme Evaluation (TAPE), the creation of former advertising executive Mike Firman. Firman built his forecasting system, used to predict ratings for all programmes, initially by tracking patterns in the popularity of films across different ITV stations. He explained:

> it suddenly hit me that if you looked up the ratings of old feature films which had already been shown in one area and balanced these with the factors of the programmes that led into them and the other programmes that were playing against them, maybe there was some formula which could enable us to know how they would do in areas where they hadn't yet played.

By comparing stars, genres and story elements against actual ratings, Firman was able to compute the likely audience appeal of films and grade them accordingly. Elkan Allan reported for the *Sunday Times Magazine*:

> When film played against film, as they did on Sunday nights, by going over old TAM records for nine areas, he [Firman] was able to set Alan Ladd against William Holden; then Burt Lancaster against Alan Ladd; then William Holden against Burt Lancaster and built up a table of relative strengths.

> Gradually a system of scoring emerged: 90 points for Burt Lancaster, Robert Mitchum, 75 for Errol Flynn, 50 for Henry Fonda, down to Charles Laughton, 25, and Judy Garland, only 10. When he started on categories, he found that he could compute 75 for British War; 70 for non-sadistic modern dress action, schools and teachers; 65 for English family comedy-dramas and Hitchcock; and so on down to 15 for politics and musicals, and 10 for stories set in newspaper offices or the Deep South. Eventually he broke up every film into seven categories, each with a score. ... While 100 is a good average score for a movie, *Carry On* films go off the graph at 200.[29]

TAPE Ltd initially offered its service in 1970 to Thames Television, which contracted with Firman's company on condition that the deal was kept secret and that it was not also offered to the BBC. Subsequently, TAPE was taken up by most other ITV companies, with the exceptions of Westward and Border.[30] Firman had so refined his system that it was able to predict ratings within three to five ratings points in 90 per cent of cases.

Although it was used to forecast the performance of other programmes too, TAPE was particularly effective with feature films. LWT's programme controller and film scheduler Cyril Bennett said of Firman: 'He is essential in scheduling of feature films because only by a scientific assessment of how movies rate in television terms can you know what is likely to be popular. How they did at the cinema box offices or my personal preference is irrelevant.'[31] Speaking to another reporter, Bennett added about TAPE:

> I find it a useful measuring instrument to evaluate the likely appeal of a film.

> By storing a body of data on films going back several years, it comes up with certain indications – some right, some wrong – some of which we take into context, some we ignore.

> Why is it necessary? I have something like 1,000 film titles in stock. I schedule two to three movies a weekend. What criteria am I going to have when programming a film? Should it be a lucky dip? Should I choose the films *I* like?[32]

When TAPE was made publicly known in 1971 through the publication of Elkan Allan's article, it drew a predictably hostile response from some quarters, with TV critic Milton Shulman describing it as 'about as useful to society as the superstitious service performed by the Greek oracles'.[33] But Shulman was hostile to the showing of films on television anyway and used TAPE as the springboard to assail broadcasters for relying on them, especially at weekends. ITV's use of the system may, however, help to explain some of the programming practices by the companies. To take one example of a film starring July Garland (scored a mere 10 out of 100 in Firman's system), the rights to *A Star Is Born* (1954/02.04.1966) were held by ITV between 1966 and 1971. In that time it received only twelve local transmissions in nine regions. Granada was the only one of the Big Five majors to show it. Was this partly a result of TAPE's predictions? Westward was another of the companies that didn't show the film and it did not subscribe to TAPE, so we cannot be certain that it was the decisive factor influencing the schedulers (the film's length, at two and a half hours, surely counted against it too). But when taking into account ITV schedulers' apparent aversion to musicals in general, TAPE cannot be ruled out as a significant factor shaping programming decisions.

The option of asking the audience what it wanted to see was exercised only rarely. Both Scottish Television (in 1966) and Granada (in 1971) constructed strands entitled 'Command Performance', based on polls of prospective viewers. In the latter case, a list of ninety-one features whose TV rights were controlled by ITV was published in the Granada edition of *TVTimes*.[34] Over 3,000 readers responded with their preferences, many of them also suggesting additional films (often of an older vintage than those on the list) they would like to see broadcast as well. In addition to scheduling a Sunday-night series of ten films based on readers' votes, Granada placed other titles from the poll in parallel strands. As a barometer of public tastes, the exercise may also have helped Leslie Halliwell choose what else to acquire in future for either his own local schedules or for the network as a whole.

Besides viewing figures, both the BBC and the IBA sought qualitative information on audience response. Questionnaires were periodically sent to representative panels of viewers, leading to the compilation of 'Reaction Indices' (BBC) or 'Appreciation Indices' (IBA) for particular programmes. However, in its 1977 report on the future of broadcasting, the Annan Committee was critical of the effectiveness of this research, finding it 'too piecemeal, too narrow and too superficial'. It judged that the broadcasters were overly preoccupied with the measurement of numbers and that the discrepancies between BBC and JICTAR figures undermined confidence in both systems. Annan noted: 'Commentators observe with some irony that the method on which each system is based consistently produces the most favourable result for those who paid for it.'[35]

Among its other recommendations, the report expressly stated that 'there should be one body responsible for carrying out the measurement of the sizes of audiences on all broadcasting outlets'.[36] Placing this responsibility on a body independent of the networks, Annan argued, would free time and resources from the broadcasters to enable them to conduct more substantial, more focused research on audiences. After several years of negotiation, on 3 August 1981 JICTAR was replaced by the Broadcasters' Audience Research Board (BARB). This was jointly owned by the BBC and Independent Television Companies Association (ITCA), with an equal number of executives from each organisation on its board. AGB retained its contract to supply the ratings, using its set-meter method with slight modifications requested by the BBC, but responsibility for qualitative research on audience reaction was given to BBC Broadcasting Research (as BBC Audience Research had been renamed). In theory, this was a more equitable arrangement, designed to avoid the unseemly public squabbles over who had won the nightly battle for viewers. But as the press pointed out, the compromises needed to gain the broadcasters' agreement meant that less information now reached the public.[37]

In its initial reports, BARB published separate charts for BBC1, BBC2 and ITV, with weekly figures listed only by region. A national top twenty was supplied monthly, not weekly, making it difficult for users to compare competing programmes' relative performance. More detailed information was provided only to paying subscribers and press outlets were allowed to subscribe only on condition that they did not compile a weekly comparative chart of their own. This was widely seen as a cover-up to protect the BBC, which usually performed badly in the monthly charts, though it maintained a healthy national share overall. It was challenged when *The Times* subscribed to BARB's service and broke the terms of its contract by publishing a top twenty for the week ending 11 October. This was the week when *Jaws* (1975/08.10.1981) achieved its near-record audience. After taking legal action against the newspaper, BARB eventually backed down and from the week ending 31 January 1982 agreed to publish viewing figures for its weekly channel top tens, along with a monthly top fifty.[38]

BARB later produced retrospective estimates of individual viewers for broadcasts that JICTAR had measured by homes tuned in. For example, the premiere of the first James Bond film, *Dr No* (1962/28.10.1975), had been seen in 10.5 million homes, according to JICTAR. BBC Audience Research had estimated an audience of 27 million viewers. BARB placed the number of viewers at 18.9 million. This figure assumed an average 1.8 viewers per household; the BBC's figure assumed 2.5 viewers per household. Thus, with three figures to choose from, it is still no clearer how many actually saw the transmission. (See Tables 7.2.1–7.2.4 for the highest-rated films according to each measuring system.)

Children's Films and the Temple 'Ban'

With fixed limits to broadcasting hours prescribed by Government until 1972, there was little reason for either the BBC or ITV to schedule feature films at off-peak times specifically for the young. The most prolific producers and distributors of films for children, Walt Disney Productions and the Children's Film

Table 7.2.1 Annual highest-rated feature films, 1961–81.

TX Year	Film	Release Year	Channel	TX Date	Homes (millions)	Weekly Position
1961	*Anthony Adverse*	1936	ITV part network	14.12.1961	5.06	9
1962	*My Forbidden Past*	1951	BBC	17.03.1962	5.53	8=
1963	*The Gold Rush*	1925	BBC	25.12.1963	5.71	9
1964	*Room at the Top*	1958	ITV network	07.07.1964	8.34	1
1965	*Jesse James*	1939	BBC1	11.12.1965	6.80	9
1966	*Daisy Kenyon*	1947	BBC1	01.11.1966	6.95	8=
1967	*Eyewitness*	1956	BBC1	09.12.1967	7.40	6
1968	*The Green Man*	1956	BBC1	14.01.1968	7.70	7
1969	*What a Carve Up*	1961	BBC1	28.01.1969	7.30	3
1970	*633 Squadron*	1964	BBC1	17.11.1970	8.20	2
1971	*The Great Escape*	1963	BBC1	28.12.1971	7.10	4=
1972	*The Blue Max*	1966	BBC1	27.12.1972	6.10	8=
1973	*El Dorado*	1966	ITV exc. STV	27.12.1973	7.10	3
1974	*Battle of Britain*	1969	BBC1	15.09.1974	7.60	1
1975	*Dr No*	1962	ITV exc. UTV	28.10.1975	10.50	1
1976	*Goldfinger*	1964	ITV network	03.11.1976	9.80	1
1977[1]	*Thunderball*	1965	ITV part network	26.02.1977	8.55	7

					Viewers (millions)	
1977[2]	*You Only Live Twice*	1967	ITV network	20.11.1977	20.80	1
1978	*Von Ryan's Express*	1965	ITV network	04.01.1978	18.75	2
1979	*Carry on Doctor*	1968	BBC1	21.09.1979	20.60	6
1980	*Live and Let Die*	1973	ITV network	20.01.1980	23.50	1
1981	*Jaws*	1975	ITV network	08.10.1981	23.25	1

Note: Chart weeks ran Monday–Sunday.

Source for Tables 7.2.1, 7.2.2 and 7.2.3: Television Audience Measurement (TAM), Joint Industry Committee for Audience Research (JICTAR) and Broadcasters' Audience Research Board (BARB), as published in the trade press.

[1] Year to 6 August.
[2] Year from 7 August.

Table 7.2.2 Highest-rated feature films, January 1961–July 1977.

Rank	Film	Release Year	Channel	TX Date	Homes (millions)	Weekly Position
1	Dr No	1952	ITV exc. UTV	28.10.1975	10.50	1
2	Goldfinger	1964	ITV network	03.11.1976	9.80	1
3	From Russia with Love	1963	ITV network	02.05.1976	9.20	1
4	The Italian Job	1969	ITV network	25.01.1976	8.80	1
5	Thunderball	1965	ITV part network	26.02.1977	8.55	7
6	Room at the Top	1958	ITV network	07.07.1964	8.34	1
7=	633 Squadron	1964	BBC1	17.11.1970	8.20	2
	Planet of the Apes	1968	ITV network	24.03.1977	8.20	8
9	The Guns of Navarone	1961	ITV network	04.04.1976	8.00	4
10	Challenge to Lassie	1949	BBC1	28.05.1975	7.85	10=
11=	Return of the Seven	1966	BBC1	18.12.1976	7.75	7=
	The Firechasers	1970	ITV network	06.03.1977	7.75	14
12	The Green Man	1956	BBC1	14.01.1968	7.70	7
13	Our Man Flint	1966	ITV network	03.12.1975	7.65	8=
14=	Battle of Britain	1959	BBC1	15.09.1974	7.60	1
	The Longest Day	1962	BBC1	26.05.1975	7.60	14
16=	The Gunfighter	1950	BBC1	07.02.1970	7.45	10
	Valley of the Dolls	1957	ITV network	26.02.1975	7.45	10=
18	Eyewitness	1956	BBC1	09.12.1967	7.40	6
19=	White Witch Doctor	1953	BBC1	17.01.1970	7.35	6
	Mosquito Squadron	1970	BBC1	20.12.1975	7.35	15

Table 7.2.3 Highest-rated feature films, August 1977–December 1981.

Rank	Film	Release Year	Channel	TX Date	Viewers (millions)	Weekly Position
1	*Live and Let Die*	1973	ITV network	20.01.1980	23.50	1
2	*Jaws*	1975	ITV network	08.10.1981	23.30	1
3	*Diamonds Are Forever*	1971	ITV network	15.03.1981	22.15	1
4	*You Only Live Twice*	1967	ITV network	20.11.1977	20.80	1
5	*Carry on Doctor*	1968	BBC1	21.09.1979	20.60	6
6	*Carry on at Your Convenience*	1971	BBC1	14.09.1979	19.95	2
7	*Carry on... Up the Khyber*	1968	BBC1	28.09.1979	19.60	10
8	*The Black Windmill*	1974	BBC1	01.09.1979	19.40	1
9	*The Poseidon Adventure*	1972	BBC1	23.12.1979	19.30	1
10	*Juggernaut*	1974	BBC1	18.11.1979	19.25	1
11	*The Belstone Fox*	1973	BBC1	08.09.1979	19.00	4
12	*Rollercoaster*	1977	ITV network	18.02.1981	18.85	3
13	*Von Ryan's Express*	1965	ITV network	04.01.1978	18.75	2
14	*The Sound of Music*	1965	BBC1	25.12.1978	18.50	2
15=	*Carry on Abroad*	1972	ITV network	08.01.1978	18.45	3
15=	*Paint Your Wagon*	1969	ITV network	01.01.1980	18.45	3
17	*The Towering Inferno*	1974	BBC1	26.12.1980	17.70	4
18=	*Skyjacked*	1972	ITV network	30.10.1977	17.50	2
18=	*Where Eagles Dare*	1968	BBC1	26.12.1979	17.50	2
20=	*Goldfinger*	1964	ITV network	12.03.1978	17.45	3
20=	*Murphy's War*	1971	ITV network	15.01.1978	17.45	6

Note: Films broadcast in August and September 1979 were shown during the ITV strike.

Table 7.2.4 Selected BBC Audience Research figures, 1963–81.

Film	Release Year	Channel	TX Date	Viewers (millions)
Live and Let Die	1973	ITV network	20.01.1980	28.0
Dr No	1962	ITV exc. UTV	28.10.1975	27.0
The Towering Inferno	1974	BBC1	26.12.1980	26.8
The Sound of Music	1965	BBC1	25.12.1978	26.5
The Poseidon Adventure	1972	BBC1	23.12.1979	26.5
The Great Escape	1963	BBC1	27.08.1979	26.0
Diamonds Are Forever	1971	ITV network	15.03.1981	26.0
Where Eagles Dare	1968	BBC1	26.12.1979	25.5
The Italian Job	1969	ITV network	25.01.1976	25.0
Goldfinger	1964	ITV network	03.11.1976	24.8
Butch Cassidy and the Sundance Kid	1969	BBC1	25.12.1975	24.7
From Russia with Love	1963	ITV network	02.05.1976	24.7
The Longest Day	1962	BBC1	26.05.1975	24.5
You Only Live Twice	1967	ITV network	20.11.1977	24.5
Battle of Britain	1969	BBC1	15.09.1974	23.0
The Guns of Navarone	1961	ITV network	04.04.1976	22.6
Goldfinger	1964	ITV network	12.03.1978	22.5
Oliver!	1968	BBC1	30.12.1978	22.5
The Gold Rush	1925	BBC TV	25.12.1963	22.0
Carry on Doctor	1968	BBC1	21.09.1979	22.0
Airport	1970	BBC1	25.12.1976	21.7
The Great Escape	1963	BBC1	28.12.1971	21.5
Ben-Hur	1959	ITV network	07.05.1978	21.5
Krakatoa, East of Java	1968	BBC1	19.08.1979	21.5
The Belstone Fox	1973	BBC1	08.09.1979	21.0
The Dirty Dozen	1967	BBC1	26.12.1977	20.8
633 Squadron	1964	BBC1	17.11.1970	20.5
Murphy's War	1971	ITV network	15.01.1978	20.5
The Wizard of Oz	1939	BBC1	25.12.1975	20.4
The Dirty Dozen	1967	BBC1	07.05.1979	20.3

Source: BBC Audience Research, as reported in the trade press.

Foundation, generally declined to make them available to television. Disney films remained commercially viable in cinemas for many years after their initial release and were regularly reissued, so there was no incentive for the company to devalue them with a TV sale. Disney eventually relaxed its own rules to the extent of allowing the BBC to transmit one or two live-action features per year, usually at Christmas or on other holidays, beginning with *Davy Crockett, King of the Wild Frontier* (1955/24.12.1972). However, the studio's animated features remained strictly off-limits for TV until the mid-1980s.

The British-based Children's Film Foundation (CFF) had been set up in 1951 specifically to draw children into cinemas and thereby induce in them a filmgoing habit. For that reason it had virtual charitable status as a beneficiary of the British Film Production Fund, or Eady Levy, the statutory scheme set up to subsidise the producers of British films with a bonus on their theatrical revenues. It would thus have been contrary to CFF's own remit to supply any of its limited stock of features, shorts and serials to television. When ITA Director General Robert Fraser enquired in 1968 about the availability of CFF films for use in children's hour, he was told: 'until such time as CFF has a stock of films surplus to the requirements of its Saturday morning matinées, it is not proposed to consider releasing any film to television. To do so would be simply cutting their own throats.'[39] Again, it was not until the mid-1980s that this position changed. Broadcasters therefore had to find suitable material for children from their regular stocks or from other sources of specialised material.

From the early 1950s, when she was an assistant in the BBC's Film Purchase Section, until about 1980, Peggy Miller was responsible for the acquisition and presentation of scores of shorts, features, serials and series made overseas. Miller had particular responsibility for children's programmes and oversaw the editing of these films to make them suitable for a British child audience. Her name may be particularly associated, by viewers of a certain age, with European fairy-tale and fantasy features that were re-edited into serialised form, usually with the addition of a voice-over narrator. They included *The Tinderbox* (1959/01.10.1964), *The Yellow Slippers* (1961/24.12.1964), *The Golden Goose* (1964/10.11.1966) and, the best-remembered and most frequently repeated of all, *The Singing, Ringing Tree* (1957/19.11.1964). The latter was broadcast seven times on BBC1 over a period of sixteen years. Between 1964 and 1969, these and many other films and series were shown under the umbrella titles 'Tales from Europe' and 'Tales from Overseas'. Even after these series rubrics had been dropped, dubbed and re-edited 'foreign' films continued to form part of regular children's programming until the early 1980s.[40]

Serialisation of films for children was not unique to the BBC. In 1967, Leslie Halliwell developed a series for Granada, provisionally called 'Great Stories of the Screen' and eventually 'Film of the Book'. A number of features adapted from prestigious literary properties were shown in twenty-minute episodes over several weeks, accompanied by 'a commentator who would not only keep narrative continuity but add comments, with visual aids, in the vein of literary and film appreciation, explaining to the children why the story, and the filming of it, are so compelling'.[41] The commentator chosen was Granada's regular station host Bill Grundy. Seven feature films were presented in this way between July 1967 and April 1968, beginning with David Lean's *Great Expectations* (1946/04.07.1965) in six episodes (see Table 7.3). The 'informative' nature of the series meant that these films were exempted from the ITA's usual quotas on foreign material and films (as a weekday station at this time, Granada was allowed only two features per week). Granada was initially given permission to show the series locally for the Authority to evaluate its quality. Evidently officers approved, as a number of other ITV stations, including Rediffusion London, later played the serialisations of *Tom Brown's Schooldays* (1951/09.01.1962) and *The Pickwick Papers* (1952/25.12.1961). One of the ITA's concerns had been that the films' directors might object to their work being treated in this way, following recent press controversies around ITV's editing of feature films (see Chapter 11), but there is no evidence of any adverse reaction along these lines.[42]

Though it was not aimed at children, a subsequent Granada series with the same producer, Peter Heinze, was based on a similar idea. 'Talking About...', networked in the Sunday early-evening 'God slot', combined serialised feature films with studio discussions about the moral issues raised by them. The series, hosted by David Steel MP, began on 26 January 1969 with Anthony Asquith's *Orders to Kill* (1958/17.06.1965), presented in three episodes of 45–50 minutes each over successive weeks and culminating in a discussion with guests including a clergyman, an army officer who had been a wartime secret agent, and an academic from Manchester Business School. Four other films were subsequently shown in like fashion over the series' five-month run (see Table 7.4).

The number of regular slots in which films meant for children could be placed was limited. Outside of holiday periods, when films were often given irregular daytime placings, they tended to be shown either on Saturday mornings – in pre-sport slots introduced in the early 1970s, before these were largely taken over by live, studio-based entertainment shows – or in the regular weekday children's hour between 4.00pm and 5.00pm. A feature film placed in one of these latter slots left little time for other programmes, so ITV companies would typically choose only one day per week for them. Thames, for example, scheduled a 'Children's Film Matinee' slot at 4.20pm on Thursdays for a number of weeks each year between 1975 and 1978, with several other companies following suit. Among the films selected were vintage comedies (Laurel and Hardy, Abbott and Costello, the Crazy Gang), adventure (Tarzan, Lassie) and Westerns (including Hopalong Cassidy).

Thames's film lists also included two Japanese creature features, *Son of Godzilla* (1967/03.03.1977) and *Ebirah, Terror of the Deep* (1966/03.02.1977), which had received BBFC 'U' certificates. The IBA officer who approved them, Dermot O'Hagan, expressed the hope that they were 'not going to frighten any adults who may be watching'. But his tongue-in-cheek memo was followed by a more serious one after *Ebirah* appeared first in ATV's own children's slot, when the Authority's Midlands monitor thought that 'very young children viewing on their own might

Table 7.3 Film of the Book (Granada), 1967–68.

Film	Year	Number of episodes	TX first episode	Shown by other stations
Great Expectations	1946	Six	03.07.1967	No
Tom Brown's Schooldays	1951	Five	14.08.1967	Yes
The Card	1952	Four	19.09.1967	No
The Maltese Falcon	1941	Five	24.10.1967	No
The Pickwick Papers	1952	Five	28.11.1967	Yes
Tunes of Glory	1960	Five	24.01.1968	No
On the Beach	1959	Seven	28.02.1968	No

Note: *TV Times* listing on 24.01.1968 bills *The African Queen*.

Table 7.4 Talking About… (Granada), 1969–70.

Film	Year	Number of episodes	TX first episode
Orders to Kill	1958	Three	26.01.1969
Life for Ruth	1962	Three	16.02.1969
Lease of Life	1954	Three	16.03.1969
Room at the Top	1958	Three	13.04.1969
Shake Hands with the Devil	1959	Three	04.05.1969

well be quite scared'. O'Hagan therefore asked for an assurance that the film was indeed suitable for children. The Thames staffer who had previewed it replied that she would not argue with the monitor's judgement on 'this particular feature film and its splendid monsters' but added: 'we do not consider that in our 4.20ish slot we are providing entertainment for very young children who, as you know, are catered for at noon'. The transmissions of both films went ahead, but Thames and ATV were the only two ITV stations to play them.[43]

A greater controversy occurred over some apparently innocuous films that the Authority considered merely dated rather than dangerous. In planning its first children's film season, Thames had submitted for approval a list that included several vehicles for 1930s child star Shirley Temple. A number of Temple films had been acquired by individual ITV stations for local use, but – with the solitary exception of *Heidi* (1937/26.12.1971) – they had not been taken for the network as a whole. Granada was the first to show them, with an extensive chronological season on Saturday mornings in 1973; STV, Border and Southern also picked them up. Thames proposed to purchase thirteen Temple titles from their current distributor, Warner Bros (which at that time handled the product of Twentieth Century-Fox, the Temple films' owners), for use in its planned Thursday matinee series of films for children. However, while approving the other choices on Thames's list, including films starring Will Hay and Old Mother Riley, IBA officers had been unhappy about the Temple films, which they thought too old-fashioned for modern youngsters. Thames's programme planner Pat Mahoney was so informed, and he in turn passed the decision on to his contact at Warner's and to Leslie Halliwell in order to cancel the proposed deal.

It was then that the *Daily Mirror* broke an exclusive story that Shirley Temple films had been banned from children's television. The newspaper quoted an unnamed IBA spokesman who said that Temple 'had no relevance to modern children' and would be 'more likely to appeal to the nostalgia of grandmothers'. An unspecified ITV executive was quoted as saying that the ban was 'ludicrous'. Over the next two days, the *Mirror* reported a 'lollipop backlash' by child viewers, including a petition against the alleged ban organised by 200 schoolgirls. The paper even tracked down Temple herself, now the US Ambassador to Ghana, to solicit her amused reaction. Other newspapers picked up the story and, not unexpectedly, ran with it. The *Daily Mail* quoted another anonymous IBA official, who denied there was a ban and said that the Authority had merely 'suggested' to Thames that 'they should surely find something less wet than Shirley Temple to fill their children's film hour'. A week after the story broke, the *Mail* carried a letter from the IBA's Deputy Head of Information, John Guinery, saying that there was no ban, that the requested withdrawal of Temple's films applied to the one company only, and that the IBA had simply recommended that Thames's children's film slot could 'be better used'.[44]

In the interim, the Authority had received dozens of protesting letters. Some were from adults, variously outraged, sarcastic or distressed, and in several cases pointing out the absurdity of such a decision when 'pornographic' and violent films were being allowed onto the air. One viewer wrote a complaint in verse, which was answered in kind by an IBA officer. But many letters were from children upset that their favourite star had been taken off their screens. Some were clearly the result of write-ins organised by schoolteachers; others were apparently composed by children as young as six. Several letters enclosed lengthy petitions demanding that the ban be overturned. Some mentioned opinion surveys that children had conducted among their classmates ('27 out of 28 voted Shirley Temple'). Some were critical of ITV, hoping that it would go bankrupt or that executives would lose their jobs. But all were in Shirley's favour and pointed out how out of touch broadcasters were with real children's tastes and interests. 'I think your ITV chiefs are a bit cracked', wrote sixteen-year-old S.R. from St Albans – 'If you don't think again I'll be converted to the BBC. Long live the BBC.' 'I think you were very wicked to ban Shirley Temple's films', said thirteen-year-old Miss K. in a four-page letter. 'I would like you to think again, stop being daft and put them back on again', wrote Caroline, eight, of Andover. 'I do not think you can know many little girls or else you would not make yourselves look so silly.' And C.H. of London commented:

> My friends and I are very, very wild with you. First you take off [the TV series] *Planet of the Apes* and then you ban the Shirley Temple films. It's all very well for the ITV programme chiefs to laugh but they wouldn't be laughing if they got sacked. ... I am not in the upper class because I am only a secondary school girl, but I have my own opinions and so do others.[45]

Further investigation by Thames failed to discover how the press 'leak' had occurred. The source was suspected as being either Warner Bros or Halliwell, but this was never proven.[46] In any event, with the IBA's repeated protestations to the press and in replies to irate correspondents, the affair proved a considerable PR embarrassment. One letter referring to the supposed ban was received a whole six years later. Towards the end of 1975 and over the next two years, Thames actually did place a number of Temple films in its schedules, though not on Thursday afternoons. Otherwise, again with the exception of *Heidi*, they did not subsequently appear on any other ITV stations and few were shown on the BBC. There may have been no official ban, but this minor scandal apparently had the effect of scaring off other programme planners.

Pre-echoes and Explosions: Films at Christmas

In Britain, the Christmas and New Year fortnight has come to be associated with a profusion of films on television, particularly blockbusters. The first feature televised on a Christmas Day was a repeat: the BBC's fourth transmission of Mickey Rooney in *Little Lord Fauntleroy* (1936/24.06.1948) in 1949. Two years later, a 'B' picture, *Wallaby Jim of the Islands* (1937/25.12.1951), was the UK's first Christmas Day premiere. Now long forgotten, it was well enough liked at the time to be revived over two successive years and was even cited in *Hancock's Half-Hour*. Better remembered is Laurel and Hardy's *Swiss Miss* (1938/25.12.1952), but for the next few years Yuletide feature films were scant.[47]

Then, in 1957, ITV networked, across the four stations then in operation, not one but three features on Christmas Day. The reason for this 'break in the accepted pattern of day-to-day programmes', explained *TV Times*, was 'to enable the people who work in the TV studios to have more time off to spend at home with their families'.[48] The first of the trio, *The Lady from Boston* (1951/25.12.1957), was placed immediately after the Queen's 3.00pm Christmas message, the first time this had been televised. It was followed in the early evening by *The Big Top* (1951/25.12.1957), a Russian circus film with English translation by Wolf Mankowitz, and later by Fred Astaire and Rita Hayworth in the musical *You Were Never Lovelier* (1942/25.12.1957). BBC Television had its own afternoon film that year, the romantic comedy *Mrs Mike* (1949/25.12.1957). On Christmas Eve, the Corporation presented the UK television premiere of *It's a Wonderful Life* (1946/24.12.1957) and on Boxing Day, the aptly-chosen pugilist melodrama *Body and Soul* (1947/26.12.1957). Over the next few years, with ITV companies mainly scheduling on a regional basis, the BBC in particular established Christmas night as a prime film slot. In annual succession, the Corporation's big holiday films were *Top Hat* (1935/25.12.1958), *High Noon* (1952/25.12.1959), *The Prisoner of Zenda* (1937/25.12.1960) and *Rebecca* (1940/25.12.1960). *The African Queen* (1951/15.01.1961), shown on Christmas Day 1962, was criticised in the press as 'only' a channel premiere, the film having previously been shown on ITV (see Chapter 4).

Festive films often drew substantial audiences. According to the BBC's own figures, *Rebecca* was seen by 12,700,000 viewers; using a different yardstick, TAM estimated that 4,258,000 homes tuned in to Hitchcock's *Notorious* (1946/26.12.1961) on Boxing Day the same year. But the BBC's biggest ratings success to date was achieved with a forty-year-old silent film. Charlie Chaplin's *The Gold Rush* (1925/25.12.1963) made the top spot on TAM's chart for Christmas Day, with 5.7 million homes tuning in; BBC Audience Research estimated up to 22 million viewers.[49] Moreover, the Corporation's film for Christmas afternoon that year, *Abbott and Costello Meet Captain Kidd* (1952/25.12.1963), placed fifth on TAM's chart. Both films helped the BBC achieve its highest audience share since the advent of ITV, with between 68 per cent (TAM figures) and 80 per cent (BBC figures) of viewers tuned to the channel that day.[50]

The press was at best sceptical, at worst scathing, of what it saw as unseasonal entertainment offerings. One newspaper speculated: 'When the children of today's TV tycoons ask: "What did you do at Christmas, 1965, Daddy, to keep the viewers happy?" the answer is bound to be: "Why, we showed a lot of old films".'[51] This commentator considered it an 'insult' that the thirty-two-year-old *King Kong* (1933/23.10.1965) should be a peak-time Christmas Sunday attraction on several ITV stations, though it was the film's premiere transmission in those areas. Noting the number of now-deceased actors in the following year's festive lineup and comparing the broadcasters' seasonal largesse to Scrooge, another columnist commented: 'I can count 15 old movies across the channels over the holiday period and TV is in danger of becoming the Ghost of Christmas Past.'[52] Nevertheless, in both 1965 and 1966, a BBC1 feature film placed second in TAM's Christmas Day ratings charts: *Road to Bali* (1952/25.12.1965) and *The Comancheros* (1966/25.12.1966).

The BBC came to dominate the annual holiday ratings more often than not, sometimes by a very substantial margin. In 1968, the Corporation claimed a combined lead for its two channels of nearly four to one over ITV, with an audience share of 79 per cent on Christmas Day and 76 per cent on Boxing Day. Among BBC1's ratings hits that year were *Some Like It Hot* (1959/25.12.1968), with over 15 million viewers according to the BBC, and *The Bulldog Breed* (1960/26.12.1968), with over 20 million.[53] JICTAR put the BBC's Christmas Day share that year at 69 per cent.[54]

The fact that most of the BBC's films were broadcast nationwide and ITV's locally undoubtedly helped the Corporation get more titles onto the ratings charts than its competitor. At Christmas 1970, the BBC had 'an almost unbeatable selection of feature films', according to one trade journal.[55] Proving the point, three of them were placed on JICTAR's chart for Christmas week, along with ITV's sole networked feature, *Invitation to a Gunfighter* (1964/24.12.1970). Throughout the following decade, the ITV companies' Christmas schedules were increasingly coordinated, with more frequent networking of films along with other programmes.

Cinemas in Britain invariably closed on Christmas Day (they still do) but the week after was traditionally a boom time at the box office. Television provided particularly unwelcome competition, as was pointed out in 1972 by a letter to a trade paper, hoping for 'some highly influential person to intercede for a reduction in the number of old films to be televised this Christmas'.

> The cinemas were literally beaten to their knees financially last Christmas by massive coverage of 'oldies' on TV culminating on the Tuesday, when we might have hoped for a let-up, with *The Great Escape*, at the vital cinema time of 6pm, thus killing a great deal of the country's evening trade.[56]

Astutely placed in the lull between the big holiday dates, *The Great Escape* (1963/28.12.1971) attracted 21.5 million viewers, according to the Corporation's figures: a record for any film on the BBC to that date. It even beat *The Morecambe and Wise Christmas Show* in the holiday ratings, while still lagging behind the Queen's broadcast.

Despite the BBC's overall dominance, ITV's Christmas film matinees often performed strongly. *King Solomon's Mines* (1971/25.12.1971), *That Riviera Touch* (1966/25.12.1972), *Those Magnificent Men in Their Flying Machines* (1974/25.12.1974), *Doctor in Trouble* (1970/25.12.1975) and *Please Sir!* (1971/25.12.1976) all gave the commercial network its best ratings of their respective Christmas Days, before the BBC scooped the evening schedules. 'Past experience has shown that where films clash it is invariably the first off the mark that gets and holds the audience', noted one observer in 1974, adding cautiously: 'But this is the year of big-big films when past rules probably count for little.'[57]

That year did indeed mark an escalation in both the number and the prestige of the films premiered on television at Christmas, as well as in the prices paid for them. Others making their small-screen debut in 1974, all on BBC1, included *Grand Prix* (1966/22.12.1974), *The Graduate* (1967/23.12.1974), *True Grit* (1969/25.12.1974), *The Bridge on the River Kwai* (1957/25.12.1974), *The Magnificent Seven* (1960/26.12.1974), *Chitty Chitty Bang Bang* (1968/26.12.1974) and *El Cid* (1961/27.12.1974). These big guns had been brought out as the Corporation's capacity to fund original programming had diminished due to budget cuts. Nevertheless, the BBC claimed a three-to-one ratings victory: 'This was the most spectacular and successful Christmas we have had for the past five years', crowed Director of Programmes Alasdair Milne. 'We not only had the best films, but we made the best programmes.'[58] According to the BBC's own figures, *The Bridge on the River Kwai* had drawn eighteen million viewers, while ITV's *Those Magnificent Men in Their Flying Machines* had nine million.[59] Both were shown on Christmas Day, albeit in the evening and afternoon, respectively, so they were not in direct competition with each other. JICTAR confirmed the Corporation's victory, with a viewing ratio of 58 per cent (BBC1) to 39 per cent (ITV) for the day and week, but gave the BBC's most popular film of Christmas week as *Ice Station Zebra* (1968/24.12.1974), with 6.3 million homes tuning in, and ITV's as *The Most Dangerous Man in the World* (1969/29.12.1974), with 6.5 million homes. Both, however, were surpassed by ITV's New Year's Day offering, Hitchcock's *Topaz* (1969/01.01.1975), seen in 7.1 million homes, according to JICTAR.

In holiday periods the IBA relaxed its usual restrictions on the number of films that could be shown in a typical week, but nevertheless held the ITV schedulers to account, demanding balanced schedules that offered a suitable range and variety of entertainment and 'no undue concentration of acquired material'.[60] Proposed schedules that failed to achieve this balance were sent back for reconsideration. The Authority considered ITV's reliance on films at Christmas 1973 to be 'excessive', and while the draft 1974 schedules were seen as an improvement, officers argued that they contained 'probably the maximum number of feature films which should be allowed'.[61] Reflecting on that year in retrospect, the IBA noted of both ITV and BBC that 'the emphasis for many peak evenings was heavily concentrated on prestigious feature films'. But the Authority pointed out:

> It is worth recalling that when the BBC scheduled *The Bridge on the River Kwai* last Christmas Day it certainly held a high proportion of those viewers who switched to it but the audience was comparatively small compared with the likely audience in a normal week. It may therefore serve the audience as a whole better to reserve ITV's limited stock of very good films for non-Christmas weeks.

The IBA's research also suggested that up to half of all viewers were away from home at this time of year and would appreciate shorter programmes rather than a profusion of 'specials'. With this in mind, the Authority considered the big film mooted for Christmas 1975, the nearly four-hour epic *Lawrence of Arabia* (1972/22 & 23.12.1975), 'excessively long'.[62] However, rather than drop it entirely, ITV split the film over two evenings in the run-up to the holiday. Another IBA paper commented: 'It will be interesting to see whether an excellent film such as this can hold an audience on two successive evenings (a method of scheduling which is used on the continent but has not so far been tried in this country for films).'[63] In fact, spreading a film over two or even three evenings had often been done by ITV in the 1950s and 1960s, albeit not with such a major title as *Lawrence of Arabia*. In this instance, rather than dividing the film at the theatrical intermission point, as was done by BBC1 with both *Cleopatra* (1963/29 & 30.12.1973) and *Gone with the Wind* (1939/26 & 27.12.1981), the break was taken slightly earlier in the film to produce two parts of roughly equal length (120 and 105 minutes, including commercial breaks). In ratings terms it was only moderately successful: JICTAR placed the two halves at chart positions 11 and 16 for the week, the first part reaching 6.15 million homes and the second having only a slight drop-off with 6.1 million. This was ITV's highest-rated film in a week again dominated by BBC1.

In a 1980 article, Michael Pilsworth elucidated some of the strategies used by schedulers to attract, retain and build audiences, as well as the arcane terms used to describe them:

The art is to build towards the climax, the audience peak, little by little as the evening progresses. Peaks and troughs are to be avoided. ... 'Hammocking' involves placing 'bankers' [reliable ratings-getters] both before and after a less popular programme, with the intention that a large audience hooked by the first popular programme will be happy to wait for the second, and will 'sit through' the intervening serious programme. This assumes an 'inheritance' effect: the serious programme is said to 'inherit' the audience from the first popular programme. Programmes that attract large audiences sometimes create the reverse of an inheritance effect; that is, they cause an increase in the audience well before the programme begins. This is known as a 'pre-echo' in scheduling jargon.[64]

The Christmas 1975 schedules provide some model examples. In *Radio Times*, Chris Dunkley explained the way that BBC1 Controller Bryan Cowgill had placed his feature films for maximum impact in relation to other programmes:

His BBC1 'build' on Christmas day, for example, started gently but compellingly with *Laurel and Hardy* at 12.20, went into a skating spectacular at 1.20, on to a *Top of the Pops* special before the Queen's Christmas broadcast, and got going in real earnest at 3.5 with *Billy Smart's Christmas Circus*. That was designed to attract a sizeable audience, hold it, and deliver much of it (the 'inheritance factor') to *The Wizard of Oz* which will also have attracted a lot of viewers.

Following the afternoon TV premiere of *The Wizard of Oz* (1939/25.12.1975) with special editions of two of the BBC's top-rated shows, *Bruce Forsyth and the Generation Game* and *Some Mothers Do 'Ave 'Em*, created a 'pre-echo' for the evening's main set pieces. The twin climax was 'the dead-cert *Morecambe and Wise Christmas Show* which developed like an atomic reaction leading into the explosion of the "world television première" of *Butch Cassidy and the Sundance Kid* at 8.45'.[65]

There were no weak spots in BBC1's lineup in need of 'hammocking'. By contrast, ITV's schedule peaked early with its own film matinee, *Doctor in Trouble*, and headed downhill from there. Its evening set piece was another film premiere, but one that seemed chosen to reach an entirely different type of viewer: Franco Zeffirelli's adaptation of Shakespeare's *The Taming of the Shrew* (1967/25.12.1975), starring Elizabeth Taylor and Richard Burton. This was the kind of 'serious' fare that pleased the IBA but not the mass audience, and it consequently appeared nowhere in the ratings charts. JICTAR put the audience for *Butch Cassidy and the Sundance Kid* (1969/25.12.1975) at 6.5 million homes and the BBC claimed 24.7 million viewers. Over the course of the day, JICTAR estimated that the BBC held 70 per cent of the audience; BBC Audience Research made it an extraordinary 88 per cent. Either way, observers agreed 'that ITV had practically opted out of the annual audience struggle'.[66]

Why hadn't the commercial network hit back, as had been widely anticipated, with one of its own big weapons of mass entertainment? Dunkley explained:

Against such a prodigious frontal assault the ITV programme controllers knew that massive retaliation was the only defence if they intended making a real fight of it: they would have had to throw in one of the James Bond films which they are holding in reserve, and this they were quite unwilling to do. 'James Bond against *Butch Cassidy* would just cancel out – we'd have been throwing it away,' said Paul Fox [Controller of Yorkshire Television]. Jeremy Isaacs [Thames Television] felt the same: 'The audience would have been split down the middle. It would have been pointless.'

What the ITV men might have added was that even if they, as programme staff, had wanted to use a Bond movie, the money men in ITV would have been more than unhappy at the idea of screening it during the Christmas period, let alone against anything as powerful as *Butch Cassidy*. They knew that ITV advertising income, which flows in unusually fast in the approach to Christmas, stops dead on the night of 23 December and stays at the lowest point of the year for the next fortnight or so.[67]

The only (partial) exception to this trend of BBC dominance was 1978, when Morecambe and Wise moved over to Thames after a decade with the BBC. On this occasion, 007 provided the build-up: their prestigious Christmas show was preceded by *Diamonds Are Forever* (1971/25.12.1978), the first screening of a Bond film on a Christmas Day. JICTAR reported that forty-one out of 100 TV sets in the London area were switched to ITV on the night. The claim was predictably disputed by BBC Audience Research, which gave the Corporation the benefit of a 60:40 split across the day and calculated the largest audience for its afternoon film, the television premiere of *The Sound of Music* (1965/25.12.1978 – see Figure 7.4). There was only a slight overlap between the two features, so viewers could easily channel-hop from one to the other. BBC figures gave the musical an audience of 26.5 million viewers and the Bond film only 15.5 million, whereas JICTAR's figures were 18.5 million and 14.35 million, respectively.[68] Nevertheless, this was a reversal of the usual pattern whereby the BBC won the evening round and left ITV with the consolation prize of the matinee.

Although the ratings established that most viewers that Christmas Day were tuned to BBC1 or ITV, there was another film premiere on offer. Those seeking an alternative to dirndls and diamonds could find it in Akira Kurosawa's

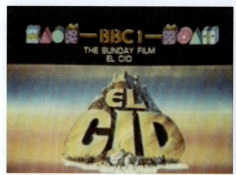

Figure 7.4a–b On-screen promotion for *El Cid* (1961) and *The Sound of Music* (1965), BBC1's 1978 blockbusters for Christmas Eve and Christmas Day, respectively. Screen grabs from a video trailer uploaded to YouTube by The TV Museum.

Russo-Japanese epic *Dersu Uzala* (1975/25.12.1978) on BBC2, as an online reader's comment for the *Guardian* recalled.

> I'm sure our house wasn't the only one disappointed but the variety show tradition had reached near its pits and I remember how the following Xmas we – my Dad (a brickie) and us kids – instead crowded around the festive council house hearth to watch Kurosawa's *Dersu Usala* [*sic*] on BBC2. Us kids complained at first but unable to make a case for the offerings on 1 and ITV, gave it a chance and really enjoyed it.[69]

Films not in the English language are the subject of the next chapter.

Notes

1　Author's interview with Sir Paul Fox, 3 September 2012. Fox also commented: 'Gordon was a wonderful, loveable, gentle, hard-working soul – you could not have had a sweeter companion to go with to Los Angeles. … Those sort of people are very, very difficult to find – people who were knowledgeable commercially about which films would work on television; secondly, had the nous to do the deal and drive a hard bargain; and thirdly, above all, to be straight about it. There was an awful lot of money involved and there were too many backhanders in that business.'

2　See Bill Gilbert, 'Early Days of TV Acquisition', *The Veteran* 136 (Autumn 2012): 18–21; and 'Overcoming FIDO', *The Veteran* 141 (Winter 2013): 15–17. Gilbert joined the BBC from Granada in November 1959.

3　Kenneth Adam, 'Yes, Let's See 14 Films a Week', *Evening News*, 12 May 1970.

4　Author's interview, 3 September 2012.

5　'Television Equivalent of the Third', *The Times*, 15 August 1964, 10.

6　The first Controller of BBC2, Michael Peacock, was forced to deny that the new schedules were 'a panic move': 'New Programmes for BBC2', *The Times*, 2 September 1964, 6; Douglas Marlborough, 'New, New, NEW, on BBC2!', *Daily Mail*, 2 September 1964, 7.

7　TAM press release, 'Film Attracts BBC2's Biggest Audience', 25 November 1964. 'The Vintage Years of Hollywood' was created and programmed by Bill Gilbert, who initially wanted to call it 'The Golden Years'. According to Gilbert, it was Gordon Smith who insisted on 'Vintage', to evoke fine wine. Bill also programmed 'The Western', 'The Love Affair' and 'The Hollywood Musical' (author's interview with Bill Gilbert, 23 January 2013).

8　Alasdair Milne, 'BBC Television: The Purchase and Transmission of Feature Films, 1978–79', n.d. (1978), BBC R78/1, 123/1.

9　'Royal Variety Slumps out of Ratings', *The Stage and Television Today*, 5 December 1974, 18.

10　Leslie Halliwell, 'Film Quality Group Visit', 19 October 1973, IBA/01023: 3996311.

11　'*News at Ten* Comes out on Top', *Campaign*, 20 August 1976; 'Top of the TV Pops – Spartacus or the News?', *Screen International*, 11 September 1976, 23.

12　Alasdair Milne, 'Film Purchasing Policy', 27 May 1976, BBC R78/1,123/1.

13　Representatives from each company described their respective services in 'Three TV Measurement Kings Line up for Your Approval', *World's Press News*, 12 August 1955.

14　Ibid.

15 Donald Dinsley, 'Are They Telling You the Truth about TV?', *Sunday Dispatch*, 11 January 1959.

16 Bedford Attwood, quoted in 'Profits, Culture and the Great God TAM', *Sunday Times*, 28 May 1961, 28.

17 'Keeping up to Date', *Dealer*, August 1968.

18 Reply to letter from John Cross, 'Working Out Viewing Habits', *TV Times*, 28 January 1971, 53.

19 'No Sharp Practice', *The Stage and Television Today*, 12 March 1970, 10.

20 Ibid.

21 *Television*, 13 February 1970.

22 'BBC Claims It Got Biggest Share Yet', *The Stage and Television Today*, 12 August 1976.

23 Arthur Sandles, 'TV Olympics Battle still Running', *Financial Times*, 10 August 1976, 7.

24 *Broadcast*, 16 June 1976, 12.

25 'Audience Research – Who's Right in the Ratings?', *Broadcast*, 25 April 1979, 6, 8.

26 'ITV Ratings Slide Worries Media Chiefs', *Campaign*, 4 December 1970.

27 Tony Gruner, 'Films Fly High', *Kine Weekly*, 19 June 1971.

28 'Feature Films – the Countdown to Action', *The Stage and Television Today*, 14 October 1976, 12.

29 Elkan Allan, 'The Professional Prophet', *Sunday Times Magazine*, 28 November 1971, 27. The score was for Potential Audience Return (PAR).

30 'How to Eliminate Failure, by TV's First Professional Prophet', *Cinema TV Today*, 11 March 1972. According to this report, Granada and Anglia used TAPE to anticipate ratings only when selling airtime; the other ten companies (excluding Channel, which largely took Westward's feed) used it to determine 'what film viewers are going to watch'.

31 Quoted in ibid.

32 Quoted in ibid.

33 Milton Shulman, 'Don't Think, Just Put on an Old Movie', *Evening Standard*, 1 December 1971.

34 See the unsigned article 'Command Performance: Your Favourite Films', *TV Times* (Granada), 11 March 1971, 18, for the full list and the poll results in 'Coming Soon: All Your Best Film Favourites', *TV Times* (Granada), 20 May 1971, 40.

35 Home Office, *Report of the Committee on the Future of Broadcasting*, 451.

36 Ibid, 454.

37 'The Birth of BARB', *Broadcast*, 20 July 1981, 24–25; 'BARB Launches New Era of Audience Research', *The Stage and Television Today*, 6 August 1981.

38 '*Jaws* Wins Monster Audience for ITV', *The Times*, 20 October 1981, 20; Peter Fiddick, 'Blackout on Top 20 Ratings Clouds the TV Picture' and 'TV Rivals Join in Audience Figures Cover Up', *Guardian*, 18 January 1982, 1, 4; '*Times* in BARB Deal', *Broadcast*, 18 January 1982, 7; David Hewson, '*The Times* Wins TV Ratings Battle', *The Times*, 22 January 1981, 2; Peter Fiddick, 'TV to Release Top Ten Ratings', *Guardian*, 22 January 1981; 'Now BARB Will Publish a New Top Fifty', *Broadcast*, 28 January 1982.

39 Stephen Murphy, quoted in Bernard Sendall to Sir Robert Fraser, 11 January 1968, IBA/00645: 3995796.

40   For a list of 'Tales from Europe' transmissions, see http://thewhitehorses.angelfire. com/002-talesfromeurope1.html. See also Robert Hanks, 'Archive TV: *The Singing, Ringing Tree*', *Sight and Sound* 31, no. 10 (October 2021): 96.

41   Halliwell to Murphy, 16 May 1967, IBA/01072: 3996262.

42   Murphy to Halliwell, 17 May 1967; note from Sendall (29 May 1967) on memo, Murphy to Sendall, 26 May 1967, IBA/01072: 3996262.

43   Dermot O'Hagan to Pat Mahoney, 3 February and 10 February 1977; Joan Elman to O'Hagan, 15 February 1977, IBA/01021: 3996313. On British television's sporadic use of these and similar films, see Sim Branaghan, 'Monsters from an Unknown Culture – Godzilla (and Friends) in Britain 1957–1980', Part 4, *SMGuariento. com*, 2018, at http://www.smguariento.com/monsters-from-an-unknown-culture-godzilla-and-friends-in-britain-1957-1980-by-sim-branaghan-part-4/.

44   Clifford Davis, 'Banned', *Daily Mirror*, 4 March 1975; Roger Todd, 'Shirley: Now the Lollipop Backlash', *Daily Mirror*, 5 March 1975; Margaret Hall, 'What a Giggle Says Shirley', *Daily Mirror*, 6 March 1975; Margaret Hinxman, 'Does Shirley Temple Frighten YOU?', and Martin Jackson, 'And the Man behind the Ban', *Daily Mail*, 5 March 1975, 6; John Guinery, 'Not Banned' (letter), *Daily Mail*, 12 March 1975, 29.

45   Letters in file 'Shirley Temple Films (1975–88)', IBA/01025: 3996309.

46   Michael Gillies, 'Shirley Temple', 5 March 1975; Donald Cullimore to George A. Cooper, 17 March 1975, IBA/01025: 3996309.

47   For a different account, see the present author's blog posts 'Films on TV at Christmas', Parts 1–3, online at sheldontimeshall.com.

48   Derek Meakin, 'Three Films for Christmas Day', *TV Times*, 20 December 1957, 11.

49   'Charlie Chaplin's *The Gold Rush*', *Radio Times*, 16 April 1964, 44.

50   'BBC "Had 80 pc of Viewers"', *Daily Telegraph*, 1 January 1964; TAM Press Release, 6 January 1964.

51   Weston Taylor, 'In the Court of Old King Kong', *News of the World*, 19 December 1965.

52   James Thomas, 'How Many Old Films Do You Want in Your Stocking?', *Daily Express*, 12 December 1966.

53   'Four out of 5 Watched BBC at Christmas', *Daily Telegraph*, 2 January 1969.

54   Peter Knight, 'BBC Scores Big Lead on Holiday TV', *Daily Telegraph*, 7 January 1969.

55   Tony Gruner, 'BBC Could Dominate Christmas Ratings', *Kine Weekly*, 12 December 1970.

56   E.O. Parker, 'Give Cinemas a Christmas Box' (letter), *CinemaTV Today*, 18 December 1972.

57   Ron Boyle, 'As the Real Life Drama behind Your Small Screen Christmas Movies Gets under Way', *Daily Express*, 24 December 1974.

58   '"Beeb" Claims Holiday Crown', *Journal*, 4 January 1975.

59   'Brave Face from ITV after Christmas KO', *CinemaTV Today*, 18 January 1975.

60   Sir Brian Young to Miles Byrne, 17 February 1977, IBA/01021: 3996313.

61   Sendall, 'Draft Christmas Schedule 1974', IBA Paper 197(74), 17 September 1974, RK/3/96, IBA/01063: 3996271.

62   Sendall, 'Christmas and New Year Programmes', IBA Paper 244(75), 11 September 1975, RK/3/21/7, IBA/01063: 3996271.

63 Sendall, 'Christmas and New Year Schedule', IBA Paper 276(75), 9 October 1975, RK/3/21/8, IBA/01063: 3996271.

64 Michael Pilsworth, '"An Imperfect Art" – TV Scheduling in Britain', *Sight and Sound* 49, no. 4 (Autumn 1980): 238.

65 Chris Dunkley, 'Scheming for a Bright Christmas', *Radio Times*, 1 January 1976, 67.

66 Richard Last, 'BBC Claims 88 pc of Viewers on Christmas Day', *Daily Telegraph*, 3 January 1976.

67 Dunkley, 'Scheming for a Bright Christmas'.

68 Diane Chanteau, 'We Scooped Festive TV Say Thames', *Evening Standard*, 28 December 1978; 'BBC Claim Clean Sweep at Xmas', *The Stage and Television Today*, 11 January 1979; 'TV Ratings', *Broadcast*, 22 January 1979.

69 Thunderbird5, comment on Joe Moran, 'Christmas TV: Five Key Moments', *Guardian*, 19 December 2014, online at http://www.theguardian.com/tv-and-radio/2014/dec/19/how-tv-shaped-the-great-british-christmas. ITV's afternoon film was *Battle for the Planet of the Apes* (1973/25.12.1978).

CHAPTER 8

The Home and the World –
Foreign-language Films on Television

Ou Est Mon Screwdriver? – The quickest way to discover that your set is not adjusted properly is to try to follow a French film like *Monsieur Alibi*. The sub-titles are out of focus, invisible (e.g. white lettering on a white tablecloth) or so large that they sprawl out of sight. Surely there must be *some* foreign films available to the BBC with the sound track 'dubbed' in English.
(John Harman, 'On My Screen', *Scan and Television News* 3, no. 4, August 1950, 21; original emphasis)

In 1970, a survey conducted by the magazine *Films and Filming* asked independent distributors ten questions about the business of releasing foreign-language films in the UK. One of them concerned the likely impact on the theatrical market of the regular showing of such films on television. Companies were asked to say whether TV 'helped to create a cinema-going audience for foreign films' or whether it was merely 'competition for the specialised cinema'.[1] Michael Chivers of Amanda Films found that broadcasts of 'Continental films' enhanced demand, 'particularly in the 16mm field, after the film has had extensive theatrical exhibition'. Charles Cooper of Contemporary Films did not think that television was the best way to see 'subtitled films', but felt that it nevertheless 'would tend to create an audience rather than diminish it'. Ian R. Jessel of Target International Pictures concurred, commenting: 'The fact that foreign films can be seen regularly on BBC2 will slowly help create a greater audience for foreign films but it will take time. I do not consider its effect harmful for the specialised cinema.'[2] While not all the ten respondents thought that subtitled films on TV stimulated demand for them in cinemas, none considered them to be a source of competition. The attitudes of these specialised distributors thus deviated strikingly from the standard views of mainstream exhibitors, whose hostility to television we have seen previously.

This chapter explores the 'specialised' field of non-Anglophone films on television, beginning with early research into the domestic audience for such films, and traces the development of dedicated broadcast strands for them – not only on the BBC channels.

Subtitled Films on Early Television

As discussed in Chapter 1, the prewar television service included a small number of feature films in foreign languages with English subtitles. These films were not always received with undiluted rapture. Assistant Director of Television R.E. Rendall reported that the first two to be shown, *The Student of Prague* (1935/14.08.1938) and *Man of the Moment* (1937/12.09.1938), 'produced considerable crops of complaints'.

> In both cases many people have said that they could not follow the film because they could not adjust their sets to make the English captions legible. They all object to our use of foreign films, and there was some quite virulent criticism of our use of a German film at that particular time.[3]

Rendall advised the Director of Television, Gerald Cock, to postpone the broadcast of further foreign-language films, as their showing was 'doing us more harm than good'. More went ahead anyway. The following year, 1939, a BBC audience survey returned 4,027 completed questionnaires from an estimated total of 20,000 set owners (see Table 8.1). Viewers were asked to express their opinion of nineteen different programme categories. Strongest approval (93 per cent of respondents) was received for outside broadcasts of plays and variety and for newsreels; particular disapproval was reserved for studio musical items (liked by only 12 per cent) and continental feature films (23 per cent). Cartoons were enjoyed by 82 per cent of viewers, live-action short films by 56 per cent and American or British feature films by 65 per cent.[4] There were requests for more of the latter but, as we have seen, very few were available to television. Reporting on the survey, *Radio Times* explained the reason why, apart from the intrinsic quality of the films themselves, foreign pictures were still being broadcast despite apparently being disliked by 77 per cent of the audience: 'the old difficulty of booking good English and American films'.[5] Clearly, the problem of film-industry opposition was now common knowledge.

With the postwar relaunch of the television service, the question of finding suitable film material again arose. An idea given careful consideration on more than one occasion was a Sunday-afternoon 'Film Society' or 'Third Programme' repertory slot, offering both foreign-language and silent films, few of which had yet been seen on television. A list of twenty-two titles suggested for the proposed slot ranged in age from *Rescued by Rover* (1905/05.05.1969) to *Kipps* (1941/01.02.1981) and included French, Italian, Russian, German and American films as well as British. Ernest Lindgren, director of the British Film Institute's National Film Library (now the BFI National Archive), was canvassed about the possibility of televising selected films from the library's large collection of material conserved for posterity. Lindgren was willing in principle to co-operate, but pointed out the difficulty of identifying and locating copyright holders, who would have to give permission before their films could be televised. Programme

Table 8.1 BBC audience survey, 1939.

Type of production	Percentage of viewers who like them	Type of production	Percentage of viewers who like them
A: Studio Production		**B: Outside Broadcasts**	
Drama: (a) Short	70	Sporting Events	88
Drama: (b) Full Length	83	Other Outside Events	89
Cabaret Variety Revue	91	Plays or Variety	93
Orchestra Soloists	45		
Musical Features	12	**C: Films**	
Ballet	25	News Reels	93
Operetta	26	Cartoon Films	82
Talks: News, Maps, etc	74	Short Films	56
Sports Demonstrations	43	Feature Films	
Other Demonstrations	80	(a) English or American	65
Picture Page	92	(b) Continental	23

Source: The Scanner, 'Television Is Grand!', *Radio Times*, 7 July 1939, 13.

Organiser Cecil Madden wanted to launch the slot with Robert Flaherty's *Nanook of the North* (1922/03.08.1958), but this was not yet available. Instead, clearance was obtained for two prewar German productions following payment to the Custodian of Enemy Property of a £20 royalty for each transmission.[6] Josef von Sternberg's *The Blue Angel* (1930/01.12.1947) was transmitted but Fritz Lang's *Metropolis* (1927/12.08.1975), while mooted, failed to appear. However, an abridged version of *The Cabinet of Dr Caligari* (1920/05.07.1948) was shown with an introduction by Roger Manvell.

The number of commercial distributors dealing in continental films was very small, though occasionally this specialised type of product was also handled by major companies. As members of the trade associations, the majors were generally reluctant to deal with television at all. But over dinner with Imlay Newbiggin-Watts, a former associate now working for the BBC, Sir David Cunynghame, Foreign Sales Director of Alexander Korda's London Film Productions, let it be known that he was willing to supply a number of the European films under the company's control. They included celebrated French and Italian productions such as *Les Enfants du paradis* (1945/03.08.1948), *Open City* (1945/24.08.1948) and *Panique* (1947/06.09.1949). The price asked for them was high by the Corporation's usual standards – £500 per title for two screenings apiece – but the quality of the films and the importance of the source (Korda having been a sympathetic contact before the war) meant that the deal was seen by BBC management as good value.[7]

Les Enfants du paradis was chosen as the first to be screened. The three-hour film was presented as a prestige event over two consecutive nights and promoted with a background article in *Radio Times* by *Sunday Times* film critic Dilys Powell.[8] But technical difficulties again became apparent. The film's second half involved a large number of darkly lit scenes, with reel 7 (of twenty) considered unsuitable for broadcast. A new copy of that reel was therefore struck, printed lighter than normal. However, the transmission of the first half was marred by sound distortion, leading not only to viewer complaints but to concerns at the Corporation about the bad impression of television's presentation standards this must have left on the film industry.[9]

A problem that to some extent affected all film transmissions in the early postwar years was the age of the equipment still in use. The prewar Mechau telecine did not render dark images very clearly, particularly shadowy or night-time scenes. Foreign films presented particular challenges, because subtitles were often printed too small to be legible on a television monitor, remained too briefly on the screen, had been printed in white type against a light background or were cropped at the bottom or sides by the TV screen borders. Ordering 'clean' (unsubtitled) prints of foreign films, for which subtitles were then made specifically for television, added considerably to costs and negatives were not always readily available for this purpose. Two other French films offered by Cunynghame, *La Belle et la Bête* (1946/15.04.1952) and *Les Portes de la nuit* (1946/29.03.1985), were rejected because of their poor subtitling and preponderance of dark shots.

The Mechau telecine was not only old, it was also temperamental, and prints that were not in pristine condition (most copies supplied by distributors being from existing stock rather than newly struck for TV were prone to breakages). This had happened several times during the first postwar feature transmission, *Marie-Louise* (1944/28.10.1946), which was interrupted three times in the first ten minutes. The first broadcast of *Open City* in August 1948 was disrupted by no fewer than five breakdowns, resulting in an order that no feature films not already scheduled should be shown during evening hours until new telecine equipment could be installed. Head of Television Films Philip Dorté ordered that all prints be rigorously inspected, rehearsed and where necessary repaired or replaced before transmission.[10]

The new telecine was not received until May 1949 and the subtitling problem not addressed until September the same year, with the introduction of a process employed by the Paris-based firm Titres that stamped subtitle captions directly onto film prints using tiny printing blocks. The licensing arrangement with London Films, having lapsed in the interim, was renewed to allow further screenings, beginning with the delayed first showing of *Panique*, followed by repeats of all three titles. This was desirable for both the BBC and the distributor, as these films had been duly banned by the Cinematograph Exhibitors' Association (CEA) from further cinema bookings and therefore no more revenue could be expected from that direction.[11] London Films was for this reason wary of offering other foreign-language pictures and the BBC itself was reluctant to seek out more than a handful from elsewhere because of the generally unfavourable audience reaction.

Strong feelings for and against foreign films were regularly displayed in the letters pages of *Radio Times*. Correspondence alternated between indignant complaints and requests for more:

I thoroughly enjoy cinema going and therefore like seeing films televised but tonight I was forced to advance to within one yard of my receiver to understand what the film *Les Enfants du Paradis* was about. As a result I am now suffering from a stiff neck, and trying to restore my eyesight to normal. Please don't show any more films with sub-titles. The average television receiver screen is too small for comfortable reading.[12]

Many people like myself enjoy foreign films, yet we have seen no fresh ones since letters of complaint appeared in *Radio Times*. They are easily understood by the average person, and as the acting and film technique reach a high level, I shall be delighted when they are televised again.[13]

I read with growing apprehension the letter of a viewer who favours foreign films. Please, not again.[14]

Some months back we were promised a series of foreign films and were, indeed, delighted with *Les Enfants du Paradis* and *Open City*. Many viewers must be wondering, like myself, whether Scattergood Baines is intended as a substitute. If so, could we not have at least one Continental film a month?[15]

I wish to protest about programmes like *Panique*. If we *must* suffer this type of programme at least let us have it in English.

Many thanks for that truly magnificent film *Panique*. Repeat, please.[16]

Could we not have some more of such films as *Panique* and *Les Enfants du Paradis*? Surely there are other viewers besides myself who, apart from enjoying these films for their own particular charm and freshness, would welcome them as a change from the everlasting Variety and ballet programmes.[17]

Other correspondents pointed out how television might come to the aid of those viewers with restricted opportunities for seeing the films that interested them:

I am disabled and unable to travel to London to see these films, but there must be many other people who for various reasons must forgo this pleasure and who would welcome the chance of seeing on television such films as *Poil de Carotte*, *Mayerling*, *The Bicycle Thieves*, and many others, which never come to our local cinemas. Could we not have a fortnightly or monthly series of foreign films?[18]

One of television's most illogical whims was the early evening showing of Carné's *Les Enfants du Paradis* recently. Films with Jean-Louis Barrault in them are riches which come only occasionally to those with the misfortune to live outside London, and such tragic outcasts deserve them at a reasonable hour. My own modest suggestion is that you show *Les Enfants du Paradis* on the first *Thursday* of every month instead of repeating the Sunday play...[19]

One viewer echoed the thoughts of BBC schedulers in hoping for a regular repertory slot:

May I support the plea for more foreign films, and may I add to that a plea for more of the classics of the cinema? As we cannot have the best of the current studio productions let us have the best from the past, more films like *Of Mice and Men*, for instance. Could we not have a 'Television Film Club,' to show the best films from all over the world, as our film societies do? ... Or, as an alternative, why not a serial 'History of the Cinema' illustrated by showings of the important films of each period?[20]

Professional commentators also had divided views. On the one hand, *Scan*'s anonymous reviewer gave their endorsement to *Panique*, 'which showed how fine even a sordid crime film can be. Expect usual adverse criticism from those who refused to switch on because "it was a foreign film." English sub-titles or not, this was an intelligent evening.'[21] On the other, *The Listener*'s Reginald Pound sympathised with the naysayers:

> No production problem bedevilled the televising of the French resistance film, *Bataille du Rail*. But the presentation was unsatisfactory in that many viewers probably gave up trying to read the English captions very soon after the film had started. Something should have been done to avoid or minimise this annoyance. No one pays £2 a year to be irritated even for two minutes.[22]

Ten years after the Corporation's first survey of its viewers, *Scan* magazine published the results of a Television Poll conducted by the British Television Viewers' Society, which collected 65,469 public responses (see Tables 8.2.1 and 8.2.2). On a chart of the most popular programme types, which respondents selected from a prepared list, 'Films – English spoken' appeared fifth, with a 66.3 per cent satisfaction rate. Twelfth and last on the chart were 'Films – foreign languages', with only 28.9 per cent satisfaction – nearly 24 percentage points below the next most popular. Even more telling was a chart of the *least* popular actual programmes, with accompanying *dissatisfaction* rates, in which foreign-language films occupied four of the top five 'unpopularity' spots. Commented the Society's K. Sampson: 'It is apparent that viewers have stated in no uncertain way that they look upon their sets as a means of bringing entertainment into their homes – not education nor culture.' The poll results were to be forwarded to the BBC, and Sampson noted:

> If the results are received in the spirit of co-operation [with] which we intend to present them the effort will be well worth while and we shall all benefit by the deletion of that small minority of programmes which at the moment are not in accord with the wishes of viewers as expressed through the Television Poll.[23]

Philip Dorté concluded with dismay that, 'with the exception of a minority of Academy and Studio One-minded viewers, second grade English-speaking films are much preferred to first grade foreign-language ones'.[24] The Academy and Studio One were West End cinemas specialising in foreign-language and 'art' films. The distribution companies that supplied them had few outlets in which to screen the films they imported other than these and a handful of other specialised showcases around the country. Television was therefore a potentially valuable client once a film had completed its initial run, as mainstream cinemas outside the capital rarely showed foreign-language films and the TV service was in any case expanding only slowly across the country. However, the attraction of selling to television was compromised not only by the danger of the CEA cutting off any possibility of future revivals, but by the low hire fees the BBC was able

Table 8.2.1 Most popular programme types, 1948–49.

Popularity	Programme	Per cent
1	Plays	80.9
2	Variety	78.3
3	Actualities	70.1
4	Musical comedy	69.3
5	Films – English spoken	66.3
6	Ballet	66.2
7	Documentary features	65.3
8	Orchestral music	63.9
9	Quiz programmes	61.1
10	Opera	56.5
11	Cultural programmes	52.2
12	Films – foreign languages	28.9

Table 8.2.2 Least popular programmes, 1948–49.

Unpopularity	Programme	Per cent
1	Bridge Demonstrations	59.3
2	*Alexander Nevsky* (foreign film)	52.2
3	*The Blue Angel* (foreign film)	47.9
4	*Life of Titan* (foreign film)	46.1
5	*Les Enfants de Paradis* [*sic*] (foreign film)	42.5
6	Crossword	37.2
7	Laurel and Hardy (short films)	36.3
8	On Your Head (about hats)	33.2
9	Eye of the Artist	29.9
10	Western films	28.4
11	Espana	25.4
12	Casa D'Esalta	24.9
	Children's Section	
1	Orchestral Concerts	26.8
2	Foreign cartoons	24.3
3	Charley Chase Comedies	20.3

Source: K. Sampson, 'Results of the Television Poll', *Scan* 1, no. 10 (February 1949): 12.

to offer. A successful release such as the Italian comedy *Four Steps in the Clouds* (1942/27.02.1951) could gross £3,000 in a West End run, but the hire fees offered by BBC Film Booking Manager Greeve del Strother rarely exceeded £300.[25]

One bright spot was that, in marked contrast to the hostility of mainstream distributors and exhibitors (with the notable exceptions of London Films and Michael Balcon's Ealing Studios), some managers of companies specialising in imports took a positive view of television. C.V. Bargate of GCT Distributors, affiliated to the Curzon Cinema in London's Curzon Street, and George Hoellering of Film Traders, linked to the Academy Cinema in Oxford Street, were both keen to help the BBC, despite fears that opposition from the trade would lead to boycotts.[26] Hoellering even offered specially to import films for joint use by the Academy and the television service, believing that more foreign-language films on TV would enlarge the audience for them in cinemas.[27] Following a meeting with Hoellering, Graham Woodford of the BBC's Film Booking Section reported:

> His line was possibly the most broad-minded of any distributor in that he considered that it was almost a prestige boost to have his films televised and that he considered it good publicity in the widest sense for foreign films which he thought would benefit in the long run by going to areas hitherto closed to films not in the English language … he is the type of man who is genuinely interested in the idea and prepared to support it for what it is rather than from what he can get out of it.[28]

As the BBC's coverage gradually widened across the country throughout the 1950s, it was able to bring films that had had very little national exposure to a much wider public than could have seen them in metropolitan showcases. When GCT's *Four Steps in the Clouds* was transmitted, BBC Audience Research reported: 'Many provincial viewers were pleased at this first opportunity of seeing a good foreign film.' Moreover, subtitled films provided a rare type of programming that could be enjoyed by viewers with hearing impairments, estimated as comprising 16 per cent of the UK population.[29]

Hoellering had his own ideas about how foreign films should be presented on television, recommending the abridgement of a long film like Roberto Rossellini's *Paisà* (1946/26.06.1951) and even offering to prepare TV versions of product from other distributors: 'I believe a film should be specially cut for television, intelligently shortened and with fewer titles, and in some cases, where it really fits, a commentary mixed in, but not the whole way through – only at certain points. Again this depends on each individual film.' He added:

> I want to assure you that I am not just keen on booking films to you. I really want to do a good job on the films so that the televising of these films is a success. This is the most important of all to us, because if it is not successful, even if we get paid, it would not be good for our special trade. Instead of creating an audience in our art cinemas, we would put the audience off seeing Continental films.[30]

When *Four Steps in the Clouds* was televised, special measures were taken to make the film more appealing and accessible for viewers. The subtitles were spoken aloud in English voice-over, delivered live during transmission by actors in the BBC studio. This type of presentation, supervised by del Strother, was subsequently used for selected parts of *Paisà*, another film with multilingual dialogue, and for the previously-rejected *La Belle et la Bête*. Reaction was once again decidedly mixed. BBC Audience Research found a generally positive response to *Four Steps in the Clouds*, with 64 per cent of viewers surveyed in favour of the presentation experiment and only 33 per cent definitely against it (see Table 8.3). It was

Table 8.3 Reaction Indices for foreign-language films on BBC Television, 1950–52.

Title	Day	Date	Time	Sets-in-use (%)	Reaction Index
The Barber of Seville	Sunday	15.01.1950	9.00pm	74	49
Panique	Sunday	26.02.1950	7.00pm	52	66
Paris, capitale de la danse	Friday	28.04.1950	10.05pm	61	46
It Concerns Us All	Sunday	21.05.1950	7.30pm	51	73
Ramuntcho	Tuesday	30.05.1950	9.00pm	59	57
Monsieur Alibi	Friday	14.07.1950	8.15pm	67	43
Four Steps in the Clouds	Tuesday	27.02.1950	8.45pm	74	66
Bataille du rail	Tuesday	17.04.1951	8.25pm	66	63
Alexander Nevsky	Wednesday	09.05.1951	9.30pm	63	46
Gitans d'Espagne	Friday	08.06.1951	9.00pm	52	38
Paisà	Tuesday	26.06.1951	8.35pm	41	61
La Belle et la Bête	Tuesday	15.04.1952	8.30pm	63	51

Source: Adapted from memo, Robert Silvey to Cecil McGivern, 1 May 1952, BBC T1/3.

particularly liked by viewers in the 'lower income group', despite the apparent unsuitability of some of the English voices: among the voice artists used were such distinctly-British performers as Valentine Dyall and McDonald Hobley.[31] *Four Steps in the Clouds* was seen by a large proportion of the potential audience, with 74 per cent of television sets thought to be tuned in during the broadcast. *Paisà* had a relatively small audience of 41 per cent of sets in use, but it drew a 'reaction index' (approval rating) of 61 and was well enough regarded to be repeated twice during the same year.[32]

Previewing *La Belle et la Bête* in *Radio Times*, the *Observer*'s film critic C.A. Lejeune commented:

> In one point *La Belle et la Bête* should prove an admirable choice for television. The story is so familiar in its main outline that everyone can follow it, even if the sub-titles should turn out to be not always legible. And the spare French dialogue appears to consist largely of the two urgent addresses – 'Belle!' and 'Bête!' – which most people can manage to interpret without any real strain at all.[33]

But *The Listener*'s Reginald Pound again offered a contrary view: 'The *poésie* of the end-product was more *bête* than *belle*!'[34] This time, audiences seemed to agree. With 63 per cent of sets in use, the film had a reaction index of only 51. A Viewer Research Report summarised the findings of a survey 'based on 364 completed questionnaires':

> The film itself did not make much of an appeal. A minority were enthralled by its magical atmosphere, and thought it a 'most poetic representation of the old fairy-tale', but most viewers either disliked its rather eerie quality, sometimes described as 'nightmarish', or were just not interested in a 'childish and rather vague story'. There was also the usual adverse reaction from those viewers who object in principle to the screening of any foreign film, though several were, it seems, not altogether averse to 'the realistic type of French film'.

The film's 'half-light' visual style also did not come across well on television and the spoken-title presentation was found to be intrusive, especially by those viewers who understood French (a greater proportion of the audience than could speak Italian) and wanted to listen to the original dialogue, which remained just audible under the English translation. The simultaneous presence of French dialogue, English voices and subtitles was found to be 'a considerable strain on those reporting, and it was roundly condemned as confusing, irritating and superfluous'.[35] This disappointing reception seems to have put paid to the notion of a repertory slot, in spite of requests from some viewers. After *La Belle et la Bête*, no more foreign-language films were shown by the BBC for more than four years.

'Late Night Film' and 'International Film Season'

Between 1956 and 1960, the BBC resumed occasional transmissions of foreign features, with a dozen overseas, non-Anglophone films shown either in their original languages with subtitles or, in a minority of cases, with an English voice track. They included recognised European classics and award winners such as *Le Jour se lève* (1939/20.12.1956), *Bicycle Thieves* (1948/05.03.1957 – see Figure 8.1), *Race for Life* (1956/02.01.1958) and *Devil in the Flesh* (1947/09.11.1959). The first Asian feature to be shown on British television also appeared in this period: Kon Ichikawa's Japanese production *The Harp of Burma* (1956/26.07.1959), better known as *The Burmese Harp*, was presented in a 'specially edited version' running about 90 minutes, shortened from its original 116.[36]

In train with its gradual increase in regular weekly film strands, the BBC launched its first midweek evening slot on Tuesdays in July 1961. 'Late Night Film' was introduced in *Radio Times* as comprising 'outstanding and off-beat international feature films'.[37] Despite the series title, transmissions usually started around 9.30pm and the strand soon moved to Fridays. It included some films that were perhaps less mainstream than would normally have been seen in the channel's peak-time Saturday and Sunday slots, though the series also featured two early Fred Astaire-Ginger Rogers musicals and other Hollywood pictures. Its first season began with an English-language Swiss production, *The Last Chance* (1945/18.07.1961), and included an English-dubbed version of the French *Isle of Sinners* (1950/15.08.1961). No film was billed as having subtitles until the trio of Sergei Eisenstein classics that ended the run: *Alexander Nevsky* (1938/21.05.1948), in a longer version than had previously been broadcast, and the two-part *Ivan the Terrible* (1944/17.11.1961 and 1958/24.11.1961). *Sight and Sound* commented:

> Startlingly, the BBC is able to claim an average audience of five million for each of the programmes, with each film attracting a slightly larger public and slightly more enthusiastic reaction than its predecessor. In television terms, five million is still a minority audience; in cinema terms, it would represent a fantastic public for these particular films.[38]

Figure 8.1 BBC Television presented a subtitled version of *Bicycle Thieves* (1948) as its main evening attraction on 5 March 1957. *Radio Times* © Immediate Media Co. Artwork © Robert Micklewright.

This, the magazine noted, was more than the average regular audience for the film-themed TV programmes *Picture Parade* and *The Cinema Today*, both concerned with new releases. A positive response also appeared in *Radio Times*'s letters column:

> I should like to express my gratitude to the BBC for showing the three magnificent Eisenstein films. Their excitement and beauty as works of art need no elaboration.
>
> I would like to take this opportunity to plead for the showing of more such films from all over the world.
>
> In Belfast – and I imagine also in most other places with the exception of London, and Edinburgh at festival time – the chance of seeing such films is practically nil, whereas one can still see American (and British) films, old and new, at any of half a dozen cinema six nights a week.[39]

Five more subtitled films subsequently appeared under the 'Late Night Film' banner: Vittorio de Sica's *Umberto D* (1951/24.08.1962) and the UK premiere of a new Dutch film, *Funfair in the Rain* (1962, 06.09.1962), followed by Andrzej Wajda's war trilogy, *A Generation* (1956/11.01.1963), *Kanal* (1957/18.01.1963) and *Ashes and Diamonds* (1959/25.01.1963). Derek Hill in *Sight and Sound* reported that the audience for the season ranged from 6½ million for *Ashes and Diamonds* to 8½ million for *Bicycle Thieves*; and Gordon Smith, who with Dora Nirva was principally responsible for the presentations, worked out that the films shown would have needed a run of at least fifty years in the average specialist cinema to clock up such an audience. More than three times as many people in Britain have now seen *Bicycle Thieves* as *South Pacific*.[40]

Moreover, and just as importantly, many viewers liked what they saw. According to Hill, '*Kanal* obtained an appreciation rating (expressed on an average enjoyment scale unrelated to the actual audience figure) almost as high as any British or American film ever shown by the BBC – despite the fact that the order of two of its reels was reversed. And *Bicycle Thieves* was still more popular.'[41]

Hill, who had written background articles on *Umberto D* and the Wajda war trilogy for *Radio Times* and who would later become a film buyer for Channel Four, noted that the purchase prices now paid by the BBC were competitive with the average returns for subtitled films from UK cinema release. This made a TV sale a more attractive proposition than heretofore. This success had its downside, however, drawing opposition from companies such as Gala. Its manager Kenneth Rive announced that as a distributor he would refuse to deal with any producer selling films less than ten years old to television and that as an exhibitor he would boycott the releases of renters like Contemporary, which had sold films to the BBC, including the war trilogy.

The Film Society movement also took notice, with Peter Armitage, editor of the British Federation of Film Societies' magazine *Film*, suggesting excitedly in 1961 that 'we are perhaps nearer than ever to the TV equivalent of a film society, which has frequently been mooted in the past'.[42] Returning to the subject two years later, however, the journal found that the 'idea of a film society of the air' was 'causing a fair amount of consternation among film societies', as they were now experiencing competition of their own. The editorial tried to reassure readers that the showing on television of films like Alain Resnais's *Hiroshima mon amour* (1959/01.02.1963) was 'wonderful publicity and could enlarge the potential film society audience'. But it also acknowledged that such broadcasts reached 'an audience 100 times larger than the total film society membership (50,000)' and that 'if TV showings become much more frequent there might be a superficial case to be made out for all film societies shutting up shop'.[43]

Midway through its run, 'Late Night Film' was rebranded as 'International Film Season', thus becoming the BBC's first regular weekly showcase specifically devoted mainly to foreign films – though the initial presentation under this rubric, *Hiroshima mon amour*, was shown in a dubbed version. The series ran for only four more weeks, ending with another UK premiere, Ermanno Omi's *Time Stood Still* (1959/22.02.1963), again in an English-language version. *Radio Times* published a selection of viewers' letters in response to the series, most though not all favourable:

May I say 'thank you' to BBC-tv for the International Film Season? We who are distant from the main centres of population have little or no chance to enjoy the Art of the Cinema and usually have access only to its more brash and commercial products.

For this reason the recent season made Friday a highlight of the week. All the films have shown how adult the cinema can be; and have been a memorable experience.[44]

Admirable though they may be, foreign films with English sub-titles are not at all suitable for the small screen.

The captions, appearing as they do in a light colour against a similar background, coupled with the fact that they are so rapidly presented, demand about ninety minutes of close concentration if the story is to be understood at all.[45]

I very much appreciate the series of sub-titled films being shown on BBC-tv every Friday.

I am sure they provide interest for many hundreds of people in this country who like myself are deaf, and thus quite unable to enjoy the great number of plays that are presented every week.

May one hope that you will continue to run this series and give pleasure to a great number of people otherwise cut off?[46]

An article in the magazine commented on 'the remarkable popularity' of the first season, which seemed to indicate that there was 'a large public for Continental films among television viewers. This is the encouraging fact underlying the second season which opens tonight and is intended to be much wider in scope than the first.'[47] This further twelve-week series appeared in July 1963 and was followed by a third, fourteen-week run in early 1965, on what was by then BBC1, despite the existence of a new 'minority' channel in the shape of BBC2. Some of the films in the third season had previously been shown in BBC2's own first regular film strand, 'Cinema 625', thus making them available to a potentially larger audience on the main channel. After this, there were no more runs of 'International Film Season'. Instead, both it and 'Cinema 625' were superseded by a new series beginning in October 1965.

'World Cinema'

For the next decade, 'World Cinema' became the BBC's regular platform for sub-titled and specialised films. It made BBC2 the main institutional home for films not in the English language and fulfilled, more than any previous strand, the ambition for a repertory cinema of the air. British and American films were included – the series' second presentation was *Brief Encounter* (1945/11.10.1965) – but the hallmark was variety of source material: the 1970 season was billed as a 'new series of outstanding feature films from more than twenty different countries'.[48] The later seasons (1970–74) included groups of two, three or more films organised around directors, actors, writers, countries, continents or themes, such as the Great War, 'The Mind of the Child', 'The Art of Compilation', 'Shakespeare round the World' and 'Heart-throbs of the 20s'. In his detailed study of the series, Ieuan Franklin identifies twenty-six countries of origin for the films shown in just its first five years.[49]

'World Cinema' was programmed by David Francis, formerly Television Acquisitions Officer of the National Film Archive. He was recruited by the BBC's Head of Purchased Programmes, Gordon Smith, after they had met on the Archive's selection committee. Francis was charged particularly with acquiring films for the planned colour service, due to start on BBC2 in 1967. He visited the film markets at Milan and Brno, picking up both new films and classics relatively cheaply by comparison with those acquired from the British and American majors. He recalled this period in a 2021 interview:

> You were aware that, at that time, the only place you could see foreign-language films was in art-house cinemas in big cities. So, it was very important, if we were to create a new audience, that they were presented in the very best possible way on television, giving a chance to those people who could never see them in the cinema and enjoy them there. We took a lot of care to make the very best presentations, including producing our own subtitles. I used to write all the programme notes that were sent out to the publicity, the critics, and things like that. ...

> An awful lot of people were brought up on world cinema because of this effort which gave them their first experience of foreign language films. I keep on meeting them even today. It made a huge impact. Because we spoke English, in Britain, we'd really only seen British and American films in the cinemas. World Cinema offered a new and unknown world, so far as most people were concerned.[50]

It is worth looking more closely at the presentation of one major film that was placed successively in three of these specialised film strands. Akira Kurosawa's *Seven Samurai* (1954/21 & 28.06.1964) was first released in British cinemas in 1955, in an abridged version running 155 minutes. The BBC had considered it for acquisition two years later, when Film Booking Assistant Peggy Miller previewed it. Her viewing report gives an indication of some of the considerations then shaping film selection:

> The black and white photography is excellent with some remarkable tracking shots. There are a number of close-ups of Japanese faces, some of which are surprisingly beautiful. The film is extremely long and runs over two hours, which will probably mean that we would have to cut but in any case, although the subtitling is very good both in content and vision, I think the Japanese language is so outlandish to our ears that it may prove to be somewhat wearing after an hour or so. There is also a certain amount of brutality which, although it does not exceed European standards of decency in this respect, nevertheless might be rather hard to take by some of the more squeamish members of the public. Again a fine film but not, I think, suitable for our purposes.[51]

The film was not taken at this time, but *Seven Samurai* eventually appeared in the first season of 'Cinema 625' in June 1964, transmitted in two parts (running approximately 80 and 75 minutes, totalling roughly the same length as the UK theatrical version) over successive weeks. A repeat showing on BBC1 in 'International Film Season' the year after followed the same pattern. But for its third transmission, this time as part of 'World Cinema', it was shown in two parts in a single evening, 14 September 1972, the parts separated only by a five-minute news bulletin coinciding with the original intermission. The advertised slot length was 185 minutes, and *Radio Times*'s film columnist Philip Jenkinson explained: 'This version is 45 minutes longer than any print previously seen in Britain and BBCtv has prepared special new subtitles for the whole film.'[52]

The achievement again did not go unnoticed in *Sight and Sound*. 'A newish print, fresh and literate subtitles, and the overwhelming flow and vigour of the narrative, helped to make this a triumph for BBC2's World Cinema series', commented John Gillett. He also quoted the impressions of a Japanese visitor:

> 'Very interesting place, London,' remarked Mr Hisakazu Tsuji, friend and scriptwriter for Mizoguchi. 'My wife and I arrived in our hotel, turned on the television and there was the complete version of *Seven Samurai* – which isn't available in Japan.'[53]

The film's audience was again estimated as five million viewers. Among them was the future filmmaker and host of BBC2's 'Moviedrome' series, Alex Cox, who recalled the screening as a formative moment.[54]

After 306 films shown between 1965 and 1974, 'World Cinema' was wound up and Francis returned to the National Film Archive. The last season was immediately followed by 'Milestones of the Film', a fifteen-week series comprising 'classic films that have influenced the development of the world cinema'.[55] In 1975, BBC2 had no specific slot showcasing foreign-language films, though almost two dozen were incorporated into other strands (see Chapter 12). But a successor series emerged the year after.

'Film International'

Seasons of 'Film International' ran annually from 1976 to 1983, with an additional final run in 1986. This series put more emphasis than its predecessor on recent releases and festival entries rather than classic revivals or linking themes. Across the eleven years, it encompassed 117 titles, though other series of foreign-language films were also broadcast in this period. In early 1979, the fourth season of 'Film International' ran into trouble over a group of major European films, each by a different director but sharing a common theme: sex. Promoting the series, *Radio Times* ran an illustrated article by critic Philip Oakes called 'Sex and the Cinema'. It included the comment: 'Certainly the season will be greeted with enthusiasm and indignation, not in equal parts, because protests are always more vocal. But it is a giant step from films like these which explore sex to those which simply exploit it.'[56] The first part proved prophetic. Two films in particular brought significant complaints: the opening presentation, Luis Buñuel's *Belle de jour* (1967/19.01.1979), and Louis Malle's *Dearest Love* (1971/02.02.1979).[57]

Unlike the subsequent titles in the season, which were shown at 10.30pm or later, *Belle de jour* started at 9.25pm, not long after the watershed. Objections came not just from the public but also the BBC's own Board of Management, members of which described it as 'a thoroughly nasty and disagreeable film' and 'about as erotic as a cold breakfast'. While not all the Board found *Belle de jour* offensive, a majority considered that it was 'a film which exploited sex'. Members held that, irrespective of the film's merits, its 'promotion and placing' had been misjudged, having 'the political effect of putting perfectly sensible, moderate people in to the same camp as Mrs Whitehouse'.[58] Indeed, the clean-up campaigner Mary Whitehouse had herself written to the *Guardian* (*The Times* being unavailable due to industrial action) to describe in lurid detail the contents of two sequences. Whitehouse's own account was taken to task by other correspondents, including a reverend gentleman who described the film as 'intensely *moralistic*'.[59]

A lengthy letter sent by another viewer to the BBC's Chairman, Sir Michael Swann, described *Dearest Love* as being 'designedly amoral and anarchistic' and 'intrinsically evil', concluding: 'If this film does not deprave and corrupt then nothing will.' Swann's reply defended the decision to show the film, citing its favourable critical reception and noting that its late-night placing and the billing in *Radio Times* 'gave a fair indication of the content so that those likely to be offended should not have stumbled upon it accidentally'.[60] But internally at the Corporation, there was still concern. Referring in particular to *Dearest Love*, a letter from the Nationwide Festival of Light described the season as 'a regular BBC "porn slot"'.[61]

The Deputy Managing Director of Television, summoned to a meeting of the BBC's General Advisory Council (GAC), was warned 'to come to that meeting well briefed about the series, to defend the party line on the subject of identifying films by their BBFC classification, and not to be too vigorous in his defence of the films in the current series'. The Director General, Ian Trethowan, considered 'that it had been a mistake to present them as a series of adult films and that it had been wrong to put *Belle de Jour* first and to schedule it at 9.25pm'.[62]

It was unfortunate that the season coincided with a debate in the House of Commons relevant to the censorship of films and television: on the Indecent Displays (Control) Bill and a proposed inquiry on Television Programmes (Scenes of Violence).[63] The BBC Board of Management noted that over 100 members of Parliament, including one of the GAC, had signed a motion calling for a ban on the broadcasting of films that had received 'X' certificates from the British Board of Film Censors (BBFC). Trethowan blamed this motion specifically on the negative publicity given to 'Film International'.[64]

The controversy also reached *Radio Times*, of course, with two selections of letters representing a range of public viewpoints. One correspondent considered *Belle de jour* 'degrading, immoral and sick', whose transmission validated Mary Whitehouse's most dire predictions. Another commented in more general terms: 'Among current euphemisms, one of the silliest is that a film is suitable for "adult viewing", when in truth it is fit for nobody's viewing.' But other viewers disagreed, describing Buñuel's film as 'brilliant' and 'marvellous' and thanking the Corporation for 'a cinematic feast', representing 'the very best of world cinema'. One added: 'All credit to the BBC for this series. Some of us have no access to viewing serious or interesting films except through the BBC.'[65]

Besides 'Film International', BBC2's other major foreign-film strands included director retrospectives: François Truffaut (ten films in 1978 – see Figure 8.2), Jean Renoir (twelve, 1979) and Claude Lelouch (four, 1979); national cinemas, including 'The Italian Cinema' (twelve, 1969–70) and two seasons of French films (no fewer than thirty-seven titles in 1969 and seven in 1980); crime in 'Murder International' (ten, 1979); and Spaghetti Westerns (seven, 1979). This last series was shown during the long ITV strike of that year and therefore proved extremely popular, achieving what BBC Audience Research claimed was the largest ever audience for any programme to date on BBC2: 18.5 million viewers for *The Good, the Bad and the Ugly* (1966/19.04.1976) on Thursday, 23 August. This was only half a million fewer than for its BBC1 premiere on Easter Monday 1976; it exceeded BBC2's previous record audience by 4.5 million.[66]

Spaghetti Westerns were of course shown in English-dubbed versions and therefore they and other such films often turned up on BBC1, which after 1965 very rarely presented subtitled films. However, a four-week Sunday-morning series on BBC1 in 1980 called 'International Success' presented three subtitled feature films and a selection of Hong Kong TV crime shows. The features – the Indian *Amar Akbar Anthony* (1977/07.09.1980), the Spanish *The Spirit of the Beehive* (1973/06.11.1976) and the Greek *Lieutenant Natassa* (1970/21.09.1980) – were not listed in *Radio Times*'s regular films column and were therefore easily missed if viewers were not alert. *Amar Akbar Anthony* was the first product of the Hindi popular cinema ('Bollywood') to be shown on British television.

In 1984, at the behest of what was by then the Programme Acquisition Department, BBC Broadcasting Research conducted a survey of public reaction to 120 films shown between January 1977 and June 1983 (see Tables 8.4.1–8.4.6).[67] The survey was partly quantitative, examining the films' ratings data and Reaction or Appreciation Indices (RIs and AIs, the difference in acronym reflecting recent changes in research methods, as discussed in Chapter 7), and partly qualitative, studying responses to specific questions asked in general interviews conducted with 987 members of the public. It found that foreign-language films were in general less popular than other programmes in the same time band on BBC2 (most were shown late on Saturday evening), in terms of both the number of viewers watching and the degree of their enjoyment. Among the survey report's main findings were these:

> The majority of viewers say they would 'never watch' a foreign language film on TV. Fewer than 1 in 10 would 'make a point of watching'. The rest may or may not do depending on the film itself or, more frequently, the competition. Despite the small numbers who would make a point of watching, around three quarters have seen a sub-titled film and only slightly fewer have seen a film they recognise as dubbed.[68]

The survey also canvassed attitudes to dubbing as opposed to subtitling. Although the majority of general viewers preferred dubbing, 'presumably because it

Figure 8.2 In the autumn of 1978, French filmmaker François Truffaut was the latest director to be recognised with a retrospective on BBC2. *Radio Times* © Immediate Media Co. Artwork © Mick Brownfield.

Tables 8.4.1–8.4.6 BBC Broadcasting Research: Foreign-language films on BBC2, 1977–83.

Table 8.4.1 Audiences for foreign-language films, January 1977–June 1983.

Average audiences for:	All foreign language films on BBC2		'Film International' Saturdays BBC2 10.00pm to close		Other programming Saturdays BBC2 10.00pm to close		BBC2 Saturdays 10.00pm to Close	
	millions	(no. of films)	millions	(no. of films)	millions	(no. of weeks)	millions	(total no. of weeks inc. films)
1977	1.2	(21)						
1978	0.9	(22)						
1979	1.4	(9)						
1980	0.8	(6)						
1981	1.3	(12)						
1982	1.3	(26)	1.2	(22)	1.7	(31)	1.5	(53)
1983 (Q. 1 & 2)	0.7	(24)	0.8	(16)	1.5	(10)	1.1	(26)
Jan 1982 – June 1983	1.0	(50)	1.0	(38)	1.6	(41)	1.3	(79)
Jan 1977 – June 1983	1.1	(120)	-	-	-	-	-	-

Note: Estimates from 1977–81 are derived from the Daily Survey. From 1982 onwards they are derived from BARB. (This footnote in the report refers to different methods of audience research used in these different periods; see Chapter 7 for background.)

Table 8.4.2 Audience composition for foreign-language films, January 1982–June 1983.

	'Film International'[a] Saturdays BBC2 10.00pm to Close		Other Programming Saturdays BBC2 10.00pm to close		BBC2 Saturdays 10.00pm to close		UK population aged 4+
	%	(no. of films)	%	(no. of weeks)	%	(total no. of weeks inc. films)	%
Age:							
4 – 15	8	(25)	6	(40)	7	(65)	19
16 – 24	8	(25)	9	(40)	9	(65)	14
25 – 34	17	(25)	17	(40)	17	(65)	14
35 – 44	33	(25)	33	(40)	33	(65)	27
55+	34	(25)	33	(40)	34	(65)	26
Sex:							
Male	50	(25)	49	(40)	49	(65)	49
Female	50	(25)	51	(40)	51	(65)	50
Social Grade:							
ABC1	34	(25)	30	(40)	32	(65)	34
C2	35	(25)	37	(40)	36	(65)	35
DE	30	(25)	33	(40)	32	(65)	31

Note:

[a] Based on the 23 films shown between January 1982 and June 1983 on Saturdays which gained an average audience of 1 million or more (footnote in report).

Table 8.4.3 Average indices of appreciation for films, January 1977–June 1983.

	All foreign language films on BBC2	
	Reaction Index / Appreciation Index	(no. of films) on base of average
1977	54	(21)
1978	62	(22)
1979	64	(9)
1980	–	(6)
1981	63	(12)
1982	68	(26)
1983 (January–June)	58	(17)
January 1977–June 1983	61	(113)

Average Appreciation Indices January–June 1983 for:-

		Appreciation Indices	(No. in category)
Films and plays on BBC		71	(–)
All films	BBC	65	(298)
	BBC1	67	(157)
	BBC2	64	(141)
Foreign language films on BBC		58	(17)

Note: All indices before Feb 1982 are reaction indices (RI), afterwards they are appreciation indices (AI) (footnote in report, referring to differing methods of research).

Table 8.4.4 Dubbing v. subtitling.

% preferring…			
Dubbed films			**54**
Because	Less demanding to watch		21
	Subtitles are distracting		20
	Can't read fast enough		11
	Subtitles illegible		7
Subtitled films			**22**
Because	Dubbing irritating		1
	Mouth and words don't match in dubbed versions		9
	Prefer original soundtrack		6
	Easier to follow		6
No preference either way			**16**
Don't know			**8**

Table 8.4.5 Preference for dubbed or subtitled films.

	All viewers	Attitude to foreign language films on TV			
	%	Positive %	Neutral %	Negative %	Varies/don't know %
Prefer dubbed	54	26	64	54	46
Prefer subtitled	22	57	29	9	38
No preference	16	15	6	23	11
Don't know	7	0	1	13	5
No response	1	2	0	1	1
Unweighted base	987	73	273	507	134

Table 8.4.6 'Black patch' v. 'plain white' subtitling.

% seeing any:	%
– Subtitled films on TV	74
– 'Black patch' subtitled films	48
– 'Plain white subtitled films	56

Reaction to:	'Black patch' subtitling	%
	– Easy to read	59
	– Clear	49
	– Irritating	15
	– Off putting	15
	– Confusing	9

'Plain white' subtitling	%
– Irritating	39
– Off putting	36
– Confusing	32
– Easy to read	18
– Clear	10
Not asked	**26**

Source for Tables 8.4.4–8.4.6: Omnibus 19, reproduced in 'Foreign Language Films on Television'.

Source for Tables 8.5.1–8.5.6: Report by Ann Rawcliffe-King (BBC Broadcasting Research), 'Foreign Language Films on Television', September 1984, BBC R9/203/1.

minimises the difference between them and other films', the small proportion (8 per cent) who made a point of watching foreign films preferred subtitling, as it was 'considered more authentic'.[69] The report even examined what type of subtitling viewers preferred: they came down strongly in favour of the BBC's practice of printing electronic subtitles on a black strip superimposed on the picture (the so-called 'black patch' method), rather than the use of 'plain white' titles which, as we have noted, had caused so much bother in the past because they were hard to distinguish from the background image. This new method seems to have been introduced experimentally with Eric Rohmer's *Love in the Afternoon* (1972/16.02.1979), one of the less contentious films in the season of 'adult' films discussed earlier.[70] Summing up, the research report concluded:

> These films generally gain small audiences. It is therefore difficult to consider reactions to them individually on very many occasions. However, all the evidence suggests that overall they appeal most, are watched by and appreciated most by younger, middle class male viewers who are likely to be highly educated and light viewers of television generally.[71]

Even so, the report pointed out, devotees of foreign films were a small minority of this demographic. The statistical data assembled for the survey indicates fluctuating patterns of popularity among individual films (both in numbers of viewers and degree of appreciation), with no evident trends other than the fact that they generally performed less well in ratings terms than other types of film. The average Reaction or Appreciation Index for foreign films was 61 across the whole period but the highest were achieved by *L'Enfant sauvage* (1970/07.10.1978) and *The Year of the Hare* (1977/24.01.1981), both with RIs of 76, and *The Driving Licence* (1974/05.06.1982) and *Diabolo menthe* (1977/27.11.1982), both with AIs of 77. As for audience size, by far the largest was recorded for *Belle de jour*, with an average 4.6 million viewers tuning in, though its RI was 57. No wonder the Board of Governors was so worried.

ITV's 'International Screen'

It was not only the BBC that broadcast films from overseas sources other than Hollywood. In the nine months following the opening of the commercial television service in September 1955, the ITV London contractors showed only eight feature films, all transmitted on weekdays by Associated-Rediffusion (A-R). Two of these, the swashbucklers *The Masked Pirate* (1949/10.10.1955) and *The Iron Mask* (1929/20.02.1956), were divided into short episodes and serialised in children's hour. The former was an English-dubbed Italian production, directed by Edgar G. Ulmer; the latter was a late silent picture starring Douglas Fairbanks Sr, presumably broadcast in the 'sonorised' version that had recently been released in cinemas, with a commentary track by the star's actor son, Douglas Jr. The other six films were shown in peak-time midweek slots under the umbrella title 'International Screen', the first named feature-film strand of any kind on British television. As this rubric suggests, most of the films shown were overseas productions, albeit most likely presented in dubbed versions rather than subtitled (*TV Times* listings give no indication but it seems likely that if subtitles had been used they would have been mentioned).

The first film presented in the 'International Screen' series, Jacques Becker's *Edward and Caroline* (1951/11.10.1955), had earlier been announced for transmission by the BBC in April 1954 before being cancelled at short notice. This was reportedly over technical difficulties with subtitling but was more likely due to the possible consequences for its distributor, Films de France, of breaking the industry ban on films for television.[72] The remaining titles in the series were: *A Tale of Five Cities* (1951/12.12.55), a British production with multiple European settings; Vittorio de Sica's *Miracle in Milan* (1951/19.12.1955); two more British independent features, *They Made Me a Fugitive* (1947/09.01.1956) and *Thunder Rock* (1942/23.01.1956); and another French comedy, *Ignace, or Marriage by Order* (1937/30.01.1956). A-R subsequently showed two more European pictures: another Becker, *Golden Marie* (a dubbed version of *Casque d'or*, 1952/16.07.1956), and the Italian *Sunday in August* (1950/20.08.1956). The latter was later presented, with subtitles, in the BBC's 'International Film Season'. Few of these films, except for the three British features, were picked up by other local ITV stations once they had begun broadcasting.

A number of English-language versions of popular European films did neverthe-less figure in ITV schedules over the next two decades and beyond. Most of these were Westerns and other action films, including several of the Karl May adaptations featuring Pierre Brice as Indian chief Winnetou and a handful of 'pepla' (sword-and-sandal epics). But they also included films by major European directors, including H.G. Clouzot's *The Wages of Fear* (1953/26.10.1968) and *The Fiends* (better known as *Les Diaboliques*, 1955/03.09.1971), de Sica's *Two Women* (1960/03.05.1970) and *Sunflower* (1970/04.09.1977), Luchino Visconti's *The Leopard* (1962/06.05.1972) and Claude Chabrol's *The Champagne Murders* (1967/01.10.1973). Most were doubtless acquired as part of packages from Hollywood distributors.

Very occasionally, an ITV company might try something bolder. When Thames Television scheduled Kaneto Shindô's *Onibaba* (1964/20.07.1970) during the sta-tion's 'Japanese Week' to mark the Expo '70 world's fair in Osaka, two viewers wrote to the ITA to complain. Though the film had been edited to match the BBFC's cuts, one letter called it 'the most disgusting, disgraceful, distasteful, obscene load of old rubbish that I have ever seen in all my life'.[73] Stephen Murphy wrote to both correspondents to defend the showing of a film he considered a masterpiece, though in an internal memo he acknowledged that 'in terms of both sex and violence it goes a great deal further than any film that has ever been shown on Independent Television'.[74] This film too was shown in a dubbed version. It was not until the 1970s and 1980s that subtitled foreign films came to ITV, and then in only a few regions.

Welsh Experiments

In July 1971, ITA Chairman Lord Aylestone was surprised to read a report in *The Times* that HTV, the contractor for Wales and the West of England, was to show, uncut and with the Authority's approval, a season of recent 'experimental' films. This scheduling idea had emerged from a chance meeting between Lord Harlech, the company founder and also president of the BBFC, and Derek Hill, now director of the New Cinema Club. The club specialised in showing experi-mental and non-commercial films of a highly specialised kind. According to

Hill in the newspaper, 'I said something like it's a pity there isn't a New Cinema season on television and he made sympathetic noises and put me in touch with Patrick Dromgoole, their programme controller.' On a previous occasion, Hill had sold Harlech the television rights to a controversial American documentary, *Warrendale* (1967/29.03.1969), which had been turned down by both the BBC and theatrical distributors. It launched the New Cinema Club and was then part-networked on ITV through HTV. Out of this conjunction of interests emerged a series initially called 'Experimental Film Season' but later billed as 'Cinema Club' (see Table 8.5).[75]

Contrary to the claims made in *The Times*, most senior members of the Authority had not even been aware of the planned series, let alone approved the six films selected for broadcast.[76] By the time regional officers got around to previewing them – three British-made documentaries on filmmakers and three works of fiction, all subtitled – they had already been scheduled and announced, so the ITA's position was to some extent a fait accompli. Most of the titles presented few problems, though Dusan Makavejev's *Innocence Unprotected* (1968/09.08.1971) and Stellan Olsson's *Close to the Wind* (1969/03.08.1971) required minor edits at the Authority's request. However, Alejandro Jodorowsky's *Tar Babies* (1968/16.08.1971) was subjected to six substantial cuts, totalling 12–14 minutes from a 98-minute running time. Even so, officers expressed the view after transmission that it 'should not have been allowed to be screened' and that it 'was basically unsuitable for television ... in parts shocking, obscene and violent, and entirely unsuitable for general public consumption'.[77] HTV's Cardiff station received forty-four viewer complaints, and though company staff continued to defend the film's inclusion in the season they accepted that the Authority's cuts were appropriate.

Despite this rocky start, HTV brought 'Experimental Film Season' back for a second run in 1973 and a third in 1975; the series then ran annually as 'Cinema Club' until 1983. Showing across the eleven seasons were works by such film-makers as Jean-Luc Godard, Akira Kurosawa, Ingmar Bergman, Rainer Werner Fassbinder, Wim Wenders and Nagisa Oshima, and films from Africa, Latin America, Eastern Europe and Australia. Each screening was introduced by an expert speaker; for the first few seasons this was art historian A.C.H. Smith, who was followed in later years by *Sunday Times* TV columnist Elkan Allan (co-author of a guide to films on television), *Observer* journalist Jennifer Selway, the long-standing head of the National Film School, Colin Young, and finally critic and historian Christopher Frayling. Frayling recalls the series' producer telling him: 'Not only are we showing some interesting films, but it's fantastically cheap broadcasting: a two-hour slot, with a short introduction, for the price of five minutes!' He added that it could usefully be cited at franchise renewal time as an example of cultural broadcasting (see Figure 8.3).[78]

The Authority continued to monitor the seasons and preview the films, requesting cuts where necessary – usually for language, including swear words in

Table 8.5 HTV film seasons, 1971–76.

Season 1: Experimental Film Season (1971)

Title	Year	Country	TX date	Presentation
Double Pisces, Scorpio Rising	1970	Austria/UK	19.07.1971	English
About 'The White Bus'	1968	UK	26.07.1971	English
Voices	1970	UK	02.08.1971	English
Innocence Unprotected	1968	Yugoslavia	09.08.1971	Subtitled
Tar Babies	1968	Mexico	16.08.1971	Subtitled
Close to the Wind	1969	Sweden	23.08.1971	Subtitled

Season 2: Experimental Film Season (1973)

Title	Year	Country	TX date	Presentation
The Switchboard Operator	1967	Yugoslavia	16.07.1973	Subtitled
Children in Conflict: Group Therapy	1967	USA	30.07.1973	English
The Theatre of Mr and Mrs Kabal	1967	France	06.08.1973	Subtitled
The Great Chicago Conspiracy Circus	1970	USA	13.08.1973	English
Millhouse, a White Comedy	1971	USA	20.08.1973	English

Season 3: Experimental Film Season (1975)

Title	Year	Country	TX date	Presentation
Here Comes Every Body	1972	USA	14.07.1975	English
The Money Order	1968	France/Senegal	21.07.1975	Subtitled
Blood of the Condor	1969	Bolivia	28.07.1975	Subtitled
Antonio das Mortes	1969	Brazil	04.08.1975	Subtitled
Maidstone	1970	USA	11.08.1975	English
La Chinoise	1967	France	18.08.1975	Subtitled

Season 4: Cinema Club (1976)

Title	Year	Country	TX date	Presentation
Lenny Bruce without Tears	1972	USA	26.07.1976	English
Dodes'ka-den, Part 1	1970	Japan	02.08.1976	Subtitled
Dodes'ka-den, Part 2	1970	Japan	09.08.1976	Subtitled
Black God, White Devil	1964	Brazil	16.08.1976	Subtitled
The Rite	1969	Sweden	23.08.1976	Subtitled

subtitles, and sexual content. It also took note of public reaction, which as well as the expected complaints included expressions of gratitude. One viewer wrote to HTV:

> For a commercial station to show, say, *Blood of the Condor* (black & white, subtitled, indifferent film quality), even late at night, seems extremely public-spirited. I have enjoyed your season of classic horror films and the Korda classics, but to show such modern films makes the present series the most interesting (on *any* channel) for a very long time, particularly for cinema-goers who would otherwise get no chance to see foreign films.
>
> Once again, thank you, and keep up the good work for as long as you are able.[79]

Figure 8.3 Christopher Frayling, last presenter of HTV's 'Cinema Club' series, in the studio to record his introduction. Photograph courtesy of Christopher Frayling. Photographer unknown.

The tone of Authority communications regarding the series also gradually changed, so that by 1977 even the regional officer who had asked for the cuts to *Tar Babies* was able to remark on 'a highly commendable season'.[80]

More controversial was a one-off series of three films broadcast not in their integral foreign languages but dubbed into Welsh. Over consecutive weeks in late-night slots, HTV Wales transmitted the Hammer production *Frankenstein Must Be Destroyed* (1969/28.09.1974) as *Mae Frankenstein yn fyw* (12.09.1978), the Hollywood Western *Shane* (1953/28.08.1972) as *Shane* (19.09.1978) and the French drama *The Sin of Father Mouret* (1970) as *Pechod y tad Moureau* (26.09.1978). All had been re-voiced by Welsh-speaking actors; English subtitles were retained for the third film but the others offered no help to viewers who were not conversant in Welsh. The Authority's regional officer considered the experiment a success, despite the fact that HTV had received some 500 calls of complaint for each of the first two films; the relative obscurity of *Mouret/Moureau* meant that it provoked little response. The officer proffered his own judgement:

In technical terms the dubbing was excellent – the dialogue was well synchronised with lip movements and in all cases (except one) voices matched the characters well. The notable exception was in *Shane* where the actor who supplied the Welsh version of Alan Ladd's voice did in fact have a very weak, muted and almost effeminate delivery. In fact one of those who wrote to HTV complaining about the film asked whether the part of Shane was supplied by Twiggy![81]

The only other documents in the IBA Archives concerning these films are contrasting letters from two local councillors, whose views must stand as representative of polarised popular opinion. One congratulated HTV on its 'encouraging start to broadening the variety of programmes produced in Welsh'. He considered *Mae Frankenstein yn fyw* (which translates literally as *Frankenstein Is Alive*) the most successful of the three and thought that despite the 'obvious difficulties in dubbing "American" into Welsh the dubbing of *Shane* was on a par if not better than films dubbed into English from Chinese, French and other languages'.[82]

His colleague from Mid Glamorgan County Council was less complimentary. Writing to both Lord Harlech and IBA Chairman Lady Plowden to demand that HTV lose its broadcasting licence, he built an eloquent case:

> For many workers in factories, coal mining and the steel industry in industrial South Wales the fact that after a hard days [*sic*] work they have to put up with such drivel is unacceptable and enough to make one throw one's licence on the back of the fire. One steelworker I spoke to was so incensed that he felt like putting a sledge hammer through his television set. A comment from an underground worker in my area who had come home after a particularly trying day at Bedwas Colliery and switching on to Frankenstein dubbed in Welsh, was that it was enough to make him put his working clothes back on and rush back down the Colliery.[83]

While this councillor did not disapprove of Welsh-language programming generally, he felt that by 'dubbing the culturally strong Welsh language on to films like Frankenstein you are prostituting the language in an unforgivable way'. In a further letter, in which he suggested that advertisers withdraw their business from HTV in protest, he referred to the 'final degradation' of *Pechod y tad Moureau* where 'we had the ridiculous situation of a French film dubbed in Welsh and with English sub-titles. The cost to process such a film by paying for research into the French equivalent of the Welsh language must be enormous.'[84] The experiment does not seem to have been repeated, though *The Sin of Father Mouret* reappeared the following year, now in its original language, on 'Cinema Club'.

Sourthern's Late, Late Shows

Besides the Authority, other ITV contractors took notice of HTV's specialised film seasons. In 1978, the trade press reported that Derek Hill, now working for art-house distributor Essential Cinema, had written 'to all the other commercial companies suggesting a similar arrangement and has received a positive response from all but two stations'.[85] Although most of this interest seems to have come to nothing, Tyne Tees picked up four of HTV's films: three in French with subtitles plus Celestino Coronado's highly idiosyncratic version of *Hamlet*

(1976/26.08.1977). One other company took up the challenge in a remarkably ambitious way, when Southern Television created its own specialised series in the form of 'The Late, Late Show'. *TV Times*'s programme billing explained the show's ethos:

> The title is no accident. This is a show for night people, adults who deliberately decide to stay up and watch what we offer in the early hours. It is not family viewing. This first season of *The Late, Late Show* features seven films. Mainly from the continent, all well-made and acted, but considered by some to be unsuitable for showing earlier in the evening.[86]

The first season actually included six features (all but one subtitled) and a programme of shorts to mark the pioneering FIAF Congress on early cinema, then being held in Brighton. A second run started in November the same year, and it was followed – without a break – in March 1979 by a variation, 'The Late, Late Premiere', showcasing films not previously seen in the UK. This season continued until the end of June. Thus, audiences in the South East were offered a non-mainstream film, generally subtitled, almost every Friday night for eight months, a run interrupted only for the Christmas holiday and occasional sporting events. Southern carried on in like manner in 1979–80 and again in 1980–81. The latter included four foreign-film seasons in immediate succession: five weeks of 'Continental Showcase', sixteen of 'The Late, Late Show', thirteen of 'The Late, Late Premiere' and finally a five-week run of *Madame le juge*, a series of French made-for-TV movies starring Simone Signoret, with directors including Claude Chabrol (see Table 8.6).

Like HTV's, the Southern series employed on-screen hosts. The initial season of 'The Late, Late Show' was presented by ITN newscaster Gordon Honeycombe, who was subsequently replaced by film critic Tom Hutchinson. The IBA approved of this type of presentation, as a presenter could warn viewers of any problematic content (Hutchinson was specifically briefed to do so) and thus head off possible complaints – what one officer described as a 'buffer effect'.[87] This was particularly important because, unlike HTV's amenable production team, Southern's programmers refused to consider making any cuts to the films. The company's Director of Programmes, Jeremy Wallington, justified this position following the Authority's receipt of a rare viewer complaint towards the end of the series' run:

> To remind you of the principles behind THE LATE LATE SHOW... it was established three years ago as a means of delivering high quality films, usually from Europe, which can normally only be seen in the few remaining art cinema houses in Britain. The experiment, which has been highly successful in providing our sales department with a cultured and valuable audience, has led to many letters of congratulations from viewers and virtually no complaints ... In dealing with films of this kind we decided at the outset that under no circumstances would we cut them. They must remain as the producer intended. If we felt a particular film was beyond the boundaries of sophisticated public taste then we would not transmit it – and have decided not to do so on many occasions.[88]

Table 8.6 Southern Television film seasons, 1978–80.

The Late, Late Show: Season 1 (1978)

Title	Year	Country	TX date	Presentation
The Sin of Father Mouret	1970	France/Italy	21.04.1978	Subtitled
And Hope to Die	1972	France/Italy/Canada	28.04.1978	Subtitled
Erotissimo	1969	France/Italy	05.05.1978	Subtitled
Blanche	1971	France	12.05.1978	Subtitled
Janice (Road Movie)	1973	USA	19.05.1978	English
Early cinema shorts + *Dressing for Pleasure* + *Switch-off*	1977	UK	26.05.1978	Silent/English
The White Wall	1975	Sweden	02.06.1978	Subtitled

The Late, Late Premiere: Season 1 (1979)

Title	Year	Country	TX date	Presentation
The Clown	1976	West Germany	23.03.1979	Subtitled
Rally	1970	Finland	30.03.1979	Subtitled
The Beach Guard in Winter	1976	Yugoslavia	06.04.1979	Subtitled
Two Heartbeats	1972	Israel	27.04.1979	Subtitled
For Your Pleasure	1978	Sweden	11.05.1979	Subtitled
Bluff Stop	1977	Sweden	18.05.1979	Subtitled
Grete Minde	1977	Austria/West Germany	25.05.1979	Subtitled
Foreigners	1972	Sweden	01.06.1979	Subtitled
Nine Months	1976	Hungary	08.06.1979	Subtitled
A City's Child	1971	Australia	15.06.1979	English
Elvis! Elvis!	1976	Sweden	22.06.1979	Subtitled
The Brutalization of Franz Blum	1974	West Germany	29.06.1979	Subtitled

Continental Showcase (1980)

Title	Year	Country	TX date	Presentation
Who Are You	1970	France/Italy	10.10.1980	Subtitled
Poitín	1979	Ireland	17.10.1980	Subtitled
Ne pleure pas (Don't Cry)	1978	France	24.10.1980	Subtitled
Hagan fuego, por favor	1979	Spain	31.10.1980	Subtitled
Madame de juge: Le Dossier Françoise Muller	1975	France/West Germany	07.11.1980	Subtitled

At the end of that same year, 1981, Southern lost its regional franchise in the IBA's latest round of renewals and reallocations. Its successor, Television South (TVS), was not so adventurous in its film choices. When TVS launched its own series of European films, 'Continental Movie', hosted by Colin Young, all eight titles in the first season were French productions with English voice tracks. So also were most of the films in the later seasons of HTV's 'Cinema Club'. This was the result of Leslie Halliwell's purchase for the network of a package of dubbed European pictures, mainly mainstream genre movies of a more conventional kind than those previously shown by HTV and Southern. They were initially programmed in the

Granada region in 1980, under the umbrella title 'The Continental', and subsequently circulated throughout the ITV system. Thus, LWT created an 'Adult Continental Movie' strand and Westward Television, 'Continental Cinema'. But when TVS's initial series drew complaints from local viewers now trained to expect authentic soundtracks, the company announced that it would in future show overseas films in their original languages.[89]

Notes

1 'Foreign Films on British Screens', *Films and Filming*, June 1970, 18.
2 Ibid, 19, 22, 26.
3 R.E. Rendall to Gerald Cock, 16 September 1938, BBC T6/138. The survey is from Listener Research Section, Public Relations Division, 'An Enquiry into Viewers' Opinions on Television Programmes Conducted in the First Quarter of 1939', 26 June 1939, BBC R9/9/3.
4 The Scanner, 'Television Is Grand!', *Radio Times*, 7 July 1939, 13.
5 The Scanner, 'French Film', *Radio Times*, 14 July 1939, 18.
6 P.M. Jenkins to Ernest Lindgren, 28 February 1946; Lindgren to Jenkins, 5 April 1946; G.D.G. Perkins to Cecil Madden, 16 October 1946, BBC T6/219. The 'Third Programme' designation (equivalent to the present BBC Radio 3) was used by Cecil Madden in a memo of 19 June 1952, BBC T6/144/4.
7 Imlay Newbiggin-Watts to Norman Collins, 28 February 1947, BBC T16/76/1; Sir David Cunynghame to Collins, 9 June 1948, BBC T6/194.
8 Dilys Powell, 'A Paris Boulevard in 1840', *Radio Times*, 30 July 1948, 25.
9 Cecil McGivern to Collins, 27 May 1949, 29 June 1948 and 13 August 1948; McGivern to E.E.Tel, 6 August 1948, BBC T6/194.
10 Philip Dorté to Greeve del Strother, 25 August 1948, BBC T6/144/1.
11 Del Strother to A/H.Tel.Pres., 30 May 1949, BBC T6/13; del Strother to Cecil McGivern, 20 October 1950, BBC T1/3.
12 A.S. Hayes, 'Sub-titled Film' (letter), *Radio Times*, 13 August 1948, 25.
13 Frances Stone, 'In Favour of Foreign Films' (letter), *Radio Times*, 19 November 1948, 25.
14 H. Capon, 'Foreign Films' (letter), *Radio Times*, 3 December 1948, 25.
15 A.G. Roberts, 'Foreign Films' (letter), *Radio Times*, 21 January 1949, 25.
16 A.T. Joel and S.G. Sewell, 'One Man's Meat' (letters), *Radio Times*, 16 September 1949, 41.
17 Kathleen Blagden, 'Plea for French Films' (letter), *Radio Times*, 2 February 1951, 48.
18 Joyce Pattison, 'Plea for Film Classics' (letter), *Radio Times*, 23 February 1951, 47.
19 Jill Anne Bowden, '*Les Enfants du paradis*' (letter), *Radio Times*, 27 January 1950, 45.
20 H. Stern, 'Plea for Film Classics' (letter), *Radio Times*, 23 February 1951, 47.
21 'Review of Recent Programmes', *Scan: the Television Journal* 2, no. 6 (October 1949): 14.
22 Reginald Pound, 'Animals on the Move', *The Listener*, 26 April 1951, 682–3.
23 K. Sampson, 'Results of the Television Poll', *Scan* 1, no. 10 (February 1949): 12. The poll had appeared as an insert in *Scan* 1, no. 8 (December 1948).

24 Dorté to Collins, 13 September 1949, BBC T6/194.
25 Record of interview, del Strother with C.V. Bargate, 20 November 1950, BBC T6/152.
26 Record of interview, del Strother with Bargate, 10 May 1950, T6/152; del Strother to McGivern, 27 May 1952, BBC T6/149.
27 Del Strother to McGivern, 27 May 1952, BBC T6/149.
28 Record of interview, Graham Woodford with George Hoellering, 28 January 1953, BBC T6/149.
29 Alec Sutherland to McGivern, 17 March 1951, BBC T6/152.
30 Hoellering to Woodford, 6 August 1954, BBC T6/149.
31 Sutherland to McGivern, 17 March 1951, BBC T6/152.
32 Chart enclosed with Robert Silvey to McGivern, 1 May 1952, BBC T1/3.
33 C.A. Lejeune, 'A Film Fairy-story', *Radio Times*, 11 April 1952, 41.
34 Reginald Pound, 'Worm's Eye View', *The Listener*, 24 April 1952, 686.
35 Viewer Research Report, 8 May 1952, BBC T6/194.
36 *Radio Times*, 24 July 1959, 9.
37 Bill Gilbert, 'Late Night Film', *Radio Times*, 13 July 1961, 26. Gilbert programmed the first season of 'Late Night Film'.
38 'Viewing Figures', *Sight and Sound* 31, no. 2 (Spring 1962): 65.
39 Gloria Symons, 'The Eisenstein Films' (letter), *Radio Times*, 14 December 1961, 39.
40 Derek Hill, 'International Film Season', 66. *South Pacific* (1958/05.11.1972) held the record at the time for the most financially successful film released in the UK.
41 Ibid.
42 Peter Armitage, 'Films on Television', *Film* 30 (Winter 1961): 16.
43 'Films on Television', *Film* 36 (Summer 1963): 35–36.
44 R.L. Jenkins, 'Foreign Films and...' (letter), *Radio Times*, 28 February 1963, 45.
45 A. Lynch, 'English Sub-titles' (letter), *Radio Times*, 28 February 1963, 45.
46 E.M. Esson, 'For the Deaf' (letter), *Radio Times*, 12 September 1963, 42.
47 Michael Williams, 'International Film Season', *Radio Times*, 27 June 1963, 44.
48 *Radio Times*, 19 March 1970, 53.
49 Ieuan Franklin, 'BBC2 and World Cinema', *Journal of British Cinema and Television* 14, no. 3 (2017): 352.
50 Quoted in Rachael Stoeltje, 'Interview with David Francis, Part I', *Journal of Film Preservation* 105 (November 2021): 100–1. Besides 'World Cinema', Francis also programmed BBC2's 'Midnight Movie' strand.
51 Peggy Miller to AHF Tel., 'Feature Films Offered by Films de France', 7 February 1957, BBC T6/152.
52 Philip Jenkinson, 'This Week's Films', *Radio Times*, 7 September 1972, 11.
53 John Gillett, 'Japanese Notebook', 27.
54 Alex Cox, 'Shutting out Subtitles', *Guardian*, 25 June 2004, online at https://www.theguardian.com/film/2004/jun/25/1.
55 *Radio Times*, 15 August 1974, 45.
56 Philip Oakes, 'Sex and the Cinema', *Radio Times*, 11 January 1979, 17, 19.
57 The other titles in the season were Vittorio de Sica's *Marriage Italian Style* (1964/26.01.1979), *Fellini's Roma* (1972, 09.02.1979), Eric Rohmer's *Love in the Afternoon* (1972/16.02.1979) and Walerian Borowczyk's *Story of a Sin* (1975/02.03.1979). A seventh film, Philippe de Broca's *Chère Louise* (1972/09.03.1979), was a late addition.

58 Minutes of the Board of Management, 22 and 29 January 1979, BBC R78/1, 123/1.

59 Mary Whitehouse, 'TV's Peephole on the Ugly Face of Sex' (letter), *The Guardian*, 31 January 1979, 10; 'A Film wherein Lies a Moral Tale for Mary Whitehouse' (letters), *Guardian*, 2 February 1979, 12; original emphasis.

60 Mr D.G.L. to Sir Michael Swann, 3 February 1979; Swann to D.G.L., 7 March 1979, BBC R78/1, 123/1. Bryan Forbes's review of *Dearest Love* in his *Radio Times* 'Films' column reads in its entirety: 'In a film that was frowned upon by the French government at the time, Louis Malle directs with humour, affection and an awareness of sexual longing' (27 January 1979, 17).

61 Alan Howden to Elizabeth Smith, 16 February 1979, BBC R78/1, 123/1.

62 Minutes of the Board of Management, 5 February 1979, BBC R78/1, 123/1.

63 See *Hansard*, Commons, 29 March 1979 and 7 December 1979.

64 Minutes of the Board of Management, 29 January 1979, BBC R78/1, 123/1.

65 Letters from B. Wye, B.M. Taylor, S. Matthew, Edwin L.P. Morgan and Peter Mark, 'BBC2 Films: Too Late or Too Filthy?', *Radio Times*, 8 February 1979, 61, and '"Adult" Films: Good, Bad or Mistitled?', *Radio Times*, 8 March 1979, 70. The present author dates his own interest in non-Anglophone cinema to the transmission in this series of *Dearest Love*.

66 'ITV Viewers Do Switch over, BBC Claims', *Guardian*, 17 September 1979, 3.

67 Ann Rawcliffe-King (BBC Broadcasting Research), 'Foreign Language Films on Television', September 1984, BBC R9/203/1. Although the report states that 'Film International' had begun in January 1977, it had in fact launched on 25 September the previous year. Though ostensibly concerned mainly with that strand, the survey covered several other seasons that had not been billed under the 'Film International' rubric.

68 'Foreign Language Films on Television', 1.

69 Ibid, 2.

70 In his response to a letter commenting that the new method was 'very easy on the eye', Alan Howden noted that reaction to it had been 'very favourable' and that it would come into general use later in the year when necessary engineering work was done 'to convert experimental equipment into an operational form' (reply to Peter Mark, 'Subtitle Problem', *Radio Times*, 8 March 1979, 70). The use of electronic subtitles is one reason why foreign-language films were usually played out from tape transfers rather than live telecine.

71 'Foreign Language Films on Television', 2.

72 Ingram Fraser to McGivern, 31 May 1954, and attached clippings from *The Times* and *Evening Standard*, 19 April 1954, BBC T6/152.

73 Letter from A.E.C., 20 July 1970, IBA/01023: 3996311.

74 Stephen Murphy to All Regional Officers, 21 July 1970, IBA/01023: 3996311.

75 'Lord Harlech's New Cinema Plunge', *The Times*, 4 July 1971, 12. Hill discusses the New Cinema Club and its successor, Essential Cinema (which also supplied films to HTV), in an interview with David Prothero, 'Derek Hill', *Journal of Popular British Cinema* 3 (2000), 133–43.

76 Bernard Sendall to Robert Fraser, 6 July 1971, IBA/01020: 3996317.

77 Lyn Evans to Joseph Weltman, 13, 18 and 19 August 1971, IBA/01025: 3996309.

78 Professor Sir Christopher Frayling, personal communication, 15 October 2022.

79 R.J.H. to HTV Programme Controller, 30 July 1975, IBA/01025: 3996309; original emphasis.

80 Clare Mulholland to Dermot O'Hagan, 20 July 1977, IBA/01025: 3996309.

81 Dennis Francis to O'Hagan, 2 October 1978, IBA/01021: 3996312. Recordings of all three transmissions reportedly survive in the Welsh National Archives.

82 Cllr P.W. to Lady Plowden, 22 September 1978, IBA/01021: 3996312.

83 Cllr R.D. to Plowden, 20 September 1978, IBA/01021: 3996312.

84 Cllr R.D. to Plowden, 27 September 1978, IBA/01021: 3996312.

85 'ITV Companies Negotiate with Essential Cinema for Minority Movies', *Broadcast*, 6 February 1978, 8.

86 *TV Times* (Southern), 13 April 1978, 69.

87 Richard King to STSO, 12 May 1981, IBA/01024: 3996310.

88 Jeremy Wallington to J.A. Blair Scott, 12 May 1981, IBA/01025: 3996309.

89 Leslie Halliwell to Chris Rowley, 28 May 1980; D.S. to Michael Gillies, 3 March 1983, IBA/01021: 3996312.

CHAPTER 9

The Rules of the Game –
Regulating Films on Television

Our monitor in the Southern area felt that a film about a three time rapist escaping from prison, shooting a woman and her lover in bed with a culminating scene involving a bloody knife fight was unsuitable for 7.55pm. I tend to agree and it is not really what we had in mind when we discussed the possibility of some worthwhile, albeit adult, films being playable at 8.00pm on Sundays.[1]

(Memo, Dermot O'Hagan to Ken Fletcher, 13 February 1975, IBA/01023: 3996311)

Broadcasters and the BBFC

Among the subjects most frequently raised in public correspondence with the broadcasting organisations was the status within television of British Board of Film Censors (BBFC) certificates. Commercial films generally had to receive a BBFC certificate as a condition for exhibition in licensed public cinemas; attached to the front of film prints, it was the first image projected on screen. Why, many enquirers wanted to know, was it not included when the film was broadcast and publicised as a guide for prospective viewers, particularly parents?

From its foundation in 1913, the BBFC issued two types of certificate for cinema films: 'U' (for universal), meaning a film was suitable for all patrons; and 'A', meaning that it was recommended for adult audiences. In 1938, the 'H' certificate was introduced for films with 'horrific' content, limiting admission to patrons aged sixteen and over. This was replaced in 1951 by the 'X' certificate, which indicated a broader range of material suitable only for adults. Following changes in the American film industry, which introduced an age-graded ratings system for the first time in November 1968, the BBFC revised its own classification rules in July 1970. The age limit for 'X' films was raised from sixteen to eighteen years and another new certificate was introduced: 'AA', restricting admission to those aged fourteen and over.[2]

The industry's increasing targeting of adult audiences meant that many films produced in this later period included material that would have been prohibitive only a few years before: in essence, sex, violence and bad language, along with the breaking of social taboos. From the early 1970s, press reports often appeared reflecting on the challenges television would face in future, as the newly permissive films became available to it.[3]

Prints supplied to the broadcasting organisations, which came from varying sources and often (especially in later years) were struck especially for TV use, did not always carry BBFC certificates, and even when they did they were usually omitted on transmission. The BBC's Film Booking Manager, Greeve del Strother, recorded in 1946 that in prewar days it had been 'the practice in all film transmissions not to fade in until the Board of Censors' certificate had run through'.[4] Three years later, the Corporation's solicitor gave advice to the Controller of Television that there was no obligation to transmit the certificates.[5] In 1952, a proposal to include 'A' certificates in transmissions of films considered unsuitable for children was rejected by the Head of Television Films, Philip Dorté, on a point of principle. Dorté argued that BBFC certification exclusively concerned the film industry and was nothing to do with television, where the rule should be 'to exercise our own judgment and use our own formula'.[6] This continued to be the BBC's position for decades to come.

The formula devised at this time was for BBC staff responsible for acquiring films to preview them prior to transmission and inform the Presentation department when a warning was deemed necessary that a film was unsuitable for children. Such warnings would be conveyed on air by an announcer immediately prior to broadcast and might also be printed in *Radio Times*'s programme listings. Four films were so designated in 1952, after which the warning policy seemed to lapse.[7] Any cuts deemed necessary were made by staff editors.

The Independent Television Authority (ITA) arrived at its own policy on films carrying the BBFC 'X' certificate, or those that had not received a certificate at all (because either they had been refused one or they had not been released in the UK and therefore had not been submitted for certification). The ITA's principal concern in this regard was to uphold Section 3(1)(a) of the Television Act 1954, which demanded that 'nothing is included in the programmes which offends against good taste or decency or is likely to encourage or incite to crime or to lead to disorder or to be offensive to public feeling'.[8] It was the Authority's duty to see that this was observed and as such it operated in lieu of an external censor. It wanted to be given advance notice of any intention by ITV companies to transmit 'X'-rated or uncertificated films. In such cases, ITA officers might request a preview of the film in question and, following that, make a recommendation on its suitability for broadcast. The 1957 memorandum setting out this policy noted that 'when proposing to show these films on television the time of their showing and the announcement with which they will be prefaced are perhaps more important than their content'. It also stipulated a crucial underlying principle: 'that television collects a large habitual audience which, unlike the audiences for the theatre or cinema, has made no conscious and deliberate decision to see the production concerned'.[9] Thus, protection for the casual, unprepared viewer was considered axiomatic (see also Chapter 11).

For all their insistence on remaining independent arbiters of their own affairs, the broadcasters often found it expedient to cite precedent in the BBFC's judgements as a defence against potential criticism. With controversial films, they also sometimes informally sought the advice of the BBFC's Secretary, John Trevelyan (1958–71), at his encouragement, though such consultations were never acknowledged publicly. This, along with the willingness of the ITA in particular to replicate the BBFC's editing of films, suggests a lack of confidence in the mechanisms developed specifically for the regulation of television, despite declarations to the contrary.

The first BBFC 'X'-certificate film to be shown on British television was Jacques Becker's crime melodrama *Golden Marie* (1952/16.07.1956). According to the *Daily Mail*, when it was transmitted by Associated-Rediffusion (A-R) at 8.00pm in London, three cuts were made and viewers were 'warned that the 90-minute film is not suitable for children or nervous people'.[10] Apparently the ITA took little notice of this broadcast, because an officer later claimed erroneously that the first 'X' film shown on ITV was *Intimate Relations* (1953/15.04.1958), a British production based on a play by Jean Cocteau.[11]

The BBC's first 'X'-rated picture was an American independent film, *The Well* (1951/29.08.1960). But a bigger stir was created by the British production *I Am a Camera* (1955/07.01.1961), whose billing in *Radio Times* stated boldly: 'When released in the cinema *I Am a Camera* was given an "X" certificate.'[12] The first transmission was at 8.40pm on a Saturday evening, but in 1966 the film was repeated at 3.30pm on a Saturday afternoon. On this occasion, the Association of Independent Cinemas (AIC) objected. BBC2 Controller David Attenborough noted in an internal memo that the film had been certificated 'X' due to 'references to abortion' and these were cut out for television. No complaints were received from the general public.[13]

Even televised excerpts from 'X'-rated films were a cause for concern. A local council objected to the transmission of clips, on the BBC and ITV respectively, from *The Wild One* (1953/26.12.1972), which was initially refused a BBFC certificate until being given a belated 'X' in 1967, and *Saturday Night and Sunday Morning* (1960/30.01.1966).[14] Similar protests were received from the AIC, which also made its concerns known both to the Home Secretary and to the BBC's Director General, Hugh Carleton Greene. The AIC – a particularly vociferous trade organisation, dismissed by the BBC's Cecil Madden as a minor breakaway group representing very few exhibitors – was concerned by the apparently inconsistent standards operated by the broadcasters, the BBFC and local authorities. It could not understand why films that had been censored and restricted or even prohibited for exhibition in cinemas could be shown, in whole or part, on television. A case in point was the social-problem drama *Cosh Boy* (1953/08.09.1961), which had been banned by Warwickshire County Council but was shown on BBC Television and subsequently by two ITV stations.[15] Greene's response to the AIC was curt: 'We apply the same standards to films as we do to other programme material and we do not have any machinery which could be described as "censorship".'[16]

Nevertheless, the unrestricted transmission of films and film extracts led to questions being asked in the House of Commons by MPs including Stephen Swingler (Labour, Newcastle-under-Lyme), who called for legislation to impose on television a system of censorship similar to that applied to the cinema (though the BBFC, as an independent trade body, at that time had no statutory powers). Postmaster-General Reginald Bevins declined, preferring to delegate judgement in such matters to the BBC's Board of Governors and the ITA. Authority officers refuted Swingler's exaggerated claims regarding the number of 'X'- films broadcast and dismissed the notion that the excerpts shown from *Saturday Night and Sunday Morning* had been the scenes that had earned it an adult certificate.[17]

This matter also resulted in a pertinent observation from film producer and Anglia Television board member John Woolf: changes in social and cinematic standards since films had been produced meant that 'the certificates of the British Board of Film Censors, issued years ago, should hardly be taken into account at all when deciding the suitability of films for Television'.[18] A commonly-cited, if extreme, example of a film's change in status between its release in cinemas and its acquisition by television was *Abbott and Costello Meet Dr Jekyll and Mr Hyde* (1953/29.12.1966), 'X'-rated by the BBFC but later broadcast in children's viewing time.

From the early 1960s, both the BBC and the ITA observed a 'watershed' of 9.00pm, separating what the Authority called 'Family Viewing Time' from the later part of the evening, when adults could be expected both to form the main audience and to take responsibility for what their children viewed. Films that had received an 'X' certificate but which were nevertheless subsequently shown on ITV before the watershed included *Quatermass 2* (1957/12.08.1965), *The Enforcer* (1951/09.10.1965), *Rebel without a Cause* (1955/30.05.1966), *A Taste of Honey* (1961/06.10.1966) and *The Bachelor Party* (1957/07.11.1966). Several of these led to expressions of concern from film-industry bodies or members of the public simply on the basis of their cinema certificates, but the ITA received no complaints from any viewers who had actually seen the films on transmission.

An indication of broadcasters' sometimes problematic relationship with the BBFC is the case of *What Ever Happened to Baby Jane?* (1962/11.01.1969). Robert Aldrich's gothic thriller had been passed with small cuts for the 'X' certificate in November 1962. But when first broadcast, by London Weekend Television (LWT) at 7.30pm on a Saturday, it was transmitted in a new, uncut print received direct from the distributor. The Authority's monitor, viewing the film as it went out, considered it unsuitable for future showing before 9.00pm.[19] John Trevelyan had not been consulted beforehand and subsequently wrote personally to the ITA Director General, Sir Robert Fraser:

> Even if it had been shown with our cuts I would have been unhappy about showing the film at a time when children would probably be viewing. The few cuts we made were for the 'X' category, and were designed to remove the worst bits of sadism. ... I would be unhappy if I thought that this kind of thing would be likely to recur.[20]

In reply, Fraser explained that the Authority had been erroneously informed by the British Film Institute (BFI) that the film had received an 'A' certificate and so had not been alerted to the potential problems. He said that the companies had been told 'of the necessity, when dealing with new prints of difficult films' of consulting the BBFC.[21] Trevelyan responded that if ITA or ITV representatives wanted 'to telephone me at any time I could give an indication of whether we had made substantial cuts in an "X" picture, and also whether I would regard this as troublesome in any way for TV transmission'.[22]

The Authority's Senior Programme Officer Stephen Murphy (who in 1971 succeeded Trevelyan as BBFC Secretary) pointed out that 'we do not follow quite the same policies as the BBFC, and it has seemed to me wise not to be too closely involved with them'.[23] But he nevertheless asked that letters be sent to each ITV company, instructing them to make permanent cuts to film prints in accordance with past BBFC certifications. The letters included the following comments: 'As you will know, we are under some pressure not to transmit "X" material at all. We have no intention of yielding to this pressure, but nevertheless it would be most unwise in the present climate to be transmitting un-cut versions of "X" certificate films.'[24]

Three executives wrote in reply. Anthony John of Thames Television commented that his company had been 'using John Trevelyan's good services for a long time' and that he was 'always most helpful. Sometime ago we found a whole batch of American prints which had not passed through his hands and so we were able to prevent an "ugly situation".'[25] The others, however, were less convinced of the wisdom of involving the film censor in TV decisions. Yorkshire Television's John Mountford believed that 'an appeal to the BBFC for details of their cuts is an unhappy situation insofar that we should be sufficiently in touch with current opinion to make our own decisions'.[26]

Granada's Leslie Halliwell was also sceptical, arguing that 'blind obedience' to the BBFC's previous judgements would lead to the making of cuts that in the present day would not have been made by it. Halliwell cited the example of *The Bachelor Party*, to which material cut by the censors had been restored for TV transmission, yet which was still permitted to be shown before 9.00pm.[27] Of the BBFC's original cuts to *Baby Jane*, he remarked:

> all that was removed was one kick by Bette Davis and a few feet of hysterics by Joan Crawford while she was strapped to the bed. I very much doubt whether either of these cuts would have been made today, and neither really comes into the categories of horror or imitative violence: they are just slightly unpleasant.[28]

Halliwell noted that the BBFC cut films in all categories, not just those with 'X' certificates, which would mean that the companies would be consulting with it over hundreds of films each year. He preferred to rely on ITV's own internal mechanisms. Responding, Murphy acknowledged instances when past BBFC cuts 'would no longer seem either necessary or right' and said that these could be rectified for transmission. But he also pointed out 'the difficult political situation.

Although the agitation to ban all X films does not seem to be gaining much support I feel we should not add fuel to the fire by putting out versions of films which have not even got BBFC approval.'[29]

The issue did not go away. In a 'supplementary memorandum', submitted to the Home Secretary following the publication of the Annan Report (1977), the Cinematograph Exhibitors' Association (CEA) advocated the complete prohibition from television of all 'X'-certificate films. The CEA was honest enough to admit that its 'members would probably stand to gain' if such a proposal were enacted, but nevertheless insisted that it was primarily 'concerned with the public interest'.[30] The same proposal was made in Parliament by Raphael Tuck MP (Watford, Labour), and again by Michael Shersby MP (Uxbridge, Conservative), each time without success.[31] The subsequent White Paper on Broadcasting (1979), while recommending the display of BBFC certificates when films were shown on television, also reasserted the broadcasters' responsibility for self-regulation. The Government did, however, establish the independent Broadcasting Complaints Commission in 1981. The following year, the 'X' disappeared altogether when the BBFC revised its own certification system and renamed itself the British Board of Film Classification.

BBC Internal Regulation

Explaining why it would be inappropriate to classify television programmes in the same way as the BBFC did cinema films, a 1968 article in *Radio Times* pointed out other important considerations:

> One big difference between television programmes and cinema films is often overlooked. Admission to the cinema is controlled; but anyone can watch television who tunes in to it. Thus unescorted children can be kept out of the 'A' film by the cinema manager, and young people can be excluded altogether from programmes with an 'X' certificate. The same rules could not, however, be enforced for television. Indeed, far from helping, to label films 'A' or 'X' might make matters worse. To watch such programmes might seem rather daring to some children, while some adults might turn on an 'X' certificate play, not to enjoy it as a drama but in the expectation of being shocked and titillated.[32]

The preferable alternative to certification, argued the unsigned article, was a combination of methods: careful scheduling, placing 'programmes with essentially adult themes' after 9.00pm and not running trails for them any earlier; indicating programme content in *Radio Times* itself; and broadcasting warnings before the transmission of programmes on 'sensitive' subjects. Reaffirming these points a decade later, the BBC's Director of Television, Alasdair Milne, articulated the Corporation's general view of BBFC certification and internal regulation:

> The original 'X' certificate, even when used by the commercial cinema, was a wayward instrument of classification. Many films awarded an 'X' certificate ten or twenty years ago would not receive such a certificate for the cinema today. A high proportion could even be suitable for late

> television viewing. The BBC's policy of selection and editorial control already ensures that no film will reach the screen unless its content has been very carefully considered in advance. This is a responsibility that must rest with the BBC and not be off-loaded to the public.[33]

The *Radio Times* article, however, had concluded on a different note: 'In the end the responsibility for deciding to watch must rest on the shoulders of the adult viewer.'[34] It was this balance of public and institutional responsibility that was often the subject of dispute in complaints.

In the second half of the 1970s, Alasdair Milne authored a number of position papers articulating the Corporation's film acquisition and scheduling policies. In November 1975, he briefed the Board of Governors on the subject of films, 'with particular emphasis on the rapidly changing standards in the contemporary cinema of the treatment of sex and violence'. Milne described the vetting procedure in the Purchasing Department:

> 1. Before being purchased, all films offered in a package are screened by a responsible member of the department's staff.
> 2. Any film carrying a Censorship 'X' classification, is seen personally by the Head of the Department before it is bought. If he is in any doubt, the film can, of course, be referred upwards to the relevant Channel Controller or the Director of Programmes in the normal way.
> 3. Before *each* transmission, the film is again screened by the Purchasing Assistant responsible for the particular strand in which the film is scheduled. Particular note is taken of the film's suitability to the time period of its transmission, of topical references likely to cause offence, etc.

He went on:

> The process of screening calls for the exercise of individual judgment in circumstances of great difficulty; the quality or artistic integrity of the film has to be weighed against the possibility that the subject matter and/or the treatment might cause outrage to the viewing public, particularly when seen in the domestic situation. Explicit sex or violence are the most frequent causes of rejection but by no means all; bad language, scenes of drug taking, reconstructions of current crimes such as bombings and hi-jackings have all posed problems recently.[35]

Milne acknowledged that it was 'likely that we are moving more slowly than the audience in accepting changing standards' but felt 'we are right to be tardy, not least because of the potential impact on our own drama output if we were seen to be less than rigorous in our scrutiny of feature films'. It was important that consistent standards were seen to be maintained over both in-house productions and acquired programmes like films. Milne reported that several recent high-profile films that had been offered to the BBC had been rejected for their unacceptable content despite their 'considerable merit'. They included *Straw Dogs* (1971/10.08.2003), *Carnal Knowledge* (1971/02.12.1983), *Last Tango in Paris* (1972/14.02.1993) and *The Killing of Sister George* (1968/28.09.1975).[36] (The last of these was bought by ITV and is discussed in Chapter 11.)

Some films that the Corporation had purchased nevertheless still caused concern, albeit often internally rather than with the public. Among them were two violent Westerns, *Heaven with a Gun* (1969/04.05.1975) and *Fistful of Dollars* (1964/01.08.1975). Staff considered that 'a mistake had been made' in showing *Heaven with a Gun*, which was never repeated. *Fistful of Dollars* had been referred to the Controller of BBC1 for permission to broadcast, but despite staff misgivings it was well received. According to BBC Audience Research, it drew 12 million viewers on first transmission in a late-night (9.55pm) slot, scoring a high audience Reaction Index and receiving only 'a handful of complaints'. Milne pointed out of this and other Clint Eastwood films: 'because they are Westerns these films fall into an accepted convention, while even within that convention they are reasonably stylised and distanced from the contemporary viewer' (see Figure 9.1).[37] This did not prevent viewers writing to *Radio Times* to complain about the violence in Eastwood's *High Plains Drifter* (1973/11.09.1978), though several others replied in its defence.[38] There was also internal criticism of the decision to transmit Michael Winner's Charles Bronson thriller *The Mechanic* (1972/15.01.1979), which was not shown again by the BBC until fifteen years after its first transmission.[39]

Figure 9.1 Spaghetti Westerns did well with audiences despite BBC schedulers' initial misgivings over violence. *Radio Times* © Immediate Media Co. Artwork © David da Silva.

In a later report, Milne explained that, on his instructions, warning announce-ments immediately before programmes were 'used sparingly, because they would quickly become devalued if too frequent'. Other means were used instead to give viewers a 'flavour' of what they were in for, such as advance trails on screen and the publicity materials prepared by Presentation staff and disseminated by Press Information, including the billings used in *Radio Times*.[40]

Regulating ITV

Rules and regulations governing films shown on the commercial network were not all concerned with content or matters that could be called censorship. The ITV companies operated under a number of restrictions, partly to appease the talent and labour unions (represented by a Safeguards Committee) and to protect in-house television production, partly to comply with the terms of the Television Act 1954. The ITA, in its capacity as regulator, policed possible violations of the Act and otherwise sought to interfere as little as possible in the companies' business. But following criticism by the Pilkington Report (1962) that it was not exercising its powers forcefully enough, the Authority adopted a more proactive, interven-tionist stance. It required that the companies submit their planned quarterly schedules in advance, scrutinising them to ensure that a 'proper balance' of pro-grammes was maintained in each company's output. More explicit and rigorous rules were developed and these were sometimes modified in the light of changing conditions. They included rules governing the scheduling of feature films.

In December 1967, following discussions with the companies, the Authority set a limit of not more than five feature films per week in any one region (including those served by two companies for different parts of the week); of these, not more than two films could be British. This was to ensure that feature films were covered by the quota of 14 per cent imported material (see Chapter 4); if more than two British films were scheduled in any one week, the excess would be counted for quota purposes as foreign. Additional films were permitted in bank holiday weeks and over the Christmas and New Year fortnight. No more than four films per week could be scheduled to start in peak viewing hours (between 6.00pm and 10.00pm). Even though it recognised the difficulties of scheduling films, the Authority did 'not like to see feature films straddling the news, and never straddling the *News at Ten*' – although this in fact happened on a great many occasions. It discouraged repeats of films after less than a two-year interval and more than two transmissions per film, and would 'not favour repeats exceeding in any one quarter more than ten per cent of the total films shown'.[41]

These rules were revised in 1970, when the limit of five films per week was raised to six, not more than three of which should be British. This adjustment was made to allow the companies to play off existing stocks of films before their hire contracts expired. The ITA also recognised that cinema films played an impor-tant role in competition for audiences with the BBC, which had no comparable restrictions on film scheduling, and that an uneven number of films created problems for the 'London split' between Thames and LWT.[42] Increasing numbers of television programmes imported from the US were of feature length, whether long-form episodes of continuing series or stand-alone made-for-TV movies; the latter, Authority staff felt, were, 'from the viewer's standpoint, indistinguishable from cinema film'.[43] A shortage of British-produced telefilm series meant that the companies were dependent on imports for this kind of material, which ate into their foreign-film allowance. Under the revised rules, the long-form American telefilms counted as feature films for quota purposes so as not to increase the proportion of feature-type material overall. When the companies asked the following year for this to be rescinded, the ITA agreed on condition that long telefilms and cinema films should not be placed next to one another in the schedules.[44]

In the spring of 1972, the Government derestricted broadcasting hours, allowing both the BBC and the ITV companies to determine their own limits on their services. In recognition of this situation and following further discussions with the companies' Programme Policy Committee and with the unions' Safeguards Committee, another new set of rules governing the use of feature films and other acquired material was drafted in May 1972. The permitted number of cinema films and made-for-TV movies was raised to seven 'in weekly schedules composed of 90 hours or more', though it remained as six for schedules of less than this (those operated by the smaller regional stations). The major companies planned to increase their broadcasting hours by offering extended daytime services from the autumn; these often included a new weekday film matinee. Thames Television had begun doing this in London in the spring of 1971, but it took deregulation for others to follow suit. The limitation of not more than three British films remained in place and new rules governed the scheduling of all long-form film material, whether made for the cinema or television:

(i) At least two hours should elapse between the finish of one film with a running time of more than sixty minutes and the start of another.

(ii) The number of these films shown between 7 pm and 11 pm should not exceed five a week and at least one of these should begin not earlier than 10.30 pm.[45]

In discharging its statutory obligations, the Authority – renamed the Independent Broadcasting Authority (IBA) in July 1972 – might appear to have been unduly doctrinaire and these various rules may seem unnecessarily restrictive; certainly some of the companies felt that way in response to certain of its regulations and decisions. But officers insisted that, despite appearances, the rules were flexible in their application and avoided being too specific about details in order to give the companies some leeway.[46]

Senior executive control of the Authority lay with the Director General and the Chairman. Below them were the fixed-term Members, who like them were appointed by Government. But day-to-day liaison with the ITV companies was generally left to permanent staff, particularly the Programme Services division.

Seniority here lay with the Deputy Director General, Bernard Sendall, succeeded in 1977 by Colin Shaw as the Director of Television; and with the Head of Programme Services, a role occupied by Joseph Weltman until 1976, when he was briefly replaced by David Glencross before the latter went on to become Deputy Director of Television and, in 1983, Director of Television. Programme Officers, dealing with the detail of content and scheduling issues, included Stephen Murphy and Dermot P. O'Hagan. Administrative Officers including Neville Clarke and Michael Gillies dealt with public complaints. Almost all complainants received a diplomatic personal reply, often drafted by the Programme Officers and sometimes written or signed by the Director General or Chairman. The number of complaints the Authority received regarding individual films was very small for the size of their audiences (doubtless the companies received more at local level); but each was taken seriously and carefully considered for its policy implications as well as the particular case.

Given the federated nature of the ITV structure, it was perhaps felt necessary to impose a degree of standardisation across the companies' scheduling, which was otherwise prone to wide variation, particularly with regard to feature films. As well as the balance of programming, the Authority also kept watch on the quality of material broadcast. Where films were concerned, this meant not just the content but the visual and sound quality as experienced by the viewer. The Authority's Engineering Division sought to maintain and improve technical standards on the network. Before a film print was accepted for transmission it was tested by technicians and rejected if found to be unacceptable. All broadcasts were monitored by staff at each regional office, who wrote daily reports containing both critical comments on programme quality and a technical grading, with 1 representing the highest standard and grades of 4 or below deemed unacceptable (though they still occurred).

Feature films brought particular technical challenges for television because they had been designed, staged, framed, lit and processed for a different medium. Prints made specifically for TV use were therefore processed differently from those originally distributed to cinemas, with less contrast between the light and dark areas of the image. Films shot in widescreen formats such as CinemaScope or Panavision were often reframed in the laboratory and supplied to TV in 'rectified' (reformatted) prints for ease of transmission, though production of these prints apparently ceased after 1976. The network stations were better equipped to 'pan and scan' a widescreen anamorphic print; occasionally a panned-and-scanned tape transfer would be made available to the smaller companies if a rectified print was not available. The stylistic trends of cinema in the 1970s also caused some problems, as the tetchy Leslie Halliwell explained: 'Many modern films (including television movies) have developed a fashion which neither engineers nor viewers like, i.e. inky black shadows, halated light sources, etc. This is intended to be realism and is even cropping up in *McCloud*.'[47] Halliwell was concerned that monitors and engineers might consider such traits to be technical flaws that would count against companies' performance in quarterly evaluative reports.

Colour was introduced to the ITV network in November 1969 (as it was on BBC1, two years after BBC2) but it took seven years before all local stations were equipped to transmit in colour; the smallest company, Channel Television, broadcast in monochrome until 1976. But once it became standard, the IBA pressed for a progressively greater proportion of colour programmes, including films, in each station's output, especially at peak-times. Local schedulers were sometimes asked to alter their selections if they were found to be unsuitable. A memorandum of December 1975 on the upcoming winter schedule noted: 'A careful check is being made of any black and white feature films in the schedule to ensure that only those which are thought to be of good quality are allowed.'[48]

By the late 1970s, it was increasingly unusual for black-and-white films to appear during peak evening hours, though it did occasionally occur. When six out of nine films scheduled for Granada over two successive weeks in February 1978 were found to be in monochrome, including three in peak-time, the IBA objected. *Danger Within* (1959/17.04.1966) had previously been shown twice by Granada as well as twice on the BBC, yet it had been pencilled in for a Sunday evening. *Topper* (1937/07.10.1952) had also been shown by the opposition, though it had not been seen on television for more than two decades; as the film was four decades old, IBA officers were unconvinced that it was appropriate for the evening slot scheduled.[49] Halliwell therefore withdrew both these films and substituted recent made-for-TV movies instead.

Halliwell also locked horns with the IBA over its determination to weed out from the network inventory what Authority officers saw as inferior films.[50] Staff compiled a master list of 150 films that had regularly received a technical grade of 4 or lower on transmission, with a view to eliminating 'between 20–40 of the least good programme quality'.[51] They solicited the film buyer's help in making the selection and he tried to be cooperative, but it proved difficult to agree on which titles were expendable. Among the first group of sixteen films selected by officers, Halliwell was nonplussed to find a Laurel and Hardy feature, *Bonnie Scotland* (1935/31.05.1971), and an all-star Ealing war drama, *The Big Blockade* (1942/05.04.1959); he insisted on reprieving these and most others.[52] In another IBA report, Hammer's war film *The Camp on Blood Island* (1958/13.10.1974) was dismissed in these terms: 'This is a British film, directed by Val Guest, the epitome of talentless British hack directors. I think it stars Peter Cushing [it does not]. I very much doubt whether this is worth keeping.'[53] (It was kept.)

Halliwell did succeed in having a concession made for films that were deemed to be of 'archival' value for reasons of artistic worth or historical interest. These could be exempted from engineers' technical evaluations, especially if they were shown in off-peak hours when standards might be 'relaxed'. But there were differences of opinion over what actually constituted archival value and which films merited that status. As Halliwell pointed out, the distinction between technical and aesthetic quality was sometimes blurred in discussions – as was, from the IBA's point of view, the distinction between films which were 'genuinely "archival"' and those that were 'merely "old"'.[54]

Halliwell submitted a list of 173 films held in stock that he considered archival; the IBA in turn drew up its own, more conservative list of sixty-three titles. Halliwell responded that the idea of such a list might have seemed

> perfectly acceptable as far as it goes, but it will be worse than useless if you regard its acceptance as some kind of promise that we will not play any other films more than twenty years old. Many of the pleasures of BBC scheduling consist of much older films which your researchers would doubtless exclude from any archival list simply because they don't figure in the right books.[55]

Whereas Halliwell knew the stock at first hand, officers were dependent for their judgements on what few reference books were available at the time; coincidentally or not, Halliwell was currently at work on the first edition of his own *Film Guide*, published in 1977. Authority officers sensed that they were caught between conflicting interests and that the notion of a definitive protected list was probably unworkable, given that films were constantly moving in and out of stock as contract terms expired and new batches were bought. They therefore agreed that titles should be submitted for exemption from quality standards on an ad hoc basis, as they were acquired or scheduled. Staff did not want to give 'blanket approval' to all films deemed archival by the buyer as this might lead to companies 'filling up the schedules with very cheap material'.[56] Halliwell found this notion depressing:

> Frankly I don't see how any system can work while one side goes on suspecting the other of base motives. I would have hoped that by now the IBA might have realised that we don't deliberately buy poor quality film on the cheap, and indeed that suppliers would not sell older material more cheaply than modern material, as they know that there is a very definite limit in the number of films that we can use and so they charge much the same for old as for new. If anything comes up which is worth more than the average money you surely have ample evidence that we are not reluctant to spend it.[57]

In 1973, a technicians' report examined inconsistencies in technical quality among the ITV stations: 'Telecine machines vary in make, type, gamma correction, scan tube phosphor, depth of focus, maintenance condition and accuracy of alignment, to suggest just a few probable causes of variations between programme companies handling the same films.'[58] To ensure greater consistency, the report therefore recommended that the companies regularly networked one or two features per week but noted that such a policy would need the Authority's active enforcement.[59]

The IBA well understood the advantages of networking, both practical and economic.[60] One was the potential saving on print costs: laboratory charges for making 35mm copies of films were increasing (around £1,000 each by 1976) and, due to their usually being shown twice in each of fourteen regions, prints suffered considerable wear and tear. Although two prints were typically acquired of each title, replacements sometimes had to be ordered before a film had completed its licence period. Halliwell pointed out that, taking into account previewing, editing and transmission, 'each print when shown locally by every station receives about

84 runs through machinery, which includes rewinding; and to this one must add other viewings [and] promotional uses'.[61] Only one print might be needed of a film intended for networking, as it would receive very few transmissions. Shipping costs would also be reduced and busy local film departments could have their labour reduced if one major station transmitted a film to the rest of the network.

Scheduling films regionally for fixed slot lengths also meant that films were subjected to cuts for time, especially in the case of long films, and this was often done inexpertly (see Chapter 11). But a film shown on the whole network could be given a slot tailored to its length, without need for cutting; or if cuts had to be made, they could be done centrally, by a single, experienced editor at the originating station rather than by local editors. Yet as we have seen, until the mid-1970s the networking of films was extremely rare (see Chapter 7). Factors that prevented it from becoming more common included local schedulers' insistence on their own autonomy and perceived variations in regional tastes and habits: 'for example, it was alleged that people go to bed earlier in Anglia territory than elsewhere'.[62] There was also a potential loss of flexibility if local advertising slots in a networked film were not fully sold, and some companies felt that scheduling different films in each region allowed them a better chance in the local ratings. Viewers in fringe areas could often receive more than one station signal and therefore had an increased choice of viewing. Following a recommendation by the Standing Consultative Committee on Quality, Halliwell began drawing up reserve lists of films intended for networking, which he submitted annually to the Authority. But some companies jumped the gun and booked films on the list for local use, depleting the stock available for networking. Although increasing numbers of films were networked each year, they remained in the minority even in peak-time until the mid-1980s, while off-peak films remained locally scheduled for much longer.

When Is a Feature Film a Telefilm?

Underlying the Authority's system of rules was its statutory obligation to maintain both programme balance and programme quality. The rules were often tested by company schedulers hoping for more flexibility, and two cases in 1968–69 illustrated the blurred lines that sometimes existed between a feature film originally made for theatrical release and a telefilm made specifically or primarily for the small screen.

Between 1960 and 1965, Anglo Amalgamated Film Distributors released a series of forty-seven crime thrillers adapted from the novels of Edgar Wallace and filmed at Merton Park Studios. These films, all around an hour long, played extensively as 'B' pictures in UK cinemas and most of them were acquired for local broadcast by Thames Television, shortly before it began operating the London weekday franchise in July 1968. The company asked the ITA to classify the series not as feature films but as telefilms, in which case they would not be counted against its film quota. According to Thames executive Howard Thomas, the company had acquired forty of the films on the understanding that they had originally been 'designed as a series for American Television'. The company had consequently paid 'a considerably higher price than the one they would have attracted as feature films'. Thomas explained that the company intended to schedule the episodes 'in place of American one-hour film series', and on that basis wanted them to be counted against the foreign quota rather than the film quota.[63]

This placed the Authority in a quandary. Another ITV company, Grampian, had also acquired the series and proposed treating them as feature films; the ITA had classified them accordingly. After viewing two sample films, Senior Programme Officer Stephen Murphy considered the series 'grey and second-rate', though not 'too bad to be shown: we cannot rule out its emergency use'. However, he felt that when the Authority was 'trying to get a bright new look in to the system' following the recent franchise reallocations, it 'should not be encouraging people to show rather old, very "B" material'.[64] Deputy Director General Bernard Sendall informed Thomas that the ITA had to consider the consequences for 'the system as a whole' of any ruling, and that a decision in favour of Thames's request might set a precedent 'for other developments in relation to "B" film material which we would not wish to see'.[65] However, after Thomas provided a signed letter from the films' producer, Nat Cohen, confirming that the series had been made with 'the American television market foremost in our minds', Sendall acknowledged that he had made his case convincingly.[66]

Conditional upon the Authority's acceptance of his proposal was Thomas's assurance that the films would not be scheduled in place of 'live or videotaped' domestic TV productions, a requirement that would also be made of any other station wishing to play the series.[67] But a further undesirable precedent threatened if domestically-produced material were offset against the foreign quota, as Thomas had proposed. This could lead to objections from American interests 'as a deliberate act of discrimination against the import of American material' and lead to trouble for the Government's General Agreement on Trade and Tariffs (GATT). Thames was therefore permitted to schedule the Wallace series instead of other telefilm material (including British) or feature films, but largely on the basis of a gentlemen's agreement rather than a general ruling.[68]

The Wallace films did not begin to appear in ITV schedules for another year: the earliest transmission appears to have been *Man Detained* (1961/26.06.1969) on Thames. Typically they were used as off-peak fillers, initially late at night and subsequently (once regular daytime programmes had begun in 1972) in weekday afternoon and morning slots. Over time, the Authority came to regret allowing the Wallace series to be shown, not because of any breach of Thomas's assurances but because of the extent of the films' use by Thames and other companies. Most ITV stations played at least some of them, but an audit halfway through 1972 revealed that Thames alone had by that point made seventy-one individual Wallace transmissions and was well into its third run of the series. Granada had played fifty-five transmissions, Yorkshire Television eighty-three and HTV forty-six; all four companies were still regularly playing the films.[69] The Authority's Head of Programme Services, Joseph Weltman, was led to wonder 'just how long we shall go on reaping the consequences' of the 1968 decision.[70]

The Wallace films disappeared from the schedules after 1975 but the question of the series' suitability arose again eight years later when Leslie Halliwell acquired it on spec for the new Channel Four, which turned it down. The films were then offered to ITV and when several stations proposed to play them – as features rather than as telefilms – the Authority queried them on grounds of quality. Correspondence suggests that its staff had confused them with the 'Scotland Yard' series of 1950s shorts fronted by Edgar Lustgarten, which had also previously been seen on ITV.[71] After viewing one of the Wallace films, officers admitted the error and acknowledged that they were 'better than we remembered them'.[72] They must also have taken into account Halliwell's valiant defence that they 'feature a whole range of splendid writing, acting and directorial talent which makes them historically interesting on these accounts alone. As for their entertainment value and technical worthiness, I am prepared to stake my own reputation on this.'[73] The films were again seen locally on ITV for some years to come and at time of writing they are still being shown daily on Talking Pictures TV.

A second example of a feature-film series being claimed as a telefilm series also concerned Thames. As the successor to Rediffusion, the company had inherited some of its older acquisitions, including the series of twelve 'B' mysteries starring Basil Rathbone as Sherlock Holmes and Nigel Bruce as Dr Watson. These had been produced in America for Universal Pictures between 1942 and 1946 on the basis of a limited licensing deal with the estate of Sir Arthur Conan Doyle. When the rights lapsed, Universal sold the films on to a TV distributor. They had first been televised in the UK by Granada in 1959–60, with A-R transmitting them in London in 1960.[74] Other companies had shown them intermittently as feature films, but when Thames took over the London weekday franchise it saw them as a telefilm series. Its Director of Programmes, Brian Tesler, claimed that they had clearly been 'made for television, not the cinema' on the strength of a company name: Motion Pictures for Television Inc. This was the TV distributor that had taken over the films from Universal and had presumably substituted its own credit for the studio logo in the opening titles. Tesler argued that acceding to Thames's request would not involve the ITA in setting 'a new and dangerous precedent' as, besides the Edgar Wallace series now already agreed to be telefilms, there appeared 'to be no other series of films in existence made specifically for television rather than the cinema'.[75]

The grounds for refusing this proposal were less than clear-cut and led to an internal disagreement. Joseph Weltman pointed out that Tesler was in fact basing his request on a recent precedent, the Wallace series, but argued that the Authority's decision should be based on the particular facts of the case. In this instance, the main issue, according to Weltman, was not whether the films were or were not telefilms, but rather quality:

> The present case is a request to accept in the schedules some 30-year-old films of not very distinguished quality. We do not give a hang whether or not they were made for television in the first instance. In our view they are just not good enough for showing on ITV in 1969.[76]

Weltman wrote to Tesler to ask what use was planned for the films in the schedules, adding tartly: 'Frankly we are surprised that you should be contemplating any use of them whatsoever on Thames Television in 1969 – or later.'[77] Tesler responded that he had no particular use in mind but explained: 'I obviously would not play them in peak time, but they are almost bound to come in handy at some time or other. Your classification of their status would in itself condition their use.'[78] However, Bernard Sendall demurred from the views of his colleague. He countered:

> The Edgar Wallace decision related to British material which could be a substitute for British television productions. This Sherlock Holmes material cannot be. Its quality cannot be directly relevant to the issue we have before us. If we are convinced that it is now totally unacceptable in anybody's schedule (even after more extra hours have arrived), then, of course, we must let this fact be known, and it will not matter whether it is regarded as feature film or television film. But (a) do we know enough about it to be able to say? and (b) have we ever before singled out any series for such an absolute ban on grounds of quality?[79]

Weltman responded that he was not proposing an 'absolute ban' on the series but merely wanted to make it 'more difficult' for Thames to use the films as an entire series rather than as occasional fillers. He returned to the question of quality: 'We accept a certain modicum of foreign material because that we believe will give us a better television service, not because it is more convenient for companies to fill air time by purchase than by production.' Films, he believed, should be chosen on the basis of 'programme merit', not mere availability.[80]

As a way of resolving the matter, Sendall suggested informing Tesler simply that the Authority did 'not feel able to depart from the present classification of these films as feature films rather than television series'.[81] Weltman did so, Tesler accepted the decision with good grace, and the Sherlock Holmes series did not get a showing on Thames. It did, however, have some off-peak repeat runs on Granada, HTV and Grampian in 1969–70 before the television rights lapsed. They were subsequently picked up by the BBC, which showed most of the films in peak-time BBC1 slots in 1977–78, launching the series with a major article in *Radio Times*. Over the following decades they enjoyed half a dozen repeat runs on BBC2 and one or two showings each on Channel Four. Films considered by one ITA officer as unsuitable for showing in 1969 continue to appear on television in the 2020s.

ITCA Film Clearance and Certification

Besides the Authority's oversight, ITV had its own regulatory procedures for handling films and telefilm series. The commercial system was more complex than the BBC's, given the federated nature of the network. Each of the companies had an officer responsible for film and programme acquisition, whose role involved vetting bought-in material and giving approval to broadcast it, procedures not dissimilar to those in the more centralised BBC setup. In the case of Scottish Television (STV), for example, 'off-duty Transmission Controllers see all the incoming film and report doubtful sections to the Director of Programmes, who then views these sections himself and decides whether or not they should be shown'.[82]

At the Authority's instigation, on 1 August 1962 a formal 'clearance and certification' routine for feature films and telefilms was introduced by the contractors' representative body, the Independent Television Companies Association (ITCA). Its aim was to ensure consistency of standards across the network, so that different regions did not play substantially different versions of a given film or series episode, or show them at times of day for which other stations had judged them unsuitable. Either the purchasing company or the first company to play a film previewed it and issued an ITCA certificate, or clearance card, indicating its suitability for showing at particular times of day (see Figure 9.2). Once a certificate had been issued, a paper copy of the card, attached to the can containing the first reel, accompanied the film print on each booking by a local station. If permanent cuts were required for reasons of content, these were made by the certificating company and the cut sections were destroyed to prevent them finding their way back into the print. If more than one print had been acquired, each print had to be edited to conform to the approved version. However, if a company needed to make cuts solely for timing purposes to fit a scheduled slot on a particular transmission, these sections were to be reintegrated after the film had been transmitted (see the discussion of editing for time in Chapter 11). If a company wanted to show a film at an earlier time than specified on the card, it could either seek the Authority's permission or make additional, temporary edits at its own risk, restoring the cuts after use. In any event, the clearance card did not absolve each company from previewing and approving a film before its local transmission.[83]

A 'history sheet' for each film was supposed to document its use. But inconsistencies in record-keeping and lack of clarity in recommended transmission times led to a revised clearance system operating from 1 July 1967. There were now three standard time bands: Suitable Any Time (SAT), Post-8.00 (meaning that the film should not begin transmission before 8.00pm) and Post-9.00. Films could also be designated as particularly suitable for children's viewing time. Gradually, however, further permutations crept in. Certain SAT films could be unofficially recommended to begin after 7.00pm. Post-8.00 films could be shown in afternoons during term time, so long as they finished by 4.00pm, when schools turned out. Both Post-8.00 and Post-9.00 films could begin earlier than these times at weekends, but particularly strong Post-9.00 films could be recommended for showing no earlier than 10.30pm. Films with scenes involving hangings or preparations for a hanging could not start earlier than 9.30pm, unless such scenes had been edited out; this was to be avoid them being seen by children who might imitate them. The Authority had insisted on the hanging rule after a spate of accidents

Film Clearance

INDEPENDENT TELEVISION COMPANIES ASSOCIATION

To: MR. L. PARKER, I.T.C.A.   From: ANTHONY JOHN

c.c. Mr. S. Murphy, I.T.A.
Mr. C. Towle, A.B.Pathe
Mr. R. Godfrey, A.B.C.
Mr. P. Mahoney, A.B.C.
File

Feature or Series Title _____ THE FRIGHTENED CITY _____

Episode No. or Title _____

    Copy No. _1 & 2_ has been viewed by _ABC TELEVISION LIMITED_

    and is considered suitable for transmission at the following times:
        (Transmission outside the recommended times must be
        cleared with the Independent Television Authority.)

ALL TIMES	POST 8.00	POST 9.00
No	Yes	Yes

                          Insert YES or NO in each box

The following excisions have been made:

Minutes In   Description

_51.00_   _Prolonged scene with man and woman in bedroom trimmed_

_70.00_   _Threatening by Police in interview at Scotland Yard trimmed_

_82.00_   _Close-ups of final fight trimmed_

_____   _____

_____   _____

_____   _____

Approximate Running Time in Minutes: _84.00_

Signed: _____   Date: _____

Source: Bournemouth University's IBA Archive
https://libguides.bournemouth.ac.uk/archives-special-collections/iba-archive
• Document in IBA Archive file: Films - Clearance Routine and Acquisition; 01-May-62 to 01-Dec-68
• File in IBA Archive box: 3996311 (https://bournemouth.on.worldcat.org/oclc/1315592032)

Figure 9.2 ITCA Clearance Card for *The Frightened City* (1961), enclosed in a letter from Anthony John to Stephen Murphy, 25 January 1967, IBA/01023: 399611.

involving children. Exceptions to the rule, otherwise rigorously enforced, could be made in the case of certain 'classic' films – though the only example ever cited in internal memos was *The Hunchback of Notre Dame* (1939/06.01.1962). In May 1972, the Post-8.00 category was changed to Post-7.30 to allow more flexibility in scheduling, but long-form American made-for-TV movies (made at a standard length) could begin at 7.15pm. Thus, a system aimed at achieving consistency and simplicity ended up being inconsistent and over-complicated in practice.

Although certificates were intended to be permanent, a good deal of negotiation took place even after they had been issued. The Authority often queried a particular classification and asked for it to be amended – not always to make it more restrictive. Regional monitors, who made daily notes on every station's transmissions, often commented on the suitability of films for particular time slots and certificates could be amended following their recommendations. For example, officers advised that *Blood Money* (1962/29.09.1968), originally certificated as Post-8.00, could safely be made SAT.[84] Conversely, *Portrait of a Mobster* (1961/14.04.1967) – misspelled 'Monster' in internal correspondence – was considered too strong for SAT and officers asked for it to be made Post-8.00 instead.[85] Sometimes senior staff made their own interventions. An early-evening transmission of *Coast of Skeletons* (1964/13.09.1970), certificated SAT, was 'watched with horror' by Stephen Murphy. In his view, the film, which had received a BBFC 'U' certificate, contained three clear breaches of the Authority's Code on Violence. He considered it should be either Post-9.00 if uncut or Post-8.00 if heavily cut. Murphy added in his memo to Thames Television: 'our choice of feature films already compares very badly with the BBC's. Let's not make the record any worse.'[86]

The advent of centralised film acquisition through the appointment, in July 1968, of Granada's Leslie Halliwell as Network Film Purchase Officer led to increased systematisation. There was considerable variance in certification practices between companies and the Authority grew to distrust the judgement of the regional stations. So did Halliwell, who commented on 'the way companies disagree with each other and issue in some cases absurd certifications'.[87] This concern was addressed from the mid-1970s, when efforts were made to centralise the clearance process too. Halliwell certificated as many films as possible at the point of purchase. Thereafter, representatives of the network companies were expected to do most of the work; regional companies issuing certificates were asked to do so in consultation with Halliwell or the Network Certification Officer, Ken Fletcher. Films containing potentially controversial material were to be certificated only by major companies and especially problematic cases could be adjudicated by the Film Clearance Committee, a group of experienced, senior personnel. These films would also be referred for approval to the Authority, which might if necessary overrule certification decisions. Content cuts had to be justified in writing and the deleted sections were no longer to be destroyed but retained in the event of later revision, in which case they could be reinstated. In January 1977, the IBA recorded some statistics for the revised system: 'In the first nine months of 1976, 198 feature films were previewed and certificated by the companies. Of these 181 (91 per cent) were certificated by the major companies and a total of 86 (43 per cent) by one company (Granada) alone.'[88]

The Authority maintained its requirement to see and approve film schedules in advance. When a film had been scheduled earlier than its certificate allowed, officers usually asked for another title to be substituted. But they could be flexible in dealing with requests for exceptions. Post-9.00 films on weekdays effectively meant a 10.30pm start if they were not to be interrupted by *News at Ten*. Weekends were more pliable and officers often allowed a Post-9.00 title to start an hour or so earlier on a Sunday if the film's 'prestige' value warranted it. But they refused requests along these lines for films deemed too adult in content, despite their acknowledged quality, such as *Georgy Girl* (1966/02.01.1972) and *Tony Rome* (1967/17.09.1973).

The appropriateness, or otherwise, of a film for the time it was transmitted was a regular cause of concern. Films certificated as Post-7.30, despite risqué language, brief nudity or mild violence, included *Perfect Friday* (1970/05.10.1975), *The Virgin and the Gypsy* (1970/05.09.1975), *There's a Girl in My Soup* (1970/07.03.1976), *The MacKintosh Man* (1973/13.11.1978) and *Ryan's Daughter* (1970/13.01.1980). All these drew public complaints but the IBA, having given its approval, did not censure the schedulers. Demand from local companies for films to be shown at different times resulted in at least one title, *100 Rifles* (1968/06.07.1975), being made available in two different prints, one more heavily edited than the other.[89] After some particularly strong Post-9.00 films had been scheduled to start too soon following the watershed, the IBA asked for subsequent showings to be recommended for post-10.30pm. These included *Sitting Target* (1972/14.10.1977) and *Man at the Top* (1973/02.09.1978). The former, a violent British crime thriller, was described by O'Hagan as 'a good candidate for the "Post 10.30" (or even later) category'. Ken Fletcher replied: 'A-hah, I knew this would happen. Now you want a category even later than "post 10.30". Maybe we should create a slot for insomniacs.' O'Hagan responded, tongue in cheek: 'Of course we do have a category later than POST 10.30. Its [*sic*] called "banned"! A-hah!'[90]

Despite the defences, in evidence submitted to the Committee on the Future of Broadcasting, made by both the BBC and the IBA of their respective regulatory systems, the Annan Report (1977) criticised the broadcasters for failing to do more to protect and warn viewers. It cited BBC research on screen violence, conducted in 1972, which 'showed that the chief offenders were imported films' (presumably including American telefilms as well as feature films), but this had not been followed up. It advocated more use of prefatory on-air announcements and urged that a film's BBFC certificate 'should be announced both in the programme journal and before the broadcast. Such announcements should make clear whether parts of the film have been removed or reinstated following the grating of the certificate.' Annan argued that ITV's own certification system was too complicated to be readily understood by viewers, whereas most people were aware of the BBFC categories.[91]

This recommendation was not adopted in the White Paper that followed. But it raised the question of how else viewers might be forewarned of potentially offensive or disturbing content. From 1 August 1973, ATV in the Midlands had trialled an on-screen warning symbol on selected programmes with explicit sexual or violent content. This took the form of a white rectangle placed in the bottom-left corner of the screen (see Figure 9.3). Programmes so designated were preceded by a verbal warning and the symbol remained in vision for the duration of the broadcast. Although dubbed a 'sex symbol' by the press, the warning sign was adopted at the instigation of the IBA's working party on screen violence.[92] The Annan Committee approved of the experiment, citing IBA research that viewers had found the symbol useful and noting the Authority's intention to extend its use to Southern Television.[93] But the IBA had reservations, as indicated by a 1976 memo:

> If anything our experiment with the warning symbol has proved that our editorial judgments work reasonably well. ... The warning symbol is the thin edge of what could be a large and possibly illiberal wedge. The wider use of such symbols for classification may provide short term public relations benefits for the broadcasting institution, but will end with poorer broadcasting and less protection for the public.[94]

The warning symbol did not become a permanent fixture as Annan had urged and seems to have been employed only rarely, but it was still being used in the ATV and Southern areas as late as 1980 for *Marathon Man* (1976/01.09.1980). The film

STEWART KNOWLES explains the significance of the new symbol which will appear occasionally on your television screen. It will be shown, as below, in the bottom left-hand corner of the screen

Bernard Sendall, left, IBA's Deputy Director General (Programme Services), is chairman of the special IBA working party which decided upon the new warning symbol

Figure 9.3 IBA Deputy Director General (Programme Services) Bernard Sendall and the on-screen warning symbol trialled in the ATV (Midlands) and Southern Television regions from 1973. *TVTimes* © Future Publishing Ltd.

was transmitted uncut, beginning at 9.00pm and with a break for *News at Ten*. The IBA received a number of complaints from viewers in other regions who had tuned in late, thus missing the verbal warning beforehand. Some complainants had changed channels due to the offence given by a competing film on BBC1, *An Investigation of Murder* (1973/01.09.1980), only to find the alternative fare even worse. One letter complained about the warning symbol itself.[95]

Deputy Director of Television David Glencross reported in early 1981 that there had recently been 'some shift towards acquired programmes as being more likely to provoke complaint than home produced ones' and that feature films were now 'likely to present us with more problems in the area of taste and offence than has usually been the case in previous years'.[96] Director of Television Colin Shaw, while acknowledging 'that a service of excellence, quality and stimulation cannot be provided without provoking complaint', did not think that the recent wave of protests at certain films was 'the result of brave and original challenges to existing orthodoxies':

> Gratuitous violence and bad language ... do not add greatly to the lustre or excellence of the service. Nor, except possibly in the very short term, do they add to the size of audience and therefore to the commercial strength of the system.[97]

The system's regulatory mechanisms came under particular stress over a pair of scheduling blunders in the autumn of the same year. Karel Reisz's *The Gambler* (1974/26.09.1981) was due to be networked on Saturday, 12 September, at 9.15pm. Just over one week earlier, ITV executives previewed the film and withdrew it because of bad language that they deemed excessive, particularly for the scheduled time. Leslie Halliwell provided a detailed account of how the film had been provisionally certificated in August 1980 (see Table 9.1) and then cleared for transmission by the Film Clearance Committee in April 1981. But the committee had seen only a sample reel, not the whole film, and by the time it was viewed by LWT – which was due to originate the transmission for the network – and referred to senior staff for a decision, it had been billed in *TVTimes* and publicised on-screen. The short-notice cancellation of *The Gambler* was widely discussed in the press, causing considerable embarrassment to both ITV and the IBA. Although the Authority had not been involved in the decision, the incident reflected badly on a system that had been designed 'to make sure that feature films are properly scheduled'. David Glencross pointed out:

> This places all of us in an indefensible position ... if the IBA, at whatever level, is to speak with any assurance and accuracy about ITV's scheduling of acquired films, it must be much more confident than it feels at the moment about inter-company procedure and the respective role of the Film Purchase Group and the Film Centre. There is a need for as much certainty in companies' knowledge of acquired film in advance of scheduling as there is about ITV's own product.[98]

The replacement film was *McQ* (1974/22.03.1979), a John Wayne detective thriller, which itself drew at least one complaint for violence: a viewer called the

Table 9.1 ITCA certification viewing report on *The Gambler*.

DATE: 27 August 1980

TITLE THE GAMBLER	SYNOPSIS A compulsive gambler's downfall.
TYPE OF FILM Drama	
SOURCE Paramount	
CERTIFICATION 2100	
REASONS FOR RESTRICTION Bad language and overtones of violence.	
SUGGESTED USE IN SCHEDULE Late peak.	RECOMMENDED CUTS Bleeping out of various words on soundtrack.
TX RUNNING TIME	(See over for examples) Reel 2 – Man's arm being broken
ADDITIONAL COMMENTS	

Reel 1   …fucking bet…
            Fuck my protection
            …wish to fuck…

Reel 2   Fuck off
            What the fuck are you trying to pull
            …kick your fucking face in
            Mother fucking…
            Scares the shit out of them

Reel 3   –

Table 9.1 (continued)

Reel 4	Give me the fucking money
	Where's the rest of my fucking money
	(Many mumbled fucks during a bath sequence)
	Do you want to fuck my girlfriend?
	I would have wiped the floor with your arse
Reel 5	The Fucking Laker game
	Mother fucker
Reel 6	Fuck gambling
	What the fuck are you doing
	This mother fucker dragged me…
	This mother fucker's crazy

Source: IBA/01024: 3996310.

substitution 'a meaningless exercise in censorship and one which I hope will not be repeated'.[99] The response from IBA Director General Sir Brian Young pointed out that many viewers did not agree, noting that the violence in *McQ* 'was comparatively muted for a film made in the mid-seventies'.[100]

The same could not be said of another film released the same year, *The Klansman* (1974). ITV had scheduled it for a network showing exactly two weeks later, at 10.15pm on Saturday, 26 September. This time it was the turn of three Authority officers to preview the film, one week before transmission. They considered it unacceptable:

> We agreed that basically it is a nasty, very violent film containing three rapes, a castration and countless killings. Aside from that, the theme – the white liberal versus the Ku Klux Klan, which was probably acceptable in the United States when the film was made, makes it difficult if not impossible to show in this country in the present social climate (Brixton, Toxteth, etc.)

> We feel that to allow this film to be shown would be irresponsible and could, indeed, be regarded as an incitement to racial violence. It would certainly be almost impossible to defend to complainants on either or both of the above scores.[101]

The Klansman was 'voluntarily withdrawn' by ITV; it has never been shown on terrestrial television. As its substitute, schedulers chose none other than *The Gambler*, whose soundtrack had now been edited to remove four uses of 'motherfucker'. However, at least twelve instances of 'fuck' (including 'kick your fucking face in') and seven of 'shit' (including 'Jesus shit') were retained. Several complaints were duly received, including one from the National Viewers' and Listeners' Association (NVALA), which had previously congratulated the Authority on the film's earlier withdrawal (inappropriately, due to its non-involvement in the action). Enclosing a monitor's report itemising each incidence of swearing, NVALA secretary Mary Whitehouse commented: 'Surely judgment let alone anything else is being corrupted.'[102] The IBA's reply defended the decision to reschedule the edited version and considered that the monitor was merely cherry-picking words that would upset NVALA members more than most other viewers:

> The catalogue prepared by your member is, frankly, no more than that and gives no indication of the context in which the words quoted appeared. As you know, the general criteria we seek to apply to language of this kind is [*sic*] that it should not be used gratuitously to shock, but should be appropriate to the characters and theme of the drama. There are bound to be strong differences of opinion about the acceptability on television of language which finds free expression in other media and, while we exercise a considerable degree of control, we nevertheless have to depend to some extent on the discipline of different placings for different kinds of material and also on the commonsense and restraint of viewers.[103]

Two major last-minute cancellations in the space of three weeks demonstrated that neither ITV's clearance and certification procedure nor the IBA's oversight of scheduling was foolproof when having to deal with the increasingly challenging material now available for broadcast. Faced with a particularly problematic film, schedulers could seek the advice of Authority staff; but there were limits to the guidance officers were able to give. After viewing part of *Death Wish* (1974/16.05.1981) at Leslie Halliwell's request, Dermot O'Hagan wrote to him to explain their general position:

> Firstly, although we are from time to time prepared to give our views on the acceptability or not of a given film or a scene in a film we would not wish this to become normal practice particularly in the case of more 'contentious' films which you might be doubtful about acquiring. Secondly, our views on film content, while given in good faith, cannot be regarded as bestowing any sort of official 'seal of approval' on a film. The Authority can at any time reverse the decisions of its staff on any programme or film should it see fit to do so.[104]

This placed the responsibility for scheduling decisions in the hands of ITV companies but located ultimate authority with IBA members; the role of programme staff could only be advisory. Halliwell's response was characteristically querulous:

> I think your second paragraph makes your first paragraph almost worthless. Surely you are our guiding light: if we can't turn to you for a seal of approval, we may well be stuck with the impossible situation of having paid a great deal of money for a programme which we are not going to be allowed to transmit. Surely the buck has to stop somewhere? and what is the point of our making our own judgement in respect of 'contentious' films if we know that you are likely to countermand our decision? It is no use playing the King if someone else is going to play the Ace.[105]

O'Hagan annotated this letter with a wry handwritten comment addressed to his colleagues: 'I don't believe that Leslie will ever really understand the system in which we operate!'

Banned, Postponed, Shelved and Withdrawn Films

Officially, the Authority did not ban films outright, but in doubtful cases it asked ITV schedulers to reconsider their choices. As we have seen in the case of *The Klansman*, this allowed the appearance of voluntary compliance with officers' recommendations, though they could have been enforced if the companies had not conceded. Several such instances arose as early as 1961–62.[106] One involved *Women of Twilight* (1952/29.02.1964), the first British film to have received a BBFC 'X' certificate. It was acquired by Associated-Rediffusion as part of the Independent Film Distributors (IFD) deal discussed in Chapter 4. A-R notified the Authority of its intention to show the film in July 1961. On the basis of a synopsis alone – the story is set in a home for unmarried mothers – Bernard Sendall declared that it 'just won't do, even after 10pm'. He reasoned that, aside from the need for compliance with the Television Act 1954, 'there is a public relations aspect to take into account'.[107] After viewing the film, A-R's scheduler Cyril Francis substituted another title. This scenario was repeated when Granada also proposed to transmit the film; but three years later, as part of its sharing arrangement with A-R, the BBC showed *Women of Twilight* on a Saturday at 10.15pm. This was its sole transmission; it was the only title from the IFD package never shown by an ITV company.

A thriller about a home invasion, *Lady in a Cage* (1964), had been denied a certificate by the BBFC but was classified Post-9.00 by ATV. When the film's censorship history was mentioned in *TVTimes*'s billing prior to its first scheduled transmission, by STV at 11.05pm on 23 June 1972, the Authority's Regional Officer for Scotland, John Lindsay, previewed it and told the company that he considered the film 'sick, obscene, excessively violent, and uncuttable'. Lindsay described the film as 'a forerunner of *Clockwork Orange* and others of the genre. If people want to pay money to go to a cinema to see this kind of thing, that is their business – in my own view it is our business to keep this film off ITV anywhere at anytime.'[108] Of course, the refusal of a BBFC certificate made seeing the film in a UK cinema difficult – further investigation revealed that, although seven local councils had allowed it to be shown, *Lady in a Cage* had never been exhibited in Scotland.[109] This precedent emboldened the Authority to ban it from the network. Dermot O'Hagan informed Leslie Halliwell: 'While agreeing with your contention that it is a serious film this, in a sense, makes it less rather than more acceptable even for late-night viewing.'[110] ATV's own scheduled transmission on 7 July was cancelled and the film was permanently withdrawn from the network.

Films were sometimes cancelled for political reasons or because of some event in the news. In early 1972, the BBC had problems finding a slot for *Wilson* (1944/02.07.1972), a Hollywood biopic of President Woodrow Wilson, partly because of its length (two-and-a-half hours) but also because it repeatedly clashed with scheduled party political broadcasts that would have necessitated interrupting it. *The Times* pointed out that 'on one particular date the break would have come just as a character holds up a placard saying "Vote for Wilson" – and that just before a party political broadcast on behalf of the Conservatives'.[111] The sitting Labour prime minister was of course Harold Wilson. Seven years later, the Labour Government was accused of having a hand in LWT's withdrawal of the industrial-relations satire *I'm All Right Jack* (1959/26.05.1969) from a scheduled transmission on 15 April 1979, in the run-up to a General Election following the 'Winter of Discontent'. The order to pull the film reportedly came from the IBA following discussions with Transport House, at that time the Labour Party HQ.[112] The Authority then instructed its regional officers to check the schedules of all ITV companies to ensure that 'no films have been scheduled which could even remotely be considered to be similarly inappropriate during the election campaign'.[113]

The volatile Northern Irish situation in the 1970s made certain films unscreenable. The BBC was put under pressure to withdraw *The Informer* (1935/28.11.1959) from a John Ford season when the Loyalist Association of Workers asked William Whitelaw, Secretary of State for Northern Ireland, to intervene in its scheduling.[114] The transmission of the IRA melodrama went ahead on 21 January 1973, but it was not shown again for nearly twenty years. Two other Irish-set films, Ford's *The Plough and the Stars* (1936/04.07.1997) and Ealing's *The Gentle Gunman* (1952/12.08.1965), were never broadcast by the BBC, although the Corporation held them both under contract and the latter had previously been shown on ITV. Two more, *Shake Hands with the Devil* (1959/25.06.1965) and *A Terrible Beauty* (1960/13.06.1965), which had also been shown locally by ITV companies, have not been seen on terrestrial channels since 1969.

It was not only domestic politics that caused concern. The BBC withdrew *Judith* (1966/25.10.1975), set in Israel in 1948, at short notice from a transmission scheduled for 7 October 1973. The film was cancelled because, according to an official comment in *Radio Times*, 'its final scenes showed hostilities between Arabs and Israelis, and it was felt that, coming immediately before the 10 o'clock News on BBC1 the day after the outbreak of the Middle East war, there was danger of confusion between fiction and fact'.[115] The former president of the Anglo-Jewish Association, Harold Sebag-Montefiore, had a different view: 'It was an extraordinary act of self-censorship. I can only assume that the BBC thought showing the film might cause disfavour to the BBC in the Arab countries.'[116] *Judith* was not rescheduled until two years later.

When a documentary, *Last Grave at Dimbaza* (1974/12.12.1974), about the living conditions of Black South Africans in a resettlement camp built by the Apartheid regime, was first offered to the BBC, it was reportedly rejected as too 'political' or 'partisan'. The 54-minute film had been made illegally, under secret conditions, by an anonymous British crew and smuggled out of the country. After it had received acclaim at the Cannes Film Festival and the National Film Theatre, the Corporation reconsidered and acquired it for the long-running series *Man Alive*.[117] For the sake of 'balance', the BBC invited a South African government representative to appear in the studio for a post-screening discussion. But the offer was declined unless the government could submit its own film by way of rebuttal and in the interests of 'British fair play'.[118] The result was that an abridged version of *Last Grave at Dimbaza* was followed immediately by the government-approved film, *Black Man Alive: The Facts*, compiled from official propaganda material. The 85-minute composite programme, including a discussion chaired by Desmond Wilcox, was entitled 'South Africa: Two Points of View'. *Radio Times*'s brief background article was called, with pointed irony, 'Looking on the White Side'. The full-length version of *Last Grave at Dimbaza* received a theatrical release the following year, when the *Monthly Film Bulletin*'s Verina Glaessner called it 'the most precisely informative and shattering indictment of the South African government's apartheid policy to have been shown in this country'. The review referred to the BBC's scheduling decision as revealing 'a discouraging political naivety and a sad disregard for television's potential as a medium for passionate reportage'.[119]

Several years later, it was reported that the BBC had refused to air another cinema documentary, *Before Hindsight* (1977/11.02.1978), about newsreel coverage of the rise of fascism, unless the makers removed a closing statement by TV journalist Jonathan Dimbleby, in which he made the point that 'in years to come historians will look back on the present media coverage of Northern Ireland and South Africa with the same incredulity as we currently regard 1930s newsreels'. According to the *Guardian*, Dimbleby argued 'that the current obsession with "balance" makes it impossible for film-makers to get the message across'.[120] In the event, *Before Hindsight* was broadcast with Dimbleby's statement apparently intact. Indeed, *Radio Times*'s billing highlighted it, perhaps in an attempt to take the sting out of the film's tail. Another studio discussion immediately followed the transmission, as part of a programme called *Was It 'Before Hindsight?'*.[121]

Sometimes cancellations occurred because of broadcasters' anxiety at possible public reactions. BBC1 had initially scheduled the anti-war musical *Oh! What a Lovely War* (1969/03.11.1974) for a peak-time premiere on Remembrance Sunday, but worries about causing offence led to its being shown the week before instead. Perhaps it was the disturbing subject matter that gave the BBC cold feet over the true-life crime drama *In Cold Blood* (1967/26/11/1977), twice announced for major peak-time strands, in 1973 and 1975, only for it to be withheld and squeak out years later, unheralded, as a 'Midnight Movie'. Other programme changes occurred for legal reasons. In almost identical situations, ITV pulled *Guns of the Magnificent Seven* (1969/29.09.1975) from a network slot on 18 January 1978 and BBC1 withdrew *Caravan to Vaccares* (1974/04.07.1982) from its scheduled transmission on 29 October 1979, in both instances after listings magazines had gone to press. The broadcasters were each convinced that they held exclusive rights to the film in question and had contracts to prove it; but this was disputed by their competitor, who argued the same. The cases went to court and both were resolved in favour of the objecting party.[122]

The purchase of package deals often led to some items being deemed unsuitable for showing. The BBC's large British Lion deal of 1968, discussed in Chapter 5,

included ten films that the Corporation declined to transmit. Often such decisions were based on age or quality grounds. In other cases, censorable content,
print problems or copyright issues may have been responsible. Only insiders can
account for the absence from the airwaves of such films as *Blackmailed* (1951),
Comin' round the Mountain (1951), *Pop Gear* (1965), *Three on a Couch* (1966), *The
Penthouse* (1967), *The Blood of Fu Manchu* (1968), *Hail Hero* (1969), *Me, Nathalie*
(1969), *King Lear* (1970), *Zachariah* (1971), *Hammer* (1972), *Rachel's Man* (1973),
Drum (1976) and *Sunday Woman* (1976). All of these were under contract to the
BBC but none has ever been shown by the Corporation or by ITV.[123] Perhaps the
most notable no-shows were three early Hitchcocks: *Murder* (1930/13.10.1989),
The Skin Game (1931) and *Number Seventeen* (1932/02.06.1985). These were
acquired by the BBC as part of a large package deal with EMI in 1976, but their
licence term was allowed to lapse without a single transmission, even as part of a
comprehensive, seventeen-film Hitchcock season in 1982. The first and last were
later shown on Channel Four, but *The Skin Game* has never been broadcast on any
terrestrial channel.

Some high-profile titles offered to broadcasters were evidently prohibitive, at
least in the period covered by this book. Besides those cited earlier, they included
A Clockwork Orange (1971/13.10.2002) and *The Exorcist* (1973/17.03.2001).
There were also films that buyers wanted to acquire but were prevented from
doing so. Leslie Halliwell was keen to have *Percy* (1971/20.05.1992), a British
sex comedy about a penis transplant, for ITV; but on the basis of a synopsis and
a *Monthly Film Bulletin* review, the IBA dismissed it as 'soft porn'. Halliwell
chided officers for their reliance on the BFI's journal of record, 'which once upon
a time was extremely reliable but has lately been run by eggheads, longhairs and
pompous twits'.[124] He insisted that Authority staff at least give the film the benefit
of the doubt by previewing it, telling Dermot O'Hagan: 'I think you and I both
have the same duty toward *Percy* as we would toward *Oedipus Rex*. They are both
subjects we propose to show to the public, and the first is likely to be seen by many
more people, and therefore be more influential, than the second.'[125] However,
despite further approaches from both Halliwell and the film's distributor, EMI,
the Authority stood its ground. O'Hagan sampled half an hour and considered
that 'all the humour in this film, both visual and verbal, is concentrated unremittingly below the waist and that 100 minutes of snigger-evoking dirty jokes would
probably be asking too much of the average television viewer even in 1977'.[126] As
films were being offered to television several years before they became available to
screen under the CEA's five-year edict, executives and officers had to anticipate
future public tastes rather than base their judgement solely on contemporary
standards. They were inclined to be conservative. *Percy* finally emerged on
Channel Four nearly two decades later, after Halliwell's death.

Problems with some films emerged only after they were broadcast, leading
them to be withdrawn later. Following Thames's premiere transmission of *Night
Hair Child* (1972/30.10.1978), an IBA monitor's report drew attention to sexual

scenes involving a child actor, Mark Lester.[127] The Authority upheld two viewer complaints and, concerned that it might fall foul of the recent Protection of Children Act 1978, asked for the film to be withdrawn from network circulation. Its distributor, Rank, had the offending scenes edited to comply with the law, but the Authority 'was not quite so confident that it is not in breach of our own IBA Act – specifically Section 4(1)(a)' and advised Halliwell to 'consider losing it'.[128] The film was not shown again.

The case of *Twisted Nerve* (1968/15.09.1974) was more complicated. The thriller was shown without incident in most ITV regions until its transmission by ATV on 5 October 1975. The company and the IBA received letters of complaint from the Movement of Practising Psychologists, the National Society for Mentally Handicapped Children, the Mental Health Film Council and the Campaign for the Mentally Handicapped. The nature of their complaints is indicated by a passage from the first of these letters:

> The film concerns the murders committed by a young man whose elder brother suffers from Down's Syndrome (Mongolism). It makes the explicit suggestion that parents who have born a mongol child are at risk through some analogous chromosomal mechanism for bearing a child who will grow up unavoidably to be a 'psychopath'. In fact, not only is there no known genetic causation for 'psychopathy', but there is no reason to link Down's Syndrome with any other transmitted condition that might affect a sibling's learning or behaviour.[129]

The letters all emphasised the distress that such misinformation could cause to people with Down's Syndrome and their families, as well as the confusion it could generate among the general public. They also pointed out that similar concerns had been expressed at the time of the film's theatrical release. ATV's investigations revealed that in response to these earlier complaints, a prefatory caption had been added to the film in cinemas, which had not been included in the two prints supplied to ITV. The company located the preamble, adding it to both the network's prints so that it would accompany subsequent transmissions in other regions, and used part of it in the script for an announcement broadcast before the following week's film on 12 October: 'For those viewers who watched last week's Big Film, *The Twisted Nerve* [*sic*], we would like to emphasise that there is no established scientific connection between Mongolism and psychotic or criminal behaviour.'[130]

The matter did not end there, however. When the film was repeated on ATV four years later, the preamble was omitted. No explanation was ever found for this omission, but it led to a further set of complaints, including some from those who had written letters in 1975. As a result, the IBA resolved that there should be no further transmissions of the film. When this decision was communicated to Leslie Halliwell, he replied that, while the network accepted the ruling as the title was near the end of its contract, he 'saw no reason to withdraw a film because of one mistake in presentation although the film in question had played satisfactorily on numerous previous occasions'. He added, on a personal note: 'if I, as the father of a mongol child, did not object to it, then I saw no reason whatever for public protest'. In a handwritten annotation on the same memo, Dermot O'Hagan commented of the indefatigable buyer: 'The man never gives up.'[131] Perhaps even more remarkable is that Halliwell's obstinate defence contradicted his own judgement on *Twisted Nerve* in his *Film Guide*, first published in 1977: 'Absurd, unpleasant, longwinded and naively scripted shocker, rightly attacked because it asserted that brothers of mongoloids are apt to become murderers. A long way behind the worst Hitchcock.'[132]

Notes

1 The film in question was *Pendulum* (1969/02.02/1975).
2 A useful guide to BBFC certificates can be found in the BFI's Screenonline pages at http://www.screenonline.org.uk/film/id/592611/index.html. A new certification system was introduced in November 1982 by the renamed British Board of Film Classification, but this lies outside the scope of the present book.
3 See, for example: James Thomas, 'Why Today's X-film Is Giving the TV Men a Headache...', *Daily Express*, 12 April 1971; Jack Bell, 'Beware the Blue Horizon...', *Daily Mirror*, 3 May 1973; Philip Phillips, 'Telly Is Running out of Old Films!', *Sun*, 1 September 1973; Jack Pitman, 'Weigh TV Chances of "Hot" Pix O'seas', *Variety*, 3 September 1975, 39, 74.
4 Quoted in Imlay Newbiggin-Watts to Philip Dorté, 7 October 1946, BBC T6/334.
5 Solicitor to Norman Collins, 17 May 1949, cited in S.J. de Lotbinière to Greeve del Strother, 26/05/1952, BBC T6/144/4.
6 Dorté to de Lotbinière, 28 May 1952, BBC T6/144/4.
7 The films in question were *Of Mice and Men* (1939/23.01.1951), *The Face at the Window* (1939/28.04.1952), *Jack London* (1943/14.12.1948) and *White Legion* (1936/01.12.1952).
8 A similar passage appeared in Section 4 of the Independent Broadcasting Authority Act 1973, which replaced the Television Act 1954.
9 Note by the Chairman, 'Section 3(1)(a) of the Television Act in Relation to Plays and Films', SCC Paper 16(57), 9 May 1957, IBA/01020: 3996317.
10 'ITV to Show X Film', *Daily Mail*, 13 July 1956. *TV Times* billed the film under the programme rubric 'Play of the Week'.
11 T.E. Brownsdon, ITA Regional Officer for Southampton, claimed erroneously that 'only one full length "X" film has ever been shown on ITV' ('"X" Films on TV' [letter], *Southern Evening Echo*, 18 February 1961).
12 *Radio Times*, 5 January 1961, 9.
13 David Attenborough to Kenneth Adam, 27 January 1966, BBC T16/72/6. The AIC's objections were reported the same day in Brian Dean, 'Cinema Chiefs Attack X Films on BBC', *Daily Mail*, 27 January 1966, 9. The first transmission was claimed to be uncut (Tom Merrin, 'X Film for TV', *Daily Sketch*, 2 January 1961). Between the two BBC broadcasts, *I Am a Camera* had also been shown on at least three occasions by ITV companies, as per the IFD sharing arrangement discussed in Chapter 4.
14 W.O. Todd to David James MP, 26 April 1960; John Trevelyan to Bernard Sendall, 2 June 1960, IBA/01020: 3996317. For further discussion of controversies around the

screening of excerpts from 'X' films on television, see Holmes, *British TV & Film Culture in the 1950s*, 230–50.

15	Cecil Madden to J.C. Thornton, 12 August 1960; A.R. Partner to R.A. Butler MP, 20 July 1960; Partner to Hugh Carleton Greene, 23 December 1960; Gerald Beadle to Greene, 4 January 1961, BBC R34/1, 245. The AIC's objections to the prospect of *Cosh Boy* being televised were reported in Leslie Mallory, 'Banned Films Can Be Seen In the Home', *News Chronicle*, 23 August 1960, and Ivor Jay in 'City Bans a Film – But Not the BBC!', *Birmingham Evening Despatch*, 8 September 1961. Both *Cosh Boy* and *Saturday Night and Sunday Morning* were cited in Parliamentary debates about broadcasting standards: *Hansard*, Commons, 1 March 1961.

16	Greene to Partner, 5 January 1961, BBC R34/1, 245.

17	*Hansard*, Commons, 15 February 1961; M. Hallett to Stephen Swingler MP, 21 February 1961, IBA/01020: 3996317.

18	John Woolf to Sir Robert Fraser, 'X Certificate Films', 6 March 1961, IBA/01020: 3996317.

19	ITA Programme Intervention Report, 17 January 1969, IBA/01020: 3996317.

20	Trevelyan to Fraser, 21 January 1969 (marked 'Private and Personal'), IBA/01020: 3996317.

21	Fraser to Trevelyan, 30 January 1969, IBA/01020: 3996317.

22	Trevelyan to Fraser, 6 February 1969, IBA/01020: 3996317.

23	Stephen Murphy to Fraser, 27 January 1969, IBA/01020: 3996317. Murphy served at the BBFC from 1971–75 before returning to his former Authority role.

24	Dermot O'Hagan to Leslie Halliwell et al, 13 February 1969, IBA/01020: 3996317.

25	Anthony John to O'Hagan, 17 February 1969, IBA/01020: 3996317.

26	John Mountford to O'Hagan, 16 February 1969, IBA/01020: 3996317.

27	Halliwell to O'Hagan, 17 February 1969, IBA/01020: 3996317.

28	Halliwell to Murphy, 6 March 1969, IBA/01020: 3996317.

29	Murphy to Halliwell, 5 March 1969, IBA/01020: 3996317.

30	Cinematograph Exhibitors' Association, 'Supplementary Memorandum to the Home Secretary on the Report of the Committee on the Future of Broadcasting (the Annan Committee): A Proposal that Cinema Films Certificated by the British Board of Film Censors in the "X" Category Should Not Be Shown on Television', 28 September 1977, IBA/01020: 3996317.

31	'Television (X Certificate Films)', *Hansard*, Commons, 30 November 1978; 'Cinematograph Films (Certification)', *Hansard*, Commons, 20 March 1980. A similar motion had previously been put by William Rees-Davies MP (Conservative, Isle of Thanet) in a debate on the Public Indecency Bill (13 April 1973). Raphael Tuck had previously raised the issue of 'X' films on television in 1968 and did so again in a debate on the White Paper on Broadcasting (the IBA Bill) in 1979: *Hansard*, Commons, 29 March 1979. In the latter, his farewell speech to the House, he admitted to 'again riding my hobby-horse'. Tuck proposed setting up an independent board to vet films and prohibiting those films unsuitable for children from being broadcast at any time.

32	'Why No "X" Certificate?', *Radio Times*, 4 January 1968, 4.

33	Alasdair Milne, 'BBC Television: The Purchase and Transmission of Feature Films, 1978–79', n.d. (1978), BBC R78/1, 123/1.

34 'Why No "X" Certificate?'

35 Milne, 'The Purchase and Transmission of Feature Films', 25 November 1975, BBC R78/1, 123/1.

36 Ibid. In his memoirs, Milne describes a 'private session' held for BBC Governors at the BBFC offices in March 1973, when chief censor Stephen Murphy (formerly of the ITA) introduced extracts from several of these films, leaving Governors 'stunned' and 'speechless' (*DG*, 64).

37 Ibid.

38 Letters, 'BBC1's Film Violence', *Radio Times*, 5 October 1978, 73; 'Violence and Certificates', *Radio Times*, 26 October 1978, 81, 83.

39 Milne, 'The Purchase of Foreign Feature Films and Series', 2 March 1979, BBC R78/1, 123/1.

40 Milne, 'Classification of Feature Films', G20/77, 28 January 1977, BBC R78/1, 123/1. The Corporation's official guidance on the portrayal of violence, first drawn up in 1972 and revised by Milne in 1979, was issued in a booklet jointly published by the BBC and the IBA. It included a paragraph specifically on purchased programmes, incorporating many of the points summarised in this section. See *The Portrayal of Violence on Television: BBC & IBA Guidelines*, 21–2.

41 'Feature Films', SCC Paper 1(68), 2 January 1968, IBA/409: 3997081.

42 'Feature Films on Independent Television', ITA Paper 2(71), 21 January 1971, IBA/409: 3997081.

43 'Feature Films on Independent Television', ITA Paper 138(70), 11 December 1970, IBA/409: 3997081.

44 'Feature Films on Independent Television', ITA Paper 148(71), 10 December 1971, IBA/409: 3997081.

45 'The Control of Films', ITA Paper 83(72), 22 May 1972, IBA/409: 3997081.

46 An IBA officer made this point forcibly in responding to a request for clarification of the 'two-hour' rule for long films in evening schedules: Chris Rowley to Halliwell, 15 November 1978, IBA/01021: 3996312.

47 Notes attached to Halliwell to David Glencross, 21 May 1976, IBA/01024: 3996310.

48 'The Winter Schedule – Final Report', IBA Paper 330(75), 9 December 1975, IBA/00014: 3997086.

49 Rowley to J. Harrison, 23 February 1978, IBA/01021: 3996312.

50 Rowley to Paul Fox (draft), 1 March 1976, IBA/01024: 3996310.

51 Rowley to O'Hagan, 19 December 1975, IBA/01024: 3996310.

52 Halliwell to Rowley, 20 February 1976, IBA/01024: 3996310.

53 David Vick to Rowley, 26 February 1976, IBA/01024: 3996310.

54 Glencross to Halliwell, 13 January 1976, IBA/01024: 3996310.

55 Halliwell to Glencross, 13 September 1976, IBA/01025: 3996309.

56 O'Hagan, 'List of Archival Films', n.d. (1976); Glencross to Halliwell, 21 September 1976, IBA/01025: 3996309.

57 Halliwell to Glencross, 23 September 1976, IBA/01024: 3996310.

58 P.J. Darby to O'Hagan, 18 November 1973, IBA/01023: 3996311.

59 Darby and P.J. Marshall, 'Further Considerations on the Problems of Feature and Series Film', 8 November 1973, IBA/01023: 3996311.

60   Halliwell, 'Film Quality Group Visit', 19 October 1973, IBA/01023: 3996311.

61   Halliwell to Glencross, 21 May 1976, IBA/01024: 3996310.

62   Darby and Marshall, 'Further Considerations'.

63   Howard Thomas to Bernard Sendall, 19 July 1968, IBA/00645: 3995796.

64   Stephen Murphy to Sendall, 12 June 1968, IBA/00645: 3995796.

65   Sendall to Thomas, 3 July 1968, IBA/00645: 3995796.

66   Nat Cohen to Thomas, 24 July 1968, IBA/00645: 3995796. Chibnall and McFarlane claim that the 'series was conceived primarily for theatrical exhibition, but was eventually shown on American television as the *Edgar Wallace Mystery Theatre*' (*The British 'B' Film*, 240).

67   Sendall to Thomas, 7 August 1968, IBA/00645: 3995796.

68   Sendall to Joseph Weltman, 12 August 1968, IBA/00645: 3995796.

69   Dermot O'Hagan to Penry Jones, n.d. (1972), IBA/00645: 3995796.

70   Weltman to Brian Tesler, 11 May 1972, IBA/00645: 3995796.

71   Chris Rowley to Colin Shaw, 8 March 1983, IBA/00645: 3995796.

72   Rowley to Halliwell, 16 May 1983, IBA/00645: 3995796.

73   Halliwell to Peter Bannister, 29 April 1983, IBA/00645: 3995796. By contrast, responding to a reader asking why the Edgar Wallace films were no longer shown on television, *TV Times*'s film columnist David Quinlan wrote: 'Unfortunately, nearly all of them are in black and white, less than 70 minutes long and badly dated. Present-day TV companies would stand to gain very little by showing them' ('Where's Wallace', Letters, *TV Times*, 13 November 1980, 36).

74   According to Bill Gilbert, the Holmes films had been sold to Granada by Irvin Shapiro's company Films Around the World ('Films on TV: Before the Flood', *The Veteran* 120, Autumn 2008, 13). See also David Pierce, '"Senile Celluloid": Independent Exhibitors, the Major Studios and the Fight over Features on Television, 1939–1956', *Film History* 10, no. 2 (1998): 141–64.

75   Tesler to Weltman, 30 December 1968, IBA/00645: 3995796.

76   Weltman to Sendall, 13 January 1969, IBA/00645: 3995796.

77   Weltman to Tesler, 14 January 1969, IBA/00645: 3995796.

78   Tesler to Weltman, 17 January 1969, IBA/00645: 3995796.

79   Sendall to Weltman, 24 February 1969, IBA/00645: 3995796.

80   Weltman to Sendall, 24 February 1969, IBA/00645: 3995796.

81   Sendall to Weltman, 26 February 1969, IBA/00645: 3995796.

82   Letter from STV, 9 July 1962, IBA/01023: 3996311.

83   'Rules Relating to Clearance of Acquired Film Programmes', 27 July 1962, IBA/01023: 3996311.

84   O'Hagan to Halliwell, 21 January 1969, IBA/01023: 3996311.

85   Television Programme Intervention Report, May/June 1969, 18 June 1969, IBA/01023: 3996311.

86   Murphy to Anthony John, 7 October 1970, IBA/01023: 3996311.

87   Halliwell, 'Agenda for Discussion of Film Administration Matters' (Network Planners Meeting, 12 March 1976), 23 February 1976, IBA/01024: 3996310.

88   'Acquired Film on Independent Television', IBA Paper 21(77), 14 January 1977, IBA/01024: 3996310.

89   'ITV's Film Buying Policy Revealed by Halliwell', *Broadcast*, 8 March 1976, 4.

90 O'Hagan to Fletcher, 1 February 1978; Fletcher to O'Hagan, 14 February 1978; O'Hagan to Fletcher, 16 February 1978, IBA/01024: 3996310.

91 Ibid, 254.

92 Peter Black, '"Sex Symbol" to Warn Viewers', *Daily Mail*, 30 April 1973, 3; 'ITV Will Try out X Certificate', *Guardian*, 30 April 1973, 1; 'Symbol on TV Screens as Warning of Violent Films', *The Times*, 3.

93 Home Office, *Report of the Committee on the Future of Broadcasting*, 254. Channel Four's similar 'Red Triangle' warning symbol was launched in September 1986.

94 Neville Clarke to Penry Jones, 25 March 1976, IBA/01024: 3996310. The warning symbol and the Authority's rulings on screen violence, including the ITV Code (1971), are discussed in the joint BBC/ITV publication previously cited: *The Portrayal of Violence on Television: BBC & IBA Guidelines*, 33–52.

95 Letters from Mrs E.W.L., Mrs A.B., Mr I.S. and Mrs P.J.H., 1–3 September 1980, IBA/01021: 3996312.

96 Glencross, 'Complaints about Home Produced and Acquired Programmes', 23 January 1981, IBA/01021: 3996312.

97 'Some Recent Viewer Responses', PPC Paper 5(81), 2 February 1981, IBA/01021: 3996312.

98 Glencross to Fox, 8 September 1981, IBA/01024: 3996310.

99 Ms M.Z. to IBA, 15 September 1981, IBA/01021: 3996312.

100 Young to Ms M.Z., 25 September 1981, IBA/01021: 3996312.

101 O'Hagan to Jones, 17 September 1981, IBA/01024: 3996310.

102 Whitehouse to Thomson, 23 October 1981, IBA/01021: 3996312.

103 Thomson to Whitehouse, 4 November 1981, IBA/01021: 3996312.

104 O'Hagan to Halliwell, 24 January 1980, IBA/01024: 3996310.

105 Halliwell to O'Hagan, 25 January 1980, IBA/01024: 3996310.

106 See also the discussions of *King Kong* (1933/23.10.1965) and *Womaneater* (1958) in Chapter 10.

107 Sendall to Jan Choyce, 26 April 1961, IBA/01020: 3996317.

108 John Lindsay to Weltman, 20 June 1972, IBA/01023: 3996311.

109 Television Programme Interventions Report, 'Scottish Television: Feature Film', 14 July 1972, IBA/01023: 3996311.

110 O'Hagan to Halliwell, 29 June 1972, IBA/01023: 3996311.

111 'Party Split', *The Times*, 1 July 1972, 14.

112 Gerald Bartlett, 'Ban on TV Showing of *I'm All Right*', *Daily Telegraph*, 16 April 1979.

113 O'Hagan to All Regional Officers, 19 April 1979, IBA/01021: 3996312.

114 'BBC in Storm over IRA Film', *Sun*, 18 January 1973.

115 Letters Editor, reply to '*Judith*: for the Record', *Radio Times*, 25 October 1973, 82.

116 Quoted in David Leigh, 'BBC Cancel Film about Earlier Conflict', *The Times*, 8 October 1973, 6.

117 Martin Walker, 'Open File: Beeb Boob', *Guardian*, 8 June 1974, 13; Michael White, 'London Letter', *Guardian*, 6 December 1974, 15.

118 Vlok Delport, Director of Information at the South African Embassy, London, quoted in 'Looking on the White Side', *Radio Times*, 5 December 1974, 4.

119 Verina Glaessner, '*Last Grave at Dimbaza*' (review), *Monthly Film Bulletin* 42, no. 496 (May 1975): 109.

120 Peter Hillmore, 'Guardian Diary', *Guardian*, 22 November 1977, 15.

121 'Was It "Before Hindsight"'?, *Radio Times*, 9 February 1978, 23.

122 'Temporary Ban on TV Film', *Financial Times*, 27 October 1979, 26.

123 A number of films contracted to the BBC but unshown by the Corporation have since turned up on Talking Pictures TV and other independent channels, including *Horrors of the Black Museum* (1959), *The 14'*, etc.

124 Halliwell to O'Hagan, 18 October 1974, IBA/01023: 3996311. In the same correspondence, officers were also asked to consider the suitability for television of *The Killing of Sister George* and *Straw Dogs*.

125 Halliwell to O'Hagan, 28 October 1974, IBA/01023: 3996311.

126 O'Hagan to Halliwell, 26 February 1975, IBA/01023: 3996311.

127 Janet Lee, Monitor's Report, 30 October 1978, IBA/01024: 3996310. Bizarrely, the monitor also recorded that the transmission had been preceded by an announcement that the film's director, James Kelley, had died the same day.

128 O'Hagan to Halliwell, 10 July 1979, IBA/01024: 3996310.

129 Letter from A.S., 6 October 1975, IBA/01023: 3996311.

130 Barrie Wood to Pat Salt, 15 October 1975, IBA/01023: 3996311.

131 Halliwell to O'Hagan and O'Hagan's note, 25 March 1980, IBA/01024: 3996310.

132 Halliwell, *Halliwell's Film Guide* (Eighth Edition), 1139.

CHAPTER 10

Appointments with Fear –
Horror Films on Television

It's easy to see why horror films suit late-night viewing. Throughout history witches and ghosts have favoured the midnight hour for their mischief, so it's only right that their celluloid relatives follow suit. And, to be honest, some films in the genre are best appreciated when critical faculties are on the wane, transforming inadequacies of the script and acting into positive virtues. Horror films viewed in the home carry an extra dimension, too, for the perambulations of the Frankenstein monster, Dracula's search for jugular veins, and the ghastly activities of werewolves, ghouls and things that go bump in the night, seem all the more fantastic when surrounded by familiar living-room clutter – the photos of Gran, the cactuses, the tax demand under the clock.

(Geoff Brown, 'Films That Go Bump in the Night', *Radio Times*,
26 June 1980, 70)

Towards a Horror Policy

Until the 1970s, horror films always seemed to present problems for British television programmers.[1] This was despite the fact that what is often claimed, erroneously, to be the very first feature film broadcast on British TV was a horror film: *The Student of Prague* (1935/14.08.1938 – see Chapter 1). Nevertheless, judging by the films transmitted over the following three decades, both the BBC and ITV were habitually wary of horror. Few such films appeared in the schedules throughout the postwar years, even after the advent of the 'five-year rule' in 1964 opened up the studio backlogs to broadcasters. Those films that we would now commonly describe as horror were often presented under other, less provocative generic rubrics.

For example, in October 1967, BBC1's new peak-time strand 'The Saturday Thriller' – comprising 'Feature films with suspense, danger, excitement', to quote the listings blurb – was launched with *The Innocents* (1961/07.10.1967), based on Henry James's ghost story *The Turn of the Screw*. This was shown at 8.30pm, between *The Val Doonican Show* and the *Horse of the Year Show*, suggesting that it was aimed at least partly at a family audience. Although *Radio Times* referred to the film's original reviews as having 'used adjectives like "ghastly, ghostly, grim" to describe it', the word 'horror' was nowhere mentioned.[2] Most other films in the season concerned crime rather than the supernatural. Similarly, the Easter

Monday premiere on BBC1 of *Psycho* (1960/15.04.1968) was also billed in *Radio Times*'s programme pages as a thriller, though elsewhere in the magazine it was described as Hitchcock's 'Gothick [sic] masterpiece'.[3]

On ITV, the showing by Granada of *Quatermass 2* (1957/12.08.1965) – the first to be seen on television of Hammer Film Productions' three big-screen adaptations of BBC TV's Quatermass serials – was billed in *TV Times* as 'The famous film thriller'.[4] The same station presented Universal's *The Wolf Man* (1941/05.02.1968) in a series called 'Late Night Thriller', described in the listings magazine as a 'series of feature films for the witching hour'.[5] Also included in this strand, among an assortment of mainly crime films, were another TV serial adaptation, *The Trollenberg Terror* (1958/19.02.1963), and *The Beast with Five Fingers* (1946/06.10.1966). Even the horror spoof *Abbott and Costello Meet Frankenstein* (1948/19.12.1966) was shown in a series called 'Crime and Mystery' and described – inevitably – as a 'comedy thriller'.[6]

The 'problem' of horror films was demonstrated most acutely in the case of *King Kong* (1933/23.10.1965). The film had originally been scheduled by ABC Television in a strand called 'Great Movies of Our Time' on the evening of Saturday, 4 April 1959. It was billed in *TV Times* but newspaper listings on the planned day of broadcast indicate that *King Kong* had been pulled and replaced by a war film, *Desperate Journey* (1942/04.04.1959). I have not found any documentation in the IBA Archives to explain this last-minute substitution, but papers from 1961–62 give some clue as to the reasons. They relate to separate scheduling proposals by ABC and ATV in London – the former wanted to show it in serial form, the latter as a late-night feature. In December 1961, a memo to Director General Robert Fraser and Deputy Director General Bernard Sendall compared *King Kong* favourably to a new monster movie, *Gorgo* (1961/26.07.1978), currently on release in London's West End. Programme Clearance Officer Jan Choyce set out explicitly the issues it raised:

> Both companies are now sorting this one out, but for us there is one question: do we want horror films on the television screen at all? It might be useful if I say that in giving an X certificate to most horror films (and there are more about than is generally known) the BBFC is aware that many older children would be entertained enormously by these pieces; the gimmicks of camera and puppets are in themselves fascinating. Some of the material is plainly U [certificate] in type. On the other hand some of it would scare the daylight out of any normal child, especially when horrific sound and violent colour add the full effects. Logically a horror film ought to horrify. This some of them do wholly, some in part, and some hardly at all. But the last named, generally the poorer ones, occasionally substitute a kind of obscenity in the monsters for lack of a better word, and this cannot be overlooked.
>
> However, alongside this is the plain fact that these films entertain. They are very good box office, and they have devotees of either sex, particularly, (so I have been informed) among older 'teen-agers (younger ones in the case of 'A' [certificate] films) and middle-aged men. The question of our accepting such material is not entirely a straightforward one about *King Kong*, and I would be glad to be advised.[7]

Sendall responded: 'I am afraid I have never seen a horror film and feel I would have to see *King Kong* ... before forming an opinion.'[8] Choyce replied with a note: 'You must, I think, see 3 or 4 of the juiciest' (presumably she meant other horror films).[9] Considering further the crucial question of whether the Authority wanted horror films on television, Sendall later added: 'The answer seems to be: – in general, no, any more than we want X [certificate] films.'[10]

On New Year's Day 1962, having by now seen *King Kong*, Sendall wrote again:

I may be an odd sort of chap, but I was utterly revolted by this film. It would take a lot of argument to persuade me that it is allowable on ITV within the terms of 3(1)(a) [of the Television Act 1954].

What particularly stuck in my throat was its avid inhumanity. Nobody shed a tear for all those brave sailors who died that the Beauty might live. The horrible fate of innocent members of the New York public was but a trivial incident and the cruel, callous perpetrator of this horror was not thought to be the least reprehensible by the Cop with whom he exchanged words after all was over. Nor did he show the slightest sense of guilt at any time. If this is funny, then there is a dimension in which I cannot operate.

Perhaps you can let ABC and ATV know that there is a complete ban on this film at my level. If they want to appeal to DG and above, let them say so.[11]

The word 'ban' was rarely used in Authority communications, except to deny that bans as such were issued, so this was an unusually strong statement, with wider policy implications. Choyce responded:

I am immensely relieved that you have taken this line over *King Kong*. The whole range of horror films is one about which I feel apprehensive; not least because there are some quite good ones. Many others are, believe it or not, far beastlier than *King Kong*, and once having admitted them at all it would have been awfully difficult to draw the line.[12]

ABC and ATV's plans to show *King Kong* were apparently dropped without an appeal, though there is no further correspondence in the archives specifically about the film. However, it did crop up in a draft paper prepared by Choyce, apparently at Sendall's behest, intended for circulation to the Standing Consultative Committee (SCC), one of the Authority's formal channels of communication with the programme companies. This paper was titled 'Horror on the Screen' (a covering note was headed 'Horror on Television', with inverted commas added by hand around the word 'Horror') and was intended to raise in a more general way the matter of the ITA's policy on horror films and indeed horror in ITV programmes generally. It observed that there had been no official ruling on the subject, but only on particular films such as *King Kong* ('a classic of its kind'), of which the paper noted: 'ABC and ATV agreed not to screen this after it had been seen by several members of the Authority Staff.'[13] Thus it implied that the companies had made a voluntary choice not to show the film, rather than its withdrawal being the result of an Authority edict.

In seeking to prepare the ground for a policy on horror, the paper suggested that the companies might 'prefer an "each on its own merit" assessment'. This had apparently worked with in-house productions such as Associated-Rediffusion's anthology series *Tales of Mystery*, about which the Authority had been consulted. The paper noted: 'In general this arrangement has worked satisfactorily, and it could be said that providing the Authority is given advance information about such a project there is no need for an overall ruling, with the clear exception that "horror for horror's sake" is inadmissible.' But it argued that such a policy would be less workable with acquired programming such as feature films, over which the ITA had had no formative influence, than with original TV productions. Nor did the existing policy on dealing with 'X'-rated films apply clearly to horror in particular:

> The arrangement by which the companies consult the Authority about the screening of 'X' films or film excerpts does not cover the situation, for the reason that the BBFC frequently puts a mild or weak or ineffectual horror film into the 'A' category rather than give it the gratuitous and unmerited advertisement it might have in the 'X' category. A recent example of this is the screening [on Granada] of *The Strange World of Planet X* an 'A' certificate film with horror sequences, which some viewers might well have found offensive.

Another recent example (unmentioned in the paper) demonstrated that the standard policy on 'X'-certificate films was not always followed. Granada had scheduled the 'X'-rated British film *Womaneater* (1958) – about a carnivorous plant but again billed as a 'film thriller' – for 10.45pm on Thursday, 15 November 1962, without consulting the Authority first.[14] An ITA officer previewed the film and considered it 'unsuitable for transmission'; although the station disagreed, it chose an innocuous replacement at short notice, after *TV Times* had gone to press. *Womaneater* was never shown anywhere on the ITV network.[15]

The paper suggested the possibility of 'an umbrella agreement that any material, imported film, British film, or homespun, which has horror as its main ingredient, or in which horror plays a substantial if subsidiary role, should not be screened without reference to the Authority'. It noted: 'Such a ruling would give an opportunity for the screening of any good horror film, and since quite undoubtedly some people enjoy horror films it might seem to be the liberal approach to the subject.' However, there remained the question of how horror could be defined with sufficient rigour to enable such an agreement to work. The paper made a valiant attempt, distinguishing between 'modern' and 'classic' horror in trying to specify their potential effects on the viewer:

> The modern horror is injected with a scientific aura, such as is sometimes seen in Space-Science fiction. It can project Beings or Things from a four dimensional universe, and they may be apparitions frightening in themselves, (including, for example, dismembered brains which have acquired mobility and seem almost obscene in doing so), in addition to being frightening in the sometimes unwholesome atmosphere in which they move. This may be said to be portrayal of physically horrible things, but equally horrific is the morbid tension in which

the ideas are propounded. More classic horror, on the other hand, is injected with Victoriana. It moves in a world of vampires, were-wolves, bedevilled maidens, witches and warlocks. Its impact can be as strong as that of modern horror. Again there is a physical portrayal of something horrific bounded by a tension of atmosphere which is intangible. Both are horrific in their impact on the mind. We might therefore say of horror material that it is created for the purpose of injecting the imagination with fear of a paralysing nature. Our concern is that the paralysis should only be very temporary.

By its very nature horror may come near to obscenity and to blasphemy. For this reason the Authority requires a very careful appraisal of any material likely to come near to that defined as horror, and would like to be consulted. We know that quite a library of horror films exists. Many of these patently defy the approval of any competent judge; some are border-line. Indeed the area between 'horror' and 'horror-comic' (the latter a product of the sick mind) is a twilight one, and the best assessment may be the work of several people.

The paper concluded by acknowledging that while 'by far the safest course would be for the Authority and the companies to agree upon a definitive ruling of "no horror"', this could be seen as unduly restrictive: 'there is, in the best horror material, a quite legitimate source of entertainment and spine-chilling enjoyment for the connoisseur, and we may prefer a liberal attitude providing the safeguards satisfy us'.

In the event, the paper was not circulated to the SCC on the advice of the Director General, who, according to Sendall, 'felt that it was a little lacking in clarity for the purposes of this body and somewhat zigzagging in argument'. Sendall blamed himself for failing to edit the 'raw material' Choyce had provided, admitting that he 'did find the problem very elusive and difficult to express in simple black and white terms'. In view of this, he advocated instead 'a pragmatic approach', in which the companies agreed to consult the Authority when they had material of a kind that could be described as horrific.[16]

In the absence of a fixed policy, a more 'liberal' view must subsequently have prevailed in the case of *King Kong*, as it was eventually transmitted by ABC on Saturday, 23 October 1965, followed by showings in other regions (including ATV in London) during the Christmas holiday that year. The ABC broadcast went out at 9.35pm and was billed in *TV Times* as 'The greatest spectacular film thriller of all time'.[17] But on this occasion, the magazine's recently added films column at last used the 'H' word: 'Horror films may come and go, but *King Kong* (Saturday) goes on for ever, it seems.'[18] This was a reference to the film's frequent cinema reissues rather than its appearance on home screens. For the subsequent transmissions at Christmas, there were regional variations in listings magazine coverage as well as in the schedules. ATV billed *King Kong* in *TV Times* as 'The world-famous and historic cinema classic',[19] while Westward Television's programme journal *Look Westward* went for 'The most thrilling monster film of all time.'[20] The latter's columnist Peter Noble commented: 'Epic films may come and go. But *King Kong*, still packs a powerful punch, thirty years after it was first shown.' He added for extra emphasis: '*Do not miss this horror classic.*'[21]

Following these initial transmissions, *King Kong* was intermittently revived locally on ITV over the next decade. Even then it did not always have an easy passage. In 1972, newspapers reported that the film had been withdrawn from a scheduled lunchtime transmission on Christmas Day following Authority objections that it was 'too horrific for children'.[22] The rights then transferred to the BBC, which gave it an early-evening slot on BBC1 on Friday, 17 December 1976, nine days before a new remake opened in the UK – a move attacked by the film industry as an attempt to sabotage the big-screen box office. *Radio Times* billed the original as 'a classic of horror movies'.[23]

The MCA-Universal Horror Package

A change in attitude within both the Authority and ITV was signalled during 1969, when horror films were definitively established as a programming staple of British television. The ground had been prepared the year before, when both broadcasting organisations had mounted productions of horror stories made directly for television: the BBC's *Late Night Horror* and ABC's *Mystery and Imagination*. The latter had been running on ITV since 1966 but in 1968 the series dramatised *Frankenstein* and *Dracula* for the first time on British television.

On the first Sunday evening of the new year, 5 January, London Weekend Television (LWT) transmitted Ealing Studios' supernatural portmanteau *Dead of Night* (1945/12.09.1964), billing it in *TVTimes* as a 'must for horror addicts' and a 'masterpiece of the macabre'.[24] On the following Saturday the same station launched a new film strand, 'Murder, Mystery and Suspense', with *What Ever Happened to Baby Jane?* (1962/11.01.1969), describing it as a 'classic horror-and-suspense story'.[25] But perhaps most significant was Thames Television's new late-night strand on Mondays, 'The X Film'. Although this was launched on 6 January with a non-horror, *The Criminal* (1960/09.06.1968), it subsequently included a number of horror films along with crime thrillers and adult dramas. Eight of the thirteen titles in the series' first season were horror and fourteen of the twenty-two in the second season. The latter included a seven-week straight run of horror classics from Hollywood's Universal Pictures, beginning with *Frankenstein* (1931/28.07.1969).

Also significant was the 1968 appointment as Network Purchase Officer of Leslie Halliwell, Granada's films booker. Halliwell was not only a hugely knowledgeable film buff but a horror enthusiast, whose published works – besides the reference books with which he became synonymous – include three volumes of short horror fiction and *The Dead That Walk*, a monograph on classic horror films and their literary sources. Within a year of taking up the network role, Halliwell concluded a deal for a group of twenty horror films with MCA Television, which handled the output of Universal (now owned by the former talent agency Music Corporation of America). The package included thirteen films made by the Hollywood studio between 1931 and 1945, as well as seven British productions (most of them in colour) made by Hammer between 1960 and 1963 for release through Universal (see Table 10.1 and Figure 10.1). The price paid for the package was £60,000, or an average of £3,000 per film: a relatively modest sum even then, when a feature could cost more than twice as much.[26]

The Authority was nervous about the public response that the films, even the older ones, might receive if played at peak time. Halliwell proposed showing the Universal titles on Granada with an 8.00pm start (most likely on Saturdays). However, Programme Officer Dermot O'Hagan asked him to reconsider:

Table 10.1 The MCA–Universal horror package (ITV, 1969).

Universal films	Hammer films
Dracula (1931)	*The Brides of Dracula* (1960)
Frankenstein (1931)	*The Curse of the Werewolf* (1961)
The Mummy (1932)	*The Shadow of the Cat* (1961)
Bride of Frankenstein (1935)	*Captain Clegg* (1962)
Werewolf of London (1935)	*Night Creatures* (1962)
Dracula's Daughter (1936)	*Kiss of Evil* (*The Kiss of the Vampire*, 1963)
Son of Frankenstein (1939)	*Paranoiac* (1963)
The Mummy's Hand (1940)	*The Evil of Frankenstein* (1964)
The Ghost of Frankenstein (1942)	
Frankenstein Meets the Wolf Man (1943)	
Son of Dracula (1943)	
House of Frankenstein (1944)	
House of Dracula (1945)	

Figure 10.1 Leslie Halliwell's 1969 purchase of a package of horror films was announced in the Granada edition of ITV's listings magazine. *TV Times* © Future Publishing Ltd.

Quite a number of these films have 'X' certificates and are admittedly quite old and while we are conscious of the fact that not all 'X' certificate films are now unsuitable for showing in the early evening, I am a little worried about the possible reaction both here and outside to, say, a season of such films at the comparatively early time of 8pm. I think we would be much happier if you had made them all 9pm.[27]

Halliwell readily complied but pointed out that in fact all the older films had been 'made before the "X" was invented' in 1952, and therefore most carried the defunct 'H' certificate once used for 'horrific' films.[28] In the event, not only Granada but all the other stations played the films even later at night, typically starting around 10.30pm or 11.00pm. This may have been as much out of practicality as consideration of audience sensibilities: showing the films at 9.00pm on a week night would have meant interrupting them for the networked *News at Ten*, something the Authority itself discouraged. Weekend news bulletins were shorter and thus more flexible for scheduling purposes, but most stations chose to play the films on Monday or Friday nights; over time, these late slots became regularly associated with horror strands.

The first ITV stations to play films from the MCA package were Granada, Thames, Anglia and Border (see Table 10.2). The first three had each created a late-night, post-10.30pm film slot capitalising on the public association of the BBFC 'X' certificate with adult themes: Granada's 'The X Thriller' (Fridays), Thames's already-mentioned 'The X Film' (Mondays) and Anglia's 'X of the Week' (Fridays). Not all the films shown in them had actually been certificated 'X' but the series titles were more opportunistic than precise, using the 'X' brand as a come-on in precisely the way that many voices in television feared would have been the case had the actual BBFC certificates been displayed (see the last chapter); surprisingly, there is no evidence in the archives to suggest that the Authority objected to this. While Thames's season, like Anglia's, included both horror and non-horror, Granada's consisted exclusively of horror films: fifteen of them, including six of the seven Hammer titles from the MCA package (the seventh was shown in a different strand while the series was running). It was thus the first dedicated horror-film season on British television.

The Monday after 'The X Thriller' concluded, Granada began a second horror series, 'Famous Monsters', including eleven of the thirteen Universal titles as

Table 10.2 Selected ITV film strands, 1969.

Thames Television	Granada Television	Anglia Television
The X Film: Season 1 (Monday)	*The X Thriller* (Friday)	*X of the Week* (Friday)
6 January – 31 March	6 June – 12 September	10 January – 19 September
13 films, including 9 horror	15 films, all horror	34 films, including 7 horror
The X Film: Season 2 (Monday)	*Famous Monsters* (Monday)	*The Horror Film* (Friday)
7 July – 15 December	15 September – 8 December	26 September – 20 February
22 films, including 15 horror	13 films, all horror	21 films, all horror

well as two that the station had previously acquired: *The Wolf Man* and *Abbott and Costello Meet Frankenstein*. Except for these two, Border Television showed the same films on the same dates, presumably taking the feed from Granada's transmissions but substituting alternative (non-Universal) titles for the area exclusives. Granada played the remaining two Universal films, *The Mummy* (1932/21.11.1969) and *The Mummy's Hand* (1942/28.11.1969), after Christmas. Not to be outdone, Anglia followed 'X of the Week' with its own dedicated series on Fridays, called simply 'The Horror Film'. This extended to February 1970 and comprised twenty-one films, including all but one in the MCA package; why *The Evil of Frankenstein* (1964/29.08.1969) was omitted is a mystery. Thames's very selective use of films from the package is more easily explained. Due to the 'London split', whereby acquired films were allocated to one or other of the two London companies, Thames had transmission rights to only fourteen of the MCA films (the Universal Frankensteins and the Hammers) while LWT had the remaining six (the Draculas and Mummies). The latter were not broadcast in London until two years after Thames's initial season, when LWT played them in its own Friday-night horror series, 'Nightmare', beginning on 9 July 1971 with *Dracula* (1931/13.10.1969).

By the end of 1969, the development of dedicated horror strands had created a branded identity for late-night horror as a distinct televisual zone. Other film genres could be programmed at any time of day, where there was less need to protect tender sensibilities; but creating a space at the end of an evening forged an association of horror with a particular part of the schedule. These just-before-bedtime slots were conceived as appropriate to the films' grown-up appeal but also offered harmless 'forbidden' pleasures to younger viewers – especially at weekends, when there was no school the next day. The artful scheduling of titles that might be inaccessible in cinemas, and otherwise read about only in books and magazines, created new generations of horror fans, offering an *ad hoc* education in genre history and heritage.

Over the course of the network's seven-year lease on the MCA horror package, the twenty titles played in almost every ITV region, often twice and in some cases three times.[29] They certainly justified their purchase price and proved the viability of the genre in terms of television audience appeal (and therefore advertising revenue). Just as much to the point, they opened the way for many more horror films to be acquired for the commercial network, feeding what was by now an established appetite among the viewing public.

The 1969 seasons did more than break new ground in television programming; they provided a template for other stations to follow in creating their own dedicated horror strands. ATV was perhaps the most prolific and inventive of the companies: its strand rubrics included 'The Monster Movie' (later the name of a Saturday-morning slot for children), 'ATV Horror Picture House', 'The Friday Film Fantastic', 'The Creature Feature', 'A Date with the Devil' and a series each dedicated to particular genre stars: 'The Price of Fear' and 'Christopher Lee –

Prince of Menace'. Yorkshire Television (YTV) paid a similar tribute with 'Cushing's Creatures', and also adopted the title of a famous horror film for a whole series: 'Night of the Demon'. Scottish Television (STV) contributed 'Don't Watch Alone' and the delightfully punning 'Night for the Screamish', while Ulster Television offered 'Movie Macabre'. HTV had 'Terror!' and Southern 'The Frighteners', as well as a number of less imaginatively named slots: 'The Late Thursday Horror Film', 'The Late Friday Horror Film', 'The Late Saturday Horror Film', 'The Sunday Horror Film' and simply 'Late Horror Film'. Tyne Tees also adopted 'The Monster Movie' as well as 'Fear on Friday', while Thames, Westward, Channel Television (which usually took Westward's feed) and Grampian all followed Anglia with 'The Horror Film'. LWT went for the simplest rubric of all: 'Horror!'

But it was Granada that really set the pace for the other stations. Besides 'Famous Monsters' (a title also subsequently used by Westward and Channel as well as Border) and the later 'House of Horrors', Halliwell created the single best-known of all the ITV horror strands. He borrowed its title from a BBC radio show of the 1940s, which he describes in his book *The Dead That Walk* while noting the BBFC's wartime ban on horror films in cinemas: 'The film censor could not prevent, but must surely have remarked on, the astonishing popularity through-out the war years of a radio series called *Appointment with Fear*, its scary stories of ghosts and long-leggedy beasties brought to the nation by a sepulchral-toned "Man in Black".'[30] Granada's first season of 'Appointment with Fear' was billed as 'a series of classic mystery thrillers from Britain and Hollywood in the Forties'.[31] It began on Saturday, 6 November 1971 with Warner Bros' Wilkie Collins adaptation *The Woman in White* (1948/12.12.1959), continuing in subsequent weeks with Ealing's *Dead of Night* and two melodramas, *The Unsuspected* (1947/29.01.1961) and *Sleep, My Love* (1948/17.09.1957). Then, on 4 December, *King Kong* made its first appearance on the station in six years. For good measure, Halliwell scheduled the sequel, *The Son of Kong* (1933/09.12.1971), on the following Thursday. Though it was not yet exclusively associated with horror or indeed with late nights – this initial season had a mid-evening slot – the 'Appointment with Fear' brand was thus established.

The following month, YTV launched a horror season under the same banner with Hammer's *The Gorgon* (1964/20.03.1971). Over the course of the next few years, other stations to adopt 'Appointment with Fear' as a series title included Thames, ATV, STV, Tyne Tees, Westward and Channel; there may have been others. It was still being used well into the 1980s, often with novel local variants such as animated titles (monster heads morphing into one another), staged pro-logues (the studio camera roaming cobwebbed crypts or laboratories stocked with smoking test tubes) and distinctively illustrated 'ad cards' heralding the commercial breaks. Tyne Tees's featured a red-painted mousetrap, which remains my own most vivid memory of the series.[32]

Midnight Movie Fantastic: Horror Double Bills

No other film strand on British television has enjoyed a popular following comparable to that of the horror and fantasy double bills broadcast annually on BBC2 from 1975 to 1981, with an additional run in 1983. These seasons, occupying the 'Midnight Movie' slot on Saturdays throughout the summer months, have inspired many articles and blog posts written by fans, most of them not professional writers or academics but lay enthusiasts whose passion for horror was first stimulated by them.[33] The double bills also have their own Wikipedia entry and at one time were the inspiration for a campaign group dedicated to bringing back 'classic horror' to the BBC.[34] They remain for many an unholy grail of television film programming.

We have already noted the paucity of horror-related films on television before the 1970s; this was especially true of the BBC, and it is therefore worth tracing the steps by which the Corporation worked its way up to providing the seminal horror strands of the decade. In 1970, BBC2 transmitted *The Phantom of the Opera* (1962/06.06.1970), a Hammer production which, although released by Universal, was somehow absent from the MCA package bought for ITV the previous year by Leslie Halliwell. Later the same month, the channel broadcast *Pit and the Pendulum* (1961/23.96.1970), one of the Edgar Allan Poe adaptations directed by Roger Corman for American International Pictures. The BBC acquired six of the eight films in this cycle, which were aired at intervals over the next few years, most often in the long-established 'Midnight Movie' slot. Repeat transmissions on BBC1 of three of these films formed a short Vincent Price season on successive Friday nights in August 1973. Brief as it was, this was nevertheless the Corporation's first horror-film season as such.

Overlapping the Price series and running from July to September was a variant on 'Midnight Movie' that laid the groundwork for the double bills that followed two years later (see Table 10.3). Over ten weeks on Saturday nights, 'Movies

Table 10.3 'Movies through Midnight' (BBC2, 1973).

TX Date	First film	Second film
14.07.1973	*China Seas* (1935)	*Farewell My Lovely* (1944)
21.07.1973	*The Thin Man* (1934) [P]	*The Hounds of Zaroff* (1932) [P]
28.07.1973	*New Moon* (1940) [P]	*My Name Is Julia Ross* (1945) [P]
04.08.1973	*Dark Passage* (1947)	*A Life in the Balance* (1955) [P]
11.08.1973	*Pat and Mike* (1952)	*The Tall Target* (1951) [P]
18.08.1973	*My Favorite Brunette* (1947)	*The Devil-Doll* (1936) [P]
25.08.1973	*The Shopworn Angel* (1938) [P]	*Force of Evil* (1948)
01.09.1973	*Captain Blood* (1935)	*The Girl in Black Stockings* (1957) [P]
08.09.1973	*Macao* (1952)	*The Mask of Fu Manchu* (1932) [P]
15.09.1973	*Babes in Arms* (1939)	*Hot Spot* (*I Wake Up Screaming*, 1942)

Note: [P] indicates a UK TV premiere.

through Midnight' paired contrasting Hollywood films from a variety of genres –
mainly crime (including several examples of what would now be called film noir)
but also comedies, musicals, action adventures and three horror films: *The Hounds
of Zaroff* (1932/21.07.1973), Tod Browning's *The Devil-Doll* (1936/18.08.1973)
and Boris Karloff in *The Mask of Fu Manchu* (1932/08.09.1973). Both *The Hounds
of Zaroff* and *The Devil-Doll* would later be included in the dual-horror seasons,
the latter twice. This series was the first time the BBC had regularly shown films in
double bills, a scheduling strategy that several ITV companies had experimented
with some years before, until the ITA's rules on programme balance forbade it.
Other major horror films broadcast by the Corporation in the first half of the 1970s
included a non-Poe Price vehicle, *House of Wax* (1953/02.01.1972), and several
more Hammer productions. *The Quatermass Experiment* (1955/17.06.1972), the
British studio's breakthrough film, was deemed historically significant enough to
merit a short article in *Radio Times*. *Dracula – Prince of Darkness* (1966/09.08.1974)
was shown to accompany a documentary on Bram Stoker's commercial legacy by
his descendant, the broadcaster Daniel Farson, which earned a more substantial
article.[35] But in addition to these and a few other one-off screenings, three more
strands formed significant antecedents to the horror double bills.

On Christmas Day 1973, BBC2's transmission of Hammer's *Quatermass and
the Pit* (1967/25.12.1973) initiated what would become an occasional series of
horror films to close holiday evenings. Only one of these films was actually billed
in *Radio Times* as 'The Bank Holiday Horror Film' – the second, *Torture Garden*
(1967/26.08.1974) – and the tradition was later revived on BBC1 with *Asylum*
(1972/28.05.1979) on Spring Bank Holiday. It seems likely that in programming
these films on these occasions, schedulers had in mind a follow-up to the annual
made-for-TV *Ghost Story for Christmas*, shown on BBC1 from 1971 to 1978. In the
autumn of 1974, BBC1 presented seven science-fiction films on early Wednesday
evenings in British television's first strand dedicated to the genre. Initially billed
in *Radio Times* as 'Science Fiction Series' before being renamed 'Sci-Fi Season'
from the second week onward, it included several titles with horror elements,
including *Them!* (1954/09.04.1967), which had a BBFC 'X' certificate. Finally, in
early 1975, 'Midnight Movie' featured a six-week run of Hammer productions,
among which four were horror-related.

The horror double bills began with the launch of 'Midnight Movie Fantastic'
in August 1975 (see Table 10.4). *Radio Times*'s billing again changed mid-run,
becoming 'Fantastic Double Bill' from the series' third week onward. Only about
half the initial selection could really be called horror films: also included were
several fantasy and science-fiction films as well as a pair of horror comedies and
even a sonorised version of the silent epic *Noah's Ark* (1928/16.08.1975). The
second season in 1976 was more emphatically called 'Masters of Terror', explained
as 'featuring some of the great stars of terror and suspense'. It began with the
pairing of Lon Chaney as *The Phantom of the Opera* (1925/14.08.1975) – billed
as 'a newly-restored version with an added musical score' – and Fredric March as

Table 10.4 BBC2 horror double bills, 1975–77.

Midnight Movie Fantastic / Fantastic Double Bill (1975)

TX Date	First film	Second film
02.08.1975	*The Cabinet of Dr Caligari* (1920)	*Quatermass 2* (1957)
09.08.1975	*The Tell-Tale Heart* (1962) [P]	*The Premature Burial* (1962) [P]
16.08.1975	*Noah's Ark* (1928) [P]	*Man and His Mate* (1940)
23.08.1975	*This Island Earth* (1955)	*Barbarella* (1968)
30.08.1975	*The Cat and the Canary* (1939)	*The Comedy of Terrors* (1963) [P]
06.09.1975	*The Beast with Five Fingers* (1946)	*The Maze* (1953) [P]

Masters of Terror (1976)

TX Date	First film	Second film
14.08.1976	*The Phantom of the Opera* (1925) [P]	*Dr Jekyll and Mr Hyde* (1931) [P]
21.08.1976	*The Devil-Doll* (1936)	*Frankenstein Created Woman* (1967)
28.08.1976	*The Hounds of Zaroff* (1932)	*The Hound of the Baskervilles* (1939) [P]
04.09.1976	*The Mad Genius* (1931) [P]	*Pit and the Pendulum* (1961)
11.09.1976	*The Walking Dead* (1936) [P]	*Dracula – Prince of Darkness* (1966)

Dracula, Frankenstein – and Friends! (1977)

TX Date	First film	Second film
02.07.1977	*Dracula* (1931)	*Frankenstein* (1931)
09.07.1977	*Bride of Frankenstein* (1935)	*The Brides of Dracula* (1960)
16.07.1977	*The Mummy* (1932)	*The Wolf Man* (1941)
23.07.1977	*Son of Frankenstein* (1939)	*The Kiss of the Vampire* (*Kiss of Evil*, 1963)
30.07.1977	*Dracula's Daughter* (1936)	*The Plague of the Zombies* (1966)
06.08.1977	*The Ghost of Frankenstein* (1942)	*The Premature Burial* (1962)
13.08.1977	*The Raven* (1935)	*The Black Cat* (1934)
20.08.1977	*Frankenstein Meets the Wolf Man* (1943)	*The Raven* (1963)
27.08.1977	*House of Frankenstein* (1944)	*The Reptile* (1966)
03.09.1977	*Son of Dracula* (1943)	*The Evil of Frankenstein* (1964)
10.09.1977	*House of Dracula* (1945)	*The Fall of the House of Usher* (1960)

Note: [P] indicates a UK TV premiere.

Dr Jekyll and Mr Hyde (1931/14.08.1976).[36] When a viewer wrote to complain that the latter was missing a key scene, Alan Howden of the Purchased Programmes Department felt obliged to say: 'we thought we had done rather well to obtain a brand new print from the original negative to give the film its first public showing in England for over 30 years'.[37] Another nine years passed before a complete, fully restored (or nearly so) version was transmitted. It was not announced as such but the additional footage was noticed by another viewer, who wrote that 'this BBC screening could quite possibly be a world "first" – and unheralded to boot!'[38] This was not the only time that the BBC, or its promotional organ, was apparently unaware that it had acquired a more complete version of a film than had been seen in decades. The 1980 season of what was by then known simply as 'Horror Double

Bill' began on 28 June with a version of *Night of the Demon* (1957/19.10.1968) longer than any that had previously been shown on British television, or indeed in cinemas. This too was 'unheralded' in advance billing, though it made the *Radio Times* cover (see Figure 10.2).[39]

At eleven weeks, the third season in 1977 was the longest, and the only one – until the belated 1983 encore reprising most of its contents – not to include any

Figure 10.2 The sixth season of BBC2's 'Horror Double Bill' series was launched with a classic *Radio Times* cover illustration in 1980. *Radio Times* © Immediate Media Co. Artwork © Mark Thomas.

television premieres. Entitled 'Dracula, Frankenstein – and Friends!', it featured all the Universal classics that had constituted ITV's 1969 MCA package, including three Hammer titles, plus three of the Corman Poe adaptations and two Hammer films previously shown on the BBC. It also included two Universal rarities, very loosely derived from Poe – *The Raven* (1935/09.02.1973) and *The Black Cat* (1934/22.06.1970) – that had otherwise been transmitted only once each by Granada. This comprehensive, mainly chronological retrospective represented, 'perhaps more than any series before or since', according to Sim Branaghan, 'a rich crash course in the genre's historic highlights'.[40]

The subsequent seasons in 1978 ('Monster Double Bill'), 1979 ('Masters of Terror' again) and 1980 ('Horror Double Bill', a title retained for the remaining two seasons) tended to pair a black-and-white film from the 1930s, 1940s or 1950s with a more recent, usually colour, film. The older title was almost always shown first, to the chagrin of some viewers eager to get to the more overtly horrific newer ones, which often began transmission after midnight.[41] This pattern was retained in 1981 but in this instance each of the earlier films came from one stable: not Universal, but RKO Radio. In 1979, as noted in Chapter 3, the BBC had acquired in perpetuity the entire RKO library but was only just beginning to place the films in its schedules. This season was therefore the first showing on *national* television for eight of the nine horror 'B' movies produced at the studio by Val Lewton between 1942 and 1946.[42] Most of them had again been broadcast only in Granada's North West region, aside from two also shown by YTV, for which Leslie Halliwell had briefly served as a scheduler.

Both the 1980 and 1981 seasons ended with a stand-alone film rather than a double bill. There was no horror season in 1982 and the last in 1983 included one single and even a triple bill. All sixteen films in this final group had been shown in previous years, suggesting that as a programming idea it had run its course and was now simply being recycled. In that fallow summer of 1982, BBC2 instead played a seventeen-film Hitchcock retrospective, occupying both Saturday and Sunday evenings; in four of those weeks, the Saturday titles were coupled with films directed by Claude Chabrol, in a parallel series called 'A Tribute to the Master'. Nevertheless, in the ensuing years, horror strands continued to appear on the BBC in various forms, including a run of double bills in 1993. Before then the dual idea had also been adopted by Leslie Halliwell for a Saturday-night series of 'Monster Horrors' on Channel Four in 1986, again reviving the canonical Universal titles alongside many archival rarities. All these, however, take us beyond the period covered by this book.

In his extensive online survey of horror films on television, Sim Branaghan pinpoints two sources of definable 'impact' that the BBC2 horror double bills had on a generation of predominantly young viewers: shared experience and a sense of occasion. Recalling excited schoolyard conversations, Branaghan says that the feeling of 'comradeship was overwhelming' among friends who had seen the same films. Besides this sense of community made possible before the fragmentation of

audiences with the advent of the VCR and later the Internet, the films thus seen
had scarcity value. As Branaghan points out, 'The blanket restricted-access of the
era is precisely what defined it, and gave the films concerned their inherent sense
of excitement. You COULDN'T see these things every day in the 70s. You were
lucky if you got to see them once every three years.'[43] Indeed, some titles in the
seasons have never been repeated since: *Voodoo Island* (1957/19.07.1978), *Black
Friday* (1940/04.08.1979) and *The Mad Ghoul* (1943/12.07.1980) were all broadcast in the BBC2 double bills for not only the first but the only time, to date, on
terrestrial television.

Concerns, Complaints and Controversies

Insofar as the Authority had cause for concern with the horror films shown by
ITV, this was as much to do with quality control as with the potential for offence,
though the two issues were not always clearly distinguishable. For example, ITA
officers found that *The Tingler* (1959/03.02.1969), included in Thames's 'The
X Film' series, was of 'poor quality'. Bernard Sendall noted that 'there is some
public concern about showing "X" films on television at all, and that this policy
can better be justified if we can point to the high quality of the films transmitted'.[44] Thames promised to look again at its other selections, but apparently
it did not look closely enough: Dermot O'Hagan considered *The Giant Claw*
(1957/03.03.1969) 'sheer garbage'.[45] O'Hagan subsequently intervened when
YTV proposed to show *The Tingler* ('a film which we could well do without') at
8.25pm, though he conceded that the Authority 'might be open to argument about
its suitability for a later time'.[46] He similarly objected to the scheduling by ATV of
The Haunting (1963/28.09.1970) at 7.00pm.[47] Both films were removed from the
schedules and subsequently shown at later hours.

The last title in Thames's second 'X Film' season of 1969 was the only one
to cause serious alarm. In correspondence following the showing of *Peeping
Tom* (1960/16.12.1969), Senior Programme Officer Stephen Murphy quoted a
comment by another officer, 'that it should never have been transmitted'. Other staff
considered that it was 'pretty sick stuff, but not "bannable"', and Murphy acknowledged that its director, Michael Powell, was 'a man of no mean calibre'.[48] Sendall
responded that, according to the ITA Director General, 'it was impossible to find
support in the [Television] Act for any decision to ban such films'.[49] No further
action was taken and the film remained in circulation on the network until 1976,
being shown by most ITV stations seemingly without controversy. *Peeping Tom* had
been certificated as Post-9.00 with a recommendation that it not be shown before
10.30pm. The same stipulation applied to *Witchfinder General* (1968/18.05.1973),
of which O'Hagan commented: 'I think it would do no harm to warn Companies
that this film is not suitable for showing before 10.30pm – at the earliest.'[50]

It is striking, however, that most of the communication regarding horror
films in the IBA Archives was internal and largely confined to Authority staff

and company representatives. Viewers were apparently less concerned about the genre than officers had initially feared. Throughout the 1970s, only a handful of hostile letters about either particular horror films or the genre in general were received from viewers (at least as registered by the Authority; local ITV stations may have had more). Staff also developed a sanguine, rather cynical approach to the occasional viewer complaints about horror. Replying to a 1974 letter, Senior Programme Officer Neville Clarke stated: 'Most of the late Monday night films which are currently being shown in the London area are somewhat old "horror" films which few people nowadays find either frightening or disturbing. They are, of course, shown at a time when only adults may be expected to be viewing.'[51] Two other viewers – a shift worker and a child of school age – were aggrieved that most horror films were shown *too* late at night; in a note to colleagues, Dermot O'Hagan remarked: 'Obviously if you have a horror film the only time at which you can reasonably place it is late night!'[52] A five-page letter complaining about Hammer's *Dracula AD 1972* (1972/14.04.1978) drew another exasperated response from O'Hagan: 'I shall never understand why people who do not like Dracula/horror movies persist in watching them – usually to the bitter end! (Perhaps so that they can write in these sort of complaints!)'[53]

There were three complaints about *Witchfinder General*, one of which was about the cuts made to the film rather than its content. Another viewer protested that Hammer's *Kiss of Evil* (1963/22.08.1969) had been drastically edited, an opinion with which Thames's Pat Mahoney readily concurred: he admitted that the station had 'obviously "boobed" on this one'.[54] *The Wicker Man* (1973/16.03.1979) attracted complaints from five viewers, two of whom were particularly upset by the ending. Some MPs forwarded letters about particular films from concerned constituents, and one of them – Norman Lamont (Conservative, Kingston-on-Thames) – wrote one himself about the psycho-thriller *Fright* (1971/25.02.1977), which was sent to a local newspaper.[55] The most intriguing missive came from a television personality, Hughie Green, who was disturbed by the violence in the Amicus portmanteau *Tales from the Crypt* (1972/07.12.1975), screened during the Balcombe Street Siege, which took place in Marylebone near to where Green lived.[56]

The pattern of correspondence changed in the 1980s, as some of the most successful and controversial recent horror films became available to television. Reports in 1980 that Leslie Halliwell was considering buying *The Exorcist* (1973/17.03.2001) for ITV led to many outraged letters, both in the press and sent to the IBA, but Halliwell later announced that he had decided against acquiring it.[57] The IBA Archives nevertheless contain correspondence between Halliwell and the Authority in which he repeatedly asks why he is not permitted to show an American TV version. The transmission of *The Omen* (1976/31.08.1981) and *Damien – Omen II* (1978/26.05.1982) brought the IBA thirteen and ten complaints, respectively. ITV had scheduled *The Omen* for 9.00pm on August Bank Holiday Monday, but five IBA officers previewed the film and found it unsuitable for this time. They would have preferred that it not be scheduled on a holiday, when more young people than usual were likely to be watching, but ultimately it was accepted for broadcast at 10.00pm.[58] Most of the complaints were from Christians worried about the occult theme and its potential for harmful influence; one was about the frequency of commercial breaks in the first hour.

The showing of the sequel was preceded by an announcement 'to the effect "that those who have seen *The Omen* will know what to expect from *Damien – Omen II*"'. Authority responses to correspondence about the sequel (repeatedly misnamed 'Damien and Omen II') noted that comparatively few complaints had been received about the original film. One of these had been from the husband of Mary Whitehouse, secretary of the National Viewers' and Listeners' Association (NVALA); one of the complaints about *Omen II* was from Mrs Whitehouse herself. She felt that the film was particularly unsuitable in the context of 'all the suffering and pain and anxiety' in the country due to the military conflict in the Falkland (Malvinas) Islands, which had begun several weeks earlier. The IBA's response stated that while schedules were under review due to the crisis, 'the horrific aspects of the Falklands situation are of a different dimension from those of the film' and that it had not been thought necessary to call for the latter's cancellation.[59]

The blockbuster status of these later titles ensured that they were networked rather than scheduled locally like older horror films. This was of course also the case with *Jaws* (1975/08.10.1981) and *Jaws 2* (1978/09.01.1983), hybrids of horror and action-adventure that were deemed suitable for early-evening showing. Both had received BBFC 'A' certificates, which were advisory and non-restrictive; ITV certificated them as Post-7.30. Despite their early starts and gory content, both films were shown uncut, although internal documentation indicates that *Jaws* had been acquired in a TV version. The premiere screening of *Jaws* began at that time on a Thursday evening (see Figure 10.3); but for the second transmission the following year, ITV sought dispensation from the IBA for a 6.45pm start on a Saturday.[60] The Authority received ten complaints for the original film's two transmissions, all but one about its suitability for these time slots. The exception concerned profane language, and this was the subject of all six complaints received about *Jaws 2*. On the other hand, a viewer commented in a newspaper letter about *Jaws*: 'I can only say that it made a pleasant change for me, and probably many others, to be able to see an entertaining film at a reasonable time.'[61]

Mary's *Baby*

The single biggest controversy regarding a horror film broadcast in this period concerned a film shown by the BBC. The Corporation's acquisition of Roman Polanski's *Rosemary's Baby* (1968/29.10.1976), in a package deal with Paramount, was widely reported in July 1974, though the film was embargoed for broadcast until 1976. According to one newspaper, 'BBC chiefs [were] in an agony of indecision on whether to show it' due to its black-magic theme, including a scene trimmed

Figure 10.3 ITV's premiere of *Jaws* (1975) on 8 October 1981 achieved the second-highest audience rating for any film ever shown on British television. *TV Times* © Future Publishing Ltd.

by the BBFC, in which the heroine is raped by the Devil.[62] The news prompted Mary Whitehouse to enquire with the Attorney General whether the showing on television of 'X'-certificated films was illegal due to the likelihood of under-age viewers tuning in. Whitehouse considered *Rosemary's Baby* 'the first of a long line of unsuitable films' and warned that *Last Tango in Paris* (1972/14.10.1993), *The Exorcist* 'and all the rest will be along soon unless action is taken now'.[63]

Eighteen months later, as the film became eligible for broadcast, she wrote to the BBC's Director General, Sir Charles Curran, and, having received assurances that there was no plan to show it, hoped this would be the end of the matter. But when the film's imminent transmission was announced on air in August 1976, in a preview of BBC1's autumn film lineup, Whitehouse claimed again 'that this is a softening-up process to get *The Exorcist* shown'.[64] In a letter to the *Daily Telegraph*, she stated:

It is so difficult to understand how any responsible broadcasting authority could decide to transmit this film through the uncontrolled medium of television that one wonders on whose authority this decision was made and who, exactly, if anyone, has viewed the film. Dealing as it does, in Roman Polanski's powerful fashion, with the occult, with Satanism, with the birth of a 'possessed' child conceived through intercourse between Rosemary and the Devil, it touches on depths of depravity, mental anguish and the psychologically unbalanced, which should arouse the greatest caution.[65]

Whitehouse found an unexpected ally in the comic actor Kenneth Williams, who wrote his own letter to *The Times*, noting that 'cruelty practised upon a pregnant woman [Rosemary, not Mary] should provoke our anger; it does mine'. He elaborated:

> Like all propagandas disguised as art, it will always find ready defenders, and liberally minded people will deplore the attempt to stifle work on which the commonality should be allowed to form its own judgment, et cetera. Alas, the commonality has no such ability; that is why we have the BBC Board of Governors. Mrs Whitehouse is right to appeal to them. They are custodians of an honourable tradition and should show the same concern as she does about things which do violence to the human spirit, and wound the conscience, not in the cause of art, but of making money.[66]

Curran later admitted in a letter of reply to Whitehouse that the August preview had been premature, as it had aired before a firm transmission date had been decided and even before the film's suitability for broadcast had been approved. According to Whitehouse, Curran had written: 'The film had to be viewed at a senior level within the television service and that has now taken place and there is no good reason why it should not now be screened.'[67] When the BBC announced one month later that it would be shown in a late-night slot on the weekend of Halloween, there were contradictory reports about whether it would be cut. One stated that the film would 'be shown in its entirety' while others suggested that the BBFC-approved version, with a fifteen-second cut to the diabolical rape scene, would be the one transmitted.[68]

Following the transmission, beginning at 10.46pm on Friday, 29 October (Halloween weekend), Whitehouse again wrote to the press: 'No warning was given before the programme, not even as to the terribly disturbing effect it might well have on pregnant women. Pregnant women! Through the early hours of the morning I received calls from *men* who were too sick and angry to sleep!'[69] The editor of a trade paper to which she had also written, regarding its leader column's claim that the film was 'neither shocking nor disturbing', challenged her statement that no warning had been broadcast: 'Was the description "a macabre and frightening excursion into the world of devils and witchcraft in modern New York" given beforehand by the continuity announcer not a warning?'[70]

Now that viewers had had the opportunity to make up their own minds, *The Times* published several letters either endorsing or disputing Whitehouse's position:

> The film *Rosemary's Baby* is in places visually repulsive and certainly it ought not to be seen by children (since it was not shown until shortly before eleven pm the fault for their being able to do so surely lies with their parents rather than the BBC), but it is difficult to concede that the film is essentially evil or blasphemous and its effect is to arouse horror and disgust at both these things. … Looked at in the large *Rosemary's Baby* is a highly moral fairy story.

All the television sets I have seen in my life have an on/off switch. Why don't Mrs Whitehouse and her 'sick and angry' men use it, instead of doing what they think to be a great favour to the vast majority of viewers. … Mrs Whitehouse's reference to the law in controlling that on/off switch is more frightening, more damaging and more disturbing than anything so far viewed on the box.

The unsuitability of many programmes appearing on television is a national scandal. It is naïve indeed to assume that parents will be able to 'censor' programmes by sending their children to bed, even when they know what kind of programme is being shown, which is anyway far from likely.[71]

One letter from a psychologist at St Bartholomew's Hospital, superficially supportive, may instead have been a tongue-in-cheek admonition:

Congratulations to Mrs Whitehouse on her timely demonstration (November 3) of the effect of satanism [sic] on our mental health. She may be interested to learn of a recent study in which I found that of 27 patients with religious delusions, three were possessed by the devil and 18 by the Holy Ghost. The importance of banning literature potentially dangerous to the susceptible mind cannot be exaggerated.[72]

It was Whitehouse herself who advocated a solution to what she saw as the problem, suggested by another film recently shown on television:

I wonder how many of your readers watched the highly perceptive and beautifully produced *The Spirit of the Beehive* shown last Saturday in Film International on BBC2? This demonstrated most movingly and tragically how a small child's mind had been affected by watching, in the village hall of a Spanish village, a showing of *Frankenstein*. A study of this film should surely be a compulsory part of every television producer's training.[73]

Rosemary's Baby is specifically mentioned in the Annan Report on the Future of Broadcasting (1977). In fact, it is mentioned twice: once in reference to Whitehouse's complaint, the other in respect of prefatory warnings. Implicitly aligning itself with the campaigner, the report found that 'more should have been done' to alert viewers to the film's disturbing content before its transmission.[74]

Notes

1 American TV broadcasters had no such inhibitions: see Heffernan, *Ghouls, Gimmicks, and Gold*, 154–79.
2 Jack Lewis, 'Saturday Thriller', *Radio Times*, 5 October 1967, 3, 8.
3 Victoria Hitchcock, '*Psycho*'s Director', *Radio Times*, 11 April 1968, 34.
4 *TV Times* (Northern), 5 August 1965, 31.
5 *TV Times* (Northern), 1 February 1968, 27.
6 *TV Times* (Northern), 15 December 1966, 35.
7 Jan Choyce to Sir Robert Fraser and Bernard Sendall, 11 December 1961, IBA/01021: 3996312.
8 Note by Sendall on Ibid, 14 December 1961, IBA/01021: 3996312.

9   Note by Choyce on ibid, 15 December 1961, IBA/01021: 3996312.

10 Sendall to Choyce, 21 December 1961, IBA/01021: 3996312.

11 Sendall to Choyce, 1 January 1962, IBA/01021: 3996312.

12 Choyce to Sendall, 2 January 1962 (IBA, IBA/01021: 3996312).

13 Draft paper, 'Horror on the Screen', 3 April 1963, IBA/01021: 3996312. Subsequent quotations in this section are also from this document unless otherwise noted.

14 *TV Times* (Northern), 9 November 1962, 37.

15 Stephen Murphy to HRS, 14 November 1962, IBA/01020: 3996317.

16 Sendall to Choyce, 14 May 1963, IBA/01021: 3996312.

17 *TV Times* (Northern), 21 October 1965, 29.

18 John E. Mann, 'Film Fare: Heroes of the Cruel Sea', *TV Times* (Northern), 21 October 1965, 12. Exactly the same words were used in London *TV Times*' films page for the ATV transmission on 26 December 1965, but this time attributed to Peter McDonald.

19 *TV Times* (London), 23 December 1965, 27.

20 *Look Westward*, 18 December 1965, 51.

21 Peter Noble, 'Films: Near Things in the Far East', *Look Westward*, 18 December 1965, 12; italics in original.

22 Martin Jackson, 'It's Not Your Night, Verdi!', *Daily Express*, 11 November 1972.

23 *Radio Times*, 9 December 1976, 66. This occasion was an example of BBC1 Wales opting out of a film transmission in favour of local programming.

24 *TVTimes* (London), 2 January 1969, 37.

25 *TVTimes* (London), 9 January 1969, 33.

26 Frank Copplestone, NPC Paper 5(70), 'Review of Network Film Purchasing Arrangements', 30 January 1970; Leslie Halliwell, NPC Paper 29(71), 'Film Purchases', 26 May 1971, IBA/01023: 3996311. Halliwell's acquisition of the horror package was reported in Ken Roche, 'Horror of Horrors! Dracula's Been Bought Up', *TVTimes* (Granada), 8 May 1969, 8–9.

27 Dermot O'Hagan to Halliwell, 25 June 1969, IBA/01023: 3996311.

28 Halliwell to O'Hagan, 29 July 1969, IBA/01023: 3996311.

29 I have been unable to locate transmission dates (if any) for *The Mummy* on ATV or Ulster, *The Mummy's Hand* on ATV or YTV, or *Kiss of Evil* (aka *The Kiss of the Vampire*) on Westward or Channel.

30 Halliwell, *The Dead That Walk*, 12.

31 *TVTimes* (Granada), 4 November 1971, 41.

32 For recollections and listings of ATV's horror seasons, see Kinsey, 'Appointment with Fear', in McNaughton, *70s Monster Memories*, and Sim Branaghan, 'Invitation to Terror – Horror Films on British Television in the 1970s & 80s', *SMGuariento.com*, 2017 (updated 2023), at http://www.smguariento.com/invitation-terror-horror-fil ms-british-television-1970s-80s-sim-branaghan/.

33 Besides Branaghan, 'Invitation to Terror', see also David Brilliance, 'Seeing Double', *The Dark Side* 179 (2016): 30–3; Meikle, 'The BBC2 Horror Double Bills', in Bryce, *Television Terrories*; and Ogley, 'Horror Double Bills', in McNaughton, *70s Monster Memories*.

34 See https://en.wikipedia.org/wiki/Horror_Double_Bills. The Classic Horror Campaign Group had its own website, now defunct, at http://www.classichorror campaign.com/about-us/.

35   Henry Fenwick, 'The Blob That Won the Queen's Award', *Radio Times*, 15 June 1972, 12; Anthony Haden-Guest, 'Dracula Revamped', *Radio Times*, 1 August 1974, 6–7. Subsequent *Radio Times* articles to accompany the horror double bills were: Angela Carter, 'Perfectly Monstrous', 30 June 1977, 4–5, 9; John Kobal, 'Review: Horror, Horror', 31 August 1978, 66; Geoff Brown, 'Films That Go Bump in the Night', 26 June 1980, 70–4; Geoff Brown, 'Tasteful Terror, Elegant Unease', 2 July 1981, 6–7.

36   *Radio Times*, 12 August 1976, 15.

37   Alan Howden, reply to John Mole, 'Incomplete Film Classic' (letter), *Radio Times*, 2 September 1976, 58.

38   Michael Dee, 'Complete Jekyll and Hyde' (letter), *Radio Times*, 4–10 May 1985, 96. It's possible that this version was still missing part of a scene in which Miriam Hopkins undresses before sliding into bed.

39   See the Indicator Limited Edition Blu-ray for the various different versions of *Night of the Demon* (Powerhouse Films, 2018).

40   Branaghan, 'Invitation to Terror'.

41   See Branaghan, 'Invitation to Terror'; Brilliance, 'Seeing Double'; and the letters from S.R. Oliver and W.T. Hoath, 'Horror in Black and White', *Radio Times*, 29 August–4 September 1981, 67, and from M. Gale and D. Dando, 'Not Horrific' and 'More Gore Please', *Radio Times*, 24–30 September 1983, 88.

42   The ninth Lewton horror film, *The Ghost Ship* (1943/11.09.1994), had been unavailable for many years for legal reasons before finally being cleared for broadcast more than a decade later.

43   Branaghan, 'Invitation to Terror'.

44   Television Programme Intervention Report January/February 1969, 21 February 1969, IBA/01021: 3996312.

45   O'Hagan to Murphy, 4 March 1969, IBA/01021: 3996312.

46   O'Hagan to Regional Officer, Yorkshire, 19 September 1969, IBA/01023: 3996311.

47   O'Hagan to H.G. Watkins, 21 July 1970, IBA/01023: 3996311.

48   Murphy to Sendall, 17 December 1969, IBA/01023: 3996311.

49   Handwritten note by Sendall on ibid.

50   O'Hagan to Graham Murray, 23 May 1973, IBA/01023: 3996311.

51   Neville Clarke to Rev. F.R.C., 9 October 1974, IBA/01023: 3996311.

52   Note by O'Hagan, n.d. (1973), IBA/01023: 3996311.

53   O'Hagan to ATAO II, 8 August 1978, IBA/01021: 3996312.

54   Letter from J.U., 9 March 1972; Pat Mahoney to O'Hagan, 14 March 1972, IBA/01023: 3996311.

55   Norman Lamont MP to Lady Plowden, 19 October 1977, IBA 01023: 3996311; 'Protest over Sex, Violence in *Fright* Film', *Surrey Comet*, 22 October 1977.

56   HOI to Joseph Weltman, 8 December 1975, and telephone call record, 9 December 1975, IBA 01023: 3996311. On the siege itself, see 'Siege of Balcombe Street' at https://stmarylebonechanginglives.org/siege-of-balcombe-street.

57   'TV May Show "Devil" Shocker', *Daily Mail*, 22 July 1980; 'No to *The Exorcist*', *Daily Mail*, 31 January 1981, 21.

58   David Glencross to Colin Shaw, 15 July 1981; Shaw to Penry Jones, 1 September 1981, IBA/01023: 3996311.

59 Christine to Lord Thomson, 26 May 1982; O'Hagan to ATAO II, 'Attached Complaint', 1 June 1982; Lord Thomson to Mary Whitehouse, 26 May 1982, IBA/01023: 3996311.

60 Chris Rowley to Shaw, 8 September 1982, IBA/01023: 3996311.

61 C.P. Moore, '*Jaws* Ban' (letter), *Daily Mail*, 20 October 1981, 34.

62 Martin Jackson, 'The Devil and the BBC', *Daily Mail*, 20 July 1974, 15.

63 Mary Whitehouse, quoted in Ivor Dean, 'Move to Keep X Films off BBC and ITV', *The Stage and Television Today*, 22 August 1974, 13.

64 Quoted in Peter Atkinson, '*Rosemary's Baby* to Be Shown by BBC', *Evening Standard*, 27 August 1974.

65 Mary Whitehouse, 'BBC and Screening of *Rosemary's Baby*' (letter), *Daily Telegraph*, 7 September 1976.

66 Kenneth Williams, '*Rosemary's Baby* on TV' (letter), *The Times*, 13 September 1976, 15.

67 Sir Charles Curran to Whitehouse, quoted in 'Film Extract Seen Too Soon, Admit BBC', *Daily Telegraph*, 28 September 1976.

68 '"Devil" Film Gets a Halloween TV Slot', *Daily Mirror*, 25 September 1976; 'BBC Boob over Devil Film', *Evening News*, 27 September 1976.

69 Mary Whitehouse, 'Films on Television' (letter), *The Times*, 3 November 1976, 17.

70 Editor's reply to Mary Whitehouse, '*Rosemary's Baby*' (letter), *The Stage and Television Today*, 18 November 1976, 20.

71 Katherine M. Thwaites, Emil M. Janson and Crispin Hill, 'Films on Television' (letters), *The Times*, 5 and 6 November 1976, 15.

72 Roland Littlewood, 'Films on Television' (letter), *The Times*, 6 November 1976, 15.

73 Whitehouse, '*Rosemary's Baby*'.

74 Home Office, *Report of the Committee on the Future of Broadcasting*, 254, 263.

CHAPTER 11

Abridged Too Far –
Editing of Films for Television

The appeal of the Big Film feature on Sunday evenings is due largely, I believe, to the fact that many viewers have already seen and enjoyed the films in the cinema.

My own enjoyment of the Big Film – and I suspect that of many others – has been blunted by the cuts. Rather than risk disappointment at finding my favourite scenes deleted, I would just as soon not watch the programme.

(G.A.V. Warwicker, 'A Film Fan's View' [letter], *TV Times*, 25 February 1965, 11)

This Film Has Been Modified to Fit Your Screen

Films are materially altered before broadcast for any number of reasons, not all of which are due to censorship. This chapter explores some of them, from purely operational matters to problematic content. Viewers who have seen a given film before, whether in a cinema or on a previous transmission, often become aware of disparities on a further viewing; others speculate about cuts by comparing transmission times with published theatrical running times. Much confusion has been caused by the fact that British television runs at a fractionally faster speed than projected film. Under the PAL (Phase Alternating Line) colour analogue system, film on television runs at 25 frames per second (fps) rather than the theatrical standard of 24fps. This means that a film running 100 minutes in cinemas will run 96 minutes on television, without cuts. For this reason, many viewers noticing variant running times assume that a film has been edited for TV when it has not. But in other instances, the difference is too great to be explained by technology alone.

Although editing to reduce length has been (and remains) common, British broadcasters have generally avoided one of the worst practices of American television: inserting additional footage – either specially filmed or rescued from the cutting-room floor – to pad out a slot longer than a film's theatrical version can fill.[1] Such expanded edits have only rarely found their way onto British TV, sometimes by accident. The version of *Earthquake* (1974/26.12.1980) shown on ITV for its network premiere was an extended-for-TV edition, featuring whole characters and plotlines not in the cinema original. So was that of *Star Trek: The Motion Picture* (1979/03.09.1984), which on first transmission overran its time slot and delayed the start of *News at Ten*, apparently because schedulers had not previewed the version supplied by the distributor and assumed it was the shorter theatrical cut.

Other, unforeseen types of 'editing' can also occur, especially during the analogue era when 35mm prints were run live on telecine during broadcast (see Figure 11.1). Breakdowns were less common than might be supposed but one occurred during LWT's transmission of *Underworld USA* (1961/09.02.1969) on 15 December 1973. This caused a two-minute interruption while the reel was loaded onto another machine; when the film resumed, 45 seconds of the climax had been lost.[2] Occasionally other errors arose. BBC2's transmission of the Marx Brothers' *A Day at the Races* (1937/01/01/1968) in the 'Midnight Movie' strand on 24 October 1979 had two reels shown in the wrong order, a mistake that might have been ruinous for a film less anarchic to begin with.[3]

Of course, it could be argued that cinema films can never be televised in their original form, simply because of technological differences between the two media. British television was for more than three decades broadcast exclusively in black and white. Feature films made in colour were therefore shown in monochrome, the first being *Western Approaches* (1944/14.12.1947). The first UK channel to transmit in colour was BBC2, beginning experimentally on 1 July 1967 and moving to a full service from 2 December the same year; the inaugural feature film broadcast in colour was *Thunder Bay* (1953/03.12.1967). BBC1 began its colour service on 15 November 1969, as did most of the major ITV companies (see Chapter 5, Table 5.3). But the transition went slowly: although colour television licences were introduced at the start of 1968, they did not outnumber monochrome licences until 1976.[4] The last ITV station to convert to colour was the smallest, Channel Television, that same year. Anticipating the launch of colour transmissions, the BBC had stockpiled Technicolor IB prints, which unlike Eastmancolor prints did not fade over time. However, prints supplied to the broadcasters were more often struck specifically for television use; as it was cheaper to make monochrome

Figure 11.1a–b BBC transmission prints were meant to be kept in pristine condition and were not physically cut. Photographs: author's copyright.

copies than colour ones, much of the stock held by ITV, in particular, comprised decolourised versions. Thus, even after the start of colour transmissions and continuing into the 1970s, ITV viewers could see such richly hued films as *Black Narcissus* (1947/09.05.1965) and *Vertigo* (1958/26.06.1966) only in black and white. Moreover, many newer television prints were processed using inferior colour systems that failed to capture the films' original palettes and were prone to rapid fading.[5]

Technological difference was most conspicuous in respect of one matter that has received much coverage over the years: the variant aspect ratios (height-to-width proportions) of projected film images and the television screen. Even before the advent of widescreen cinema formats in the mid-1950s, there were disparities between the shape of theatrical film images and their broadcast equivalents (see Figure 11.2). In 1950, *Scan and Television News* explained what viewers would see differently henceforward:

> On April 3rd the BBC made a permanent change in the aspect ratio of the television picture. Up to that date the ratio had been 5:4, but now the ratio is 4:3. This decision was only taken after full consultation with the trade, which recognises the change as an advancement, in that the new ratio will be in line with 35 and 16 mm films. Formerly it was impossible to transmit a film without the side edges being cut off, but the change in ratio has overcome this.[6]

With films made from 1953 onwards, even more of the sides were cut off. Widescreen processes such as Todd-AO, CinemaScope, Panavision and MGM Camera 65 had aspect ratios ranging from 2.20:1 to 2.76:1. ITV film buyer Leslie Halliwell explained the challenges they posed to broadcasters, which were at once technical, aesthetic and economic:

> A moment's thought will show that these films cannot possibly fit on to the TV screen in their original form, except as a strip across the middle of it. If they are magnified to fill the screen, most of the original picture is lost at the sides, and with it much essential action, so that the viewer is likely to see two noses pointing at each other across an empty space.
>
> The usual solution is to take the negative back to the laboratory and make a new 'television version', selecting from each shot the action which will best fit into the television ratio. This can never give the original impression, especially in the case of spectaculars like *The Great Race* and *Battle of the Bulge*, but it's the best television can do, and to do it costs at least ten thousand dollars a film.[7]

The first anamorphic widescreen film to be shown on British (and possibly world) television was *Storm over the Nile* (1955/29.10.1960), filmed in CinemaScope (see Chapter 4, Figure 4.2).[8] This was a full year before the more celebrated case of *How to Marry a Millionaire* (1953/06.11.1970) on US television. Anecdotal evidence suggests it may have been transmitted in what we would now call 'letterboxed' format, unlike the American film. In response to researcher Julian Upton's queries on an online discussion forum about the historical presentation of widescreen films on television, 'Film Man' contributed this recollection:

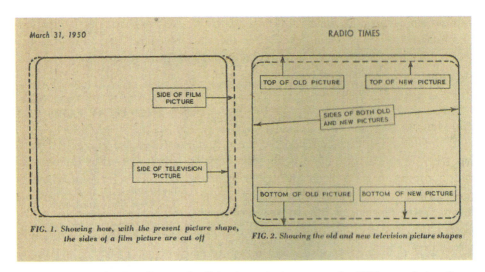

Figure 11.2a *Radio Times* illustrated a slight change in the aspect ratio of TV transmissions from March 1950. *Radio Times* © Immediate Media Co.

Figure 11.2b The visible picture area is marked in the leader of a 35mm transmission print. Photograph: author's copyright.

I remember way back on a Saturday evening in October, 1960, when I was 13 and a half, the BBC showing the CinemaScope film *Storm over the Nile* full width, probably as an unannounced experiment and, with the thick black bars over the top and bottom of the image, it really was like looking through a letterbox on our 14 inch screen. I remember my dad complaining because he thought his picture had been reduced in height. It took me quite a while to get him to realise that if you put an oblong into a square, you have to make the oblong smaller... hence the gap at the top and bottom of the screen. The funny thing was that he had seen widescreen films at the cinema, but somehow couldn't relate to them on television. This showing of a 'Scope film full width was a rare occurrence in those days and I don't remember it happening again until Granada ran *To Hell and Back* around 1968. Every few minutes, they put the words 'This is a CinemaScope film' across the top black band and 'Do not adjust your set' across the bottom black band.[9]

In contrast to this account, BBC Purchasing Assistant Bill Gilbert later recalled supervising the 'panning and scanning' of both *Storm over the Nile* and a second CinemaScope film from the IFD package (see Chapter 4), *Three Men in a Boat* (1956/12.04.1961). Gilbert claimed a place in the record books:

I was first to physically pan and scan two reels at a time onto tape. It was difficult to rehearse and very much a wing and a prayer.

Storm over the Nile presented a further problem as much of the action footage had been taken from the earlier *The Four Feathers* [1939] and had been blown up and cropped to fit the new width – we were now cropping the blow-up.

It was difficult to pan and scan *Three Men* as in many scenes there were the three men in close-up in the boat. The pan/scan operation meant we would lose in the picture one or more of the characters, perhaps when they were talking.[10]

More commonly, either the distributor supplied a ready-made 'rationalised' version in the form of a 35mm print processed in 4 x 3 format; or a pan-and-scan videotape transfer of a widescreen print was prepared in advance of transmission after telecine camera positions and movements had been carefully planned, rehearsed and computerised. In the period covered by this book, letterboxing was a rare exception rather than a regular practice, though it was common for 'hard-matted' widescreen films in non-anamorphic ratios (typically 1.66:1, 1.75:1 or 1.85:1) to be presented with a sliver of black matting at top and bottom. When this was not the case and films that had been filmed 'open matte' were presented in fullscreen format on television, more was in shot than would have been seen in cinemas. Thus, microphone booms and other intrusions were made unintentionally visible in the broadcasts of such films as *Night Moves* (1975/16.11.1980).[11]

Viewers generally accepted panning and scanning as the norm, only rarely writing in to complain, either out of principle or when it was badly done. Most were probably unaware of the practice, but could not help noticing when a broadcaster varied the standard presentation. The most notorious instance was the premiere transmission on BBC1 of *2001: A Space Odyssey* (1968/01.01.1982), filmed in Super Panavision 70. The majority of the film was shown fullscreen, panned and scanned in the usual manner, but the space sequences were letterboxed with the electronic addition of extra stars on the black matting at top and bottom, sometimes spilling over onto the film image. *Radio Times* printed four sample letters of complaint and the experiment was not repeated.[12]

'Defamation of Talent': Editing for Time

The BBC earned a deserved reputation for seeking to present the most complete version of a film possible. When, on occasion, an abridged print was supplied, the Corporation's buyers asked the distributor for a full-length one and only accepted the short version if the original was definitively confirmed to be unavailable. Mistakes and oversights were also usually addressed for further showings. For decades after its first release, Michael Powell and Emeric Pressburger's *The Life and Death of Colonel Blimp* (1943/26.12.1972) was only available commercially in drastically abridged prints. On its first transmission, BBC2 showed, with Powell's approval, a re-edited version the director had prepared for reissue in 1948, running 130 minutes. According to film historian Jeffrey Richards, the BBC had uncharacteristically overlooked the full-length version held by the BFI.[13] But for its first repeat, launching a Powell and Pressburger season on 11 September 1980, *Radio Times* reported that the film was to be shown in its 'full original version' for the first time since 1943.[14] This was five years before *Blimp* was restored and re-released by the BFI. The BBC also often restored material cut by the British Board of Film Censors (BBFC): the broadcast version of *Cape Fear* (1962/12.07.1969), for example, was longer than any seen in British cinemas.[15]

The Corporation's policy was due partly to its dedicated and knowledgeable purchasing staff but it was also facilitated by the nature of its operation. With a national service (except for occasional regional opt-outs) over two channels and no commercial breaks, the BBC's schedules were flexible enough to allow films to be placed in slots long enough to accommodate them without cuts. Although films were sometimes interrupted by news bulletins, as happened on weeknights in the late 1960s, schedules could generally be adjusted to avoid this. Paul Fox, Controller of BBC1 (1967–73), recalled: 'We had the great advantage of running feature films without any breaks and at their proper length. They were untouched – truly untouched; if they were two hours and ten minutes, the slot was two hours and ten minutes, or there was an overrun. What was not done ever, ever, was to cut the film to suit the slot, which was done at ITV – for perfectly good commercial reasons.'[16]

The federated ITV network system, by contrast, was relatively rigid. As discussed in Chapter 7, local stations were programmed independently by each contractor, but their schedules had to coincide at certain points for networked programmes, such as news bulletins and other live shows. With slots of fixed length and no capacity to overrun, feature films in particular – among the longest items in a schedule, with no standardisation in running time – were often trimmed to fit rather than chosen for the precise time available. The alternative, substituting a film of shorter length, sometimes after billing had been published in the event of other schedule changes, was reportedly more annoying to viewers, who might not be aware of cuts unless they had seen the film before. Moreover, companies had to insert commercial breaks. The Television Act 1954 called for 'natural breaks' but, unlike TV-originated material, cinema films had not been designed with ad breaks in mind, as critics often pointed out.

Editing of films, often by very substantial amounts, was therefore so common as to be the norm on ITV from its very beginning. In 1961, ABC Television presented Sunday-afternoon seasons of war films ('Impact!') and comedies ('If It's Laughter You're After') that had all been edited to a slot length of around one hour, inclusive of both commercial breaks and on-screen introductions. The first 'Impact!' presentation was Ealing's *Convoy* (1940/01.03.1959) on 26 March 1961, introduced by its star, John Clements. At full length, the film should have run 75 minutes; the slot allocated was 55 minutes, including introduction. This was far from the worst case. The Western *The Big Country* (1958/17.10.1965) ran an integral 160 minutes. ATV's premiere transmission, also on a Sunday afternoon, occupied a slot of 120 minutes, including commercials. The company's film buyer and scheduler, Lew Grade, admitted that it was 'a tragedy to have to cut some of these epics as drastically as we do', but argued that the solution was to rejig the network schedules to allow longer screening slots, rather than blaming schedulers for working within the space they had available.[17]

Examples of poor editorial decisions are legion and were often gleefully reported in the press. *To Have and Have Not* (1944/13.09.1958) was robbed of its most famous line, Lauren Bacall's 'You know how to whistle, don't you, Steve? You just put your lips together and blow.' The titular production numbers of *Dames* (1934/20.07.1960) and *Blues in the Night* (1941/18.07.1964) were deleted but the pedestrian plots left intact.[18] Entire characters were removed but the actors' billing was retained, on screen and in publicity. Listings magazines mentioned highlights that had been lifted out and on-air promotion used scenes that could not be seen in the films themselves. The reasons for such cutting could be extremely arbitrary. Scottish Television (STV) cut five minutes from *The Bramble Bush* (1960/05.07.1966) because late-night staffing problems meant closing down earlier than scheduled. Rediffusion cut *The Gentle Gunman* (1952/12.08.1965) by over ten minutes because of 'lack of broadcasting hours' under Government-imposed restrictions.[19]

Unsurprisingly, some viewers noticed. A notorious instance is ATV London's presentation of *The Secret Life of Walter Mitty* (1947/22.10.1964) on 31 January 1965 (the feed was shared by both Southern Television and Anglia Television). In its original version, the Danny Kaye comedy included six dream sequences visualising the hero's fantasy life. ATV cut 27 minutes, including three of the dreams in their entirety. Complainants accused the company of perpetrating a 'confidence trick' in promoting the film heavily on air but giving no indication that it would be an abridged version; indeed, advance trails had included part of one of the deleted scenes. The ITA defended ATV's editorial decision on the grounds that the programme following the film was a live, networked drama and so the company was left with no choice other than to cut the film; but it acknowledged that the mistake was to schedule it for that evening in the first place. One viewer questioned the legality of failing to declare that *Mitty* was abridged, but the Authority explained that ATV was acting within its rights: 'Mr Grade acquires the films on contractual terms which do not limit him to screening them entirely whole, unabridged or unedited, nor has he advertised his intention of doing this. You have, therefore, no right of presumption that you will see them entirely whole.'[20]

It was not only viewers who felt short-changed; filmmakers objected too. In July 1965, five distinguished directors, producers and screenwriters – Anthony Asquith, Sidney Cole, Paul Dehn, Anthony Havelock-Allan and Ivor Montagu – wrote a joint letter to *The Times*, drawing attention to the practice of editing films for television. It was followed by further correspondence, including letters from former Ealing studio head Michael Balcon and director Charles Frend endorsing its position. The joint letter made no distinction between the BBC and the ITV companies, but the examples cited – *Scott of the Antarctic* (1948/20.12.1964), *The Cruel Sea* (1953/24.06.1965) and *Orders to Kill* (1958/17.06.1965) – had all recently been transmitted by ITV. The first two (both directed by Frend) had been cut by 29 minutes each, the third (directed by Asquith) by 26 minutes (see Figure 11.3). The letter argued:

> Many viewers are seeing [the films] for the first time and justifiably assume that they are seeing the best of which we are capable. Not only do we and everyone else associated with these films lose our reputations, we may well also lose our means of earning a living. For who, judging by these mangled travesties of the originals, would employ or finance such glaring incompetence?
>
> Television is guilty of what we can only describe as 'defamation of talent'.

The signatories added that, if they as filmmakers had been 'victims of misrepresentation, the viewers have been victims of what amounts to fraud', and demanded: 'If, for some cogent reason, cuts have to be made, the cuts must be announced and the cutting be done under the supervision of the original producer, director, or someone appointed by them.'[21]

The high profile of the filmmakers and the force of their complaint ensured that the letter was given wide coverage in other newspapers. The ITA also took notice. After receiving a missive from the Association of Cinematograph, Television and Allied Technicians (ACTT) and meeting a delegation led by Asquith, the Authority, through its Deputy Director General, Bernard Sendall, asked each of the four major programme companies (ATV, ABC, Rediffusion and Granada) for written statements of their editing policies and practices.

Cecil Bernstein at Granada deferred to his company's resident film expert, Leslie Halliwell. Halliwell claimed to fit films as closely as possible to the available

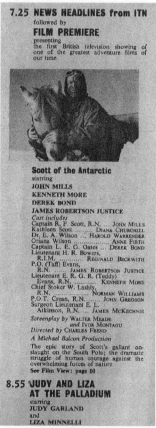

Figure 11.3a–b ABC Television's transmission of Ealing's *Scott of the Antarctic* (1948) on 20 December 1964 stirred the blood of the film's makers when it was cut by half an hour to fit a 90-minute time slot. *TV World* © Aston Publications Ltd.

slot and 'where this is impossible the film chosen is usually slightly too short rather than too long'. He admitted that cuts of up to seven or eight minutes might still occasionally be necessary, and in these cases he personally suggested the edits but said, 'If the film will not cut smoothly, it is not used.' However, Halliwell was based in London and had to relay instructions in writing to editors based at the company's Manchester studio; he was not on hand to see the results. He added:

> Occasionally features are cut for a different reason, namely because at their original length, they would, in my view, be dated and boring. Here even greater care is taken in deciding what is to go and the most we have eliminated is about 15 minutes from a 100 minute film. We would certainly not cut a well known film by an important director, only the more routine feature and second feature films.[22]

Memoranda from ITA officers indicate that at least some Authority staff shared these sentiments, as did schedulers at other companies. Lew Grade argued:

> Feature films were made with an entirely different transmission medium in mind and in many instances have long drawn out sequences which although eminently suitable for a cinema audience are totally unrealistic and unrelated when transmitted on a television screen. The technique of production and requirements of television are as far apart from those of the cinema industry as film production is from theatrical direction.[23]

Three of the four company executives consulted felt that it was impractical to involve a director or producer in re-editing their own work. Despite assurances to the ACTT that they were willing to do so, subsequent correspondence indicates not a single instance of this happening. As for legal authority, most hire contracts allowed leeway for films to be cut to fit time slots or to accommodate ad breaks. In only one case, regarding a small number of titles from the Rank Organisation, was there a condition that the distributor had to be consulted before cuts were made. Here Rank had itself supplied shortened versions of the films with a contractual stipulation not to cut them further without prior approval. Grade explained that such approval was easily sought and received but Halliwell thought that 'this instruction is more honoured in the breach than the observance'.[24]

Of the three films mentioned in the filmmakers' joint letter, Asquith's *Orders to Kill* posed particular problems because of content. At the time of the complaint, it had been shown by only two stations: Rediffusion in London and ABC (which had acquired the film for the network) in the Midlands and North. On both occasions it was heavily cut, by 26 and 21 minutes, respectively; some of the cuts were intended to be permanent rather than temporary. ABC's editing had involved substantially reducing a scene in which the hero, on an undercover mission in wartime France, assassinates a suspected Nazi collaborator. Besides length cuts to the film, this sequence had been edited in order to comply with the Authority's rules on excessive violence. Asquith's objections to the cuts focused on a single word uttered by the victim near the beginning of the sequence: 'Why?' Deleting this, he argued, robbed the scene and the film of its point (the victim is innocent).

Leslie Halliwell agreed that this cut harmed the film and believed that 'Asquith has every right to carp'.[25] The Authority therefore approved further re-editing of the sequence to restore the key utterance while eliding some of the brutality. This delivered a sop to Asquith's complaint, achieved without setting a precedent for direct interference in broadcasting by the film industry. ITA Director General Sir Robert Fraser stated, in agreeing to the revisions, 'Here I think we would be wise to give ourselves one notch of credit, so that we have something to say if the question [of cutting] is raised again.'[26]

It was, of course. By my count, the IBA Archives contain complaints related to cuts in at least sixty-five named films shown on ITV between 1965 and 1981. More than two-thirds of these concern cuts for time rather than for content. These were just the films where viewers noticed and wrote in. The Authority's papers indicate that a great many more abridged films appeared in the schedules, more than were ever complained about, although there were also many letters complaining in general terms about ITV's treatment of films. Between 1966 and 1968, the ITA conducted several studies of film editing across the network in order to build up a clearer picture of what was happening at local levels (this coincided with the increasing systematisation of film clearance and certification discussed in Chapter 9). They produced illuminating results.

A survey of forty films transmitted by two or more companies between late May and early July 1966 revealed that, with one exception, no transmissions of a given film by any two stations on different dates had exactly the same running time. Indeed, the differences could be quite marked. The original running time of *Alexander the Great* (1956/17.10.1965), at telecine speed, was 135 minutes. On both Granada and ATV in London the film ran 120 minutes (this was the exception). On ATV in the Midlands, it ran 96 minutes – a cut of 39 minutes, or more than one quarter of its length.[27]

Summarising the survey, Senior Programme Officer Stephen Murphy noted that 'the vast majority of the instances we looked at disclosed only small variations (under two minutes)', with the biggest deviations coming from ATV and Granada. But as he pointed out with reference to *Orders to Kill*, the emphasis on timings alone was misleading as 'an unskilful editor could well ruin a film with a cut of only a few seconds'. Murphy drew the conclusion that the 'statistical exercise was not as significant as I had at one time thought; it does reveal, though a generally ruthless attitude to film'.[28]

In September the same year, all companies were asked by the Authority to state 'the procedures followed for the cutting of feature films', identify which company employee was responsible for it and give their qualifications for doing so, and explain the reasons why cuts were made.[29] Lew Grade responded on behalf of ATV:

We view films acquired by us immediately they are received and then, where necessary, delete any excessive violence and sex in conjunction with our experienced film editors. Then, when requested, we inform purchasing contractors whether the films are suitable for the slots for which they require them ...

Apart from this first original editing action, the feature films are also re-edited by the Head of our Film Editing Department, Mr Fred Pullen, to the required length, i.e. for the time period intended for our own transmission. The actual final editing is made approximately two weeks prior to our transmission date ...

Once the film has been edited for a particular time slot, it is then viewed again to be absolutely sure that it is acceptable. When there is a drastic reduction in the length of the film, the actual transmission is preceded by an announcement to the effect that 'This film is specially adapted for television', though the exact wording of the announcement varies from time to time.[30]

Whether all these procedures were followed in every instance is open to question, given the evidence available in other documents. Southern Television recorded having transmitted 182 films in the first nine months of the year, proudly claiming that '67 were not cut at all' – or put another way, that 115 *had* been cut.[31] Besides providing factual and statistical information, a number of the companies presented the rationale for their editing, including Granada via Halliwell, who admitted removing fifteen minutes from *A Night to Remember* (1958/27.02.1966) to improve it – not the kind of 'B' feature he had previously said was 'improved' by cutting.[32]

In April the following year, the four major companies were further asked to provide 'full details of all feature film cuts made since September 1966'; the regional companies were asked to do the same 'if they had this information readily available'.[33] ATV supplied a list of ninety-two films transmitted in its two franchise regions, of which only twenty-one had not been cut; the longest reduction was of 22½ minutes to *Ivy* (1947/03.01.1967), shown in the Midlands on 30 March 1967. Granada did not provide a full list but reported only one case where more than two minutes had been removed from a film: eighteen minutes from *The Charge of the Light Brigade* (1936/25.12.1959) on Boxing Day 1966, 'owing to its excessive length and slow pace'.[34]

A survey of 180 films shown during January 1968 produced a table of comparative figures. According to Stephen Murphy, 'The method was to take the total cinema running time of films shown in January by each company, and to express the actual transmission time (*not* slot time) as a percentage of it.' Data were not available for all stations, samples for some companies were small and the cinema running times were not adjusted for telecine speed. Figures were rounded up to the nearest minute and Murphy acknowledged that some of the information on original running times might be unreliable. Nevertheless, he argued, the results presented a valid picture of variant practices across the network (see Table 11.1). The average cutting rate among the companies was 8.3 per cent, but ATV London's was nearly twice the average at 16.2 per cent.[35] In an exchange of correspondence with Lew Grade, Bernard Sendall commented:

Table 11.1 Percentage cutting of feature films by ITV companies, January 1968.

Company	Percentage
ABC	8.6
Anglia	7.5
ATV London	16.2
ATV Midlands	6.6
Grampian	6.2
Granada	6.9
Rediffusion	4.2
Southern	6.4
STV	6.6
Tyne Tees	9.2
Ulster	8.6
Westward and Channel	11.8
Network Average	**8.3**

Source: Attachment to memo by Stephen Murphy, 'Cutting of Feature Films', 26 February 1968, IBA/01023: 3996311.

> This represents a real problem for us. As you know, the Authority has always defended the companies' right to edit films slightly. Inevitably, it is by the London output that our critics judge us: and they have a good case, as long as ATV is putting out films like *The Fugitive Kind* on February 18th. The original running length was 119 minutes: the transmission was 86 minutes. After making the usual allowances for telecine, over a quarter of the film had been removed. No film editor, however skilled, can retain all the essential elements of the original film if he has to cut to this extent; and indeed the transmission inevitably showed signs of it.[36]

Grade made familiar noises about films not being 'made specifically for any slot' but he promised penitently that 'this will be watched very carefully in the future'.[37] A few months later, ATV surrendered its London franchise to London Weekend Television (LWT), while taking over the full week in the Midlands. Its successors' record turned out to be almost as erratic as Grade's had been. Screenwriter Harold Pinter wrote to the *Sunday Times* to point out that LWT's premiere transmission of his *The Pumpkin Eater* (1964/02.11.1969) was 'mutilated' by cuts totalling twelve minutes. In fact, an ITA memo states that it was cut by 19½ minutes.[38]

Meanwhile, Grade was still up to his old tricks. In the same newspaper in 1971, Hunter Davies's profile of the ATV mogul included an overheard conversation between Grade and his scheduling assistant, Olive Hennessy:

> 'I'll tell you what you do here, Olive. Olive, you take this Alan Ladd out of here. So now we need 107 minutes. My God, Olive. Is that one 152? I don't mind a repeat. You got me a repeat?'
>
> 'What about Breakfast at Tiffany's?'
>
> 'When did we do it last?'
>
> 'December 6, 1969.'
>
> 'Too soon, Olive, too soon.'

'It's jolly good.'

'What's this? A Dean Martin. That will do.'

'It's too long. Here's one. It says sordid, preferable after 9.'

'Put it in. Cut it by 21 minutes. Anything else?'

'There's still a gap here. What about Breakfast at Tiffany's?'

'OK, put it in. Great Olive.'[39]

This passage, particularly Grade's offhand cutting instruction, was widely cited elsewhere.[40]

Having learned from the Asquith and Pinter affairs, the Authority became wary of offending filmmakers who took a particular interest in the treatment of their work. When Carl Foreman was observed 'gently enquiring around the place' about what cuts were to be made in his very long war film *The Victors* (1963/08.02.1970), Stephen Murphy issued a directive to regional officers:

> This is an exceptionally good film. Carl Foreman does happen to be president of the Screenwriters' Guild. These two circumstances taken together will, I hope, suffice to convince all regional companies that the film will be treated with tender care.[41]

LWT transmitted *The Victors* uncut, though the print the network had acquired was the shortened general-release version, re-edited by Foreman himself. But when ATV scheduled the same film for a 7.00pm start despite its Post-8.00 ITCA certificate, planning to make cuts to ensure it was suitable for the early slot, Programme Officer Dermot O'Hagan wrote to Olive Hennessy to dissuade her. Hennessy replied that, although they were 'not so irresponsible as to run a film that has been mutilated by editing', ATV intended 'to cut the offending passage since we could afford to lose 16 minutes'.[42] The extent of editing that would have been needed to ensure suitability finally determined that a different film had to be chosen.

Formal representations from the film industry had abated by the 1970s, allowing the Authority to believe that the situation had improved, despite occasional public complaints about incidents such as LWT cutting out the climax of *Pony Express* (1953/12.09.1965) on 4 April 1970 and Granada deleting 20 minutes from *The Big Country* on 24 May 1970 (including another scene that had been used in trailers).[43] But the issue bubbled up again in a different forum. Allen Eyles's monthly 'TV Films' column in *Films and Filming* featured regular reports on cutting catastrophes, often sent in by readers. In 1971, Eyles wrote directly to the Authority to ascertain its official position on the subject. In his first reply of a lengthy correspondence, Dermot O'Hagan asserted: 'Provided such editing is done with the proper technical skill and with proper regard for the aesthetic qualities of the film the ITA accepts that it is necessary.' He also disclosed that in the most recent network survey, conducted between March and April 1971, 'out of a total of 570 feature film transmissions during a period of eight weeks the average length of cuts was seven minutes'.[44] O'Hagan seemed to consider this a modest amount, eminently justifiable; that is not how it was construed when his comment was printed in Eyles's column and repeated in other press reports.[45]

There was considerable regional variation in cutting practices; particular stations had their own local idiosyncrasies. Eyles reported a reader's observation that 'STV have a persistent habit of cutting right in the middle of a scene for a commercial break but not picking it up again. Instead they take up a completely new scene.'[46] Southern habitually cut out the opening credits of films and replaced them with its own captions. This was technically in breach of standard hire contracts, which specified that credits and copyright declarations should not be removed. But the company's press officer argued in its defence that it was 'better to cut the credits rather than the action'.[47]

In 1973, a group of ITV executives (including Leslie Halliwell) and engineers toured five regional stations to study the handling of film at local levels. They found that films were cut even when shown in open-ended slots late at night so that stations could close down earlier and thereby avoid making staff overtime payments. Their draft report noted: 'One station last week appears to have cut a Hitchcock thriller by 12 minutes for this reason: the result is unlikely to be a happy one.'[48] A sampling of films shown on the evening of 14 October 1973 revealed that seven films had each been cut by between four and ten minutes, including one, *Shane* (1953/28.08.1972), which a recent missive had stipulated was not to be cut at all.[49] The report found that films bore the brunt of local economies because they were more malleable than other programmes. 'The only thing you can fiddle is a film', its authors explained.

> This was the excuse given to us, in one form or another, by every region as a justification for cutting. Films, especially feature films, are used by all companies as a variable to help balance the evening's advertising. In other words, film is cut because it *can* be cut. Prints are edited, usually hastily, in anticipation that advertising breaks will be fully sold. If they are not, bits of the edited film are replaced at the last moment. This is obviously the kind of procedure that should be done with great care if at all. In our view a busy station editor has no time to do it even reasonably well. Furthermore, planners admit that they manage very well in evenings when no feature film is scheduled, so that obviously more careful and considerate scheduling would eliminate the need for cutting.[50]

A second 1973 report, by technical officers from the IBA's Quality Control Section, provided further details of the extent as well as the variability of film cutting that took place locally:

> Most companies readily admitted cutting by up to five minutes in an eighty-five minute slot to accommodate different feature length. Some companies treated each film on its merits and quoted examples where they had obtained replacement films rather than cut a particular film at all. However, an investigation of quoted running against scheduled time reveals that cutting is far more widespread than is admitted. It was admitted by some companies that they cut up to twenty minutes from a film to avoid running into penalty overtime payments after midnight.

> Whilst cutting down of features was regarded as a skilled job, many cases were quoted where essential parts of the story were removed (such as the musical numbers being cut of a musical). It is common for films to be returned to Anglo-EMI with parts missing, or in the wrong place and, on several occasions, companies have transmitted films in this state without realising it.[51]

Besides impairing the viewer's experience, the practice of fourteen companies all editing films differently led to substantial wear and tear on the stock. The executives' report therefore recommended that more films should be networked, especially in peak-time slots, so that any necessary editing could 'be done centrally once and for all and with care' and so that feature films, 'which are in short supply, can be carefully scheduled to realise their maximum potential'. As a way of regulating local cutting, it suggested that 'note should be taken of any scenes which might usefully be edited to bring the film down to a length which is likely to be required'. Films made for the cinema did not of course take into account the scheduling needs of commercial broadcasters, who preferred standardised running times in order to fit fixed slots. For an 85-minute slot, a running time of 78 minutes allowed sufficient space for advertisements; 105-minute and 120-minute slots entailed film durations of 95 and 108 minutes, respectively. The report therefore proposed that 'a cutting sheet be made out indicating possible individual cuts, the total amount by which the film is considered cuttable, or (where appropriate) the fact that it is not cuttable at all'. Each film's cutting sheet would accompany the print as it was sent out to stations. But the report also recognised the possibility that companies would schedule a film 'not for the slot which they are obviously cut to fit but for the next one, thus resulting in even more editing!'[52] The proposal was not followed.

The increased networking of films from the mid-1970s onwards did not eliminate editing for length. As late as 1981, network transmissions of *Rollercoaster* (1977/18.02.1981), *The Return of the Pink Panther* (1975/14.09.1980) on 28 July and *Paint Your Wagon* (1969/01.01.1980) on 26 December were cut to fit time slots: the first by around eleven minutes, the second by seven and the third by around sixteen. In the case of *Paint Your Wagon*, this involved removing four entire songs from the musical.[53] Meanwhile, at local level the same year, Southern Television admitted to cutting eleven minutes from *The Happiest Days of Your Life* (1950/04.07.1972) on 7 December. On 30 December, Southern's Director of Programmes, Jeremy Wallington, told a complainant: 'I agree with you that such radical cuts should not be permitted in any film, not only a British comedy classic of this kind.' He added an even more candid explanation:

> The reasons for the savage cuts on this occasion, were partly due to the fact that Southern Television is going out of business shortly, that arrangements had been made to transfer most of the film stocks to the incoming tenants and no alternative film, appropriate to the slot and of the right length, was available. My apologies.[54]

Perhaps Wallington was mindful that, with the company's franchise set to expire the following day, there was nothing left to lose by being honest.

Bob & Carol & Ted & Alice and George

Although the IBA Archives contain extensive internal correspondence, among staff officers and between them and the ITV companies, discussing matters of concern regarding films, the Authority received very few complaints from viewers about film content until the second half of the 1970s. In that period, there was a significant rise in three kinds of complaint: that certain films had been cut too heavily; that certain films had not been cut enough; and that certain films had been shown at all, cuts or no cuts. This development was precipitated by the nature of the material that was increasingly becoming available to television. It only got worse over time.

In the 1975 autumn season, most of the ITV companies moved their regular Sunday-night film slot from 7.55pm, in Family Viewing Time, to 9.10pm, after the watershed and following the evening news (the news bulletin was shorter and earlier at weekends than on weeknights). This allowed the films to run uninter-rupted, except of course by advertisements. During the week, titles certificated Post-9.00 would either have had to straddle *News at Ten* (a practice discouraged by the IBA but often accepted as an inevitable consequence of scheduling restric-tions) or start at 10.30pm or later. The change of time slot was reflected in the more adult nature of the films selected. Several of the companies had reservations about showing some of these films so soon after the watershed. The IBA, too, was wary without being actively opposed, one officer commenting: 'whether or not 9.10pm on Sunday is a suitable point of time at which to place comparatively recent and sometimes *very* adult and controversial films, albeit outside the family viewing period, is still perhaps a matter of debate'.[55]

The Authority hoped that the companies would not schedule their most con-tentious films on successive weeks but would intersperse them with less risky material: older films, such as *From Here to Eternity* (1953/02.02.1969) and *What Ever Happened to Baby Jane?* (1962/11.01.1969). These had once posed content problems (see Chapter 9) but now, in the light of changing standards, seemed relatively innocuous. None of the films shown in the Sunday slot that season was fully networked, but several were part-networked. They often performed strongly in the ratings: sample figures showed that viewing figures exceeded expectations in every time band, often by a substantial margin. Moreover, the films tended to hold their audiences to the end instead of losing them in the later bands (see Table 11.2). Several titles nevertheless generated complaints; there were also many letters expressing general concern about the number of 'X'- or 'AA'-rated films that were now being shown on TV. Two films in particular attracted a higher than usual number of letters and phone calls: *Bob & Carol & Ted & Alice* (1969/14.09.1975) and *The Killing of Sister George* (1968/28.09.1975). Both were broadcast simulta-neously in ten of the fourteen ITV regions. The IBA received a total of eighteen complaints regarding one or both, as well as copies of ten more letters sent to one particular station, exhorting it not to show *Sister George*. These numbers may

Table 11.2 Ratings for ITV Sunday-night films in three regions, September 1975.

Bob & Carol & Ted & Alice (14 September)

	21.30		22.00		22.30	
	Actual	Expected	Actual	Expected	Actual	Expected
London	31	31	29	28	30	21
Lancashire	35	33	26	29	35	20
Yorkshire	35	31	33	28	31	19

The Executioner (21 September)

	21.30		22.00		22.30	
	Actual	Expected	Actual	Expected	Actual	Expected
London	38	31	34	28	33	21
Lancashire	37	31	36	27	36	19
Yorkshire	34	31	32	28	33	19

The Killing of Sister George (28 September)

	21.30		22.00		22.30		23.00	
	Actual	Expected	Actual	Expected	Actual	Expected	Actual	Expected
London	36	32	32	29	27	22	24	16
Lancashire	41	33	38	29	36	20	33	16
Yorkshire	35	31	33	28	29	19	29	14

Source: Memo, Joseph Weltman to Brian Young, '"X" Films on Sunday Evening', 20 October 1975, IBA/01020: 3996317.

appear small given the size of audiences, but each complaint was taken seriously by the Authority and the norm was none.[56]

Directed by Paul Mazursky, *Bob & Carol & Ted & Alice* is an American satire on contemporary sexual mores and middle-class Californian lifestyles, including newly-fashionable sex therapy. Letters complained that it was a 'sordid, vulgar film' and 'a useless, shocking and unnatural display', that its 'sexual frankness was quite offensive', and that it 'should never have been passed for a television screening'. One, more sympathetic, viewer, while acknowledging the film's serious intent, challenged its 'unrealistic' and 'psychologically inadequate' view of group therapy and free sex.[57]

Mary Whitehouse, Secretary of the National Viewers' and Listeners' Association (NVALA), argued that the film's 'transmission raises questions of legality'. Reminding the IBA of its statutory obligation 'to ensure that "nothing gives offence to public feeling" or "offends against good taste and decency"' and expressing 'surprise at the deterioration of standards', she added: 'It would now appear that the Authority is prepared to condone material which clearly offends in those terms.'[58] The IBA disagreed, and in its standard reply to complainants (quoting the film's favourable review in the BFI's *Monthly Film Bulletin* for support) emphasised that it found *Bob & Carol & Ted & Alice* acceptable under its Family Viewing Policy, though not for family viewing time:

> This policy aims to ensure that nothing is transmitted before 9.00 pm that would be considered unsuitable for viewing by the young, whether on their own or in the family circle. After 9.00 pm we think it reasonable to expect parents to exercise some of their proper responsibilities and to decide whether their young children should continue to watch television. We do not say that all programmes shown after 9.00 pm will be unsuitable for 'family viewing' but as a national broadcasting service we believe we should be failing in our responsibilities to the viewing public if we decided that at no time would responsible programmes on serious adult themes be transmitted. At the same time we recognise a duty to parents who are prepared to exercise responsibility, to make it clear when we propose showing material that they might not wish their children to see.[59]

One lengthy chain of correspondence concerned not the film itself but a promotional trailer for it. A viewer who had seen a preview at 7.25pm on STV considered this too early to show excerpts from an adult film. Whitehouse's letter also mentioned the trailer, and the Authority acknowledged the challenges of 'making clear' the nature of a Post-9.00 film in previews broadcast before the watershed:

> We do our best to see that promotions for programmes which appear at a time when children may be viewing in large numbers are suitable for that particular time whatever the subject of the film itself. In this particular case two different trailers were made, one specifically for showing before 9.00 pm, which contained one of the more comic scenes from the film, and one for showing after 9.00 pm.[60]

Despite its London setting, *The Killing of Sister George* is also an American production. Directed by Robert Aldrich, it concerns the relationship of a lesbian TV soap-opera actress and her younger lover. In the US, it had been one of the first films awarded an 'X' rating by the Code and Ratings Administration (CARA), the censorship board established in November 1968 by the Motion Picture Association of America (MPAA). Even so, it had been prosecuted for obscenity in Boston, where a cinema manager was given a six-month jail sentence for showing it. When submitted to the BBFC, the film had initially been refused a certificate, but the censorship board of the Greater London Council (GLC) had issued a local 'X' certificate, allowing it to be released, with minor cuts, in London. The BBFC had subsequently relented and granted an 'X' after requiring a three-minute cut to remove a bedroom seduction scene involving partial nudity. Some local authorities still banned it anyway.[61]

The IBA had been consulted prior to Leslie Halliwell's purchase of the film and raised no objection in principle. The print previewed by Yorkshire Television (YTV) was the uncut version, which the company planned to show in its entirety as the 'problem' scene, towards the end of the film, would not be broadcast until around 11.25pm. But after internal discussion it was decided to edit the scene to 'take out some of the explicitness' (Southern Television would not agree to take the transmission unless this was done). Programme Officer Dermot O'Hagan remarked that 'if the full version is shown we may well get complaints that we allowed a film originally certificated for London only to be shown in areas outside London'.[62]

The editing was done by LWT, which eventually originated the transmission for the network rather than YTV. The available documentation is inconsistent about how much was cut: some memos state that it was edited to match the BBFC-approved version, whereas others are more vague. Deputy Director General Bernard Sendall consented to the transmission, provided the version broadcast was not more explicit than the one passed by the BBFC, but it is not clear if this was in fact the case. O'Hagan commented: 'I think that LWT may argue that five years is a long time and public standards have changed.'[63]

Several of the public complaints came via local Members of Parliament, including one who told a constituent that it was 'absolutely deplorable that such evil films should be shown on television when it is impossible to restrict the audience'.[64] Another was made by an MP, Trevor Skeet (Conservative, Bedford), writing on his own behalf. Descriptions of the film ranged from 'sickening' and 'unsavoury' to 'sheer porn' and 'filth'. One complainant, a schoolteacher, enclosed a list of forty-nine 'AA' and 'X' films shown on all channels in the past two months, commenting:

> I can see no sound reason why a film like *The Killing of Sister George* (or any other 'X' film, for that matter) should be shown on television. Those who wished to see this film have already had ample opportunity of doing so in a cinema. Those who wish to see it again could always request their cinema manager to book it again. But to show such material on television is sheer irresponsibility.[65]

One of the stations that did not show the film on its first, part-networked broadcast was Westward Television. Ten letters sent to the company chairman, Peter Cadbury, and copied to the Chairman of the IBA, Lady Plowden, were clearly part of an orchestrated campaign, as they all made substantially the same points, in the same order and with similar wording. They too included an expression of concern at the 'proliferation' of 'X' and 'AA' films on television and the fact that the BBFC certificates were not shown on screen. Their standard wording included the following:

> My special plea is that *The Killing of Sister George* is not shown on Westward TV unless the lesbian love scene is cut out. The moral of the story would thereby be unaffected. I appeal to you for the sake of our young people – the future adult generations – and for the sanctity of the good and pure aspects of our national heritage.[66]

The film was nevertheless shown in the Westward region on 26 October, apparently with no further cuts. The IBA's replies to these letters also had a standard wording, one which emphasised the film's prestige through its basis in a play that had received critical acclaim:

The film is admittedly a powerful and, in many ways, disturbing film on a theme which some people may well have found distasteful but it is also a seriously intentioned and well written film (adapted from an original stage play) dealing, perhaps at times realistically, but not in a gratuitously sensation seeking manner, with a controversial area of human relationships.[67]

The replies also mentioned that all advance promotion had presented *Sister George* as an adult film, that discussions had taken place with the ITV companies beforehand, and that the film had been 'carefully edited'. Besides the complaints sent or copied to the Authority, local stations may have received some of their own, although Granada's Leslie Halliwell claimed to have received only one, 'from a woman who complained that in one scene a budgie was shown in a cage far too small for it!'[68]

The following year, *Sister George* had the distinction of being cited in a parliamentary debate about film censorship. Bob Cryer MP (Labour, Keighley) used it to draw attention to the fact that films with an 'X' certificate shown in cinemas to restricted audiences were later 'shown on television with no guidance whatsoever'. He proposed that 'some sort of statutory force should be given to the BBFC certificates' so that broadcasters, like cinemas, were required to display them. The Home Secretary, Brynmor John, seemed in principle to agree, commenting: 'Since television is in our homes, it is in many ways a more obvious way in which films can be seen by people to whom they are not suited, particularly children – and all parents have experienced that from time to time.' But rather than act on Cryer's proposal, John merely pointed out that the Annan Committee was looking into it.[69]

Rough Summer Nights: 'The Savage West' and Other Westerns

In the summer seasons of 1976 and 1977, the ITV companies adopted a new scheduling strategy: a regular late-night, networked film slot aimed at adult audiences. Networked films of any kind were still relatively rare on ITV, and while these series were superficially a positive response to the IBA's calls for more networking, the choice of films was not greeted by the Authority with unreserved enthusiasm. The 1976 series was called 'The Savage West'; 1977's, 'For Adults Only'. Both seem to have been conceived as a way of packaging minor titles that, scheduled locally, might have attracted little notice. But giving them prominent network programming in this way brought more attention to them than they might otherwise have received.

'The Savage West', scheduled at 10.30pm on Mondays, comprised nine Westerns from the 1960s and 1970s. This was one of three networked film strands in ITV's 'Summer Festival' that year, a coordinated attempt to counter the BBC's exclusive coverage of the Olympic Games.[70] The other two series – 'The Saturday Action Film' and 'The Thursday Adventure Film' – mainly comprised peak-time repeats of older blockbusters, most of which had previously been networked as holiday specials. Westerns had long been a TV staple, but the fact that most modern films in the genre could only be shown after the watershed was in itself a sign of changing times. Those selected for the series were, with one exception, television premieres, but few were well-known and their content ensured that all were certificated Post-9.00. Indeed, the IBA was not convinced that they were all suitable for broadcast even in a 10.30pm slot. 'Looks like being a rough old Monday night in the summer!', commented Programme Officer Dermot O'Hagan of the advance schedule. He considered the 'nasty *and* violent' *The Desperados* (1968/18.11.1974) to be 'a film which we could well do without'. On the basis of a synopsis, O'Hagan thought that *A Town Called Bastard* (1971/09.08.1976) made '*The Wild Bunch* sound like *Mary Poppins*'.[71] An IBA monitor later commented of *A Man for Hanging* (1972/16.08.1976): 'This mindless rubbish just about manages to fill the time between the ads. Pretentious; painful. *Don't* show it again.'[72]

Despite these internal reservations, the Authority received only four public complaints: three were about the late hour at which the films were shown and one concerned the cuts made to the first, *Two Mules for Sister Sara* (1970/28.06.1976). This film was later cited in two *TV Times* articles explaining the challenges ITV's editors faced with violent films and giving different accounts of what had happened with it.[73] The film had been acquired in a version pre-censored for American television (a 'TV version') and further cuts were made by Leslie Halliwell to make it suitable for what had initially been envisaged as a 9.00pm start. An ATV officer, responding to a local complainant, remarked that he did not know why these cuts had not been restored when the film – certificated 'A' by the BBFC – was rescheduled for the later slot.[74] Another viewer wrote to the London *Evening Standard* to opine that the series should have been retitled 'The Censored West', noting that *Two Mules for Sister Sara* 'had every mild swear word deleted and every scene of violence removed, destroying any sense of continuity'.[75]

Otherwise, the series as a whole was well received (see Table 11.3). The IBA noted that ratings were particularly strong for the only two titles with significant reputations, *Two Mules for Sister Sara* and *Bandolero!* (1968/12.07.1976); Appreciation Indices had also been high for most of them. Viewing panels surveyed by the Authority's research arm, Audience Reaction Assessment (AURA), gave their endorsement to *Two Mules for Sister Sara*, with eight favourable comments ('a very high number in relation to the normal level of comments'). Two critical comments were made on the violence in each of *The Desperados* and *Dirty Little Billy* (1972/02.08.1976).[76]

Two years later, a second season of 'The Savage West' was networked during the 1978 World Cup, though this time it comprised only three films. The series' title was also borrowed by several companies, including Granada, HTV and YTV, for locally-programmed slots. In between the two seasons, ITV networked three other major Westerns that might otherwise have found a place in the series, each of which posed its own challenges for schedulers and regulators.

Table 11.3 Ratings and Appreciation Indices for 'The Savage West' (ITV, June–August 1976).

Film	Year	TX Date	Stations	Rating	A.I.
Two Mules for Sister Sara	1970	28.06.1976	ITV Network	27	83
The McMasters	1970	05.07.1976	ITV Network	15	73
Bandolero!	1968	12.07.1976	ITV Network	24	75
The Desperados	1968	19.07.1976	ITV Network	18	67
Cry Blood, Apache	1970	26.07.1976	ITV exc. HTV	17	79
Dirty Little Billy	1972	02.08.1976	ITV exc. HTV	16	55
A Town Called Bastard	1971	09.08.1976	ITV exc. HTV	19	55
A Man for Hanging	1972	16.08.1976	ITV exc. HTV	n/a	n/a
Minnesota Clay	1964	23.08.1976	ITV exc. HTV	n/a	n/a

Source: Adapted from memo, Desmond J. Vick to Bernard Sendall, 23 August 1976, IBA/01024: 3996310.

Some viewers who saw *The Wild Bunch* (1969/29.07.1976) on its initial British release later recalled it as the full, original version running 145 minutes, the one approved by director Sam Peckinpah.[77] But evidence from the time suggests otherwise. As passed by the BBFC on 29 July 1969, the official UK running time was 138 minutes, 21 seconds. According to the current BBFC website, the censors made seven small cuts to the version submitted; other sources claim that cuts were also made to another scene, in all totalling ten seconds. It can be concluded, therefore, that the film had been shortened by the distributor, Warner-Seven Arts, even before it reached the BBFC, though not by as much as the ten minutes cut for the US release.[78]

The UK television rights were acquired by ITV in 1975 and the print supplied was another pre-edited American TV version. Leslie Halliwell and LWT's scheduler, Cyril Bennett, made additional cuts of 'close-up shock moments', totalling around ninety seconds.[79] They provisionally scheduled the networked premiere for 8.15pm, in the 'Saturday Action Film' strand during the Olympic summer. But after previewing it, the IBA ruled that it was completely unsuitable for family viewing time, even with cuts, commenting: 'The film has no message; is if anything immoral and illustrates Peckinpah's preoccupation with violence for its own sake.' Bennett replied to defend both his judgement and the film, declaring: 'The "message" is that violence, in any form is anti-life. I'm truly sorry the point was lost at Brompton Road.' Bernard Sendall subsequently dismissed this as 'twaddle' and the film was duly rescheduled to start at 9.00pm.[80] According to one programme controller, on transmission it ran 129 minutes, 25 seconds, which equated to about 135 minutes at cinema speed.[81]

Even before the broadcast, the Authority had received a five-page letter from an irate viewer complaining about the rumoured cuts. Several more letters were received soon after it went out and another the following year. Only one viewer complained about the film itself, referring to it as 'sick and degenerate' trash that should never have been shown. The others all objected to the cuts, on the grounds that they marred the film's artistic integrity.[82] The controversy extended to the press, one persistent correspondent writing to at least three trade papers, as well as directly to the IBA, to insist that ITV's version of the film had run up to seventeen minutes short of its full length and complaining that no attempt had been made to acquire the longer version(s).[83] The Authority's stock response, in both private and public correspondence, was that less than two minutes of material had been removed by ITV before transmission and that this was not sufficient to harm the film significantly. However, the credibility of its position was marred by persistent misinformation about the length of the version originally seen in Britain and the provenance of the cuts made to it in the US. With Halliwell as its source, the IBA claimed that these cuts had been made by the film's original editor, 'presumably' with Peckinpah's knowledge and approval, rather than by the distributor. Halliwell himself admitted that he had not seen the film prior to previewing the TV version, making his account of its troubled history less than persuasive.[84]

The film critic of the *Evening Standard*, Alexander Walker, also joined in the attack. Walker had an additional reason to feel aggrieved: he had been commissioned to write an article for *TVTimes*, used as the magazine's cover story in the week of transmission, in which he defended the film's violence against criticisms that it was gratuitous (see Figure 11.4).[85] Yet when he came to view the broadcast version he found that much of what he had been defending had been removed. 'Perhaps I should have received fewer complaining letters,' mused Walker, 'had the IBA insisted on altering *The Wild Bunch*'s credits to: Directed by Sam Peckinpah, with additional cuts by Leslie Halliwell.'[86]

For the film's second transmission, part-networked at Christmas 1978, Halliwell located a version 'eight minutes longer' and then 'cut half a minute of a throat-slitting scene', commenting: 'We don't have to have that sort of thing in the living-room.'[87] Unlike the premiere, the repeat brought no complaints to the IBA. As Ed Buscombe recalled in his *Sight and Sound* review of the 1995 'restored' theatrical reissue, subsequent broadcasts included all the scenes that had been cut from the US version. Only Halliwell's trims remained missing from ITV's print, as Buscombe explained: 'so for example when Mapache cuts Angel's throat, we don't actually see the blood spurt in the TV version, as we do on the big screen'.[88] Otherwise, the new version restored relatively little that British television viewers had not seen already.

Soldier Blue (1977/18.09.1977) was, if anything, even more notorious for extreme violence than *The Wild Bunch*. The print acquired by ITV was a US reissue version that had been re-edited by the distributor to achieve a 'PG' rating, reportedly removing around four minutes of footage from the climactic massacre by cavalrymen of an Indian village. When ITV's scheduling plans were first announced in the press, the film's director Ralph Nelson was quoted as saying that this version was a 'misrepresentation' of his work: 'ITV are capitalising on the title of a successful film. They are guilty of false advertising.'[89] No additional cuts were made when *Soldier Blue* was transmitted at 10.00pm on a Sunday

Figure 11.4a–b *TVTimes* prepared viewers for the network premiere of *The Wild Bunch* (1969) on 31 July 1976 but didn't mention the cuts. *TVTimes* © Future Publishing Ltd. Artwork © Giannetto Coppola.

evening; despite the late hour, JICTAR placed it in the ratings top ten for the week.

The IBA received three letters of complaint, all about the cuts made to the original film. Both an ITV executive and an IBA officer privately expressed some sympathy with these complaints. Mansel Lloyd, Head of Film Clearance at YTV, disapproved of the film's pre-censorship by its distributor, saying that 'the editorial responsibilities for purchased programmes should not be delegated to outside bodies'.[90] Dermot O'Hagan agreed in principle, commenting that if films had to be edited, 'this is better done by "us" rather than by "them"', though in this case he did not think that the distributor had done 'all that bad a job'. But he also sympathised with a complainant who said that viewers should have been warned beforehand that the film had been edited from its theatrical version and that it should not have been promoted as if it were the original.[91] Programme Officer Michael Gillies's reply to this viewer admitted: 'It might have been helpful if the films page of TV Times had indicated which version was to be shown.'[92] The question of whether advance billing should indicate when a film had been edited, for any reason, was one that had lain around the ITV system for many years without being resolved. This was perhaps the first time it was acknowledged internally that broadcasters might have a responsibility to declare in advance billing that a film was not the original version seen in cinemas.

Sergio Leone's *Once upon a Time in the West* (1968/01.05.1978) had been on ITV's books for several years before it was finally scheduled. Its length (165 minutes, or 158 minutes at telecine speed) and a climactic scene involving a hanging, which meant that under IBA rules it could not be shown starting before 9.30pm, combined to keep it off the air until the UK's first May Day Bank Holiday.[93] The IBA consented to a 9.15pm start and though it had asked ITV staff to pay 'due attention' to 'violent sequences', the film was shown uncut. Leslie Halliwell set out the companies' position:

> The Film Clearance Committee looked at it yesterday and decided there is nothing which can or should be cut. The shooting of the boy is not seen, and is indeed the subject of a rather callous joke; the hanging sequence comes extremely late and is done as a dream flashback with 'poetic' music, which means that it cant be trimmed [*sic*]. The rest of the violence is no worse than one would encounter in an average western, or indeed in our own homes…[94]

ITV's transmission was the first public showing of the full-length version in the UK; the original 1969 theatrical release, with a BBFC 'A' certificate, had run 144 minutes. The only letter received by the IBA was, for once, one of praise: a viewer who had previously complained of cuts to films including *Two Mules for Sister Sara*, *The Wild Bunch* and *Soldier Blue* wrote that he had been taken aback by the 'complete (almost) version' presented, adding only a request that the widescreen film subsequently be shown letterboxed, 'so that more of the picture may be seen'.[95]

Sex before Bedtime: 'For Adults Only'

Announcing ITV's 1977 summer film series to the press, Leslie Halliwell made the connection to the previous year's late-night strand: 'They were heavy Westerns. These films will be heavy dramas.' He elaborated: 'We have sex films – what I would call adult melodrama. They are sexy, but not terribly explicit. Anything they contain has been seen on television plenty of times before.'[96] He probably didn't expect any fuss. Locally for Granada, Halliwell had been programming film strands under the title 'For Adults Only' almost every year since 1968; ATV had used it too, with nothing more than an occasional raised eyebrow from the Authority. But the promise of sexy adult films was too easy a target for the national press to miss. The series received more column inches than was normal for a TV publicity launch, accompanied by headlines such as 'Naughty Nights on ITV', 'ITV to Show "Mostly Sex" X-films', 'A Sizzling Summer of Sex Films on STV', 'Monday Is Sex Cert Night on ITV' and 'TV Porn Shocker: Sit Back for Sex Films before Bedtime'.[97]

The IBA was unsurprised at the furore. When first informed of ITV's scheduling plans in April, officers had expressed some reservations, which continued to mount as details of the series became clearer. Authority staff had three areas of concern: the general quality of the films selected; the problematic nature of some of their contents; and the idea of presenting them under the umbrella title 'For Adults Only'. Dermot O'Hagan had at first been in favour of the latter but soon changed his mind.[98] Noting that ATV was also 'uneasy' about the title, David Glencross made an oblique reference to pornography: 'Such a title might be interpreted as a breakthrough for the kind of feature film which has not been previously shown on Independent Television.'[99] Director of Television Colin Shaw added that it was 'worth asking whether the use of the series title is going to confer upon the films a cachet which might prove somewhat embarrassing and might harm the interests of a rather more considerable series of films on another occasion.'[100] ITV's Programme Controllers Group, which had programmed the series, dug in its heels, arguing that the title served as 'a warning to the audience of the nature of the films' rather than, as the IBA saw it, a 'come-on'. The Authority reluctantly consented, noting that while the films added nothing to ITV's reputation, they were 'not so extreme that it would be reasonable to ban them en bloc'.[101]

Of the eight films initially chosen for the series, all network premieres, IBA staff considered only the first, Clint Eastwood's *Play Misty for Me* (1971/04.07.1977), to be at all 'distinguished' (see Table 11.4). Finding that their reviews in the BFI's *Monthly Film Bulletin* made 'depressing' reading, officers asked to preview several other titles before giving their consent to broadcast. They approved *Assault* (1971/18.07.1977), *Doctors' Wives* (1971/25.07.1977), *The Seven Minutes* (1971/08.08.1977) and *No Blade of Grass* (1971/15.08.1977) only after editing had removed shots of rape victims, a surgical operation, frank sexual language and extensive scenes of violence, respectively. *No Blade of Grass* was a borderline

Table 11.4 'For Adults Only' (ITV, July–August 1977).

Film	Year	TX Date	Stations
Play Misty for Me	1971	04.07.1977	ITV Network
The Chase	1966	11.07.1977	Thames, Anglia
Hustling (TVM)	1975	11.07.1977	ATV, YTV, TTT, UTV, WTV, CTV, BTV
Police Woman: The Trick Book (TVM)	1976	11.07.1977	Granada, STV, HTV, Southern, Grampian
Assault	1971	18.07.1977	ITV Network
Doctors' Wives	1971	25.07.1977	ITV excluding STV
Little Ladies of the Night (TVM)	1977	01.08.1977	ITV Network
The Seven Minutes	1971	08.08.1977	ITV excluding HTV
Willard	1971	08.08.1977	HTV
No Blade of Grass	1971	15.08.1977	ITV Network
The Beguiled	1971	22.08.1977	ITV Network

Note: Most stations carried the films on Monday nights on the dates shown, except for Anglia Television, which showed them on Friday nights in the same weeks. TVM = made-for-TV movie.

case that staff, considering it 'one of the most violent films that any of us can recall seeing for some time', thought fell fowl of the ITV Code on Violence.[102]

Ultimately only one film was rejected: Roger Vadim's *Pretty Maids All in a Row* (1971/02.06.1978). Its withdrawal at a relatively late stage, after it had been announced, created other problems besides the loss of prestige. One of the film's stars, Angie Dickinson, had been chosen as *TV Times*'s cover star for the week, and it was too late to change the cover image. Consequently, Thames and Anglia filled the gap with a repeat of an older Dickinson film, *The Chase* (1966/10.10.1971), and several other stations substituted a feature-length episode of her current TV series, *Police Woman*. Although *Pretty Maids All in a Row* was later accepted for broadcast with substantial editing, O'Hagan considered the film 'basically second rate soft-core porn with more than its fair share of nudity, murders (with vague hints of sado-masochism) and phallic references'.[103] Its proposed presentation in a prominent networked slot was one of the factors that led officers to 'query the wisdom of showing it under this generic title'. Staff also felt that the series as a whole raised wider concerns:

> In a more general context, what we so-far know and have seen of these films does seem to us to put a question mark against ITV's whole policy of feature film purchase. It also questions the wisdom of networking these sort of film [*sic*] – since they are not the sort of material which the Authority had in mind when it urged the companies to consider more networking of feature films. Finally, these films seem to us to add weight to the adjective used in the Annan Report to describe ITV's choice of feature films – 'deplorable'.[104]

At the launch, Halliwell had virtually admitted that the films had been programmed simply because they were available and had been paid for. 'As we buy films we tend to collect them in packages and these are some we have collected recently', he said. 'I would not describe them as the greatest films ever made, but they are interesting and worth showing.'[105] He acknowledged that they would need to be edited, but added: 'we will not be cutting the films so much that we will ruin them'. Referring to *Assault*, Halliwell explained: 'In one film we will be cutting out the last scream of a girl as she is raped. So instead of there being three screams, there will only be two.'[106]

Prospective viewers were not encouraged. The IBA recorded that in June, before the series started, it had received thirty-one complaints about 'For Adults Only', among the half-dozen largest critical postbags received for any programme in the past two-and-a-half years.[107] Ultimately, there were more: I counted fifty-six letters and records of phone calls related to the series in the IBA Archives. The overwhelming majority based their complaints on nothing more than the press reports, many believing that ITV planned to show pornography. Only one criticised the content of a film (*Play Misty for Me*) after viewing it. Four correspondents welcomed the series but complained about the late hour; three other letters came from the landlord of a seaside guest-house whose residents had come back to their lodgings early to see the films and gone to bed disappointed by the lack of truly adult material; and one, written by the future horror novelist Stephen Laws on behalf of himself and twelve other viewers, criticised the cutting of *No Blade of Grass*. That film had been heavily cut by the BBFC on its theatrical release at the behest of the distributor, MGM-EMI, and in consultation with its director, Cornel Wilde, so that it could receive an 'AA' certificate instead of an 'X'. The version received by ITV was, for a change, the full-length original. Halliwell was therefore able to reply quite honestly that, even with extensive editing (the IBA requested seven specific cuts), ITV had shown a more complete version than had been seen in UK cinemas.[108]

Despite their own reservations about the series, Authority officers were nevertheless obliged to defend their decision to allow the films to be shown. Responding to one complainant, the Chairman, Lady Plowden, pointed out:

> The facts do not seem to bear out your belief that the series has given offence to the vast majority of people. Although our research is not yet complete, it appears that, despite extensive publicity about the films to be shown, larger numbers of people than usual chose to watch at 10.30 pm on Mondays. I agree that the nature of some of the films shown could give offence to some people, but their numbers were perhaps not so great as early newspaper reports had suggested.[109]

Expletives (Sometimes) Deleted: Bad Language

In a 1978 paper, BBC Controller of Programmes Alasdair Milne discussed the problems posed by some recent acquisitions:

> In judging feature films great care is taken not to create any double standard as between such films and BBC-originated output. In general it is the BBC's policy as a matter of scholarship

to put films out as works of art, i.e. as originally made for the cinema. The BBC does not trim or edit to save time. However, it has been recently forced to cut more than it used to do. The reason has generally been to get rid of bad language. It is clear that for the immediate future the language used in many of the more recent feature films is the factor that presents the greatest difficulty when judging the film's suitability for television. The Television Service continues to feel that an absolute ban must be placed on the transmission of certain words.[110]

In an earlier paper, Milne gave the example of *Five Easy Pieces* (1970/30.12.1976), which had received a BBFC 'AA' certificate and was edited by the BBC to delete 'half a dozen words'. A dozen letters of complaint were still received from viewers.[111] Leslie Halliwell, sensitive to the common criticism that ITV regularly cut films, offered a journalist his own views on BBC policy:

> I saw last week in some paper that the BBC, of course, never cut films. Don't you believe it – the BBC do cut films, otherwise they wouldn't be able to play them. They cut the best line out of *The Owl and the Pussycat*, where Barbra Streisand asks some fellows to fuck off. The line had just gone, making no sense of the scene. They cut the fuck song out of *Taking Off* – just gone completely.[112]

The BBC's chief in-house editor during his thirty-year stint at the Corporation, Ken Locke, became renowned for his ability to edit soundtracks seamlessly, often by taking substitute words from other parts of the film to replace unusable dialogue. In his interview for the British Entertainment History Project, Locke recalled being described as the Corporation's 'fuck remover'.[113]

Complaints to the IBA about bad language, like those about sex and violence, mounted after the mid-1970s. In 1975, viewers complained about the expression 'balling a chick' in *Bob & Carol & Ted & Alice* and about 'the worst of the four letter words' being used in *The Killing of Sister George* (though in fact 'fuck' is mouthed silently rather than spoken aloud).[114] But much milder terms could also cause offence. Later the same year, one viewer complained that in *Lawrence of Arabia* (1962/22 & 23.12.1975), 'the American newsman is made to exclaim "Jesus wept" as an oath, immediately followed by the expletive "bloody" on at least two occasions'.[115]

Casual blasphemy and common vulgarity were regular causes of concern, but more serious problems could occasionally arise. Perhaps the earliest major example was the film adaptation of James Joyce's novel *Ulysses* (1967/05.09.1973). Director Joseph Strick had retained the graphic sexual language of Molly Bloom's soliloquy, including a single use of the word 'fuck'. When it was submitted for cinema certification, the BBFC asked for a number of deletions, including twenty-nine specific lines of dialogue. Strick reluctantly complied in order to meet contractual conditions laid down by the distributor; but he had also submitted the film to the more lenient Greater London Council (GLC) censorship board, which passed it uncut. Many other local authorities banned *Ulysses*, but in 1970, following the changes made that year to its certification system, the BBFC accepted it uncut for the 'X' category.[116]

The BBC acquired the film in 1968 as part of its British Lion package deal (see Chapter 5). After the usual five-year embargo was up, the Corporation proposed to show the uncut version. Mary Whitehouse demanded that the film, which she described as 'quite unacceptable in the homes of the vast majority of people', be previewed by the BBC's Board of Governors and General Advisory Council so that they could make any cuts believed necessary.[117] The broadcast went ahead, the Governors reportedly having been informed of it 'some time' before. Whitehouse, who 'had deliberately missed part of her dinner to watch the film at 9.05 pm', commented: 'I have no hesitation in saying that the soliloquy by Molly was the most obscene scene shown on television.'[118]

It is very likely that the film's basis in a literary classic, albeit a controversial one, accounted for the BBC's liberal treatment. It was scheduled as the second of two Joyce adaptations shown in BBC2's 'World Cinema' strand. No specific advance warning appeared in *Radio Times*, though Philip Jenkinson's review in his weekly film column referred to the soliloquy, 'which predictably had puritans foaming at the mouth and which now – equally predictably – makes one wonder what, conceivably, all the fuss was about'.[119] If the BBC received complaints, none subsequently appeared in *Radio Times*. JICTAR's minute-by-minute ratings chart showed that, throughout its duration in London, *Ulysses* achieved a TVR ranging between 9 and 13 (average 11, or a 24 per cent share of the potential audience). These were by far the channel's highest viewing figures of the day.[120]

Both the BBC and the IBA required films to be held to the same criteria as in-house TV productions. Until the late 1960s, these had generally remained on a par, but thereafter the film industry streaked ahead of (or dropped below, depending on viewpoint) domestic standards. This was made clear when films adapted from television series took advantage of the greater permissiveness enjoyed by the cinema. *The Alf Garnett Saga* (1972/21.11.1977) is a case in point. This was the second of two films based on the situation comedy *Till Death Us Do Part*. Although the series had been made by the BBC – which acquired the first spinoff film, also called *Till Death Us Do Part* (1968/09.10.1978) – the sequel was bought by ITV and scheduled for a Saturday-night summer network slot, beginning at 9.15pm, following the 1978 World Cup quarter-final playoff. The IBA received at least twenty-four complaints, 'centred on language, racial slurs and sexual innuendo'. Authority staff broadly agreed with the complainants, having had reservations about the film's placing in a prominent slot following the football, 'which would presumably have carried over a sizable proportion of young viewers'.[121]

There had been advance notice that such problems might occur. On the film's only previous transmission, by Border Television the year before, the local IBA monitor had diligently noted 151 instances of swearing: 'bloody' was used 106 times, 'bleeding' fourteen, 'bollocks' eleven, 'sod' ten, 'piss' six, 'guit' (*sic*) twice, and 'bastard' and 'ass' once each.[122] The 'racial slurs and sexual innuendo' were apparently not considered serious enough to record in detail. The film had been certificated Post-9.00 by LWT's Margaret Walker, who had done so believing 'that the expletives are all second class swearing, i.e. no four letter unmentionables'. Dermot O'Hagan, noting that the Authority received 'more complaints about bad language' than about violence or sex, requested that the certificate be changed to Post-10.30. But Network Certification Officer Ken Fletcher pointed out that Post-10.30 was by agreement only a recommendation, not a formal category, which would have amounted to a second watershed. A note by O'Hagan to his Authority colleagues suggested that an additional such category might yet be considered; at that time, 'given the strong incidence of strong "X" films at the moment', there was 'no alternative' but to insist on Post-10.30 for some titles. He conveyed this to Fletcher, pointing out that some ITV productions such as plays and documentaries had also been placed after *News at Ten* 'because of content problems'. In the case of *The Alf Garnett Saga* (which had received a BBFC 'AA' certificate), the recommendation was clearly not followed, although O'Hagan had repeated his caution when the network scheduling was announced.[123]

Stephen Murphy resolved in future to 'harden up' the film's certificate to Post-10.30. But in setting out the Authority's 'agreed line' on it he remarked:

> We are, however, a little surprised that the title itself did not remind people of the Alf Garnett character. It was a six year old movie based on an eleven [actually twelve] year old television series *Till Death Us Do Part*, and had many of the original characteristics. (The language was a bit worse – though no more frequent.) This may suggest to some people that standards on television are *not* dropping – rather the reverse.[124]

As the decade wore on and language (among other things) in films became stronger, broadcasters were faced with increasingly tough choices: to cut or not to cut? Perceived quality and creative integrity often made the difference. When ITV acquired *Deliverance* (1972/07.10.1978), there was some doubt at the IBA that the film could be shown at all. There were two particular areas of concern: several uses of strong language, including in voice-over dialogue during the opening sequence; and a scene of prolonged homosexual rape and sexual assault. As Secretary of the BBFC when the film was released theatrically, Stephen Murphy had supervised the editing of the rape scene to achieve an 'X' certificate, but neither he nor the director, John Boorman, had been satisfied with the results. Recalling this experience, Murphy commented to his colleagues at the Authority: 'I have seen nothing on television approaching this scene.'[125] Other staff agreed that *Deliverance* 'pushes the frontiers a little further back'.[126] Adding to the IBA's worries was the fact that ITV schedulers proposed to show the film in a networked slot during the 1977 Christmas period, starting at 9.15pm after an abbreviated news bulletin. The Authority rejected it for such an early hour at any time and particularly at Christmas, but considered that the film could be approved for a later slot if suitably edited. A memo instructing an officer accordingly remarked: 'We suggest you say 22.30 was our ruling, but allow yourself to give in to pressure for 22.00 if they insist. (It is an excellent and prestigious film.)'[127]

Seven instances of swearing were 'blooped' from the soundtrack without physical cuts to the print and the rape scene was carefully edited. Officers felt 'that congratulations are due for a highly professional and sensitive editing job on a very difficult film'.[128] When *Deliverance* was eventually transmitted on the network, at 10.15pm on an autumn Saturday, the Authority apparently received no complaints. But three years later, a part-networked repeat at 9.20pm, again on a Saturday, brought eight letters of protest, mainly at the language rather than the rape. Investigation revealed that the blooping ink used to remove the swear words had been partially washed off when the 35mm print was cleaned, inadvertently restoring two uses of 'fuck'.[129] The fact that these came in the opening minutes meant that some viewers were so offended that they switched off before even getting to the rape scene. Responding to one complainant, Director General Sir Brian Young explained the Authority's difficulties:

> I am sorry that you were offended by some of the language in this film. It illustrates very sharply the dilemma we face in deciding whether to show on television some of the more recent productions for the cinema. The IBA accepts that many viewers are offended by the use of bad language on television but on the other hand viewers object to what they call the mutilation of films which results from editing. There is no solution to this problem which will satisfy everyone, but in general our view is that provided a film is of sufficient merit, and provided it is shown at a sufficiently late hour in the evening so as to ensure that children are not viewing in any large numbers, it would be wrong to insist that all bad language should be edited out. These are, however, difficult areas of judgment and I would not wish to pretend that our decision will always be the right one.[130]

Coming Clean

As several of the cases discussed in this chapter demonstrate, broadcasters realised that with certain films they would inevitably receive complaints whether or not they chose to edit them for content. The more popular or well-regarded the film, the more criticism they were likely to get if they cut it. In the autumn of 1979, following a ten-week hiatus from August to October caused by the longest period of industrial action in its history, ITV resumed transmissions in a week 'front-loaded' with major film premieres. But all four networked films suffered cuts: *Chinatown* (1974/24.10.1979) lost the crucial part of the scene in which Jack Nicholson's character has his nose slit; a bloody amputation and a bathtub love scene were omitted from *Gold* (1974/27.10.1979), even though the latter had been used in advance promotions; and both *The Last Detail* (1973/27.10.1979) and *Walking Tall* (1973/30.10.1979) were shown in US TV versions that removed their original bad language and violence, respectively. Messages of complaint said that viewers should have been informed beforehand that they were about to see edited versions, not the cinema originals.

The following year, ITV tested the limits of what was permissible with three films, all broadcast at 9.00pm on Mondays: *Marathon Man* (1976/01.09.1980),

California Split (1974/22.09.1980) and *The Mean Machine* (1974/27.10.1980). *Marathon Man* was transmitted uncut, preceded by a verbal warning announcement; viewers in the ATV and Southern areas saw the IBA's onscreen warning symbol throughout the transmission (see Chapter 9). *California Split* was also shown intact, but without a warning of any kind; apparently the decision not to cut it was based on a misunderstanding between Leslie Halliwell and an IBA Regional Officer. The bad language in *The Mean Machine* was edited out of the first hour, shown before *News at Ten* (all three films straddled the news bulletin), but retained for the remainder, giving viewers of the first part a false sense of civility.[131] Halliwell later acknowledged that these films contained 'the kind of language which would have been unthinkable twelve months earlier'. He went on:

> The Authority has generally encouraged the playing of adult feature films which include a measure of sex, violence and profanity, providing that the films can be seriously defended as adult in the full meaning of the word. ... On the whole it does no harm to any film to have moments of violence or sex toned down by editing, but language is more difficult, as well as being, apparently, the most offensive to viewers. Sometimes we elect to go for a television version but then run the risk of being accused of emasculating the film. All of us would like to transmit good films intact, but we must be sure that they deserve this favoured treatment.[132]

The IBA received thirteen complaints about *Marathon Man*, twenty-four about *California Split* and at least four about *The Mean Machine*.[133] One viewer, who noted that *California Split* contained the word 'motherfucker' in its first ten minutes, referred approvingly to the BBC's practice of cutting out such words. Several other letters about *California Split* invoked the kind of vivid invasive imagery often deployed by complainants (emphases mine):

> 'I write to ask to please stop *raping our living room* with your filth and obscenities.'

> 'In these days one can hear such words anywhere, but it appals me to think they can *invade my home* through the medium of television.'

> 'If I used that language in the street I could be prosecuted for obscenity – yet you *push it into my house*, where my family is listening.'[134]

The first of these comments may have been triggered by an article in the *Daily Mail*, 'The Rape of Your Living Room', prompted by the broadcast of *Marathon Man* and cited by several complainants. Its author wrote to the Authority to say that he had received 'well over 100' letters of support from readers, the strongest response to any article he had written in his twenty-year career.[135]

The complaints went higher than the IBA, which was sent copies of all relevant correspondence received by Government. A local councillor wrote to the Chief Constable of his area and to the Home Secretary about *California Split*. A viewer incensed by *The Mean Machine* wrote to his local MP, who forwarded the letter to 10 Downing Street and received a personal reply from Prime Minister Margaret Thatcher.[136] Another Member of Parliament, Norman Tebbit, wrote to Home

Office minister Leon Brittan on behalf of two of his own constituents who had sent him a clipping of the *Daily Mail* article. Fortunately, the Home Office had its own standard response to requests for intervention: 'responsibility for programme content rests with the broadcasting authorities' and it was governmental policy that 'the broadcasting authorities should be assured their independence in matters of programme content and scheduling, taking relevant factors into account, including the time when children might normally be expected to be viewing'.[137]

IBA staff held the line. Of these three films, officers were most vigorous in their defence of *Marathon Man*, which had enjoyed particularly high viewing figures and Appreciation Indices. They were less forthright in defending *California Split*, while acknowledging that the film, directed by Robert Altman, had received some critical acclaim:

> We would accept that some of the language in the film was not completely justified by the quality of the theme or its treatment, neither of which seemed strong enough to bear the weight of words placed on it. That is in contrast to the film *Marathon Man*, shown a little while before and which earned a very high appreciation from the audience.

The Authority again pointed out the problems inherent in modern films:

> The cinema in the past decade or so has made much greater use of both language and subject-matter which could not then have found a place on television, but which may, with the passing of time and the changing of standards, become more acceptable as programmes for television. Deciding where to draw the line is a matter for judgment in each individual case, and we are almost certain to make a wrong choice from time to time, erring on the side of caution unnecessarily in some cases, going too far in the other direction in other cases.[138]

The following year, ITV networked *Death Wish* (1974/16.05.1981) at 9.20pm on a Saturday. The opening rape-and-murder scene was heavily edited (or as Leslie Halliwell put it, 'cut to ribbons'); yet multiple instances of swearing, including not only four-letter words but also 'the multi-syllabled variety' (Halliwell again), were retained.[139] The IBA received eight complaints: six about the language and two about the cutting. Officers were however forearmed with audience research which showed that not only had the film topped the ratings for the week with nearly 16 million viewers (twice the number expected for the time of transmission), but it had also enjoyed an unusually high Appreciation Index of 85, with 206 viewers out of 238 surveyed describing it as either 'Very' or 'Extremely' interesting and/or enjoyable.[140] Among the complaints was one from Mary Whitehouse, enclosing an NVALA monitor's report. Filling a typewritten page, the latter concluded:

> The film, at 9.20pm, could have been acceptable family viewing as the violence, even that of the original mugging was subdued, but the language simply made family viewing an embarrassment. It was a pity that a film dealing with a theme that has become part of modern life, i.e. the mugging of the helpless, and treating it in an exciting and novel way was disfigured by the unnecessary and repetitive use of disgusting language.[141]

In her covering letter, Whitehouse raised an issue that prompted the Authority to seek legal advice: she claimed that the word 'motherfucker', used liberally in the film, had 'been found obscene by the courts', therefore ITV was in breach of the law. A legal opinion confirmed that the claim was misleading. Replying to Whitehouse, IBA Chairman Lord Thomson of Monifieth commented:

> It does seem to us that this question raises a more important issue than the question which is concentrated on by your monitor and others who have complained about this film, namely, whether it is justifiable when portraying the actions of evil people to also depict the language which they use themselves and provoke in others.[142]

Nevertheless, the Authority took the complaints seriously and asked for the offending word to be edited out of the film's repeat transmission. Conversely, it allowed the reinstatement of material previously cut from *The Wild Bunch*, *Chinatown* and *Gold*, whose removal had upset many viewers.

Despite their sympathy with viewer complaints, IBA officers were doubtful about both the wisdom and the practicability of advertising the fact that a film had been cut. However, they eventually consented to a brief notice, jointly written by the Authority's Director of Television, Colin Shaw, and *TVTimes* editor Peter Jackson, being placed on the magazine's film page. It explained ITV's internal certification system and advised that BBFC certificates were not used in promotion because they did not always 'refer to the version shown on television'.[143] This item, headlined 'Putting You in the Picture', appeared at irregular intervals from late 1979, presumably when space considerations allowed. But it was not until 1981 that David Quinlan's film reviews first identified particular films as being shown in abridged versions. *Saturday Night Fever* (1977/29.07.1981) was transmitted in an early-evening slot on the Prince and Princess of Wales's wedding day in the edited version that had been released in UK cinemas with a BBFC 'A' certificate, subsequent to the original 'X'-rated release. This was flagged in Quinlan's column; so, later, was the fact that rape-revenge drama *Lipstick* (1976/07.11.1981) was to be broadcast in an American TV version. The reviewer also thoughtfully advised readers that the networked repeat of *Chinatown* in June 1981 included 'a scene you'll find intact in this fuller version of the film than that previously screened on television'.[144] Such liberalisation was not to last in the following years, when sanitised TV versions became more commonplace.

Notes

1 See John Gillett, 'Film into Detergent', *Sight and Sound* 40, no. 1 (Winter 1970–71): 22. The examples cited here, disowned by their directors, are Joseph Losey's *Secret Ceremony* (1968/27.11.1974) and Peter Hall's *Three into Two Won't Go* (1969/04.12.1974), both released by MCA-Universal, neither of which was broadcast in its re-edited form in the UK.

2 Margaret Walker to Dermot O'Hagan, 3 January 1974, IBA/01023: 3996311.

3 'A Reel Clanger', *Daily Star*, 26 November 1979.

4 'UK Television Licences', *Terramedia*, online at https://www.terramedia.co.uk/reference/statistics/television/television_licences.htm.

5 Aside from an occasional rare instance, computer colourisation of black-and-white films has never been accepted as a standard practice on British television.

6 'Different Aspect Gives a Better View', *Scan and Television News* 3, no. 1 (May 1950): 7. The change is also discussed in D.C. Birkinshaw, 'The Shape of Your Television Picture', *Radio Times*, 31 March 1950, 43. The author was BBC Television's Superintendent Engineer.

7 Leslie Halliwell, 'How We Buy the Films for ITV and What the Problems Can Be', *The Stage and Television Today*, 10 July 1975, 17.

8 Su Holmes claims that Twentieth Century-Fox's CinemaScope production *Black Widow* (1954/12.04.1969) was broadcast on ITV in London at Christmas 1956 (*British TV & Film Culture in the 1950s*, 228). In fact, the film in question was Hammer's pre-'Scope British 'B' picture *The Black Widow* (1951/23.12.1956).

9 Film Man, comment on 'Broadcasting Films on Television', 13 October 2011, at www.britmovie.com. I am grateful to Julian Upton for sharing his MA research on this topic. The earliest transmission date on Granada I can find for *To Hell and Back* (1955/02.12.1971) is 26 January 1973, so Film Man may be thinking of another film.

10 Bill Gilbert, 'Early Days of TV Acquisition, *The Veteran* 136 (Autumn 2012), 20. *Storm over the Nile* was repeated on BBC2 on 05.02.1966, so perhaps this was the panned-and-scanned transmission. *Three Men in a Boat* was shown by BBC Television on 27.10.1962.

11 Tony Bennelick, 'Booms, Boats and Boobs' (letter), *Radio Times*, 11 December 1980, 83.

12 Letters from Roy Arblaster, Philip Billinge, Peter J. Brown and Lee Menham, '"2001" Wasn't Good Enough…', *Radio Times*, 21 January 1982, 76.

13 The cuts made to this version are described, quoting Richards, in Allen Eyles, 'On TV', *Film and Filming* 19, no. 6 (March 1973): 74–5.

14 Programme listing and Geoff Brown, 'Archers on Target', *Radio Times*, 4 September 1980, 17, 65.

15 Allen Eyles, 'Cinema TV', *Film and Filming* 17, no. 2 (November 1970): 68.

16 Author's interview with Sir Paul Fox, 3 September 2012. Fox later also worked for ITV.

17 Lew Grade to Lord Hill of Luton, 16 February 1965, IBA/01023: 3996311.

18 Richard Roud, 'Big Pictures on the Small Screen', *Guardian*, 11 March 1966, 11; 'Cut out This Butchery of Old Favourites', *Express and Star*, 10 November 1966.

19 John McMillan to Bernard Sendall, 3 August 1965, IBA/01023: 3996311.

20 Hill to Mr R.P., 8 March 1965, IBA/01023: 3996311.

21 Anthony Asquith, Sidney Cole, Paul Dehn, Anthony Havelock-Allan and Ivor Montagu, 'Defamation of Talent' (letter), *The Times*, 23 July 1965, 13. See also the letters, printed under the same heading, from Michael Balcon and Charles Frend in the issues of 27 and 30 July 1965, respectively. Both *Scott of the Antarctic* and *The Cruel Sea* were directed by Frend and produced by Balcon. Cole was the associate producer and Montagu the co-writer of the former. *Orders to Kill* was directed by Asquith, produced by Havelock-Allan and co-written by Dehn. The BBC's Gordon

Smith also wrote to *The Times*, to exempt the Corporation from the filmmakers' charges (24 July, 7).

22   Leslie Halliwell, quoted in Cecil Bernstein to Sendall, 3 August 1965, IBA/01023: 3996311.

23   Grade to Sendall, 2 August 1965, IBA/01023: 3996311.

24   Halliwell to Bernstein, 7 June 1966, IBA/01023: 3996311.

25   Ibid.

26   Fraser to Sendall, 24 June 1966, IBA/01023: 3996311.

27   'Running Times of Feature Films', n.d. (1966), IBA/01023: 3996311.

28   Stephen Murphy, 'Film Editing', 5 September 1966, IBA/01023: 3996311.

29   Minutes of the 111th Meeting of the Standing Consultative Committee, 'The Arrangements for Editing Feature Films', 14 September 1966, IBA/01023: 3996311.

30   Grade to Sir Robert Fraser, 15 September 1966, IBA/01023: 3996311.

31   Southern Television Limited, 'Feature Films Transmission Year to 18th September, 1966', 22 September 1966, IBA/01023: 3996311.

32   Halliwell, 'Scheduling and Editing of Feature Films', 20 September 1966, IBA/01023: 3996311.

33   Minutes of the Meeting of the Standing Consultative Committee, 'The Cutting of Feature Films', 12 April 1967, IBA/01023: 3996311.

34   Ken Brierley to W.A.C. Collingwood, 12 June 1967, IBA/01023: 3996311.

35   Murphy, 'Cutting of Feature Films', 26 February 1968, IBA/01023: 3996311.

36   Sendall to Grade, 27 February 1968, IBA/01023: 3996311.

37   Grade to Sendall, 29 February 1968, IBA/01023: 3996311.

38   Harold Pinter, 'Pinter Cut' (letter), *Sunday Times*, 16 November 1969, 8; O'Hagan to Murphy, 17 November 1969, IBA/01023: 3996311.

39   Hunter Davies, 'The Mogul of Mass Taste', *Sunday Times*, 5 December 1971, 33.

40   See, for example, Peter Waymark, 'Never Mind the Story Feel the Width', *The Times*, 24 December 1971, 10.

41   Murphy to All Regional Officers, 9 February 1970, IBA/01023: 3996311.

42   O'Hagan to Olive Hennessy, 3 December 1971; Hennessy to O'Hagan, 6 December 1971, IBA/01023: 3996311.

43   Letters from Mr V.C.T., 7 April 1970, and Mr R.H.L., 28 May 1970, IBA/01023: 3996311.

44   O'Hagan to Allen Eyles, 1 October 1971, IBA/01023: 3996311.

45   Allen Eyles, 'TV Cinema', *Films and Filming* 18, no. 3 (December 1971), 68–9; Waymark, 'Never Mind the Story Feel the Width'.

46   Allen Eyles, 'The Mutilators', *Films and Filming* 16, no. 6 (March 1970): 76.

47   Quoted in Allen Eyles, 'Brighter Viewing', *Films and Filming* 16, no. 8 (May 1970): 74.

48   'Film Quality Group Visit' (draft), 19 October 1973, IBA/01023: 3996311.

49   *Shane* had been transmitted by YTV (one of the stations visited on the Film Quality tour) and Tyne Tees. The unlucky Hitchcock film appears to have been *Rebecca* (1940/25.12.1961), transmitted by ATV as part of a late-night Hitchcock season on 12 October 1973.

50   'Film Quality Group Visit'.

51   P.J. Darby and P.J. Marshall, 'Further Considerations on the Problems of Feature and Series Film', 8 November 1973, IBA/01023: 3996311.

52 'Film Quality Group Visit'.

53 Letters from Mr R.H., 18 February 1981, and Mr J.P., 29 July 1981; record of phone call from Mr H., n.d.; Barrie Wood to O'Hagan, 17 August 1981 and 22 January 1982, IBA/01021: 3996312.

54 Jeremy Wallington to Mr. R.B., 30 December 1981, IBA/01023: 3996311.

55 Joseph Weltman to Sir Brian Young, '"X" Films on Sunday Evening', 20 October 1975, IBA/01020: 3996317; original emphasis.

56 The films were shown on subsequent occasions by ATV, Westward and Channel. I have been unable to locate transmission dates for UTV.

57 Letters from Mrs N.W., Mrs E.H., Mr J.C.G., Mrs E.G., Mr C.J.C. and Mr J.S., 15-16 September 1975, IBA/01023: 3996311.

58 Mary Whitehouse to Young, 2 October 1975, IBA/01023: 3996311.

59 Neville Clarke to Mrs E.G., 31 October 1975, IBA/01023: 3996311. This viewer had written separate letters of complaint about *Bob & Carol & Ted & Alice* and *The Killing of Sister George*, both of which were addressed in Clarke's response. Variations on his standard wording were used in many replies to complainants.

60 Young to Whitehouse, 24 October 1975, IBA/01023: 3996311.

61 According to the BBFC's website there are three folders of archival material on the film, suggesting a complex case: https://bbfc.co.uk/case-studies/killing-sister-george.

62 O'Hagan to Weltman, 16 September 1975, IBA/01023: 3996311.

63 Sendall to Young, 17 September 1975, IBA/01023: 3996311. O'Hagan's annotation is hand-dated 22 September 1975. The version subsequently shown five times on Channel Four (initially on 25 November 1983 in a series called 'What the Censor Saw') was cut by about one minute forty seconds, substantially less than the BBFC's three minutes, and retains the majority of the problematic scene. It seems likely that this was the same print approved by the IBA in 1975.

64 N.W. MP to Mr G.B.H., 2 October 1975, IBA/01023: 3996311.

65 Mr P.C.M. to Lady Plowden, 28 September 1975, IBA/01023: 3996311.

66 Mr N.P. to Plowden, 27 October 1975, IBA/01023: 3996311.

67 Plowden to T.H.H. Skeet MP, 21 October 1975, IBA/01023: 3996311.

68 Peter Knight, 'War of the Old Films Goes Reeling On', *Daily Telegraph*, 20 December 1976.

69 'Film Censorship', *Hansard*, Commons, 22 July 1976.

70 The strand was carried by all ITV stations except HTV, which opted out of the last five films in favour of its local series, 'Cinema Club' (see Chapter 8). It showed most of the remaining titles in early 1977.

71 O'Hagan to Halliwell, 20 November 1974, IBA/01023: 3996311; O'Hagan to DHPS and HPS, 27 April 1976, IBA/01024: 3996310.

72 Jack Smith, Headquarters Monitor Report, 16 August 1976, IBA/01024: 3996310. Only one company, ATV, repeated the film after this first showing.

73 Peter Genower, 'Does TV Make the Kindest Cuts of All?', *TV Times*, 12 August 1976; Malcolm Jenkins, 'Guardians – or Butchers?', *TV Times*, 16 February 1978, 10–11.

74 Jean Morton to Mr D.L., 4 August 1976, IBA/01023: 3996311. The complainant, a high-school teacher of film studies, later became a Labour MP.

75 Michael Fisher, 'Censored' (letter), *Evening Standard*, 1 July 1976. The complainant in this instance, a friend of the present author, was an Odeon cinema manager.

76 Desmond J. Vick to Sendall, 'The Savage West', 23 August 1976, IBA/01024: 3996310.

77 On 25 January 1985, the BFI's National Film Theatre showed a French-subtitled 70mm print, with which it claimed to present 'for the first time in Britain the uncut version of *The Wild Bunch*' (National Film Theatre programme booklet, January 1985, 22).

78 The BBFC case study of *The Wild Bunch* is at https://www.bbfc.co.uk/education/case-studies/the-wild-bunch.

79 Leslie Halliwell, '*The Wild Bunch*' (letter), *Sunday Times*, 1 August 1976, 11.

80 Penry Jones to David Glencross, 2 April 1976; Bennett to Sendall, 9 April and 26 August 1976, IBA/01024: 3996310. The Authority's headquarters were at 70 Brompton Road, SW3.

81 David Johnstone, 'Films on TV' (letter), *Glasgow Herald*, 7 August 1976.

82 Letters from Mr R.P-E., 27 July 1976, Mr N.S., 31 July 1976, Mr C.A-S., 31 July 1976, Mr D.N.R., 1 August 1976, and Mr J.F, 3 March 1977; replies from Michael Gillies, 2 and 18 August 1976 and 14 March 1977, IBA/01023: 3996311; Sendall to Berkeley Smith, 13 August 1976, IBA/01024: 3996310.

83 Letters from John Fleming, 'The Film, the Whole Film and Nothing But...', *Campaign*, 11 March 1977; 'Butchering of *Wild Bunch*', *Screen International*, 12 March 1977, 8; and *Time Out*, 14 March 1977.

84 Halliwell to O'Hagan, 11 November 1975, IBA/01024: 3996310; Brian Davies, 'Buying for the Small Screen', *Campaign*, 25 February 1977.

85 Alexander Walker, 'Sam's Bloody Ballet', *TV Times*, 29 August 1976, 5–7.

86 Alexander Walker, 'Why Cut the Pick of the Bunch?', *Evening Standard*, 12 August 1976.

87 Quoted in Tom Hutchinson, 'Your Bidder in the Stalls' (interview), *Sunday Express Magazine*, 27 December 1981.

88 Ed Buscombe, '*The Wild Bunch*' (review), *Sight and Sound*, October 1995, 62.

89 '*Soldier Blue* Gets a Whitewash', *News of the World*, 23 January 1977. All versions of the film released in the UK, theatrically and on video, have been cut by the BBFC.

90 Mansel Lloyd to O'Hagan, 27 September 1977, IBA/01023: 3996311.

91 O'Hagan to Lloyd and note from O'Hagan, 4 October 1977, IBA/01023: 3996311.

92 Gillies to Mr J.G., 11 October 1977, IBA/01023: 3996311.

93 Pat Mahoney to O'Hagan, 21 September 1976, IBA/01024: 3996310.

94 Halliwell to O'Hagan, 24 February 1978, IBA/01024: 3996310.

95 Letter from Mr M.R.P.A., 21 May 1978, IBA/01021: 3996312.

96 'It's Sex – But No Violence Please', *Birmingham Evening Mail*, 21 June 1977. The same or similar words were quoted in numerous other press reports.

97 Respectively: *Daily Express*, *Daily Telegraph*, *Glasgow Daily Record*, *Western Daily Press* and *Daily Mirror*, all 22 June 1977.

98 O'Hagan to Jones and Chris Rowley, 4 April 1977, IBA/01024: 3996310.

99 Colin Shaw to Glencross, 26 April 1977, IBA/01024: 3996310.

100 Shaw to Smith, 3 June 1977, IBA/01024: 3996310.

101 Shaw to Young, 22 June 1977, IBA/01024: 3996310.

102 O'Hagan to Shaw, 'For Adults Only', n.d. (1977), IBA/01024: 3996310.

103 O'Hagan to Jones, 26 May 1977, IBA/01024: 3996310. When the re-edited film was later scheduled locally and drew a single complaint, the IBA's Director of Television

replied disingenuously: 'I cannot agree that it could really be regarded in any sense as "soft porn"' (Shaw to Mr H.G.R., 1 December 1981, IBA/01022: 3996312).

104 Ibid.

105 Quoted in Peter Atkinson, '"Adult" Movies of Seventies on ITV', *Evening Standard*, 21 June 1977.

106 Quoted in Ken Irwin and Mary Malone, 'TV Porn Shocker', *Daily Mirror*, 22 June 1977.

107 Michael Gillies, 'Aspects of Family Viewing', CRB Paper 14(77), 12 July 1977, IBA/01024: 3996310.

108 O'Hagan to Shaw, 6 July 1977; Stephen Laws to Halliwell, 16 August 1977; Halliwell to Laws, 25 August 1977, IBA/01024: 3996310.

109 Plowden to Mr S.N.B., 31 August 1977, IBA/01024: 3996310.

110 Alasdair Milne, 'BBC Television: The Purchase and Transmission of Feature Films, 1978–79', n.d. (1978), BBC R78/1, 123/1.

111 Milne, 'Classification of Feature Films', G20/77, 28 January 1977, BBC R78/1, 123/1.

112 Quoted in Davies, 'Buying for the Small Screen'.

113 Ken Locke, interview 444, *The British Entertainment History Project*, 1999, at https://historyproject.org.uk/interview/ken-locke.

114 Letters from Mr J.C.G., 15 September 1975, and Mr G.B.H., 29 September 1975, IBA/01023: 3996311.

115 Letter from Dr G.F.N., 26 December 1975, IBA/01024: 3996310.

116 The details of the *Ulysses* case are discussed by former BBFC Secretary John Trevelyan in his memoir *What the Censor Saw*, 113–15. The changes required by the Board are detailed in an appendix (243–5).

117 Quoted in Hugh Davies, 'Mrs Whitehouse Urges BBC Cuts in *Ulysses*', *Daily Telegraph*, 29 August 1973.

118 'Film Shock for BBC Governors', *Sunday Telegraph*, 9 September 1973.

119 Philip Jenkinson, 'This Week's Films', *Radio Times*, 30 August 1973, 9.

120 'A Day's Television Audience', in Croston, *ITV 1974*, 127. This book refers erroneously to *Ulysses* as a play.

121 Glencross to Michael Grade, 30 June 1978, IBA/01024: 3996310.

122 A.A. Dane, Regional Monitoring Report Form, B/287/77, 21 November 1977. The monitor commented: 'The fact that it was shown at 22.30 was to Border's credit but the bad language could well offend some viewer [sic] particularly if it was shown with a 9.00 pm start time.'

123 O'Hagan to Ken Fletcher, 29 November 1977; Fletcher to O'Hagan, 6 December 1977, and note by O'Hagan, n.d. (1977); O'Hagan to Fletcher, 15 December 1977; O'Hagan to Glencross, 3 May 1978, IBA/01024: 3996310.

124 Murphy to Margaret Escott, July 1978, IBA/01024: 3996310; original emphasis.

125 Murphy to O'Hagan, 8 September 1977, IBA/01024: 3996310.

126 Jones to Glencross, 21 September 1977, IBA/01024: 3996310.

127 Shaw to Rowley, 9 February 1978, IBA/01024: 3996310.

128 O'Hagan to Ken Bellini, 16 November 1977, IBA/01023: 3996311.

129 Paul Fox to Shaw, 18 November 1981, IBA/01024: 3996310.

130 Young to Mr D.W.M., 27 July 1981, IBA/01022: 3996312.

131 O'Hagan to Halliwell, 30 September 1980, IBA/01021: 3996312. The three films were all fully networked except for *The Mean Machine*, which was dropped by ATV.

132 Halliwell, 'Draft Guidance Notes for Company Certificators', 23 June 1981, IBA/01024: 3996310.

133 Glencross, 'Complaints about Home Produced and Acquired Programmes', 23 January 1981, IBA/01021: 3996312.

134 Letters from Dr P.D.F., Mrs D.L., Ms M.H. and Mr G.W.H., 22–4 September 1980, IBA/01021: 3996312.

135 Brian James, 'The Rape of Your Living Room', *Daily Mail*, 15 September 1990, 6; James to Plowden, 20 October 1980, IBA/01021: 3996312. Selected readers' responses to the article, including one from Sir John Mills, were published in 'Your Verdict on TV: Guilty', *Daily Mail*, 18 September 1980, 6.

136 Letters from Cllr E.J.M., 7 October 1980, Mr T.A., 28 October 1980, and Margaret Thatcher MP, 28 November 1980, IBA/01021: 3996312.

137 Norman Tebbit MP, 30 September 1980, and Home Office reply, 27 October 1980, IBA/01021: 3996312.

138 Gillies to Mr D., 16 October 1980, IBA/01021: 3996312.

139 Halliwell to O'Hagan, 6 April 1981, IBA/01024: 3996310; Halliwell, 'Draft Guidance Notes'. Documents are ambiguous about whether ITV made the cuts or if it had shown an American TV version. Given the incidence of swearing, the former seems more likely.

140 Murphy to Lord Thomson of Monifieth, 2 June 1981; DHOR to Thomson, 10 June 1981, IBA/01021: 3996312.

141 'Monitoring Report on the Film *Death Wish*', enclosed with letter, Whitehouse to Thomson, 28 May 1981, IBA/01022: 3996312.

142 Thomson to Whitehouse, 21 July 1981, IBA/01022: 3996312.

143 Shaw to Glencross, 2 August 1979, IBA/01021: 3996312. This notice, whose final wording differed slightly from Shaw's draft, seems to have first been used in editions published 29 November 1979.

144 David Quinlan, '*Chinatown*' (review), *TV Times*, 11 June 1981, 26.

CHAPTER 12

Witnesses for the Prosecution –
Report on Reports

If most people have any sense of cinema's past, they get it from *television* – both in terms of films transmitted and of programmes about the cinema.

Now both the BBC and the IBA should impose criteria other than purely commercial, consumerist ones on the broadcasters. So audiences have a right to take them to task (in a way that would be inappropriate with a purely commercial organisation) if they fail to live up to these criteria.

In my view, the BBC and ITV film policies do fail. Their treatment of the cinema is dominated by consumerist concerns and falls far short of what responsible film policies might be.
(Colin McArthur, '*The Hollywood Greats*, or How to Trivialize the Cinema', *Tribune*, 11 August 1978; reprinted in *Dialectic! Left Film Criticism from 'Tribune'*, 76)

At the start and end of the 1970s, two independently-authored reports provided wide-ranging critical assessments of the treatment of feature films by British broadcasters. The first, *Films on TV* (1971), was written by Edward Buscombe for a conference organised by the United Nations Education, Scientific and Cultural Organization (UNESCO) on 'the worldwide relationship' between films and television.[1] Buscombe was at the time a lecturer in film studies at Acton College and for the British Film Institute (BFI), and a regular contributor to *Screen*, the journal of the Society for Education in Film and Television (SEFT). His study, subtitled 'British Television and the Cinema – A Report', was published by *Screen* as a 64-page booklet.[2]

The second analysis, 'The BBC and the Film Industry' (1979), was by Lynda Myles, then director of the Edinburgh Film Festival and a member of the BBC's General Advisory Council, to which the report was submitted as a discussion paper. Unlike Buscombe's, her eleven-page paper focused (inevitably, given its provenance) on the BBC exclusively. Myles was concerned not only with the showing of films on television and with TV programmes about the cinema, as Buscombe had also been, but with the extent to which television should become involved in financing film production, a topic that would assume growing importance in the following decade.[3]

Between these two interventions, several other writers took up the same topic in articles for newspapers and magazines. So did the Annan Report on the Future of Broadcasting (1977), and it was also the subject of a public panel discussion at the BFI's National Film Theatre. In this chapter, the claims made by each of these commentators (along with those of their respondents) will be summarised and then tested by applying them to a detailed examination of one particular year's film scheduling.

Films on TV (1971)

The first part of Ed Buscombe's booklet, 'The Transmission of Cinematographic Films on Television', included extensive factual information on the acquisition and programming practices of the BBC and ITV. But it also made both swingeing criticisms of those practices and a number of recommendations to remedy them. As much of the present book has already explored the practical matters Buscombe discusses, I will focus particularly on his criticisms and recommendations. The booklet's second part, 'Television Programmes about the Cinema', does not directly concern us here, though I will touch on this section when dealing with Lynda Myles's report further below.

Noting that feature films were both a relatively cheap form of TV programming and very popular, Buscombe lamented that 'the view of the cinema which television presents is in many ways an unsatisfactory one'. This he attributed in part to the fact that 'In Britain the cinema has still to gain acceptance as a legitimate art form with those who form cultural tastes.'[4] He argued that both the BBC and ITV 'lack a spirit of adventure in their buying policy. The BBC are especially faint-hearted in this respect. "World Cinema" is safely tucked away on BBC2, late at night where it can do no harm.'[5] He contrasted this with the prominence given to classics of the theatre, such as BBC1's Sunday-night *Play of the Month* series; why, he asked, couldn't foreign-language films be played at peak-time too? With the exception of HTV's then-recent first series of experimental films (see Chapter 8), ITV had never been known to show a non-Anglophone film in its original language. The federated structure of ITV made it 'extremely difficult to do any coherent planning in the showing of films, and impossible to tie in screenings with programmes about the cinema'. The 'package deal system' was blamed for the number of 'extremely bad films' that were broadcast.[6] Buscombe admitted that, with rare exceptions, the technical quality of broadcast prints was good, but he noted the ongoing problem of showing CinemaScope films and the lesser one that many viewers with monochrome TV sets were still seeing colour films in black and white. He anticipated that in time this situation would remedy itself, but also foresaw that censorship of films on television would likely increase.

Perhaps the report's most interesting section concerns patterns in film programming. Buscombe argued that it 'must be obvious to anyone who reflects upon it, that the way in which television companies actually schedule the films they buy must have a far-reaching effect upon the way the films are received'. He elaborated:

Over the last few years it has been more and more the tendency of both the BBC and ITV to arrange their films in what they like to call 'seasons'. By this is meant a grouping together of a number of films with some kind of a connecting link between them. Films are rarely shown on their own any longer, without any sort of attempt to put them into a series.[7]

However, according to Buscombe, in practice such seasons either tended to be too short or merely opportunistic, due to the limitations on available material when films were divided between the two broadcasting networks:

The justification of showing films in groups is that this adds something to the audience's appreciation, that the viewer might be able to discern a development or contrast different styles within the work of a particular artist. Seasons are one of the most valuable ways of increasing awareness of how the cinema works. Current series on both BBC and ITV, however, achieve little of this...[8]

Films were grouped on TV mainly by star and genre, which reinforced common-sense thinking about films either as star vehicles or as belonging to a thematic category. Generic grouping was preferred by ITV as it permitted more flexibility, whereas a given actor's body of work might be split between the networks, making an ideal selection of titles difficult. The BBC had more seasons built around actors, but Buscombe criticised these for including only three or four titles each. He cited a run of four Paul Newman films on BBC1 earlier in the year. But he might also have been thinking about BBC1's current Sunday-night series 'The Great Stars' (1971–72), which typically comprised groups of three films per actor. At the time, BBC1 had only once screened a season of films around a particular director ('The Films of Alfred Hitchcock' in 1969), though other filmmakers had been showcased in BBC2's 'World Cinema' strand. Buscombe commented that directors, actors and genres were not 'the only way films might be programmed'.

They can be grouped by subject matter, or according to the period in which they were made, or by style, or by scriptwriter. The possibilities for intelligent and imaginative programming are wide, but the programmers seem reluctant to depart from a safe policy of reliance upon stars and the old categories of Western, comedy, musical, etc.[9]

He also noted that 'television companies when buying films keep an eye open for possible future seasons. So the way in which films are programmed affects which films may be bought: another reason for adventurous film schedules.'[10]

The report's strongest criticisms were reserved for ITV's interruption of films with advertisements and its habit of cutting arbitrarily for length. Of the former, using the term mentioned in the Television Act 1954, Buscombe opined that it was 'difficult to see how anyone could find a natural break in a film designed for continuous exhibition'. He argued that the common defence of this practice, 'that there would be no films at all [on ITV] were it not for the advertising', was disproven by the existence of certain programme types (religious, educational and sporting events) that were free of ad breaks.[11] Regarding editing for length, the author commented:

> I have been assured by people in ITV that cuts are always replaced as soon as the particular transmission for which they were made has occurred, and this will have to be accepted, but the danger remains that cut prints *could* get into circulation; and the surest way to make sure they don't is to stop cutting them.[12]

Buscombe bemoaned the fact that, instead of presenting silent films in full and at the correct speed, broadcasters preferred facetious clip shows such as the BBC's recent series *Golden Silents* (see Figure 12.1). This was described as an 'exercise in blood-sucking', one which 'distorts what the silent cinema was really like' and destroys 'the sense of rhythm and timing that was the basis of their art'.[13] In fact, the ratings success of *Golden Silents*, hosted by comedian Michael Bentine with audience reactions to film extracts recorded at the BFI's National Film Theatre in the manner of a sitcom laughter track, eventually led to a series of full-length silent features being broadcast in the same way. Half a dozen such films were shown by BBC1 on early Saturday evenings in the summer of 1973, all introduced by Bentine from the NFT.

Looking to the future, Buscombe anticipated increasing numbers of old films being televised, as was the case in America, but cautioned against complacent optimism. He argued that

> unless something can be done now to impress upon television companies, especially ITV, that the cinema is worthy of being treated as more than product, to fill a time slot, the past, (and hence, inevitably, the present,) of the cinema will be seriously distorted. For every film which is rescued from rotting in some studio vault there will be several which will come to exist only in special television versions, either with CinemaScope 'rationalised' in a special print, or with whole sections missing, or even re-shot. And it is not only in this physical way that the cinematic heritage is damaged. Who can measure the harm done to those whose understanding of the cinema is warped by the way television distorts it? To some this may not appear of very much consequence; yet the situation is at least comparable to one in which Shakespeare is available in abridged versions only, with modernised spelling.[14]

Among Buscombe's concluding recommendations were the following:

1. Both the BBC and ITV should be more adventurous in their choice of films shown. Foreign-language films, films made by independent producers, and even silent films should have regular slots.
2. Both ITV and the BBC should break out of the present straitjacketed programming policy, which groups films only by genre or star.
3. ITV must stop interrupting films with commercials, and stop cutting them.
4. Television companies should look into the possibility of donating prints to the National Film Archive.[15]

'Above all', he ended, 'television should adopt a much more independent attitude to the industry, it should be less dazzled by its glamour and more interested in its genuine achievements. This doesn't sound like much to ask. Unfortunately it is asking for a revolution.'[16]

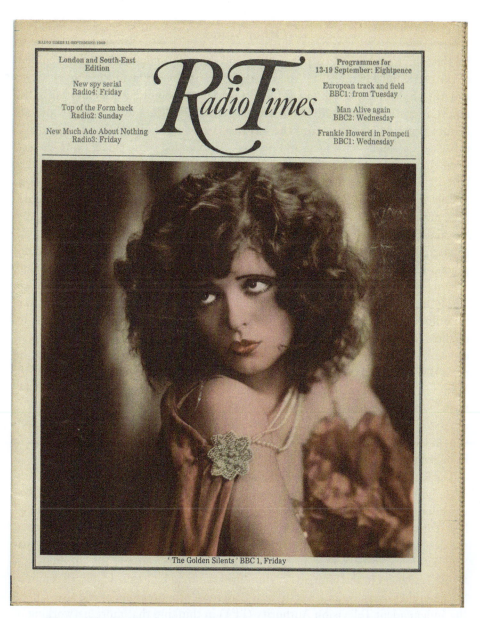

Figure 12.1 Clara Bow was among the stars appearing in Michael Bentine's series *Golden Silents* (1969–70), a celebration of pre-sound cinema presented in the absence of full–length silent features. *Radio Times* © Immediate Media Co. Cover photograph from the Kobal Collection.

Other Voices

Ed Buscombe's UNESCO paper was seen and generally endorsed by other members of the press, notably by Elkan Allan in the *Sunday Times*, David Pirie in *Time Out* and Allen Eyles in *Films and Filming*. In his newspaper column, Allan emphasised the report's negative points, calling it a 'stinging attack on BBC and ITV policy towards feature films', which 'condemns the way they are selected, bought, and shown, and is backed up solidly with facts and figures'. Allan added some evidence of his own from the current week's schedules (5–11 December 1971). He considered that BBC1's Sunday-night film, the Rommel biopic *The Desert Fox* (1951/05.12.1971), 'hardly compares with last week's [play] *Tartuffe* in weight'. The 'World Cinema' presentation on BBC2, the Swedish *Who Saw Him Die?* (1968/09.12.1971), was 'far and away the best film of the BBC week' but was 'sadly buried' late at night (it started at 10.10pm). As support for Buscombe's criticism of ITV's scheduling practices, Allan adduced Thames Television's cutting of ten minutes from *Ocean's Eleven* (1960/27.08.1966) and the interruption of LWT's transmission of *The Chase* (1966/10.10.1971) by a news bulletin. He noted approvingly that the report was 'scornful of the habit of grouping films under spurious seasons' and the buying of films in packages, which he agreed led to the acquisition of bad films as well as good. Among the 'many qualifying for opprobrium' in the week of writing, he cited BBC2's 'grisly' British comedy *As Long as They're Happy* (1955/06.10.1970). However, Allan's example of a widescreen film being broadcast with only an 'arbitrary portion of the action in frame', Yorkshire Television's transmission of *The Devil at 4 O'Clock* (1961/13.12.1968), was ill-chosen. The film had not in fact been shot in CinemaScope or any other anamorphic process and was therefore unlikely to have been substantially compromised in the way that he suggested.[17]

David Pirie was more nuanced in his appraisal of the report. He referred to what he called the 'wholesale cannibalisation of one medium by another' but considered that Buscombe had been 'slightly harsh on the BBC', which he argued had 'consistently managed its films with more integrity than ITV'. He criticised the decentralised programming of films by the commercial companies, noting that 'the difference in presentation is absolutely enormous' among the different stations. Audiences in the Granada region (programmed by Leslie Halliwell) enjoyed 'much higher overall standards in films than most other regions'. Pirie also echoed the Independent Television Authority (ITA) in thinking that more networking of films would 'make certain that the maximum attention is given to selection and presentation, as opposed to the "slot something in" philosophy of many planners at the moment'. He acknowledged 'at least one' BBC season 'of real importance', overlooked by Buscombe: 'The Movie Crazy Years' (1971), dedicated to the classic films of one particular studio, Warner Bros (see Introduction, Figure 0.2).[18]

In his monthly column on films shown on TV for *Films and Filming*, Allen Eyles broadly agreed with Buscombe's main arguments but added a number of caveats. He commented:

Mr Buscombe argues very strongly that neither the BBC nor ITV show enough respect for the cinema as an art form. I think he is rather unfair towards the BBC and tends to accept too readily the idea that ITV shouldn't be expected to do as much because it is programmed for the profit of the individual companies. The ITA exists to assert the public interest in ITV programmes, especially where minority interests are concerned. In feature films, I think it is not doing enough...

Eyles was sceptical about Buscombe's claim that 'World Cinema' could profitably have been given a more prominent peak-time slot on BBC1 instead of late at night on BBC2. He pointed out that BBC1's Sunday-evening *Play of the Month* slot, with which Buscombe compared it, was a gesture towards 'prestige' that regularly lost the channel viewers. They turned instead to ITV's competing attraction – usually a film. Placing 'World Cinema' or its equivalent in such a slot, argued Eyles, would probably have the same result. He also corrected the report on various points of fact, adding information of which Buscombe had apparently been unaware; for example, the BBC already donated its used prints to the National Film Archive where contracts permitted. On programming, Eyles argued that 'TV's "patterning" of films under genres and stars does make some little more sense than not doing that'. Countering the claim that not buying films in packages would help to remove bad films from the air, he argued the opposite case: 'a vast number of films that are bad in terms of artistic quality but good as far as ratings are concerned would be eagerly bought and many important films that would be reluctantly accepted as part of a package could then be dropped.'[19]

Two years after the publication of Ed Buscombe's report, both Allen Eyles and Elkan Allan were among the panellists, along with ITV's Leslie Halliwell and the BBC's Senior Assistant (Films and Series), Purchased Programmes, Alan Howden, in a public discussion at the National Film Theatre. The panel on 'Films on Television' (5 October 1973) had been arranged as part of a season, 'Films That Nearly Got Away', programmed by Halliwell and consisting predominantly of titles that had not received a UK cinema release but which had been picked up by ITV (see Chapter 6).[20] Reporting on the event for *Film* magazine, Peter Armitage commented that both the film buyers had 'made a good showing' in the discussion, commending Halliwell in particular for rising to the challenge of defending ITV's record despite the restrictions of the network's system. Criticism was reserved for Elkan Allan's 'misconceptions about the iniquities of "packaging"' in film acquisition. Armitage explained that, contrary to Allan's assumptions, buyers did not simply accept packages exactly as offered to them by distributors; they were able to select their preferred titles and leave out those for which they had no use. In a newspaper article promoting his new reference book, *The Sunday Times Guide to Films on Television*, Allan had disclosed the contents of a package comprising seventy-four titles that he claimed the BBC had recently bought from Screen Gems, Columbia's television arm, applying to each of them the ratings used to evaluate films in his book.[21] But Armitage pointed out that, although the package had indeed been 'offered to the BBC well over a year ago and a deal was done', the Corporation had not bought its entire contents: it had selected fifty films and rejected the rest. He commented:

> Since the mid-sixties, film purchase for tv has been a buyers' market. Whereas long lists of films are offered and packages are put together, the buyer picks and chooses and is under no obligation to take any particular film. ...

> Obviously, Allan has fallen hook, line and sinker for some salesman's yarn for he retailed that a couple of good old movies are sometimes thrown in to ease the sale of American-made situation comedy and thriller tv series. In fact the shoe is on the other foot. The networks can use their willingness to take such series as leverage to get at some of the films they want.

Armitage also dismissed Allan's claims about the fees reportedly attached to particular titles by distributors, explaining that these were interpreted differently by their customers:

> When a deal is done for a batch of films, quite different assessments may be made for the individual items by the seller and the buyer. The accountancy practice of the seller is likely to undervalue a film which is already showing a handsome profit and to overvalue one which is still showing a thumping loss. These valuations will probably differ widely from those made by the tv company which is concerned with the film's future pulling power on the box.

Coming down decisively in favour of the TV buyers' arguments over the critic's, Armitage concluded: 'Demonstrably they know more about the cinema than Allan, and on the evidence I would sooner trust their taste than his.'[22]

In a 1975 article for another magazine, *Films Illustrated*, editor David Castell made a number of points similar to Buscombe's, elaborating on the notion (echoing Pirie) that television 'cannibalises the industry voraciously':

> The attempts to rationalise screenings into some kind of informative or educational season are minimal. Half a dozen films starring a particular actor, played out of chronological sequence, will pose as 'a season,' and then be neither topped nor tailed with informed critical comment.

> Until television can rationalise its love-hate relationship with the cinema – and vice versa – we have a sterile state of checkmate. The experiments of opening films on television before cinema release (*Akenfield, Stavisky*) must be accounted failures; the breaking of the five-year embargo before television screenings (*The Ruling Class*) fizzled out quietly; the television screening on BBC2 of hitherto unreleased movies (*One is a Lonely Number, Goin' Home* [sic], *The Breaking of Bumbo*) only scratches the surface of the work that is to be done towards harmony between the media.[23]

The same month that this issue was published, Castell appeared for the first time as co-presenter of BBC2's series *Film Night* (in what turned out to be its last run before cancellation the following year), though he did not mention this in his article. It appeared alongside a guest piece written by filmmaker Bryan Forbes, offered as a 'personal view' and consisting in the main of unremitting bile and scorn directed against television in general and TV film critics in particular. Forbes was also surprisingly uninformed, assuming that films were bought by networks 'on an outright-sale basis' or hired for unlimited transmissions, when both of these were very rarely the case.[24] Four years later, he replaced Philip Jenkinson as *Radio Times*'s film columnist, just as Castell had replaced Jenkinson as a *Film Night* co-host, and for an even shorter duration.

'The BBC and the Film Industry' (1979)

The BBC's General Advisory Council (GAC) was a body made up of external policy advisors, of whom Lynda Myles was one. Myles was then Director of the Edinburgh Film Festival, and her subsequent professional roles included curator of the Pacific Film Archive, Senior Vice-President at Columbia Pictures, Commissioning Editor for Drama at the BBC, Head of Fiction at the National Film and Television School, and a producer of independent films. In her own words, she served on the GAC to represent 'most of the minorities'.[25] She began her report on the BBC's treatment of films by referring to a more general problem than the 'attitudes of television management'. Echoing Ed Buscombe's earlier argument, this was 'the lack of seriousness with which cinema is regarded throughout Great Britain. For various reasons, those who dictate cultural taste in Britain have denied the cinema cultural acceptance as a legitimate art form.' Myles attributed this situation to the cinema's very popularity as a medium of entertainment; she pointed out that in the Annan Report, 'film was not included in the section dealing with the relationship between television and the arts' (it occupied a separate chapter). She considered that the BBC was 'in a unique position to make a major contribution to changing this situation'.[26]

Myles acknowledged that some in the film industry still opposed the showing of films on television due to the threat of competition with cinemas. But she pointed out that in the previous year, 1978, the British theatrical box office had taken an unprecedented upturn (and as it turned out, one not to be repeated until nearly a decade later) due to the release of a number of Hollywood blockbusters. Television could not be said to draw audiences away from such 'event' movies or, at the opposite end of the commercial scale, from 'avant-garde/experimental' films; instead, it was 'a competitor for the "middle-ground" of cinema'.[27] Nevertheless, Myles argued, the decline of cinema overall was one of the reasons why

> television now affords one of the only [*sic*] opportunities for a young cinephile to acquire any knowledge of film culture. Given the decreasing number of cinemas in Britain showing anything other than the latest Hollywood release, it is extremely difficult for a young cineaste to build up an understanding of the development of the medium other than by watching films on television.[28]

This was not the only area of commonality between Myles and Buscombe, whose report she cited in the course of her own. She noted that 'the way in which the BBC schedules feature films will affect the way in which they are received', in particular the practice of programming films in seasons. Where Buscombe had emphasised groupings based on genres and stars, Myles focused on directors and stars, perhaps reflecting changes in schedulers' selection patterns over the intervening years. She acknowledged, too, the 'obvious limitations of the market: many seasons may prove impossible if the desired films have been purchased by ITV'. Nevertheless, she advocated extending the thematic basis of seasons to 'ideas of national cinema, genre or studio'.[29] Also like Buscombe, Myles wanted the BBC to 'be more adventurous in scheduling' and found it lacking in its treatment of silent films and the avant-garde. She wanted the Corporation to 'make a key cultural contribution by screening a larger number of European films, to which few people in Britain have access', and wondered if 'the current emphasis on ratings' was a factor in holding back the showing 'of more challenging or difficult films'.[30]

Myles made specific recommendations that would help 'to change the attitude of the British public to the cinema'. One was to reconsider the approach to films evident in *Radio Times*, through which the BBC disseminated programme promotion. She used the same word as Buscombe to describe the attitude of its (now former) films columnist, Philip Jenkinson: 'camp' (flippant and fundamentally unserious). Jenkinson had recently been replaced in the magazine by the film director and screenwriter Bryan Forbes. Myles asked: 'But why not have a critic? Why should this rather "amateur" approach be permissible for the cinema in a way which would not be permitted in the other arts?'[31]

Her second suggestion was for films to be preceded by a brief on-screen introduction, as was done on French television, placing the films 'in their historical context' and with some 'information about their production'.[32] Myles referred to a recent BBC2 series, 'My Kind of Movie', in which each week a celebrity was featured in a five-minute interview about a favourite film to be broadcast the following evening. Here she echoed, consciously or otherwise, comments made by film critic Colin McArthur, who had written scathingly of this series in his review for the socialist newspaper *Tribune*.[33] Myles for her part argued:

> To criticise this [series] does not mean that anecdotes or reminiscences are invalid, but rather that they do not offer an acceptable alternative to a more informed introduction to the films concerned. What is being proposed is not an aggressively academic or highly theoretical approach to the subject, but simply some attempt (by a well-informed individual) to contextualise the feature being shown.[34]

Like Buscombe, Myles asked for more serious TV programmes to be made about the cinema; like McArthur, she pointed to BBC2's series *Arena: Cinema* as a positive model and an exception to the general rule. In asking for more 'discussion of the films which viewers are going to see on television', she may have had in mind the sole example cited by Buscombe of a television series coordinated with films currently being broadcast. This was *Cinema*: not the long-running ITV series of the same title but a 1968 educational programme for schools and colleges, written by the critic and teacher V.F. Perkins and made in collaboration with the Schools Broadcasting Council and the BFI. Buscombe had explained:

> The great innovation of the programme was that each of the eight parts was linked to a film to be shown in that week during the BBC's normal transmission hours. This meant, first, that viewers could actually be told things about a film they had seen recently – almost a unique experience in television programmes about the cinema – and second, the serious study of the cinema was not removed from the students' ordinary viewing experience into a rarified atmosphere belong[ing] exclusively to [education].[35]

However, this direct relationship of the programme to current schedules also meant that the series was never repeated after its initial broadcast. As Buscombe pointed out three years later, nothing similar had subsequently been attempted; nor had it been by 1979, when Myles asked:

> Would it not, therefore, be possible to achieve a greater degree of coherence between the films scheduled and the programmes on the cinema? This could also allow the development of programmes which could deal with ideas of genre, authorship, the studio system etc but which would also be linked to films which the audience would be able to view without difficulty.[36]

The third and final section of Myles's report was concerned with the possibility of the BBC financing feature films for theatrical release. The models for doing so were provided by European networks, principally ZDF in West Germany and RAI in Italy, which had sponsored the work of major and emerging directors in an arrangement allowing for the transmission of the films either in advance of cinema showings or after a relatively brief interval (much shorter than the five-year embargo imposed in Britain by the CEA).[37] In proposing the BBC as a potential patron of film production, Myles noted that the huge acquisition fee paid the previous year for *The Sound of Music* (1965/25.12.1978) could have been used to finance six films instead. She acknowledged the restrictions placed on in-house productions due to agreements with unions, but asked: 'Could the BBC Charter not be changed to allow for the production of feature films for the [cinema] screen and for television, plus the subsequent release of other productions?'[38]

Right of Reply

When presented to the GAC, the Myles report was accompanied by a lengthy written response from Gunnar Rugheimer, the BBC's chief film buyer, on behalf of the Corporation. Rugheimer's nine-page rejoinder addressed each of Myles's main points in twenty-one numbered paragraphs. He accepted all her compliments on his department's best efforts, but conceded none of her criticisms. The response opened by stating of the report: 'We have found it extremely helpful in the clarification of our own minds and are happy now to try and clarify the BBC's own position in what is a very complex area of programming.'[39] This emphasis on 'clarification' – that is, a restatement of current policy and practice – was an early indication that nothing much would be changing.

Rugheimer did not 'accept the suggestion that films are better treated in cultural terms in France than they are on British Television, certainly not by the BBC'.

He felt that the treatment of films by French television did not reflect the cinema's apparently more 'culturally respectable' status in that country, considering that one network's 'cine-club strand' presented films in 'no particularly organised way'. Another used televised discussions to explore 'some social or political topic raised by the film rather than its cinematic merits'. Against this he offered BBC1's regular film reviewer and star biographer, Barry Norman, who, 'because of his own scholarly approach, deals with films, old and new, in a penetrating and sensible way' (see Figure 12.2).[40] More generally, Rugheimer argued:

> Whether the cinema in Britain is – or is not – held 'in low esteem' in the country generally, this is certainly not true of the BBC, which broadcasts an exceptionally wide range of films, tries to present them intelligently and to promote them in an informative way through billings and articles in *Radio Times*. Moreover, the BBC has built up a tradition of using new prints of feature films for transmission, which are sometimes more complete and of better quality than those seen, after the first general release, in the cinema. It could be argued, in fact, that the BBC treats cinema films with more respect than the cinema itself does or ever did.[41]

According to the recollection of 'members of staff who were young cinephiles in the nineteen-fifties', it had been possible at that time to see 'only a very limited selection of films that were not recent releases' in cinemas, and these usually in 'poor prints for one day bookings on Sundays'. Rugheimer contrasted this with the present day, when young film buffs could 'see several hundred films a year on television'. He reiterated Myles's own point, that 'most pre-1952 feature films would by now have perished' through neglect or decay, were it not for their use by television.[42]

Somewhat surprisingly, given the BBC's manifest programming practices, Rugheimer asserted: 'We are not convinced of the value of scheduling films in seasons.' This was partly because of the difficulty, alluded to by Myles (and before her, Buscombe), of acquiring all the desirable films on a particular theme; but he explained further:

> The idea of treating themes historically is attractive at first sight. But we should not want to be too didactic in our presentation. Those who are most familiar with the history of the cinema can probably manage without excessive sign-posting. And for the general audience this might not be the best way of encouraging an interest in the early cinema. Lengthy exposure to works of one director or of a particular genre might discourage those people who happen not to be interested in films of a certain kind.[43]

Here Rugheimer seemed to be contradicting his own logic: presumably the same principle would apply if such films were seen singly rather than in series. He did not consider how seasons might address viewers who *were* 'interested in films of a certain kind' or who needed more 'sign-posting' to find a path through the many films that television presented.

Rugheimer emphasised the difficulties in acquiring silent films in 'good sound versions' as well as the cost of preparing new soundtracks, claiming that 'although

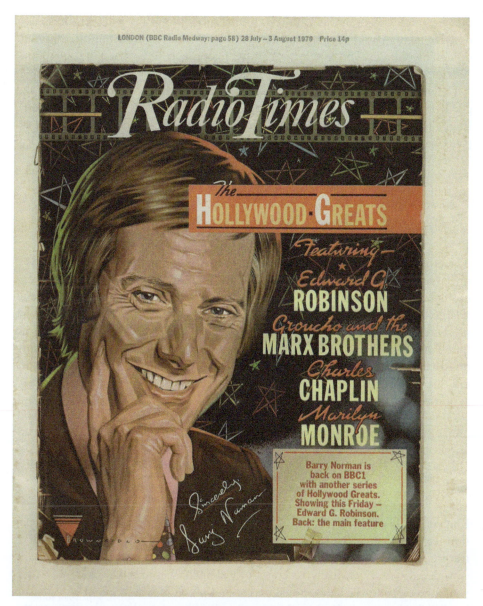

Figure 12.2 *The Hollywood Greats* (1979) was one of many BBC series on the cinema hosted by Barry Norman, who often drew sharp criticism for his journalistic approach. *Radio Times* © Immediate Media Co. Artwork © Mick Brownfield.

silent films appeal to cinephiles, we always get a number of complaints from the general audience when they are shown'. With regard to foreign-language films, he said that BBC2 had transmitted around forty such films a year since the channel's inception; while the Corporation 'could perhaps do more', it was 'not held back by anxiety over ratings, but rather by its obligation to home-produced drama and to actors and writers in this country'. Rugheimer did not say whether films from other countries could have replaced some of the American films the BBC showed, though he did point out that buyers looked for suitable films made in Canada and Australia.

Defending the purpose of *Radio Times*'s films column as being 'to bring out the good, or bad, points in a film and to give an indication of style, subject and period', Rugheimer commented, echoing the words of Gordon Smith many years before (see Chapter 5):

> Some of the films reviewed may be works of art, but others, more modestly, will be entertain-
> ment. More space and a different brief would be required if the notes were to attempt 'to
> change the attitude of the British public to the cinema'. We are not sure that should be the aim
> of the BBC, and we believe that the present, individualistic style is appreciated by readers of
> *Radio Times*.[44]

The other way of mediating films proposed by Myles, the broadcasting of spoken introductions, Rugheimer found 'interesting'; but he felt that 'even five minutes of "talking heads", while they may enhance the enjoyment of some, may send a larger number away to look at another channel'. He preferred instead to let presenters Barry Norman and Gavin Millar (the host of *Arena: Cinema*) make 'intelligent cross-references, by way of introduction, to films that are appearing on BBC television in the current or following week'. How or whether they actually did this was not detailed. Rugheimer was 'puzzled' by the criticism often levelled at Norman:

> It is true that he has a certain brightness of style. But this is at least one reason why he has
> built up a big following among ordinary viewers. He is an independent and outspoken critic.
> His judgment is sound, and his sharpest remarks are usually reserved for comments about
> the purely commercial aspects of much modern film-making. He would certainly share Miss
> Myles's concern for cinema as an art form.[45]

Rugheimer disputed the figure of £6,000 quoted by Myles as a typical acquisition fee, stating that the BBC would 'expect to pay about £50,000 for a modern feature film that has been moderately successful in the cinema'. This sum was, he considered, fair given likely revenues of £200,000 from British cinemas, which would be earned over an extended period and much of which might be eaten up by distribution costs. Against this, he stated: 'The immediate advantage to the distributor who sells to television is obvious. He receives his money immediately. The payment is substantial, and he is saved not only outlay, but effort also, which can be used to back other films.' Rugheimer gave the impression that distributors should deal with television rather than the theatrical market.[46]

With regard to film financing, Rugheimer pointed out that much of the BBC's own drama output, when shot on 16mm film, 'would, elsewhere in the world, be construed as low-budget feature film production'. Comparison with the films financed by RAI in Italy was inapposite, he suggested, because much of that funding had come from the state and simply been disbursed via the channel; it was therefore more comparable in function to the UK's National Film Finance Corporation rather than the BBC.[47] He acknowledged the necessary financial limitations on the BBC's investment in theatrical films, given its obligation to produce drama directly for television, but referred to the policy, introduced several years prior, of providing 'seed money' amounting to £250,000 annually for feature films intended for cinema release that would ultimately be seen on BBC television. This scheme had been successful in assisting 'some fifteen projects', of which only two had yet been completed, but had recently 'run into difficulties, because the cinema trade has refused to book *Agatha* so long as the BBC holds to its contractual right to show the film on television within three years of release' (see Chapter 6).[48]

Unlike Buscombe's report, 'The BBC and the Film Industry' does not appear to have been published in full externally, though Myles had summarised some of its main points in an interview with *Broadcast* magazine that appeared two months before the GAC discussion of her paper.[49] To their credit, at least some members of the BBC's Board of Management considered Rugheimer's response 'rather complacent and unyielding', though the Board conceded 'that Miss Myles was asking for rather more than the BBC could give'. One executive claimed that 'it was an uncontrovertible [*sic*] fact that Lynda Myles started out with a lot of very inaccurately based ideas'. The BBC's dilemma, he added, was: 'How do you answer the points and convince people that you know what you are doing, without appearing too defensive?'[50]

In a covering note attached to Myles's paper, presenting it for discussion, the GAC's secretary John Wilkinson posed six questions for members' consideration:

1. Should the BBC do more than it is doing at present to encourage appreciation of the cinema as an art-form?
2. Should there be more programmes about the cinema?
3. In what ways might the scheduling of films on television be improved?
4. Should the present balance of American films and films from other countries, including Europe, be changed?
5. Does *Radio Times* provide the right kind of information about films?
6. What role should the BBC play as a producer or sponsor of films?[51]

If Rugheimer's response left something to be desired, the GAC debate on Myles's report was, if the available extracts are representative, even less satisfactory. It failed to take up any of her substantive points or even to answer Wilkinson's questions in detail. Myles's own view of Rugheimer's rejoinder was summarised in the GAC minutes:

As a whole, the BBC's reply was 'a superb defence of the *status quo*'. She had not expected many of her criticisms to be accepted, but regretted nevertheless that there was no indication of any future change. The film world itself, and the demands of audiences, were changing constantly, yet the BBC's position remained appropriate to the situation some 10 years previously.[52]

If this was true, the situation described in Buscombe's report still obtained at the time Myles made hers, with little immediate prospect of significant progress.

A Sample Year: 1975

The choice of 1975 for a case study was not an arbitrary one. The year is exactly midway between the Buscombe and Myles reports. It also marked some significant developments in the scheduling of films. The challenges posed by the permissive films of the late 1960s were increasingly evident, while the blockbusters acquired by both broadcasting organisations were prominent in the schedules.

My discursive account should be read in conjunction with the accompanying tables (see Tables 12.1.1–12.1.4). They chart the broad scheduling patterns of the year for the films shown by BBC1 and BBC2 and in three representative ITV regions: Anglia, Yorkshire and London (Thames and LWT). The tables cover a period of fifty-three weeks, consecutively numbered according to the standard designation used by schedulers. Thus, the week including New Year 1974–75 is Week 1 and Christmas 1975 is in Week 52. For the sake of completeness, so that the entire calendar year 1975 is included in the survey, I have also included the New Year week for 1975–76, spanning 27 December to 2 January and numbered Week 53 (it would be Week 1 of 1976).

As explained in Chapter 7, the 'television year' is broken down into quarterly seasons. Following the convention adopted by listings magazines from the mid-1960s onward, I take the 'television week' to run from Saturday to Friday. Thus, the calendar for 1975 looks like this:

Winter: Weeks 1 to 13 (28 December 1974 to 28 March)
Spring: Weeks 14 to 26 (29 March to 27 June)
Summer: Weeks 27 to 35 (28 June to 29 August)
Autumn: Weeks 36 to 52 (30 August to 26 December)

In addition to the bracketing New Year and Christmas holidays, it should be noted that Week 14 in 1975 included Easter (hence Week 13 ended with Good Friday), marking the transition from winter to spring, and Week 35 included the August Bank Holiday, signalling the end of summer. The Spring Bank Holiday appeared in Week 22. These milestones are important because new seasons typically meant periodic changes in the schedules and bank holidays marked temporary deviations from regular scheduling patterns. In terms of feature films, a new season might include the introduction of regular strands, variations in the identity of existing ones or the dropping of some film strands in favour of other programming. A bank holiday might involve the addition of one-off 'special presentations' such as a blockbuster in peak-time, a child-friendly matinee, a BBC2 double or triple bill as an alternative to afternoon sport on BBC1 and ITV, or a late-night horror film. All of these are evident in the schedule charts, which, as well as documenting regular strands according to the series titles billed in *Radio Times* and *TVTimes*, also identify stand-alone presentations by film title. It will be seen that these tend to cluster around holiday weeks.

A further set of divisions in the tables indicates the structure of the 'television day'. For convenience, I have divided each weekday into four four-hour blocks: Morning (actually 9.00am to 1.00pm), Afternoon (1.00 to 5.00pm), Evening (5.00 to 9.00pm) and Late Night (9.00pm to 1.00am).[53] Film strands and titles are thus allocated to one or other of these four columns based on their scheduled start time (in this year, no films were scheduled to start between 1.00am and 9.00am). Here too, patterns are readily discernible: a concentration in peak-time (Evening and Late Night) hours; Morning matinees only at weekends or in holiday periods; and Afternoons similarly for the BBC, ITV stations offering regular matinees on Mondays and Fridays (budget cuts had stopped BBC1 programming regular daytime films from the previous year).

There were, broadly, two types of film strand: those determined by nothing more specific than a regular day and time slot; and those organised around a particular theme or common element. Instances of the former included BBC1's 'Saturday Night at the Movies', 'Film Matinee', 'The Monday Film' and 'The Wednesday Film'; and BBC2's 'Midnight Movie', 'Sunday Cinema', 'Tuesday Cinema' and 'Midweek Cinema' (the choice of 'film' for strands on the main channel and 'cinema' for the minority channel may in itself be indicative of the different taste regimes being addressed). Similar patterns are identifiable in the three sample ITV regions: Saturday evenings featured 'The Saturday Night Film' or 'Saturday Night Movie' (Anglia), 'The Saturday Film' (London) and 'The Main Feature' (YTV), while Sunday afternoons offered 'Sunday Matinee' (Anglia), 'The Family Film' (London) and 'Sunday Cinema' (YTV). The London companies were less inclined than others to give their regular film strands umbrella titles, but Anglia's seemed particularly to emphasise days and times: 'Monday Afternoon Film', 'Monday Late Film', 'The Tuesday Film', and so on.

The generic nature of these labels is indicated by the number of duplications among the different services. This is true not only among the commercial stations – all three of which featured a strand called 'The Big Film', for instance (a ubiquitous umbrella title on ITV) – but also between the BBC and ITV. In some regions, both the rival networks had slots named 'Saturday Night at the Movies', 'Film of the Week' (both these two in the Anglia region), 'Sunday Cinema', 'The Friday Film' (both in Yorkshire) and 'The Wednesday Film' (in both Anglia and Yorkshire). This must have been very confusing for viewers trying to distinguish between their local channels' offers.

Themed strands were far more common at the BBC than on ITV (see Table 12.2). In 1975, the Corporation's two channels between them featured no fewer than thirty-four themed seasons, variously structured around stars (nine),

Table 12.1.1 BBC film scheduling, 28 December 1974–2 January 1976.

Day (Channel)	9.00am–1.00pm	1.00–5.00pm	5.00–9.00pm	9.00pm–1.00am
Saturday (BBC1)	[Morning matinees] (1, 23, 27*, 27*, 31*, 33*, 38, 39, 49–51, 53) [*double bills]		*On the Beat* (1) Saturday Night at the Movies (2–30, 35–53) Robert Mitchum (31–34)	
Saturday (BBC2)		Saturday Cinema (1–36, 52–53) The Saturday Western (37–51)	*Born to Swing* (40) *Frankenstein: The True Story* [TVM] (53)	Midnight Movie (2–19, 21–31, 38–53) Fantastic Double Bill (32–37)
Sunday (BBC1)		*North West Frontier* (1) Film Matinee (2–10, 12, 19–28, 30–33) Fred and Ginger (13–18) The Sunday Adventure Film (35–53)	Play of the Month: *Robinson Crusoe* [BBC TVM] (1) Film of the Week (2–3, 5–7, 9–14, 22–39, 41–53) A Wartime Screen (15–20)	*Dr Jekyll and Mr Hyde* [1941] (1)
Sunday (BBC2)		Religious Film Festival (2–9) *White Christmas* (52)	*Shadow of the Thin Man* (1)	*Presley at Forty* (2–3) Murder at the Movies (4–12) *Brother, Can You Spare a Dime?* (13) *Point Blank* (14) Louis Malle's *A Human Condition* (36) Sunday Cinema (15–45, 47–52) *Demolition Man* [BBC TVM] (53)

Monday (BBC1)	Enchanted Island (14)	Postman's Knock (1) Miracle on 34th Street (52) Cinderella – Italian Style (53)	Charlie Chaplin in *The Gold Rush* (1) *Marooned* (14) *The Longest Day* (22) Walt Disney's *The Monkey's Uncle* (35) *Born Free* (52) *Kes* (53)	*The 39 Steps* [1935] (1) The Monday Film (27–40, 42–52)
Monday (BBC2)		Jolson Double Bill (14) Leaders of the Band (22) Comedy Hat Trick (35)	*Futtocks End* (14)	*Dr Terror's House of Horrors* (14) *The Deadly Bees* (22) *Dr Crippen* (35) *The Night That Panicked America* [TVM] (52) *For a Few Dollars More* (53)
Tuesday (BBC1)		The Endless Summer (1) Road to Bali (53)	*Star!* (1) The Tarzan Adventures (32–47) *The Mouse on the Moon* (49) Christmas Carry On: *Carry on… Up the Khyber* (52)	
Tuesday (BBC2)		The Odd Couple (53)	*The Devil Rides Out* (1) Tuesday Cinema (2–16, 27–38, 41–44) Images of Childhood (17–25) *James Dean: The First American Teenager* (40) Action: *The October Crisis of 1970 in Quebec* (44) Christmas with Bogart: *Casablanca* (52)	

Table 12.1.1 (continued)

Day (Channel)	9.00am–1.00pm	1.00–5.00pm	5.00–9.00pm	9.00pm–1.00am
Wednesday (BBC1)		*Jumbo* (52) Charlie Chaplin in *Modern Times* (53)	*Custer of the West* (1) The Wednesday Film (2–33) *The Red Balloon* (35) What a Carry On! (43–46) *Ice Cold in Alex* (50) Walt Disney's *The Great Locomotive Chase* (52) *Just My Luck / Trapeze* (53)	Christmas with Kojak: *A Question of Answers* [TVM] (52)
Wednesday (BBC2)		Marx Brothers Double Bill (1) *Oliver Twist* (52)	*Three Men in a Boat* [BBC TVM] (53)	*The Charge of the Light Brigade* [1968] (1) *The Evacuees* [BBC TVM] (10) *Diane* [BBC TVM] (28) *Daft as a Brush* [BBC TVM] (39) *The Whip Hand* [BBC TVM] (47) Globe Theatre: *F. Scott Fitzgerald in Hollywood* [TVM] (51) Christmas with Bogart: *Beat the Devil* (52)
Thursday (BBC1)	*Pack Up Your Troubles* (52)	*Oh! Mr Porter* (1) *The Wizard of Oz* (52) *The Court Jester* (53)	*Butch Cassidy and the Sundance Kid* (52) *Chisum* (53)	*The Missiles of October* [TVM] (1) *Hurry Sundown* (13) *The Man Who Skied Down Everest* (36) *Switch* [TVM] (42) *Run a Crooked Mile* [TVM] (53)
Thursday (BBC2)		*Swan Lake* [1966] (52) *Bells Are Ringing* (53)	*The Yearling / The Evacuees* [BBC TVM] (52)	Midweek Cinema (45–51) *Guys and Dolls* (52)

Friday (BBC1)	Let It Be (52)	The Birds and the Bees [1948] (1) tom thumb (52) Abbott and Costello in On the Carpet (53)	The Little House on the Prairie [TVM] (1) [Westerns] (9–12, 14–17, 19) Around the World in Eighty Days (13) The Invisible Man [TVM] (40) Son of Lassie (51) The Railway Children (52)	[The Friday Film] (1–21, 30–32, 35, 37–51) Hitchcock's… (22–29) The Kojak Movies [TVM] (33–34) The Lion in Winter (52)
Friday (BBC2)		Ring of Bright Water (52)	A Forest Tale: Friends for Life (13) Five Minutes to Midnight (36) The Magic Flute [TVM] (52) The Autobiography of Miss Jane Pittman [TVM] (53)	The Revivalist [BBC TVM] (13)

Notes:

Week 39: all BBC2 films were directed by Howard Hawks ('The Men Who Made the Movies').
Week 44: all BBC2 films were directed by William A. Wellman ('The Men Who Made the Movies').
Week 49: all BBC2 films were directed by Frank Capra ('The Men Who Made the Movies').
Weeks 52–53: late-night 'Christmas with Bogart' season on BBC2 spanned several regular strands, including 'Midnight Movie' and 'Sunday Cinema'.

Table 12.1.2 Film scheduling on Anglia Television, 28 December 1974–2 January 1976 (networked and part-networked titles in bold).

Day	9.00am–1.00pm	1.00–5.00pm	5.00–9.00pm	9.00pm–1.00am
Saturday	Saturday Morning Film (3–18, 20–21, 23–36)		Saturday Night at the Movies (1–2); The Saturday Night Film (3–35); The Big Film (36); Saturday Night Movie (37–53)	*The Mercenaries* (1); Mystery Movie [TVM] (18, 34); Saturday Late Film (19–33)
Sunday	*The Borrowers* [TVM] (14); *Michelangelo Antonioni's Chung Kuo (China)* (37)	Sunday Matinee (2); *Alfred the Great* (14); Sunday Afternoon Film (16–20, 22–53); Mystery Movie [TVM] (21)	*The Most Dangerous Man in the World* (1); Sunday TV Movie (2); Star Movie (3–4, 6–13, 15–31, 33–36, 53); *Akenfield* (5); *Camelot* (14)	Film of the Week (37–45, 48–52)
Monday	Morning Matinee (2); *Laurel and Hardy's Laughing 20's* (14)	Monday Matinee (1–2); Monday Afternoon Film (3–13, 15–26, 28–34, 37–39, 41, 45, 52–53); *The Drum* (14); *The Thief of Bagdad* [1940] (35); Mystery Movie (42)	*Battle of the Bulge* (14); *Lawrence of Arabia*, **Part 1** (52)	Mystery Movie [TVM] (1–6); Monday Night Film (7–11, 15); Monday Late Film (16–20, 24–35, 49–53)
Tuesday		*The Young Country* [TVM] (52)	*The Good Guys and the Bad Guys* (1); Mystery Movie [TVM] (3–22, 24–28, 53); The Tuesday Movie (29–35, 41–43, 45–51); **Tuesday Star Movie:** *Quo Vadis* (36); The Tuesday Film (37–40); **The James Bond Film:** *Dr No* (44); *Lawrence of Arabia*, **Part 2** (52)	*The Prison* [ITV TVM] (11)

Day				
Wednesday		*Monte Carlo or Bust!* (1) *Miracle on 34th Street* [TVM] (52)	*Topaz* (1) *Return to Peyton Place* (22) [TV Movie] (30–33) The Wednesday Film (34–35) *Tully* [ITV TVM] (48) *Our Man Flint* (49) *Wait until Dark* (53)	*Valley of the Dolls* (9) *Tully* [ITV TVM] (22) *Who Killed Julia Wallace?* [ITV TVM] (44) *The Naked Civil Servant* [ITV TVM] (51)
Thursday	Morning Matinee (1) *Harold Lloyd's World of Comedy* (52) *The 3 Worlds of Gulliver* (53)	Mystery Movie [TVM] (22, 24, 26, 33–35, 39) *Doctor in Trouble* (52) *Yours, Mine and Ours* (53)	Mystery Movie [TVM] (23) Thursday Night Film [TVM] (49) *The Taming of the Shrew* (52) *Carry on Again Doctor* (53)	The Late Movie (2)
Friday	Morning Matinee (2) Boxing Morning Film (52)	Friday Matinee (2) Friday Afternoon Film (14–16, 20, 22, 25–26, 29–30, 34, 47–51) *David Copperfield* [TVM] (52)	*The Devil and Miss Sarah* [TVM] (1) *The Robe* (13) *The Virgin and the Gypsy* (36) *All the Way Up* (37) *The Great Bank Robbery* (52)	Appointment with Fear (2) Mystery Movie [TVM] (1, 34–35) The Friday Late Film (45–51)

Table 12.1.3 Film scheduling on LWT/Thames Television, 28 December 1974–2 January 1976 (networked and part-networked titles in bold).

Day	9.00am–1.00pm	1.00–5.00pm	5.00–9.00pm	9.00pm–1.00am
Saturday			The Saturday Film (1) *Carry on Camping* (**8**) *The Magnificent Showman* (**13**) The Adventure Film (16–23, 31) Big Adventure Film (24–29) [Feature Film or TV Movie] (30, 32–35, 51–53) The Big Film (36) Saturday Mystery Movie [mostly TVM] (37–50)	[Feature Film or TV Movie] (1–2, 4–7, 15–23, 31–35, 37–53)
Sunday	*Thunderbird 6* (22) *Mr Bug Goes to Town* (37) *The Lone Ranger and the Lost City of Gold* (53)	*Alfred the Great* (**14**) The Family Film (24–29, 37–53) *Treasure Island* [TVM] (36)	*The Most Dangerous Man in the World* (**1**) [Feature Film or TV Movie] (3–4, 6–13, 15–36, 53) *Akenfield* (5) *Camelot* (14)	[Feature Film or TV Movie] (37–46, 48–52)
Monday	[Feature Film] (13–14, 16, 26, 29) Tales of Edgar Wallace (28, 30, 37–38) Shirley Temple in… (50–52)	[Feature Film or TV Movie] (1–13, 15–21, 23–26, 28–34, 37–39, 41–53) *The Drum* (**14**) *The Thief of Bagdad* [1940] (35)	*Battle of the Bulge* (**14**) *Lawrence of Arabia, Part 1* (**52**)	The X Film (1–11, 13) *Masterson of Kansas* (29) *Tony Rome* (35) Late Night Movie (51, 53)

Tuesday	Left, Right and Centre (2)		The Good Guys and the Bad Guys (1) The Tuesday Film (3–5) Mystery Movie [TVM] (6–13, 27–35) Tuesday Star Movie (14–22, 24–26, 36 [*Quo Vadis*]–43, 45–51) **The James Bond Film: *Dr No*** (44) *Lawrence of Arabia*, **Part 2 (52)** Tuesday Mystery Movie (53)	*The Prison* [ITV TVM] (11)
Wednesday	Tales of Edgar Wallace (2, 27) [Feature Film or TV Movie] (22, 26, 28–38, 50–52)	*Monte Carlo or Bust!* (1) *The Guns of Fort Petticoat* (18) *Ride the High Iron* (21) *Miracle on 34th Street* [TVM] (52)	*Topaz* (1) *Yours, Mine and Ours* (22) [Feature Film or TV Movie] (29–35) *Tully* **[ITV TVM] (48)** *Our Man Flint* (49) *Wait until Dark* (53)	*Valley of the Dolls* (9) *Tully* **[ITV TVM] (22)** The X Film (36–43, 45–48, 50) *Who Killed Julia Wallace?* **[ITV TVM] (44)** *The Naked Civil Servant* **[ITV TVM] (51)**
Thursday	[Feature Film] (1–2) Tales of Edgar Wallace (37–38) *Harold Lloyd's World of Comedy* (52)	Comedy Classics (18–20, 23–25) [Feature Film or TV Movie] (22, 26, 33–35, 38–39) Children's Film Matinee (36–51) *Doctor in Trouble* (52) *Take Her, She's Mine* (53)	[TV Movie] (23, 28, 49) *The Taming of the Shrew* (52) *Carry on Again Doctor* (53)	
Friday	[Feature Film or TV Movie] (13–16, 26–38)	[Feature Film or TV Movie] (1–11, 15–16, 20, 22, 25–26, 29–30, 34, 38) *David Copperfield* [TVM] (52)	*The Robe* (13) *The Virgin and the Gypsy* (36) *All the Way Up* (37) *The Great Bank Robbery* (52)	The Friday Film (1–12, 18–23, 26–35) The Korda Classics (14–17)

Table 12.1.4 Film scheduling on Yorkshire Television, 28 December 1974–2 January 1976 (networked and part-networked titles in bold).

Day	9.00am–1.00pm	1.00–5.00pm	5.00–9.00pm	9.00pm–1.00am
Saturday	Saturday Morning Cinema (24–36) *Thunderbird 6* (53)		[Feature Film or TV Movie] (2–7, 11–14, 47–53) [Carry On] (8–10) The Main Feature (15–35) Saturday's All Action Western (36–46)	*The Mercenaries* (1) Movie through Midnight (18–36) [TV Movie] (37–46)
Sunday	*The Falcon in Hollywood* (22) *The Falcon's Alibi* (23) *A King's Story* (53)	*The Three Musketeers* [1948] (14) Sunday Cinema (1, 15–19, 30–53) The British Film Comedy (20–29)	*The Most Dangerous Man in the World* (1) *Death Race* [TVM] (2) *Akenfield* **(5)** The Big Star Film (6–14 [*Camelot*], 53) The Big Film (15–21) Sunday's Star Film (22–36)	The Big Star Film (37–46, 48–52)
Monday	*A Connecticut Yankee in King Arthur's Court* [TVM] (35)	Monday Matinee (1, 12, 14–20, 22–25, 27–33, 36–38, 40–50, 52) [Doris] Day-time (2–6) *Greer Garson* (7–12) *The Drum* **(14)** *The Thief of Bagdad* [**1940**] (35) *The World of Hans Christian Andersen* (52)	**Battle of the Bulge (14)** *Lawrence of Arabia*, **Part 1 (52)**	*Prudence and the Pill* (35) *A Case of Rape* [TVM] (36) *Queen of the Stardust Ballroom* [TVM] (37) Wicked Women (38–51) *Move Over, Darling* (53)

Tuesday		The London Nobody Knows (11)	**The Good Guys and the Bad Guys (1)** Mystery Movie [TVM] (3–22, 24–35, 37–38) _Quo Vadis_ (36) [Feature Film or TV Movie] (39–43) **The James Bond Film: _Dr No_ (44)** The Tuesday Film (45–51, 53) _Lawrence of Arabia_, **Part 2 (52)**	_The Prison_ [ITV TVM] (11)
Wednesday	_Donald of the Colours_ (53)	_Monte Carlo or Bust!_ (1) The Wednesday Film (15, 18, 21) _Miracle on 34th Street_ [TVM] (52)	_Topaz_ (1) _Houseboat_ (22) [Feature Film or TV Movie] (29–35) _Tully_ [ITV TVM] (48) _Our Man Flint_ (49) _Wait until Dark_ (53)	Mystery Movie [TVM] (1) _Valley of the Dolls_ (9) _Tully_ [ITV TVM] (22) _Who Killed Julia Wallace?_ [ITV TVM] (44) _The Naked Civil Servant_ [ITV TVM] (51)
Thursday	_Harold Lloyd's World of Comedy_ **(52)**	[Feature Film or TV Movie] (22, 24, 26, 33–35, 39, 53) _Doctor in Trouble_ (52) An American in Paris (53)	Mrs Sundance [TVM] (23) Midweek Movie [TVM] (49) _The Taming of the Shrew_ (52) _Carry on Again Doctor_ (53)	
Friday	_Laurel and Hardy's Laughing 20's_ (13) _Gulliver's Travels_ (52)	Friday Matinee (1–2, 7–11, 13) Agatha Christie Mysteries (3–6) The Friday Film (14–16, 20–22, 25–26, 29–30, 34, 39) _David Copperfield_ [TVM] (52)	_Steel Town_ (1) _The Robe_ (13) _The Stalking Moon_ (36) _Cactus Flower_ (37) _The Great Bank Robbery_ (52)	Korda Greats/The Korda Season (1–16) The Friday Night Film (17–35, 53)

Table 12.2 BBC film strands in 1975.

THEMED STRANDS

Subject	Month	Day	Time	Channel	No. films
STARS					
Presley at Forty	January	Sunday	Late Night	BBC2	2
Fred and Ginger [musicals]	March–April	Sunday	Afternoon	BBC1	6
Cary Grant (TC)	March–April	Tuesday	Evening	BBC2	4
Randolph Scott [Westerns]	April–May	Friday	Evening	BBC1	5
Bette Davis (FM)	May–July	Sunday	Afternoon	BBC1	7
Robert Mitchum	July–Aug	Saturday	Evening	BBC1	4
Burt Lancaster (FW)	July–Aug	Sunday	Evening	BBC1	5
James Dean (SuC)	Sept–Oct	Sunday, Tuesday	Evening	BBC2	3
Christmas with Bogart	December	Various	Late Night	BBC2	5
GENRES					
Murder at the Movies	Jan–March	Sunday	Late Night	BBC2	9
[Westerns]	Feb–March	Friday	Evening	BBC1	4
[The Bank Holiday Horror Film]	April, May, August	Monday	Late Night	BBC2	3
A Wartime Screen	April–May	Sunday	Evening	BBC1	6
Hollywood musicals (TC)	July	Tuesday	Evening	BBC2	4
Midnight Movie Fantastic (Fantastic Double Bill)	Aug–Sept	Saturday	Late Night	BBC2	12
The Sunday Adventure Film	Aug–Dec	Sunday	Afternoon	BBC1	19
The Saturday Western	Sept–Dec	Saturday	Afternoon	BBC2	14
Hollywood hoofers [musicals] (TC)	October	Tuesday	Evening	BBC2	3
SERIES					
Fu Manchu (TWF)	March	Wednesday	Evening	BBC1	3
The Tarzan Adventures	Aug–Nov	Tuesday	Evening	BBC1	12
What a Carry On!	Oct–Nov	Wednesday	Evening	BBC1	4
DIRECTORS					
Alfred Hitchcock	May–July	Friday	Late Night	BBC1	8
Orson Welles (SuC, MC)	Aug–Sept	Sunday, Tuesday	Evening	BBC2	5
Howard Hawks	September	Various	Various	BBC2	4
William A. Wellman	October	Various	Various	BBC2	4
Frank Capra	Nov–Dec	Various	Various	BBC2	4
WRITERS					
George Bernard Shaw (TC)	Jan–Feb	Tuesday	Evening	BBC2	4
Raymond Chandler (TC)	September	Tuesday	Evening	BBC2	3

Table 12.2 (continued)

THEMED STRANDS					
Subject	**Month**	**Day**	**Time**	**Channel**	**No. films**
STUDIO					
Hammer (MM)	Jan–Feb	Saturday	Late Night	BBC2	6
OTHER THEMES					
Religious Film Festival	Jan–Feb	Sunday	Afternoon	BBC2	8
Images of Childhood	April–June	Tuesday	Evening	BBC2	9
Films for all the family (TWF)	April–Aug	Wednesday	Evening	BBC1	20
Movie Pacemakers (SuC)	Oct–Dec	Sunday	Late Night	BBC2	6
Britain's knights of the stage (MC)	Nov–Dec	Tuesday	Evening	BBC2	6
MADE-FOR-TV MOVIES					
Made-for-TV movies (SaC)	Jan–March	Saturday	Afternoon	BBC2	10
Made-for-TV movies (TFF)	April–May, July–Nov	Friday	Late Night	BBC1	18
The Kojak Movies	August	Friday	Late Night	BBC1	2
GENERAL STRANDS					
Subject	**Month**	**Day**	**Time**	**Channel**	**No. films**
Saturday Cinema	Jan–Aug, Nov–Dec	Saturday	Afternoon	BBC2	38
Saturday Night at the Movies	Jan–July, Aug–Dec	Saturday	Evening	BBC1	48
Midnight Movie (excluding Fantastic Double Bills)	Jan–July, Sept–Dec	Saturday	Late Night	BBC2	43
Film Matinee	Jan–March, May–Aug	Sunday	Afternoon	BBC1	24
Film of the Week	Jan–Dec	Sunday	Evening	BBC1	41
Sunday Cinema	May–Aug	Sunday	Late Night	BBC2	38
The Monday Film	June–Dec	Monday	Evening	BBC1	25
Tuesday Cinema	Jan–April, July–Oct	Tuesday	Evening	BBC2	32
The Wednesday Film	Jan–Aug	Wednesday	Evening	BBC1	31
Midweek Cinema	Nov–Dec	Thursday	Evening	BBC2	7
The Friday Film	Jan–May, Aug–Dec	Friday	Late Night	BBC1	36

genres (nine), film series (three), directors (six), writers (two), a studio (one) or a common thematic element (four). This simplified list is slightly misleading in that, by virtue of their particular talents and iconographic associations, several of the featured stars, directors and writers tended to be linked with certain genres. Thus, 'Fred and Ginger' equated to musical comedies (see Figure 12.3), Randolph Scott

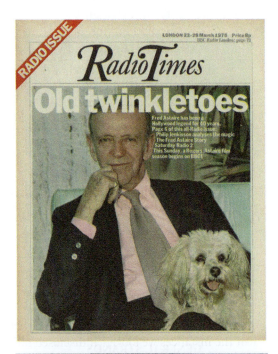

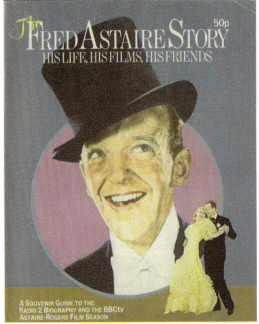

Figure 12.3a–b In the spring of 1975, Fred Astaire was the subject of both a six-film BBC1 season and a thirteen-part Radio 1 biography, written and presented by Philip Jenkinson. In addition to a profile article by Jenkinson in the regular magazine, *Radio Times* published a 68-page special on Astaire to accompany the shows and films. *Radio Times* © Immediate Media Co. Photograph © Ellen Graham.

to Westerns, and Alfred Hitchcock and Raymond Chandler to different types of thriller. Several strands were designed to spotlight a number of particular individuals within a generic or thematic context: thus, a group of three musicals each featuring a different male 'hoofer' (dancer), a season of films starring 'Britain's knights of the stage in some of their most distinguished film performances', and 'Movie Pacemakers', a series 'featuring the work of some of the most influential directors of the contemporary international cinema'.[54]

Another notable feature of the BBC's programming is that a number of these themed seasons were placed *within* established strands, forming sub-sets of otherwise non-thematic series. For example, the last three seasons just mentioned were placed within the series 'Tuesday Cinema', 'Midweek Cinema' and 'Sunday Cinema', respectively, while for a time 'The Wednesday Film' was devoted to 'films for all the family'.[55] A further variant of this was to 'strip' films on a particular theme across all the established slots in a given week, rather than confining them to a single dedicated slot over a number of weeks. In 1975, BBC2 offered four mini-seasons of this kind. One of these was 'Christmas with Bogart', the first of what became an annual trend of showcasing a particular star over the holiday period (the following year offered 'Christmas with Cagney').[56] The other three involved one-week, four-film tributes to directors featured in the imported American documentary series *The Men Who Made the Movies*: Howard Hawks, William A. Wellman and Frank Capra. Hitchcock was the first subject of this series but his season instead played weekly at peak-time on BBC1.[57]

Thematic strands were in the minority on ITV stations, but they were not completely absent. YTV, for example, devoted daytime seasons to Doris Day, Greer Garson, 'Agatha Christie Mysteries' and 'Wicked Women', Thames to Shirley Temple, and both YTV and LWT to producer-director Alexander Korda (several other regional stations followed suit thanks to Leslie Halliwell's reacquisition of the Korda library for the ITV network). Anglia completed its latest 'Appointment with Fear' horror season at the beginning of the year, Thames created 'Children's Film Matinee' and resumed 'The X Film' (moving the latter strand from Monday to Wednesday), and LWT offered adventure films on Saturday evenings, a time when YTV favoured Westerns. Both Thames and YTV mounted seasons of vintage comedies, the latter also placing two more Carry On films around the part-networked *Carry on Camping* (1969/15.02).[58] BBC1 had its own four-week Carry On season, partially reprising a longer one from the previous year.

Networking and part-networking were more in evidence at ITV this year than they had ever been before (see Tables 12.3 and 12.4). This was a trend that would increase in years to come; besides complying with the IBA's wishes for more coordinated scheduling and addressing the ongoing issue of print wear and tear (see Chapter 9), it may have been spurred by the increasing scarcity of new films suitable for peak-time slots. This consideration was also partly responsible for the later placing in the autumn of Sunday-evening film slots, which moved from a typical 7.25 or 7.55 to 9.10pm (see Chapter 11). Major box-office hits were scheduled in prominent network

Table 12.3 Film transmission statistics, 1 January–31 December 1975.

ITV films only	No. films
Total film transmissions	3,952
Total individual titles	1,517
UK TV premieres	147
Films first shown by BBC	130
Films fully networked	16
Films part-networked	9
Dubbed overseas films	13
Subtitled foreign-language films	4
Documentaries	7
Compilation films	5

All channels:

Channel	No. films
BBC1	319
BBC2	233
Anglia	261
ATV	347
Border	311
Channel	307
Grampian	282
Granada	389
HTV Wales & West	328
London (LWT/Thames)	332
Scottish	261
Southern	279
Tyne Tees	307
Ulster	257
Westward	307
Yorkshire	291
All stations (films)	2,060
All stations (premieres)	374
All stations (transmissions)	4,497

Note: Made-for-TV films not released in UK cinemas are excluded.

slots, supported by extensive editorial coverage in *TV Times*. Thus, the TV premieres of *Valley of the Dolls* (1967/26.02), *The Robe* (1953/28.03), *Dr No* (1962/28.10) and *Our Man Flint* (1966/03.12) were all promoted by cover features in the magazine (see Figures 6.2 and 12.4). Doing battle in the ratings war, *Camelot* (1967/30.03) and *Battle of the Bulge* (1965/31.03) led the charge at Easter, while *Quo Vadis* (1951/02.09) fronted the autumn season and the two-part *Lawrence of Arabia* (1962/22 & 23.12) Christmas week. These films generally placed highly in the ratings, but industrial action affecting most ITV stations in May's Spring Bank Holiday week gave a boost to the BBC's presentation of *The Longest Day* (1962/26.05) at what would usually have been a competitive time (see Tables 12.5.1 and 12.5.2).

Table 12.4 ITV networked and part-networked films (simultaneous transmission in seven or more regions), 28 December 1974–2 January 1976.

Film	Year	TX date	No. regions
The Most Dangerous Man in the World	1969	29.12.1974	14
The Good Guys and the Bad Guys	1969	31.12.1974	14
Monte Carlo or Bust!	1969	01.01.1975	14
Topaz	1969	01.01.1975	14
Akenfield	1974	26.01.1975	14
Carry on Camping	1969	15.02.1975	12
Valley of the Dolls	1967	26.02.1975	14
The Magnificent Showman	1964	22.03.1975	7
The Robe	1953	28.03.1975	14
Camelot	1967	30.03.1975	14
The Drum	1938	31.03.1975	14
Battle of the Bulge	1965	31.03.1975	14
The Thief of Bagdad	1940	25.08.1975	7
Quo Vadis	1951	02.09.1975	13 (excluding STV)
Bob & Carol & Ted & Alice	1969	14.09.1975	10
The Executioner	1970	21.09.1975	9
The Killing of Sister George	1968	28.09.1975	10
Dr No	1962	28.10.1975	13 (excluding UTV)
Our Man Flint	1966	03.12.1975	14
The Virgin Soldiers	1969	07.12.1975	8
Lawrence of Arabia	1962	22 & 23.12.1975	14
Harold Lloyd's World of Comedy	1962	25.12.1975	14
Doctor in Trouble	1970	25.12.1975	14
The Taming of the Shrew	1967	25.12.1975	14
David Copperfield	1970	26.12.1975	14
The Great Bank Robbery	1969	26.12.1975	14
Wait until Dark	1967	31.12.1975	14
Carry on Again Doctor	1969	01.01.1976	14

Following the cancellation of 'World Cinema' the previous year, and prior to the launch of 'Film International' the following year, there was no dedicated BBC2 slot for foreign-language films in 1975. Instead, these were integrated into existing strands, whether themed – such as 'Murder at the Movies', 'Religious Film Festival' and 'Images of Childhood' – or otherwise. In addition, two Ingmar Bergman productions made for Swedish television but released in UK cinemas were also given prominent slots: the series *Six Scenes from a Marriage* (1973) was shown in six weekly parts from 7 February, albeit in an English-dubbed version at the director's insistence (it even merited a *Radio Times* cover feature); and the opera *The Magic Flute* (1975/26.12) was BBC2's main attraction on Boxing Day.

Other types of specialised film were also shown on BBC2. No fewer than three silent features appeared in August: *Metropolis* (1927/12.08), *The Cabinet of Dr Caligari* (1920/02.08) and *Noah's Ark* (1928/16.09), the latter two among the double bills in the 'Midnight Movie Fantastic' season (see Chapter 10). Also on

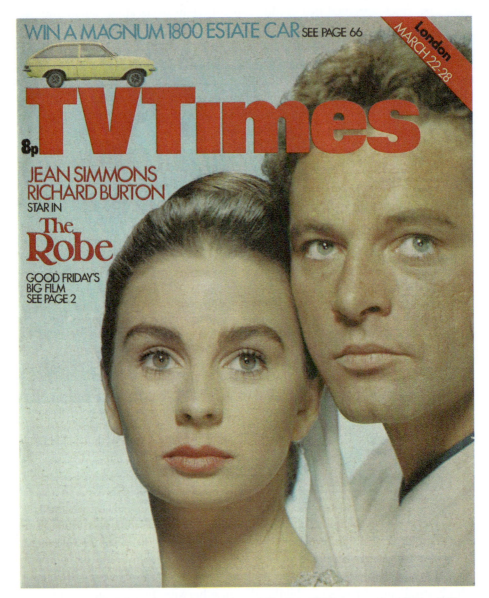

WIN A MAGNUM 1800 ESTATE CAR SEE PAGE 66

London
MARCH 22-28

TVTimes

8p

JEAN SIMMONS
RICHARD BURTON
STAR IN

The
Robe

GOOD FRIDAY'S
BIG FILM
SEE PAGE 2

Figure 12.4 ITV's belated television premiere of *The Robe* (1953) was on Good Friday 1975. Note that this issue is for the same dates as *Radio Times*'s Fred Astaire cover, a rare instance of both magazines having film-related cover stories in the same week.
TVTimes © Future Publishing Ltd.

BBC2 and outside the feature realm, *The Magic Moving Picture Show* (25.01, 24.12), a one-off programme hosted by film historian John Huntley, anthologised early shorts by the Lumière brothers and Georges Méliès; and the thirteen-part series *The First Picture Show* (beginning 20.09), fronted by director and critic Gavin Millar, showcased new short films 'made by young film-makers at art

Table 12.5.1 JICTAR ratings for selected film transmissions, 28 December 1974–2 January 1976.

Film	Year	Channel	TX date	Homes viewing (millions)	Ratings place
Dr No	1962	ITV exc. Ulster	28.10.1975	10.50	1
Challenge to Lassie	1949	BBC1	28.05.1975	7.85	10=
Our Man Flint	1966	ITV network	03.12.1975	7.65	8=
The Longest Day	1962	BBC1	26.05.1975	7.60	14
Valley of the Dolls	1967	ITV network	26.02.1975	7.45	10=
Mosquito Squadron	1970	BBC1	20.12.1975	7.35	15
Topaz	1969	ITV network	01.01.1975	7.05	10
Dodge City	1939	BBC1	24.05.1975	7.05	12
The Last Voyage	1960	BBC1	06.12.1975	6.85	18
Butch Cassidy and the Sundance Kid	1969	BBC1	25.12.1975	6.65	4
The Most Dangerous Man in the World	1969	ITV network	29.12.1974	6.50	6
The Robe	1953	ITV network	28.03.1975	6.45	17=
Monte Carlo or Bust!	1969	ITV network	01.01.1975	6.25	19=
Lawrence of Arabia, Part 1	1962	ITV network	22.12.1975	6.15	11=
Lawrence of Arabia, Part 2	1962	ITV network	23.12.1975	6.10	15=

Source: JICTAR, as published in the trade press.

Table 12.5.2 BBC Audience Research figures for selected film transmissions, 1 January–31 December 1975.

Film	Year	Channel	TX date	Viewers (millions)
Dr No	1962	ITV exc. Ulster	28.10.1975	27.0
Butch Cassidy and the Sundance Kid	1969	BBC1	25.12.1975	24.7
The Longest Day	1962	BBC1	26.05.1975	24.2
The Wizard of Oz	1939	BBC1	25.12.1975	20.0
Carry on Doctor	1968	BBC1	22.10.1975	17.0
The FBI Story	1959	BBC1	09.11.1975	17.0
Around the World in Eighty Days	1956	BBC1	28.03.1975	14.0
Spring and Port Wine	1970	BBC1	02.03.1975	14.0
'A Wartime Screen' (series)		BBC1	April–May	Av. 13.0
A Fistful of Dollars	1964	BBC1	01.08.1975	12.0

Note: JICTAR/AGB estimated 16 million viewers for *Butch Cassidy and the Sundance Kid*; a memo from BBC Television Managing Director Alasdair Milne (2 January 1976, BBC R78/1, 123/1) claimed 25.5 million viewers.

Source: BBC Audience Research, as published in the trade press.

colleges, film schools and polytechnics throughout Britain'. In a *Radio Times* 'Preview' column, Philip Jenkinson praised the latter as 'television's first attempt to give independent film-making the exposure it deserves'.[59] Acquired documentaries were included only rarely in Jenkinson's regular films page, usually being placed in the schedules as if they were television productions, even when they had received theatrical release. In 1975 these included *Brother, Can You Spare a Dime?* (1975/23.03), *The Double Headed Eagle* (1973/01.07), Louis Malle's *A Human Condition* (1974/31.08), *The Man Who Skied down Everest* (1975/04.09) and *James Dean: The First American Teenager* (1975/30.09).

The European children's films acquired by BBC producer Peggy Miller were also not acknowledged in *Radio Times* as theatrical features (see Chapter 7). With the addition of English narration and re-edited into episodic form, four such films were serialised throughout the year as part of children's programming on BBC1. A Soviet animal adventure, *A Forest Tale: Friends for Life* (1972/26.12.1974), was similarly presented with an English soundtrack as a holiday special on BBC2. Albert Lamorisse's featurette *The Red Balloon* (1956/27.08), whose storytelling was sufficiently visual not to need either subtitles or a voice-over, earned a place at peak-time on the main channel, despite its being the film's fifth transmission on British television. Several other popular European productions were shown in dubbed versions on BBC1, including the television premieres of Sergio Leone's *Fistful of Dollars* (1964/01.08) and *For a Few Dollars More* (1965/30.12) and Francesco Rosi's *Cinderella – Italian Style* (1967/29.12).Their equivalents at ITV included *Ulysses* (1954/17.12), *Flaming Frontier* (1965/10.05) and *The Champagne Murders* (1967/24.03), all shown that year in London; *The Treasure of Silver Lake* (1962/25.10) and *Among Vultures* (1964/27.09), both shown in Yorkshire; and *Babette Goes to War* (1959/22.08, 11.10), shown by both YTV and Anglia.

Both the BBC and ITV acquired a number of mainstream features whose UK distributors had not deemed them sufficiently commercial to merit a theatrical outing. Unreleased films shown in one or more of our three sample ITV regions included *The Uncle* (1966/23.06) and *Revenge Is My Destiny* (1971/13.04) in London, *Mara of the Wilderness* (1965/07.06) and *Kenner* (1968/12.07) on Anglia, *Molly and Lawless John* (1972/30.09) on YTV, *The Day of the Wolves* (1971) in both London (04.01) and Yorkshire (27.07), and *The Picasso Summer* (1969) on both Anglia (28.06) and YTV (19.07). Those shown by the BBC included *Change of Habit* (1969/11.01), *Number One* (1969/03.08), *The Breaking of Bumbo* (1970/17.08), *Going Home* (1971/13.07) and *One Is a Lonely Number* (1972/29.06).

Although this book is primarily concerned with theatrical films, it is important to acknowledge those made directly for the small screen because they increasingly came to take the place of feature films. ITV was more heavily committed to showing made-for-TV movies than the BBC, though both networks acquired a substantial number. First seen on British television in 1969, American TV movies acted as a substitute for the new cinema films considered too sexually explicit or too violent for the domestic medium, and could safely be placed in both peak-time and daytime slots. Most in evidence on ITV were detective stories, collectively presented under the rubric 'Mystery Movie' and incorporating several series built around recurring characters, such as *Banacek*, *Columbo*, *Hec Ramsey*, *McCloud* and *McMillan and Wife*. Of our three sample stations, Anglia made the most extensive use of such films, often placing them on several different days in the same week. LWT's 'Saturday Mystery Movie' alternated TV movies with cinema films.

The BBC, by contrast, tended to confine made-for-TV features to a few particular slots: Saturday afternoons on BBC2 for the first ten weeks of 1975, then late Friday nights on BBC1 for the rest of the year. In addition, 'pilot' films launched several acquired American series, including *The Little House on the Prairie*, *The Invisible Man* and *Switch*, while feature-length episodes of *Kojak* (a ratings topper) were also given prominent slots. So too were a number of prestige TV movies presented as one-off specials, including two that had received a limited UK theatrical release: *Frankenstein: The True Story* (1973/27.12) and *The Autobiography of Miss Jane Pittman* (1974/02.01.1976).

A number of British-produced TV dramas, shot on 16mm or 35mm, which would in other countries have been identified as films, were instead typically billed as plays or dramatised documentaries. They include the BBC's *Robinson Crusoe* (29.12.1974, a rare *Play of the Month* episode made on film), *The Evacuees* (05.03, repeated on Christmas Day) and *Three Men in a Boat* (31.12). On ITV, there were two episodes of the occasional *Armchair Cinema* anthology series made by Thames's subsidiary Euston Films, *The Prison* (11.03) and *Tully* (28.05, repeated on 16.11), plus YTV's docudrama *Who Killed Julia Wallace?* (29.10) and another Thames production, *The Naked Civil Servant* (17.12). All four ITV-produced films were networked, the latter two presented under *The Wednesday Special*, an umbrella strand that embraced drama, documentary and sport. None of these productions, or other filmed dramas made as part of BBC1's ongoing *Play for Today* series or as occasional specials on BBC2, had any kind of theatrical release, due to agreements with unions that also restricted the number of times they could be broadcast and the period in which they could be repeated.

Mr Lucifer's Advocate

How does the film scheduling for 1975 stack up against the critical cases made by Edward Buscombe and Lynda Myles? Both recommended more adventurous programming policies, with more foreign-language and silent films, more independent and avant-garde films, and more imaginative choices of themed season. In general, they also asked for a more serious approach to the presentation of films as a step towards helping a more sophisticated film culture develop in Britain. To what extent did the films and film series broadcast in 1975 meet these challenges or bear out the criticisms?

It should be clear from my detailed summary that the selection of topics for film strands was more varied than the reports would suggest. Besides stars, directors and genres they included a studio (Hammer, in a six-film season included in 'Midnight Movie'), writers (Shaw, Chandler, Christie), a producer (Korda), several series (including the first UK transmissions of the MGM Tarzan films), and such themes as religion, childhood, female villains and the screen performances of theatrical knights. Granted that in most cases these strands comprised on average half a dozen titles each (some even fewer), but that was comparable to what a repertory cinema could reasonably have been expected to offer. Prints were, as even Buscombe and Myles acknowledged, likely to have been in far superior condition to those typically seen in such theatres, even assuming they had the access to distributors' back catalogues enjoyed by the broadcasters. In the case of genres, the wider range of titles possible allowed for much longer seasons, including nineteen weeks of 'The Sunday Adventure Film' on BBC1, fourteen of 'The Saturday Western' on BBC2 and thirteen of YTV's 'Wicked Women'. Yorkshire also scheduled sixteen Korda productions.

If the avant-garde was indeed under-represented, the same could not be said of popular cinema of the past. Besides four films from the 1920s (three silents and an early sound feature), during the calendar year the BBC transmitted forty-six films from the 1930s and 102 from the 1940s. Collectively, the fifteen ITV companies broadcast eighty from the 1930s and 168 from the 1940s. In local terms, considering only our sample regions, the London companies showed seventeen from the 1930s and thirty from the 1940s; Anglia, eight and thirty, respectively; and Yorkshire, twenty-one and thirty-one. In total, excluding made-for-TV films, more than 2,050 individual titles were transmitted by all UK stations in calendar 1975. Precisely 400 were made before 1950 – a respectable number. Though they tended to predominate in the afternoon and late at night, these older films were not all consigned to off-peak slots: BBC1's 'A Wartime Screen', comprising six British films of World War Two, all new to television, was placed at peak-time on Sunday evenings. The same channel's Tarzan season, twelve films made between 1934 and 1953 (many of them also new to television), had a prime Tuesday-evening slot. Even on ITV, Korda's *The Drum* (1938/31.03) and *The Thief of Bagdad* (1940/25.08) were, respectively, networked and part-networked as holiday specials.

On BBC2, many of the films in the peak-time 'Tuesday Cinema' and 'Midweek Cinema' strands were of like vintage, including a version of *Major Barbara* (1941/28.01) several minutes longer than any that had been seen theatrically. Among the features shown in BBC1's early-evening 'Wednesday Film' series was a recently-rediscovered Will Hay comedy, *Where's That Fire?* (1939/11.06). Indeed, the identification of that film's long-forgotten negative in Twentieth Century-Fox's Hollywood vault was precisely the result of enquiries made by the BBC's Alan Howden. The version of *Joan of Arc* (1948/12.01) presented in BBC2's 'Religious Film Festival' had been painstakingly reconstructed to its original length for a previous transmission after successive reissues had reduced the running time by some forty-five minutes.[60] These are concrete examples of films owing not just their physical preservation but their restoration and public availability directly to television's intervention.

Ten theatrical feature documentaries were shown by the BBC and seven more by local ITV channels, including *Michelangelo Antonioni's Chung Kuo* (1972/07.09), a documentary about China, on Anglia and in other regions. Although there was no dedicated BBC foreign-language strand in 1975, twenty-three such films nevertheless appeared in its schedules. This was, however, fewer than in any year for the past decade (see Appendix 1). The absence of a dedicated slot akin to 'World Cinema' also limited audience access to non-western cinema more heavily than in previous years. The only films broadcast that year made outside North America and Europe were shown exclusively in HTV's latest 'Experimental Film Season': *The Money Order* (1968/21.07) from Senegal, *Blood of the Condor* (1969/28.07) from Bolivia and *Antonio das Mortes* (1969/04.08) from Brazil.[61]

I want to end this chapter on a personal note. The year 1975 is significant for me because it was the first of which I was fully aware as a viewer. At the age of nine, I had begun buying *Radio Times* the previous September and added *TV Times* in January, specifically to keep track of what films were due to be shown on television. I kept notes and lists of the films broadcast in my region, the North East of England. I could then plan what films to watch, rather than just happening upon them randomly, and I tried to see as many as I could. There were restrictions. Lacking any means of recording, I had to miss any film that clashed with a programme my parents wanted to see, or indeed with a rival film. Because of school, I could not stay up too late or see weekday matinees. Sent to bed, I missed many endings, including the hero's auto-enucleation in *The Man with the X-Ray Eyes* (1963/21.07). But I still managed to take in quite a lot: according to my typewritten records, I saw, in part or whole, 333 films on TV that year, out of 857 notionally available to me. This compared with eleven cinema visits in the same period.

In that formative period, this impressionable child saw, besides many of those already mentioned: *My Darling Clementine* (1946/25.01), *The Gospel According to Matthew* (1964/02.02), *The Producers* (1967/25.05), *Kes* (1969/03.06), *The Prisoner of Zenda* (1937/16.07), *Citizen Kane* (1941/26.08), *The Adventures of Robin Hood* (1938/14.09), *The Private Life of Sherlock Holmes* (1970/07.12), *The Treasure of the Sierra Madre* (1948/21.12) and *Casablanca* (24.12). Not all of these I appreciated on first encounter, but that didn't put me off trying again on the next transmission.

A run of blockbusters on Sunday nights fed my nascent interest in the epic. Thanks to BBC1's placing of its Hitchcock season on Friday evenings (when there was no school the following day), I saw *Psycho* (1960/30.05), *Dial M for Murder* (1954/06.06) and five others. Thanks to Tyne Tees' 'Appointment with Fear' also being on Fridays, I saw *Bride of Frankenstein* (1935/02.05), *Dracula* (1931/16.05) and other Universal horrors, even if in a random order. The Tarzan series, however, I saw in the right order. I don't know if it was half term or a convenient illness that allowed me to see for the first time Basil Rathbone and Nigel Bruce in *The Adventures of Sherlock Holmes* (1939/20.10) one Monday afternoon. On Saturday, 11 October, I was forced invidiously to choose between *She Wore a Yellow Ribbon* (1949) and *Bad Day at Black Rock* (1955). But on lucky weekends, or bank holidays, I could see four or five movies in one sitting. For nothing.

Christmas Day and Boxing Day each offered a choice of nine films, of which I saw seven over the two days. On August Bank Holiday Monday, I managed four and a half out of eight. Sunshine be damned.

These and many other small-screen film-viewing experiences, around this time and in the years that followed, gave me a dawning awareness of cinema history that was supplemented by my first reference books, which included Angela and Elkan Allan's *The Sunday Times Guide to Movies on Television* and Leslie Halliwell's *The Filmgoer's Companion*. I was not alone. Responding to a *Radio Times* column quoted in the Introduction to this book, in which Chris Dunkley referred to the 'dilution' and 'distortion' of cinema films when seen on television, reader Jacqui Atkins spoke for me when she wrote a letter citing the incomparable opportunities television offered to see classic films:

> A whole generation like myself, interested in cinema, doesn't have a glowing memory of those films being shown in cinemas on their original release, and without television we would have missed out completely. …
>
> Of course, there are those which need size to convey a feeling of space, but a truly great film or brilliant performance doesn't need physical size.
>
> Films such as *Casablanca* and *All About Eve*, such stars as Judy Garland and Humphrey Bogart, and there are many others, would be compelling on any scale. Doesn't the enthusiasm of many people like myself, who have seen them almost entirely on television, testify to this?
>
> Where films do gain from television is in the very intelligent organisation applied to them.
>
> The short seasons of specific stars and themes, accompanied by *Radio Times* articles, and now the excellent *Radio Times Fred Astaire Special* – an idea to be repeated, I hope, with future seasons – give the films a perspective denied to them on original release.[62]

Atkins may have been replying directly to Dunkley, but in spirit she was answering Buscombe and Myles too.

Notes

1 Elkan Allan, 'Report Slams TV Movie Policy', *Sunday Times*, 5 December 1971, 52.
2 Buscombe, *Screen Pamphlet* 1: *Films on TV*.
3 Lynda Myles, 'The BBC and the Film Industry', 21 March 1979, BBC R78/1, 123/1.
4 Buscombe, *Films on TV*, 9–10.
5 Ibid, 12–13.
6 Ibid, 14–15, 18.
7 Ibid, 23.
8 Ibid, 25–6.
9 Ibid, 26.
10 Ibid, 27.
11 Ibid, 27–8.
12 Ibid, 29.

13 Ibid, 30.

14 Ibid, 31–2.

15 Ibid, 61.

16 Ibid, 62.

17 Allan, 'Report Slams TV Movie Policy'.

18 David Pirie, 'Electric Cinema', *Time Out*, 24–30 December 1971. A second Warner Bros season was broadcast on BBC2 in 1979.

19 Allen Eyles, 'TV Cinema', *Films and Filming* 18, no. 6 (March 1972), 68. Besides his regular column, Eyles had earlier written his own, rather more positive, reports on the subject: 'The Film on TV', in Speed, *Film Review 1968–1969*, 157–60; and 'TV Survey', in Speed, *Film Review 1969–1970*, 46–7.

20 Leslie Halliwell, 'Films That Nearly Got Away', National Film Theatre programme booklet, September–November 1973, 50–2. The season was reviewed in Mansel Stimpson, 'Films on Your Own Screen', *Film* 2, no. 10 (January 1974): 22.

21 Elkan Allan, 'Guess What's Coming on Television', *Sunday Times Magazine*, 21 October 1973, 100, 102; Allan and Allan, *The Sunday Times Guide to Movies on Television*.

22 Peter Armitage, 'Films on Television', *Film* 2, no. 9 (December 1973), 7–8. See also Armitage's brief survey of TV film-buying, 'Peaceful Coexistence between Films and Television', *Film* 2, no. 4 (July 1973): 20.

23 David Castell, 'The Cannibal in the Corner', *Films Illustrated* 8, no. 50 (October 1975): 67.

24 Bryan Forbes, 'A Personal View', *Films Illustrated* 8, no. 50 (October 1975): 66.

25 Quoted in Doreen Taylor, 'Films, TV and Lynda Myles', *Broadcast*, 29 January 1979, 5.

26 Myles, 'The BBC and the Film Industry', 1–2.

27 Ibid, 2.

28 Ibid, 3.

29 Besides the case of Warner Bros, mentioned earlier, other studios had been the subjects of BBC seasons: Twentieth Century-Fox (1972), Columbia (1976), Paramount (1976), Elstree (1976) and, most impressively, Ealing (1977). The latter comprised nineteen titles, each preceded by an edition of Gaumont-British News for the film's month of release.

30 Ibid, 3–4.

31 Ibid, 5. Forbes was in turn soon replaced by Sheridan Morley, better known for his writings on theatre than cinema. Philip Jenkinson had earlier written of his own dissatisfaction with film critics in 'Whatever Happened to Opinion or How I Learned to Stop Criticising and Love the Movies', *Film* 50 (Winter 1967): 7–9. Despite this, in his *Radio Times* column he was regularly critical of the films shown by the BBC, often drawing attention to their perceived defects. See Hall, '"So Much More than TV Times": Film Coverage in *Radio Times* and *TV Times*'.

32 Ibid, 5. On French practices in the televising of films, see for example Robert Aarons, 'French Television', *Film* 61 (Spring 1971): 17.

33 'Critics and teachers working hard to lead their readers and students towards more adequate ways of discussing the cinema will get no help at all from *My Kind of Movie*' (Colin McArthur, 'The BBC's Cinema Policy – Whose Kind of Movie', *Tribune*, 20 October 1978, reprinted in *Dialectic!*, 79).

34 Myles, 'The BBC and the Film Industry', 5.

35 Buscombe, *Films on TV*, 57.

36 Myles, 'The BBC and the Film Industry', 7.

37 On the sponsorship of Italian and West German films by television, see John Francis Lane, 'Italian TV as Super-Producer', *Sight and Sound* 40, no. 2 (Spring 1971): 76–7; Vincent Porter, 'TV Strategies and European Film Production', *Sight and Sound* 43, no. 3 (Summer 1974): 163–5, 175; Porter, 'Television and Film Production in Europe', *Sight and Sound* 46, no. 4 (Autumn 1977): 205–7, 251; and, contrasting the European and American scenes, John Russell Taylor, 'Movies for a Small Screen', *Sight and Sound* 44, no. 2 (Spring 1975): 113–15. Michael Radford made the case for a European-style integration of cinema and television production from a filmmaker's point of view in 'Television and Movies', *Sight and Sound* 45, no. 4 (Autumn 1976): 227.

38 Ibid, 10.

39 Gunnar Rugheimer, 'Response from the BBC', 22 March 1979, 12 (pagination continued from Myles's paper), BBC R78/1, 123/1.

40 Ibid, 12.

41 Ibid, 13.

42 Ibid, 13–14.

43 Ibid, 14.

44 Ibid, 15.

45 Ibid, 16. Compare Rugheimer's remarks with Colin McArthur's *Tribune* review of Norman's 1978 series *The Hollywood Greats*, whose view of cinema he described as 'trivializing' and which, he argued, had the effect of pre-empting 'more serious programmes about the cinema' ('*The Hollywood Greats*, or How to Trivialize the Cinema', in *Dialectic!*, 77).

46 Ibid, 17.

47 Ibid, 18.

48 Ibid, 19.

49 Taylor, 'Films, TV and Lynda Myles'.

50 Minutes of a meeting of the Board of Management, 'The BBC and the Film Industry', 26 March 1979; Roger Cary to the Chairman, 'GAC Paper on the Film Industry', 9 April 1979, BBC R78/1, 123/1.

51 John Wilkinson to General Advisory Council, 'The BBC and the Film Industry', GAC 569, 11 April 1979, D371-4, BBC R78/1, 123/1.

52 Minutes of a Meeting of the General Advisory Council, 'The BBC and the Film Industry', 18, BBC R78/1, 123/1.

53 *TV Times*'s films page used these four designations rather than actual start times, though in its case 'Morning' meant actual morning and 'Late Night' after 10.00pm.

54 *Radio Times*, 30 October 1975, 57; 16 October 1975, 27.

55 *Radio Times*, 27 March 1975, 51.

56 Subjects of other festive seasons included Elvis Presley (1977), Fred Astaire and Ginger Rogers (1978), Jack Lemmon (1978, 1981), The Beatles, Gene Kelly (both 1979), Astaire solo, Clark Gable, Walter Matthau (all 1980), William Holden, Harold Lloyd and Cliff Richard (all 1981).

57 Directors featured in subsequent episodes of *The Men Who Made the Movies* and similarly treated to week-long BBC2 tributes were George Cukor (1976), Vincente

Minnelli, King Vidor and Raoul Walsh (all 1977). Other Hollywood directors previously featured in BBC seasons were Alfred Hitchcock (1969), John Ford (1972), Billy Wilder (1972) and Preston Sturges (1973). They were followed by Fritz Lang, Fred Zinnemann (both 1977), Henry King, William Wyler (both 1978) and Douglas Sirk (1979). Some of these were the subjects of further retrospectives in the 1980s.

58 Unlike in other parts of this book, all bracketed transmission dates mentioned in this section are for 1975 unless otherwise noted.

59 *Radio Times*, 30 October 1975, 21, 17.

60 Armitage, 'Films on Television', 7; 'News', *Radio Times*, 8 June 1975, 4; Allen Eyles, 'TV Cinema', *Films and Filming* 18, no. 5 (February 1972): 68.

61 *The Money Order* and *Antonio das Mortes* were co-produced with European countries.

62 Jacqui Atkins, 'TV Films Are OK…' (letter), *Radio Times*, 10 April 1975, 69.

Things to Come – Into the Eighties

Film-makers used to write in sand: their work was all too short-lived. Television has given some films a continuing lease of life for which I, for one, am grateful.

(Sir Michael Balcon, 'A Bouquet from Balcon', Letters, *Radio Times*, 11 August 1977, 51)

New Horizons, New Providers

Although the internal reception given to Lynda Myles's 1979 report did not bode well for progressive change at the BBC, significant developments did take place in the years immediately following. Whether these were at all due to her intervention is impossible to say. But films on television had lost none of their popularity in the 1980s, when most of the all-time highest ratings for broadcast films were recorded. According to a 1982 poll conducted for the *Sunday Times* by Market and Opinion Research International (MORI), a majority of viewers favoured the showing of more films on TV. This was especially the case with viewers aged between eighteen and twenty-four (57 per cent).[1] They were to get their wish.

In this period, and for the next two decades, film strands, on BBC2 in particular, became more extensive and the choice of topics more ambitious. 'The Great American Picture Show', celebrating the 'New Hollywood' of the previous decade, was launched in 1980. This first of three seasons included twenty films, most of them network premieres. In early 1982, finally delivering on Gunnar Rugheimer's assurance that his team had their eyes on the Dominions, BBC2 ran its first 'Australian Film Season', with sixteen titles. Five more such seasons were to follow in the next few years, and the Antipodes were henceforth to become a regular source of English-speaking films on all channels. Director retrospectives grew in size and ambition. A ten-film BBC2 tribute to Michael Powell and Emeric Pressburger in 1980 contributed significantly to the critical and public rediscovery of the writer/producer/director team. At Christmas 1981, the silent and early-sound features of Harold Lloyd were televised in their entirety for the first time in a fourteen-film retrospective. Most of them had previously been glimpsed only in the clip shows that so irritated Ed Buscombe. The following year featured mammoth BBC2 seasons devoted to Orson Welles (all thirteen of his completed features), Alfred Hitchcock and John Ford (seventeen films apiece). They sent this teenage viewer scurrying to his local library to read up on these filmmakers' careers and achievements.

In 1979, Purchasing Assistant Alan Howden had acquired for the Corporation the entire RKO library, in perpetuity – the offer of which had been refused in 1957. Films from this deal began to appear in the schedules in 1981 and for the next three decades they became a mainstay of off-peak programming, until the BBC's use of vintage movies began to dwindle (see Figure 13.1). No doubt due to the unavailability of suitable materials for a large number of the more obscure titles, only about half the RKO inventory of 740 features was ever transmitted and, though the Corporation retains the UK broadcast rights for the whole library to this day, only around forty are regularly revived, on air or on iPlayer.

At ITV, continuing a trend from the late 1970s, peak-time films were increasingly networked or part-networked. In pursuing new acquisitions, Leslie Halliwell and the Film Purchase Group were often successful in beating the BBC to major packages. In 1981, an internal memorandum sought to redress the common complaint among IBA staff 'that the BBC has often in the past obtained the better feature films'. For 'almost the first time', it argued, ITV now had the better stock. The memo listed thirty-five recent acquisitions, including such blockbusters as *Jaws* (1975/08.10.1981), *Saturday Night Fever* (1977/29.07.1981), *Shampoo* (1975/11.11.1981), *A Star Is Born* (1976/14.12.1981), *The Way We Were* (1973/14.01.1982), *Alien* (1979/11.07.1982) and *Heaven Can Wait* (1978/03.01.1983). But it also included a number of prestige films of the kind that would not normally be considered typical ITV fare. Among them were *California Split* (1974/22.09.1980), *The Duellists* (1977/12.08.1982), *Equus* (1977/28.12.1982), *An Unmarried Woman* (1977/23.07.1983) and *Carnal Knowledge* (1971/02.12.1983).[2] Most of these titles were networked on ITV over the next few years, but *Carnal Knowledge* and *Equus* were held back as more suitable for the forthcoming alternative service for which the Authority had also assumed regulatory responsibility.

Channel Four began broadcasting on 2 November 1982; its Welsh-language counterpart, Sianel Pedwar Cymru (S4C), commenced transmissions the day before. It quickly transformed the TV landscape. Not the least of its interventions was the scheduling of a wider range of films than had ever before been seen on British television. Feature films, often of an older vintage than usually seen on ITV as well as more foreign-language, independent, experimental and non-commercial films than the BBC was prepared to transmit, were a major part of its offer from the very beginning. Deliberately or otherwise, the new channel succeeded in addressing many of the complaints and concerns voiced by the likes of Buscombe and Myles. But besides the new terrestrial broadcaster, other competing forces also made their presence felt. In a 1980 article for *Sight and Sound*, Michael Pilsworth foresaw that 'change is on the way, and it is coming not from the schedulers, but from the audience'.

Figure 13.1 The BBC's acquisition in 1979 of UK TV rights to the entire library of
RKO Radio Pictures made possible a six-part documentary series, *The RKO Story* (1987), to
accompany a season of the studio's films. *Radio Times* © Immediate Media Co.
Artwork © Jeff Cummins.

The audience's real tastes will be revealed by technological developments that will end forever that monopoly of the means of television distribution which has played such a central role in determining the nature of television broadcasting. Individual viewers will be able to watch selected programmes, when they want to watch them, through the use of time-shift technology (video-cassette recorders). They will also be able to view television material that they have purchased from retail outlets in the form of video-discs.[3]

The availability, from 1978 onwards, of affordable domestic video player-recorders using the cassette technologies Betamax, VHS and Philips 2000 turned viewers into schedulers. As Johnny Walker has explained, 'time-shift' off-air recording enabled 'individuals to construct their own television schedules at a time when television networks ceased broadcasting in the evening, when one of the main networks was striking, and when discussions abounded between various parties about the launch of a fourth television channel'.[4] Many of the companies entering the new field of video distribution dealt in pre-recorded feature films, made available on cassette or even laserdisc for sale or, more often, rental. The films released in these formats were often of a kind that mainstream broadcasters would not have contemplated transmitting.

However, Pilsworth argued, the 'most far-reaching changes will undoubtedly result from the twin developments of satellite distribution and cable television'.[5] Following the granting of licences in 1972, five independent cable-TV operations had opened in the mid-1970s, all with a limited lifespan. But these were community television services, addressed specifically to local residents, not commercial systems offering feature films.[6] The Annan Report (1977) took a discouraging view of toll-TV, describing it as 'a ravenous parasite' feeding off existing material (including films) rather than being an originator of new programming.[7] But in November 1980, the Government authorised a new wave of toll-TV experiments, involving twelve pilot schemes over a two-year trial period. Among other programme material, they were permitted to show films twelve months after their registration with the Board of Trade. These films had to have received a BBFC certificate and 'X'-rated titles could only be shown after 10.00pm. Quotas on British or EEC-originated material for cinemas and local-authority rulings on particular films would apply to cable services in those areas also, but unlike films in cinemas no levy would be charged. All the services to which licences were granted had feature films at their core. Their licences ran initially until 31 December 1982, with an option for the holders to extend them by a year on payment of a renewal fee.[8]

The first such service, Rediffusion's Starview, opened in Reading, Tunbridge Wells, Pontypridd, Hull and Burnley in September 1981, with monthly subscription charges ranging from £7.95 to £11.95. These charges were reported to be 50 per cent higher than expected because of the rental prices demanded by Hollywood film distributors, as represented by the Motion Picture Exporters Association of America. All five towns could see the same programmes, mainly films. The first month offered sixteen features in a 'revolving programme', launched with the Rank Organisation's *The Sea Wolves* (1980). Reporters noted that another of Starvision's initial titles, Rank's *The Wild Geese* (1978), was also included in ITV's current autumn lineup. With the CEA's embargo now reduced to three years, there was little to separate the attractions on toll-TV and free-TV.[9]

The second UK service to launch, Visionhire's Showcable, opened on 15 October with yet another Rank release, *The Thirty Nine Steps* (1978), whose conventional broadcast rights were owned by ITV. The service reached around 170,000 homes, each paying £7.95 per month. Visionhire was the renamed British Relay (see Chapter 5) and its partner in Showcable was none other than the BBC, which was also involved with cable subscription services in the US. Showcable's films were selected and transmitted by BBC Enterprises, the Corporation's commercial trading arm, 'responsible for the purchase, scheduling and presentation of the programmes which will originate from Television Centre in London from the equivalent of a conventional continuity suite'. Among the fifty-four titles in Showcable's initial lineup was the BBC's most expensive buy: *Gone with the Wind* (1939), first shown on 31 October, nearly two months before its much-vaunted terrestrial premiere on BBC1. SelecTV opened in Milton Keynes on 29 October with *The Electric Horseman* (1979) and *The Rose* (1979), followed one week later by Radio Rentals' Cinematel service in Swindon, opening with *Grease* (1978). In addition to showing two films nightly, Cinematel also relayed the ITV services for the ATV, HTV and Southern Television areas. These cable channels were described in one trade journal as 'the first step towards de-regulation' of British broadcasting.[10]

Channel Four, S4C, Starview and Showcable marked the first wave of what was ultimately to be a torrent of new stations, including terrestrial, cable, satellite and later digital providers, as the established BBC/ITV duopoly gave way to a multi-channel, multi-platform array of alternatives. These developments are too complex and far-reaching to be dealt with here. Instead, they will be the subject of a second volume, intended to pick up where we have left off and complete the story of feature films on British television.

Televisual Cinephilia

I began this volume by asking why the subject of films on television has historically received so little attention from scholars, and suggested that this was fundamentally because they were seen as neither one thing (cinema) nor another (television). For purist cineastes and cinephiles, their not-cinema status can be nothing but a compromise; for broadcasting professionals and media historians, their not-television status makes them of inferior interest to TV originations. Perhaps only the viewers appreciate their value.

In Chapter 5, I quoted ITV film buyer Leslie Halliwell's comment, 'We've never bought a film that didn't have a reasonable function.'[11] Through a detailed examination of the shifting relationships between the institutions of broadcasting and the film industry, and through a synoptic study of the changing use of feature films as programme material, I have tried to demonstrate the range of functions films performed. They include, inter alia: giving studio crews a break from live broadcasting; providing a cheap alternative to original drama; adding to the variety of programme types and textures; offering an opportunity to catch up with hard-to-see releases unavailable in local cinemas; supplementing income by exploiting licensing rights; capturing, building and retaining audiences; establishing regular viewing patterns through fixed programme slots; competing with the opposition in the battle for ratings; attracting bids from advertisers; and satisfying a cultural remit by appealing to minority or specialised groups. As can be seen from this (far from exhaustive) list, the functions of films on TV vary according to the different constituencies involved – programme-makers, schedulers, distributors, viewers – and according to context and situation. One thing remains constant, however – a principle I gleaned from the first interview I conducted for the book, with Steve Jenkins, the BBC's outgoing Head of Films, in 2012: once a cinema film enters television, it becomes television, not cinema. The integration of films within television practices and the adaptation of films to television purposes therefore become central to understanding their place in the economy of broadcasting. If films on TV primarily serve the interests of television, does television also have a responsibility – economic or cultural – to the cinema? That is a question which, as we have seen, filmmakers, broadcasters, labour unions, critics and legislators have often wrestled with, but the answer again depends on viewpoint and vested interest.

Besides suggesting the richness of the topic as a subject for further research, I also want the book to be seen as paying tribute to the under-appreciated, little-known work of those many television executives who have been responsible for the acquisition, selection and placing of films in schedules. They created film strands that, for all the criticisms levelled at them, were often remarkable for their ambition, scope and sophistication. I have generally avoided the now-overused term 'curation', which for some of the more workaday scheduling might seem a rather hifalutin term; but in the best instances that is certainly what it was. The constraints on schedulers, particularly in the commercially-driven, federated structure of ITV, have tended to preoccupy critical commentators and prevent recognition of the very real achievements made possible within, often despite and sometimes, perhaps, even because of those constraints. The technological limita-tions of analogue, 4×3 transmission and the distractions of the domestic viewing environment have also been unduly emphasised. The proof that these necessary compromises were not fatal for the films thus presented lies in the several gen-erations of viewers whose awareness, knowledge and appreciation of cinema were cultivated, not just in cinemas themselves, but also through the agency of their supposed rival and nemesis. The present author's love of movies is as much the product of domestic television viewing as it is of visits to the pictures. I am not alone.

Another reason why this history needed to be written is that the kind of viewing experience with which it is concerned is an ephemeral one. All viewing experiences are, of course, in taking place on particular occasions, in particular locations and in situations that are personal to the viewer; experiences that cannot be recaptured except through remembrance. There have been a number of studies in recent years of cinemagoing and popular memory; some also of early home-video viewing.[12] But the audience for broadcast television is the largest of all, and the 'folk memory' of viewing films through that medium is in urgent need of documentation. A future study on the present subject might well focus on the audience experience in particular. I might even write it.

Not only is the viewing experience ephemeral: so too are the television schedules that delivered films to viewers. In the article quoted earlier, Michael Pilsworth described scheduling as an 'imperfect art'. It may also be increasingly a lost one, as the past requirements of balance and variety in any given evening schedule are no longer superintended by proactive regulators. By comparison with the IBA's, Ofcom's is a light-touch form of policing. The sheer proliferation of broadcast channels, often highly specialised, means that this balance may no longer be required: a schedule does not any longer have to offer something for everyone as there are specialised providers catering for different tastes. Linear schedules themselves may eventually disappear: for the children of the twenty-first century, streaming is the consumption mode of choice, with the viewer positioned as scheduler and the viewing platform little more than an online library. Seen from this vantage point, the severe limitations on choice in the period covered by this book may seem absurd, especially to anyone who wasn't there at the time. Yet these limitations had their advantages, not only for ratings performance – with less competition, each programme claimed a much larger share of the potential audience – but also for viewers themselves and even for the films.

Christian Keathley notes in his 2006 study *Cinephilia and History*, subtitled *The Wind in the Trees*, that the 'death of cinephilia' coincided with the rise of television, especially pay-cable TV and home video. He argues that cinephilia depends on scarcity, on the difficulty of seeing films, if they are to retain their unique 'aura' (in Walter Benjamin's sense, usually applied to fine art). With video – and one might add, especially today the Internet – availability cancels out aura: 'The knowledge that a film can always be caught a few months hence on video makes movies subject to us rather than us being subject to them. Their existence as events is weakened.' Keathley, an American born the year before the present author, contrasts this with his experience of the cinema: 'I can recall times when I was watching a movie and the pleasure became so great that I would consciously say to myself, "You'd better enjoy this now, take in all you can, because soon it'll be over and gone."'[13] Eventually, however, there was a 'change of habits in perception brought on by the conditions of modernity: faced with an abundance of stimuli – or in this case, an abundance of availability, of choice – one closes down, sets up boundaries where seem to exist, retreats into what one already knows instead of seeking out what is new.' As a result, Keathley claims, 'For the post-cinephile generations, this shift to virtual accessibility has resulted, quite paradoxically, in a certain loss of history due to the "televisualization" of cinema.'[14]

Anyone who teaches film studies to young people, as I do, will have noticed the pattern by which an ever-increasing plenitude of choice produces an ever-narrower range of viewing experience. Students today have more cinema at their disposal than any generation in history; yet they generally come to university having seen fewer films and with a more limited range of cinematic interests than any of their predecessors. This is not a contradiction, but entirely predictable: as Keathley suggests, infinite choice is intimidating, so – often with the nudging of algorithms – people tend to seek out what they already know and watch what their peers are watching.

But the very restrictions placed on British television in the three-channel, pre-video era, I would argue, gave the films broadcast in that period some of the same aura of scarcity associated with those caught fleetingly in repertory cinemas. With few to choose from – an average of fourteen per week in any given region in the 1970s – one could, with a little effort and even without a video recorder, see almost everything; and with so few opportunities to see them, each screening was precious.[15] The BBC and ITV generally observed a two-year interval for film repeats, if titles were repeated at all. Today, licensing deals allow a film to be rerun in the space of a week; the BBC operates a six-month cycle for repeats on its main channels while the digital channels, free-to-air or otherwise, often show a film half a dozen times in the space of a year. Streaming platforms, of course, allow films to be seen at the viewer's convenience, at least until they are taken down. With such luxury, it is easy to become blasé and not bother watching a film at all, as we imagine it will always come around again. The conveniences of digital recording and downloading mean that a film may sit unviewed on a hard drive for months or even years. But with no means of preserving it (except perhaps for a reel-to-reel or audio-cassette recorder placed under the telly and competing with noises in the room) and little chance of revisiting it anytime soon, a 'live' transmission had to be caught on the night. The particular advantage of trying to watch almost every film as it came along, seizing every opportunity, was that a viewer – this viewer, for one – would see an extraordinarily wide range of films which, with greater freedom, they might otherwise have overlooked. Limited choice can indeed be liberating, and this applies as much to broadcast television as it does to cinema.

On Sunday, 23 October 1977, I saw for the first time, in BBC2's 'Screen 2' series, *Harold and Maude* (1971/23.10.1977), a film about liberation. I was just shy of my thirteenth birthday. The fact that the transmission started at 11.00pm now makes me think that the following week was half term, though I saw a good many other films in the same slot that autumn, so perhaps it wasn't. There were a dozen films on television in my region that week, excluding made-for-TV movies, and I saw nine of them. Some I hated, some I liked, but this was the one that stood out. There was no big splash in *Radio Times*, no illustration to pull me in or tell me it

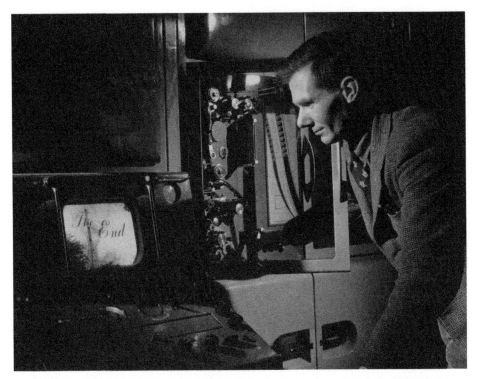

Figure 13.2 Televising film on one of the telecine machines at Alexandra Palace, March 1951. The engineer makes an adjustment to the machine while watching the closing caption on the screen. BBC Photo Library © BBC.

was something special, and Philip Jenkinson's review was iffy. I watched it just because it was on. It instantly became, if not quite my all-time favourite film, at least my favourite made since it was made. I saw its two subsequent BBC repeats, in 1980 and 1982, and in 1990 I recorded it on VHS from Channel Four. Later still I bought the DVD and then the Blu-ray. I have taught the film many times to students, almost always with favourable results. In 1977, I would not have been able to see it in a cinema, even in the unlikely event that it had been shown at my local, because it carried a BBFC 'AA' certificate, barring under-fourteens, and I didn't look old enough to pass. Nevertheless, I think I was the right age to see it. I would not have found it alone. Television brought it to me.

Notes

1 'Anatomy of a National Habit: What Turns You On – and Turns You Off', *Sunday Times Magazine*, 7 November 1982, S1 2–3.
2 Memo from STSO, 'Feature Films', 10 June 1981, IBA/01021: 3996312.
3 Michael Pilsworth, '"An Imperfect Art" – TV Scheduling in Britain', *Sight and Sound* 49, no. 4 (Autumn 1980): 239.

4 Walker, *Rewind, Replay*, 18.

5 Pilsworth, '"An Imperfect Art"', 239.

6 Lewis, *Community Television and Cable in Britain*, 26–35; Bernard Davies, 'Cable', *Broadcast*, 20 September 1976, 7–8. Peter Lewis was himself the manager of Rediffusion's Bristol Channel. According to Lewis's figures, 8.6 per cent of the channel's output consisted of films, but these were locally-made amateur films or extracts from current cinema releases, not full-length features.

7 Home Office, *Report of the Committee on the Future of Broadcasting*, 220.

8 'Two Year Trial for Pay TV', *The Stage and Television Today*, 13 November 1980, 15, 17; 'Cleared Line for Cable', *Broadcast*, 16 March 1981, 7.

9 'Starview to Burst Forth in September', *Broadcast*, 17 August 1981, 9; Elkan Allan, 'Manna for the Five Towns', *The Times*, 19 September 1981, 16. To avoid confusion between terrestrial and cable, no transmission dates are given for films cited in this section.

10 'Kicking off in London with Fifty-four Films', *The Stage and Television Today*, 15 October 1981, 18; 'Untwisting London Cable Plans', *Broadcast*, 20 July 1981, 14–15; Adrian Hodges, 'Three More Cable Firms Are Set for the Off', *Screen International*, 17 October 1981, 141; 'Cable Pilots – HO Will Not Make Value Judgments', *The Stage and Television Today*, 17 September 1981, 25.

11 'More Movies to Be Shown on TV', *Sunday Times*, 31 January 1971, 40.

12 See, for example, Kuhn, *An Everyday Magic*; Smith, '*The Exorcist* in the Home: Remembering Parental Regulation', and Egan, 'Childhood Memories of Horror Films in the Home: Questions, Patterns and Contexts', both in Egan, Smith and Terrill, *Researching Historical Screen Audiences*, 203–38.

13 Keathley, *Cinephilia and History*, 21–2.

14 Ibid, 24.

15 Geoffrey Nowell-Smith also makes this point: 'And early television was ordered too: when there were limitations on the number of films shown on the box, each one was an event, which had its particular place in everyday cultural life' ('On History and the Cinema', *Screen* 31, no. 2 [Summer 1990]: 167).

Appendix 1: BBC Film Statistics

Table A1.1 Feature film transmissions on BBC Television, 1937–63.

Year	Premiere transmissions	Repeat transmissions	First BBC TX ex-ITV	Subtitled films	Total transmissions
1937	1	1	0	0	2
1938	7	11	0	8	18
1939	6	5	0	3	11
1946	1	0	0	1	1
1947	10	4	0	3	14
1948	47	40	0	6	87
1949	90	82	0	4	172
1950	57	91	0	7	148
1951	23	82	0	4	105
1952	39	54	0	1	93
1953	26	62	0	0	88
1954	16	45	0	0	61
1955	9	12	0	0	21
1956	17	17	0	1	34
1957	18	14	0	1	32
1958	43	23	0	3	66
1959	49	17	0	3	66
1960	32	53	0	2	85
1961	60	51 inc. ex-ITV	1	7	111
1962	54	55 inc. ex-ITV	9	2	109
1963	58	66 inc. ex-ITV	13	17	124
Totals	660	786	23	73	1,446

Note: TX = transmission.

Table A1.2 Feature film transmissions on BBC1 and BBC2, 1964–81.

Year	BBC1 TV premieres	BBC2 TV premieres	BBC1 repeats	BBC2 repeats	BBC1 total	BBC2 total	Total TV premieres	Total repeats	1st TX ex-ITV	Subtitled films	Total transmissions
1964	54	24	46	126	100	150	78	172	6	22	250
1965	90	84	52	20	142	104	174	72	7	48	246
1966	125	90	74	53	199	143	215	127	0	47	342
1967	114	110	80	48	195	157	225	128	2	46	352
1968	123	111	76	55	199	166	234	131	3	39	365
1969	128	88	92	116	220	204	216	208	6	48	424
1970	123	90	104	93	227	183	213	197	3	33	410
1971	126	121	109	99	235	220	247	208	9	36	455
1972	86	133	148	93	234	226	219	241	11	40	460
1973	92	114	215	123	307	237	206	338	44	36	544
1974	107	92	244	120	351	212	199	364	65	34	563
1975	119	110	199	124	318	234	229	323	84	24	552
1976	106	101	220	132	326	233	207	352	79	27	559
1977	97	105	220	158	317	263	202	378	111	36	580
1978	75	101	201	165	276	266	176	366	67	32	542
1979	68	68	189	235	255	303	136	424	79	41	560
1980	87	96	199	220	286	316	184	418	96	26	602
1981	57	92	211	253	269	344	149	464	106	23	613
Totals	1,777	1,730	2,679	2,233	4,456	3,963	3,507	4,912	778	638	8,419

Appendix 2: ITV Film Statistics

Table A2.1 ITV networked films, 1964–81.

Year	Networked premieres	Networked repeats	All networked films
1964	3	0	3
1965	0	0	0
1966	0	0	0
1967	0	0	0
1968	8	8	16
1969	1	1	2
1970	0	0	0
1971	2	0	2
1972	3	1	4
1973	7	0	7
1974	18	0	18
1975	15	1	16
1976	21	10	31
1977	28	7	35
1978	24	8	32
1979	19	9	28
1980	31	7	38
1981	43	22	65
Totals	223	74	297

Note: The year 1968 is an anomaly: for two weeks during a period of industrial action (5–18 August), the London companies transmitted a national service, including films.

Table A2.2 Average programme time devoted to feature films on ITV, 1956–82.

Year	Average weekly transmission hours (all programmes)	Average weekly transmission hours (feature films)	Percentage of programme time (feature films)
1956	47 hours	1 hour 15 minutes	3.7
1959	63 hours	3 hours 45 minutes	6
1962	64 hours	4 hours 00 minutes	6.25
1965	66 hours	6 hours 42 minutes	10
1968	69 hours	6 hours 53 minutes	10
1970–71	71 hours 47 minutes	8 hours 40 minutes	12
1971–72	74 hours 18 minutes	9 hours 40 minutes	13
1972–73	88 hours 54 minutes	10 hours 38 minutes	12
1973–74	96 hours 40 minutes	10 hours 11 minutes	10.5
1974–75	98 hours 02 minutes	9 hours 29 minutes	10
1975–76	92 hours 55 minutes	9 hours 44 minutes	10.5
1976–77	99 hours 34 minutes	8 hours 42 minutes	9
1977–78	102 hours 25 minutes	8 hours 27 minutes	8
1978–79	100 hours 41 minutes	8 hours 00 minutes	8
1979–80	102 hours 53 minutes	8 hours 27 minutes	8.25
1980–81	104 hours 00 minutes	7 hours 23 minutes	8.25
1981–82	102 hours 02 minutes	8 hours 06 minutes	8

Note: Programme years ran from April–March. The figures do not include made-for-TV movies.

Sources: Memorandum by the Television Staff, 'Changes in the Balance of ITV's Schedule 1970–1975', IBA Paper 273(75), 9 October 1975, IBA/00014; and the ITV yearbooks published by the ITA and IBA, edited by Eric Croston.

Appendix 3: FIDO Filmography

The Film Industry Defence Organisation (FIDO) acquired television rights to 974 distinct films (including twenty-three titles covenanted twice) in covenants signed between March 1959 and February 1965. These covenants represent deals with 106 vendors, thirteen of which had more than twenty films covenanted. The packages in respect of each covenant are listed here alphabetically by vendor and chronologically for each vendor by date of covenant. The sum in brackets after each group was paid by FIDO for all the titles covered by that particular covenant; the films could be reclaimed by the vendors or copyright owners on repayment of this fee. Titles or groups annotated with an expiry date had not been reclaimed by their owners as of August 1970, meaning they would still be under embargo for broadcast until the specified date unless the covenants were subsequently bought out. These 531 films involved a total outlay by FIDO of £615,285.

Source: FIDO Collection, BFI Special Collections, Box 17, Item 3 (undated), and Box 18, Item 1 (November 1968, amended August 1970).

* film screened on television before the end of 1964
** separate covenants issued to two different vendors on different dates

Ace Distributors Ltd
Trinity House (1942) (£750) (21 December 1960)

Adelphi Films Ltd (C.D. Dent)
Bless 'em All, Skimpy in the Navy (1949), *A Ray of Sunshine* (1950), *Penny Points to Paradise* (1951), *The Kilties Are Coming* (1952), *Hands of Destiny* (1954), *You Lucky People* (1955), *Fun at St. Fanny's* (1956), *Stars in Your Eyes* (1957) (£17,750) (24 November 1961)
My Death Is a Mockery*, Song of Paris* (1952), *Is Your Honeymoon Really Necessary?** (1953) (£2,000) (12 January 1962)

Advance Films Ltd (C.D. Dent)
Father and Son (1934), *Law and Disorder* (1940), *Comin' thro' the Rye* (1947), *High Jinks in Society, Melody in the Dark, The Nitwits on Parade* (1949), *Bait* (1950) (£4,000) (4 January 1960)

Albany Film Productions Ltd (Julian Wintle)
Tread Softly* (1952) (£1,250) (12 July 1960)

Almanak Film Productions
Small Town Story (1953) (£975) (3 June 1960)

Ambassador Film Productions Ltd (Gilbert Church)
Scrooge (1935), *Broken Blossoms, Murder by Rope** (1936), *Incident in Shanghai** (1938), *Black Memory* (1947), *The Temptress* (1949) (£4,600) (12 March 1959)

Lord of the Manor (1933), *Dangerous Ground, Faces, The Way of Youth* (1934), *Jubilee Window, Once a Thief* (1935), *The Early Bird, House Broken, Love at Sea, Show Flat* (1936), *The Elder Brother, The Luck of the Irish, Lucky Jade* (1937), *Irish and Proud of It* (1938), *Full Speed Ahead*[1] (1939) (£1,500) (21 January 1960)

The Ghost Camera, His Grace Gives Notice, The Lost Chord, A Royal Demand (1933), *Say It with Flowers* (1934), *Admirals All [Admiral's Secret?], Annie Leave the Room!, A Fire Has Been Arranged, Inside the Room* (1935), *Eliza Comes to Stay, In the Soup, Juggernaut, Midnight at Madame Tussaud's**, Murder at the Cabaret, The Secret Voice* (1936), *Beauty and the Barge, First Night, Landslide, The Last Curtain**, Missing Believed Married** (1937) (19 May 1960) (£2,000)

*The Man in the Mirror**, Spy of Napoleon* (1936), *Down to the Sea in Ships/The Last Adventurers**, The Vicar of Bray* (1937), *The Curse of the Wraydons* (1946), *The Mysterious Mr. Nicholson* (1947), *The Greed of William Hart* (1948), *King of the Underworld, Murder at Scotland Yard* (1952) (£900) (25 November 1960)

Condemned to Death, The Marriage Bond, When London Sleeps (1932), *Called Back, I Lived with You, The Iron Stair, Mannequin, The Medicine Man, The Roof, Shot in the Dark, The Umbrella* (1933), *The Black Abbot, The Lash, Lily of Killarney, Open All Night, The Pointing Finger, Tangled Evidence, Whispering Tongues* (1934), *The Ace of Spades, Checkmate**, Department Store, In a Monastery Garden, Lazybones, Squibs* (1935), *The Belles of St. Clements**, The Last Journey**, Wednesday's Luck** (1936), *Alibi Breaker/Double Exposures**, The Angelus, Lancashire Luck**, Loaded Dice/Cross My Heart**, Under a Cloud**, Underneath the Arches* (1937) (£3,400) (19 April 1961)

Andick Films Ltd (A.E. Andrews)
*Captain's Orders** (1937) (£75) (26 November 1959)
Too Many Husbands (1938) (£450) (21 February 1961)
A Sister to Assist 'er (1948) (£300) (30 June 1963)
Sweet Beat (1959) (£900) (22 January 1964)

Anglo Amalgamated Film Distributors Ltd (Gordon Rayner)
The Floating Dutchman (1952), *Counterspy, Noose for a Lady, Street of Shadows* (1953) (£13,000) (3 July 1962)

*Assassin for Hire**, Mystery Junction** (1951), *Ghost Ship**, Wide Boy** (1952) (£3,000) (20 July 1962)

Dangerous Voyage (1954) (£3,000) (2 February 1964)
The Sleeping Tiger (1954) (£6,000) (2 February 1964)
The Brain Machine, Little Red Monkey (1955) (£6,000) (6 May 1964)

---

[1] Listed in F.I.D.O. file as *Full Steam Ahead*

Anglofilm Ltd
Shadow of the Past (1950) (£2,750) (26 February 1962)

Archway Film Distributors Ltd (A.M.G. Gelardi)
Return to the Desert (1956), *Black Ice, The House in the Woods, Light Fingers* (1957) (£7,500)
  (23 August 1961)

Associated British Pathé Ltd/Corsair Films Ltd
The Night Won't Talk (1952), *Three Steps in the Dark* (1953) (£2,000) (7 July 1959)
The Harassed Hero, Meet Mr. Malcolm (1954) (£2,000) (7 June 1961)

Associated British Pathé Ltd/Marble Arch Productions Ltd
Father's Doing Fine (1952), *The Weak and the Wicked* (1954) (£9,900) (21 November 1960)

Associated British Pathé Ltd/Mayflower Pictures Corporation Ltd
Cairo Road (1950) (£5,500) (19 April 1961)

Associated British Pathé Ltd/Summit Film Productions Ltd
Golden Ivory (1954) (£3,250) (10 February 1961)

Associated British Picture Corporation Ltd
My Irish Molly (1938), *Black Eyes, Dead Men Are Dangerous, The Gang's All Here, Lucky
  to Me, Me and My Pal, Murder in Soho, The Outsider, Poison Pen* (1939), *The Door with
  the Seven Locks, The Flying Squad, The House of the Arrow, The Middle Watch, Return to
  Yesterday, She Couldn't Say No* (1940), *East of Piccadilly, The Farmer's Wife, My Wife's
  Family, Spring Meeting, Tower of Terror* (1941), *Banana Ridge, The Night Has Eyes,
  Suspected Person* (1942), *Thursday's Child, Warn That Man, Women Aren't Angels* (1943)
  (£68,500) (26 February 1962; expiry year 1983)
*The Ware Case** (1938), *Cheer Boys Cheer*, Come On George, The Four Just Men*, Let's Be
  Famous*, There Ain't No Justice*, Trouble Brewing** (1939), *Convoy*, Let George Do It!*,
  The Proud Valley*, Sailors Three*, Saloon Bar*, Spare a Copper*, Young Man's Fancy**
  (1940), *Black Sheep of Whitehall*, Ships with Wings*, Turned Out Nice Again** (1941),
  The Big Blockade, The Foreman Went to France*, The Ghost of St. Michael's*, The Goose
  Steps Out*, The Missing Million*, Went the Day Well?** (1942), *The Bells Go Down*,
  Headline*, My Learned Friend, Nine Men*, San Demetrio London*, Undercover** (1943)
  (£55,000) (2 April 1962)
Champagne Charlie, Dreaming*, Fiddlers Three*, For Those in Peril*, The Halfway House*,
  It Happened One Sunday, Return of the Vikings* (1944) (£15,000) (15 February 1963)
Dead of Night, I Live in Grosvenor Square, Johnny Frenchman, Man from Morocco, Painted
  Boats*, Pink String and Sealing Wax** (1945) (£20,000) (6 August 1963)
The Captive Heart, The Overlanders** (1946) (£8,400) (9 September 1963)
Night Boat to Dublin, Piccadilly Incident, Quiet Weekend (1946) (£21,000) (16 September
  1963)
Knave of Hearts (1954) (£4,000) (29 May 1964)
Here Comes the Sun (1946) (£1,200) (5 August 1964)
Frieda, Hue and Cry, It Always Rains on Sunday*, Nicholas Nickleby* (1947) (£12,600)
  (5 August 1964)

The Loves of Joanna Godden (1947) (£3,000) (5 August 1964)
Against the Wind*, Another Shore*, Saraband for Dead Lovers*, Silver Darlings (1948)
    (£9,100) (5 August 1964)
Brighton Rock (1947) (£6,000)

Associated British Picture Corporation Ltd/Associated British-Pathé Ltd
Laughter in Paradise (1951), *Top Secret* (1952), *Happy Ever After* (1954), *Now and Forever*
    (1956) (£21,000) (12 January 1962)

Bayford Films Ltd (Francis Searle)
Ticket to Paradise (1961) (£2,500) (21 February 1964)

B.E.T. Investments Ltd
Anna Karenina*, Bonnie Prince Charlie (1948) (£4,500) (29 December 1959)

Blakeley's Films (M/c) Ltd
Trouble with Eve (1960), *Rag Doll* (1961) (£4,000) (20 January 1964)

Border Film Productions Ltd (Mrs. O. Negus-Fancey)
Shamus (1947), *Forces' Sweetheart* (1953), *Flight from Vienna, They Never Learn* (1956)
    (£2,000) (19 May 1960)
Down among the Z Men (1952), *Johnny on the Spot** (1954) (£600) (29 July 1960)
Action Stations (1956), *Men of Tomorrow* (1959), *Climb Up the Wall, Girls of the Latin
    Quarter, Shoot to Kill* (1960), *Old Mac* (1961) (£2,400) (2 April 1962)
Let the People Laugh/Sing as You Swing (1937), *The Body Vanishes, Mistaken Identity* (both
    produced 1939, released 1942), *Up with the Lark* (1943), *The Night Comes Too Soon**
    (1947), *Hangman's Wharf* (1950), *Behind the Headlines* (1952), *Calling All Cars* (1954),
    The Missing Scientists (1955) (£3,000) (21 March 1964)
The Traitor (1957) (£500) (8 June 1964)

Brandon Fleming, Esq, c/o Eric L'Epine Smith Ltd
Alive on Saturday (1957) (£300) (21 July 1961)

British Aviation Pictures Ltd (George King)
The First of the Few* (1942), *Tomorrow We Live** (1943), *Candlelight in Algeria** (1944)
    (£3,000) (12 November 1959)

British Lion Films Ltd (total £417,506.15s.11d.)
*The Courtneys of Curzon Street, An Ideal Husband, A Man about the House, Mine Own
    Executioner, Night Beat, White Cradle Inn* (1947), *The Fallen Idol, Spring in Park Lane,
    The Winslow Boy* (1948), *The Cure for Love, Elizabeth of Ladymead, The Last Days of
    Dolwyn, Maytime in Mayfair, Saints and Sinners, The Small Back Room, That Dangerous
    Age, The Third Man* (1949), *The Angel with the Trumpet, The Happiest Days of Your Life,
    My Daughter Joy, State Secret* (1950) (£115,500) (7 September 1960)
The Elusive Pimpernel, Odette, Seven Days to Noon, The Wooden Horse (1950) (£30,000)
    (18 October 1960)

Forbidden (1949) (£3,000) (3 November 1960)

The Small Voice (1948) (£4,000) (17 November 1960)

The Long Dark Hall (1951) (£5,906.15s.11d.) (17 November 1960)

Children of Chance (1949) (£3,000) (23 December 1960)

The Teckman Mystery (1954) (£3,000) (23 December 1960)

Into the Blue (1950), *Flesh & Blood, The Tales of Hoffmann* (1951) (£14,000) (30 December 1960)

Honeymoon Deferred (1950), *The Lady with the Lamp* (1951), *Derby Day, Trent's Last Case* (1952) (£20,000) (19 April 1961)

Lady Godiva Rides Again, The Magic Box, Mr. Denning Drives North, Outcast of the Islands, The Wonder Kid (1951), *Cry, the Beloved Country, The Holly and the Ivy, Home at Seven, The Ringer, The Sound Barrier, Who Goes There?* (1952) (£60,000) (20 April 1961)

The Captain's Paradise, Folly to be Wise, The Heart of the Matter, The Man Between, The Story of Gilbert and Sullivan, Twice upon a Time (1953), *The Belles of St. Trinian's, Hobson's Choice, Malaga, The Stranger's Hand* (1954), *The Constant Husband, The Man Who Loved Redheads, Stolen Assignment, Three Cases of Murder* (1955) (£79,500) (1 December 1961)

Eight O'Clock Walk, Front Page Story, The Intruder, They Who Dare (1953), *Aunt Clara, Bang! You're Dead, Beautiful Stranger, Devil Girl from Mars, The Green Scarf* (1954), *The Colditz Story, Geordie, Raising a Riot* (1955), *Operation Malaya / Terror in the Jungle* (?) (£73,000) (1 December 1961)

Around the Town, I've Got a Horse (1938), *Home from Home* (1939), *All at Sea* (1940) (£1,000) (24 February 1962)

Yangtse Incident (1956) (£6,000) (9 September 1963)

Butcher's Film Distributors Ltd (John Phillips)

Music Hall Parade (1939), *Garrison Follies* (1940), *Bob's Your Uncle, Gert and Daisy Clean Up, Gert and Daisy's Weekend* (1942), *It's in the Bag* (1944) (£1,200) (12 March 1959)

*Old Mother Riley, M.P.*** (1939), *Somewhere in England** (1940), *Sheepdog of the Hills** (1941), *Old Mother Riley in Paris**, Somewhere in Camp** (1942), *I'll Walk beside You*, Somewhere on Leave*, Variety Jubilee** (1943), *Home Sweet Home*** (1945), *Demobbed*, Send for Paul Temple*, Under New Management / Honeymoon Hotel** (1946), *Calling Paul Temple** (1948), *Scarlet Thread*** (1951), *Emergency Call*, Hammer the Toff*, Salute the Toff** (1952), *The Broken Horseshoe**, Operation Diplomat*, There Was a Young Lady** (1953), *The Black Rider*, Roadhouse Girl / Marilyn** (1954), *Stock Car** (1955) (£13,000) (29 July 1959)

Facing the Music (1933 or 1941), *Danny Boy* (1934 or 1941), *Rose of Tralee* (1937 or 1942), *Stars on Parade* (1936), *Night Journey* (1938), *Sword of Honour* (1939), *The Girl Who Forgot, Jailbirds, Pack Up Your Troubles, Three Silent Men* (1940), *Front Line Kids* (1942), *For You Alone, My Ain Folk* (1945), *The Hangman Waits* (1947) (£2,800) (4 August 1959)

Somewhere in Civvies (1943), *I'll Turn to You* (1946), *The Hills of Donegal* (1947), *When You Come Home* (1948) (£2,400) (14 February 1960)

*Dark Secret*** (1949), *Paul Temple's Triumph, Something in the City*, The Story of Shirley Yorke** (1950), *Madame Louise*, There Is Another Sun / Wall of Death** (1951), *Paul Temple Returns* (1952) (£5,000) (7 June 1961)

Assignment Redhead (1956), *Man from Tangier, You Pay Your Money* (1957), *Blind Spot, The Golden Disc, Mark of the Phoenix* (1958) (£9,000) (27 October 1961)
Undercover Girl (1958) (£2,000) (29 May 1963)
Life in Danger, Naked Fury (1959) (£4,000) (29 May 1963)
The Gentle Trap (1960) (£1,500) (October 1964)

Butcher's Film Distributors Ltd/Chelsea Films Ltd
Them Nice Americans (1958) (£2,000) (18 February 1964)

Carisbrooke Films Ltd
The Flamingo Affair (1948) (£400) (2 October 1962)

Chancellor Film Productions Ltd (B.M. Ostrer)
Idol of Paris (1948) (£3,500) (5 April 1961)

Charles Deane Productions Ltd
Stolen Time (1958) (£1,250) (31 December 1962)

Columbia (British) Productions Ltd
Rhythm Serenade, We'll Meet Again (1943) (£3,100) (18 October 1960)
29 Acacia Avenue (1945) (£3,000) (24 January 1961)

Columbia Pictures Corporation Ltd
South American George (1941), *Get Cracking, Much Too Shy* (1942), *Bell-bottom George* (1943), *He Snoops to Conquer* (1944) (£8,750) (4 April 1961)
One Exciting Night (1944) (£1,550) (5 April 1961)
I Didn't Do It (1945), *George in Civvy Street, This Man Is Mine* (1946) (£6,500) (19 September 1961)

Columbia Pictures Corporation Ltd/Warwick Productions Ltd
The Red Beret (1953), *The Black Knight, Hell below Zero* (1954) (£22,500) (24 January 1961)
A Prize of Gold (1955), *The Cockleshell Heroes, Safari* (1956) (£22,500) (19 April 1961)

Conqueror Films Ltd
Waterfront (1950) (£5,500) (30 November 1960)

Constellation Films Ltd (Anthony Havelock-Allan)
*Never Take No for an Answer/The Small Miracle** (1951) (£5,000) (21 July 1961)

Coronado Productions (England) Ltd (Gordon W.G. Rayner)
Your Witness (1950), *Circle of Danger* (1951), *Saturday Island* (1952) (£13,000) (18 October 1960)
Sea Devils (1953) (£6,000) (4 March 1963)

Crescent Productions Ltd (Steven Pallos)
The Crowning Touch, In the Wake of a Stranger (1959) (£2,500) (1964)

Cross Channel Film Distributors Ltd
More Deadly than the Male (1960) (£500) (2 April 1962)

David MacDonald Productions Ltd
Noose (1948) (£3,000) (20 November 1962)

Embassy Pictures (Associated) Ltd (George King)
Men of Steel (1932), *Little Stranger, Oh No Doctor!* (1934), *Gay Old Dog, Lend Me Your Husband, The Man without a Face, Windfall* (1935), *It's Never Too Late to Mend* (1937), *John Halifax, Gentleman, Sexton Blake and the Hooded Terror** (1938), *Gaiety George** (1946) (£4,200) (12 November 1959)
The House of Silence, Riding High, When the Poppies Bloom Again (1937) (£1,450) (15 March 1960)

Emmet Dalton Ltd
Professor Tim (1957) (£1,250) (19 April 1961)

Emmet Dalton Ltd/British Lion Films Ltd
Home Is the Hero, This Other Eden (1959) (£6,000) (12 July 1963)

Equity British Films Ltd
Servant of the People (?) (£225) (26 November 1959)

Eternal Films Ltd (Stanley J. Wilson)
Jackpot, The Price of Silence, The House on Marsh Road (£6,000) (2 April 1962)

Excelsior Film Productions Ltd (Marcel Hellman)
Talk about Jacqueline (1942), *Wanted for Murder* (1946), *Meet Me at Dawn* (1947), *This Was a Woman* (1948) (£15,000) (19 May 1960)
Jeannie (1941) (£5,000) (17 April 1963)

Exclusive Films Ltd (A. Lawrence)
The Dark Road (1948) (£2,000) (30 July 1962)
Someone at the Door (1950) (£2,000) (20 July 1962)
Dick Barton – Special Agent (1948), *The Adventures of PC 49, Dick Barton Strikes Back** (1949), *Dick Barton at Bay* (1950), *A Case for PC 49* (1951) (£13,000) (22 January 1963)
Death in High Heels (1947) (£1,500) (22 March 1963)
River Patrol (1948) (£2,500) (20 May 1963)
Life with the Lyons (1954), *The Lyons in Paris* (1955) (£9,000) (14 February 1964)

Exclusive Films Ltd/Bee Films Ltd
The Jack of Diamonds (1949) (£2,000) (22 January 1963)

Fine Arts Films Ltd
The Case of Charles Peace (1949), *The Girl Who Couldn't Quite* (1950) (£2,000) (4 August 1959)

Francis Searle Productions Ltd
Murder at Site 3 (1959) (£2,200) (17 July 1964)

Graham Rowlandson & Co
Dr. Morelle: the Case of the Missing Heiress (1949) (£600) (3 November 1960)

Grand National Pictures Ltd (Maurice J. Wilson)
The Right Age to Marry (1935), *The Marriage of Corbal* (1936), *Father Steps Out, Jericho, Mademoiselle Docteur, Pearls Bring Tears, Right Strange Adventures of Mr. Smith* (1937), *Easy Riches, Merely Mr. Hawkins, Miracles Do Happen, Romance à la Carte, Second Best Bed* (1938) (£5,750) (26 November 1959)
Not So Dusty*, When Knights Were Bold (1936), *Farewell to Cinderella* (1937), *Darts Are Trumps, His Lordship Regrets* (1938), *His Lordship Goes to Press* (1939) (£2,750) (4 January 1960)
Four Days*, Smart Alec*, A Tale of Five Cities**, Two on the Tiles* (1951) (£1,400) (3 November 1960)
Under Your Hat* (1940) (£500) (2 April 1962)
The Turners of Prospect Road** (1947) (£750) (2 April 1962)

Grove Film Productions Ltd
It's a Great Day (1955) (£1,500) (20 February 1962)

Herbert Wilcox, Esq
The Beggar's Opera (1953) (£6,000) (expiry year 1986)

H.H. Films Ltd (Harold Huth)/Baker, Todman & Co (Chartered Accountants)
Blackmailed (1951) (£4,000) (5 April 1961)
Sing along with Me (1952) (£1,400) (18 February 1963)

Holbein Films Ltd/Ingram Films Ltd
The Master of Bankdam* (1947) (£2,000) (4 May 1962)

Independent Sovereign Films Ltd
Obsession (1949) (£2,500) (18 February 1960)
Valley of Eagles (1951) (£3,950) (12 January 1962)

International Motion Pictures Ltd (Stuart Levy)
House of Darkness (1948) (£2,500) (23 August 1961)
The Large Rope (1953) (£3,000) (20 July 1962)

Javelin Films Ltd
The Woman in Question (1950) (£4,750) (4 May 1962)
The Browning Version (1951) (£7,500) (8 August 1964)

J. Phillips Film Distributors Ltd (ex-Butcher's)
The Armchair Detective, Distant Trumpet* (1952) (£2,000) (18 August 1960)

Leinster Films Ltd
My Hands Are Clay (1948) (£575) (30 September 1960)
The Missing Princess (1954) (£300) (30 April 1963)

Leontine Entertainments Ltd
A Killer Walks (1952) (£2,250) (9 May 1962)

London and Overseas Film Services Ltd/Film Studios (Bermuda) Ltd
(in liquidation)
Bermuda Affair (1956) (£3,000) (20 November 1962)

London and Overseas Film Services Ltd/Southern International Films Pty Ltd
King of the Coral Sea (1953) (£2,500) (20 July 1964)

London Film Productions Ltd
The Private Life of Don Juan*, *The Scarlet Pimpernel** (1934), *The Ghost Goes West**, *Sanders of the River** (1935), *Men Are Not Gods** (1936), *Elephant Boy** (1937) (£10,000) (9 October 1961)
The Man Who Could Work Miracles*, *Things to Come** (1936), *The Squeaker** (1937), *The Challenge**, *The Divorce of Lady X**, *The Drum** (1938), *Over the Moon** (1939), *21 Days** (1940) (£12,500) (9 October 1961)
Wedding Rehearsal (1932), *The Private Life of Henry VIII** (1933), *The Rise of Catherine the Great** (1934), *The Conquest of the Air, Forget Me Not**, *Rembrandt** (1936), *Knight without Armour** (1937), *Return of the Scarlet Pimpernel** (1938), *The Four Feathers, The Lion Has Wings, Q Planes**, *The Spy in Black** (1939), *The Thief of Bagdad** (1940), *Lady Hamilton**, *Lydia** (1941), *Jungle Book** (1942) (£22,500) (4 May 1962)

London Independent Producers Ltd (cc. Monarch Film Corporation)
The Happy Family (1952) (£2,476.5s.8d.) (28 October 1960)

Major Productions (London) Ltd (John Temple-Smith)
The Girl on the Pier* (1953) (£500) (5 April 1961)

The Mancunian Film Corporation Ltd (John F. Blakeley)
Boots! Boots! (1934), *Off the Dole* (1935), *Holidays with Pay* (1948), *Somewhere in Politics* (1949) (£1,150) (14 August 1959)
International Circus Review, Showground of the North (1948), *School for Randle, What a Carry On!* (1949) (£1,250) (27 October 1959)
Let's Have a Murder, Over the Garden Wall (1950), *Love's a Luxury** (1952) (£1,500) (23 March 1960)
Cup-Tie Honeymoon (1948) (£200) (23 June 1960)
It's a Grand Life (1953) (£1,250) (23 June 1960)

Mark III Scope Productions Ltd
Escape in the Sun (1956) (£2,500) (10 September 1962)
No Rain at Timburi (£1,600) (4 April 1964)

Marksman Films Ltd (Maxwell Setton)
*St. Martin's Lane** (1938) (£1,750) (1 December 1961)

Mayflower Pictures Corporation Ltd
The Adventurers (1951), *Appointment in London* (1953) (£12,000, of which only the first
instalment of £4,000 was paid) (14 September 1964)

Monarch Film Corporation Ltd (W.V.A. Gell)
Circumstantial Evidence*, *Night Was Our Friend** (1952), *House of Blackmail** (1953),
The Blue Parrot*, *Burnt Evidence**, *Dangerous Cargo**, *Delavine Affair**, *Devil's
Point**, *Final Appointment**, *Profile** (1954), *Room in the House** (1955) (£5,500)
(September 1964)

Monarch Productions Ltd (W.V.A. Gell)
*Hindle Wakes** (1952) (£750) (4 May 1961)
And the Same to You (1960) (£4,000) (1 December 1961)

National Film Finance Corporation (Group 3)
Brandy for the Parson, *The Brave Don't Cry*, *Judgment Deferred*, *Miss Robin Hood*, *Time
Gentlemen Please!*, *You're Only Young Twice* (1952), *Background*, *The Conquest of Everest*,
Laxdale Hall, *The Oracle* (1953), *Child's Play*, *Conflict of Wings*, *Devil on Horseback*,
Make Me an Offer, *Orders Are Orders* (1954), *The Blue Peter*, *John and Julie*, *The Love
Match* (1955), *The Angel Who Pawned Her Harp*, *Doublecross*, *Man of Africa* (1956), *The
End of the Road* (1957) (£70,000) (23 August 1961)

National Telefilm Associates Inc (UK) Ltd
I Met a Murderer (1939) (£2,500) (5 May 1960)

Orb Productions Ltd (Nat Miller)/Fortune Films Ltd
Big Fella (1937) (£925) (30 December 1960)

Orb Productions Ltd/Forward Films Ltd
The Secret Tent (1956) (£1,600) (20 April 1960)

Orb Productions Ltd/M. & A. Alexander (British National)
*Turn of the Tide** (1935), *Meet Mr. Penny**, *Mr. Reeder in Room 13** (1938), *Old Mother
Riley Joins Up**, *What Would You Do, Chums?* (1939), *Spies of the Air** (1940), *The
Common Touch**, *The Seventh Survivor** (1941), *The Lady from Lisbon**, *One of Our
Aircraft Is Missing**, *Penn of Pennsylvania**, *Sabotage at Sea** (1942), *The Dummy Talks**
(1943), *Heaven Is round the Corner**, *Murder in Reverse** (1944), *The Agitator**, *Battle
for Music*, *The Echo Murders**, *Give Me the Stars**, *Meet Sexton Blake**, *Twilight Hour**,
Waltz Time*, *The World Owes Me a Living** (1945), *Dual Alibi**, *Spring Song**, *Woman to
Woman** (1946), *The Ghosts of Berkeley Square**, *Mrs. Fitzherbert** (1947), *Counterblast**,
*No Room at the Inn** (1948) (£15,000) (13 September 1960)
Debt of Honour (1936), *The Street Singer* (1937), *Old Mother Riley in Society**, *The Second
Mr. Bush** (1940), *Love on the Dole**, *Old Mother Riley's Circus**, *Old Mother Riley's
Ghosts**, *"Pimpernel" Smith**, *This England** (1941), *Let the People Sing*, *Salute John*

Citizen*, Those Kids from Town* (1942), *The Butler's Dilemma*, Old Mother Riley Detective*, When We Are Married* (1943), *Medal for the General*, The Shipbuilders*, Strawberry Roan** (1944), *Latin Quarter** (1945), *Appointment with Crime*, The Laughing Lady*, Lisbon Story*, Meet the Navy** (1946), *Green Fingers** (1947), *The Three Weird Sisters*, Uneasy Terms** (1948) (£9,250) (23 August 1961)

Lassie from Lancashire* (1938), *Laugh It Off*, Old Mother Riley in Business** (1940), *Asking for Trouble, We'll Smile Again** (1942), *Old Mother Riley Overseas*, Theatre Royal** (1943), *Candles at Nine*, The Trojan Brothers/Murder in the Footlights*, Welcome Mr. Washington** (1944), *Don Chicago*, Old Mother Riley at Home** (1945) (£3,563.9s.6d.) (20 July 1962)

Orb Productions Ltd/X Productions Ltd
Don't Say Die (1950) (£250) (12 January 1962)

Pax Films Ltd (cc. Monarch Film Productions; Steven Pallos)
The Fake (1953) (£2,000) (20 February 1960)

Pendennis Pictures Corporation Ltd (Steven Pallos)
Action for Slander*, Dark Journey*, Dinner at the Ritz*, Fire over England*, The Green Cockatoo*, Under the Red Robe* (1937), *South Riding** (1938), *Call of the Blood** (1948) (£2,500) (30 November 1960)
The Diamond (1954) (£3,000) (11 March 1964)

Pennant Picture Productions Ltd (George King)
The Face at the Window* (1939), *The Chinese Bungalow*, Crimes at the Dark House* (1940), *The Shop at Sly Corner** (1947) (£3,800) (12 November 1959)

Periclean Films Ltd/Trinity Productions Ltd (J.G. Saunders)
The Weapon (1956) (£3,500) (6 June 1963)

Plantagenet Films Ltd/Baker, Todman & Co (Chartered Accountants)
Give Us This Day (1949) (£1,500) (23 August 1961)

Premier Stafford Productions Ltd (John Stafford)
Spring in the Air (1934), *Admirals All, The Crouching Beast, There Goes Susie* (1935), *Beloved Impostor, Wings over Africa* (1936), *The Avenging Hand, Wake Up Famous, The Wife of General Ling* (1937), *Return of the Stranger* (1947) (£4,000) (4 November 1959)
The Woman with No Name (1950) (£4,500) (2 March 1961)

Present Day Productions Ltd
Dark Interval** (1950), *Chelsea Story** (1951), *Blind Man's Bluff**, Come Back Peter** (1952) (£1,000) (20 July 1962)

Producers Representations Ltd (Steven Pallos)
The Golden Madonna* (1949) (£500) (19 September 1962)

Rank Film Distributors Ltd (total: £450,000)
The Day Will Dawn (1942) (£4,500) (20 April 1960)

Curtain Up (1952) (£2,500) (23 December 1960)

The Dark Man (1951) (£3,000) (19 April 1961)

The Gentle Sex, The Lamp Still Burns (1943) (£5,000) (7 June 1961)

The Clouded Yellow (1950), *The Beachcomber, Street Corner* (1953), *Forbidden Cargo* (1954), *Above Us the Waves* (1955) (£25,000) (30 June 1961)

Band Waggon (1938), *The Arsenal Stadium Mystery, The Frozen Limits, On the Night of the Fire, A Window in London* (1939), *For Freedom, Gasbags, Neutral Port* (1940), *Back Room Boy, Cottage to Let, Freedom Radio, The Ghost Train, Hi Gang!, I Thank You, The Man at the Gate, Old Bill and Son* (1941), *The Great Mr. Handel, Hard Steel, In Which We Serve, King Arthur Was a Gentleman, Secret Mission, Unpublished Story* (1942), *The Flemish Farm, It's That Man Again, The Life and Death of Colonel Blimp, The Man in Grey, Miss London Ltd., The Silver Fleet, They Met in the Dark, We Dive at Dawn* (1943) (£76,500) (11 August 1961)

Fame Is the Spur (1947) (£6,000) (20 July 1962)

Top of the Form (1953) (£4,000) (20 July 1962)

The Demi-Paradise, Millions like Us (1943), *Bees in Paradise, A Canterbury Tale, Don't Take It to Heart, English without Tears, Fanny by Gaslight, Give Us the Moon, Love Story, Madonna of the Seven Moons, Mr. Emmanuel, Tawny Pipit, Time Flies, Two Thousand Women, The Way Ahead* (1944) (£67,500) (9 April 1963)

I Know Where I'm Going!, I'll Be Your Sweetheart, A Place of One's Own, The Rake's Progress, They Were Sisters, Waterloo Road, The Way to the Stars (1945), *They Knew Mr. Knight* (1946) (£41,000) (30 June 1963)

Beware of Pity, Carnival, I See a Dark Stranger, London Town, The Magic Bow, A Matter of Life and Death, Men of Two Worlds, School for Secrets, The Way We Live (1946) (£38,000) (12 July 1963)

The Brothers, Dear Murderer, The End of the River, Holiday Camp, Hungry Hill, Jassy, The Man Within, The October Man, Odd Man Out, The Root of All Evil, Take My Life, Uncle Silas, The Upturned Glass, When the Bough Breaks, The Woman in the Hall (1947) (£59,000) (7 February 1964)

Colonel Bogey, Esther Waters, London Belongs to Me, One Night with You (1948) (£10,500) (6 May 1964)

Blanche Fury, Daybreak, Fly Away Peter, The Fool and the Princess, Good Time Girl, It's Hard to Be Good, Love in Waiting, The Mark of Cain, Mr. Perrin and Mr. Traill, Once a Jolly Swagman, Penny and the Pownall Case, A Piece of Cake, Sleeping Car to Trieste, A Song for Tomorrow, To the Public Danger, Trouble in the Air, Vice Versa, The Weaker Sex, The Woman Hater (1948) (£57,500) (1964)

The Blind Goddess, Broken Journey, The Calendar, Easy Money, Here Come the Huggetts, My Brother's Keeper, Portrait from Life (1948) (£28,000) (1964)

Appointment with Venus (1951), *Desperate Moment* (1953) (£10,000) (19 June 1964)

Rank Film Distributors Ltd/Gaumont British Ltd

Uncensored (1942) (£1,500) (7 June 1961)

Dear Octopus (1943) (£3,000) (13 June 1961)

Rank Film Distributors Ltd/L.P. Enterprises (Films) Ltd

Morning Departure (1950) (£7,500) (22 November 1963)

Raymond Stross Productions Ltd
The Man Who Watched Trains Go By (1952) (£2,750) (24 February 1960)
*The Tall Headlines/The Frightened Bride*** (1952), *Star of India* (1954) (£5,500) (17 November 1960)

R.B. Wainwright, Esq
Wolf's Clothing (1936) (£1,250) (2 February 1960)
*Secret of Stamboul** (1936), *School for Husbands** (1937) (£3,000) (14 February 1960)

Remus Films Ltd (Ralph S. Bromhead)
Carrington V.C. (1954) (£6,000) (1 January 1963)

Saturn Films Ltd (formerly Stratford Films Ltd.; A. Lawrence)
*Celia**, *Meet Simon Cherry** (1949), *The Lady Craved Excitement**, *The Man in Black**, *Room to Let**, *What the Butler Saw** (1950), *The Black Widow**, *Cloudburst**, *The Dark Light**, *Death of an Angel**, *The Rossiter Case**, *To Have and to Hold** (1951), *The Gambler and the Lady**, *Lady in the Fog**, *The Last Page**, *Never Look Back**, *Stolen Face**, *Whispering Smith Hits London**, *Wings of Danger** (1952), *Blood Orange**, *The Flanagan Boy**, *The Saint's Return** (1953) (£10,000) (10 February 1961)
*36 Hours**, *Face the Music**, *Four Sided Triangle**, *Mantrap** (1953), *Five Days**, *The Glass Cage*, *Mask of Dust*, *Murder by Proxy*, *The Stranger Came Home*, *Third Party Risk* (1954), *Women without Men* (1956) (£20,000) (2 April 1962)

Sheldrake Films Ltd (Lewis Gilbert)
*They Made Me a Fugitive** (1947) (£2,350) (31 December 1962)

Stratford Films Ltd (J.G. Saunders)/Kenilworth Film Productions
Third Time Lucky (1949) (£3,700) (22 October 1964)

Television Programmes (Distributors) Ltd (S.L. Simpson)
Love in Exile (1936), *For Valour*, *Millions**, *Return of Old Mother Riley/Old Mother Riley**, *Splinters in the Air**, *Talking Feet** (1937), *Old Mother Riley, M.P.*** (1939), *The Stars Look Down** (1940), *You Will Remember** (1941), *Old Mother Riley in Paris*** (1942), *Home Sweet Home***, *Journey Together** (1945), *School for Danger*, *The Turners of Prospect Road*** (1947), *Daughter of Darkness*** (1948), *Dark Secret*** (1949), *Dark Interval***, *Lilli Marlene** (1950), *Death Is a Number**, *The Lady from Boston**, *Private Information**, *Scarlet Thread***, *A Tale of Five Cities*** (1951), *Blind Man's Bluff***, *Circumstantial Evidence***, *Night Was Our Friend***, *The Tall Headlines/The Frightened Bride*** (1952), *Black 13**, *The Broken Horseshoe***, *House of Blackmail***, *Men against the Sun**, *The Wedding of Lilli Marlene** (1953), *The Blue Parrot***, *Burnt Evidence***, *Dangerous Cargo***, *Delavine Affair***, *Devil's Point***, *Final Appointment***, *Profile***, *Solution by Phone* (1954), *Barbados Quest*, *Breakaway*, *Room in the House***, *A Yank in Ermine** (1955), *High Terrace* (1956) (£32,300) (20 April 1960)

Theatrecraft Ltd
*The Seventh Veil** (1945) (£4,500) (2 April 1962)

Tower Films Ltd (Steven Pallos)
Hotel Sahara (1951) (£6,000) (27 October 1961)

Triangle Films Ltd
*Midnight Episode** (1950) (£1,200) (23 February 1960)

Twentieth Century-Fox Film Co Ltd
Keep Smiling (1938), *A Girl Must Live, Inspector Hornleigh, Shipyard Sally, So This Is London* (1939), *Inspector Hornleigh on Holiday, They Came by Night, Where's That Fire* (1940), *Inspector Hornleigh Goes to It, Kipps, Once a Crook* (1941), *The Young Mr. Pitt* (1942) (£51,000) (19 April 1961)
The Girl in the News, Night Train to Munich (1940) (£9,000) (9 October 1961)
Wings of the Morning (1937) (£4,000) (20 July 1962)
We're Going to be Rich (1938) (£3,000) (20 July 1962)
Dark World, The White Lilac (1935), *The Big Noise, Find the Lady, Highland Fling, Rhythm in the Air, Troubled Waters, Under Proof, Wise Guys* (1936), *Against the Tide, The Black Tulip, Catch as Catch Can, Concerning Mr. Martin, Double Alibi, East of Ludgate Hill, The Five Pound Man, Jennifer Hale, Passenger to London, Strange Experiment, There Was a Young Man, Variety Hour* (1937), *Dial 999, Father o' Nine, The Last Barricade, Second Thoughts, The Villiers Diamond* (1938) (£3,250) (10 September 1962)
*Escape** (1948) (£5,000) (1 January 1964)

Twickenham Film Productions Ltd
Lucky Mascot/Brass Monkey (1948) (£3,750) (4 May 1962)
*The Years Between** (1946) (£1,500) (20 July 1962)

Twickenham Film Studios Ltd
Star of My Night (1954) (£1,500) (10 September 1962)
*Daughter of Darkness*** (1948) (£500) (15 February 1965)

Unifilms (Feature Productions) Ltd/Newberry-Clyne Associates Ltd
Crosstrap, Stork Talk (1962) (£3,500) (6 May 1964)

Universal Securities Ltd (Raymond Stross)
Rough Shoot (1953) (£5,250) (24 February 1960)

Vic Films (Joseph Janni)
White Corridors (1951) (£5,000) (10 October 1962)

Walter Tuckwell & Associates Ltd/Filmée S.A./Eurafilm Anstalt
The Saint in London (1939), *The Saint's Vacation* (1941), *They Flew Alone* (1942), *The Saint Meets the Tiger, Yellow Canary* (1943), *Great Day* (1945) (£17,000) (8 July 1964)

Warner Bros Pictures Ltd
The Briggs Family, Confidential Lady, Dr. O'Dowd, George and Margaret, His Brother's Keeper, Hoots Mon!, Murder Will Out, That's the Ticket, Two for Danger (1940), *Fingers*

(1941), *The Dark Tower, The Night Invader, The Peterville Diamond* (1943), *The Hundred Pound Window* (1944), *Flight from Folly* (1945) (£18,500) (23 August 1961)

Welbeck Films Ltd
The Third Visitor (1951) (£3,000) (20 February 1962)
Desert Mice (1959), *Beyond the Curtain, Faces in the Dark, Too Young to Love* (1960), *The Night We Dropped a Clanger* (1961) (£20,000) (15 February 1963)

Zelstro Films Ltd (Raymond Stross)
Hell Is Sold Out* (1951) (£1,000) (18 March 1964)

Appendix 4: List of Abbreviations

AAP: Associated Artists Pictures
ABFD: Associated British Film Distributors
ABPC: Associated British Picture Corporation
ACC: Associated Communications Corporation
ACT: Association of Cinematograph Technicians
ACTT: Association of Cinematograph Television and Allied Technicians
ADP: Association of Directors and Producers
AFM: American Federation of Musicians
AGB: Audits of Great Britain
AIC: Association of Independent Cinemas
AIP: Association of Independent Producers
A-R: Associated-Rediffusion
ASFP: Association of Specialised Film Producers
ATP: Associated Talking Pictures
ATV: Associated TeleVision
BARB: Broadcasters' Audience Research Board
BBC: British Broadcasting Corporation (formerly British Broadcasting Company)
BBFC: British Board of Film Censors (later British Board of Film Classification)
BFI: British Film Institute
BFPA: British Film Producers' Association
BHE: British Home Entertainment
BIP: British International Pictures
BRTA: British Regional Television Association
BTV: Border Television
CEA: Cinematograph Exhibitors' Association
CFC: Cinematograph Films Council
CFF: Children's Film Foundation
COI: Central Office of Information
CRT: cathode-ray tube
CTV: Channel Television
EMI: Electric and Musical Industries
FBFM: Federation of British Film Makers
FBI: Federation of British Industries

      FFU: Federation of Film Unions
      FIC: Film Industry Council
     FIDO: Film Industry Defence Organisation
      FPA: Film Production Association of Great Britain
     FPCI: Film Production and Cinema Industries
      FPG: Film Purchase Group
      GAC: General Advisory Council
     GATT: General Agreement on Trade and Tariffs
      G-B: Gaumont British Picture Corporation
      HTV: Harlech Television
      IBA: Independent Broadcasting Authority
      IFD: Independent Film Distributors
      ITA: Independent Television Authority
      ITC: Incorporated Television Company
     ITCA: Independent Television Companies' Association
      ITV: Independent Television
   JICTAR: Joint Industry Committee for Audience Research
      KRS: Kinematograph Renters' Society
      LWT: London Weekend Television
      MCA: Music Corporation of America
     MORI: Market and Opinion Research International
       MU: The Musicians' Union
    NATKE: National Association of Theatrical and Kine Employees
    NARAL: Net Advertising Revenue After Levy
     NFFC: National Film Finance Corporation
      NFI: Network Film Information
      NPC: Network Purchase Committee
    NVALA: National Viewers' and Listeners' Association
      PAL: Phase Alternating Line
      PAR: Potential Audience Return
      RCA: Radio Corporation of America
      REP: Renters', Exhibitors' and Producers' Committee
      RTÉ: Raidió Teilefís Éireann
      SCC: Standing Consultative Committee
      STV: Scottish Television
      TAC: Television Advisory Committee
      TAM: Television Audience Measurement
     TAPE: Television Audience Programme Evaluation
      TTT: Tyne Tees Television
      TVS: Television South
      TWW: Television Wales and West
      UTV: Ulster Television
      VAF: Variety Artistes' Federation

VTR: videotape recording
WTV: Westward Television
WWN: Wales West and North
YTV: Yorkshire Television

Appendix 5: List of Personnel

*Names marked with an asterisk appear in more than one list.

BBC: Senior Executives

Kenneth Adam: Controller of Programmes, Television, 1957–61; Director of Television, 1961–68

David Attenborough: Controller, BBC2, 1965–69; Director of Programmes, 1969–72

George Barnes: Director of Television; Director of Television Broadcasting, 1950–56

Donald Baverstock: Assistant Controller of Programmes, Television; Controller BBC1, 1963–65

Gerald Beadle: Director of Television Broadcasting

Gerald Cock: Director of Television, 1935–39

Norman Collins: Controller, Television, 1947–50

Bill Cotton: Controller, BBC1, 1977–81

Brian Cowgill: Controller, BBC1, 1973–77

Charles Curran: Director General, 1969–77

*Paul Fox: Controller, BBC1, 1967–73

Maurice Gorham: Head of Television Service; Controller, Television, 1946–47

Sir Hugh Carleton Greene: Director of Administration, 1956–58; Director General, 1960–69

Sir William Haley: Director General, 1944–52

Alan Hart: Controller, BBC1, 1981–84

Cecil Madden: Programme Organiser, Television; Television Programme Officer; Assistant to Controller of Television Programmes

Cecil McGivern: Head of Television Programmes; Controller, Television Programmes, 1950–57; Deputy Director of Television Broadcasting, 1957–61

Alasdair Milne: Director of Programmes, Television; Managing Director, Television

Michael Peacock: Controller, BBC2, 1964–65; Controller, BBC1, 1965–67;

Sir John Reith: Director General, 1927–38

Robin Scott: Controller, BBC2, 1969–74; Deputy Managing Director, Television, 1977–80

Dennis Scuse: General Manager, Television Enterprises, 1963–72

Aubrey Singer: Controller, BBC2, 1974–78

Joanna Spicer: Programme Organiser, Television; Film Booking Section; Assistant Controller (Planning) Television; Assistant Controller, Television Developments

Ian Trethowan: Director General, 1977–82

Ronald Waldman: Business Manager, Television Programmes, 1958–60; General Manager, Television Promotions; General Manager, BBC Television Enterprises, 1960–63

Brian Wenham: Controller, BBC2, 1978–82

Huw Wheldon: Managing Director, Television, 1968–75

BBC: Film Acquisition, Operations and Scheduling

L.G. (Leslie) Barbrook: Film Booking Manager, 1936–39

Philip Dorté: Head of Television Outside Broadcasts and Film Supervisor; Head of Films, Television

David Francis: Assistant, Programme Purchasing, Television Enterprises, 1965–74

William Gilbert, Peggy Miller, June Morrow, Dora Nirva, Graham Woodford: Assistants, Film Booking Section

Alan Howden: Assistant, Programme Purchasing, Television Enterprises; Head of Purchased Programmes, Television, 1983–99

Ken Locke: Editor, Head of Film Examination, Programme Acquisitions

J.H. Mewett: Administrative Assistant, Films, Television; Head of Film Operations, Television; General Manager, Film Operations and Services, Television

Gunnar Rugheimer: Head of Purchased Programmes, Television; General Manager, Programme Acquisitions, Television, 1970–83

Gordon Smith: Assistant Head of Films, Television; Film Booking Manager; Head of Purchasing, Television Enterprises, 1957–70

Greeve del Strother: Film Manager; Film Shorts Manager; Film Booking Manager, 1946–56

Norman Swallow: Assistant Head of Films, Television

Daphne Turrell: Assistant to Film Booking Manager; Acting Film Booking Manager

David K. Wolfe-Murray: Television Liaison Officer

ITV: Company Executives

Paul Adorian: Managing Director, Associated-Rediffusion

Cyril Bennett: Controller of Programmes, London Weekend Television

Cecil Bernstein: Managing Director, Granada Television

Peter Cadbury: Chairman, Westward Television

Joan D. Elman: Associated-Rediffusion, Rediffusion Television, Thames Television

Ken Fletcher: Television Wales & West; British Regional Television Association (Manager, Film Purchasing Consortium); Granada Television; Network Certification Officer

*Paul Fox: Head of Programmes, Yorkshire Television, 1973–77; Managing Director and Director of Programmes, Yorkshire Television, 1977–88; Chair, Network Purchase Committee

Cyril Francis: Assistant Controller of Programmes – Planning, Associated-Rediffusion

A.J. (Tony) Gorard: Company Secretary, Anglia Television; Managing Director, HTV

Lew Grade: Director, Associated TeleVision; Deputy Chairman and Joint Managing Director, ATV Network

Michael Grade: Director of Programmes, London Weekend Television

Leslie Halliwell: Granada Television; Network Film Purchase Officer

Lord Harlech: Chairman, Harlech Television (HTV)

Jeremy Isaacs: Director of Programmes, Thames Television, 1974–78

Anthony John: Programme Liaison Officer, ABC Television/Thames Television

David Johnstone: Assistant Controller of Programmes/Director of Programmes, Scottish Television

Mansel Lloyd: Head of Film Clearance, Yorkshire Television

Pat Mahoney: Film Schedules Executive, Thames Television

Graham Murray: Granada Television; Network Certification Officer (see https://historyproject.org.uk/interview/graham-murray)

Berkeley Smith: Programme Controller, Southern Television; Director, Programme Planning Secretariat

Brian Tesler: Director of Programmes, ABC Television/Thames Television; Programme Controller, Thames Television; Chairman, Network Purchase Committee

*Howard Thomas: Managing Director, ABC Television; Deputy Chairman, ABC Television; Managing Director, Thames Television; Chairman, Thames Television

Ward Thomas: Managing Director, Yorkshire Television

Margaret Walker: Manager, Film Services, London Weekend Television

Jeremy Wallington: Director of Programmes, Southern Television

Barrie Wood: Film Schedules Manager/Deputy Programme Planner, ATV Network

ITA/IBA: Senior Executives

The Baron Aylestone: Chairman, 1967–75
Sir John Carmichael: Acting Chairman, 1962–63
Sir Kenneth Clark: Chairman, 1954–57
Sir Robert Fraser: Director General, 1954 –70
*The Baron Hill of Luton: Chairman, 1963–67
Sir Ivone Kirkpatrick: Chairman, 1957–62
Sir Ronald Matthews: Acting Chairman, September–December 1957

Baroness Plowden: Chairman, 1975–80
A.W. (Anthony) Pragnell: Secretary; Deputy Director General
The Baron Thomson of Monifeith: Chairman, 1981–88
Sir Brian Young: Director General, 1970–83

ITA/IBA: Programme Staff

Peter Ashforth: Assistant Television Administrative Officer
Jan Choyce: Programme Clearance Officer
Neville Clarke: Programme Administrative Officer
Margaret England: Assistant Programme Administrative Officer
Margaret Escott: Assistant Programme Administrative Officer
Michael Gillies: Programme Administrative Officer; Television Administration Officer
David Glencross: Senior Programme Officer, 1970–76; Head of Programme Services, 1976; Deputy Director of Television, 1977–83; Director of Television, 1983–90
Michael Hallett: Information Officer
Penry Jones: Deputy Head of Programme Services
*Stephen D. Murphy: Senior Programme Officer
Anne Nethercott: Television Administration Officer
Teresa Newberry: Assistant Television Administrative Officer
Dermot P. O'Hagan: Programme Officer; Television Programme Officer
Christopher Rowley: Senior Programme Scheduling Officer; Senior Television Scheduling Officer (see https://rhombus-dove-5pn6.squarespace.com/about)
Bernard Sendall: Deputy Director General (Programme Services), 1955–1977
*Colin Shaw: Director of Television, 1977–83
Noel Stevenson: Principal Liaison Officer
Judy Strang: Assistant Television Administrative Officer
Dorothy Viljoan: Assistant Administrative Officer
Joseph Weltman: Head of Programme Services

ITA/IBA: Regional Officers

G.W. Alcock: South East (Southampton)
F.W. Bath: North West (Manchester)
T.E. Brownsdon: South East (Southampton)
Dr H.R. Cathcart: Northern Ireland (Belfast)
Frank Copplestone: Head of Regional Services; Programme Planning Secretariat
Lyn Evans: Wales and West England (Cardiff)
J.N.R. Hallett: East of England
J.E. Harrison: North West (Manchester)
W.A. Jamieson: Assistant Officer, Scotland

John Lindsay: Scotland (Glasgow)
R.F. Lorimer: North East (Newcastle)
*Stephen D. Murphy: North West (Manchester)
Clare Mulholland: Bristol
G.S. O'Brien: Assistant Officer, Scotland
G.G. Percy: South West (Plymouth)
J.A. Blair Scott: South (Southampton)
A. Stringer: Yorkshire (Leeds)
W.H. Wilson: Northern Ireland (Belfast)

Film Industry: Principal Affiliations

Baron (George) Archibald: Federation of British Film Makers
R.P. (Reginald) Baker: Ealing Studios; British Film Producers' Association
Sir Michael Balcon: Ealing Studios; Bryanston Films
C.V. Bargate: GCT Distributors
*Cecil Bernstein: Granada Theatres
John Boulting: British Lion Films
R.S. (Robert) Camplin: Director, Cinematograph Exhibitors' Association
James Carreras: Exclusive Films; Hammer Film Productions; Saturn Films
Ian Crémieu-Javal: Gaumont British Picture Corporation
Sir David Cunynghame: London Film Productions
John Davis: The J. Arthur Rank Organisation
Cyril Edgar: Walt Disney Mickey Mouse
G.H. (George) Elvin: Association of Cinematograph Technicians, Association of
    Cinematograph, Television and Allied Technicians
J.S. Fairfax-Jones: Denning Films
E.J. Fancey: The E.J. & S.A. Fancey Syndicate
Ingram Fraser: Films de France
Sir Henry French: British Film Producers' Association
Joseph Friedman: Columbia Pictures
W.R. Fuller: Cinematograph Exhibitors' Association
J.C. Graham: Paramount Film Service
Sir David Griffiths: Kinematograph Renters' Society
R.J. Hanbury: Radio Pictures
K.N. (Kenneth) Hargreaves: J. Arthur Rank Film Distributors
George Hoellering: Film Traders
Sir Arthur Jarratt: British Lion Film Corporation
David Kingsley: National Film Finance Corporation
Alexander Korda: London Film Productions
Ernest Lindgren: National Film Archive
S. Maurice Livingston: International Optima Corp.
A.W. Mallinson: Cinematograph Films Council

John Maxwell: British International Pictures
*Stephen D. Murphy: British Board of Film Censors
J.B. Myers: London Film Productions
Sir Tom O'Brien: National Association of Theatrical and Kine Employees
Hugh Orr: Association of Independent Cinemas
David Ostrer: Gaumont British Picture Corporation
Isidore Oster: Gaumont British Picture Corporation
Lawrence G. Parker: Association of Specialised Film Producers
A.R. (Aubrey) Partners: Association of Independent Cinemas
Peter Plouviez: British Actors' Equity Association
J. de Quidt: Cinematograph Film Council
J. Arthur Rank: The J. Arthur Rank Organisation
W.G. (Gordon) Rayner: Associated British Film Distributors
J.E. Ricketts: Walt Disney Mickey Mouse Ltd
David Sarnoff: Radio Corporation of America
W.J. (Bill) Speakman: Film Industry Defence Organisation
F.L. (Fred) Thomas: The J. Arthur Rank Organisation
Howard Thomas: Associated British-Pathé
John Thorpe: London & Overseas Film Services
John Trevelyan: British Board of Film Censors
Arthur W. Watkins: British Film Producers' Association

Bibliography

Primary Sources

BBC Written Archives Centre, Caversham (cited in endnotes as BBC, followed by the file number). BBC copyright content reproduced courtesy of the British Broadcasting Corporation. All rights reserved.

R12/217/2: Copyright: Television Films.

R44/1,238/1 and R44/1,350/1: RKO Film Library.

R78/1,123/1: Purchase of Feature Films.

T1/3: TV Audience Research – Foreign Films.

T6/13: TV Films: Associated British Film Distributors.

T6/40: TV Films: British Lion Film Corp.

T6/110: TV Films: Denning Films.

T6/122: TV Films: Ealing Films Ltd.

T6/135/1: TV Films: Exclusive Films Ltd.

T6/138: TV Films: Feature Films.

T6/144/1–5: TV Films: Film Memos.

T6/149: TV Films: Film Traders.

T6/151: TV Films: 16mm Films.

T6/152: TV Films: Films de France.

T6/169: TV Films: Hire of Films from Outside Sources.

T6/194: TV Films: London Film Productions.

T6/219: TV Films: Old Time Films.

T6/240: RKO Radio Pictures Ltd.

T6/334: TV Films: Walt Disney Mickey Mouse Ltd.

T6/360/1: TV Films: Film Industry Relations with the BBC.

T16/72/4: TV Policy: Films.

T16/73: TV Policy: Films – Gaumont-British Pictures.

T16/75/1: TV Policy: Film Industry Relations.

T16/76/1–3: TV Policy: Film Industry Relations with the BBC.

T16/311/1-2: BBC Governors – D.Tel.'s Report, Film Statistics.

T36/5: Commercial Television – Associated-Rediffusion – Purchase of Feature Films.

BFI Reuben Library Special Collections, FIDO Collection (cited in endnotes as FIDO, followed by the box number).

Boxes 12–14: Letters to Vendors

Box 14, Items 2–5: Minutes of the Negotiating Committee, Purchasing and Finance Committee, General Purposes Committee and Executive Committee

Box 17, Items 4 and 5: Minutes of Board Meetings, Balance Sheets
Box 18, Item 4: Questionnaire

BFI Reuben Library Special Collections, Michael Balcon Collection (cited in endnotes as MBC, followed by the file number).
MBC 1/91c: FBFM Council Report no. 4, 10 December 1957, Minutes of the Federation of British Film Makers.
MBC 1/92: 'Control of Supply of Feature Films to Television: Proposals of CEA for Discussion with Other Sections of the Trade', 18 December 1957.

ITA, IBA and Cable Authority Archives, Bournemouth University (cited in endnotes as IBA, followed by the archive reference number and file number). All materials from the IBA Archives are available in Bournemouth University library: https://libguides. bournemouth.ac.uk/archives-special-collections/iba-archive.
IBA/00007: 3997080 – Feature Films Straddling the News.
IBA/00008: 3997081 – Feature Films on Independent Television.
IBA/00014: 3997086 – Proposed Levy on Cinema Films Shown on Television.
IBA/00644: 3995785 – Foreign Films – Negotiations with Unions.
IBA/00644: 3995785 – Foreign Films – Future Plans for Television Films.
IBA/00645: 3995796 – Edgar Wallace Series.
IBA/00645: 3995796 – Sherlock Holmes Films.
IBA/01020/01021: 3996317 – TV Act – Possible Breaches of Section 3(1)(a) – X-certificate Films.
IBA/01021: 3996313 – TV Act – Possible Breaches of Section 3(1)(a) – Horror Films.
IBA/01021/01022: 3996312 & 3996313 – Films on Television – General.
IBA/01022: 3996312 – X-certificate Films.
IBA/01023: 3996311 – Films on Television – Cutting of Feature Films.
IBA/01023/01024: 3996311 & 3996310 – Films – Clearance Routine & Acquisition.
IBA/01025: 3996309 – Films on Television – Archival Classification.
IBA/01025: 3996309 – HTV Experimental Films.
IBA/01025: 3996309 – Shirley Temple Films.
IBA/01063: 3996271 – Christmas Schedules.
IBA/01072: 3996262 – Films for Children – Children's Programmes.
IBA/034: 3997074 – Feature Films in Television.
IBA/389: 3997082 – The Control of Films.
IBA/409: 3997081 – Feature Films on Independent Television.
IBA/422: 3997073 – Use of Imported Films – Final Agreement at Last.

Books

Aldridge, Mark. *The Birth of British Television: A History*. Basingstoke: Palgrave Macmillan, 2012.
Allan, Angela, and Elkan Allan. *The Sunday Times Guide to Movies on Television*. London: Times Newspapers, 1973; revised edition, London: Severn House, 1980.
Alvarado, Manuel, and John Stewart. *Made for Television: Euston Films Limited*. London: Methuen, 1985.

Andrews, Hannah. *Television and British Cinema: Convergence and Divergence since 1990*. Basingstoke: Palgrave Macmillan, 2014.

Anon. *John Logie Baird: A Pictorial Record of Early Television Development 1924–1938*. Tiverton: Kelly Publications, 2001.

Bailey, Kenneth, ed. *The Television Annual for 1950/51*. Long Acre, London: Odhams Press, 1950.

Bailey, Kenneth, ed. *The Television Annual for 1954*. Long Acre, London: Odhams Press, 1953.

Baird, John Logie. *Sermons, Soap and Television*. London: Royal Television Society, 1990.

Barr, Charles. *British Cinema: A Very Short Introduction*. Oxford: Oxford University Press, 2022.

Binder, Mike. *Halliwell's Horizon: Leslie Halliwell and His Film Guides*. Lulu Publishing, 2011.

Briggs, Asa. *The History of Broadcasting in the United Kingdom, Volume 2: The Golden Age of Wireless*. Oxford: Oxford University Press, 1965.

Briggs, Asa. *The History of Broadcasting in the United Kingdom, Volume 4: Sound and Vision*. Oxford: Oxford University Press, 1979.

Briggs, Asa. *The History of Broadcasting in the United Kingdom, Volume 5: Competition*. Oxford: Oxford University Press, 1995.

Burns, Russell W. *John Logie Baird, Television Pioneer*. IET History of Technology Series, no. 28; Stevenage: Institute of Engineering and Technology, 2000.

Buscombe, Edward. *Screen Pamphlet 1: Films on TV*. London: Society for Education in Film and Television, n.d. [1971].

Chibnall, Steve. *Quota Quickies: The Birth of the British 'B' Film*. London: BFI Publishing, 2007.

Chibnall, Steve, and Brian McFarlane. *The British 'B' Film*. London: BFI/Palgrave Macmillan, 2009.

Croston, Eric, ed. *ITV 1974: Guide to Independent Television*. London: Independent Broadcasting Authority, 1974.

Currie, Tony. *The Radio Times Story*. Tiverton: Kelly Publications, 2001.

Davis, Anthony. *Television: The First Forty Years*. London: Independent Television Publications, 1976.

Docherty, David, David Morrison and Michael Tracey. *The Last Picture Show? Britain's Changing Film Audiences*. London: BFI Publishing, 1984.

Edinburgh International Film Festival. *What Is a Television Film? An Edinburgh Festival Conference*. Contrast, 1964.

Egan, Kate, Martin Ian Smith and Jamie Terrill, eds. *Researching Historical Screen Audiences*. Edinburgh: Edinburgh University Press, 2022.

Eyles, Allen. *Gaumont British Cinemas*. Burgess Hill: Cinema Theatre Association/BFI Publishing, 1996.

Eyles, Allen. *The Granada Theatres*. London: Cinema Theatre Association/BFI Publishing, 1998.

Falk, Quentin, and Dominic Prince. *Last of a Kind: The Sinking of Lew Grade*. London and New York: Quartet Books, 1987.

Forman, Denis. *Persona Granada: Some Memories of Sidney Bernstein and the Early Days of Independent Television*. London: André Deutsch, 1997.

Glancy, Mark. *Hollywood and the Americanization of Britain: From the 1920s to the Present*. London: I.B. Tauris, 2014.

Gomery, Douglas. *Shared Pleasures: A History of Movie Presentation in the United States*. London: BFI Publishing, 1992.

Halliwell, Leslie. *The Dead That Walk. Halliwell's Moving Pictures*; London: Grafton Books, 1986.

Halliwell, Leslie, and Graham Murray. *The Clapperboard Book of the Cinema*. London: Hart-Davis, MacGibbon, 1975.

Hanson, Stuart. *From Silent Screen to Multi-Screen: A History of Film Exhibition in Britain since 1896*. Manchester: Manchester University Press, 2007.

Heffernan, Kevin. *Ghouls, Gimmicks, and Gold: Horror Films and the American Movie Business, 1953–1968*. Durham and London: Duke University Press, 2004.

Hill, John, and Martin McLoone, eds. *Big Picture, Small Screen: The Relations between Film and Television*. Acamedia Research Monograph 16; Luton: John Libbey Media/ University of Luton, 1996.

Hilmes, Michele. *Hollywood and Television: From Radio to Cable*. Urbana: University of Illinois Press, 1999.

Holmes, Su, *British TV & Film Culture in the 1950s: Coming to a TV near You*. Bristol: Intellect, 2005.

Hoyt, Eric. *Hollywood Vault: Film Libraries before Home Video*. Berkeley: University of California Press, 2014.

Jacobs, Jason. *The Intimate Screen: Early British Television Drama*. Oxford: Oxford University Press, 2000.

Jewell, Richard B. *Slow Fade to Black: The Decline of RKO Radio Pictures*. Oakland: University of California Press, 2016.

Keathley, Christian. *Cinephilia and History, or: The Wind in the Trees*. Bloomington and Indianapolis: Indiana University Press, 2006.

Kelly, Terence, with Graham Norton and George Perry. *A Competitive Cinema: An ILEA Research Report*. London: Institute of Economic Affairs, 1966.

Kermabon, Jacques, and Kumar Shahani, eds. *Cinema and Television: Fifty Years of Reflection in France*. New Delhi: Orient Longman, 1991.

Kerzoncuf, Alain, and Charles Barr. *Hitchcock Lost & Found: The Forgotten Films*. Lexington: University Press of Kentucky, 2015.

Klinger, Barbara. *Beyond the Multiplex: Cinema, New Technologies, and the Home*. Berkeley, Los Angeles and London: University of California Press, 2006.

Kuhn, Annette, *An Everyday Magic: Cinema and Cultural Memory*. London: I.B. Tauris, 2002.

Lewis, Peter M. *Community Television and Cable in Britain*. London: British Film Institute, 1978.

Macnab, Geoffrey. *J. Arthur Rank and the British Film Industry*. London: Routledge, 1993.

Martin, Andrew S. *Sound & Vision: Television from Alexandra Palace (And Some Other Places) – A Programme Guide 1928–1939, Volumes 1–7*. Handsworth Wood: Kaleidoscope Publishing, 2021.

Mayne, Laura. *Channel 4 and the British Film Industry, 1982–1998*. Edinburgh: Edinburgh University Press, 2024.

McArthur, Colin. *Dialectic! Left Film Criticism from Tribune*. London: Key Texts, 1982.

Medhurst, Jamie. *The Early Years of Television and the BBC*. Edinburgh: Edinburgh University Press, 2022.

Milne, Alasdair. *DG: The Memories of a British Broadcaster*. London: Hodder & Stoughton, 1988.

Moran, Joe. *Armchair Nation: An Intimate History of Britain in Front of the TV*. London: Profile Books, 2013.

Norman, Bruce. *Here's Looking at You: The Story of British Television 1908–1939*. London: British Broadcasting Corporation/Royal Television Society, 1984.

Ostrer, Nigel. *The Ostrer Brothers & Gaumont British*. Lulu Publications, 2010.

Paulu, Burton. *British Broadcasting in Transition*. London: Macmillan, 1961.

Pilling, Jayne, and Kingsley Canham, eds. *The Screen on the Tube: Filmed TV Drama* (Cinema City Dossier Number 1). Norwich: Cinema City, 1983.

Political and Economic Planning. *The British Film Industry: A Report on Its History and Present Organisation, with Special Reference to the Economic Problems of British Feature Film Production*. London: PEP, 1952.

Porst, Jennifer. *Broadcasting Hollywood: The Struggle over Feature Films on Early TV*. New York: Rutgers University Press, 2021.

Potter, Jeremy. *Independent Television in Britain, Volume 3: Politics and Control, 1968–80*. Basingstoke: Macmillan, 1989.

Potter, Jeremy. *Independent Television in Britain, Volume 4: Companies and Programmes, 1968–80*. Basingstoke: Macmillan, 1990.

Robertson, Patrick. *The Guinness Book of Film Facts and Feats*. Enfield: Guinness Superlatives, 1980.

Segrave, Kerry. *Movies at Home: How Hollywood Came to Television*. Jefferson, NC: McFarland, 1999.

Sendall, Bernard. *Independent Television in Britain, Volume 1: Origin and Foundation, 1946–62*. Basingstoke: Macmillan, 1982.

Sendall, Bernard. *Independent Television in Britain, Volume 2: Expansion and Change, 1958–68*. Basingstoke: Macmillan, 1983.

Slater, Jim, and Grant Lobban. *All Shapes and Sizes: An Illustrated History of Film in Cinema and Television*. Salisbury: AG Books, 2019.

Spraos, John. *The Decline of the Cinema: An Economist's Report*. London: George Allen & Unwin, 1962.

Stokes, Jane. *On Screen Rivals: Cinema and Television in the United States and Britain*. Basingstoke: Macmillan, 1999.

Sulik, Boleslaw. *A Change of Tack: Making* The Shadow Line. London: British Film Institute, 1976.

Swift, John. *Adventures in Vision: The First Twenty-five Years of Television*. London: John Lehmann, 1950.

Trevelyan, John. *What the Censor Saw*. London: Michael Joseph, 1973.

Walker, Johnny. *Rewind, Replay: Britain and the Video Boom, 1978–92*. Edinburgh: Edinburgh University Press, 2022.

Williams, Raymond. *Television: Technology and Cultural Form*. London: Fontana/Collins, 1974.

Chapters in Books

Aubrey, Anthony. 'Is There a Future for Pay TV?' In *Film Review 1964/*1965, edited by F. Maurice Speed, 60–3. London: Macdonald, 1964.

Auty, Martyn. 'But Is It Cinema?' In *British Cinema Now*, edited by Auty and Nick Roddick, 57–70. London: BFI Publishing, 1985.

Buscombe, Edward. 'All Bark and No Bite: The Film Industry's Response to Television'. In *Popular Television in Britain: Studies in Cultural History*, edited by John Corner, 197–209. London: BFI Publishing, 1990.

Caughie, John. 'Before the Golden Age: Early Television Drama'. In *Popular Television in Britain: Studies in Cultural History*, edited by John Corner, 22–41. London: BFI Publishing, 1990.

Christie, Ian. 'A Beginner's Guide to the Telefilm Jungle'. In *The Screen on the Tube: Filmed TV Drama*, edited by Jayne Pilling and Kingsley Canham, 10–11. (Cinema City Dossier Number 1). Norwich: Cinema City, 1983.

Clarke, Michael. 'Television Prospect: Some Reflexions of a Documentary Film-maker'. In *The Cinema 1952*, edited by Roger Manvell and R.K. Neilson Baxter, 174–87. Harmondsworth: Penguin, 1952.

Eyles, Allen. 'The Film on TV'. In *Film Review 1968–1969*, edited by F. Maurice Speed, 157–60. London: W.H. Allen, 1968.

Eyles, Allen. 'TV Survey'. In *Film Review 1969–1970*, edited by F. Maurice Speed, 46–7. London: W.H. Allen, 1969.

Francis, David. 'The Film and Television'. In *Film Review 1970–1971*, edited by F. Maurice Speed, 33–5. London: W.H. Allen, 1969.

Gorham, Maurice, with R.K. Neilson Baxter. 'Television: A Medium in Its Own Right?' In *The Cinema 1951*, edited by Roger Manvell and Baxter, 131–46. Harmondsworth: Penguin, 1951.

Hall, Sheldon. '"So Much More than TV Times": Film Coverage in *Radio Times* and *TV Times*'. In *Film Critics and British Film Culture: New Shots in the Dark*, edited by Sheldon Hall and Robert Shail. Edinburgh: Edinburgh University Press, 2024.

Hall, Stuart. 'Technics of the Medium'. In *Television Times: A Reader*, edited by John Corner and Sylvia Harvey, 3–10. London: Arnold, 1996.

Hayward, Anthony. 'Films on TV'. in *Film Review 1983–1984*, edited by F. Maurice Speed, 29–37. London: W.H. Allen, 1983.

Kael, Pauline. 'Movies on Television'. In *Kiss Kiss Bang Bang: Film Writings 1965–1967*, 217–26. London: Marion Boyars, 1970.

Kinsey, Wayne. 'Appointment with Fear'. In *70s Monster Memories*, edited by Eric McNaughton, 381–8. Brighton: Buzzy Krotik Productions, 2016.

Lafferty, William. 'Feature Films on Prime-Time Television'. In *Hollywood in the Age of Television*, edited by Tino Balio, 235–56. Boston: Unwin Hyman, 1990.

Leader, Raymond. 'Why We Never See Their Films on Television'. In *Film Review 1964/1965*, edited by F. Maurice Speed, 47–9. London: Macdonald.

Litman, Barry R. 'The Economics of the Television Market for Theatrical Movies'. In *The American Movie Industry: The Business of Motion Pictures*, edited by Gorham Kindem, 308–21. Carbondale and Edwardsville: Southern Illinois University Press, 1982.

Meikle, Denis. 'The BBC2 Horror Double Bills'. In *Television Terrors: A History of Horror on the Small Screen*, edited by Allan Bryce, 129–38. South Cheam: Ghoulish Publishing.

More O'Ferrall, George, Mary Adams, Michael Gough, R.K. Neilson Baxter and Roger Manvell. 'Television's Challenge to the Cinema'. In *The Cinema* 1950, edited by Roger Manvell, 170–85. Harmondsworth, Penguin, 1950.

Noble, Peter. 'Television and the Movies'. In *Film Review 1960–61*, edited by F. Maurice Speed, 27–9. London: MacDonald & Co., 1960.

Ogley, Neil. 'Horror Double Bills'. In *70s Monster Memories*, edited by Eric McNaughton, 299–309. Brighton: Buzzy Krotik Productions, 2016.

Porter, Vincent. 'Television and Film Production Strategies in the European Community'. In *Entertainment: A Cross-cultural Examination*, edited by Heinz-Dietrich Fischer and Stefan Reinhard Melnik, 258–72. New York: Hastings House, 1979.

Rolinson, Dave. 'The Last Studio System: A Case for British Television Films'. In *Don't Look Now: British Cinema in the 1970s*, edited by Paul Newland, 163–74. Bristol and Chicago: Intellect, 2010.

Stuart, Frederic. 'The Effects of Television on the Motion Picture Industry'. In *The American Movie Industry: The Business of Motion Pictures*, edited by Gorham Kindem, 257–307. Carbondale and Edwardsville: Southern Illinois University Press, 1982.

Thompson, Howard. 'TV Favorites'. In *Favorite Movies: Critics' Choices*, edited by Philip Nobile, 246–53. New York: Macmillan, 1973.

Todd, Kenith, and Jayne Pilling. 'The Trodd Index'. In *The Screen on the Tube: Filmed TV Drama*, edited by Jayne Pilling and Kingsley Canham, 53–65 (Cinema City Dossier Number 1). Norwich: Cinema City, 1983.

Ware, John. 'TV Launches a Film Offensive'. in *Movie Stars: A Film World Book*, edited by Peter Noble, 10. n.d. [1949].

Journal Articles

Aarons, Robert. 'French Television'. *Film* 61 (Spring 1971): 17.

Allan, Elkan. 'The Professional Prophet'. *Sunday Times Magazine*, 28 November 1971, 27.

Allan, Elkan. 'Guess What's Coming on Television'. *Sunday Times Magazine*, 21 October 1973, 100, 102.

Anon. 'What Viewers Are Saying'. *Radio Times*, 26 March 1937, Television Supplement, 4.

Anon. 'Showing How It's Done'. *Radio Times*, 14 October 1938, 17.

Anon. 'Latest Equipment for Televising Films' *Scan* 1, no. 4 (August 1948): 11.

Anon. 'Don't Waste Time on These Films!' *Picturegoer*, 9 April 1949, 15.

Anon. 'An Insight into the Cinema-Television Conflict'. *Scan* 2, no. 1 (May 1949): 15.

Anon. 'Television and the Children'. *Scan* 2, no. 2 (June 1949): 13–14.

Anon. 'Mass Observation and Television'. *Journal of the Television Society* 5, no. 11 (September 1949): 334.

Anon. 'Review of Recent Programmes'. *Scan* 2, no. 6 (October 1949): 14.

Anon. 'Four BBC Engineers Made TV Recording Possible'. *Scan and Television News* 2, no. 9 (January 1950): 12.

Anon. 'Is This the Best They Can Do?' *Television Weekly* 1, no. 53 (17 February 1950): 11.

Anon. 'Television's Effect on the Film Industry'. *Television Weekly* 1, no. 53 (17 February 1950): 3.

Anon. 'Your Guide to Television's Future'. *Scan and Television News* 3, no. 11 (March 1951): 12–15.

Anon. 'Film Trailers Are on the Way'. *Scan and Television News* 3, no. 12 (April 1951): 18.

Anon. 'No TV Or...!' *TV News* 6, no. 18 (16 October 1953): 7.

Anon. 'The Front Page: How Goes the Enemy?' *Sight and Sound* 23, no. 4 (April–June 1954): 175.

Anon. 'The Front Page'. *Sight and Sound* 27, no. 1 (Summer 1957): 3.

Anon. 'In the Picture: Action Stations'. *Sight and Sound* 29, no. 2 (Spring 1960): 67–8.

Anon. 'In the Picture: Viewing Figures'. *Sight and Sound* 31, no. 2 (Spring 1962): 65.

Anon. 'Ten Bests'. *Film* 33 (Autumn 1962): 24–5.

Anon. 'Films on Television'. *Film* 36 (Summer 1963): 35–6.

Anon. 'Charlie Chaplin's *The Gold Rush*'. *Radio Times*, 16 April 1964, 44.

Anon. 'Oscar! (editorial). *Film* 49 (Autumn 1967): 4, 6.

Anon. 'Why No "X" Certificate?' *Radio Times*, 4 January 1968, 4.

Anon. 'Foreign Films on British Screens'. *Films and Filming* 16, no. 9 (June 1970): 18–26.

Anon. 'Command Performance: Your Favourite Films'. *TV Times* (Granada), 11 March 1971, 18.

Anon. 'Coming Soon: All Your Best Film Favourites', *TV Times* (Granada), 20 May 1971, 40.

Anon. 'Looking on the White Side'. *Radio Times*, 5 December 1974, 4.

Anon. 'Was It "Before Hindsight"?' *Radio Times*, 9 February 1978, 23.

Anon. 'Anatomy of a National Habit: What Turns You On – and Turns You Off'. *Sunday Times Magazine*, 7 November 1982, S1 2–3.

Archdeacon, John. 'Television and the BBC Charter...' *Scan* 2, no. 6 (October 1949): 4–6.

Archdeacon, John. 'The Function of Film in Television'. *Scan* 2, no. 8 (December 1949): 5–6, 8.

Armitage, Peter. 'Films on Television'. *Film* 30 (Winter 1961): 16.

Armitage, Peter. 'Peaceful Coexistence between Films and Television'. *Film* 2, no. 4 (July 1973): 20.

Armitage, Peter. 'Films on Television'. *Film* 2, no. 9 (December 1973): 7–8.

Ayres, John D. 'The Two Screens: FIDO, RFDA and Film vs. Television in Post-Second World War Britain'. *Journal of British Cinema and Television* 14, no. 4 (2017): 504–21.

Barry, Christopher. 'We're Not Doomed Yet'. *Television Weekly* 5, no. 7 (October 1952): 23.

Beadle, Gerald. 'Opening the Window on the World'. *Radio Times*, 25 October 1957, 3.

Birkinshaw, D.C. 'The Shape of Your Television Picture'. *Radio Times*, 31 March 1950, 43.

Bower, Dallas. 'Television and the Films'. *Radio Times*, 15 January 1937, Television Supplement, 5.

Boyd, Kelly. 'Cowboys, Comedy and Crime: American Programmes on BBC Television, 1946–1955'. *Media History* 17, no. 3 (2011): 233–51.

Braine, John. 'Life at the TV Top'. *TV Times* (Northern), 26 October 1962, 9.

Brilliance, David. 'Seeing Double'. *The Dark Side* 179 (2016): 30–3.

Brown, Geoff. 'Films That Go Bump in the Night'. *Radio Times*, 26 June 1980, 70.

Brown, Geoff. 'Archers on Target'. *Radio Times*, 4 September 1980, 17–18.

Castell, David. 'The Cannibal in the Corner'. *Films Illustrated* 8, no. 50 (October 1975): 65–7.

Cave, William. 'Television and the Cinema'. *Scan* 1, no. 9 (January 1949): 4–5.

Clair, René. 'Television and Cinema'. *Sight and Sound* 19, no. 9 (January 1951): 372.

Cock, Gerald. 'Looking Forward: A Personal Forecast of the Future of Television'. *Radio Times*, 23 October 1936, 7.

Corke, Hilary. 'Not Quite Innocent Deceptions'. *The Listener*, 31 December 1959, 1172.

Cross, Peter D. 'Television – the End of Film?' *Sight and Sound* 17, no. 67 (Autumn 1948): 131–2.

Crow, Duncan. 'From Screen to Screen: Cinema Films on Television'. *Sight and Sound* 27, no. 2 (Autumn 1957): 61–4.

Crow, Duncan. 'Pay Television'. *Sight and Sound* 30, no. 2 (Spring 1961): 96–7.

Daney, Serge. 'From the Large to the Small Screen'. *Libération*, 16 November 1987; translation available online at *Serge Daney in English*, http://sergedaney.blogspot.co.uk.

Davis, Blair. 'Small Screen, Smaller Pictures: Television Broadcasting and B-Movies in the Early 1950s'. *Historical Journal of Film, Radio and Television* 28, no. 2 (2008): 219–38.

Desmond, Shaw. 'Seeing round the World: What Television Will Mean to YOU', *Television* 1, no. 6 (August 1928): 11–14.

Dinsdale, A. 'Television at the Berlin Radio Exhibition', *Television* 2, no. 20 (October 1929): 379–89.

Dorté, Philip. 'Feature Films for Television'. *Radio Times*, 11 January 1952, 42.

Dunkley, Chris. 'Scheming for a Bright Christmas'. *Radio Times*, 1 January 1976, 67.

Ellis, John. 'The Future of the British Film Industry'. *Screen* 17, no. 1 (Spring 1976): 84–93.

Elvin, George. 'How Cinema Might Die'. *Films and Filming* 1, no. 11 (August 1955): 8.

Eyles, Allen. 'Boxed-in'. *Films and Filming* 11, no. 10 (July 1965): 38.

Eyles, Allen. 'The Mutilators'. *Films and Filming* 16, no. 6 (March 1970): 76.

Eyles, Allen. 'Brighter Viewing'. *Films and Filming* 16, no. 8 (May 1970): 74.

Eyles, Allen. 'Cinema-TV'. *Film and Filming* 17, no. 2 (November 1970): 68.

Eyles, Allen. 'TV Cinema'. *Films and Filming* 18, no. 3 (December 1971): 68–9.

Eyles, Allen. 'TV Cinema'. *Films and Filming* 18, no. 5 (February 1972): 68.

Eyles, Allen. 'TV Cinema'. *Films and Filming* 18, no. 6 (March 1972): 68.

Eyles, Allen. 'On TV'. *Film and Filming* 19, no. 6 (March 1973): 74–5.

Eyles, Allen. 'Classic Repertory Cinemas'. *Picture House* 45 (2020): 3–51.

Forbes, Bryan. 'A Personal View'. *Films Illustrated* 8, no. 50 (October 1975): 66–7.

Forbes, Bryan. 'Films'. *Radio Times*, 25 January 1979, 17.

Forbes, Elliot, and David Pierce. 'Who Owns the Movies?' *Film Comment* 30, no. 6 (November–December 1994): 43–50.

Franklin, Ieuan. 'BBC2 and World Cinema'. *Journal of British Cinema and Television* 14, no. 3 (2017): 344–60.

Genower, Peter. 'Does TV Make the Kindest Cuts of All?', *TV Times*, 12 August 1976.

Gilbert, Bill. 'Late Night Film'. *Radio Times*, 13 July 1961, 26.

Gilbert, Bill. 'Films on TV: Before the Flood'. *The Veteran* 120 (Autumn 2008): 11–14.

Gilbert, Bill. 'Early Days of TV Acquisition'. *The Veteran* 136 (Autumn 2012): 18–21.

Gilbert, Bill. 'Overcoming FIDO'. *The Veteran* 141 (Winter 2013): 15–18.

Gillett, John. 'Film into Detergent'. *Sight and Sound* 40, no. 1 (Winter 1970–71): 22.

Gillett, John. 'Japanese Notebook'. *Sight and Sound* 42, no. 1 (Winter 1972–73): 27.

Gordon, David. 'Ten Points about the Crisis in the British Film Industry'. *Sight and Sound* 43, no. 2 (Spring 1974): 66–72.

Gordon, David. 'British National Pictures Rides Again'. *Sight and Sound* 45, no. 2 (Spring 1976): 81–2.

Gradenwitz, Dr Alfred. 'Mihály's Tele-Cinema'. *Television* 2, no. 14 (April 1929): 59–62.

Hall, Stuart. 'Television and Culture'. *Sight and Sound* 45, no. 4 (Autumn 1976): 246–52.

Halliwell, Leslie. 'Films That Nearly Got Away'. National Film Theatre programme booklet, September–November 1973, 50–2.

Halliwell, Leslie. 'Top of the Film Pops'. *TV Times*, 11–17 February 1984, 55.

Hanks, Robert. 'Archive TV: *The Singing, Ringing Tree*'. *Sight and Sound* 31, no. 10 (October 2021): 96.

Harman, John. 'On My Screen'. *Scan and Television News* 3, no. 4 (August 1950): 21.

Hill, Derek. 'Defence through FIDO'. *Sight and Sound* 28, no. 3/4 (Summer–Autumn 1959): 183–4.

Hill, Derek. 'International Film Season'. *Sight and Sound* 32, no. 2 (Spring 1963): 66.

Hill, Derek. 'New Cinema Club' (interview). *Film* 49 (Autumn 1967): 7–9.

Hitchcock, Veronica. '*Psycho*'s Director'. *Radio Times*, 11 April 1968, 34.

Hoddinott, Derek. 'Celluloid – Servant of Television'. *Scan and Television News* 3, no. 10 (February 1951): 6–7.

Houston, Penelope. 'Time of Crisis'. *Sight and Sound* 27, no. 4 (Spring 1958): 166–75.

Houston, Penelope. 'Working Party'. *Sight and Sound* 44, no. 4 (Autumn 1975): 219.

Houston, Penelope. 'Annan and the Cinema'. *Sight and Sound* 46, no. 3 (Summer 1977): 150–1.

Houston, Penelope. 'Interim Inaction'. *Sight and Sound* 50, no. 3 (Summer 1981): 150.

Howkins, John. 'Report on Annan'. *Sight and Sound* 46, no. 3 (Summer 1977): 139–42.

Hunter, Alan. 'Television Is for the Home'. *Radio Times*, 10 February 1939, 10.

Hutchinson, Tom. 'Your Bidder in the Stalls'. *Sunday Express Magazine*, 27 December 1981.

Jackson, Michael. 'Cinema versus Television'. *Sight and Sound* 49, no. 3 (Summer 1980): 178–81.

James, Robert. 'TV's Untouchables'. *Film* 31 (Spring 1962): 29.

Jenkins, Malcolm. 'Guardians – or Butchers?' *TV Times*, 16 February 1978, 10–11.

Jenkinson, Philip. 'Letters: CinemaScope on 16mm'. *Film* 30 (Winter 1961): 38.

Jenkinson, Philip. 'Whatever Happened to Opinion or How I Learned to Stop Criticising and Love the Movies'. *Film* 50 (Winter 1967): 7–9.

Jenkinson, Philip. 'This Week's Films'. *Radio Times*, 7 September 1972, 11.

Jenkinson, Philip. 'This Week's Films'. *Radio Times*, 30 August 1973, 9.

Jones, Andrew Miller. 'Television and Cinema'. *The Penguin Film Review* 6 (April 1948): 45–52.

Jones, Gareth. '*Akenfield*'. *Sight and Sound* 42, no. 4 (Autumn 1973): 192–3.

Julian, Trevor. 'How Do Films Get Seen on TV?' *Films Illustrated* 9, no. 100 (December 1979): 134–6.

Kackman, Michael. 'Nothing on but Hoppy Badges: *Hopalong Cassidy*, William Boyd Enterprises, and Emergent Media Globalization'. *Cinema Journal* 48, no. 4 (Summer 2008): 76–101.

Lane, John Francis. 'Italian TV as Super-Producer'. *Sight and Sound* 40, no. 2 (Spring 1971): 76–7.

Lejeune, C.A. 'Films and Plays in Television'. *The BBC Quarterly*, February 1950.

Lejeune, C.A. 'A Film Fairy-story'. *Radio Times*, 11 April 1952, 41.

Lejeune, C.A. 'Korda as I Knew Him'. *TV Times*, 6 September 1957, 6–7.

Lewis, Jack. 'Saturday Thriller'. *Radio Times*, 5 October 1967, 3, 8.

Lindgren, Ernest. 'Television'. *Sight and Sound* 19, no. 7 (November 1950): 302.

Lindgren, Ernest. 'Television'. *Sight and Sound* 19, no. 8 (December 1950): 340.

Mann, John E. 'Film Fare: Heroes of the Cruel Sea'. *TV Times* (Northern), 21 October 1965, 12.

McGivern, Cecil. 'New Pattern in BBC Television Programmes'. *Radio Times*, 16 September 1955, 15.

Meakin, Derek. 'Three Films for Christmas Day'. *TV Times*, 20 December 1957, 11.

Monkhouse, Bob, and Willis Hall. 'A–Z of Television', Part Five. *TVTimes*, 11 November 1971, 21.

Moseley, Sydney A. 'The Future of Television', *Television* 2, no. 20 (October 1929): 407–8.

Moseley, Sydney A. 'The First Tele-cine Broadcast'. *Television* 4, no. 38 (April 1931): 48–9.

Nicolson, Norman J. 'Tele-cinematography'. *Television* 2, no. 19 (September 1929): 361–3.

Noble, Peter. 'Films: Near Things in the Far East'. *Look Westward*, 18 December 1965, 12.

Nowell-Smith, Geoffrey. 'On History and the Cinema'. *Screen* 31, no. 2 (Summer 1990): 160–71.

Oakes, Philip. 'Sex and the Cinema'. *Radio Times*, 11 January 1979, 17, 19.

Ottaway, Robert. 'Look What Happened in the Old Days'. *Radio Times*, 2 October 1986, 16.

Perry, Simon. 'Finance for Local Talent'. *Sight and Sound* 49, no. 3 (Summer 1980): 144–8.

Peters, Francis. 'Those Old Films on TV and What the Stars of Them Really Think'. *Photoplay*, December 1966, 42–3, 56.

Pierce, David. '"Senile Celluloid": Independent Exhibitors, the Major Studios and the Fight over Features on Television, 1939–1956'. *Film History* 10, no. 2 (1998): 141–64.

Pilsworth, Michael. '"An Imperfect Art" – TV Scheduling in Britain'. *Sight and Sound* 49, no. 4 (Autumn 1980): 237–9.

Pirie, David. 'Electric Cinema'. *Time Out*, 24–30 December 1971.

Porter, Vincent. 'TV Strategies and European Film Production'. *Sight and Sound* 43, no. 3 (Summer 1974): 163–5, 175.

Porter, Vincent. 'Television and Film Production in Europe'. *Sight and Sound* 46, no. 4 (Autumn 1977): 205–7, 251.

Pound, Reginald. 'Animals on the Move'. *The Listener*, 26 April 1951, 682–3.

Pound, Reginald. 'Worm's Eye View'. *The Listener*, 24 April 1952, 686.

Powell, Dilys. 'A Paris Boulevard in 1840'. *Radio Times*, 30 July 1948, 25.

Pringle, Ashley. '*Films on TV*' (review), *Screen* 13, no. 1 (Autumn 1972): 89–92.

Prothero, David. 'Derek Hill' (interview). *Journal of Popular British Cinema* 3 (2000): 133–43.

Purser, Philip. 'The Pally Pioneers'. *Radio Times*, 2 July 1981, 11.

Quéval, Jean. 'Cinema and Television'. *Sight and Sound* 19, no. 3 (May 1950): 141–2.

Radford, Michael. 'Television and Movies'. *Sight and Sound* 45, no. 4 (Autumn 1976): 227.

Rainbow, Nigel A. 'First Hand Report of the J. Arthur Rank Big Screen Test'. *Scan* 1, no. 10 (February 1949): 9.

Rotha, Paul. 'Documentary: Is Television Affecting Its Future?' *Film* 2 (December 1954): 14–15.

Sampson, K. 'Results of the Television Poll'. *Scan* 1, no. 10 (February 1949): 12.

The Scanner. 'News for Televiewers'. *Radio Times*, 3 July 1937, Television Supplement, 1.

The Scanner. 'Prelude to Radiolympia'. *Radio Times*, 13 August 1937, 16.

The Scanner. 'Film Comedy That Was Banned'. *Radio Times*, 11 March 1938, 24.

The Scanner. 'Television Is Grand!' *Radio Times*, 7 July 1939, 13.

The Scanner. 'French Film', *Radio Times*, 14 July 1939, 18.

Silvey, Robert. 'The BBC Looks into Viewing'. *Scan and Television News* 2, no. 12 (April 1950): 4–6.

Stimpson, Mansel. 'Films on Your Own Screen'. *Film* 2, no. 10 (January 1974): 22.

Stoeltje, Rachael. 'Interview with David Francis Part I'. *Journal of Film Preservation* 105 (November 2021): 88–103.

Summers, Sue. '*The Sailor's Return*'. *Sight and Sound* 47, no. 1 (Winter 1977–78): 26.

Sussex, Elizabeth. 'Buyer's Market'. *Sight and Sound* 34, no. 2 (Spring 1965): 62.

Sylvester, Cyril. 'Talkies versus Television'. *Television* 2, no. 16 (June 1929): 169–70.

Taylor, John Russell. 'Movies for a Small Screen'. *Sight and Sound* 44, no. 2 (Spring 1975): 113–15.

Thompson, T.A. 'Television in the Cinema'. *Picture House* 6 (Spring 1985): 3–9.

Vallance, Tom. 'Soundtrack: The Musical Returns'. *Film* 49 (Autumn 1967): 35–7.

Walker, Alexander, 'Sam's Bloody Ballet', *TV Times*, 29 August 1976, 5–7.

Williams, Michael. 'International Film Season'. *Radio Times*, 27 June 1963, 44.

Woods, S. John. 'Looking at Television'. *Radio Times*, 23 July 1937, 10.

Government Publications

Home Office. *Report of the Television Committee*. Chair: Lord Selsdon, Cmnd. 4793, London: HMSO, 1935.

Home Office. *Report of the Broadcasting Committee, 1949*. Chair: Sir William Beveridge, Cmnd. 8116, London: HMSO, 1951.

Home Office. *Report of the Committee on Broadcasting, 1960*. Chair: Sir Harry Pilkinngton, Cmnd. 1753, London: HMSO, 1962.

Home Office. *Future of the British Film Industry: Report of the Prime Minister's Working Party, 1976*. Chair: Sir John Terry, Cmnd. 6372, London: HMSO, 1976.

Home Office. *Report of the Committee on the Future of Broadcasting*. Chair: Lord Annan, Cmnd. 6753, London: HMSO, 1977.

Unpublished Dissertations

Keene, Rachael. 'Channel 4 Television: Film Policy and Film Programming, 1982–2011'. PhD. Diss., University of Portsmouth, 2014.

Mayne, Laura. 'Channel 4 and British Film: An Assessment of Cultural Impact, 1982–1998'. PhD. Diss., University of Portsmouth, 2014.

Schnapper, Amy. 'The Distribution of Theatrical Feature Films to Television'. PhD Diss., University of Wisconsin-Madison, 1975.

Sexton, Max. 'Celluloid Television Culture – the Specificity of Film on Television: The Action-Adventure Text as an Example of a Production and Textual Strategy, 1955–1978'. PhD diss., Birkbeck, University of London, 2013.

Upton, Julian. 'A Framing Liberty? The BBC's Transmission of Anamorphic Widescreen Feature Films in the First Years of Full-Colour Television'. MA Diss., University of Leicester, 2012.

Woods, Anne. 'A Critical Survey of BBC Films, 1988–2013'. PhD. Diss., University of Portsmouth, 2015.

Websites and Online Sources

Anon. 'James Bond on TV'. *MI6: The Home of James Bond 007*. 13 October 2007 (updated 5 April 2011). https://www.mi6-hq.com/sections/articles/history_bond_on_tv.

Anon. 'Pre-War Television'. *Radio Times Archive*. http://www.radiotimesarchive.co.uk/television.html.

Associated Artists Productions catalogue (1957). https://archive.org/details/moviesfromaappro1957asso/page/n73/mode/2up.

Branaghan, Sim. 'Invitation to Terror – Horror Films on British Television in the 1970s & 80s'. *SMGuariento.com*, 2017 (updated 2023). http://www.smguariento.com/invitation-terror-horror-films-british-television-1970s-80s-sim-branaghan/.

Branaghan, Sim. 'Monsters from an Unknown Culture – Godzilla (and Friends) in Britain 1957–1980', Part 4. *SMGuariento.com*, 2018. http://www.smguariento.com/monsters-from-an-unknown-culture-godzilla-and-friends-in-britain-1957-1980-by-sim-branaghan-part-4/.

Buxton, Roddy. 'Cinema for Television'. *Transdiffusion Broadcasting System*, 8 January 2008. https://www.transdiffusion.org/2008/01/08/cinema_for_tele.

Hall, Sheldon. 'Films on TV at Christmas'. Parts 1–3, 2016–17. http://sheldontimeshall.com/.

Hall, Sheldon. 'The First 50 Feature Films Broadcast on British Television'. 2016. http://sheldontimeshall.com/the-first-15-feature-films-broadcast-on-british-television-v2/.

Hall, Sheldon. 'Pre-launch Feature Films on BBC2'. 13 July 2017. http://sheldontimeshall.com/pre-launch-feature-films-on-bbc2/.

Hansard. 'Films'. 12 March 1963. https://hansard.parliament.uk/Commons/1963-03-12/debates/e75baf1a-86c8-4062-a4eb-a2bc0761cdff/Films.

Harper, Kevin. 'James Bond on the Small Screen'. *Double-O-Seven Magazine*, n.d. http://www.007magazine.co.uk/bond_on_tv.htm.

Hogben, Julius. 'Ken Locke' (obituary). *Guardian*, 9 April 2019. https://www.theguardian.com/media/2019/apr/09/ken-locke-obituary?fbclid=IwAR2A1wpRxdjQe75kLMXMr7LnEPPNDoNO_l1ZqH6f4O-BfYa8AhFf1D4x-7Y.

Laine, David. 'Pay-TV – 1960s Style'. *Transdiffusion Broadcasting System*. 23 November 2006. https://www.transdiffusion.org/2006/11/23/paytv_1960s_sty?fbclid=IwAR33rDx_obb5WFa1sJZbLw7ixC9xoPnOoFoCSVsYeJYScvURHYNpChqS7tY.

Locke, Ken. Interview 444. *The British Entertainment History Project*, 1999. https://historyproject.org.uk/interview/ken-locke.

Teletronic. 'The Day the BBC Closed Down'. http://www.teletronic.co.uk/bbcclosedown.htm.

Film Index

Films cited in the text are listed below, generally under the titles used on transmission or as billed in contemporary listings magazines, though in some instances I have amended them to reflect their onscreen billing. Alternative titles and theatrical release dates, followed by the earliest known dates of free-to-air terrestrial broadcast in the UK, are noted in brackets. The absence of a broadcast date indicates that no transmission is traceable, but this is not a guarantee that the film has never been shown on British television. Page numbers in **bold** refer to illustrations and captions; titles in tables are not indexed.

General Index

Note: Titles of television film strands and television programmes are indexed under those terms. Entries in tables are not indexed but figures and captions are (indicated by page numbers in **bold**). Organisations are listed under their full names; acronyms and abbreviations are mentioned in brackets and listed in Appendix 4.

Printed and bound by CPI Group (UK) Ltd, Croydon, CR0 4YY

21/11/2024

01792238-0001